AUSTRALIAN TOTEMISM

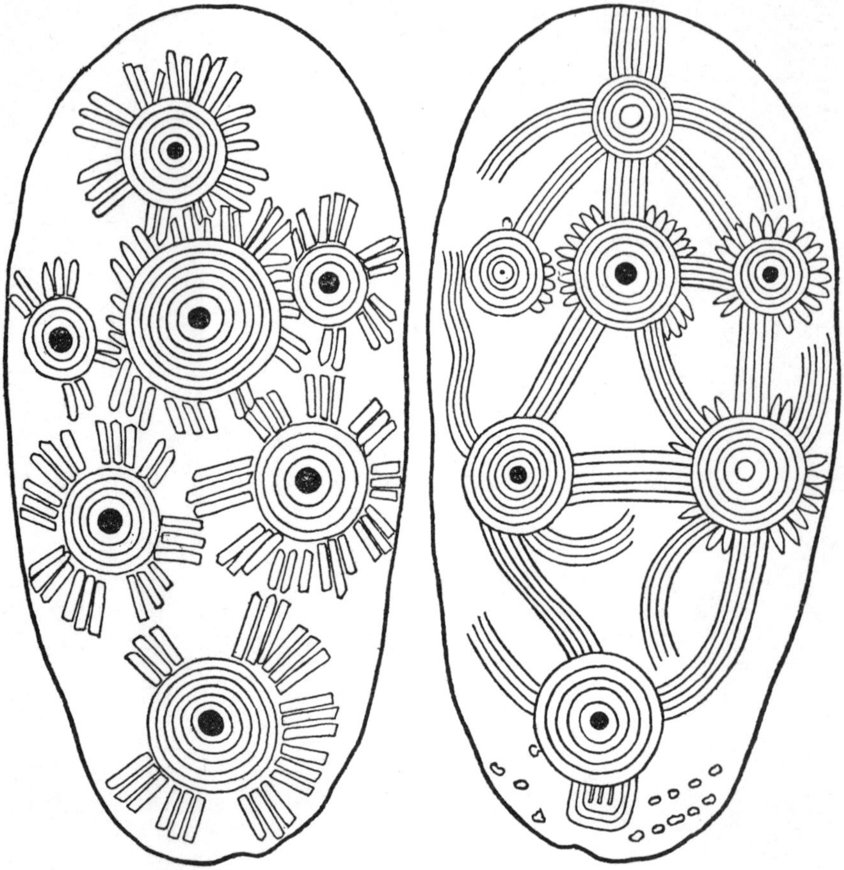

Churinga of the Unmatjera tribe. Published by permission of the Berlin Ethnographical Museum, No. VI. 35, 559. Collected by Missionary Liebler. (Number of his note: 784/12.) Flat slab of slate red-ochred and ornamented on both sides. Length, 22.5 cm.; width, 11 cm. The stone is black and red, the latter colour predominates in the ornamented part, except when marked black. The dots on No. 1 are holes in the stone. This is a Rhadapa (= ratapa, spirit-child) dalkara (= talkara, stone churinga), and belonged to the Unmatjera woman Naderintja. Liebler's note: "The Aranda contradict themselves, because they say that the human embryos (ratapa) dwell in the air and enter women, but here they point to the side where the concentric circles are connected with stripes (No. 1), as the ovary of the mother with the embryos." No. 2, the reverse side of the same churinga, represents the seven children; "the strokes round the head are the hair of the child." Of course, the same ornamental pattern is found in connexion with other secondary explanations (Cf. Strehlow, *A. & L.*, Vol. I, Tables I, II; Spencer and Gillen, *N. T.*, 146–49). Concentric circles have been interpreted recently as representing the fœtal situation by O. Rank, *Das Trauma der Geburt*, 1924, 147.

AUSTRALIAN TOTEMISM

A Psycho-Analytic Study in Anthropology

BY

GÉZA RÓHEIM

With an Introduction by

M. D. EDER

NEW YORK

HUMANITIES PRESS

Published by
FRANK CASS AND COMPANY LIMITED
67 Great Russell Street, London WC1B 3BT
by arrangement with George Allen & Unwin Ltd.

First published
in the United States of America 1971
by Humanities Press Inc.
303 Park Avenue South
New York 10, N.Y.

ISBN 391 00196 5

First edition	1925
New impression	1971

Printed in Great Britain

TO

MY BELOVED WIFE

INTRODUCTION

If, as there is no reason to doubt, the sciences of anthropology and psychology are as happy in the closer contact they have recently established as other departments of science, for instance, chemistry and physics, have become in drawing near to one another, this new relationship should become fruitful to both.

Dr. Róheim applies, in this book, the results obtained from the psycho-analytic study of individuals to the problems of anthropology, elucidating those which have hitherto baffled understanding and illuminating what has remained obscure or bizarre in the behaviour of savage man.

The data so laboriously acquired by the field anthropologist can no longer be regarded as merely freakish manifestations of savages living in outlandish parts of the world, nor merely as curiosities of behaviour to be covered by some resounding phrase which makes the mind of the savage something utterly alien from that of civilized beings. It is found that there is an intimate relationship between the observances, the ritual of primitive man and our own mental mechanisms, whilst primitive customs and modes of thought stray into our own civilized life in the form of folk-lore and fairy story.

Anthropology renders a return service to psychology by which the psycho-analyst is ready enough, some think too ready, to profit. Some of the possible objections that may be made to Dr. Róheim's methods, the use of psycho-analytic data in explanation of Australian customs, may be briefly discussed. It is well to point out in the first place that the psychological data obtained by Freud and his followers are clinical results gained from exact observation carried out for nearly a generation on a great number of persons in Europe and the New World. The data of psycho-analysis garnered from patients and from the direct observation of children rest on as solid a foundation as the phenomena of other sciences. Freud's theory of the libido summarizes the phenomena to which we refer, including the sexual life of the child, the ambivalent emotional relationship to the parents, the non-appearance in consciousness of impulses and ideas which are nevertheless springs of conduct and underlie traits of characters.

The term "unconscious" has been employed to describe these impulses, ideas, thoughts which do not permeate into consciousness and are incapable under ordinary conditions of mental life of becoming conscious—they remain entirely unconscious. That this realm of mental life is absolutely unknown to the individual's consciousness must be emphasized.

When all this is admitted the objection is sometimes raised that, though psycho-analytic findings may hold good in explanation of the minds of neuropathic persons from whom the material has been obtained, the results are not valid for normal psychology.

Waiving any consideration of the fact that the theory of the libido has been confirmed by the analysis of a considerable number of persons who were not neuropathic, it must be pointed out that an objection of this kind would equally invalidate the results of the whole of our experimental sciences. Addison put the position so clearly, so tersely, over two generations ago, that I should like to think a quotation might for ever dispose of this kind of objection :

"Although pathology, therefore, as a branch of medical science, is necessarily founded on physiology, questions may, nevertheless, arise regarding the true character of a structure or organ, to which occasionally the pathologist may be able to return a more satisfactory and decisive reply than the physiologist—these two branches of medical knowledge being thus found mutually to advance and illustrate each other."[1]

So far as the mental life of the individual and of the individual in relationship to his first groupings are concerned, we can claim a definite body of evidence, admitting of no second interpretation. Different hypotheses can be, of course, advanced in explanation of these facts ; but it will be found, I believe, that Freud's is the only theory which can lay claim to scientific validity, as it accounts for all the facts and assigns them in Newton's language *a vera causa* in explanation of the data and experience.

When we come to apply the data obtained from the investigation of individual minds to the problems of social anthropology, to the problems which Dr. Róheim solves, we have to make certain assumptions. We cannot directly verify our conclusions about man in the dawn of history, nor does an investigation of primitive man as he exists to-day help us. "Anyone," remarked Rivers, "who has attempted to discover explanations of rude rites and customs from those who practise them will have no hesitation in accepting their origin in the unconscious. If explanations are forthcoming, they are given by sophisticated members of the community who have usually been influenced by external culture. They are the wholly untrustworthy results of a recent process of rationalization."[2]

[1] *On the Constitutional and Local Effects of Diseases of the Supravenal Capsules.* A collection of the published writings of the late Thomas Addison. The New Sydenham Society, 1868.

[2] W. H. R. Rivers, "Dreams and Primitive Culture," *Bulletin of the John Rylands Library*, 1918, 25.

The hypothesis must be framed that the unconscious of a person of lowly culture is in quality the same as that of persons of the higher culture, and that the unconscious, strictly unconscious, motives which influence both alike are those discovered in the laboratory of the psycho-analyst.

An analogous assumption, of course, underlies all the sciences. The geologist also attempts to explain the past by the present: "Only in proportion," says Geikie, "as we understand the present, where everything is open on all sides to the fullest investigation, can we expect to decipher the past, where so much is obscure, imperfectly preserved or not preserved at all." [1]

To illustrate this application of psycho-analytic results to anthropology, I will take one of the factors that psycho-analysis has shown to play a great rôle in the psychic constitution of man. This is the existence of a phase of psycho-sexual development where the libidinal impulse is directed towards the self and is hence termed narcissism in psycho-analytic literature. The partial impulses which build up what finally develops into the genital impulse are pleasurable sensations experienced purely autistically, owing nothing to a second living organism. At this primary psycho-sexual level the object of the libidinal impulse is the individual's own body.[2]

Narcissism is the summation of the component autoerotic impulses and precedes the stage of object-love.

It has been found that in cases of obsessional neurosis there is always a basic conflict between the narcissistic ego and object-love; a patient suffering from this neurosis is ever seeking for objects on which to rivet his (her) libidinal impulses, but the search is for ever vain, since he (she) cannot sufficiently overcome the libidinal self-love.

His own person threatens to absorb all his interest and to cut him off from the external world. He is balancing between two mental worlds; between the world of an embryonic and infantile past, with the mental attitude proper to that phase of life, and the world where object-love makes its demands and requires fulfilment. The asylum patient may be said to have made the plunge into the past; for him the outer world has ceased to exist or it has become more or less completely merged in and swallowed up by the libidinal magnified ego.

Now, savage life offers interesting parallels to this state of things. The fear of the other sex so characteristic of the neurotic is equally prominent in primitive man. "In Malekula men and women cook their meals separately, and even at separate fires, . . . all female animals . . . and even . . . eggs are forbidden articles of

[1] Geikie, *Text-book of Geology*, 4th edition, 1903, 3.

[2] See Freud, "Zur Einführung des Narcissmus," *Sammlung kleiner Schriften*, vol. iv., 1918, 78.

diet."[1] In New Zealand every man eats by himself; "men may not eat with their wives nor wives with their male children lest their *tapu* or sanctity should kill them."[2] The fear may extend to the whole external world. The case of the Bakaïri, who are ashamed of eating in public,[3] is another well authenticated instance. This tendency to isolation through fear of the external world is seen again in the dread experienced at leaving food over or the care taken to destroy hair-clippings, nail-parings, etc., lest these fall into the hands of inimical sorcerers. Everybody is a potential enemy for the primary attitude of the ego to the outer world is that of repulsion or hatred. The individual who when eating must shut out the external world like those African kings who at meals are divided by a curtain from their guests,[4] regresses to the infantile attitude.

That one of the components in fear of the other sex is the conflict between narcissism and object-love is shown by those instances where contact with woman is regarded as fatal to the "mana" or magical will-power of man. In a Pawnee tale, "Coming-Sun" loses his magical power as soon as a woman enters his *tipi*.[5] In a Wichita myth "Little Man" enjoins the Coyote not to marry lest by marrying he should lose his powers.[6]

An Arunta medicine man who is being initiated must keep a fire burning at night between himself and his wife, for his magic power might leave him were he to have intercourse with her.[7] The source of magical power is the belief in the power of one's own wishes, in what Ferenczi has called the happy infantile delusion of omnipotence. This belief is a common neurotic trait and the sign of an archaic phase of psycho-sexual evolution. This over-estimation of one's own desires and ideas is the attitude of the narcissistic individual whose whole libidinal interest is concentrated in and on the ego and who will not allow it to flow into the outer world.

The power which the Arunta medicine man fears to lose by cohabitation is in substance his seminal fluid: or more correctly, what he fears to lose is the fixation of his libido in his own person. If he loves a woman, and not only himself, he will cease to over-estimate his own person, to believe in his supernatural power, and like ordinary mortals he will be subject to fears and to death. . . .

The Boy who preferred Woman to Power (the title of the before-mentioned Pawnee tale) is taking the common path of mankind: he is giving up his narcissistic attitude in favour of ordinary object-love and becoming, from a magician, an ordinary human being.

[1] Crawley, *The Mystic Rose*, 1902, 173.
[2] Crawley, 174.
[3] Steinen, *Unter den Naturvölkern Zentral-Brasiliens*, 1894, 66–67.
[4] Crawley, 151.
[5] G. A. Dorsey, *The Pawnee*, 1906 (Part I), 104.
[6] G. A. Dorsey, *The Mythology of the Wichita*, 1904, 254.
[7] Spencer and Gillen, *Native Tribes of Central Australia*, 1899, 529, 530.

This attitude, the conflict between object-love and the narcissistic ego, which we have learnt to understand in the psycho-analytic laboratory, seems characteristic of primitive man in general and furnishes clues to many of his peculiarities. The savage, as Frazer insists, apprehends some danger from sexuality at puberty, and it is this apprehension which prompts him to seek refuge for his soul in some object outside the body.[1] This soul which takes to its heels in escaping from sexuality is the narcissistic ego escaping from the demands of libido. For libido which cannot find an object becomes converted into fear. But here, having begotten the Devil and all his host, it is time to break off.

In attempting to decipher man's past from man's present by following up the clues supplied by the psycho-analysis of contemporary human material, we follow the method of science and use this method with the same caution as, for instance, Geikie demands on the part of the geological observer.

The conception of the primitive horde, the Cyclopean family, is admittedly a speculation, as Freud himself calls it. The deductions which Dr. Róheim draws from this hypothesis must not be regarded as of the same value as those resting upon the psycho-analyst's clinical observations. The hypothesis of the Cyclopean family is helpful since it gives a simple and satisfactory explanation of the phenomena under consideration; I have not met any criticism of the Cyclopean family which instances any phenomena that cannot be brought under that hypothesis. The concept is framed in accordance with the rules governing scientific thought where "the steps to scientific knowledge consist in a series of logical fictions which are as legitimate as they are indispensable in the operations of thought, but whose relations to the phenomena whereof they are the partial and not infrequently symbolical representatives must never be lost sight of" (Stallo, *Concepts of Modern Physics*).

It may be well to point out that Dr. Róheim uses the term "symbolism" throughout this book in the strictly technical sense in which it has come to be employed in psycho-analytic literature, as the psychic mechanism by which an unconscious sexual impulse or idea, meeting with resistance on the part of the endopsychic censor, becomes repressed and represented in consciousness by a non-sexual equivalent, the symbol. Mr. Flügel has suggested the term "cryptophor" for "symbol" in this psycho-analytic sense.

There may be, I am aware, varying opinions as to the extent to which Dr. Róheim has proved his case, but no one can deny the skill with which he has presented his vast wealth of material: the patience and persistence with which he has sought to substantiate every statement; no detail is regarded as too trivial or too obscure

[1] J. G. Frazer, *Balder the Beautiful*, 1913, ii. 277.

to escape adequate notice ; every statement receives corroboration from all available sources. Every theory advanced is based upon an exhaustive and unprejudiced exposition of the facts, and of all the facts. Dr. Róheim is always careful to point out gaps in our knowledge and weaknesses in the structure that require strengthening or even replacement.

Dr. Róheim brings zeal, a rich store of knowledge, a trained scientific imagination to bear upon the solution of the seemingly baffling problems found in this strange story of man. He follows up every clue with a penetrating insight that, without losing any detail, never gets out of touch with the main issues.

The work is not a translation, having been written in English by Dr. Róheim himself ; I have limited myself to the making of alterations in language and punctuation when the sense was not quite clear.

1925 M. D. EDER.

AUTHOR'S PREFACE

THE deficiencies to be found in this book must be classed under two headings. Those of a theoretical nature are due to the limitations of the author's abilities, but there are others for which he feels he cannot with justice be blamed. Working in Budapest after the Great War upon a book dealing with Australian Ethnology is no easy matter. The student can hope for next to nothing from the public libraries, and had I not already collected a small library of my own and taken notes, so far as the necessary publications were available, in German museums and libraries (Frankfurt, Leipzig, Berlin), before 1914, this book could never have been written. But the notes had not been taken with a view to writing a book on Australian Totemism, and the extracts (chiefly concerned with funerary customs) often proved inadequate after a lapse of years, more especially as they had been taken from a completely different point of view. The only choice I had was to make the best of it or leave the book unwritten, and I accepted the former alternative. Through the kindness of Dr. John Rickman I received some recent anthropological books, and I owe him many thanks for his disinterested aid in this matter. I must also express my grateful thanks to Dr. Eder for revising the typescript and for his help in many ways with the publication of the book.

As to scientific debts, first and foremost are those which the author, and all anthropologists, owe to the epoch-making discoveries of Professor Freud in his book on *Totem and Taboo.* I am convinced that the historian of Anthropology in future ages will note three great years in our science: 1871 for *Primitive Culture,* 1890 for *The Golden Bough,* 1912 for *Totem and Taboo,* and it is only with the third that we have begun to see behind the curtain of the stage on which the great Drama of Mankind is acted. Psycho-analysis opens the road for a dynamic point of view; we see savage behaviour in the making, we see the moulding forces at work. Important steps in the same direction have also been made by the school of ethnologists who direct their attention chiefly to the migrations of customs and the formation of peoples. Although I started out on this book from a totally different viewpoint, I have now come to the conclusion that we cannot neglect the problems of culture-contact if we wish to reconstruct the historic sequence in the transformation of custom, or attempt to get a glimpse into the prehistoric period of humanity. It is in the psychological deductions drawn from the facts established by themselves that the new school in Ethnology frequently misses the mark. I think that the controversy should not be "history versus evolution," "culture-contact versus psychology," but from the history of races to the prehistoric period of mankind, through a correct psychological interpretation of the data afforded by the study of cultural areas. And it is psycho-analysis alone that can account for the phenomena as we find them or that can help us to obtain this correct psychological interpretation.

Authors vary in their spelling of proper names, e.g. Bunjil, Bundjil ; I adopt the spelling used by the source I quote from, so that the names will be found in my text with different spellings.

GÉZA RÓHEIM.

BUDAPEST,
Spring, 1924.

CONTENTS

CHAPTER II

CHAPTER III

CHAPTER IV

contracted by this crime; they thus openly avow the very crime they are disclaiming; the responsibility for killing the Father was originally shared by the Horde of Brothers, and stones were used because they were the most effective weapon to be used by a multitude to overpower an individual with whom they did not care to come to close quarters. The Alcheringa ancestor and the hero of the punishment tales is the Father of the Primeval Horde, who was buried under a pile of stones hurled at him, and under the huge rock finally rolled over the corpse to prevent it from rising. Freud has shown that a repressed feeling of guilt characterizes the mourning customs of primitive tribes; it is the unconscious sins of the living which transform the dead into a vengeful demon. They regularly arrange an inquest; their search for the murderer, the wizard, shows that they are all unconsciously guilty of the same sin. To primitive man every death is the result of a murder because the first death which left an ineffaceable trace on his psychic system was actually and really a murder, the death of the father who was killed by his own sons. Mourning customs are the result of a compromise between the attitude of object-love which refuses to relinquish a position once occupied and repression, which is directed against the revival of the memory of the Primeval Conflict and First Death. The Stone which prevents the body from arising stands for repression, and the very object which ought to keep the body out of sight is transformed into a memorial column, an image of the dead, by a return of repressed elements. But the stone is not only shaped in human form, thereby indicating its identity with the dead man, it is also identified with the male member, thus showing the sexual origin of the conflict which leads to the death and subsequent apotheosis of the father-god. The worship of phallic gravestones is a reaction formation against the wish to castrate the Jealous Sire who selfishly usurps all the women of the horde. The ancestor who impregnates all the women of the horde, or fertilizes the fields, is the Primeval Father regaining the very object after his death for which war was waged against him by his sons as long as he was alive. Throwing stones at a grave or a god as a symbol of procreation; the leader of the horde had to be stoned before the young males could proceed to procreation, and hence the magical power of stones as the weapons of the first rebellion. The memory of the first conflict survives in the ritual use of stone, which must be regarded as the precursor of the Stone Age. This stone-culture may have been developed in various independent centres, and from these centres it must have spread over large connected areas, probably whole continents; for Oceania this starting-point of the stone-using immigrants lies in Indonesia, in the south-eastern parts of the Asiatic continent. All through Oceania stone-circles and monuments are associated with burial, human sacrifice and cannibalism, which is very natural if they originated in the murder and burial of the Paternal Tyrant whose flesh was devoured in the first act of communion by his successors. But death is a return to the maternal womb, the grave a symbol of the uterus, and the churinga in the ertnatulunga not only the corpse in the grave, but also the embryo (the penis) in the womb. This is why children are born from the rock; in Central Australia all children are born like this; in Indonesia it is only the first ancestors of the race who emerged from rocks or stones. Stone-born beings belong to the past in Indonesia, but to the present in Australia, thus pointing to the degree of evolution attained by Indonesian culture at the period in which the ancestors of the Central Australian tribes started on their migrations. For Central Australia we have already shown that the incest-complex lies at the root of the idea of children born from stones; the inhabitants of Tikopia trace their descent to two stones who married each other, and to their descendants, born of brother and sister marriage.

In Indonesia and elsewhere blood of sacrificed animals is poured on stones; the Malagasy women perform this rite at tombstones if they wish for children. In Australia it is human blood which is poured on the rock, but the animal species which is multiplied instead of the human clan. Blood has to flow in grim reality before procreation is possible; hence it becomes a symbol of procreation. The more prominent a member of a savage community is, the longer will last his mourning ceremonies, at which blood is poured over his grave, and the oftener will they be repeated, but no common mortal of modern date can vie in importance with the semi-bestial figure of the Father of the Horde, the great hero of the Heroic Age of humanity. His tragic death is the real ascent to Olympic honours; his death-rites are still perpetuated in the Intichiuma of Central Australian savages. But if the totemic intichiuma is a mortuary ritual, this seems to favour the hypothesis which derives totemism (or, in this case, Central Australian totemism) from the cult of the dead, from the belief in metempsychosis. In Indonesia we find that the animals which haunt the grave are regarded as sacred, in Australia we have the watch kept up over the grave for the totem animal of the murderer. The hours or days which follow the murder are the psychological moment for the projection of the father imago into an animal species; the conscience-stricken murderer is haunted by the vision of the dead father, whom he identifies with the animal found at the grave. The animals which gathered round the graves were carrion-eaters attracted by the smell of the putrefying corpse; that is, they were doing the same thing as the mourners, the murderous brothers—they were eating the dead father. The hawk is tabooed by the Central Australians on account of its carrion-eating nature, but the same bird is a symbol of the Supreme Being in South-East Australia, and a messenger of the Supreme Being in Borneo. The hawk is imbued with the essence of the corpse which has been left behind in their panic-stricken flight by the rebellious brothers, and thus stands for the father, but it also represents the Brother Horde, as it helped them to kill and devour the father. Eating the animal to which the child attributes its conception is regarded as a kind of cannibalism in the Banks Islands, and some Arunta traditions seem to indicate that it is really a substitute for anthropophagy. Central Australian tribes who are cannibals still taboo human flesh for the women; at an earlier period the women must have been supposed to conceive, not from eating the totem but from eating human flesh. This was equivalent to having intercourse with the murdered father (transposition upwards); and by this custom the flesh of the dead man really gets back into the inside of a woman, thus repeating as far as possible the prenatal life of the embryo. The taboo against eating human flesh is really a later repression of the Oedipus complex; the women are not to eat the flesh of their father, i.e. not to have intercourse with him. When this taboo came into force the positive aspect of the rite still survived in the taboo on eating the totem and in the belief that totem-eating resulted in conception. Thus our investigations point to the roots of intichiuma and totem-eating in mourning ritual. Many mourning rites contain an orgiastic element, and we must try to account for this co-existence of mourning and procreation by going back to the phylogenetic past, the time when procreation was only possible in the mourning period after the death of the Primeval Sire. As long as the Father was alive there could be no procreation for the Young Males; and, on the other hand, they would only attack him in the rutting season, when sexual desire compelled them to take the risks of the fray. After many attempts the young males would be successful, and a period of awe-struck panic at what they had done would ensue. They were paralysed by their victory—this was the prototype

MAPS

For the use of Map 11 *(from "Kinship Organizations and Group Marriage in Australia") the author and publishers have to thank Mr. N. W. Thomas and the Cambridge University Press; for Map* 12 *Dr. Gräbner and Messrs. A. Asher & Co., Berlin.*

LIST OF TRIBES

1. Melville tribe.
2. Bathurst tribe.
3. Larrakia.
4. Puneitja.
5. Wulna.
6. Djovei.
7. Warrai (Woolwonga).
8. Norweleimil.
9. Brinken.
10. Mulluk-mulluk.
11. Wulwullam.
12. Iwaidji.
13. Gnorbur.
14. Unalla.
15. Umoriu.
16. Kulunglutji.
17. Geimbio.
18. Kakadu.
19. Koarnbut.
20. Watta.
21. Djauan.
22. Airiman.
23. Allura.
24. Waduman.
25. Bulinarra.
26. Yungman.
27. Mungarai.
28. Nullakun.
29. Yukul.
30. Walkona.
31. Mara.
32. Anula.
33. Leeanuwa.
34. Karawa.
35. Binbinga.
36. Gnuin.
37. Kallaua.
38. Willingura.
39. Allaua.
40. Goarango.
41. Gnanji.
42. Umbaia.
43. Tjingilli.
44. Bingongina.
45. Mudburra.
46. Walpari.
47. Warramunga.
48. Kaitish.
49. Wulmala.
50. Unmatjera.
51. Ilpirra.
52. Arunta.
53. Undekerebina.
54. Yaroinga.
55. Illiaura.
56. Luritja.
57. Winnanba.
58. Pitala.
59. Mangiri.
60. Waiangara.
61. Jumu.
62. Ngali.
63. Ullparidja.
64. Wilrunerra.
65. Karkurerra.
66. Alinjerra.
67. Wonkamala.
68. Wonkatjeri.
69. Yelyuendi.
70. Karanguru.
71. Ngameni.
72. Ngurawola.
73. Marula.
74. Yaurorka.
75. Wonkanguru.
76. Dieri.
77. Urabunna.
78. Willara.
79. Kuyani.
80. Mardala.
81. Yantrawunta.
82. Kukata.
83. Hilleri.
84. Nauo.
85. Parnkalla.
86. Wiranga.
87. Narranga.
88. Kaurna (or Meyu).
89. Narrinyeri.
90. Baluk-mergen.
91. Doen bauraket.
92. Buandik.
93. Gourmditch Mara.
94. Mukjarawaint.

95. Wotjobaluk.
96. Yupagalk.
97. Yayaurung.
98. Wadthaurung.
99. Kurung.
100. Wurunjerri (Yarra R. Woewo-rung).
101. Bunurong.
102. Waring illam.
103. Ngaruk willam.
104. Gunung willam.
105. Nira-balluk.
106. Buthera-balluk.
107. Yaung illam.
108. Kurnai.
109. Biduelli.
110. Ya-itma-thang.
111. Yuin.
112. Wolgal.
113. Baraba-baraba.
114. Ballung-karab.
115. Bangerang.
116. Mogullumbitch.
117. Nourallung-baluk.
118. Wamba-wamba.
119. Bura-bura.
120. Burappa.
121. Wathi-wathi.
122. Weki-weki.
123. Leichi-Leichi (Laitu-laitu, Brown, *Journal*, 1918, 249).
124. Keramin.
125. Ta-ta-thi.
126. Muthi-muthi.
127. Wi-thai-ja.
128. Ita-ita.
129. Dhuduroa.
130. Wiradjuri.
131. Marowra.
132. Tongaranka.
133. Milpulko.
134. Naualko.
135. Barkinji.
136. Beri-ait.
137. Wongibon.
138. Ngeumba.
139. Wailwun.
140. Bulalli.
141. Kongait.
142. Wilya.
143. Pariunji.
144. Barunga.
145. Wombelbarra.
146. Kurnu.
147. Barrumbinya.
148. Murrawari.
149. Wollaroi.
150. Euahlayi.
151. Bigambul.
152. Kombaingeri.
153. Kamilaroi.
154. Geawegal.
155. Awabakal.
156. Chepara.
157. Turrbal.
158. Kaiabara.
159. Kabi.
160. Wakka.
161. Warbaa.
162. Tarbibelung.
163. Maryborough bura-tribes.
164. Thibura.
165. Emon.
166. Mundainbura.
167. Yakunbura.
168. Tilbabura.
169. Auanbura.
170. Terbabura.
171. Wakelbura.
172. Bithelbura.
173. Kongulu.
174. Kuinmurbura.
175. Various bura-tribes (Kuke-bura, Yarubura, etc.).
176. Yetti-marala.
177. Ungorri.
178. Badjeri.
179. Unghi.
180. Buntamurra.
181. Dirityangurra.
182. Kurnandaburi.
183. Babingurra.
184. Tarumbura.
185. Muthlerabura.
186. Dorobura.
187. Boanbura.
188. Mutabura.
189. Kumbukabura.
190. Munkibura.
191. Bingabura.
192. Dalebura.
193. Goa.
194. Wonamurra.
195. Yerrunthully.
196. Pitta-pitta.
197. Miorli.
198. Mallanpara (Tully River).
199. Kunganji (C. Grafton).
200. Koko-yellanji (Bloomfield River).

201. Kia (Proserpine River).
202. Koko-Yimidir.
203. Koko-lama-lama.
204. Koko-wara.
205. Koko-rarmul.
206. Gudang.
207. Kowrarega (Prince of Wales Island).
208. Yaraikanna.
209. Ngerrikuddi.
210. Kundara.
211. Koko-minni.
212. Koogobatha.
213. Karandee.
214. Myngie.
215. Mygoodano.
216. Miubi.
217. Mykoolon.
218. Gilbert River tribe.
219. Oboroondi.
220. Injilinji.
221. Workobongo.
222. Workia.
223. Kalkadoon.
224. Mitakoodi.
225. Mumandil.
226. Cowrana.
227. Yamandil.
228. Ewenyoon.
229. Niol-niol.
230. Nangamada.
231. Ngarla.
232. Kariera.
233. Widagari.
234. Namal.
235. Ngaluma.
236. Mardu-dhunera.
237. Injibandi.
238. Bailgu.
239. Targudi.
240. Ngadari.
241. Panjima.
242. Wirdinya.
243. Ngala-wonga.
244. Ina-wonga.
245. Churoro.
246. Bini-gura.
247. Noala.
248. Talainji.
249. Buduna.
250. Jiwali.
251. Tenma.
252. Warienga.
253. Baiong.
254. Maia.
255. Targari.
256. Ingarda.
257. Mălgăna.
258. Wajeri.
259. Watchandie.
260. Nooun.
261. Whajook and Perth tribe.
262. Kojonup and Eticup tribe.
263. Kokar.
264. Meenung.
265. Weel.
266. Meeraman.
267. Kunyung.
268. Muliarra.
269. Peedong.
270. Natingero.
271. Wonunda mining.
272. Yircla minung.
273. Tidni.
274. Tangara.
275. Wonkamarra.
276. Ngarra.
277. Eugoola.
278. Mayagoondoon.
279. Naungann.
280. Oonoomurra.
281. Yelina.
282. Yanda.
283. Moorloobulloo.
284. Karawalla.
285. Birria.
286. Kungerri.
287. Kungarditchi.
288. Mirkin.
289. Hinchinbrook tribe.
290. Granite Range tribe.
291. Walsh River tribe.
292. Ikelbara and other bara tribes (Halifax Bay).
293. Breeaba.
294. Cleveland Bay.
295. Mount Elliot tribe.
296. Mungerra.
297. Pegulloburra.
298. Bumbarra.
299. Owanburra.
300. Yuiperra and other burra tribes (Port Mackay).
301. Kaargooloo.
302. Yambeena.
303. Yangeeberra.
304. Torraburi.
305. Bimurraburra.
306. Kanoloo.
307. Toolooa.

308. Mooloola.
309. Goenpul.
310. Noonukul.
311. Wogee.
312. Maranoa tribe.
313. Balonne and Moonie River tribe (a sub-group of the Wollaroi).
314. Peechera.
315. Wonnarua.
316. Mount Gambier tribe.
317. Yendakarangu.
318. Thurrawal.
319. Wogait.
320. Pongo-pongo.
321. Ngarigo.
322. Ominee.
323. Bathurst district tribe.
324. Wuku-Wuku (Burnett River).
325. Karingbool (Mackenzie River).
326. Nimbalda.
327. Cammeraygal.
328. Wiimbaio.
329. Herbert River tribes.
330. Nannine tribe.
331. Gringai (Port Stephens tribe).
332. Annan River tribe.
333. Muruburra.
334. Wapio-burra.
335. Rawlinson Range tribe.
336. Clarence River tribe.
337. Rockhampton tribe.
338. Broadsound tribe.
339. New Norcia tribe.
340. Minnal Yungar tribe.
341. Newcastle tribe.
342. Perth tribe.
343. Pinjarra tribe.
344. Geographe Bay tribe.
345. Kargadar.
346. Peopleman.
347. Warrangoo.
348. Ngokwurring.
349. Macleay tribe.
350. Hastings tribe.
351. Roebuck Bay tribe.
352. Mungaberra.
353. Kudenji.
354. Wanji.
355. Kadjerong.
356. Limba Karadjee.
357. Wellesley Island tribe.
358. Birdhawal.
359. Towerhill tribes.
360. Koko Wangara (Mitchell River tribes).
361. Yidinyi.
362. Yindi tribe.
363. Milya uppa.
364. Mulya napa.
365. Ooloopooloo.
366. Plinara.
367. Tjiras.
368. Wommana.
369. Kisha (Hall's Creek tribe).
370. Nigena.
371. Keha.
372. Lunga.
373. Mayoo.
374. Wolmaharr.
375. Gundungurra.
376. Thornborough tribe.
377. Castleton tribe.
378. Koko-olkulo.
379. Koko-tabul.
380. Koko-manjoen.
381. Koko-wansin.
382. Ringa-Ringa.
383. Thangati.
384. Pikumbul.
385. Chauan.
386. Mt. Margaret tribes.
387. Angardie.
388. Quearriburra.
389. Goonine.

For tribes 370–74, see R. H. Mathews : *Division of some West Australian Tribes*, American Anthropologist N.S., II. 186, and id., *The Wombya Organization*, ibid., 497. The localization given by Matthews is approximate, he only tells us that these (and other tribes) inhabit the territory indicated on his map, but we cannot ascertain the relative position of the tribes.

According to R. H. Mathews, *Vocabulary of the Ngarrugu Tribe*, Journal and Proceedings of the Royal Society of New South Wales, 1908, 335, No. 358 (Birdhawal) would be the same tribe as No. 109 (Biduelli), which is, of course, possible if the tribe extended farther inland from the coast than indicated by Howitt.

The line of division indicates territories occupied by North and South Australian languages according to P. W. Schmidt.

ABBREVIATIONS

FRAZER, J. G.: Totemism and Exogamy, 1910 = *T. & E.*
FRAZER, J. G.: Folklore in the Old Testament, 1919 = *F. O. T.*
FREUD, Sigm.: Totem and Taboo, 1919 = *T. & T.*
HOWITT, A. W.: The Native Tribes of South-East Australia, 1904 = Howitt: *N. T.*
International Journal of Psycho-Analysis = *I. J. P. A.*
Internationale Zeitschrift für Psychoanalyse = *I. Z. Pa.*
Jahrbuch für psychoanalytische und psychopathologische Forschungen = *Jahrbuch.*
Journal of American Folk-Lore = *J. A. F.-L.*
Journal of the Royal Anthropological Institute = *J. R. A. I.* or *J. A. I.*
Journal of the Royal Geographical Society = *J. R. G. S.*
MATHEWS, R. H.: Ethnological Notes on the Aboriginal Tribes of New South Wales and Victoria, 1905 = Mathews: *E. N.*
MATHEWS, R. H.: Folklore of the Australian Aborigines, 1899 = Mathews: *F. A. A.*
RIVERS, W. H. R.: History of Melanesian Society, 1914 = Rivers: *H. M. S.*
ROTH, W. E.: Superstition, Magic and Medicine, 1903 = Roth: *S. M. M.*
SPENCER, B.: Native Tribes of the Northern Territory of Australia, 1914 = Spencer, *N. T. N. T. A.*
SPENCER AND GILLEN: Native Tribes of Central Australia, 1899 = Spencer and Gillen: *N. T.*
SPENCER AND GILLEN: Northern Tribes of Central Australia, 1904 = Spencer and Gillen, *Nor. T.*
STREHLOW: Die Aranda und Loritjastämme in Zentral-Australien, 1908 = Strehlow: *A. & L.*
TAPLIN, G.: Folklore, Manners, Customs and Languages of the South Australian Aborigines, 1879 = Taplin: *F.-L., etc.*
Zeitschrift für Ethnologie = *Z. E.*

ABBREVIATIONS USED IN LEGENDS OF MAPS

(*Cf. the Abbreviations used in the Text.*)

ANGAS = G. F. Angas, *Savage Life and Scenes in Australia and New Zealand*, London, 1847.
BRAIM = Th. H. Braim, *History of New South Wales*, 1846.
C. = E. M. Curr, *The Australian Race*, 1884–86, I.–III.
F.L. = *Folk-Lore.*
FRASER = J. Fraser, *The Aborigines of New South Wales*, Sydney, 1892.
H. = A. W. Howitt, *The Native Tribes of South-East Australia*, 1904.
MATHEW, TWO TRIBES = J. Mathew, *Two Representative Tribes of Queensland*, 1910.
MITT. D. ANTHR. GES. = *Mittheilungen der anthropologischen Gesellschaft in Wien.*
OLDFIELD = A. Oldfield, "On the Aborigines of Australia," *Transactions of the Ethnological Society*, III.
PARKER = K. L. Parker, *The Euahlayi Tribe*, 1905.
ROTH, E. S. = W. E. Roth, "Ethnological Studies among the North-West Central Queensland Aborigines," 1897.

All the other papers published by Roth are included in the North Queensland Ethnography, Bulletin, Records of the Australian Museum. They are quoted either as " Bull." (adding the number) or with short title, as for instance, " Initiation," " Burial."

SP. I. = Spencer and Gillen, *N. T.*

SP. II. = Spencer and Gillen, *Nor. T.*

SP. III. = Spencer, *N. T. N. T. A.*

STR. = Strehlow, *A. & L.*

THOMAS = N. Thomas, *Kinship Organizations and Group Marriage in Australia*, 1906.

AUSTRALIAN TOTEMISM

CHAPTER I

THE PROTO-TOTEMIC COMPLEX IN SOUTH-EAST AUSTRALIA

Definition of totemism.

AFTER the great synthetic effort represented by Frazer's "Corpus" of totemism a marked tendency in the other direction has been recognizable in anthropological literature. The unity of the problem is questioned and a separate solution proposed for each geographical area.[1] This is a view to which I do not subscribe, and it is merely for convenience that the scope of inquiry will be limited to the classical land of British totemistic controversy. The solutions proposed are psychological, and as such, naturally, are not limited to any geographical area or race; if valid at all, they must be valid for humanity in general.

By totemism I mean, with Frazer, an intimate relation supposed to exist between a group of kindred people on the one side and species of natural or artificial objects on the other side,[2] or, expressed more psychologically, the self-projection of a social unit in a natural unit.[3] Although this definition or similar ones are generally stated at the outset of the inquiry, the necessary inference is seldom drawn, that the first thing to be accounted for in totemism is the group-to-group (viz. human group to animal group) character of the magical bond. This is clearly emphasized by Ankermann who, following Gräbner and Reuterskiöld, comes to the conclusion that totemism originates in the sympathy felt by man towards the animal species inhabiting the same geographical area.[4] We must

[1] Cf. A. van Gennep, *Tabou et Totémisme à Madagascare*, 1904, 321. Gennep, *Religions, Mœurs et Légendes*, 1911, IV. 99. A. M. Hocart, "Notes on Fijian Totemism," *Anthropos*, 1914, 737. J. R. Swanton, "The Social and Emotional Element in Totemism," *Anthropos*, 1914, 289. A. A. Goldenweiser, "Totemism, an Analytical Study," *J. A. F.-L.*, 1910, 267. Robert H. Lowie, "A New Conception of Totemism," *American Anthropologist*, 1913, 189. F. Boas, "The Origin of Totemism," *American Anthropologist*, 1916, 319.

[2] Frazer, *T. & E.*, IV. 3.

[3] Cf. Goldenweiser's psychological definition, l.c., 275.

[4] B. Ankermann: "Das Problem des Totemismus," *Korrespondenzblatt*, 1910, 80; E. Reuterskiöld, *Die Entstehung der Speisesakramente*, 1912, 80. Lays stress on the importance of animals for the self-sustenance of the savage. Id., *Anthropos*, 1914, 650; Gräbner, *Anthropos*, 1915, 16, 255.

not forget that the conditions of mutual distribution between the human groups and animal species to be argued from are not those in existence to-day, even in Australia. In that far-remote period the semi-human groups of our ancestors must have been scattered over the surface of the earth with much greater intervening distances than is the case at present, and the area claimed by each of these small groups must have been correspondingly larger. In this state of things the limits of a human group and animal species would be much more likely to coincide than they do at present. Thus we come to interpret certain savage myths as self-perceptions of the unconscious processes,[1] lying behind the totemic complex. "One origin frequently assigned by natives to these family names is that they were derived from some vegetable or animal being very common in the district which the family inhabited and that hence the name of this animal or vegetable became applied to the family."[2] Similarly the Arunta imagine that water-holes containing plenty of fish are inhabited by the spirit children of the fish-totem.[3] In North-Western Australia "it would seem that the totemic centre or ceremonial ground of many of the totems is in a part of the country where the totem species is plentiful. Thus the ceremonial grounds of the White Cockatoo and the Marsh Fly are in the creek at Balla-Balla, where these two species are numerous."[4]

At the root of totemism; the "psychical survival" of a biological unity with environment.

According to the Lillooet Indians, "the Upper Bridge River Country was inhabited by the Deer people who were afterwards transformed into deer: therefore deer are most plentiful in that country at the present day."[5] This original feeling of unity with environment as represented by its most conspicuous animal species is again in itself a self-perception of really existing unity, a psychical repetition of mimicry and other organic adaptations found in the animal world. As in material culture, it is man who begins to replace organic by super-organic evolution. Whilst the animal physically adopts or imitates the form of another animal species or the colour of its environment,[6]

[1] Cf. Ferenczi, *Contributions to Psycho-Analysis*, 184.

[2] G. Grey, *Journals of Two Expeditions to North-West and Western Australia*, 1841, II. 229; cf. id., *Vocabulary of the Dialects of South-Western Australia*, 1840, 4; R. Brown, "Description of the Natives of King George's Sound," *J. R. G. S.*, I. 43.

[3] C. Strehlow, *A. & L.*, II. 52, "Animals and plants which are prolific are the totems of a greater number of men than those which are more or less scarce"; R. H. Mathews, *E.N.* of New South Wales, 1905, 60. With regard to these myths see Haddon's theory in the *Proceedings of the British Association*, 1902.

[4] A. R. Brown, "Three Tribes of Western Australia," *J. A. I.*, 1913, 167.

[5] J. Teit, "The Lillooet Indians," *Jesup North Pacific Expedition*, V. 275. Cf. Róheim, "Primitive Man and Environment," *I. J. P.-A.*, II. 157–160.

[6] Ch. Darwin, *The Descent of Man*, 1898, I. 495. Hesse-Doflein, *Tierbau und Tierleben*, 1914, 376–415.

the savage identifies himself with the totem either by ceremonial or imaginative imitation.[1]

However, in totemic matters a difficulty solved means a fresh difficulty raised. If totems were originally local they must have been patrilinear, supposing marriage to be patrilocal, which is the rule at present in Australia.[2] But if we take the tribes that really possess this postulated system into account—the Yerkla—mining,[3] the Narrinyeri,[4] the Narrang-ga,[5] the Kurnai, [6] the Yuin [7]—it is contrary to the general opinion of anthropologists to suppose that these should have retained the original form of the totemistic complex.[8] It is frequently assumed that this is a secondary localization of the totem groups, an outcome of the change from matrilinear to patrilinear reckoning of descent.[9] However, this is far from certain and we shall see that this question is susceptible of a different interpretation from an ethnological point of view. At any rate, the period of human history in which the first origin of totemism must be placed hardly took into account descent as the word is now understood. There seems good reason to suppose that humanity inherited from its semi-brutal ancestors the form of society which has been called the Cyclopean family; a number of young males, young and adult females roaming about on a restricted area under the leadership of a single full-grown male.[10] In this state of society, tribe, clan and family are co-extensive units: or rather, the Cyclopean family (or horde) is the germ out of which these institutions are differentiated in the course of evolution. Legend seems to have conserved the traces of this stage of social origins. Nurunduri is represented as having led his sons, i.e. his tribe, down the southern shore of the lakes.[11] Similarly the Kulin report that Bunjil went up to the sky-land with all his people; the legend says his "sons."[12]

[1] Frazer, *T. & E.*, I. 25, 37, II. 8, III. 55.

[2] Cf. A. Lang, *The Secret of the Totem*, 1905, 121, who goes on to show that the non-local character of totemism must have been brought about by patrilocal marriage and female descent (p. 144).

[3] Howitt, *N. T.*, 129. See also Curr, *The Australian Race*, I. 402 (W. Williams).

[4] G. Taplin, *The Narrinyeri*, 1878, 63. Howitt, *N.T.*, 1904, 130, 131. T. Moriarty, *The Goolwa Clan of the Narrinyeri Tribe*. G. Taplin, *F.L., etc.*, 50.

[5] Howitt, *N. T.*, 130. Fison and Howitt, *Kamilaroi and Kurnai*, 1880, 285.

[6] Howitt, *N. T.*, 135. For the Chepara, ibid., 86.

[7] Howitt, *N. T.*, 133. Compare the discussion between Schmidt, "Die soziologische und religiös-ethische Gruppierung der australischen Stämme," *Z. E.*, 1909, 329, and Gräbner, "Zur australischen Religionsgeschichte," *Globus*, 96, 341.

[8] But see Gräbner, "Kulturkreise in Ozeanien," *Z. E.*, 1905, 28.

[9] Cf. Howitt and Fison, "From Mother-right to Father-right," *J. A. I.*, 1882. E. B. Tylor, "On a Method of Investigating the Development of Institutions," ibid., XVIII. 1889.

[10] Lang-Atkinson, *Social Origins and Primal Law*, 1903. N. W. Thomas, *Kinship Organizations and Group Marriage in Australia*, 1906, 63.

[11] G. Taplin, *The Narrinyeri*, 1878, 61.

[12] Howitt, l.c., 891.

The next stage in the evolution of humanity is the conflict between Old and Young, between the jealous Father and the grown-up Son, the prize of the victor—the cause of the conflict—being the women of the horde, the mothers, sisters and daughters. Now there is a class of myths in Australia termed the conflict myth, and hitherto interpreted as the survival of a primeval contest between antagonistic people or races,[1] the details of which seem to be explicable by this great primeval battle of social evolution.

The conflict myth.

According to the natives of North Victoria the world was created by beings called Nooralie, who existed a very long time ago. A very old man they call Nooralpily. The Murray natives also believe that beings called Nooralle created the world. Some of these had the shape of a crow, others lived as eagle-hawks. The two groups were incessantly at war with each other till they made peace and decided that the black-fellows should be divided into the classes of Eagle-hawk and Crow. In memory of this combat there is a song, "Strike the crow at the knee, I will pierce his father."[2] This wound on the leg is a sign that may serve as a clue to the inter-relationship of Australian myths. We find Bunjil fighting with Karwien (the Blue Heron) and spearing him on the thigh so that his legs shrivelled up and became very thin and always hang down as he flies.[3] Conversely, the identity of the actors is needed to prove the identity of the action. Now, Bunjil is the Eagle-hawk,[4] and a variant of the myth proves Karwien to be the Crow.

According to the natives of the Yarra River, Bundjil was the

[1] J. Mathew, *Eagle-hawk and Crow*, 1899, 14. A. Lang, *The Secret of the Totem*, 1905, 151. J. Mathew, *Two Representative Tribes of Queensland*, 1910, 34.

[2] R. Brough-Smyth, *The Aborigines of Victoria*, 1878, I. 425.

[3] Howitt, *N. T.*, 486.

[4] P. W. Schmidt, *Der Ursprung der Gottesidee*, 1912, 284, note 3. Bunjil changes himself into an eagle when he creates the world. Lauterer, *Australien und Tasmanien*, 1900, 286. I cannot make sure whether Lauterer has got his statement from some printed source, or possibly through settlers and missionaries. He mentions Schürmann as supplying him with information (p. 264). In South-West Australia the Walja, or Eagle-hawk, is supposed to be Mamangur, or father of all, whilst Wordung and Manytch (crow and cockatoo) are his nephews. There used to be a small tribe of Waljuk (that is, Eagle-hawks) in the neighbourhood of Beverley and York. The Eagle-hawk was supposed to have made all things into *noyyung* and *ngunning* (the two primary moieties), he himself being both *noyyung* and *ngunning*. His wife was the squeaker crow. Daisy M. Bates, "The Marriage Laws and some Customs of the Western Australian Aborigines," *Victorian Geographical Journal*, XXIII, XXIV. 47, 58. Quoted by Frazer, *T. & E.*, I. 563. The conflict between father and son was afterwards overlaid by the memory of the conflict between various groups of tribes, and this side of the question has not escaped the notice of anthropologists (J. Mathew, *Eagle-hawk and Crow*, 1899). Id., *Two Representative Tribes of Queensland*, 1910, 33. Schmidt, *Der Ursprung der Gottesidee*, 1912, 320. The learned editor of the *Anthropos* explains these myths both by a racial and an astral hypothesis. The latter rests on the usual constructions of the mythological school, and is, like the whole edifice, built up by these authors without the slightest foundation.

first human being. He created everything, including the second man Karwien (Crow) and his two wives. He did not create any wives for himself, but stole those belonging to Karwien. The possession of the two wives was then decided in single combat. Bundjil wounded his adversary's knee so that Karwien fell ill and shrivelled up like a skeleton. Then Bundjil changed him into a crow, took his wives and had many children by them.[1] If we take as our starting-point the assumption that Bundjil, the "All-father," represents really the all-father, the Jealous Sire of the primeval group, the conflict seems to reflect the sexual rivalry of Father and Son at the dawn of humanity. In our myths we find one of the *dramatis personæ* as the creator of the other—and on the other hand we have variants narrating the battle between Pundjel and his sons.[2] Is the second protagonist of the combat, the defeated party, a son, or what amounts to the same thing, a brother of Pundjel? The brother or son of Pundjel is called Pallyan, and is the guardian of the waters from whence he fishes the first women, Kunner-warra and Kuurouk.[3] On the other hand, the Crow figures as the originator of a flood,[4] at Lake Condah he sends the first rain.[5] The same myth mentions Eun-newt, the bat, as the first man. Now, Pallyan, the brother-son of Pundjil, is, in his relation to the god Pundjil, certainly the first man and his name means bat.[6] W. Schmidt is thus fully justified in identifying Karwien, the adversary of Bundjil, with his son and brother Pallyan.[7] The first fight of Australian mythology seems to be a family broil between father and son, and as to the cause: *cherchez la femme*! [8]

In trying to interpret the unconscious meaning of these myths, we must remember that they relate the victory of the father, which, as it is a reversal of the natural and inevitable course of events, can only be understood if we suppose them to be told from the point of view of the father. We have learnt from Freud the empiric rule that in the interpretation of dreams reversals go usually by pairs: and we find our text speaking of Bundjil as stealing his sons' wives and begetting children by them—a reversal of the racial and infantile Oedipus complex.

The myth of the Murray Blacks, in which Crow kills the son of Eagle and is killed in his turn by the Eagle, after which he comes

[1] Brough-Smyth, *The Aborigines of Victoria*, 1878, I. 425.
[2] Id., l.c., I. 446.
[3] Id., I. 427.
[4] Id., I. 430.
[5] Id., I. 462.
[6] Howitt, *N. T.*, 484.
[7] Schmidt, *Ursprung des Gottesidee*, 1912, 288, 302, 314. Id., "L'Origine de l'Idée de Dieu," *Anthropos*, 1909, IV. 285.
[8] The typical doubling of the women in Australian myths is probably to be accounted for by the two original marriage classes (phratries). Cf. Curr, *The Australian Race*, 1886, II. 165. The first man had two wives called Keelpara and Mookwara, hence the phratry names.

to life again, seems to belong to the same cycle.[1] The text of the myth is probably the result of a secondary elaboration; in the latent content we should have Crow as the son of Eagle, killing his father (brother). Remorse and retaliation follow; the murdered father comes to life again and kills his son. Crow is split into two mythic figures, Crow himself and the son of Eagle. This made it possible to transfer the animosity felt by Crow from the Eagle to Eagle's son, who is a mythical double both of the Eagle himself and of Crow. Crow killed by Eagle and coming to life again, corresponds to the initiates who revive after having been killed by the father—an hypothesis for which we shall find sufficient proof below in the connexion of initiation with the conquering of an eagle-monster. These views as to the original meaning of the Eagle-hawk–Crow myth are strikingly confirmed by a variant from the Kariera tribe in Western Australia, which shows the incest-complex at the root of the myth, with as slight displacement as might well be expected. "In the times long, long ago, there were two Eagle-hawks who were brothers and had for their wives two galahs. The Eagle-hawks were mothers' brothers to the Crow. The Eagle-hawks and their nephews always went out hunting together, the Eagle-hawks always taking the fattest animals that were killed. The Crow one day hid the fattest kangaroo and as the Eagle-hawks suspected this, they went into a cave near by to look for the meat. The Crow sealed up the entrance, went home to the camp, and cohabited with the Eagle-hawk's wives, who were the 'toa' (mothers-in-law) of the Crow, and with whom he was naturally forbidden even to speak." If we remember that the mother's brother is often invested with the social function of the father in primitive societies and that the mother-in-law-avoidance is really a repressed form of an incest-wish,[2] the Oedipus complex as the central element of the animal conflict myths comes out pretty clearly.[3] The Kariera tribe has at the present time what Brown calls Type I of Australian marriage systems, that is, a man marries the daughter of his mother's brother or some woman who stands to him in an equivalent relation.[4] It seems possible that the "daughter" is a substitute for the "mother" in these cases; that the action of the Crow represents something forbidden from the point of view of a later stage of society which, however, was permitted in a previous phase of evolution. "In Mota, in the Banks Group and

[1] R. Brough-Smyth, *The Aborigines of Victoria*, 1878, T. 451. Cf. for a parallel, T. Mathew, *Two Tribes*, 1910, 191, Fight of Crow and Hawk; and W. E. Roth, *S. M. M.*, 1903 (Boulia District). In Gippsland the same myth is told, only the mopoke takes the part of the crow.

[2] Freud, *Totem and Taboo*, 1919.

[3] A. R. Brown, "Three Tribes of Western Australia," *J. A. I.*, 1913, 169, 170. Subsequent punishment inflicted on returning eagle-hawks by the crows.

[4] Id., ibid., 190, 191.

in Pentecost in the New Hebrides, the term used for the wife of the mother's brother is one such as 'mateima' or 'lalagi,' which is applied to other potential wives, and where this kind of nomenclature exists, there is clear evidence of marriage with this relative."[1] If, in some islands, the wife of the mother's brother is classed with the mother, this certainly may mean non-marriageableness from the present point of view,[2] but in a still earlier phase of evolution may have meant identity: so that we should have a brother-sister marriage with a son of this incestuous union trying to have sexual relations with his own mother. Brother and sister marriage must have come about after the victory of the Brother Horde over the Paternal Tyrant and when it fell into disuse there still survived an incestuous desire for the father's sister (Cf. the custom of marrying the father's sister and the hostile attitude towards the father's sister's husband[3]) as a substitute of the mother. (Father's sister and mother designed by the same term.)[4] Thus social nomenclature seems to confirm the results of myth-analysis.

To return to Bundjil: the Eagle-hawk is certainly "Mamingorak," "Our Father," as the Wotjobaluk tell us,[5] the supernatural projection of the leader and father of the Cyclopean horde-family. His wives are the Ganawarra ("Black-Swan" double),[6] probably identical with the Ngalalbal ("Emu" double), the wives of Daramulun.[7] Daramulun again is another representative of the same mythical concept as Bunjil; he is the Eagle-hawk,[8] he is "Our Father."[9] Now, Howitt has another account seemingly contradictory to the first, and here Ngalalbal is the mother of Daramulun.[10] But we know better than to look for a contradiction where there is none, for the Father-Son conflict presupposes a state of things in which the concepts of mother and wife overlap one another.

Freud's view of totemism.

We must now consider another theory as to the origin of totemism. In *Totem and Taboo* Freud has pointed out that taboo is but the negative, inhibited form of a wish-fulfilment.[11] Thus Freud explains totemic exogamy as an exaggerated reaction against original incest; the taboo against killing the totem-animal as a displaced reaction against parricide.[12] The totem is directly spoken of as father,[13] more frequently as ancestor, which is a slightly veiled expression of the same complex.

[1] Rivers, *H. M. S.*, II. 1914, 18.
[2] Id., bid., 19.
[3] Rivers, Id., ibid., II. 21, 22.
[4] Id., ibid., II. 23.
[5] Howitt, *N. T.*, 49, 490, 491.
[6] Id., l.c., 491.
[7] Howitt, "The Jeraeil, or Initiation of the Kurnai Tribe," *J. A. I.*, 1884, XIII. 450.
[8] Cf. Schmidt, *Ursprung*, 346, 364.
[9] Howitt, *N. T.*, 494.
[10] Id., l.c., 495, "The two Ngalalbal, the mothers of Daramulun," p. 546. As to the doubling, see above.
[11] Freud, *Totem and Taboo*, 1919. Cf. Marett, "Is Taboo a Negative Magic," *The Threshold of Religion*, 1909, 85. Róheim, *Spiegelzauber*, 1919, 6.
[12] Freud, *Totem and Taboo*, 1919.
[13] Frazer, l.c., I. 9, 13, 423; IV. 278.

The sacrificial killing of the totem is interpreted by Freud as an unconscious symbolic repetition of parricide, the commensal union is a survival of the original anthropophagous feast. As the present-day totems are not direct survivals of their ancient prototype, the rudiments of this complex are rather to be looked for in inter-tribal myth and ritual than in the elements restricted to one of the totem clans. At the initiation ceremony on Melville Island a Yam ceremony is performed at the same time. The Yam called Kolamma has little roots called hairs, and is thus associated with the initiation rite of making hair grow and depilation.[1] When the Yams that are to be eaten are being cooked, the men keep on singing: "Yams, you are our fathers."[2]

Phratric totemism.

Undeniably the phratry organizations Eagle-hawk and Crow (similarly those of Emu-Kangaroo and the other animal-named phatries) have two of the three orthodox tests of totemism: exogamy and the animal as ancestor or eponymous hero. The wide geographical distribution seems to argue in favour of a survival from a period before the present tribes broke off from the parent stock.

Initiation ritual.

One of the manifest objects of the initiation rite is to remove the youths from the influence of their mothers. Thus amongst the Yuin it is a rule that during the period of probation the novice is absolutely prohibited from holding any communication with a woman, even his own mother. He must not even look at one, and this prohibition extends to the emu, for the emu is Ngalalbal, the mother of Daramulun.[3] All this is inculcated in the boys at the initiation ceremony. Moreover, as we already have seen and shall continue to see, fragments of quasi-totemistic ritual and belief are found constantly associated with these ceremonies.

The origin and the unconscious content of these rites has been elucidated by Reik in an ingenious essay.[4] According to his theory the monster or spirit who, in the exoteric myth, swallows the boys is the "eject"[5] of the inimical tendencies unconsciously felt by the elder generation against the younger, whilst the feelings of sympathy become manifest in the protective attitude assumed by the initiators towards the novices. This inimical tendency lies at the root of the various trials, tortures and mutilations to which the youths are subjected. The fictive killing and various mutilations have been in the course of evolution substituted for actual murder, whilst the rite of circumcision is an attenuated castration. The whole ritual originates in the unconscious fear of retribution on the

[1] B. Spencer, *N. T. N. T. A.*, 1914, 92, 93
[2] Id., ibid., 102, 103.
[3] Howitt, l.c., 560.
[4] Th. Reik, "Die Pubertätsriten der Wilden," *Imago*, IV. 125, 109.
[5] Cf. Baldwin, *Mental Development in the Child and the Race*, 1911.

part of the elders; they themselves were unconscious rebels against their fathers in youth and now they wish to forestall the breaking out of similar feelings on the part of their sons. Thus the primeval conflict for the women of the horde is reacted in the initiation ritual, but the unconscious psychical material is subjected to a rearrangement from the viewpoint of the elders. In the real conflict the younger generation was victorious; they murdered the Father whose imago was afterwards resuscitated in their own psyche. Here we find the youths killed by the ancestral spirit and then brought to life again. The circumcision as symbolical castration marks the nature of the offence for which the youths were punished according to the law of talion. The amnesia for the past which the youths have to mimic on returning to the camp is symbolic of the repression of the feelings of childhood: they are to forget the nature of their feelings toward their mother, the first object of their infantile desire.[1] It has not escaped the notice of Reik that we have here the same psychic complex that Freud found at the root of totemism,[2] the difference being mainly in the rearrangement and the secondary elaboration to which the unconscious material has been submitted.

The Emu and Daramulun.

Returning now to the part played by the emu in these ceremonies, we find it constantly represented as a bird which is: (*a*) taboo to the novices,[3] (*b*) hunted by Daramulun, Baiamai, etc. As we generally find that social rites have like neurotic symptoms, corresponding positive and negative aspects, it seems probable that one and the same meaning must underlie the

[1] Reik, *Imago*, IV. 197.

[2] Id., ibid., 131, 140, 192. This theory of the origin of initiation rites is corroborated by Australian evidence. The ritual is always instituted by the "All-father," and is frequently traced to a conflict between the Father and his disobedient Son. Cf. R. H. Mathews, "The Bŭrbŭng of the Wiradthuri Tribes," *J. A. I.*, 1895, XXV. 297. K. L. Parker, *The Euahlayi Tribe*, 1905, 67. In relation to the novices, Baiame represents the sublimated benevolent type of paternal feelings, whilst the aggressivity is transferred to and objectivated in the figure of Daramulun. Daramulun is said to have feasted on some of the novices instead of initiating them; here we have the unconscious meaning and aggressive tendency of the mutilation, which is repressed in reality, thus returning to consciousness in myth. The cycle of legends in which circumcision with the stone knife is said to have been introduced by the culture heroes, and supplanted the rite of circumcising the novices with the fire-stick, and thus causing their death (Howitt, l.c., 646, 650; Spencer and Gillen, *N. T.*, 394, 397, 398. Id., *Nor. T.*, 425), points in the same direction. The rite is here also represented as the mitigation of a previous, purely aggressive action: the boys who were circumcised by fire all died in consequence.

[3] "Emus they kill for their fathers only; these birds being reserved and held sacred for the sole use of the old men and women."—J. Ph. Townsend, *Rambles and Observations in New South Wales*, 1849, 116, quoting Mitchell, p. 305. "None of the natives would eat of the emu, and the reasons they gave were that they were young men, and that none but older men who had 'gins' were allowed to eat it, adding that it would make young men all over boils and eruptions."—T. L. Michell, *Three Expeditions into the Interior of Eastern Australia*, 1838, II. 29 (crossing the Lachlan, near Goulburn Range, 60, 346). "No young men are allowed to eat the flesh or eggs of the emu." After this lapse of the time they may eat any-

f the bird to the youths and its use by the spirit of initiation. .oria the fat of the emu is held sacred; it is forbidden to throw y because it is believed once to have been the fat of a woman.[1] e Bŭrbŭng of the Wiradthuri tribes various mythical scenes emonstrated by drawings, paintings or carvings to the novices. Baiamai is said to have been hidden in a tree surrounded by bushes, waiting near a water-hole, according to the native custom for the emu to come and drink. He then speared it with his long spear and it ran away some distance before it fell. Baiamai ran after it, tripped over a log and fell in the position delineated.[2] Evidently the same episode is alluded to on the Bora ground of the Kamilaroi, where we see the figure of an emu with a spear sticking in its body.[3] In another account of the Wiradjuri ceremonies the emu is hunted, not by Baiamai, but by Daramulun. We see two footprints of an emu represented at a little distance from each other, made when trying to escape from Daramulun, besides the figure of the emu where it fell when he killed it.[4] At the initiation ceremonies of the Yuin we again have the emu, only acted instead of drawn. Gliding through the scene are two figures who represent the two Ngalalbal, the mothers of Daramulun.[5] We remember that the mothers are also the wives of Daramulun and we know that hunting, chasing, pursuing often symbolize coitus in the unconscious.[6] Evidently we have in the pictures of the emu-hunt a representation of the central complex of the initiation rites and totemism: the emu symbolizes the mother who is incestuously speared by her own son. That is why the novice must not look at a woman, not even at his own mother, and this prohibition extends to the emu, the mother of Daramulun.[7] This explains the taboo on emu fat as the fat of

thing except emu flesh, which must always be brought to the old men in camp and never eaten by young men at all.—W. E. Roth, "On Certain Initiation Ceremonies," *North Queensland Ethnography*, Bull. 12, 1909, 185). Emu fat: penalty —abnormal development of the penis (vulva).—Spencer and Gillen, *N. T.*, 1899, 471, 472; id., *Nor. T.*, 366, 611, 614.

[1] R. Brough-Smyth, *The Aborigines of Victoria*, 1878, I. 450. "The sacred pieces . . . can only be eaten by the very old men."—A. W. Howitt, *N. T.*, 1904, 763. Ceremony at killing of first emu.—K. L. Parker, *The Euahlayi Tribe*, 1905, 24. Emu-flesh taboo for pregnant women.—H. Klaatsch, "Schlussbericht ueber seine Reise nach Australien," *Z. E.*, 1907, 656 (Niol-Niol). Spencer and Gillen, *N. T.*, 617 (Warramunga, Gnangi, Binbinga). Boys who are about to be initiated are forbidden to eat emu and kangaroo.—A. R. Brown, "Three Tribes of Western Australia," *J. A. I.*, 1913, 174. Byama says his sons should be made young men so that they might be free to marry wives, eat emu "flesh" (cf. the emu-wives).—K. L. Parker, *Australian Legendary Tales*, 94.

[2] R. H. Mathews, "The Bŭrbŭng of the Wiradthuri Tribes, *J. A. I.*, 1895, XXV. 300.

[3] Id., "The Bora, or Initiation Ceremonies of the Kamilaroi," *J. A. I.*, 1894, XXIV. 416. Cf. note 1.

[4] Howitt, l.c., 585, 586.

[5] Id., l.c., 546.

[6] Cf. W. Stekel, *Die Sprache des Traumes*, 1911, 144, 147.

[7] Howitt, l.c., 360. If we accept the undoubtedly ingenious, though unproven conjectures of Father Schmidt, we get further points of interest for psycho-analytical

a woman, and also that the breaking through of his taboo, the first emu hunt of the young initiate, should be the occasion of a special ceremony.

These conclusions may appear somewhat strained, especially to those who are not acquainted with the methods of psycho-analysis, but a remarkable legend of the Narrinyeri, which seems to close the chain of argument, should give these interpretations the benefit of the doubt. We shall try to explain the myth of the elopement and recapture of two women by a later extension of the Oedipus complex, accounting for the doubling of the women by the extension of the family-complex to the dichotomous tribe.

Nepelle and Wyungare.

The Narrinyeri relate how Wyungare was produced by his mother's excrements without a father:[1]

> He was a "narumbe" or kaingani, that is, a novice from the beginning. He lived among the reeds at Oulawar; Nepelle's two wives admired his handsome form and fell in love with him. So they seized the first opportunity to visit his hut and finding that he was asleep they made a noise with their feet outside, like two emus running past and awoke the hunter, who jumped up and ran out expecting to see some game. He took them as his wives. Nepelle set fire to the hut and they were awakened by the burning flames. They ran along the shore of the lake pursued by fire till at last they saved themselves by plunging into the water. Wyungare, trying to escape the vengeance of Nepelle, then tied a line to a spear and hurled it at the heavens; by means of a line attached to the spear he pulled himself and afterwards the two women up. He is said to sit up there and fish for men with a fishing spear, and when people start in their sleep it is said to be because he touches them with the point of his weapon.[2]

interpretation. He equates Birrahngooloo, the favourite wife of Baiamai, with the emu (l.c., p. 363), and supposes Daramulun to have lost one foot in the fight with Baiamai, who challenged him as he hunted the emu, which was sacred to Baiamai. Schmidt, l.c., 347. "Als ein Grund des Gegensatzes zwischen beiden wird angegeben, dass Daramulum das dem Baiamai heilige Emu gejagt, *d.h. der Frau des Baiamai nechgestellt habe*" (l.c., 366. The italics are mine. This sentence contains also the correct psycho-analytical interpretation of the unconscious meaning of the chase.) If Father Schmidt is on the right track with his conjectures, we have here the complete Oedipus complex. Baiamai is the father, Ngalalbal the mother, Daramulun the son, with the subsequent castration (represented as the loss of a leg; cf. the knee-wound in the Eagle-hawk and Crow myths) as the well-known talion-punishment of incest.

[1] Cf. Origin of the blacks out of the fæces of Anjea. W. E. Roth, *S. M. M.*, 15. On these well-known infantile sex theories see below. Possibly there is also some connexion between the birth of this deified novice and eating human ordure as an initiation ceremony. Before being made a young man a youth is called Kurno, i.e. excrement by the Wiimbaio (Howitt, l.c., 739).

[2] G. Taplin, *The Narrinyeri, an Account of the Tribes of South Australian Aborigines*, 1878, 56–58.

So much for the myth itself; the conclusions will follow. Two points must be emphasized in this myth. First, there is some connexion between the legends of the elopement type and the ritual of initiation. On the surface of the affair, Wyungare is the initiate who breaks through the principal taboo of the ritual and elopes with the wives of the elders, a sin for which he is punished by death. But this death involves the unconscious admiration of the sin committed—it is a species of apotheosis. Unconsciously both the initiation ritual and the elopement legend turn on the Oedipus complex. Second, the two women of the elopement legend are emus, identical with the animal hunted by Baiamai and with the mother of Daramulun. It is the last point that indicates the direction for the further analysis of the myth. As its principal hero is actually made responsible for a dream experience we may try and explain the legend according to the principles of dream-interpretation.

The escape from fire with the subsequent plunge into water is evidently the closing episode of a vesical dream and is determined by urethral eroticism.[1] This interpretation enables us to discriminate the parallel versions of the legend. Nurundere dwelt at Tulurrug with four children and two wives. His two wives ran away from him, he pursued them with his children to Encounter Bay, and there, seeing them at a distance, he exclaimed in anger, "Let the waters arise and drown them." So the waters arose in a terrible flood and, overtaking the fugitives, they were overwhelmed and drowned. Nepelle was transported by the flood to heaven; the dense part of the Milky Way is said to be the canoe of Nepelle floating in the heavens. Its owner ascended by the same means as Wyungare had done.[2] This parallel version replaces the Nepelle of the former variant by Nurundere and Wyungare by Nepelle so that Nurundere, Nepelle and Wyungare might, if such efforts of systematization were allowable, be taken for representatives of three descending generations. At any rate, it helps us to understand the unconscious meaning of the legend if we substitute Nurundere, the Narrinyeri All-father, for the hazy and ill-defined figure of Nepelle: we thus obtain Wyungare, the initiate, the youth at the

[1] These easily recognizable dreams nearly all contain the elements of *water* (rain, flood, sometimes fire: all symbolical of urine), and *running* or hurried motion in general, which represents an effort to escape from enuresis, according to Rank, *Die Symbolschichtung im Wecktraum Jahrbuch*, IV. 69, but certainly over-determined in the same sense as hunting is (see above), and symbolical of coitus. This and the parallelism between the elements of vesical and birth-dreams (Rank, ibid., 80) explains the connexion between the elopement and the flood-episode. Cf. also, Havelock Ellis, *The World of Dreams*, 1911, 88, 89, 96, 165. As to the connexion between flood-legends and the birth of the hero, see Rank, *Der Mythus von der Geburt des Helden*, 1909; Gerland, *Der Mythus von der Sintflut*, 1912, 94. The river Mayanga was said "to have taken its rise from the spot where a princess gave birth to a child, and to have been caused by a birth-flood" (T. Roscoe, *The Baganda*, 1911, 318).

[2] Taplin, l.c., 57, 58.

age of puberty, stealing the emu-wives of the All-father. The next version contains proof that Wyungare is Nurundere's son, and is furthermore clear evidence of the urethral-erotic origin of the flood-episode. Nurundere was a tall and powerful man, who lived in the east with two wives and had several children. His two wives ran away from him and he went in search of them. Continuing his pursuit, he arrived at Freeman's Nob and there made water, from which circumstance the place is called Kainjenauld (kainjamin—to make water). At length he found his two wives at Toppong. He beat them, but they escaped again and he was now tired of pursuing them, so he ordered the tide to rise and drown them. Nurundere, when he arrived at his journey's end, did not find his son; he made fast one end of a string to his spear, threw the other end which his son caught hold of, and so helped himself along to his father. This line is still the guide by which the dead find their way to Nurundere. When a man dies, Nurundere's son, who first found the way by means of the line to his father, throws it to the dead man, who is conducted to him in like manner.[1] The "spear-chain or the heaven-line" clearly proves Wyungare to be Nurundere's son.

If we interpret the animal-named phratries or matrimonial classes as survivals of what may be termed the proto-totemic complex, we may search for further traces of this complex on the lines indicated by them.

Kangaroo and Emu.

Another animal pair named Kangaroo-Emu seem to be next in importance to Eagle-hawk and Crow.[2] There is good reason to believe that the anthropocentrical complexes projected into the animal world were riveted at a comparatively early period on these two species. For instance, in the Kariera, Namal and Injibandi tribes, a hunter, when he has killed a kangaroo or an emu, takes a portion of the fat of the dead animal, placing the fat aside. This turns into a spirit-baby, which is directed by him to enter a certain woman, who thus becomes pregnant. This animal or plant is not the totem of the child: in a very large number of cases that animal is either the kangaroo or the emu.[3] In the so-called "Yungar" languages the word "yungar" means both "man" and "kangaroo."[4] Again at King George's Sound we find the belief

[1] H. E. A. Meyer, "Manners and Customs of the Aborigines of the Encounter Bay Tribes in Woods," *Native Tribes of South Australia*, 1879, 205, 206.

[2] Cf. Schmidt, "L'origine de l'Idée de Dieu," *Anthropos*, 1909, 240, 241. N. W. Thomas, *Kinship Organizations and Group Marriage in Australia*, 1906, 83.

[3] A. R. Brown, "Beliefs Concerning Childbirth in some Australian Tribes," *Man*, 1912, No. 96. Id., "Three Tribes of Western Australia," *J. R. A. I.*, 1913, 168.

[4] Schmidt, "Die Gliederung der Australischen Sprachen," *Anthropos*, 1912, 474. Curr, *The Australian Race*, 1886, I. 276, 322–63. R. Brown, "Description of the Natives of King George's Sound (Swan River Colony)," *J. R. G. S.*, 1831, I. 50.

that if women eat a lot of kangaroo flesh they will bear children.[1] According to Bonwick the more western portion of aboriginals in Tasmania had no idea of a future existence. They thought they were like the kangaroo.[2] Amongst the Wailwun of the Upper-Hunter River the word "Buba" (father) is used as the name of an old kangaroo—father of the whole race of kangaroos whose thigh bone (4 feet long and 8 inches round) is preserved and carried about by the members of the kangaroo totem.[3]

The Manning, Hastings and Mackay tribes tell a myth of two brothers named Byama, who change themselves into big, strong kangaroos.[4] The personality of Baiamai seems to form a natural link between the mythical cycles of the kangaroo and emu. Amongst the Wiradthuri, Baiamai is also called Nguruin-dinang-ganang, that is the one with emu-feet.[5]

Traces of Baiamai's emu-footedness appear also in a myth of the Kamilaroi. A man decided to go towards the setting sun, to the home of Baiame, the ancestor of the tribe. After having travelled several days, he came to a place inhabited by a tribe of Blacks who had the bodies of men and the legs and feet of an emu. They were called Dhinnabarruda, owing to their forked feet, and they always tried to touch the feet of the passers-by, which, if they succeeded, would be transformed into emu's feet like their own.[6]

This peculiarity of Baiamai is shared by two of his colleagues in Central Australia. The Altjira of the Arunta is called Altjira iliinka (ilia=emu, inka=feet) and is described as a great big, red-skinned man with long hair and emu-feet.[7] The western Luritja

[1] R. Brown, l.c., 30. The eating of kangaroo flesh is, for these tribes, who have the same word for man and kangaroo, an unconscious equivalent for cannibalism. On eating human flesh as a cause of supernatural birth, see E. S. Hartland, *The Legend of Perseus*, I. 87.

[2] H. Ling Roth, *The Aborigines of Tasmania*, 1899, 57.

[3] Honery, "Australian Languages and Traditions, Wailwun," *J. A. I.*, 1877, VII. 250. Cf. "Bubu" as the name of the bull-roarer. R. H. Mathews, "The Bŭrbŭng of the Wiradthuri Tribes," *J. A. I.*, 1895, XXV. 297; and H. Hale, *United States Exploring Expedition*, 1846, 113. E. M. Curr, *The Australian Race*, III. 328, 384.

[4] R. H. Mathews, *F. A. A.*, 1899, 23. On the kangaroo as culture-hero: "Tamda—a large reddish kangaroo—a fabulous person from whom the usage of tattooing is derived, and who was afterwards transformed into a kangaroo." G. Teichelmann and C. W. Schurmann, *Outlines of a Grammar, Vocabulary and Phraseology of the Aboriginal Language of South Australia*, 1840, 44.

[5] Günther, *Grammar and Vocabulary of the Aboriginal Dialect called Wirradhuri*, in Threlkeld, *An Australian Language as Spoken by the Awabakal*, 1892, 94.

[6] R. H. Mathews, *F. A. A.*, 15. On supernatural beings with emu-feet, cf. Leonhardi, "Über einige religiöse und totemistische Vorstellungen der Aranda und Loritja," *Globus*, XCI. 28*f*. Basedow, "Über Felsgravierungen in Zentral-Australien," *Z. E.*, 1907, 716.

[7] C. Strehlow, *A. & L.*, I. 1. Cf., "Ulthaana (spirit), a gigantic man in the sky with an immense foot like that of an emu." F. J. Gillen, "Notes on Some Manners and Customs of the Aborigines," *Horn Scientific Expedition*, 1896, IV. 183.

give the same description of their Tukura.[1] The emu is forbidden to the Wiradjuri novices on account of its being Baiame's food.[2] At the initiation ceremonies of the Yuin the dance of Ngalalbal, mother and wife (see above) of Daramulun, is performed.[3] The latter account contains two further pregnant hints as to the unconscious meaning of these beliefs: (*a*) the animal species on which the proto-totemic complex is riveted is connected with the initiation ceremonies, (*b*) the emu is represented as the mother of the spirit of initiation. It is more than a coincidence that the name of the emu-footed supreme being of the Arunta should be Altjira, the same word meaning also the mother's totem.[4]

The eschatological significance of the emu is certainly connected with its function in the initiation ritual as well as with its meaning as a mother symbol. (Cf. on the connexion between the entrance into Heaven and initiation: "The custom of knocking out their two front teeth is connected with their entry into Heaven."[5]) A number of emus are driven past the newly arrived spirit in the realm of Tha-tha-pulli; at one of these the weapon is hurled and the emu stricken down. When they see a shooting-star they believe it to be the passage of such a nulla-nulla through space and they say: "Tha-tha-pulli is trying the strength of some new spirit."[6]

In former times the emu was a blackfellow, now he is a constellation and holds two strings which are joined to the earth to keep it balanced.[7] The Euahlayi say that the moon, when wishing to escape from the spirits who stand round the sky holding it up, to take part in the important work of baby-manufacturing, takes the shape of an emu.[8] This may be compared to the part played by emu fat as a cause of conception and to the general meaning of the emu as a mother-symbol. The emu-hunt of the soul corresponds to the emu-tabu of the novices and the emu-hunt of the initiation-spirit. (On the connexion between initiation and the other world see below.) Traces of the magico-religious importance of the emu can be found all over Australia. "A mixture of human fat and emu is applied to the wound."[9] "Emu fat and ochre is the universal remedy

[1] Strehlow, *A. & L.*, 1908, II. 1.

[2] Howitt, *N. T.* 588.

[3] Howitt, l.c., 546. On Ngalalbal as Daramulun's wife, see above.

[4] Strehlow, l.c., II. 57.

[5] E. Palmer, "Notes on some Australian Tribes," *J. A. I.*, XIII. 291.

[6] A. L. Cameron, "Notes on Some Tribes of New South Wales," *J. A. I.*, 1884, XIX. 365. Id., "Traditions and Folk-Lore of the Aborigines of New South Wales," *Science of Man*, 1903, 46.

[7] A. T. Peggs, "Notes on the Aborigines of Roebuck Bay, Western Australia," *Folk-Lore*, XIV. 362.

[8] K. L. Parker, *The Euahlayi Tribe*, 1905, 98.

[9] Shaw, *Overland Corner Tribe, River Murray, Rankbirit.* Taplin, *F. L., etc.*, 1879, 29.

for wounds. The medicine man imitates the cry of the emu when touching the sick with his magical instrument." [1]

The proto-totemic complex.

Our position thus is that the widespread therio-morphic elements of the initiation ritual on the one hand, and of mythology on the other, are to be regarded as the divergent survivals of what we call the proto-totemic complex, that is of a quasi-totemic organization resembling the present totem clans in certain respects, which also survives in a more direct line in the animal-named marriage classes. We have shown that one of the eponymous heroes of these marriage classes, the Eagle-hawk, symbolizes the Fathers, the elder generation in mythology: it is in accord with our theory to find the Eagle-hawk playing an important part in initiation ritual. Important differences between the two types of totemic complexes cannot be overlooked. In the proto-totemic organization postulated by our hypothesis, clan and horde must have been co-extensive, and a dual organization with two totems (Eagle-hawk and Crow) symbolizing the Fathers and Sons (and thus allies in certain respects yet enemies in others) must have existed. As to the theory of a connexion between marriage-classes and age-grades, see Cunow.[2] Our views agree in some measure with Rivers,[3] though we have a completely different theory to explain the origin of the dual system and lay more stress on psychic factors of evolution and less on culture contact. Nevertheless, as remarked above, it is evident that both factors have contributed their share to the origin of the Eagle-hawk and Crow myths. With Frazer, we think the dual organization to have been once universal in mankind, a step in the evolution of society, and to have been universally connected with some form of totemism.[4] We also follow Frazer in regarding the dual organization as the result of a fission, but not as something that was deliberately instituted by the elders of the tribe. If our theory is correct, it must have originated in inhibitions with regard to certain women, which arose as the psychical after-impression of innumerable conflicts between the Fathers and the Sons of the tribe.

The Eagle-hawk in initiation ritual.

The tribes within fifty miles of Maryborough held a Dora (initiation ceremony), when some old man announced that he had had a vision of the Murang (Eagle-hawk), which is the fighting bird.[5] The tribes practising the Dolgarrity ceremony have performances in which either the

[1] H. Basedow, "Anthropological Notes made on the South Australian Government North-West Prospecting Expedition," *Transactions of the Royal Society of South Australia*, 1904, XXVIII. 23, 27.

[2] *Die Verwandtschaftorganisationen der Australneger*, 1894.

[3] *H. M. S.*, 1914, II. 56.

[4] Cf. Frazer, *F. O. T.*, 1919, II. 223.

[5] A. W. Howitt, *N. T.*, 1904, 599. As W. Schmidt remarks, the same word means also "snake" (sex-symbol), "animal," "flesh," and also totem in the Wakka language. Schmidt, *Ursprung der Gottesidee*, 1912, 364. J. Mathew, *Two Representative Tribes of Queensland*, 1910, 195, 228, 231.

Eagle-hawk or the Crow is imitated.[1] It is well known that a prominent feature of initiation ceremonies all over the world is the death and resurrection of the novices. But if we take into account the unconscious elements on which the ceremony is founded we come to regard this as the result of a fore-conscious rearrangement. The ceremony originally commemorates the death of the paternal tyrant with his subsequent (endo-psychical) resurrection. This throws a new light on the Song of Yibai in the Yuin initiation ceremonies. The song refers to Malian, that is Eagle-hawk, in connexion with Yibai (one of the marriage classes), Daramulun being also Malian. The death, burial and resurrection of a man named Yibai of the totem Malian was acted,[2] and as there is habitually a close connexion between the persons acting and the scenes enacted,[3] we may suppose that the death and resurrection of the Eagle-hawk was meant.

The Eagle-hawk as cannibal monster.

Before we continue the analysis of the connexion between the Eagle-hawk and initiation we must comment on the different rôle the Eagle-hawk plays in certain legends from the one which he plays in the myths that account for the institution of the matrimonial classes. In the latter the Eagle-hawk-hero plays the part of the respected father; in the legends we are about to analyse he is an inimical power, a monster who must be destroyed by the paternal hero-god of the Baiame-type, the culture hero of puberty ceremonies. The Wailwun of the Upper Hunter River tell us about a bad spirit called Mullion (eagle) who lived on a very high tree at Girra on the Barwon and came down devouring men. They tried to drive him away by setting fire to the tree; but the wood they piled up at the foot of the tree was pushed back by invisible hands. At last Baiame told a man to get a red mouse and, putting a lighted straw in its mouth, let it run up the tree. This set fire to the tree; it blazed up and in the midst of the smoke they could see Mullion fly away.[4] The same part is played by the woodpecker and the climbing rat in an Euahlayi version. They climb the tree inhabited by Mullyan the Eagle-hawk, a redoubted cannibal, and destroy him by means of a smouldering fire-stick that makes the hut blaze up, when Mullyan throws himself down to rest. Mullyan's arm was burnt off and he now lives in the sky as Mullyangah, the morning star, on one side of which is a little star, which is his own arm.[5]

1 R. H. Mathews, *E. N.*, 131.

2 Howitt, *N. T.*, 557–56.

3 "Whenever possible the men who represented animals were of those totems." "When it is a kangaroo-hunt, it is a kangaroo-man who performs, and the wild-dog men hunt him."—Howitt, l.c., 545.

4 Honery, "Wailwun, Australian Languages and Traditions," *J. A. I.*, 1877, VII. 250.

5 K. L. Parker, *Australian Legendary Tales*, 1897, 62–64. Id., *The Euahlayi Tribe*, 1905, 102.

This altered part which the Eagle-hawk plays in the legend may be attributed to and is certainly determined by a variety of causes. To begin with, we must take the clash of cultures or people into account that makes the hero of one people the monster of the other.[1] But the further study of the legend points to a deeper psychical motive. According to the tribes at Wellington Valley, Piame is the Father of their race, and formerly lived amongst them. Mudjegong, on the other hand, is an evil spirit who, after having derived his existence from Piame, declared war upon him and now endeavours with all his power to frustrate Piame's undertakings. The offspring of Piame were numerous; all but two were destroyed by Mudjegong, who converted them into different wild animals. The two remaining children, named Melgong and Yandong, were the progenitors of the present race. Piame initiated one of them into the mysteries and directed him to extract a front tooth from each of the young men.[2] The sequel of the myth is contained in the dramatic representations performed at the initiation ceremonies, the principal one being emblematic of the destruction of the Eagle-hawk by Piame.[3] The two survivors from the attacks of the Eagle-hawk seem to correspond to his two conquerors in the former legends. The unconscious meaning of Baiame here undergoes a slight alteration: he corresponds to the always benevolent grandfather of the family circle (the father of the fathers of the human race), whilst the inimical component of the father-complex is, as usual in Australian mythology, projected into a second person[4]—Mudjegong the Eagle-hawk. He plays the part of the rebellious son to the supreme deity of mankind, but in his relation to the novices he corresponds to the paternal tyrant.[5]

This explains the prominent part played by the legend of the conquering of the Eagle-hawk in the initiation ritual, as the Eagle-hawk means the inimical; the deity of the Baiame type, the benevolent aspect of the father-complex. The initiation ritual may rightly be described as a victory of the latter over the former. At the Bŭrbŭng of the Wiradthuri tribes an eagle's nest was represented.[6] At the Kamilaroi ceremonies at a short distance from the image of Baiamai was the imitation of an eagle-hawk's nest in a tree. The blacks said there was an eagle-hawk's nest near Baiamai's first home and that he chased the eagle-hawk away.[7]

[1] Cf. Schmidt, *Ursprung*, 362. Cf. Frazer, *F. O. T.*, III, on the myth of Samson.

[2] W. Henderson, *Observations on the Colonies of New South Wales and Victoria*, 1832, 146, 147.

[3] Henderson, l.c., 148.

[4] Cf. my article on "St. Nikolaus im Volksbrauch und Volksglauben," *Pester Lloyd*, 1919, XII. 191.

[5] The usual function of the bullroarer spirit. Mudjegong = bullroarer = Daramulun. Schmidt, *Ursprung*, 365.

[6] R. H. Mathews, "The Bŭrbŭng of the Wiradthuri Tribes," *J. A. I.*, 1895, XXIV. 299, 301.

[7] Mathews, "The Bora, or Initiation Ceremony of the Kamilaroi Tribe," *J. A. I.*, 1894, 417.

The Eucla tribe have the following tradition on the origin of the rite of circumcision: A long time ago the Blacks were very numerous and much troubled with two birds of prey, considerably larger than eagle-hawks, which devoured large numbers of the tribe. There was a small group consisting of three men and one woman, and two of. these men attacked and killed these monster birds, and then went up into the sky, where they still dwell in the dark patches of the Milky Way. The remaining man and woman were attacked by a neighbouring tribe, but finally they also ascended into the Milky Way and were lost sight of.

An ascent of this sort is called walyeyooroo.[1] During circumcision the lad has to keep his eyes fixed on the two spots where dwell the slayers of the gigantic birds.[2] According to another account the lads are left lying on the ground after circumcision till the Milky Way is seen in the sky. Then the lad is asked, "Can you see the two black spots?" When he has seen them he is allowed to go to his camp, and then the medicine men tell him the following legend:

> A very long time ago, a great bird came and devoured all the people excepting three men and one woman. These were one Budera (root), one Kura (dingo), one Wenung (wombat) and a Kura woman. The men fought the bird and killed it, but after it was dead only two spears were found in the body, one belonging to the Kura and one to the Wenung man. Then they went up to the Milky Way, and the name given to the two black spots to which they went is "far-away-men." After the Budera man, who remained behind, had grown old, he also went up to the stars; but he is only seen when he walks across the moon (explanation of an eclipse or of the interlunary days?) and then he is angry.[3] Budera's children were boys, and they went inland a great distance and were absent a long time. On their return, each boy brought back with him a captured wife. The Budera, before he died, marked them with their class marks.[4]

[1] Wilyaru means initiation ceremony in various South Australian languages. Is this a mere coincidence?

[2] E. M. Curr, *The Australian Race*, 1886, I. 403. Two black spaces in the Milky Way are two old men who were speared at a Bora near the Taldora, on the Saxby River, by a race who owned this country a very long time ago. They were translated to heaven. The Milky Way is the road to heaven.—E. Palmer, "Notes on some Australian Tribes," *J. A. I.*, 1883, XIII. 293.

[3] For the account of a lunar eclipse, A. J. Peggs, "Notes on the Aborigines of Roebuck Bay, Western Australia," *Folk-Lore*, 1903, XIV. 340. H. Klaatsch, "Schlussbericht über seine Reise nach Australien," *Z. E.*, 1907, 668.

[4] Howitt, l.c., 665, 666. Cf. ibid., 129. Sub-classes (animal-named) which seem to be localized totems at the same time; ibid., 745, 746. (These sub-classes or totems are distinguished by various scars.) It is remarkable that the only other trace of what looks like totemic or tribal crests should be found in the far north

Not only the initiation ceremonies, but also—as is to be expected in accordance with Atkinson's theory of social evolution—the origin of exogamy is by this legend connected with the death of the Eagle-hawk, the tyrannous father. Another version is given by Williams:

> Long ago an immense bird larger than the brown Eagle-hawk killed and devoured all the tribe except two men and one woman, who killed the bird. Afterwards they were attacked by a hostile tribe but could not be speared because they would jump up and appear somewhere else. Finally they jumped so high that they never came down again, and the two men are dark spots in the Milky Way.[1]

The dual heroes' conquest.

The Nauo version contains many important traits. The tribe was once entirely cut off by a great and powerful warrior styled "Willoo" (Eagle-hawk), who attempted to possess himself of all the women (nucleus of the Father-Son conflict) and destroyed every man except two who escaped by climbing into trees. Their names were Karkantya and Poona ("two smaller species of hawks"). Willoo climbed after them, but they broke off the branch upon which he sat and he fell to the ground. That instant a dog deprived him of his virility, whereupon he immediately died and was transformed into an Eagle-hawk.[2] The two heroes who kill the monster thus appear in their true light: they are smaller hawks, which in the language of myths and dreams means that they are the sons of the larger one. The reason of the conflict is the intention of the large Eagle-hawk to possess all the women of the tribe: his punishment (castration) the usual neurotic aspect of incest as wish-fulfilment. The next version, in common with the Nauo myth, contains the *motif* of the small hawk who is instrumental in vanquishing the large one, whilst it is nearest to the Yircla variant as it is also explanatory of body-scars. In the Dieri tribe the initiation ceremony that comes next to the Karaweli-Wonkana is called Wilyaru.

in conjunction with paternal descent, and with traces of the myth of the vanquished Eagle-hawk. (As to the latter, see above, the myth of the two old men translated to the Milky Way at a Bora.) W. E. Armit tells us that many tribes have crests or totems, and gives the following instances: "Ngarra—a tribe on the Leichardt River, whose crest is a shell on each cheek; the Eugoola, Nicholson River, hooks on each arm; Myabi, on Saxby River, snake painted on shield, etc." Curr, l.c., II. 300, 301. We shall see below that the Urabunna and Dieri also connect the myth of the Eagle-hawk-monster with the custom of cicatrization.

[1] Howitt, *N. T.*, 744.

[2] G. F. Angas, *Savage Life and Scenes in Australia*, 1847, I. 109. The bull-roarer hero is torn to pieces, or his head is cut off by two wild dogs. Spencer and Gillen: *Nor. T.*, 1904, 420, 421, 434, 435, 493, 500, 501. Tearing asunder and decapitation are both symbolical equivalents of castration; the initiation ritual is but a mitigated castration. Cf. above on Mudjegong the Eagle-hawk, who is also the bull-roarer.

The old men let streams of their own blood flow on the young man, and then make incisions on the nape of his neck with a sharp flint. These, when healed into raised scars, denote that the person wearing them has passed through the Wilyaru ceremony.[1] We find the same ceremony combined with a fire ordeal amongst the neighbouring Urabunna, who account for the scars by an aetiological myth:

> In the Alcheringa there lived two hawks, Irritja and Wantu-wantu. The latter was a cannibal and compelled the former to hunt blackfellows for him. Irritja always let as many natives escape as he could, and gave usually only one to Wantu-wantu. Once on coming home from a hunting expedition they found a small hawk Kutta-kutta in their camp, who, to escape from Wantu-wantu, changed himself into a piece of bark and was put on the fire by Wantu-wantu in this shape. Kutta-kutta was badly burnt, but he managed to flutter out and run away chased by the old bird. Kutta-kutta escaped to the camp of the bell-bird, who had married his sister. The bell-bird (*Oreoica-cristata*) led the attack and succeeded in killing Wantu-wantu.

The cuts now made on the bodies of the Wilyaru men are supposed to represent the marks on the back and on the neck of the bell-bird. The natives will not eat the hawk Irritja because it helped their ancestors to escape from the Wantu-wantu.[2] The seemingly meaningless detail about the burning of the Kattu-kattu contains the key to the whole myth. In the Wilyaru ceremony "the novice is taken and placed in a doubled-up attitude upon a steaming and smoking mound. In this position the man remains for a short time, but sometimes long enough to burn him severely, and is then assisted off by the older men," who then make the cuts on his body.[3]

[1] Howitt, *N. T.*, 658. Gason in Curr, l.c., II. 58. Another phase of the initiation rite, the extraction of two front teeth, is also brought into connexion with the Eagle-hawk. The teeth are smeared with fat and kept for about twelve months, because, if thrown away, the Eagle-hawk would cause larger ones to grow in their place. Gason, l.c., 55. The wild-cat seems, probably for historical reasons (enmity with a group of wild-cat men), to have replaced the Eagle-hawk in the Arunta tribe Spencer and Gillen, *Nor. T.* 336.

[2] Spencer and Gillen, *Nor. T.*, 1907, 751–54. The episode of "breaking off branches" is found here as in the Nauo variant. Boys are often struck on the leg with the leg-bones of the Eagle-hawk (irritja), to pass strength from the bone into the boy. Both this species and the Brown Hawk (irkalangi) are taboo to novices. The latter is also "ekirinja" (taboo) to young women; if one of them is suckling a child and she sees one of these birds, she turns so that her breast cannot be seen by the bird, because if this should happen, or if the bird's shadow should happen to fall upon her breast, the milk would fail and the breast would swell and burst. Spencer and Gillen, *N. T.*, 472, 473. As to the carrion-eating habits of the eagle, see Fountain and Ward, *Rambles of an Australian Naturalist*, 1907, 17.

[3] Spencer and Gillen, *N. T.*, 641.

1. THE PROTO-TOTEMIC COMPLEX

I. The Eagle-hawk as All-Father, Creator, Culture Hero.

52 (p. 57), 110, 111 (H. 555), 112 (H. 564), 261, 262, 263, 264, 265, 266, 267, 339–348 (p. 38), 321 (H. 563), 328 (p. 38).

II. Bundjil.

(*a*) Word denoting man.

217, 218, 276, 280 (*Anthropos*, 1914, 991. P. W. Schmidt: *Ursprung der Gottesidee*, 1912, 285).

(*b*) Means eminent man, elder, 108. Fison and Howitt: *Kamilaroi and Kurnai*, 1880, 210.

(*c*) The Master in Heaven.

94, 95, 97, 98, 99, 100, 101, 102, 103, 104, 105, 106, 107 (H. 484–86).

III. Eagle-hawk as Phratry Name.

100, 109, 110, 112, 121, 122, 123, 124, 125, 126, 127, 128, 132, 133, 135, 136, 140, 141, 142, 143, 321, 328 (Thomas, 48, Howitt: *N.T.*, 97, 100, 126).

IV. Magician or Demon as Eagle-hawk

88 (C. G. Teichelmann and C. W. Schürmann: *Outlines of a Grammar, Vocabulary and Phraseology of the Aboriginal Language of South Australia*, 1840, 9). 211 (W. E. Roth: *Superstition*, 29), 297 (C. II, 475), 352 (Sp. I, 533).

V. Eagle-hawk as Cannibal Monster vanquished at Initiation. Eagle-hawk and Circumcision.

52 (p. 55), 76 (p. 54), 77 (p. 55), 82 (p. 55), 84 (p. 55), 85 (p. 57), 130, 139, 150, 153 (p. 51), 217 (p. 53), 272 (p. 53), 326 (p. 57).

VI. Eagle-hawk Taboo to Novices.

(*a*) 47 (Sp. II, 611), 48 (Sp. II, 612).

(*b*) Taboo for women.

25, 29, 31, 32, 41, 42, 43, 44, 45, 47, 49, 50, 51, 52, 55, 222 (Sp. II, 612).

(*c*) Childbirth taboo.

47, 48 (Sp. II, 614).

VII. Eagle-hawk and Crow. Conflict Myths.

100 (p. 38), 108, 114, 115 (p. 38), 159, 160, 196 (p. 38), 232 (p. 40), 328 (p. 38).

VIII. Identical Word for Eagle-hawk and Man.

156 (C. III, 231, 240).

IX. Eagle-hawk and Crow Represented in Initiation Rites.

90, 91, 94, 95, 96 (p. 50), 102, 106 (p. 268), 111 (pp. 50, 268), 114, 115, 116, 117 (p. 268), 119, 121, 122, 123, 124 (pp. 51, 268), 129 (p. 268), 163 (p. 50), 328 (p. 50, 268).

X. Crow as Tribal Symbol.

108 (H. 134, 374).

XI. Emu as Mother-Wife to All-Father, Hunted by Him.

89 (p. 45), 111 (p. 44), 130, 153 (p. 44).

XII. All-Father has Emu-Feet.

52, 56, 130, 153 (pp. 48, 49).

XIII. Emu Taboo.

(*a*) Novices.

35 (Sp. II, 612), 47 (p. 44), 48 (p. 44), 52 (p. 44), 89, 130, 150 (pp. 44, 49), 163 (H. 606), 235 (p. 44), 337 (p. 44).

(*b*) Childbirth.

35, 41, 47, 77 (Sp. II, 614), 229 (p. 44).

XIV. Emu in Other-World.

121, 125 (p. 49), 351 (*Folk-Lore*, XIV, 362).

XV. Kangaroo and Emu Connected with Conception.

(*a*) 232, 234, 237 (p. 47), 264 (p. 47).

(*b*) Magical use of emu fat.

65, 89 (p. 49).

XVI. Kangaroo as Class Name.

48, 130, 135, 138, 139, 148, 149, 150, 153, 154, 157, 158, 159, 163, 179, 314 (Thomas, 42, 43).

XVII. Kangaroo Connected with Supreme Being or Culture Hero.

88 (p. 48), 139 (p. 48), 152, 249, 350 (p. 109).

XVIII. Identical Word for Kangaroo and Man, or Symbolic Equivalent.

30 (C. I, 277), 108 (H. 515), 261, 263, 264, 270, 339, 340, 341, 342, 343, 344, 345, 346, 348 (p. 47).

XIX. Kangaroo Taboo.

(*a*) Novices.

35 (Sp. II, 612), 52 (Sp. I, 471), 235 (Brown: *J.R.A.I.*, 1913, 174).

(*b*) Childbirth.

35, 41, 77 (Sp. II, 614).

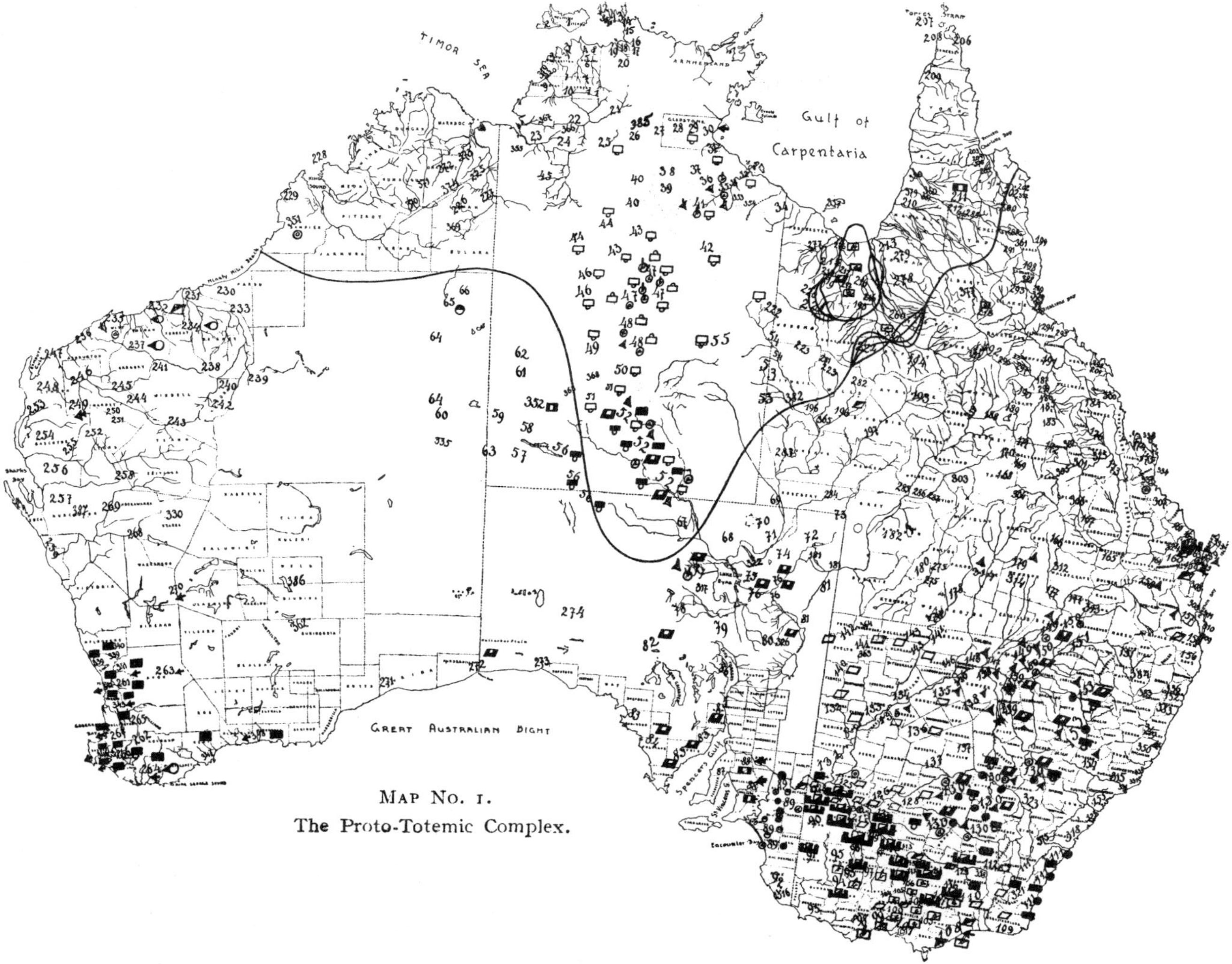

MAP No. I.
The Proto-Totemic Complex.

The small hawk instrumental in bringing about the death of the larger one stands for the novices, the generation of sons. The two larger hawks may be identified with the two currents of feeling represented in the Baime and Daramulun (Mudjegong, Gayandi) type, the benevolent and the malevolent elements in the father-complex. Possibly the explanatory turn of the legend, connecting the scars made on the novices with the defeat of the Eagle-hawk, may have something to do with the castration suffered by the Eagle-hawk in the Nauo variant, as scars and other mutilations (circumcision, tooth extraction, etc.) form one complex with castration in the unconscious.[1] It is also worthy of remark that the scars are made in imitation of the marks on the body of the Bell-bird who is the conqueror of the Eagle-hawk. Thus the novice is identified with the hero who kills Eagle-hawk, with the Son who conquers the Father. Both myth and ritual seem to have a more general significance than is visible at first sight. The name of the rite Wilyaru is certainly connected with the Willoo (Eagle-hawk) of the Nauo legend. The third stage of the Parnkalla and Nauo initiation ritual with blood-letting and scarification, thus corresponding exactly to the Wilyaroo, is called Wilyalkanye.[2] In Maroura, Bilara means Eagle-hawk.[3] The Nimbalda tribe has the word willyaroo for circumcision,[4] and according to Arunta tradition the "little hawk" men are responsible for the introduction of circumcision and class names.[5]

Summary.

We are approaching the end of the first part of our investigations. This part has been devoted to the survivals of what we have called the proto-totemic complex; that is, the projection into the environment of those unconscious concepts and feelings which have arisen out of the situation determined by the so-called "Cyclopean" family, thus making certain animal species symbolically representative of the father-mother-etc. complexes. These proto-totemic organizations must have been local, were neither patri- nor matrilineal in the sense these terms are now understood, one animal species representing the horde and more especially its leader. Later on this species must have been dupli-

[1] Th. Reik, "Das Kainszeichen," *Imago*, 1917, 31.

[2] Ch. Wilhelmi, *Manners and Customs of the Australian Natives*, 1862, 18–20. G. F. Angas, *Savage Life and Scenes in Australia and New Zealand*, 1877, I. 115.

[3] R. W. Holden, "The Maroura Tribe," in G. Taplin, *F. L.*, etc., 1879, 21.

[4] H. O. Smith, "The Nimbalda Tribe," ibid., 87. Cf. also Ch. Provis, "Kukatha Tribe," ibid., 100. On the legend in general, cf. N. W. Thomas, "Baiame and the Bell-bird," *Man*, 1905, 52, who identifies Baiame with the Bell-bird.

[5] Spencer and Gillen, *N. T.*, 394, 418, 421. A tribe of Waljuks exists (Eagle-hawks) near York. Daisy M. Bates, "The Marriage Laws and Customs of the West Australian Aborigines," *Victorian Geographical Journal*, XXIII, XXIV. 47. Frazer, *T. & E. I*, 563. Bilyara, Eagle-hawk as totem always in the Mukwara class. Howitt, l.c., 98, 99. Probably the name of the Wilja Tribe is connected with the same root.

cated, as the gradual check of uncontrolled impulses made it possible for the old and the young generation of men to go on living in the same horde. Now we have two totems for each horde, Eagle-hawk and Crow probably representing those of the parent horde from which a number of south-east (and south-west) Australian tribes branched off.[1] The Kangaroo, the Emu, and probably other animals may have been introduced at the same time.

We regard the animal-named marriage classes that extend over many of the modern totem clans and even tribes as the survivals of these ancient hordes and their beliefs.[2] This is further corroborated by the animals figuring in initiation ritual and by the myths which can only be comprehended in conjunction with this ritual. Reik's explanation gives the key to many often-noticed features in initiation rites which connect these with totemism; and we find the same animal species prominent in these as in the class names.

Whilst the Eagle-hawk and Crow symbolize the horde or any-other collective unit made up out of men, women and children, and must be derived from the parent-complex, the origin of the sex-totems is to be searched for in a not very distinct source. A variant of the Welu legend may serve to connect the two complexes.

[1] The assumptions put forth in the text are partly modified in the final chapter. I would now suppose that the Hawk was the original Father-substitute, later duplicated by making a smaller species of hawk represent the Son, but this phase has been obliterated by introducing a darker bird (Crow), the representative of another race, as opponent of the national or racial totem (Eagle-hawk). To-day the Crow is a condensed symbol of the Eagle-hawk's opponents and subsequent allies, representing both the Younger Generation and an Alien Race.

[2] In South-West Australia the names of the marriage classes have totemic meaning. See Frazer, *T. & E.*, I. 563. Amongst the Mukjarawaint and other tribes it is difficult to decide whether we have to do with totems and sub-totems, or marriage classes and totems. See Frazer, l.c., I. 462.

CHAPTER II

SEX-TOTEMS

The myth of the eagle-hawk-monster (continued).

AN aboriginal named Welu, celebrated for being a furious warrior as also a great woman-lover, made the resolution to exterminate the whole tribe of Nauos. He succeeded in killing all the males by throwing one spear through all of them as they stood in single file. Two young men, however, escaped, having sought refuge in the top of a tree. Welu followed them to kill them likewise, but they broke the branch upon which their enemy had climbed; he fell to the ground and was attacked and torn to pieces[1] by a tame dog. Thereupon Welu was changed into a bird called in English the "curlew" and the youths who had escaped his wrath were transformed into little lizards, the male of which is called Ibirri and the female Waka: this is said to have occasioned the distinction between the human sexes.

This procedure did not seem to have been approved of by the aborigines, as each sex formed a fruitless hatred against the opposite sex of this little animal, the men amidst jokes and laughter striving to kill the Waka and the women the Ibirri.[2]

[1] Symbolical substitute for castration. Cf. the myth of Osiris torn asunder and his missing phallus. See Frazer, *Adonis, Attis, Osiris*, 1907.

[2] Ch. Wilhelmi, "Manners and Customs of the Australian Aborigines," *R. S. T.*, 1862, 37. Cf. Angas, *Savage Life and Scenes in Australia and New Zealand*, 1847, I. 109. "A small lizard is supposed to be the originator of the sexes. The men distinguish it by the name of 'ibirri,' the women call it 'waka.' The men destroy the male lizards, and the women the females." As to the last detail, the account given by Wilhelmi is the correct one, as it is corroborated by Schürrmann and by the general evidence on sex-totems. C. W. Schürrmann, "The Aborigines of Port Lincoln in South Australia," in T. D. Woods, *The Native Tribes of South Australia*, 1879, 241. Cf. Tarrotarro—a species of lizard. A fabulous person who divided the sexes. C. G. Teichelmann and C. W. Schürrmann, *Outlines of a Grammar, Vocabulary and Phraseology of the Aboriginal Languages of South Australia*, 1840, 45. In the version we gave above, the cannibal bird's name was translated as Eagle-hawk, but both Wilhelmi and Schürrmann (followed by N. W. Thomas in the article quoted above) render Welu as curlew. Cf. A. L. P. Cameron, "Notes on a Tribe speaking the Boontha Murra language," *Science of Man*, 1903, 91. "They are very much afraid of the curlew." However, Schürrmann tells us that the conquerors of the monster were two kinds of hawks, as in the version quoted above. Probably the curlew is a later local innovation for the Eagle-hawk.

We have demonstrated by comparative analysis of this type of myth that the conquerors of Welu represent a later generation and thus the legend might be taken as markedly exemplifying the relative antiquity of the human complexes projected into totemism (Eagle-hawk) and sex-totemism (small hawks, son-hero).

The function attributed to the lizard reappears in Central Australia, where Mangarkunjerkunja, the Alcheringa hero of the Arunta lizard totem, transformed the "inapertwa" into real human beings. (He was the originator of subincision, fire-making and marriage regulations.[1]) The transforming of the "inapertwa" is also the subject of a myth of the Yuin, the eastern neighbours of the Kurnai. Before there were men there were creatures somewhat like human beings but without members. Muraurai, the Emu-wren, turned them into men and women by splitting their legs, separating the arms from the sides, and otherwise perfecting them.[2] The originator of sexes is at the same time their personification. There are two birds which the Kurnai reverence: the Emu-wren and the Superb Warbler, which are the sex-totems, and no man would think under any circumstances of injuring his "elder brother" Yiirung or any woman her "elder sister" Djiitgun.

The fights between the sexes.

In the Kurnai tribe sometimes ill-feeling arose between the men and the women, and then some of the latter went out and killed one of the men's "brothers" to spite them. On their return to the camp with their victim the men attacked them with their clubs and they defended themselves with their digging-sticks. Or the men might go out and kill a "woman's sister," whereupon the women would attack them.[3] Heavy blows were struck, heads were broken and blood flowed, but no one stopped them. Only those young men fought who might get married, not the newly initiated; these were supposed to stand back, not liking to see the women's blood. One fight follows the other, each party beginning the quarrel by killing the other's "sister" or "brother." In a week or two the wound and bruises were healed, and then, when one of the eligible young men met one of the marriageable women, he looked at her and said "Djiitgun," and she said "Yiirung! What does the yiirung eat?" The reply was, "He eats kangaroo," etc. Then they laughed, and she ran off with him without telling anyone.[4]

The horror the younger men feel at the women's blood may serve as a starting-point of interpretation. A well-known infantile

[1] C. Strehlow, *A. & L.*, I. 6. They stand in awe of the lizard. Strehlow, l.c., II. 73. The sky would fall down upon the earth if somebody were to kill the Mangakunjarkuna. W. Planert, "Aranda Grammatik," *Z. E.*, 1907, 566. The large lizard is taboo to the novices, the penalty being an *abnormal craving for sexual intercourse*. Spencer and Gillen, *N. T.*, 471.

[2] Howitt, *N. T.*, 484, 485.

[3] Howitt, l.c., 1904, 149.

[4] Fison and Howitt, *Kamilaroi and Kurnai*, 1880, 203.

concept of coitus is that this is an attack, a murderous attempt, upon the woman, the vagina being a bleeding wound that marks the feminine sex as the victim of masculine aggression.[1] Menstruation, the sexual purport of which is, if not consciously known, at least unconsciously felt by the savage, is accounted for in this way. At the first menstruation of a Chiriguano girl old women run about the house with sticks, "striking at the snake which has wounded her."[2] In Saibai and Yam the moon is held responsible for the appearance of the catamenia, the first period at puberty being due to actual connexion during sleep with the moon in the shape of a man.[3] In the Aru Islands the evil spirit called Boitai takes the semblance of the woman's husband and has intercourse with them whilst traversing the forest, shown afterwards by bleeding from the vagina.[4] This infantile and sadistic concept of coitus is demonstrated in the brutal treatment to which women are frequently subjected previous and preparatory to marriage (usually called "marriage by capture"[5]). It is perhaps not an illegitimate conjecture if we think the symbolic equation murder-coitus found by psycho-analysis in dreams and other products of the unconscious is also valid in the case of the Kurnai custom. Thus we should have a veiled, that is symbolic, coitus as the magical preliminary to actual coitus (marriage),[6] conforming to the general rule in the realm of magic and the unconscious that like produces like. In an Australian tribe all the eligible men are the woman's "husbands" according to the classificatory system; these men reciprocally use the term "brother" when speaking to each other.

The sex-totem represents the brother.

If the woman has symbolical connexion with the bird as "elder brother" of the man, we may say that the sex-totem stands for the whole marriage-class or age-grade; it may be regarded as an eject of a group of "brothers," as potential husbands, into nature. At present, of course, the "brothers" of a woman in the classificatory sense are non-eligible as husbands, but the sex-totem probably belongs to a state of social organization in which something like brother and

[1] Cf. S. Freud, "Tabu der Virginität," *Sammlung kleiner Schriften zur Neurosenlehre, Vierte Folge*, 1918, 229.

[2] E. Crawley, *The Mystic Rose*, 1902, 192, quoting *Lettres édifiantes et curieuses*, VIII. 333. E. Nordenskiöld, *Indianerleben*, 1912, 210.

[3] *Reports of the Cambridge Anthropological Expedition to Torres Straits*, 1904, V. 206. "The girl dreams it is a man, but really it is the moon, who embraces her." On the connexion of the moon with dreams see W. H. R. Roscher, *Selene und Verwandtes*, 1890. The part played by the moon is determined both by the monthly recurrence of the catamenia and by the erotic dreams of women at this time. Cf. Henning, *Der Traum*, 1914, for recorded cases of these dreams.

[4] Riedel, *De Sluik en Kroeshaarige Rassen tuschen Selebes en Papua*, 1888, 252.

[5] The resistance of the bride must be conquered by force. Edward M. Curr, *Recollections of Squatting in Victoria*, 1883, 143. On marriage by capture, see Avebury, Westermarck, Crawley, Kohler, Post, etc.

[6] I have given the same explanation for the love oracles of European folklore. Róheim, *Spiegelzauber*, 1919, 136.

sister group-marriage prevailed. We suppose this phase of society to have existed for a time after the breaking down of the Patriarchal Horde, but before the Dual Division was developed; we must leave the details of this question for another essay.

The representatives of the proto-totemic complex stand for the Sire in onto- and phylogenetic evolution, the sex-totem, the "elder brother" of the men (the "elder sister" of the women) represents the secondary fixation of the infantile libidinal impulse in the family circle; the parents being the objects of the first fixation, it personifies the (elder) brother or sister.

The Loritja call the plant belonging to the men and the youths mulati, and that belonging to the women and girls okara, and both tease each other with the words "This is thy twin brother" ("sister").[1] The Yuin sex-totems are the Bat and the Emu-wren as the men's brother, and the Tree-creeper as the women's sister.[2] These sex-totem fights arose in the Wotjobaluk tribe in a similar way as among the Kurnai. The men would kill an owlet-nightjar and boast about it in camp. The women in their turn would kill a bat, and carry it to the camp on the point of a stick with a piece of wood to keep its mouth wide open. This was held up in triumph to the men and proved sufficient provocation for a fight. These sex-totems were called yaur (flesh) ngirabul or mir, just like the totems proper. The bat was the brother of all the men, the owlet-nightjar the sister of all the women: the "Bat" was the man's brother and the "Nightjar" was his wife.[3] Speaking of the Western districts of Victoria, Dawson says that the grey bandicoot belongs to the women and is killed and eaten by them, but not by men and children. The common bat belongs to the men, who protect it against injury, even almost killing their wives for its sake. The fern owl, or large goatsucker, belongs to the women, and although a bird of evil omen, creating terror at night by its cry, is jealously protected by them. If a man kills one they are as much enraged as if it was one of their children and will strike him with their long poles.[4] At Port Stephens the Bat and the Tree-creeper are the Gimbai or "friends" of the men and women respectively. The men took the bat under their protection and woe betide any woman who dared to injure one. The bat was also called Kuri, that is "man."[5] In the Ta-ta-thi tribes and Wathiwathi, if a woman killed a bat there used to be a great row, in which the women sometimes got hurt. Similarly, the women reverenced a species of small owl and attacked the men if they tried to kill one of these birds.[6]

[1] C. Strehlow, *A. & L.*, IV. I. Abt. 1913, 98.
[2] Howitt, *N. T.*, 150.
[3] A. W. Howitt, "Further Notes on Australian Class Systems," *J. A. I.*, XVIII. 1889, 57. Id., *N. T.*, 150.
[4] James Dawson, *Australian Aborigines*, 1881, 52.
[5] Howitt, *N. T.*, 150.
[6] A. L. P. Cameron, "Notes on some Tribes of New South Wales, *J. A. I.*, XIV. 1885, 350.

The Ta-ta-thi call the bat "Rakur" and the small owl "Dhrail," and men and women speak to each other as "Rakur" and "Dhrail" respectively.[1] The Wathiwathi call this pair "Benalongi" and "Yeraleri." In the Turrbal tribe it was said that the small bat made the men and the night-hawk the women. The men would kill a woman's sister out of mischief, and then there would be "a sort of jolly fight like skylarking."[2] Amongst the Dieri both the men and women have a plant as "Ngambu," that is "Protector," and when they wish to tease each other the men root up the protector of the women and the women the protector of the men; showing it to the other sex they say, This is your "Ngambu."[3] The Arunta and Loritja have a small black bird as symbol of the men, and a small pigeon as symbol of the women. If an Arunta kills a pigeon he will show it to a woman, saying "nana unkwangatuja" (this belongs to you). There is also the flower worrakaljialjia as symbol of the men and the kwarakaljikaljia as symbol of the women; its milky juice is rubbed by girls on their breasts to make them grow quickly. The teasing goes on here just as in all the other cases.[4] The sex-totems are, as we have already seen, connected with the creation of sex in mankind: a function natural enough for beings who are themselves the personifications of the libido. Amongst the Awabakal the bird tilmun (a small bird the size of a thrush) is supposed by the women to be the first maker of women, or to be a woman transformed after death into a bird. These birds are held in veneration by the women only, and the bat is held in veneration on the same ground by the men.[5] The Wotjobaluk account of the creation of man says that long ago Ngunung-ngunnut the bat, who was a man, lived on the earth, and there were others like him, but there was no difference between the sexes. Feeling lonely, he wished for a wife, and he altered himself and one other so that he was the man and the other the woman. Then he made fire by rubbing a stick on a log of wood.[6] W. Schmidt very aptly remarks that the fire-making can, under these circumstances, mean nothing other than the sexual act.[7]

Our knowledge of unconscious symbolism makes it possible to

[1] Cameron, "Traditions and Folklore of the Aborigines of New South Wales," *Science of Man*, 1903, 46. Sex-totems occur as far as the Buandik on the coast, and the Wonghibon northwards. Howitt, *N. T.*, 150.

[2] Howitt, *N. T.*, 150, 151.

[3] O. Siebert, "Sagen und Sitten der Dieri und Nachbarstämme in Zentral-Australien," *Globus*, 97, 1910, 49.

[4] Strehlow, *A. & L.*, IV. 98.

[5] A. L. Threlkeld, *An Australian Language as Spoken by the Awabakal*, 1892, 79. Cf. R. H. Mathews, *E. N.*, 1905, 137.

[6] Howitt, *N. T.*, 484.

[7] W. Schmidt, *Ursprung*, 289. A variant of the fire-myth is found among the Wathi-Wathi: they say that Rakur (the bat) was the first to put fire in the wood, and he was also the first to show them how to make it. A. L. P. Cameron, "Traditions and Folklore of the Aborigines of New South Wales," *Science of Man*, 1903, 46.

discover the same meaning underlying another myth of the sex-totems also referred to by this author. The Dhiel is a small night-jar which remains in the hollow sprouts of the trees during the day and comes out at night. This bird was a woman, a being of mystery, in the far-away past, and the soldier-ant and the leech were her dogs.[1] She superintended the initiation of women and was friendly to all the beings of her own sex, but would kill and eat boys and men. This she managed to do by means of her magical water-trough:

> When the men came for a drink of water she said there was very little water in the trough so they had better put their heads in to drink. As soon as they did this the trough closed around their necks and made them fast: then she would dispose of them with her dogs and eat them. At last the crow came with a charmed shield, and when he bent his head in the trough he held the shield in front of him and prevented it from closing. Now he chased the nightjar till he overtook her as well as her dogs and killed them, breaking the magic trough. Her voice went into all the trees round which she was chased, and it is heard in the small bullroarer, the "munibear," at the initiation ceremonies. When the old women hear the small bullroarer they say, "That is our play-mate calling to us!"[2]

We may begin the interpretation of this myth with that part of it which is quite evident. Dhiel personifies woman as such. Her water-trough, then, must stand for the vagina, the men who put their heads into it perform a coitus symbolically expressed by a displacement upwards. The fear of Dhiel is the fear of the vagina with its corollary, the castration-complex and the mythical hero, the crow, personifies the psychical process by which this fear was overcome at the successful performance of the first coitus. The meaning will be made quite clear by the parallel "vagina dentata" motive of north-west American mythology: the woman with teeth in her genitalia kills all her would-be lovers till the hero inserts a stone wedge instead of his penis and breaks the charm.[3] The castration-complex is usually found to be derived from an incestuous complex as a talion-punishment on account of the fulfilment of these unconscious wishes; we may comment on the

[1] "Dogs" frequently accompany supernatural beings, and these are usually dangerous animals. They are just the reverse of man's dogs. Bahloos dogs are snakes. K. L. Parker, *Australian Legendary Tales*. Cf. S. T. Rand, *Legends of the Micmacs*, 1894, 5, 6.

[2] R. H. Mathews, *E. N.*, 153–55.

[3] Cf. F. Boas, *Indianische Sagen von der Nord-pazifischen Küste*, 24, 25, 66, 76, 77. R. H. Lowie, "The Northern Shoshone," *Anthropological Publications of the Am. Mus. Nat. Hist.*, Vol. II, P. II, 1909, 237, 238. B. H. Chamberlain, "Aino Folk Tales," 1888 (Folk Lore Soc., XXII), 37–39.

fact that Dhiel is the sex-totem, the "elder sister," and also the ancestress, the mother, of the tribe.

A myth of the Koko-minni is of very great interest in this connexion, because it shows the libidinal setting of the castration-complex as a punishment for incestuous desire, and at the same time confirms our interpretation of the wound on the leg as a symbolic castration :

> A very long time ago the Bat used to be of a very amorous disposition, and as he got tired of his wife (the bandicoot) he began to press his attentions first upon the iguana and then upon the frilled lizard. But these, instead of satisfying, seemed only to inflame his passions. He subsequently asked the Eagle-hawk for the loan of his sister. (Here the idea of sexual intercourse between the Bat—who represents the Son—and a woman belonging to the Eagle-hawk-Father, connects the myth with the proto-totemic complex.) Finally returning home, the Bat turned his wife out. Meeting his mother-in-law soon after, he proved himself guilty of incest, and feeling at last a bit tired and hungry, proceeded to look for some honey. In peering up a hollow tree, he struck his eye against a projecting piece of bark and so got his eye damaged.[1]

The Bat, whose blindness is here attributed to a similar reason to that of Oedipus, is really blind, and this must have been an additional reason for riveting the incest and castration-complex on this animal, whilst it also determined its choice as a male sex-symbol. Here, as well as in the Boulia District, the development of blindness, when not explicable by visible traumatic causes, is accounted for as a punishment for continued persistence in raping married women when alone and unprotected in the Bush. Anybody can inflict this punishment (except a woman), and it is generally of course the men injured by the rape committed on his wife who, by binding opossum claws to his little fingers and clawing the air in the direction of the offender's eye (magic of the "pointing bone" type), gets his revenge. The culprit is totally unconscious of what has been done to his visual organs and yet gets blind and can see no more women to assault.[2]

On the Bloomfield River, if somebody has sore eyes, this is because he has cut down the upper branches of a certain tree where a special kind of honey is found which has been made taboo. The hollow tree seems to be a symbol of the mother's womb[3]; this would account for these trees being sacred to the All-Father, Baiame,[4] and for the part played by the bees in the Euahlayi paradise.[5]

[1] W. E. Roth, *S. M. M.*, 5, 1903, 15.

[2] Roth, l.c., 22.

[3] Cf. Róheim, *Spiegelzauber*, 1919, 497. Id., "Das Selbst." *Imago*, 1921, 11.

[4] K. L. Parker, *More Australian Legendary Tales*, 1898, 84, 85.

[5] Parker, *Euahlayi Tribe*, 114.

The legend which attributes the origin of death (see below) to breaking the taboo set on trees (mother-symbol) and causing the Bat (masculine libido) to fly away, thus becomes intelligible. In one variant (Murray River) the woman sets out collecting fuel, in another (Euahlayi) the woman who disturbs the Bat is after the honey found in the hollow tree (see below). The account of the numerous amorous adventures of the Bat, which end in incest, illustrates Freud's theory of series-formation (Reihungbildung) as a flight from and a search after the incestuous object. The mother-in-law is of course a representative of the mother-imago, a substitute for the mother. The whole series of avoidance-customs may perhaps have been transferred to the mother-in-law at a time when the exchange of sisters was substituted for the marriage with a man's own sister, and thus the person of the mother-in-law became separate from that of the mother.

In its older form the avoidance of the mother (who was also mother-in-law) would come into operation only after having married the sister and thus relinquished all claims to the mother. At any rate, in our myth we find that the Bat peers into hollow trees after having committed incest with his mother-in-law and thus repeats the same thing in a symbolic fashion. The blindness is of course castration displaced upwards.

To return to Dhiel, it must be noted that there is a corresponding myth for the male. Dhuramoolan also killed all the initiates till he was killed and his voice put into the larger bullroarer by Baiamai. Now Dhuramoolan had a wife named Moonibear, who watched over all matters relating to women, and at the ceremony of the Bŭrbŭng she is represented by the small bullroarer.[1] The concept of the ancestral pair who in their turn are generally represented as the children of the All-Father and are personified in the two bullroarers at initiation, is intimately bound up with that of the sex-totems. The Kurnai perform the ceremony of initiation as handed down by their ancestors, the mystic pair Yiirung and Djiitgun.[2] This pair is evidently identical with the "man Tundun" and the "woman Tundun," the former of these bullroarers being the larger one, also called Wehntwin (Grandfather) or Muk-brogan (Arch-Comrade). Brogan means those who are initiated at the same time.[3] We here get a clue to the fact that the libidinal complexes are generally personified in Australian religion and mythology by a separate "Abspaltung," who appears by the side of or as created by

[1] R. H. Mathews, "The Bŭrbŭng of the Wiradthuri Tribes," *J. A. I.*, XXV. 1895, 298.

[2] Fison and Howitt, *Kamilaroi and Kurnai*, 1880, 194.

[3] Howitt, *N. T.*, 628–30. Cf. the remarks and data of P. W. Schmidt, "Die Stellung der Aranda," *Z. E.*, 1908, 893. The reference to Mathews, *E. N.*, 176, is a misprint for p. 116. Schmidt, *Ursprung*, 262.

the All-Father, although the same unconscious elements are at the bottom of both complexes: this is the first Man, the Elder Brother, the Sex-Totem. The creation of this "Abspaltung" is the consequence of a general tendency, corresponding to the infantile negation of sexuality towards the parents; since all erotic elements undergo a repression in connexion with the person of the All-Father[1] they must by the law of the return of repressed elements (Wiederkehr des Verdrängten, Freud) create a new libido object in the person of the first Man.

Repression of libidinal concepts in connexion with the All-Father, and return of these concepts in the sex-totem.

Eun-newt, the Bat, was the only one of the primeval race that stopped on the earth when the others climbed to the sky, he is the ancestor of humanity.[2] Pallian the Bat was the brother, or, as some say, the son, of the creator Bundjil. Bundjil made everything excepting women; these were fished out of the water by the Bat with his crooked stick. The stick symbolizes the penis, the water refers to the intra-uterine position of the embryo. It was also the Bat who told the Blacks to marry.[3]

Further traces of the sex-totems are also connected with symbolical representations of the sexual functions. According to the Niol-niol, who also have the two bullroarers and say that these are connected with sexuality, the Bat and the Duck were the first to be circumcised.[4] As the larger bullroarer is called Mirnbor (Duck-Man), the smaller is probably the Bat. This function of the Bat, its connexion with sexuality on the one hand, death on the other (for the sex-totems are the external souls of the men), may help to explain the following myth of the Murray River natives.

The first man and woman were forbidden to go near a certain tree where the Bat lived. Once the woman was collecting fuel (see above on the unconscious symbolic meaning of fire) and approached the tree. The Bat flew away, and this is how death came into the world.[5]

The evident similarity with the Biblical legend[6] does not seem to be the consequence of a native adaptation of missionary teachings, but rather to have been developed independently on corresponding lines of sex-symbolism. The Bat who ought not to be

[1] This is the psychological explanation of the "ethical" nature of the All-Father, which is undeniable, and has been justly emphasized by Father Schmidt.

[2] R. Brough-Smyth, *The Aborigines of Victoria*, 1898, I. 462.

[3] Id., ibid., I. 427. Howitt, l.c., 484. Wurunjerri.

[4] H. Klaatsch, "Schlussbericht ueber seine Reise nach Australien," *Z. E.*, 1907, 652, 654.

[5] Brough-Smyth, *Aborigines of Victoria*, I. 428. For the Euahlayi version, see K. L. Parker, *The Euahlayi Tribe*, 1905, 98.

[6] See the analytical interpretations as given by Levy, "Sexualsymbolik in der biblischen Paradiesgeschichte," *Imago*, V. 16.

2. TABOO, SEX-TOTEM AND INDIVIDUAL TOTEM

I. Taboo to Kill and Eat the Totem.
7 (Sp. III, 194), 41, 42, 43, 50 (p. 75), 89 (H. 135, 146), 108 (H. 135, 176), 111 (p. 73), 171 (p. 73), 180 (p. 73), 283 (C. II, 366), 318 (p. 73), 323 (p. 77).

II. Taboo to Kill and Eat Totem in a Relaxed State. (Kill and Eat only under certain Conditions, Apologize for Killing, etc.)
48, 50, 52, 56 (p. 74), 146 (p. 74), 192 (p. 74), 261, 262, 263, 264, 265, 266, 267 (p. 73), 344, 345, 346 (p. 73).

III. The Taboo only Refers to the Killing not to Eating of the Totem.
24 (Sp. III, 197), 121, 122, 123, 124, 125, 126, 228 (p. 68), 131 (Brown: *J.R.A.I.*, 1918, 248).

IV. The Taboo Refers only to Eating and not to Killing.
47 (Sp. II, 327), 77 (p. 74), 193, 194, 196, 204, 210, 223, 224 (p. 74).

V. Absence of the Totemic Taboo; Eating and Killing Permitted.
76, 150, 232, 235, 236, 319 (p. 76, Parker: *Euahlayi*, 20), 89 (Brown: *J.R.A.I.*, 1918, 229, 248–50).

VI. A Natural Species is Reserved to the Use of a Human Group.
170, 171, 183, 188, 299, 325 (pp. 88, 89, Curr, III. 27), 264 (Brown; Description of the Natives of King George's Sound, *Journ. Geog.*, I, 43).

VII. The Totem Sacrament.
24, 45, 48, 50, 52, 56, 222 (pp. 244–254).

VIII. Absence of Totemic Exogamy.
4, 6, 13, 17, 18, 19, 20, 48, 50, 51, 52, 55, 56 (Sp. I, II, III, Strehlow). The existence of the totemic taboo among the Narrinyeri (89) is sometimes affirmed, then again denied by our authorities.

IX. Sex Totems.
52, 56, 76 (pp. 62, 63), 84, 85 (p. 59), 92, 93 (p. 62), 95 (p. 62), 108, 109 (p. 60), 111 (pp. 60, 62), 118 (p. 63), 121, 122, 123, 124, 125, 126 (p. 63), 130 (p. 63), 137 (p. 64), 150 (p. 67), 155, 157 (p. 63), 202 (p. 65).

X. The Bat.
93 (p. 62), 95 (p. 62), 100 (Howitt: *N. T.*, 150), 111 (p. 62), 118 (p. 63), 121, 125 (p. 63), 150 (p. 65), 155 (p. 63), 209 (p. 324), 211 (p. 65), 229 (p. 67), 331 (p. 62).

XI. The Lizard.
52 (p. 60), 84, 85 (p. 59).

XII. Fire and Sex Totem.
95, 121 (p. 63).

XIII. Male and Female Bull-Roarer.
85, 100, 106, 108, 114, 115, 116, 117, 129, 132, 140, 141, 142, 156, 157, 229 (pp. 66, 67), 232 (Brown: *J.R.A.I.*, 1913, 168).

XIV. Individual Totems: Congenital
89 (p. 80), 163 (p. 80), 180 (p. 80), 198 (p. 80), 261, 262, 263, 264, 265, 266, 267 (p. 193).

XV. Individual Totem Received at Initiation.
24 (p. 91), 111 (p. 80), 208 (p. 80).

XVI. Individual Totem of Shaman.
89, 118 (p. 80), 150 (p. 81).

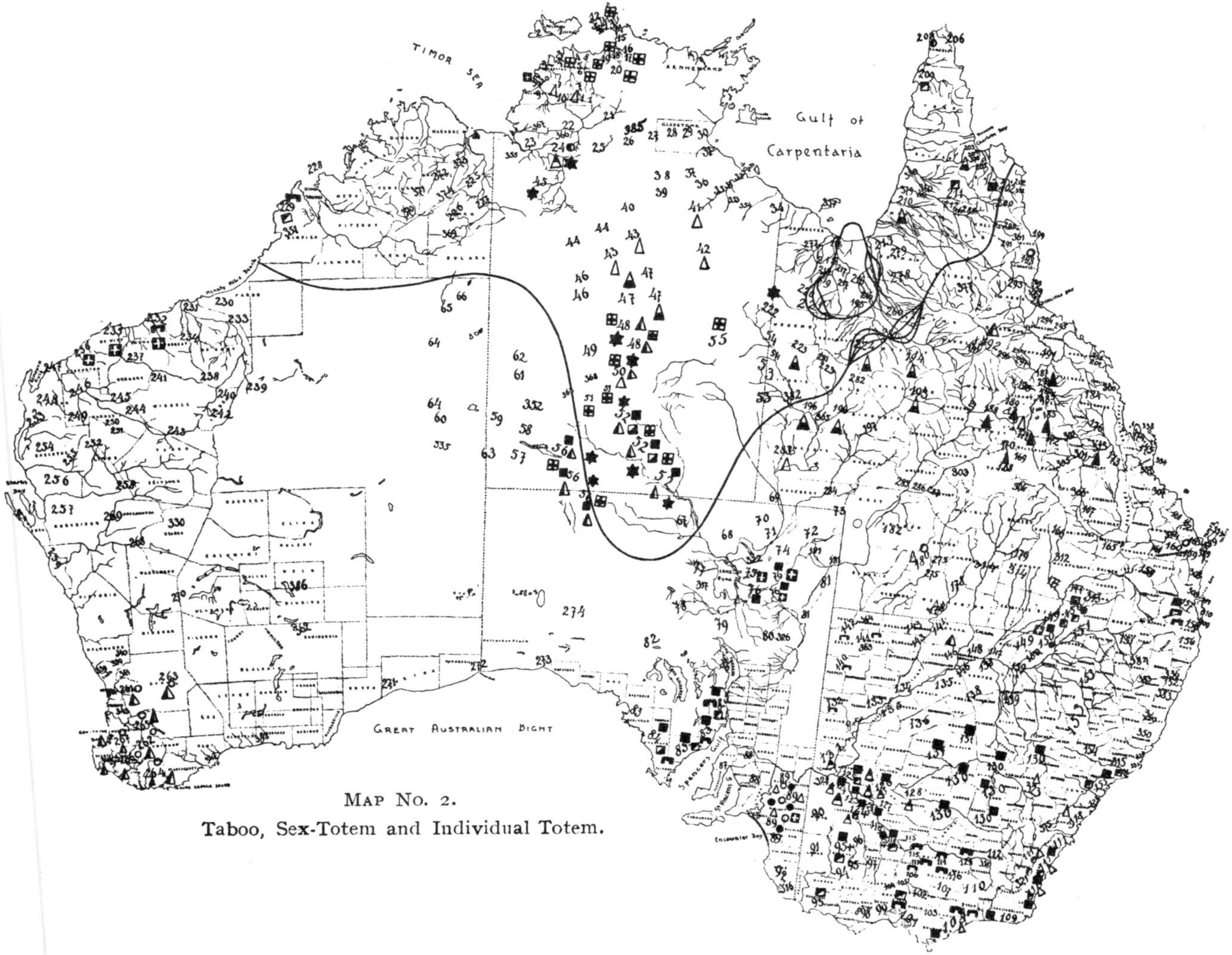

MAP No. 2.

Taboo, Sex-Totem and Individual Totem.

disturbed is the male sex-totem (a woman is responsible for letting it out !), the masculine impulse, the libido. It is the life-impulse which results in death.[1]

The part played by the Bat in Australia is in a certain sense similar to its function in European folklore. It is nailed to the door as an amulet against witches and is used in love-charms.[2] If an unmarried person chances to see one flapping its wings he will be married within a year.[3] Cutting off its head with a piece of silver and burying it is a charm to get rich.[4] Its bones are used as a talisman.[5] It figures as a love-charm, together with the frog (masculine and feminine symbols).[6] In both Continents we find the Bat as a symbol of the sexual functions and an ambivalent attitude (killing in Australia, nailing to the doorpost in Europe) towards this animal. As to the owlet, which is the sex-totem of the women, "in several villages of North and South Wales, when an owl hoots in the midst of houses, a maiden inhabitant will loose her chastity." [7]

The fear of the bat often observed in women is probably analogous to the reactions they show at the sight of other unconscious sex-symbols, such as frogs, toads, mice. The choice of the Bat as a phallic symbol is determined by its flight as well as its connexion with twilight, with the psychic twilight of the fore-conscious and the unconscious, the twilight opening the gates of dreamland, the land of a relatively uncensored wish-fulfilment for reality-stricken humanity.

The phobia of the bat getting entwined in the long hair of women is a repressed wish, the head being substituted for the female genital organ (displacement upwards) and the bat for the penis. The beliefs regarding conception are, as we shall see below, merely veiled representations of the sexual functions. The natives at Cape Bedford say that babies are made where the sun sets and in their original condition are full-grown, but in their passage into their maternal homes take the form of the curlew if a girl, of a pretty snake if a boy.[8] Bird and snake are both symbolic of the penis that effects the passage of the baby into its mother's womb, and may be paralleled by the Crow, who inserts the girl babies, and the Lizard, who inserts the boy babies, into their Euahlayi mothers.[9] The identity of the sex-totems with the spirits of

[1] For similar myths, see Róheim, *Spiegelzauber*, 1919, 122, 123.

[2] Wuttke, *Der Deutsche Volksaberglaube*, 1900, 124.

[3] M. Trevelyan, *Folk Lore and Folk Stories of Wales*, 1908, 108.

[4] P. Sebillot, *Le Folk Lore de France*, 1906, III. 45.

[5] F. S. Krauss, *Volksglaube und religiöser Brauch der Südslaven*, 1890, 147. G. F. Abbott, *Macedonian Folk Lore*, 1903, 110.

[6] Wlislocki, *Volksglaube und religiöser Brauch der Zigeuner*, 1891, 133.

[7] Trevelyan, l.c., 83.

[8] W. E. Roth, *S. M. M.*, V. 23.

[9] Parker, *Euahlayi Tribe*, 1905, 50, 61. Both are assisted by the moon, who is responsible for the origin of the sexes on the Proserpine River. Roth, l.c., 16.

initiation, their rôle as "Arch-comrades," calls attention to a further unconscious current of feeling represented by them; as demonstrated by the battles fought between the sexes, they stand for the solidarity of those of the same sex, for sexual antagonism.[1] The Dieri call the sex-totems Ngambu, "Protector," the same term being applied to the men who are entrusted with the novices during initiation.[2] That this period in the life of the Australian aboriginal is often not free from manifestly homoerotic tendencies is amply proved,[3] and we must remind the reader of Freud's conjecture that after the murder of the primeval Sire the cohesion of the clan must temporarily have been upheld by the homoerotic feelings of the brothers.[4] Now the sex-totem is the "brother," and if it stands for the feelings that are, if not utterly repressed, at least rejected by the moral code of the aboriginals, we may understand the element of "tease" evinced in the pointing out of the sex-totem.[5]

The sex-totems as representatives of the homoerotic impulse.

The following are the explanations usually given by the aboriginals themselves as to the possible origin of these concepts. At Gunbower Creek on the lower Murray the natives called the bat "brother belonging to black fellow," and would never kill one; they said that if a bat were killed one of their women would be sure to die.[6] The Wotjobaluk say that the life of a bat is the life of a man, meaning that to injure a bat is to injure some man, while to kill one is to cause some man to die. The same saying applies to the owlet-nightjar with respect to women.[7] The sex-totem is, then, an external soul; it must be here noted that psycho-analysis finds the origin of the animistic duplicate of man in the narcissistic phase of psycho-sexual evolution.[8] It is also a specific development of the narcissistic fixation which lies at the bottom of the homoerotic attitude.[9] Thus we may agree with Father Schmidt, who sees a similarity between sex-totems and soul-birds,[10] the part played by

The sex-totem as external soul. Soul and narcissistic double.

[1] See W. Heape, *Sex Antagonism*, 1913.

[2] O. Siebert, "Sagen und Sitten der Dieri und Nachbarstämmen in Zentral-Australien," *Globus*, 1910, 97, 49.

[3] Strehlow, *A & L.*, IV, vol. I, 1913, 98. W. E. Roth, "Notes on Government, Morals and Crime," *N.Q. Bull.*, No. 8, 1906, 7. Hardman, "Habits and Customs of the Natives of the Kimberley District," *Proc. Roy. Soc. Aust. I.*, Sec. III. 74. Cf. for New Guinea, T. Chalmers, "Notes on the Bugilai, British New Guinea," *J. A. I.*, 1903, XXXIII. 109.

[4] Freud, *T. & T.*, 1919, 239.

[5] Pointing out, or referring to, the sex-totem is the beginning of a row or quarrel. Nothing similar is found in connexion with the clan-totem.

[6] Frazer, *T. & E.*, 1919, I. 18. Quoting *Trans. Phil. Soc. N.S.W.*, 1862–65, 959.

[7] Howitt, *N. T.*, 149–51.

[8] Cf. Rank, "Psychoanalytische Beiträge zur Mythenforschung, 1919," *Der Doppelgänger*. Róheim, *Spiegelzauber*, 1919; id., "Das Selbst.," *Imago*, VII.

[9] Freud, "Zur Einführung des Narcissmus," *Jahrbuch* VI. 1914.

[10] Schmidt, *Ursprung*, 293.

small birds in these complexes indicating the possibility that the sex-totem also stands for the child as a narcissistic duplicate of the Self.[1]

[1] Cf. above, Dawson's remark, " They are as much enraged as if it was one of their children," and also, on the snake and curlew as prenatal incarnations of the boy and girl infant. On the connexion between narcissism, animism and the beliefs with regard to children see Róheim, *Spiegelzauber*, 1919.

CHAPTER III

THE NEGATIVE TOTEMISM OF THE SOUTH-EASTERN TRIBES

Various types of totemism.

It lies in the nature of all human attitudes and modes of behaviour to create and recreate others after their own image:[1] the proto-totemistic complex that is the psychical reaction to environmental stimuli[2] as embodied in the ejection of the father-complex[3] into an animal species,[4] continues to produce offshoots under varying social conditions;[5] these offshoots always retain the salient features of the parent type: unity with the totem[6] and the animal projection of the father imago. It is these offshoots that we actually find amongst the various stocks of humanity and that are classifiable as the various types of totemism.

In Australia we find the two main types of totemism as classified by Wundt with various intermediary and mixed forms; we will call negative, the type of totemism found in the southern and eastern tribes and embodied principally in a series of taboos; positive totemism, the type found in the central, northern and western areas and embodied in the reincarnation belief and the intichiuma ceremonies. We begin our analysis with the former, the negative type.

The main difference between the state of society found in these, an Australian tribe, and in that I suppose to have existed in the

[1] Cf. Freud, *Beyond the Pleasure Principle*, 1922, on the principle of eternal repetition; or Baldwin, *Mental Development in the Child and the Race*, 1911, on circular reaction. With regard to totemism, we have here what Goldenweiser has called the "pattern theory."

[2] The psychical reaction being, as emphasized above, merely the human and super-organic survival of animal tropism.

[3] And other components of the family complex which are, however, of secondary importance.

[4] The father being the ontogenetic root of the concept of society. See Durkheim, *Les formes élémentaires de la vie religieuse*, 1912; and also, for a similar but biological theory, Trotter, *The Herd Instinct in Peace and War*, 1919.

[5] The varying social conditions play the same part as the variety of individual and accidental experiences in the determination of the "Neurosen-wahl" (the specific form the neurotic content takes in any particular case).

[6] As the endopsychical apperception of the life-unit which man forms with his environment.

primeval horde, is the existence of a double organization:[1] the tribe and the clan. The ejective representative of the former is to be found in certain modified forms of the totemic complex as embodied in the tribal ceremonies of initiation, in the tribal belief in the All-Father, in the animal named matrimonial classes, while the clan as the smaller unit conserves certain traits of the proto-totemic complex in clan totemism. When exogamy begins to prevail in the original horde totemism may either originate as a copy of the proto-totemic complex that distinguishes the various groups of children who are born from the same extra-tribal mother, or again, the idea of fatherhood underlying the totemic complex may continue to prevail, and then we get the patrilineal and local totemic groups.[2]

Totemism of the clan and the horde.

(*a*) The Totemic Taboo

In these patrilineal clans the taboo aspect of totemism is especially prominent. Amongst the Boontha Murra a person may never on any account eat of his own totem.[3] Among the Yuin a man might not kill or eat his "Yimbir" (or Budjan). The Narrinyeri might not kill or eat their (patrilineal) totem, although another person might do so.[4] In other cases the taboo is not absolute. In south-western Australia (West Australia, 30–35° southern latitude) a certain mysterious connexion exists between a family and its kobong (matrilineal, exogamic totem), so that a member of the family will never kill an animal of the species to which the kobong belongs should he find it asleep . . . indeed, he always kills it reluctantly and never without affording it a chance to escape. . . . Similarly, a native who has a vegetable for his kobong may not gather it under certain circumstances and at a special period.[5] When a man is out hunting (Thurrawal and perhaps Thoorga tribe) he will not kill his totemic animal or plant, no matter what opportunity he may have of doing so. It is believed that by thus allowing the animal to escape or by leaving the plant unplucked, he will

It is taboo to kill the totem.

[1] Not reckoning further complications.

[2] Cf. the "major" and "minor" totems; the former is nearer to the original form. A. Lang, *The Secret of the Totem*, 1905, 144, 145. For instance, in the Goolwa clan of the Narrinyeri, the clan totem is the pelican (this the major totem), every family having its own symbol (the minor totem). T. Moriarty, in G. Taplin, *Folklore, etc.*, 1879, 50. In Western Victoria, "Every individual in the community claims some animal, plant or inanimate object as his own special totem, which he inherits from his mother." R. H. Mathews, *E. N.*, 1905, 89, whilst in all the tribes of Eastern Victoria boys and girls alike inherit the father's totem, ibid. 99.

[3] A. L. P. Cameron, "Notes on a Tribe speaking the 'Boontha Murra,'" *Science of Man*, 1904, 180.

[4] Howitt, l.c., 147. But Taplin says: "No man or woman will kill her ngaitye, *except* if it happens to be an animal which is good for food." Taplin, *Narrinyeri Tribe*, 1879, 63

[5] G. Grey, *Journal of Two Expeditions*, 1841, II. 225.

augment the supply or increase the fruitfulness of the game or vegetable.[1]

The Wotjobaluk would not harm his totem if he could avoid it, but at a pinch, in default of other food, he would eat it.[2] In the Buandik tribe a man would not kill or use for food any of the animals of the same subdivision as himself, excepting when compelled by hunger, and then he expresses his sorrow for having had to do so. A Kurnai will not kill or injure his thundung, nor willingly see another do so ; but there are exceptions to this rule.[3]

Again, the taboos to kill and to eat may be separated from each other. The Tatathi, Keramin and Wathi-wathi will not kill their own totem, but they have no objection to eating it when killed by someone else.[4] In the Waduman tribe the objection is only against killing the totem, but not against eating it if killed by a member of another totem.[5] In Queensland we have one report on a system of taboos associated with marriage classes that may be a separate type of totemism,[6] whilst another observer lays stress on the duty of the members of a clan to protect their totem animals from being killed.[7] Cases of the taboo-attitude are not totally lacking in the incarnation area either. Amongst the Urabunna no member of any totemic group eats the totem animal or plant, but there is no objection to his killing it and handing it over to be eaten by men who are not members of the totem group.[8] An Arunta will eat only very sparingly of his totem and even if he does eat a little of it he will not eat the best parts, for instance the fat. The fat and the eggs of the emu are more ekirinja (taboo) than the flesh.[9] The taboos are not enforced as strictly as in the southern area, the inhibition has been transferred from the "what" to the "how." A man of the kangaroo totem may kill a kangaroo, but not brutally by hitting it on the nose and making the blood splash about, but he must deal him a stroke on the nape of the neck. He can only eat the less valuable parts of the animal and must distribute the rest to his friends. A man of the Emu totem who has killed an emu must carefully wipe the blood away, as the sight of it is supposed to make him sad. A member of the Fish totem may only eat a little of the fish unless they are stinky, then

Taboos in Central Australia.

1 R. H. Mathews, *E. N.*, 59.
2 Howitt, *N.T.*, 145.
3 Howitt, l.c., 146.
4 A. L. P. Cameron, "Notes on some Tribes of New South Wales," *J. A. I.*, 1884, XIV. 350.
5 Spencer, *N. T. N. T. A.*, 1914, 199.
6 Roth, *Ethnological Studies*, 57. Id., "Social and Individual Nomenclature," *Bull. of N. Q. E.*, No. 18, 102.
7 E. Palmer, "Notes on some Australian Tribes," *J. A. I.*, XIII. 300.
8 Spencer and Gillen, *Nor. T.*, 1904, 149. Cf. Id., *N. T.*, 467, and Frazer, *T. & E.*, I. 185. "For example, an emu man or woman must in no way injure an emu, nor must he partake of its flesh, even when he has not killed it himself," Spencer and Gillen, *N. T.*, 467.
9 Spencer and Gillen, *N. T.*, 202.

he may eat as much as he likes. A member of the Water totem may not drink much water and is not allowed to seek shelter in the hut when it rains, but must stand out in the storm with nothing but his shield to protect him. A Mosquito man may drive the mosquitoes away with his hand if they sting badly, but he must not kill them, and a member of the Moon totem may not look at the full moon for a long time or he is liable to be killed by an enemy.[1] These facts taken together with the ceremonial eating of the totem in these tribes point to some relaxation of the inhibitory aspect of the totemic complex. In the Kaitish (and Unmatjera) tribes, under normal conditions a man does not eat his totem except ceremonially; if he were to do so freely he would be stoned by the men of the other moiety, as this would prevent him from successfully performing intichiuma.[2] In the case of the Water totem we again have a restricted taboo: men of this totem are not allowed to draw water for themselves, but they must have it drawn for them by men of the other totem.[3] When we come to the tribes north of the Kaitish, that is the Warramunga, Tjingilli, Umbaia and Gnanji tribes, we again find the absolute taboo in force.[4]

Parallelism between the two cardinal taboos of totemism.

The parallelism between the two essential taboos of totemism, not to marry a woman belonging to the same totem and not to eat (kill) the totem animal is quite remarkable if we remember that amongst the Arunta the totems are not distributed between the moieties; among the Kaitish the division of the totems between the moieties is nearly complete, whilst amongst the Warramunga, Wulmala, Walpari, Tjingilli and Umbaia the same division is absolutely complete.[5] Thus class exogamy implicitly involves totemic exogamy in these tribes. The two principal taboos (exogamy and not eating the totem) behave so far like concomitant variations, which proves that they are at least intimately bound up with one another, or perhaps that they are one and the same thing. But if we follow the path of these taboos to the north and the north-west this seeming harmony comes to an end; we have a group represented by the Larakia, Worgait and Wulwullam, with patrilineal totem groups divided between the two moieties, a second group consisting of the Djauan, Mungarai, Warrai, Yungman, Mara and Nullakun, with patrilineal totems divided between the sub-classes, then the Waduman, Mudburra, Ngainman and Billianera, with matrilineal totems found on both sides of the tribe. In all these tribes and among the Iwaidji and Melville Island tribes who have female descent the totems are strictly exogamous.[6] We are insufficiently informed as to the extent of the totem food-taboo amongst these tribes. In the

[1] Strehlow, *A. & L.*, 1908, II. 58, 59.
[2] Spencer and Gillen, *Nor. T.*, 3.
[3] Id., ibid., 325.
[4] Id., *Nor. T.*, 326.
[5] Spencer and Gillen, *Nor. T.*, 475.
[6] B. Spencer, *N. T. N. T. A.*, 179.

Worgait tribe until a child has successfully teethed it must on no account partake of the particular food to which it owes its conception.[1] In the Warrai tribe, when their old customs were in force, they never killed their own totemic animal; were they to see anyone else killing it they became angry and asked: "Why have you killed my mumulbuk?"[2] In the Waduman tribe a man will not kill his totem, but will eat it freely if given to him by another man.[3] In the North-Western Territory we have, for instance, the Kariera tribe with totem exogamy but with absolutely no eating and killing taboos, and the same obtains as to the Mardudhunera, and probably also as to the Ngaluma tribe.[4] We come to the conclusion that there certainly does exist a connexion between the two principal taboos of totemism, but that the more real of the taboos (exogamy) tends to overlap the boundaries of its more symbolic derivative (eating and killing taboo).

The Dieri, amongst whom the extension of clan solidarity in the form of the second taboo is lacking, but who preserve it in a very stringent form amongst the human members of the same totem clan (exogamy, solidarity between the members of the totem clan), are a case in point.[5]

After this geographical survey we shall try to apply the principles of psycho-analytic interpretation to these taboos.

As a starting-point, we may consider that every taboo is an inhibited wish-fulfilment,[6] and then the two taboos would correspond to the wish to kill and eat the totem and to marry women of the same clan. Or again, we may begin with what the savages themselves say: that the totem is a father symbol. Not to kill the totem means not to kill the Primeval Father, the Head of the Horde, and not to marry the mother, both being inhibited forms of the Oedipus complex.[7]

We will next turn to the reasons assigned by the savages themselves for the respect they show to the totem and see how far these fit in with the psychological theories. In the Wakelbura tribe the totem animal is spoken of as "father." A man of the Frilled Lizard totem holds that reptile sacred, and he not only refrains

[1] H. Basedow, "Anthropological Notes on the Western Central Tribes of the Northern Territory of South Australia," *Trans. Roy. Soc. S. A.*, XXXI. 1907, 4.

[2] Spencer, *N. T. N. T. A.*, 194.

[3] Spencer, l.c., 197.

[4] A. R. Brown, "Three Tribes of Western Australia," *J. A. I.*, 1913, 160, 172, 189.

[5] A. W. Howitt, "The Dieri and other Kindred Tribes of Central Australia," *J. A. I.*, XX. 1891, 41. S. Gason, "Of the Tribes, Dieyerie, Auminie, Yandrawontha, Yarawuarka, Pilladapa," *J. A. I.*, XXIV. 169. O. Siebert, "Sitten und Sagen," *Globus*, 97, 48.

[6] Cf. Freud, *T. & T.*, 113. Róheim, *Spiegelzauber*, 6.

[7] "If the totem animal is the father, then the two main commandments of totemism, the two taboo rules which constitute its nucleus—not to kill the totem animal and not to use a woman belonging to the same totem for sexual purposes—agree in content with the two crimes of Oedipus," Freud, *T. & T.*, 219.

from killing it, but would prevent others doing so in his presence. He goes so far as to seek revenge for the killing of his own totem by killing the man's "father" who did it.[1] George Bennett tells us: "In one instance a native of the Béran Plains (Bathhurst District) desired a European not to kill a 'gunar' which he had been chasing, but to catch it alive as it was 'him brother.' The animal, however, was killed, at which the native was much displeased and would not eat of it, but unceasingly complained of the 'tumbling down him brother.'"[2] In North-Western Queensland the aboriginals have a great reverence for the particular animal symbolizing their respective classes, and if anyone were to kill a bird belonging to such a division in sight of the bearer of the family name, he might be heard to say, "What for you kill that fellow? That my father!" or "That brother belonging to me you have killed; why did you do it?"[3] In Western Australia the respect paid to the totem arises from the belief that some one individual of the species is their nearest friend, to kill whom would be a great crime and to be avoided with all care.[4] The Buandik express their sorrow for having to eat his "Wingong" (friend) or Tumung (his flesh). When using the latter word the Buandik touch their breasts to indicate close relationship, meaning almost a part of themselves. Nor is the death of a "part" without dire results for the "whole." One of the tribe killed a crow and three or four days afterwards a man of the Crow clan died. He had been ailing for some days, but the killing of his wingong hastened his death.[5] A Wotjobaluk would kill the person's totem whom he wanted to injure.[6] Amongst the Kurnai the men are the "younger brothers," the women the "younger sisters," of the totem.[7] Among the Yuin the identity of the totem and the man is expressed forcibly by the totem being in the man. A member of the Lace-lizard totem changes into his totem animal, goes down the throat of a member of the Black Duck totem, and nearly kills him by attacking the Black Duck in his inside.[8] Again, amongst the Arunta the totem is the elder brother of the man,[9] and the tjurunga (own secret one) is regarded as the

[1] A. W. Howitt, *N. T.*, 147.

[2] G. Bennett, *Wanderings in New South Wales*, 1834, I. 131. Bennett's opinion is that this taboo is due to a belief in the transmigration of souls.

[3] E. Palmer, "Notes on some Australian Tribes," *J. A. I.*, XIII, 1884, 300.

[4] G. Grey, *Journals of Two Expeditions*, II. 228.

[5] Howitt, *N. T.*, 146. Cf. the expression "flesh" for totem, 145.

[6] Id., l.c., 145.

[7] Id., ibid., 146. There has been a lively discussion on the subject of Kurnai totemism between Schmidt, "Die soziologische und religiös-ethische Gruppierung der australischen Stämme, *Z. E.*, XLI. 330, and Graebner, "Zur australischen Religionsgeschichte," *Globus*, XCVI, 341, with a rejoinder by the former. Schmidt, "Die soziologischen Verhältnisse der südostaustralischen Stämme," *Globus*, XCVII. 158. But since the "thundung" are inherited and localized, we can see no reason to doubt their totemic character.

[8] Howitt, l.c., 147.

[9] Strehlow, l.c., II. 1908, 58, 60.

common body of the man and the totem ancestor.[1] It represents the spirit whose reincarnation its owner is,[2] and we may thus defer the analysis of these concepts till we come to the beliefs about child-birth. The reasons given for abstaining from killing and eating the totem fall under three distinct headings—(1) because the totem is the father, (2) the totem is the (elder) brother, (3) the totem is the external soul, a part of his own self. The second of these concepts is perhaps the most frequent, although its ontogenetic origin is later than that of the first: the (elder) brother being the first to displace the father in childish imagination. The relation of a savage to his totem is usually more that of a brother to a brother, whilst the father-complex is projected back into the abyss of time and finds its embodiment in those semi-human, semi-animal creatures of the Alcheringa, who are regarded as the progenitors of the present human and animal members of the clan. There is a natural tendency in the child to identify itself with its father, and this superadded to the original feeling of psychical and biological unity with environment leads to the identification with the totem.[3] This idea of similarity finds yet more adequate expression for the childish mind in the person of the brother, who is the true riveting-point of the narcissistic tendencies. The concept of the animal "brother" overflows into the narcissistic animal "double" or "wraith" of the third concept. This third concept, at the same time, shows the double structure of these beliefs.

The death the totemite fears as the consequence of the death of his totem animal, is really the punishment for his own unconsciously aggressive tendencies, primarily against the father, and then against the whole totem species, including himself. Killing the totem animal is an "Erzsatzunghandlung" (a vicarious action) for killing the person and thus equivalent to it from the standpoint of the Unconscious which, as already noticed, is sometimes not very far removed from the conscious ideas of an Australian.

The totem or external soul is thus simply the symbol of the man; this is especially evident from the part played by it in dream-life. According to the Euahlayi, for instance, one of the greatest warnings of coming evil is to see your totem in a dream; this is a herald of misfortune to the dreamer or one of his immediate kin.[4] According to the Arunta and Loritja the animal in the dream symbolizes a human member of the clan.[5]

To dream of his own totem means to a Wotjobaluk that someone is doing something to it for the purpose of harming the sleeper or one of his totemites. If he dreams it a second time, it means himself,

[1] Strehlow, *A. & L.*, II. 76. [2] Spencer and Gillen, *N. T.*, 643.

[3] For the importance of these identifications, cf. Freud, *Group Psychology and the Analysis of the Ego*, 1922.

[4] Parker, *Euahlayi Tribe*, 28, 29. [5] Strehlow, l.c., II. 58, 61.

and if he thereupon falls ill, he will certainly see the wraith of the person who is trying to "catch" him.[1] The explanation of this vision will be found in the autosymbolical category of phenomena as described by Silberer:[2] the vision really originates from an endopsychic knowledge of his own unconscious will—will against the person in question projected in a "contrary" form as the "dooming" intention of his adversary into the outer world. According to the Arunta and Loritja the totem ancestor's apparition in a dream means that his guardian spirit is warning him or foretelling his future. If a man of the kangaroo-totem dreams of a kangaroo with broken legs, he expects soon to break his own legs, and if he sees a kangaroo covered with blood approaching him he believes that death at the hands of an enemy is his doom; a concept that can hardly be explained in any other way than as unconscious self-punishment for aggressive tendencies (Wendung gegen die eigene Person) for the attempt to kill the father-kangaroo. Similarly, when a Moon-man looks at the full moon for a longer time than he ought (see above) it is in consequence of his own unconscious aggressive tendencies against his totem,[3] that he dreads death at the enemies' hands. Again, the eating of the totem at the intichiuma is a victorious outbreak of the repressed aggressive tendencies followed by neurotic feelings of compulsion, as clearly shown in the fear of the Arunta head-man at the intichiuma that eating too much of their totem animal might cause the extinction of the whole species:[4] this being the unconscious intention of the rite.

(b) The Individual Totem

We must here branch off into a discussion of the individual totems, for these show the greatest similarity, in their psychical content, to the clan totem in what we may term the narcissistic and brother-concept phase of its evolution.

[1] Howitt, *N. T.*, 147.

[2] Cf. Silberer, "Lekanomantische Versuche," *Zentralblatt für Psychoanalyse*, II. 383, 438, 518, 566.

[3] On the taboo against looking at the full moon, cf. Th. Harley, *Moon Lore*, 1885, 125, 149, 207. A. Goodrich-Freer, "Folk-Lore from the Hebrides," *Folk-Lore*, XIII. 190, 233. A. Strausz, "Bolgár Néphit," *Bulgarian Folk-Beliefs*, 1897, 252. H. Ankert, "Der Mond im Glauben des nordböhmischen Landvolkes," *Zeitschrift für österreichische Volkskunde*, I, 1889, 137. K. Schwenck, *Die Mythologie der Slawen*, 1850, 432. R. Fr. Kaindl, *Die Huzulen*, 1894, 97 (Looking at his own shadow by moonlight as a method of overcoming fear). B. W. Schiffer, "Alltagglauben galizischer Juden," *Am Urquell*, 1893, 118. F. J. Wiedemann, *Aus dem Inneren und Aeusseren Leben der Ehsten*, 1876, 458. Tóth, "Kiskunfélegyháza vidéki néphiedelmek" (Popular Beliefs from Kiskunfélcgyhaza), *Ethnographia*, 1906, 231. (If anyone looks into the moon for an hour a string will snap on the violin of King David—who is supposed to be the man in the moon—and strike out the eyes of the impolite starer. Here the aggressive tendency of the gazing is still preserved in the destroyed string, for which the talion-punishment instantly follows.)

[4] Spencer and Gillen, *Nor. T.*, 322, 323

To avoid misinterpretation, I may say that I do not regard the narcissistic current of feelings as derived from the feelings with regard to the father and brother, but rather to be independently derived from autoerotic sensations, and as such to be represented in primitive consciousness by the concept of the soul, which also develops into "individual totems" or "guardian spirits." The tender side of the ambivalent attitude towards the father and brother consists in the transference of the narcissistic attitude to these nearest kin.[1]

In the tribes fifty miles of Maryborough each boy has a totem called "Pincha," which is given to him by his father and which he calls Noru, that is "brother." A man does not kill or eat his Pincha. Moreover, he is supposed to have some particular affinity to his father's Pincha and is not permitted to eat it.[2] In the Boontha-Murra tribe every native has, in addition to the ordinary totem, a "brother," which might either be a bird, animal or fish.[3] The Narrinyeri applied the same term of ngaitye, meaning friend, to their personal totems and to their clan totems, which shows how closely the two different sorts of totems were associated in their minds.[4] The Yuin also called both budjan.[5] Especially medicine men amongst the Kurnai[6] and Narrinyeri[7] have personal totems acquired in dreams by the former.

In the Yaraikanna tribe, when an old man dreams of anything at night, that object is the ari of the first person he sees next morning, the idea being that the animal is the spirit of the first person met on awakening. The ari of a lad is usually determined by the resemblance to a natural object of the clot of blood formed when the tooth is knocked out at the initiation ceremony.[8] Thus the lad's own blood spilt at the symbolic castration ceremony of tooth-expulsion corresponds to the blood of the totem that he ought to be reluctant in spilling, and it is submittance to this symbolic castration that brings him the protection of the ari that is the fathers and elder brothers.[9] On the Tully River we have the calling upon "namesakes" before going to sleep that leads to their warning their human

[1] Cf. Róheim, "Das Selbst," *Imago*, VII 1, 192.

[2] Howitt, *N.T.*, 147.

[3] A. L. P. Cameron, "Notes on a Tribe speaking the Boontha-Murra," *Science of Man*, 1903, 91.

[4] H. E. A. Meyer, "Manners and Customs of the Aborigines of the Encounter Bay Tribe," in Woods, *Native Tribes of South Australia*, 1879, 197.

[5] Howitt, *N. T.*, 147.

[6] Id., "On Australian Medicine Men," *J. A. I.*, XVI. 34. Id., *N. T.*, 347.

[7] Taplin, *Narrinyeri*, 63. Meyer, l.c., 197.

[8] A. C. Haddon, *Cambridge Anthropological Expedition to Torres Straits*, V. 193.

[9] The totem obtained at the initiation ceremony in exchange for the foreskin (or tooth) must be equivalent to the object for which it is exchanged—that is, a libido symbol. Like all unconscious concepts, it is adequately explained only by a double interpretation: it means both the relinquishing of certain libidinal desires, the protection gained by this sacrifice from the "fathers" (brothers), and also the gratification of these desires.

namesakes of approaching danger in dreams or by body-sensations, whilst again on the Proserpine River it is the animals of the particular groups division that are thus called on.[1]

Whilst these statements correspond to an infantile projection of the brother concept, we see the purely narcissistic element preponderating in the yunbeai of the Euahlayi. Some people, principally wizards or men intending to become such, have an individual totem or yunbeai. This they must never eat or they will die.[2] Any injury to his yunbeai hurts the man himself, and when in danger he has the power to assume its shape. The yunbeai is a sort of *alter ego* ; a man's spirit is in his yunbeai and his yunbeai is in him.[3] A wizard often keeps his in his "minggah," that is, spirit stone or tree. This spirit gives extra strength and extra danger, for any injury to the animal hurts the man too.[4]

On the whole, the individual totem in Australia may be regarded as a hypostasis of the clan totem that branched off at the above indicated phase in the evolution of the concept. Whilst the libidinal components of the narcissistic stage together with the homoerotic tendencies involved therein, found an adequate form of ejection in the sex-totem, the personal totem seems to be rather the representative of the egoistical elements (help, warning in danger and so on) of the narcissistic attitude (self-preservation) together with the auto-symbolic corollaries of this stage of evolution.[5] From the latter point of view the personal totem may be regarded as a sort of projection of the "personalité double," and it is significant that it should be especially found amongst medicine men whose vocation evidently depends upon the neurotic or hysterical traits in their character. In the southern and eastern area with which we have been hitherto chiefly concerned, the prominent features of totemism may be characterized as checks upon individual action, both of the egoistical (food taboo) and the libidinal (matrimonial taboo) type. This second regulative function is common to totems and matrimonial classes, and this is certainly more than a coincidental agreement of these two institutions.

(c) Marriage Classes, Totems and Sub-Totems

The Narrang-ga of Yorke Peninsula are divided into four classes, called Emu, Red Kangaroo, Eagle-hawk and Shark, and the

[1] W. E. Roth, S. M. M., *N. Q. Bull.* V. 1903, 20.

[2] In this connexion it may be remarked that the absence of any taboo in connexion with the clan totem amongst the Euahlayi points to the transference of the taboo from the "Dhe" (clan totem) to its late offshoot, the yunbeai.

[3] Parker, *Euahlayi Tribe*, 21.

[4] Id., ibid., 29, 30.

[5] The individual totem represents what Freud has recently called the "Ego ideal," as contrasted with the Ego. Freud, *Group Psychology and the Analysis of the Ego*, 1922. Ferenczi has described the relationship between narcissism and the auto-symbolic functions (*Hungarian Psycho-analytic Society*, January 1920).

peninsula is divided into four parts between them. The Emu people have the north, the Red Kangaroo the east, the Eagle-hawk the west, and the Shark the south of the peninsula. There cannot be the slightest doubt in this case that the localization is the result of a secondary process, which was perhaps aided by the tribe inhabiting a limited area with natural boundaries.[1] Without the localization we should have a normal four-class system with animal-named subclasses. Another report gives us a two-class system (Eagle-hawk and Seal), with a number of totems for each class.[2]

The four localized totems of the Yercla-Mining have also a certain resemblance to matrimonial classes.[3] Dawson gives five matrimonial classes: Long-billed Cockatoo, Pelican, Banksian Cockatoo, Boa-Snake, and Quail,[4] but closer investigation proves this to be a mistake, and the usual four-class system to obtain here also.[5] Anyhow, we have here a second matrimonial institution besides the clan-totems that is named after animals.

As to the Wotjobaluk, Buandik, Gournditch-Mara, and all the tribes who have the Krokitch-Gamutch system, it is in general difficult to distinguish between classes, subclasses, totems and subtotems. They are all animal-named and merge into one another.[6]

The object of the matrimonial classes is to prevent marriage between those who are of " one flesh." The first " Great-great-grandfather " was called Kuurekeetch (Long-billed Cockatoo): his wife's name was " Kappatch " (Banksian Cockatoo). Their children were Banksian Cockatoos. As the laws of consanguinity forbade marriage between these, it was necessary to introduce " fresh flesh "; the sons and their sons got wives from a distance and thus the Pelican, Boa-snake, and Quail were introduced.[7] The number (five) of these groups, and the fact that the children take the mothers' group-name, points to totems. On the other hand, Cameron got four groups from the natives near Mortlake within the boundaries of the same territory: White Cockatoo (Krokage), Pelican, Black Cockatoo (Kubitch), and Whip Snake. He says that Pelican is supplementary to White Cockatoo and Whip Snake to Black Cockatoo. This would give us the same state of things as that reported by Dawson: Krokitch and Gamitch as the names of the primary divisions, the same names again as the names of the subclasses, Pelican and Whip Snake as the two others. The subclasses,

[1] Howitt, *N. T.*, 67, 129, 130. In the Warramunga tribe, who have also male descent, the north of the country belongs to the Kingilli, the south to the Uluuru. Spencer and Gillen, *Nor. T.*, 26.

[2] T. Kuehn, in Fison and Howitt, *Kamilaroi and Kurnai*, 285.

[3] Howitt, *N. T.*, 129.

[4] J. Dawson, *Australian Aborigines*, 1881, 26.

[5] Howitt, *N.T.*, 125.

[6] Cf. Howitt, l.c., 121–26. Frazer, *T. & E.*, 451–72.

[7] Dawson, *Australian Aborigines*, 1881, 26.

again, were arranged in pairs, as White Cockatoo could only marry Black Cockatoo or Whip Snake, but not the supplementary Pelican.[1] Following the lead of the two primary subdivisions we come to the Gournditch-Mara. Here we have the White Cockatoo (Krokitch) and the Black Cockatoo (Kaputch), these as class-names with only this totem, but a number of subtotems in the respective classes. Moreover, amongst the subtotems, we find the Pelican in the White Cockatoo class (or totem) and the Whip Snake in the Black Cockatoo division.[2] Passing on to the Buandik, we have corresponding classes (White Cockatoo, here called Karaal, and Black Cockatoo, called Wila) as totems, besides a number of others. Each totem again has its own subtotem: for instance, the White Cockatoo has the Summer and the Sun, the Black has the Moon and the Stars,[3] and a similar system exists among the Wotjobaluk.[4]

The Karingbool on the Mackenzie River and the Wuku-wuku on the Burnet River have four classes: (1) Binjoo, with the totems Wood-duck and Gum-tree; (2) Kiarra, totems Black Duck and Coolabah-tree; (3) Bunyart, totems Porcupine and Short Brigalow-tree; (4) Thadbine, totems Yellow-beaked Eagle-hawk and Tall Brigalow-tree.[5] Again, in Queensland we have four exogamous divisions, and each of these has interdictions regarding certain animals forbidding its members to eat, kill or touch these animals; if by totemism pure and simple is to be understood a certain relationship between an individual and an animal or group of animals, then these divisions must certainly be called totemic.[6] The taboo animals vary with each locality, and the same class has not always the same taboos. Every individual, as soon as he or she arrives at the necessary age, is forbidden to eat—but not necessarily to kill—certain animals, each subclass having its own particular group of things that are tabooed. Upon this point the aboriginal seems to be extremely particular, he is firmly convinced that sickness probably of a fatal character would overtake him and that the tabooed thing would certainly not satisfy his hunger. Should the delinquent be caught red-handed he would probably be put to death;[7] these animals "symbolizing the classes" are called the "fathers" and "brothers" of the class members.[8]

Hitherto we have dealt with totemic subclasses in the area in which the inhibitory aspect of the totemic attitude is more

[1] Howitt, *N.T.*, 125. "Children belong to the mother's totem" probably means that they belong to her class, but to the supplementary subclass.

[2] Id., l.c., 124. [3] Id., l.c., 123.

[4] Id., l.c., 121.

[5] A. L. P. Cameron, "On two Queensland Tribes," *Science of Man*, 1904, 27.

[6] W. E. Roth, "Social and Individual Nomenclature," *North Queensland Ethn. Bull.*, No. 18, 1910, 102. W. E. Roth, *E. S.*, 57.

[7] W. E. Roth, l.c., 1897, 57.

[8] E. Palmer, "Notes on some Australian Tribes," *Journ. Anthr. Inst.*, 1884, XIII, 300.

prominent, but analogous phenomena can also be shown to exist amongst the central and western tribes. In North-West Australia the intichiuma ceremonies are connected with the subclasses: if, for instance, the head-man of the Kangaroo tarlow may be a Ballieri, it is the other Ballieri men that help in the intichiuma. Should the head-man die, the control over the Kangaroos passes with his son into the next subclass.[1] In the Mungarai tribe the totem groups are associated with the subclasses. A remarkable feature of the totemic system of this tribe is that, while, as usual, a man must marry a woman belonging to a totemic group different from his own, the children pass into one which is not the same as that of either their father or mother, but is associated with the subclass to which they belong on the father's side of the tribe. The same system seems to be practised by the Yungman tribe.[2] In the Djauan tribe the totems are divided between the subclasses in such a way that those to which parents and children belong have them in common and the descent of the totem is strictly paternal.[3]

The Mara, Anula and Nullakun system is not quite easy to comprehend. We are told that in the Mara tribe the totems are divided between the four classes, as follows: (1) Murungun: Eaglehawk, Yellow Snake, Hill-kangaroo, etc.; (2) Mumbali: Whirlwind, Poisonous Snake, White Hawk, Crow, etc.; (3) Purdal: Blue-headed Snake, Big Kangaroo, Crane, Wallaby, etc.; (4) Kuial: Emu, Turkey, Goanna, and others.[4] A Mara man of the Mumbali class who had a snake called Daual as totem (perhaps the poisonous snake mentioned above), inherited it from his father, as his children will inherit it from him. His wife was a Purdal woman, with the Euro as totem.[5] The remarkable thing in these tribes, however, is that they do not have the usual indirect system of descent, that is, the son does not belong to the subclass which is complementary to his father's subclass; here we have direct male descent; the son belongs to the same class as his father. These are, therefore, not subclasses at all as we understand the word, so that the idea of the same totems remaining in the same divisions all through presents no difficulty.

But that there is some connexion or assimilation between totem and class is evident from what follows: the wife is a Purdal woman of the Euro totem, his mother a Kuial woman of the Goanna totem. His son will be like himself, a Mumbali of the "Daual" totem, but he must marry, like his father did before him, a Kuial of the

[1] E. Clement, "Ethnographical Notes on the West Australian Aborigines," *Internat. Archiv für Ethnographie*, 1904, XVI. 6, 7. A. R. Brown, "Three Tribes of Western Australia," *J. A. I.*, 1913, 172, 191. As to inherited rights to certain ceremonies, cf. Spencer and Gillen, *N. T.*, 278. Id., *Nor. T.*, 750.

[2] Spencer, *N. T. N. T. A.*, 205–7.

[3] Id., ibid., 208.

[4] Spencer and Gillen, *Nor. T.*, 172.

[5] Spencer, *N. T. N. T. A.*, 208.

Goanna totem.[1] The Anula[2] and the Nullakun[3] have the same system.

Sometimes, as mentioned above, it is not quite clear whether we have to do with subclasses and totems or totems and subtotems. The Kaiabara have the classes Kubatine and Dilebi and the subclasses Bulkoin, Bunda, Baring and Turowain, with two or three totems for each subclass.[4] But according to an earlier report of the same author, Kubatine means flood-water and Dilebi lightning, which in the second report are given as totems in the Kubatine class (Baring subclass) respectively. Again, in the first report we have Bulkoin rendered as "Carpet Snake," Bunda as "Native Cat," Baring as "Turtle," Turowain as "Bat," all of which figure in the second report as totems in the respective subclasses.[5] It is not quite certain which of the two reports is correct, for in South-West Australia we have the classes Wordung-mat (Crow) and Manytchmat (Cockatoo), with the subclasses Ballaruk (Pelican), Nagarnook (Emu), Tondarup (Fish-hawk) and Didarruk (The Sea). The Nagarnooks are also called Wejuks, which seems to be the ordinary word for emu, and are supposed to be able to transform themselves from men to emus at will.[6] In the Annan River tribe we have two classes named after different sorts of bees, and subclasses in these meaning Eagle-hawk, Bee, another sort of Bee, and Salt-water Eagle-hawk.[7] The boundaries between class, subclass and totem tend to become confused. In the Wiradjuri tribe we have Red Kangaroo (Murri) as a totem, in the Red Kangaroo subclass, Black Duck as a totem in the class Black Duck.[8] Amongst the Kamilaroi and Buntamurra we have a division of the totems between the subclasses. As this contradicts the general rule since the subclasses alternate with the generations, whilst the totems do not, critics have found a difficulty in allowing that the totems which follow either the father or the mother should be fixed in one subclass. However, we do not like to doubt the accuracy of our native informants, and Spencer's detailed statements in his last book, quoted above, make it clear how such a system can operate. Either we must suppose that the Kamilaroi and Buntamurra had the same system, the totems being arranged in corresponding lists under the headings of the various subclasses, so that "a Ngapalieri man of the Water-plant totem marries a Nakomara

[1] Spencer, *N. T. N. T. A.*, 208.

[2] Spencer and Gillen, *Nor. T.*, 172, and Mara, cf. id., ibid., 119. Cf. these systems with the southern Arunta. However, these four classes are again subdivided into two each, thus giving an eight-class system, in which every second class is anonymous, and in which the normal rule of indirect male descent prevails.

[3] Spencer, *N. T. N. T. A.*, 208, 209.

[4] Howitt, *N. T.*, 115.

[5] Howitt, *J. A. I.*, XIII. 336.

[6] Daisy M. Bates, l.c., XXIII–XXIV, 47, 58, quoted by Frazer, *T. & E.*, I. 563, 565.

[7] Howitt, *N. T.*, 118.

[8] Id., ibid., 107.

woman of the Paddy-melon totem and their children are Ngabullan and Poison-snake, etc.," or it is possible that there was no such system in these southern tribes. The subclass may have changed without the totem changing and, nevertheless, there may have been a misty idea that certain totems belonged to the animal-named subclasses in the same sense as the subtotem " belongs " to the totem.[1]

The path of inquiry into Australian sociology is beset by a number of difficulties at this point. Why do the classes in all the tribes correspond to each other ?[2] Why do we find the right totem in the right class and never find one totem in both classes ?[3] The first question is settled if we attribute the origin of the dichotomy to the father-son conflict, when each tribe would unconsciously feel which of the two primary divisions was the son and which the father division. But probably the dichotomy took place before the separation of the tribes, and we have here survivals of the totemic complex as it existed in the Primeval Australian Horde. This proto-totemic complex was transferred to the subclasses (originating out of a further splitting of the original classes) that perhaps in a certain measure corresponded to local divisions. The development of the present totems, the transference of the taboo to these from the original class and subclass totems, has in all probability been reached through the medium of those primitive efforts at classification that probably set in in the two-class phase and reached their full development in the four-class phase of society: in the so-called subtotems. The unconscious meaning underlying the division of society into two primary classes is fraught with such a preponderant importance for primitive man that this division is extended beyond the bounds of society and is projected into the universe, the " discharge " of this over-tension being attained by an introjection of all natural phenomena[4] into one of the two divisions. The World is divided between the Father and the Son ; that is, Man can only perceive Nature from the dominating attitude of the Family complex.

The subtotems.

The Euahlayi have a considerable number of subtotems for each totem. The Bohrah (Kangaroo), which is " friends " with the Emu, has Top-knot Pigeon, various parrots and trees and the north-east wind as subtotems. All clouds, lightning, thunder, and rain that is not blown up by the wind of another totem belong to

[1] Howitt, *N. T.*, 104, 226, 227. The Kuinmurburra have the Barrimundi, Hawk, Good-water and Iguana as sub-classes. Howitt, ibid., 111. Cf. Frazer, *T. & E.*, I. 408, 409, 433. Spencer, *N. T. N. T. A.*, 1914, 207.

[2] Cf. N. W. Thomas, *Kinship Organizations and Group Marriage in Australia*, 1906.

[3] Cf. A. Lang, *The Secret of the Totem*, 1905, 154, 171.

[4] The primary attitude of repulsion (hatred and fear) towards the outward world in general is only overcome by the psychic process of identification. Nature is dangerous, except so far as it enters into the social system.

Bohrah. The Black Snake totem claims the Sun amongst its subtotems, the Opossum totem has, besides many others, the Moon.[1] A man of the Maira (Paddy-melon) totem will never be drowned, for the rivers are one of his subtotems. Some of the totems which appear as subtotems in one part of the country are original totems in other parts, and all totems are divided between the two moieties of the tribe.[2] Amongst the Wotjobaluk, who, as mentioned above, have animal-named classes, the totems are distributed between these classes, and each totem again contains a number of subtotems. In the Ngeumba tribe, not only the people themselves but everything in the universe belongs to one or other of the two phratries Ngurrawun and Mumbun.[3] The subtotems amount to a complete subdivision of the universe between White and Black Cockatoo. A man who belongs to the Krokitch moiety and the Sun totem claimed the kangaroo as belonging to him, another claimed Bunjil. " The true totem owns him, but he owns the subtotem." [4] The system of " mortuary totems " shows how space as such is divided between the clans ; every clan claims a portion of the compass.[5] The same phratry names, with the same subdivisions of the universe, exist along the coast from the Glenelg River to Geelong, reaching inland approximately to the main dividing range. Amongst the Ta-ta-thi, Wathi-wathi and allied tribes the universe is divided between the different members of the tribe ; some claim the trees, others the plains, others the sky, stars, wind, rain, and so on. The same subdivision of the universe is also reported from the tribes of North-Western Queensland,[6] and from the Chingalee.[7] According to the Port Mackay tribe [8] (Queensland), everything in Nature is divided between the classes. The wind belongs to one class and the rain to the other. The Sun is Wutara and the Moon is Yungaree. The stars are divided between them, and if a star is pointed out, they will tell you to which division it belongs. Amongst the natives from Cape Julien to Esperance the terms noyyung and ngunning [9] are applied to every tree, shrub, root, to every thing in Nature. For instance, the Red-gum is a

[1] According to the Arunta, the Moon is a man of the Opossum totem. Spencer and Gillen, *N. T.*, 564. Opossums are usually hunted by moonlight.

[2] K. L. Parker, *The Euahlayi Tribe*, 1905, 16–20.

[3] Mathews, *E. N.*, 6.

[4] Howitt, *N. T.*, 121–23. R. H. Mathews speaks of clans, each having a list of totems, consisting of animals, plants, the heavenly bodies, the elements, and so on. In other words, all creation, animate and inanimate, is divided between Gurogity and Gumaty. R. H. Mathews, *E. N.*, 1905, 84.

[5] Howitt, *N. T.*, 454.

[6] Edward Palmer, " Notes on some Australian Tribes," *J. A. I.*, XIII. 300.

[7] R. H. Mathews, " The Wombya Organization of the Australian Aborigines," *American Anthropologist*, 1900, 494.

[8] F. Bridgeman and Rev. H. Bucas, *Port Mackay and its Neighbourhood.* Curr, *The Australian Race*, III. 45. Brough-Smyth, *The Aborigines of Victoria*, 1878, I. 91.

[9] These are the relationship-terms which denote the two primary divisions.

male and belongs to the Manytchmat division, it is ngunning for a woman of the Wordungmat division. The White-gum is female and belongs to the Wordungmat. "In fact, the primary classes Wordungmat and Manytchmat divide all natural objects between them, and every living thing and every tree, root and fruit is noy-yung or ngunning."[1] At Mount Gambier not only mankind but things in general are subject to these divisions. No reasons are assigned for the arrangement, but the divisions evidently originated out of a specially fixed chain of associations. When a native was questioned to what division a bullock belonged, he replied, after a pause, that, as it eats grass, it must belong to the Wirie (Tea-tree) division.[2] Man begins to take possession of Nature conceptually before he does so actually; the "(platonic) idea" precedes its own realization. This is evidently confirmed by the fact that in some of these primitive efforts at classification the wish-fulfilment attitude has not yet been inhibited and become negative in the totemic taboo; a "totem" is not the object a man must avoid, but a part of nature reserved for his own and his group's use. Certain animals are the especial game of each class. Obu, for instance, claims as his game emu and wallaby, and if he wishes to invite his fellows of the same subclass in a neighbouring tribe to hunt the common game, he must do this by means of a message stick made from the wood of a tree which is, like himself, of the Obu subclass.[3] Like the tribe itself, game is divided into two divisions—Mallera and Wutera, and certain classes are only allowed to eat certain sorts of food. The Banbey are restricted to opossum, kangaroo, dog, honey of small bee, etc. The Wongoo have emu, bandicoot, black duck, black snake, brown snake, etc.; the Oboo have carpet snakes, honey of the stinging bee; the Kargilla, porcupine, plain turkey, and so on. The latter division also possesses water, rain, fire and thunder, and they enjoy a reputation of being able to make rain at pleasure.[4]

The Karingbool on the Mackenzie River have four classes: Binjoo, with the totems Black Duck and Coolabah-tree; Kiarra: Wood-duck and Gum-tree; Bunyart: Porcupine and Short Brigalow-tree; Thadbine: Yellow-backed Eagle-hawk and Tall Brigalow-tree. Birt says: "I believe that among the Central Queensland tribes the aboriginal's totem is held sacred by him, but here the opposite seems to be the case. For instance, Black Duck or Wood-Duck can only be killed by either a Binjool or a Kiarra to which they belong, and must be held sacred by Bunyart or Thadbine. In like manner, the Porcupine and Yellow-backed Hawk

[1] Daisy M. Bates, *Victorian Geographical Journal*, XIII. XXIV. 1905, 1906, 48, 49. Quoted by Frazer, *T. & E.*, I. 567.

[2] Fison and Howitt, *Kamilaroi and Kurnai*, 1880, 168, 169. Howitt, *N. T*, 124.

[3] Howitt, l.c., 113.

[4] Curr, l.c., III. 27.

are exclusive property of Bunyart and Thadbine, and the same thing applies in the case of the trees of each class: Brigalow-trees are the best and the most generally used for making weapons, and should Binjoo or Kiarra want a spear from that tree, he has to apply to Bunyart or Thadbine to get it for him; whilst with regard to the gum, coolibah or box-tree, from which the bark used in making their camps is generally stripped, Bunyart and Thadbine would have to go without it unless it were given to them by Binjoo or Kiarra. Opossums are seldom found in a Brigalow-tree, and may not be taken unless it can be done without cutting the tree or injuring bark in any way. Thus Bunyart and Thadbine are often under obligation to Binjool and Kiarra for the opossums they need as food. It is obvious that, while the former couple have the advantage in obtaining weapons, the latter hold the balance of power in getting bark and catching opossums." [1]

These systems correspond exactly to that reported by W. E. Roth on the distribution of animals between the subclasses, only here we have possession instead of avoidance. The fact that the members of the one moiety had to ask for permission to use the natural objects classed under the heading of the other moiety reminds us of the "liberation" ceremonies in Central Australian intichiuma. It seems that the possession-aspect survives in ceremonies after the inhibition-aspect has become dominant in reality,[2] but this might be an additional reason to ascribe an archaic character to the totems of the dual organization.[3] However, the inhibition on the animals of the man's own phratry must have originated before clan totemism existed in the dual phase of society as a direct consequence of the inhibition to phratry incest, that is, of the existence of phratries as such. In Western Victoria every thing in the universe is divided between the phratries Gurogity and Kappaty.[4] A hunter carries weapons made from the wood of each phratry. If he throws at a Gamaty animal he uses a Gurogity missile and vice versa.[5] The multiplex totems of the phratries seem to be the material of which the multiplex subtotems of the

[1] A. L. P. Cameron, "On Two Queensland Tribes," *Science of Man*, 1904, 28.

[2] "It is understood that when a certain dance is being performed, for instance, the Tortoise dance, the members of that clan are in the position of hosts to the others, taking pride in having them dance the dance to their totem.—Speck, *Ethnology of the Yuchi Indians*, 1909, 113.

[3] We are substantially in agreement both with A. C. Haddon, *Proceedings of British Assoc.*, 1902, who thinks that the totem was originally the principal food-animal of the clan, and with Werner, "Ich werde anderwärts die Auffassung begründen dass jedenfalls eine Art des Totemismus aus dem Tabu desjenigen Tieres hervorgegangen sein dürfte das ursprünglich Jagdtier einer Stammesgruppe von Jägern war" (H. Werner, *Die Ursprünge der Metapher*, 1919, 216). As to the relation of the primitive positive aspect of totemism to the secondary inhibition, see below in connexion with the Alcheringa myths of the Arunta.

[4] R. H. Mathews, *E. N.*, 94.

[5] Id., l.c., 92.

clans were formed, and these again may develop into real totems if the process of fission lasts long enough.

The Wotjobaluk have subtotems that are in the process of gaining a sort of independence : a man who belongs to class Krokitch and totem Hot-wind claimed all the five subtotems of Hot-wind (three snakes and two birds), yet of these there was one which he especially claimed as belonging to him, namely carpet-snake. Thus his totem Hot-wind seems to have been in process of subdivision into minor totems, and this man's division might have become hot-wind-carpet-snake had not civilization rudely stopped the process by almost extinguishing these tribes.[1]

Besides the subtotems, we must mention some similar variants of Australian totemism, in which the systematic character of the subtotems (the division of the universe) is lacking, although they may possibly represent similar systems in a nascent state. To begin with, we have the linked totem system of the Melville Islanders, where the totem groups are divided into three pairs and the totems belonging to the same " pukui " (skin) regard each other as " mates " and do not intermarry. So that from the point of view of marriage, this amounts to a certain number of clans, with more than one totem for each, only these totems are co- and not sub-ordinate to each other.[2] Something similar is found amongst the Arunta, although as their totems are not co- but sub-ordinate to each other, their system may be regarded as an intermediate one between the Melville Islanders in the north and the tribes with subtotems in the south and the east. Around each of the Ilthurra or sacred holes of the Witchetty Grub totem, at which a part of the intichiuma ceremony is performed, there are certain stones standing on end which represent special birds called Chantunga. These birds are looked upon as the " ilqualthari," or the mates of the Witchetty people, because certain grubs in the Alcheringa changed into these birds. The Witchetty men will not eat this bird.[3] This food taboo is absent in the other cases mentioned by Spencer and Gillen ; all the mates they give are birds, excepting the " Big Lizard " people, who call a smaller variety of lizard their mate.

Strehlow gives a fuller list of these associated totems in which the number of plants seems nearly to equal that of birds, whilst mammals, reptiles, fishes, insects and other natural phenomena are comparatively rare.

Leonhardi thinks that this system is nearer kin to the " linked totems " of New Guinea and the Melanesian cases than to the subtotems of the southern tribes.[4] But it must be remarked that

[1] Howitt, *Smithsonian Report*, 1883, 818. Frazer, *T. & E.*, 80. Cf. Howitt, *N. T.*, 122.

[2] Spencer, *N. T. N. T. A.*, 1914, 200.

[3] Spencer and Gillen, *N. T.*, 447, 448.

[4] C. Strehlow and U. von Leonhardi, *A. & Z.*, vol III. ; *Die totemischen Kulte*, 1910, 12, 17.

the characteristic features of this "linked totem" system are absent in Central Australia.

The members of each clan have as totems (amongst the Massim) a series of associated animals belonging to different classes of the organic kingdom; ordinarily these linked totems are a bird, a fish, a snake and a plant, but a four-footed vertebrate (such as the monitor lizard or the crocodile) may be added to each series of linked totems.[1]

Less systematic representatives of the same idea are found in Melanesia and Polynesia.[2]

Mammals are conspicuous by their absence, whilst they have the dominant position in Central Australia. Possibly we may have to do with the fusion of two different systems in the case of the Arunta; normal totemism with mammals, on the one hand, and, superadded to it a system like the New Guinea one, which was relegated to a subordinate position and gave rise to the "mate" totems. In this case the predominance of birds amongst the "mate" totems would correspond to the first place occupied by them in New Guinea and elsewhere. The Waduman have a different system. In addition to the main totem, each individual has one or more accessory totems. The main one is that associated with the totemic group into which he is born, whilst the others are given to him when he is initiated. He is first of all, during the initiation ceremonies, told his main totem, which is that of his mother, and at a later period, the accessory totems.[3] This looks like a combination of the ideas of "accessory" and "individual" totem. In the Worgait tribe each individual may be associated with more than one totemic group. A man may, for instance, belong to the Frog, Shark and Sugar-bag totems. The first was his main totem and the others came afterwards.[4]

In these facts I think we have the answer to the second question,[5] and we can try to account for the fact why the totems are divided between the classes or subclasses. If we imagine the Eagle-hawk phratry to be in possession of a tract of hunting grounds and to have a number of subtotems, a time must come when over-population compels a group to leave the restricted boundaries of the phratric hunting grounds. As soon as the group that thus swarms off becomes conscious of a new collective life it will project this new unity into nature in the form of a new totem. But as all psychical processes run in preformed channels the new symbol will be chosen from the natural object previously introjected into the original phratry-concept, that is, it will be one of the subtotems of the phratry.

[1] C. G. Seligmann, *The Melanesians of British New Guinea*, 1910, 9; cf. 439.
[2] W. H. R. Rivers, *The History of Melanesian Society*, 1914, II. 338.
[3] Spencer, *N. T. N. T. A.*, 196, 197.
[4] Id., ibid., 204.
[5] "Eagle-hawk totem regularly in Eagle-hawk class."

3. ANIMAL NAMED CLASSES, PHRATRIC TOTEMS AND SUB-TOTEMS

I. Animal Named Local Organization.
87, 272 (pp. 81, 82).

II. Animal Named Phratries.

(*a*) White and black cockatoo.
92, 93, 94, 95, 96 (p. 82).

(*b*) Cockatoo and crow.
261, 262, 263, 264, 265, 266, 267 (p. 85).

(*c*) Eagle-hawk and crow.
98, 99, 100, 101, 102, 103, 104, 105, 106, 107 (H. 126), 109, 110, 112, 121, 122, 123, 124, 125, 126, 127, 128 (H. 97–100), 131 (C. Richards: "The Marran' Warree' Tribes," *Science of Man*, 1903, 126), 132, 133, 135, 136, 140, 141, 142, 143, 321, 328 (H. 97–100) (cf. Thomas: l.c. 48).

(*d*) Two species of bees.
332 (p. 85).

III. Animal Named Classes.
92, 93, 94, 95, 96 (p. 82), 98, 99, 100, 101, 102, 103, 104, 105, 106, 107, 112 (H. 111), 130, 138, 139, 148, 149, 150, 153, 154, 157, 158, 159, 163 (Thomas: l.c. 42) 174 (H. 111), 179 (Thomas: l.c. 42), 261, 262, 263, 264, 265, 266, 267 (p. 85), 314, 315 (Thomas: l.c. 42), 321 (H. 111), 332 (Thomas: l.c. 42).

IV. Totems or Animals Taboos Distributed between the Classes.
21, 26,27, 28, 31, 32 (p. 84), 153 (p. 85), 158 (p. 85), 180 (p. 85), 193, 196, 204, 210, 223, 224 (p. 83), 232, 235, 236 (p. 84), 324, 325 (p. 83).

V. The Same Word in Use to Designate Both the Class and the Totem.
67, 71, 74, 75, 76, 81 (H. 91), 92, 93, 95 (H. 122), 182 (H. 96, 97), 317 (H. 93).

VI. Sub-Totems.
43 (p. 87), 92, 93, 94, 95, 96 (pp. 82, 90), 121, 122, 123, 124, 125, 126, 127, 128 (p. 87), 131 (Brown: *J.R.A.I.*, 1918, 248), 138, 150 (pp. 86, 87), 195, 215, 216, 217, 218 (p. 87), 261, 262, 263, 264, 265, 266, 267 (p. 87), 300, 316 (pp. 87, 88).

VII. Linked Totems.
1 (Sp. III, 200).

VIII. Associated Totems.
24, 52, 56 (pp. 90, 91), 319 (p. 91).

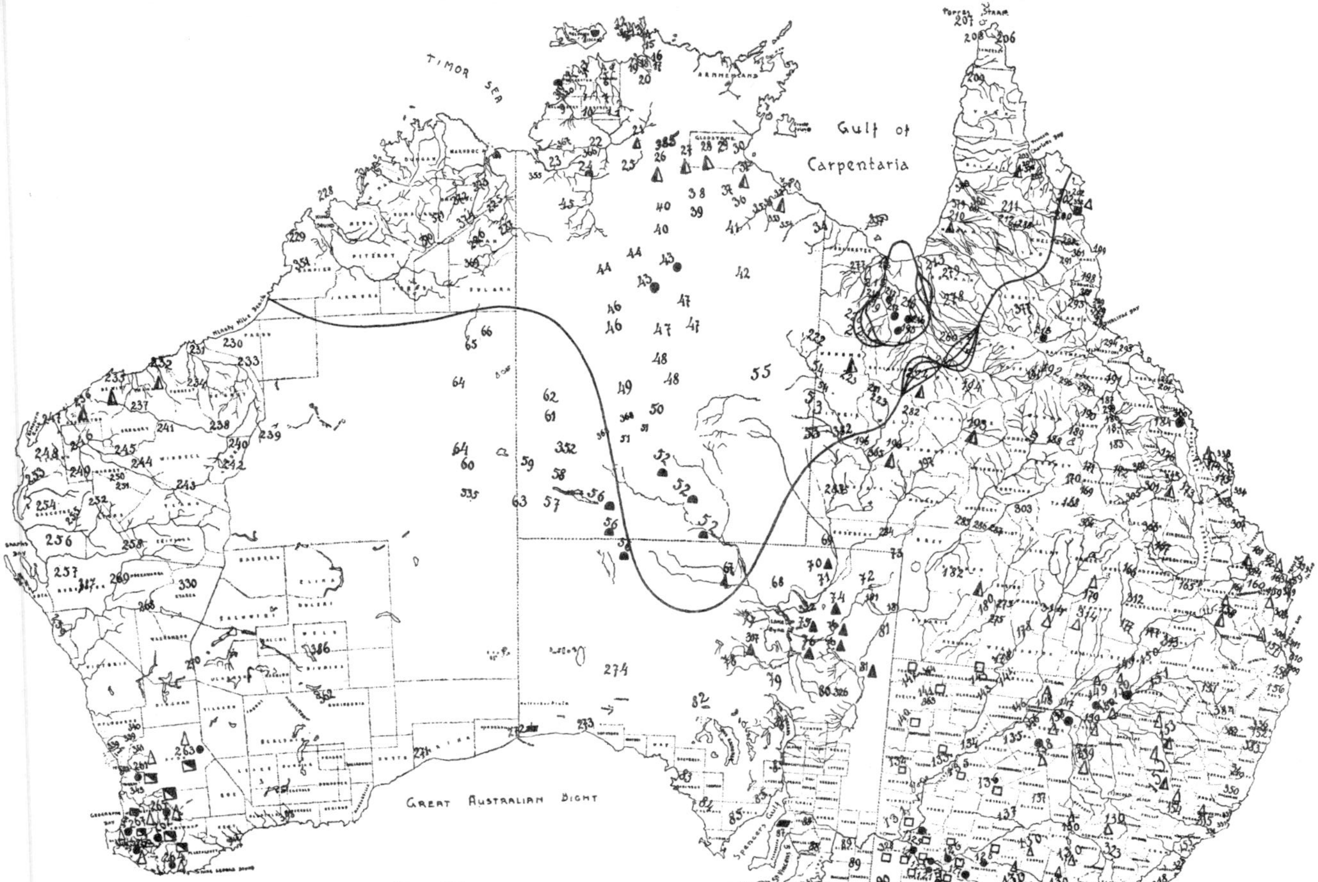

MAP No. 3.
Animal-named Classes, Phratric Totems and Sub-Totems.

Which of these subtotems is to receive an additional emphasis is probably determined by the new environment or perhaps the choice of locality is determined by the subtotem, and this is what we mean by our supposition that introjection of nature comes before possession, that man possesses nature in his collective ideas before he possesses it in fact. As Eagle-hawk phratry would only choose from Eagle-hawk, Crow from Crow subtotems,[1] evidently the same totem could not occur on both sides of the tribe. In the process of evolution the individuality of the new groups would be more and more distinct and the totemic taboo and cult would after some generations be transferred from the phratry (or sub-phratric [2]) totems to the new clan totems.[3]

[1] The group which was the last to leave the original dwelling-place where the swarming began would retain the phratry symbol as its own clan totem, and this is why we usually find an eagle-hawk clan in the eagle- hawk phratry. Cf., for instance, A. L. P. Cameron, "Notes on some Tribes of New South Wales, *J. A. I.*, 1884, 348.

[2] Phratric totems are recognized by Frazer in his original treatise (see *T. & E.*, I. 76), but the idea seems to have been dropped by him later on.

[3] My views presuppose all totemic groups to have been originally localized: contiguity in space being the starting-point of the group-concept of contiguity in thought. On the subtotems in general, cf. E. Durkheim et M. Mauss, "De quelques formes primitives de classification," *L'Année Sociologique*, VI. especially p. 67.

CHAPTER IV

THE ALCHERINGA MYTH

The living animal regarded more as brother than father by the human totemite. The father-concept projected into a mythical period.

We have already noticed the fact that the mental attitude which dominates the relation of an aboriginal to his totem-animal is characterized rather by the "brother" or "elder brother" complex than by the father-concept; this latter idea is projected into the past in the shape of semi-human mythical heroes, the common ancestors of the present human and animal totem-brethren. This is the myth by which many Australian tribes account for totemism as well as for the rest of their social institutions, and this myth forms the connecting-link between the phenomena that are chiefly characteristic of the Negative and Positive Areas of Australian Totemism. There is a tradition very widespread among the tribes of New South Wales that the earth was originally peopled by a race much more powerful, especially in the magic arts, than that which now inhabits it. The Wathi-wathi call these people Bookomurri, and say they were famous for hunting, fighting, etc., and were eventually changed into animals by Tha-tha-pulli, who then created the present race. Others say that the Bookomurri effected the change themselves, and that as animals they felt an interest in the new race that succeeded them and imparted to it much valuable knowledge. A belief exists that the magical powers of the doctors, disease-makers and rain-makers has been handed down to them from the Bookomurri.[1] The Encounter Bay tribes have no story of the origin of the world, but they suppose nearly all animals originally to have been men who performed great prodigies and at last transformed themselves into different kinds of animals and stones. Thus the Raminjerar point out several large stones or points of rock along the beach whose sex and name they distinguish.[2] With the Kurnai certain animals, birds and reptiles are known as

[1] A. L. P. Cameron, "Notes on some Tribes of New South Wales, *J. A. I.*, 1884, 368.

[2] H. E. A. Meyer, *Manners and Customs of the Aborigines of the Encounter Bay Tribe*. J. D. Woods, *The Native Tribes of South Australia*, 1879, 202.

Mukjiak, that is, "excellent flesh," while other creatures used for food are merely "jiak" (flesh). In all the tales in which a bird-man or reptile-man or animal-man takes part, in a twofold character it is a Muk-kurnai. This may be translated as "eminent man," the Kurnai of the legend being thus distinguished from the Kurnai of the present time. Besides the Muk-kurnai the Muk-rukut (Rukut-women) figure in these legends, and as they are regarded not merely as the predecessors but also as the "grandfathers" of the Kurnai, the term may be translated as "eminent ancestors."[1] The Euahlayi have their legend of the golden age when man, birds, beasts and elements spoke a common language.[2] The legends of the Lake Eyre tribes relate to the Mura-muras who were the predecessors and prototypes of the blacks who believe in their former and present existence.[3] At present these Mura-muras are supposed to inhabit trees, which are, therefore, sacred. Only the medicine men are able to see them, and it is from these Mura-muras that they obtain their magical powers.[4] In some tribes we find special names to designate this mythical "aurea aetas"; the Waduman speak of the far past as the Yabulungu,[5] the Warramunga, Walpari and Wulmala call this period Wingara.[6] In the Mungarai tribe we have the traditions of a mythic epoch called Kurnallan[7]; the Nullakun call the old times during which the ancestors walked about the country Musmus;[8] the Mara myths refer to it as Djidjan,[9] and the Anula call it Raraku,[10] the Binbinga and Tjingilli call it Mungai.[11]

"Dream times" and wish-fulfilment.

These names do not give us any clue to the interpretation of the myth as their meaning is unknown; but the Arunta whose myths on this golden age are better known than those of all the other tribes put together, afford us some information on the matter. They (and the Kaitish, Unmatjera) call the epoch in which these mythical ancestors lived Alcheringa, and as alcheri means dream this would signify "dream times."[12] Strehlow has his doubts as to this etymology, but his emendations hardly make much difference from a psychological point of view. He says to dream is "altjirerama," from altjira (totem or totem-ancestor) and "rama," to see. The

[1] Howitt, *N. T.*, 487.
[2] Parker, *Euahlayi Tribe*, 83.
[3] Howitt, op. cit., 475.
[4] Id., l.c., 482.
[5] Spencer, *N. T. N. T. A.*, 1914, 315, 332.
[6] Spencer and Gillen, *Nor. T.*, 427, 765.
[7] Spencer, *N. T. N. T. A.*, 266.
[8] Id., l.c., 267.
[9] Id., l.c., 268. However, a previous account tells us that the Mara call the Alcheringa Intjitja.—Spencer and Gillen, *Nor. T.*, II. 223.
[10] Spencer and Gillen, ibid., II. 223.
[11] Id., ibid.., 438, 754. In the Warramunga tribe the name mungai means the totem-animal and the local totem-centre.
[12] Id., ibid., 745.

Loritja have the expression for dreaming tukura nangani: to see a tukura.[1] But altjira is not the own totem of the Arunta; it is his mother's totem which he respects in addition to his own and which is supposed to warn him in dreams of impending danger.[2] This seems to show that there is a psychical relationship between the Alcheringa myths and dream-life. The Wichita myth tells us of the first man and woman and then says, "After the man and the woman were made they dreamed that things were made for them, and when they woke they had the things of which they had dreamed."[3] This is as much to say that the dream is to be viewed principally in the light of an infantile type of wish-fulfilment, and it is this regressive element which, to begin with, evidently connects the Alcheringa myths with dream-life.

Absence of totemic taboos in the Alcheringa.

The two cardinal taboos of totemism are entirely absent in these traditions, so that we may be said to have here the original wish-fulfilment type of this institution.[4] "There is not a solitary fact which indicates that a man of one totem must marry a woman of another; on the contrary we meet constantly and only with groups of men and women of the same totem living together, and in these early traditions it appears to be the normal condition for a man to have as wife a woman of the same totem as himself."[5] This state of things, which, by the way, is nothing but a projection of custom as it actually exists in the Arunta tribe,[6] is rather *sous entendu* than emphasized in the legends; not so with the positive aspect of the other taboo: the Alcheringa ancestors deliberately and systematically eat their own totem.

[1] Strehlow, *A. & L.*, I. 2, 4. As to the existence of the expression Alcheringa as a mythical period, I do not think that Strehlow's negative evidence can outweigh Spencer and Gillen's positive data, especially if we take the analogous terms of other central and northern tribes into account. As to the "altjira," this looks like a survival of matrilineal descent in a patrilineal tribe. Or, perhaps, we may have to do with two strata, one with uterine descent having been assimilated by a tribe which counted descent through the males.

[2] Id., II. 58.

[3] G. A. Dorsey, *The Mythology of the Wichita*, 1904, 25. The gods are spoken of as "dreams," ibid., 20.

[4] Cf. the discussion on this subject between Frazer, *T. & E.*, I. 238, and A. Lang, "The Historicity of Arunta Traditions," *Man*, 1910, 120.

[5] Spencer and Gillen, *N. T.*, I. 419.

[6] But "according to traditions of the middle Alcheringa there were no restrictions to marriage such as now obtain." "A Purula man and a Kumara woman are represented as having been found together." "Groups of hawk men and women, all of the Purula and Kumara classes, who may not marry one another, are represented as living together."—Spencer and Gillen, ibid., 418. "The Achilpa men meet an Achilpa woman; they perform the rite of subincision on her, and then they cohabit with her."—Id., ibid., 107. The present state of things in the Arunta tribe is that marriage is only regulated by classes, and as the totems are not distributed between these, there is no reason why a man of the kangaroo totem should not marry a woman of the same totem. But in the Alcheringa totemic endogamy, which is still a possibility, *seems to have been the rule.*

The Witchetty men eat witchetty grub at their own totem-centre.[1] The Plum men eat plums[2]; the Snake women eat their own totem, the snake,[3] and we hear of a man of the Carpet-Snake totem who lived entirely upon carpet-snakes.[4] The Moon-man, who belongs to the opossum totem, hunts opossum.[5] The Snake-Poison (ntjikantja) men kill and eat the mythical water-snake.[6] Two big renina snakes are pursued by Renina-Snake men.[7] The Grey-Kangaroo men kill and eat grey kangaroos.[8] Kangaroo-Rat men hunt kangaroo rats.[9] The Euro men have a "mate" in the form of the painted finch, which in the Alcheringa was an Euro man. These Euro men are said to have been great eaters of euro, and their bodies were drenched with blood which dripped from the bodies of the euros which they killed and carried with them, and that is why the painted finch is splashed with red.[10]

Eating the totem in the traditions of the Arunta tribe.

The Wild-Cat men change into Plum men and henceforth they eat plums just as the woman who was a Hakea-flower, and later on is a Bandicoot, eats bandicoots.[11] A man of the Euro totem eats euro and on changing his totem and becoming a Kangaroo man he eats kangaroo.[12] Plum women eat plums, Fish man goes fishing, Grub people feed on grubs.[13] The eating of the totem extends to the associated totems or "mates": out of friendship the tnelja and mbangara bushes and the kemba-flower let themselves be eaten by the Red Kangaroo in the Alcheringa, and hence these are now the "mates" of the Red Kangaroo totem.[14] The Grey Kangaroo feeds on the grass *Triodia irritans*, and we find this plant among the associated totems.[15] Perhaps the grass seed eaten by the Pigeon man ought to be mentioned in this connexion.[16] The men of the Lizard totem (*Varanus giganteus Gray*) eat the grass seed ebalanga: this is their associated totem,[17] and the same applies to the Raven man feeding on latjia roots.[18] A Grey Kangaroo man hunts the grey kangaroo (*Macropus robustus Gould*) but he cannot overtake it. Young men stop the animal in its flight and kill it. They try to roast it, but they cannot even move the corpse. The Kangaroo man lifts it easily. He keeps the tail and the fat, and gives the rest to the youths. He goes to a water-hole and on coming back he sees that flesh has again covered the bones of the

[1] Spencer and Gillen, *N. T.*, 430, 431.
[2] Id., ibid., 208, 403, 404.
[3] Id., ibid., 400.
[4] Id., ibid., 409.
[5] Strehlow, I. 17.
[6] Id., I. 23.
[7] Id., I. 48.
[8] Id., I. 29, 30, 40–42.
[9] Id., I. 63, 64.
[10] Spencer and Gillen, *N. T.*, 448.
[11] Spencer and Gillen, *N. T.*, 208, 433. Frazer, *T. & E.*, I. 238.
[12] Id., ibid., 208, 446, 449. Frazer, I. 239.
[13] Id., ibid., 208, 403, 404. Witchetty men eat witchetty grubs at a witchetty totem-centre.—Ibid. 430, 431.
[14] Strehlow, III., xii, I. 36, 37, 39, 40.
[15] Id., I. 40–42; III. xii.
[16] Id., I. 72, 73; III. xvi.
[17] Id., I. 78, 79; III. xvi.
[18] Id., I. 76; III. xv.

Kangaroo.[1] The Loritja tribe is not very far removed in social and religious organization from the Arunta, and we find the same episodes in its legendary lore. The two brothers Neki (another name of the root wapiti) and Wapiti gather and eat wapiti roots.[2] The Lizard men swallow live lizards and snakes, after which they perform the lizard intichiuma.[3] The Emu men eat emu.[4] Especially the Kangaroo men eat chiefly kangaroo flesh.[5] Among the northern neighbours of the Arunta, the Kaitish and Unmatjera, we find the same motive. There is a story of the Emu man Ululkara, who came to Central Mount Stuart in the Kaitish country and there found a lot of Emu men eating emu, after which he asked them to give him some.[6] Some lubras of the Yelka (*Cyperus rotundus*) totem lived at a place called Illipa in the Kaitish country and constantly walked about gathering the bulb to eat.[7] A young Atnunga (rabbit-kangaroo) man travelling over the country came across an old man of the same totem who was too old and infirm to get about, and so the old man gave the young one an Atnunga Churinga, telling him to go and hunt for Atnunga all day and dig them out with his Churinga. He did so, and brought the animals which he caught back to the old man, who cooked and ate them.[8] The legend of the Opossum men finds it necessary to state in so many words that they did not eat opossum but allia, the seed of the gum tree,[9] showing that opossum would be regarded as their natural and normal food. Similarly, the Kaitish legend tells us that the Eagle-hawk men hunted wallaby as they did not eat eagle-hawk for fear of turning prematurely grey if they did so.[10] Now there is a tribal taboo on the eagle-hawk,[11] and the legend seems to affirm the existence of this tribal taboo in the Alcheringa as the only reason for the Eagle-hawk men not eating eagle-hawk.

Eating the totem in the Alcheringa myths of the Loritja, Kaitish and Unmatjera.

Other legends are of interest, as they form the connecting-link between the present neurotic (taboo) aspect of totemism[12] and the positive wish-fulfilment side of the same attitude, which, instead of being realized in practice, is partially realized in mythical phantasy and ritual.[13] The Unmatjera tradition says:

The neurotic side of the wish-fulfilment.

[1] Strehlow, *A. & L.*, I. 40–42. The legend proves that this class of myth is a projection of the ritual into the past: eating of the totem, and thus giving the non-totemites permission to feed on it with subsequent re-birth (multiplication of the animal) are all well-known features of the ritual. See infra.

[2] Id., II. 10.

[3] Id., II. 37, 38.

[4] Id., II. 32.

[5] Id., II. 23, 24.

[6] Spencer and Gillen, *Nor. T.*, 394.

[7] Id., ibid.

[8] Id., ibid., 321, 322, 397. Cf. the existing custom in connexion with the emu totem in the Arunta tribe.—Spencer and Gillen, *N. T.*, 202.

[9] Id., *Nor. T.*, 413, 414.

[10] Id., ibid., 398.

[11] Id., ibid., 611, 612. As to the meaning of this previous existence of the eagle-hawk taboo, see above on the eagle-hawk myths as representative of a proto-totemic complex.

[12] The term is used in comparison with the state of things in the Alcheringa. It is more positive than the totemism of the south-eastern area.

[13] As to the ritual, see below.

that the ancestor of the Idnimita totem called Idnimita used to think within himself, "What shall I eat to-day? I have no brother or son to get idnimita for me; I will gather it for myself. If I do not eat idnimita I shall die." At that time there was nothing in the country but idnimita, and a little bird called Thippa-thippa. Idnimita said to another old man of the Idnimita totem, "I have been eating idnimita." Then another old man jumped up and said, "I have been eating idnimita also: If I eat it always it might all die." After this Idnimita, who had been eating big grubs, performed the sacred ceremony of the Idnimita totem. Then he walked some distance away and performed another one, and then he went on and gathered idnimita and returned to his camp where once more he performed a ceremony and sent a man out to secure the grubs which arose after he had thus performed ceremonies. Later on he again painted himself with down, performed Intichiuma, and went out to collect the grubs. After this boils appeared on his legs. He went out and gathered more grubs, and then he became so ill that he could not walk and had to lie down all day in his camp. He grew very thin, his throat closed up, and before daylight he burst open and died.

When the natives make Intichiuma at the present day they pass between the legs of the old Idnimita man, which are represented by stones.[1] The Kaitish variant says that one of the two Idnimita men, when they had as usual been eating the Idnimita grub, said to himself, "Suppose I eat more grubs, then perhaps they might all die." However, he went out and gathered some more and ate them, but again he said to himself, "No good: suppose I go on eating too much, they might be frightened and go away to another country." "Then he again performed Intichiuma and sang the grubs, and went out and saw the young *idnimita* rising out of the ground." "Very good, I have seen them." Accordingly he continued to make Intichiuma and to eat the grubs produced from these ceremonies.[2]

A third tradition that belongs to this group relates how a Kaitish man, called Murunda, continually gave grass-seed to another man who like him was called Murunda and also belonged to the grass-seed totem. He told him also that by and by, when he (the old Murunda man) was dead, the grass-seed was to be given to the men of the other moiety (and consequently other totemic group) of the Kaitish tribe. Accordingly, when the old

[1] Spencer and Gillen, *Nor. T.*, 324, 325. Evidently a rebirth-ritual (cf. Róheim, "Die Bedeutung des Uberschreitens," *I. Z. Pa.*, VI. 242), this would fit the general tendency of the intichiuma (see below).

[2] Spencer and Gillen, *Nor. T.*, 322, 323.

Murunda died the younger man told the other men to gather plenty of grass-seed and first of all to show it to him and then they might eat it. He was afraid that if he himself ate too much he might swell up.[1]

These myths afford us some insight into the unconscious mechanism of Arunta ritual and tradition. The narcissistic doubles ("Abspaltungen") of the same person (of the two men called Murunda of the same totem, evidently father and son) arise out of an ambivalent attitude towards a given complex: it is the neurotic doubt of the Idnimita man as to the fitness of his behaviour in eating idnimita. We also get a glimpse at the reason why totem-eating should be taboo. The neurotic doubt whether eating the totem may not lead to the extinction of the whole species points to the original meaning and intention of this action: eating the totem is an attempt to annihilate the whole totem-species, the sign of a hostile, revolutionary attitude towards the father.[2] In the Intichiuma ceremonies we have a reaction formation against the original tendency to kill the animal, for killing the animal is regarded as the right way to make it multiply. The ambivalent feelings connected with totem-eating find an abreaction in the narcissistic, imitative identification with the animal-ancestor; the tendency of the totem to multiply in consequence of the ritual corresponds to the tendency to form doubles of the Ego which is characteristic of narcissism in general, as well as to a feeling of contrition for having killed the father.[3]

The Idnimita man begins to perform Intichiuma when his doubts arise, but this does not prove a sufficient means for the repression of his scruples. The neurotic aspect of the totem-eating that creeps up into conscience as the "atra cura" following the wish-fulfilment, seems somehow to be connected with the death of an old man of the totem: it is the young Murunda man who first performs the ceremonies and institutes the totem-taboo with the survival of the positive aspect in the "showing" of the grass-seed after the death and according to the command of the old one. This "showing" is a survival of ceremonial eating, as we shall see below. In the Waduman tribe, if a man of any totemic group dies, the animal or plant is taboo to all members of that totemic group until after the performance of a certain ceremony. The brother of the dead person brings the totemic animal or plant into camp. A fire is made and the head man of the totem passes

[1] Spencer and Gillen, *Nor. T.*, 322. Another tradition mentions an old grass-seed man who always fed on grass-seed.

[2] It is when these aggressive impulses become inhibited that they turn against the subject ("Wendung gegen die eigene Person"). The act may either lead to the extinction of the species or to the death of him who commits it.

[3] Many "fathers" arise in the place of the dead one. On the sexual significance of these rites, see below. The young idnimita grubs of the second legend may be compared to the idnimita man who "jumps up" in the first.

the body of the animal or plant through the smoke arising from the fire, after which it may be eaten. All members of the totemic group must put their heads into the smoke of the fire in which the animal is cooked.[1] The death of a totemite is a repetition of the Primeval Murder that necessitates a renewal of the Primeval Sacrament. Compare the sacramental eating of the totem animal in burial ceremonies.[2]

Freud regards totemic cult as a post-mortem apotheosis of the murdered father, originating out of the feeling of contrition that followed the bloody deed and consequently produced the symptoms of a post-mortem or subsequent obedience (" Nachträglicher Gehorsam ") shown towards the totem as a father-substitute.

The Murunda myth contains an express statement of the latter: the cult is instituted in obedience to the bequest of the dying totem-father. Now we come to see a deeper meaning in the fact of the Alcheringa ancestors eating their own totem. They represent a phase of totemism prior to the contrition which followed the great prehistoric parricide: indeed, this can not well be otherwise, as they themselves are the " Fathers " and their positive totemism is primarily but a psychical reflection of the physical feeling of unity with environment.

Yet we cannot doubt that innumerable strata of human development are superposed on each other in these myths: the " Fathers " of the present race are also the " Primeval Sons " who have killed and devoured the " Primeval Sire " and who now continue to repeat the deed in sacramentally [3] eating the totem.

The various phases of the onto- and phylogenetic Oedipus complex are thus likely to be represented in these myths.

The Oedipus complex in the Alcheringa myths and the meaning of totem-eating.

> In ancient times when all the kangaroos and wallabys were blind, two Grey-Kangarooo men lived in the Northern MacDonnel Ranges with an old blind " goddess " who was their aunt. They lived on the kangaroos they killed, but they only gave their aunt one bit of flesh from the ribs and a very little fat. One day the younger brother gave her some of the caul-fat (ibarkna), she smelt it and whilst the men were asleep smeared it all over her face. This gave her eyesight: she began to blow and spit all over the kangaroo-bones that were lying about in the camp, with the result that they all became alive again and could see to run away. When the men heard all the kangaroos jumping away they knew what had happened and

[1] Spencer, *N. T. N. T. A.*, 1914, 198, 199.

[2] J. G. Frazer, *T. & E.*, II. 590. Quoted in this connexion by Freud, *T. & T.*, 1919, 232.

[3] As to the sacramental character of the eating see infra, and in connexion with the ceremonies.

> decided to kill their aunt. But next day she had intercourse with her two nephews, who gave her spears and she showed them how to use them so that they could kill kangaroos, although these could see now. Next night there was a hurricane that robbed the men of their senses so that they ran about on the top of their hill and howled like the storm. Their aunt ran after them and bound them together with a cord, whereupon all three were turned to stone.[1]

The myth turns on the blindness and on the identity of the blind "goddess" and the blind kangaroo. She is evidently a sort of genius of the kangaroo species: an anthropomorphic symbol of the same complex. The blindness is the blindness of the embryo before birth: when the dead kangaroos are reborn they first obtain eyesight. As in many parallel cases killing is equivalent to coitus, the intended punishment equivalent to the means chosen for averting it. A rearrangement of the episodes according to the principles of dream-interpretation is needed to make the unconscious meaning of the myth apparent. As we have already seen, killing (and eating the totem) is equivalent to having intercourse with a woman of the totem class, with the "aunt," the "mother" as representative of the whole species.[2] There is a reversal of cause and consequence in the myth: it is this incestuous intercourse that causes the dead kangaroos to be reborn and gives them their eyesight. Nor in the unconscious is it the men who inflict punishment; it is rather they who undergo punishment as a consequence of their incest: they go mad and howl about on the mountain-tops.[3] The myth gives us a pregnant hint as to the meaning of the jumping about of the kangaroo after an intichiuma: it is probable that the same unconscious tendencies are present in the abreaction-form (the dancing) of the ceremony.

That the eating of the totem animal is by the usual mechanism of the "transposition upwards," equivalent to endototemic incest, will be amply proved in the subsequent chapter. The interpretation given to this myth may suffice for the present, and also facilitate the comprehension of "The Wanderings of Three Wild-Dog Men" inasmuch as we here find the same motive in a less symbolic form:

> In the Alcheringa there dwelt at Chilpma three men of the Wild-Dog totem. One was an old Bulthara man and two

[1] Strehlow, *A. & L.*, I. 29, 30. A variant of the myth in connexion with emus.—Ibid., 30, 31.

[2] Grown-up children call their mother "banga," i.e. the old one, the blind one.—Strehlow, l.c., IV. 67. The kangaroo was originally blind—according to a myth of the Perth tribe.—E. W. Landor, *The Bushman, or Life in a New Country*, 1847, 210 (Armstrong in the *Perth Inquirer*).

[3] The howling of the storm is an eject of their own state of mind.

were young men, both Panunga. The young men stole the old one's bag with two Churinga in it and ran away, followed by the old man with a great stabbing-spear. They came to Uchirka, where they found an old woman of the Wild-Dog totem, with a newly-born child, both of whom they killed and ate, leaving some meat for the old man. They travelled on and came to Itnuringa, where they found some Oruncha men with whom they were afraid to interfere and camped at Ulkupira takima. Here they found another old woman of the Wild-Dog totem, whom they killed and proceeded to eat, and while thus engaged the old man came in sight. They gave him meat, but he only ate a very little of it, being sulky. That night they were afraid to sleep lest the old man should kill them, and before daylight they ran away and came to Pilyiiqua. Here they camped and found some small Wild-Dog men, some of whom they killed and ate. The old man again overtook them and again they gave him meat of which he would only eat a little, being still very sulky and on the lookout for the opportunity of killing them. Once more they ran away before daylight and came to Mount Gillen, where they camped on top of the range and found an old woman of the Wild-Dog totem, whom they killed and ate. The old man came up later on, but the two young men had hidden themselves. He saw, however, a lot of Wild-Dog men who originated here (this lies in a Wild-Dog locality at the present day), and thinking the two might be in their midst, he attacked them with his great spear and killed several, after which they all combined together and killed him. The local men were very angry, and so the two young men, being afraid to join them, went up into the sky, taking the bag with them.[1]

"The Wanderings of Three Wild-Dog Men."

The myth brings the two heroes down again from the sky, and it continues with a series of repetitions of the original motives. At Ulthirpa they found a man of the Wild-Dog totem (another representative of the father-imago in the light of the friendly component of the ambivalent attitude) who lived on wild-dog flesh, of which he consumed large quantities. He had a Nurtunja (a ceremonial implement) and a quabara undattha (a totemic ceremonial), which he showed to the two young men. They go on to Erwanchalirika, where they found a Bulthara Wild-Dog man, whom they killed and ate. (Open realization of the Oedipus wish.) After eating him their faces became suffused with blood, producing a most uncomfortable feeling, so that they relieved each other by sucking one another's cheeks. (Hysterical conversion as a consequence of contrition: the bloody deed is symbolized in their faces.)

[1] Spencer and Gillen, *N. T.*, 434.

Now, according to the four-class system which still exists in the southern part of the tribe, and which must have preceded the present eight-class system in the whole tribe,[1] a Bulthara man marries a Purula woman and their children are Panunga,[2] that is to say, the two younger men may be regarded as the sons of the old one. The theft they commit seems to be the Original Sin: they steal his Churinga—his other self, the symbol of his reproductive powers. He keeps the Churinga in a bag (uterine symbol) and pursues them, with his great spear (penis). The flight is a flight from the father-imago and the halting-places are a series of repetitions of the incestuous act (eating the old woman and children of the Wild-Dog totem: the human ones this time, not the animals). The truly infantile sulkiness of the old man in accepting only a little meat is very characteristic of the whole setting of the myth, while the ambivalent attitude of the youths who always repeat the incestuous act, and the futile attempts at reconciliation with the father, are also responsible for the repeated delay of the open conflict that is brought about by the dream-mechanism of repeated flights.[3] When it does come to the conflict, which is a remarkably realistic description of what must have taken place between the injured Sire and the Brothers in the Primeval Horde (the victory of the brothers is achieved by their uniting their forces in their utmost need), the outbreak is hidden from consciousness (the two heroes hide themselves) in so far as the other Wild-Dog men who originated there "are not at first recognizable" as so many duplications of the dual Son-Heroes. From the point of view of psycho-analysis the old Wild-Dog man is not deceived in his judgment when he charges the group, expecting to find his sons amongst them. After the parricide the contrition felt at the deed is projected out of the personality of the Son-Heroes in the anger of their doubles against them, whilst the ascent to the sky, which appears a talion-punishment of the parricidal act, is really death veiled by a sort of apotheosis. The following myth shows the Son as the aggressor, and may serve to elucidate a further characteristic feature of the Alcheringa traditions:

[1] Cf. N. W. Thomas, *Kinship Organizations and Group Marriage in Australia*, 1906, 78. Strehlow, *A. u. L.*, IV. 632. Spencer and Gillen, *N. T.*, 83. The movement which spread the eight-class system over Australia seems to have stopped mid-way in the Arunta tribe, for their northern neighbours all have eight classes, whilst the tribes to the south have only four. In Arunta tradition, all reforming movements come from the north.

[2] However, even in the southern part of the tribe each of the four subclasses is in reality divided into two divisions, but these divisions are nameless.—Spencer and Gillen, *N. T.*, 71. As to nameless divisions, cf. A. R. Brown, "Note on Systems of Relationship in Australia," *J. A. I.*, 1913, 193.

[3] The Oruncha men are, as usual, ejects of the inimical feelings of the actors of the drama and repetitions of the dreaded father-imago.

The kangaroo and the initiates.

A big grey kangaroo lived at a place near Finke George; it ate porcupine grass and slept in a cave. There came one day from the west a man belonging to the totem of the Grey Kangaroo who was called Lakalia (the Pursuer); and he came to kill the grey kangaroo with a big stick. The kangaroo ran away, hotly pursued by the Kangaroo man, who tried to kill it with his pointing-stick, but the kangaroo quietly turned round and looked his pursuer in the face. Both of them saw a demon in the shape of an Echidna that lifted its stone axe to kill the kangaroo, but the animal escaped and continued its flight. It ran on to the east, and everywhere where it stopped to feed or sleep there is a totem-centre at the present day. At last it came to Tanginta (Ironwood-tree place), where a rukuta (a young man after circumcision who must keep hidden) noticed the kangaroo and tried to stop its flight. The rukuta threw a stick at the kangaroo but missed it: the animal charged and squeezed the rukuta so that he remained there in a helpless state with broken bones. Lakalia came up and dressed his wounds. The kangaroo met a lot of women, stopped, and wanted to lie down there, but the women compelled him to continue his flight. He came to Tjuntula, where there were many rukuta. One of them stood in the way of the animal and broke the kangaroo's legs with a stick. Then all the young men united to kill the kangaroo and take the Churinga from his head. They could not move the corpse when wanting to roast it: Lakalia, who had arrived in the meantime, managed this with ease. After consuming the flesh it reappeared again on the bones and was cut off a second time. Lakalia felt tired, and before the entrance of the cave he put his "tnatantja" into the earth and both he and the Kangaroo Totem God are turned to stone Churinga.[1]

In some respects this legend is a counterpart of the Wild-Dog myth: the demon as eject of the repressed aggressive tendencies and the flight being points in common. "Pursuer," a member of the Kangaroo totem, seems to stand in the relation of son to the "Old Man Kangaroo." The legend would thus represent the flight of the Primeval Sire from the Horde. The inimical attitude between the Sire and the Sons is exemplified by the fights between him and the rukuta as typical of the younger generations: in the first instance he is successful but in the second, when a number of "rukuta" combine in the attack (like the Wild-Dog men above) they break his leg (castration),[2] cut him to pieces and take his

[1] Strehlow, *A. & L.*, I. 40–42.

[2] The appearance of the Echidna, who, as we shall see below, represents the castration complex, corroborates this interpretation.

4. THE ALCHERINGA AND THE ALL-FATHER

Cf. pp. 94–142, 434 for the data contained in this map,
unless indicated otherwise below.

I. The Alcheringa.

4, 6, 12, 13, 17, 18, 19, 20, 24, 27, 28, 31, 35, 41, 42, 43, 46, 47, 48, 49, 50, 51, 52, 55, 56, 67, 74, 75, 76, 77, 222 (cf. II, III, same map), 108, 121, 122, 123, 124, 125, 126, 128 (cf. VII), 261, 262, 263, 264, 265, 266, 267 (Frazer: *Totemism and Exogamy*, I, 555), 375 (R. H. Mathews: "Some Mythology of the Gundungurra Tribe, N.S.W.," *Z.E.*, 1908, 203), 385 (R. H. Mathews: "Notes on Some Native Tribes of Australia," *Journ. Roy. Soc. N.S.W.*, 1906, XL, 108).

II. A Single Alcheringa Ancestor for each Totem Group.

35, 41, 42, 43, 46, 47, 48, 222.

III. Alcheringa Beings Travel about in Groups.

50, 51, 52, 55, 56, 67, 74, 76, 77.

IV. The All-Father.

(*a*) Baiamai, 130, 138, 139, 150, 152, 153, 349, 350 (pp. 48, 49).
(α) Baimai as culture hero, 214 (*The Australasian Anthr. Journal*, 1896, I, 19).
(*b*) Daramulun, 110, 111, 112 (H. 564), 321 (H. 563).
(β) Daramulun as bullroarer spirit, 130 (H. 587), 137 (H. 589).
(*c*) Bundjil, 94, 95, 97 (Braim: l.c. 244), 98, 99, 100, 101, 102, 103, 104, 105, 106, 107.
(*d*) Nurundure, 89.
(*e*) Pirnmeheeal, 93.
(*f*) Mungan-ngaua, 108.
(*g*) Tha-tha-pulli, 121, 122, 123, 124, 125, 126, 128.
(*h*) Maamba, 156.
(*i*) Koin, 155, 315, 329.
(*k*) Birral, 163.

Number IV without any letters refers to other Supreme Beings of the same type, 324, 325 (A. L. P. Cameron: "On Two Queensland Tribes," *Science of Man*, 1904, 27).

V. Otiose Supreme Beings.

3, 8, 48, 52, 56, 232 (John G. Withnell: *The Customs and Traditions of the Aboriginal Natives of North-Western Australia*, 1901, 1).

VI. The All-Mother.

4, 6, 13, 17, 18, 19, 20, 24, 45.

VII. Supreme Being in Conflict with Alcheringa Ancestors.

108, 121, 122, 123, 124, 125, 126, 128.

VIII. Petrifaction.

3, 4, 6, 8, 13, 17, 18, 19, 20, 24, 47, 50, 52, 56, 67, 74, 76, 77, 89, 138, 139, 150, 153, 324, 325.

IX. The Fugitive Wives.

84, 85, 89, 155.

X. The Two Heroes.

24, 27 (Sp. III, 216), 45, 48, 50, 52, 56, 69, 70, 71, 73, 74, 76, 81, 84 (pp. 112–117), 85 (p. 59), 130 (R. H. Mathews: *F.A.A.*, 1899, 11, 12), 150, 153 (pp. 51, 52).

XI. Inapertwa Myth.

48, 50, 52, 56, 74, 75, 101.

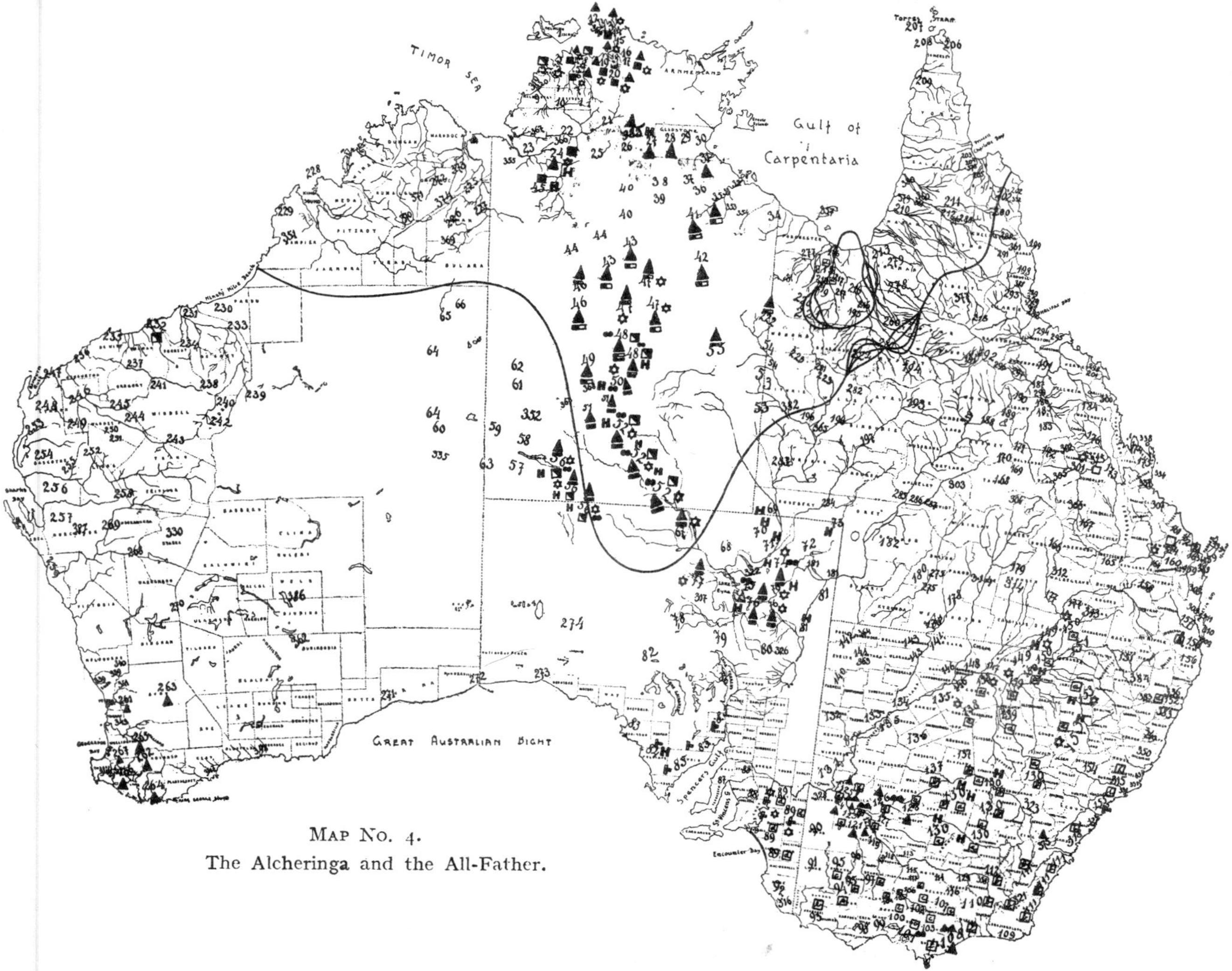

MAP NO. 4.
The Alcheringa and the All-Father.

magical power from him. In vain the Sire expects to find a resting-place with the women of the Horde; they, too, side with victorious youth. The "Pursuer," the ally of the rukuta, is a sort of functional personification of their wishes. The Father is reborn after the flesh has been taken from the bones in the totem sacrament: this event typifies the multiplying ritual to be performed at the totem-centre. The ritual must evidently be the result of a compromise between the Son and the Father aspect of the Oedipus complex, as both the Pursuer and the Old Kangaroo are turned into Churinga, from which the present human and animal members of the totem are re-incarnated. The Dieri legend on the origin of the Lake Eyre is a variant of the same theme.

> Once a pregnant woman caught sight of a kangaroo and said, "O! if I could only have that kangaroo for food." The child in her womb said, "H'm!" This is repeated three times and then her son is born. He immediately jumps up and pursues the kangaroo with his mother's digging-stick. The kangaroo runs away and comes to a place where a number of men are holding a circumcision ceremony. They kill him with their boomerangs, skin him and distribute his flesh among all who are present. The boy comes up in breathless haste, but they all say that nobody saw the kangaroo. He says it must be there: they are at least to give him the skin. He gets the skin and says, "What shall I do now? I will peg the skin out." One back leg he made fast towards the south-east, the other to the south-west, tail to the south, the forelegs, head and neck to the north-west, north and north-east. This is the origin of the hill called Duturunna.[1]

The end of the legend looks as if it had once been meant to account for the origin of the sky-vault: at any rate the Arunta and Loritja call the blue sky the "flesh," the night sky with the stars the "bones," the vault the "stomach" of the sky and behind these they believe in the existence of a "back" of the sky.[2]

The legend is thus connected with a class of myths in which the universe is fashioned out of the body of the dead father or mother. But the legend professes to account for the origin of Lake Eyre, called Kati-tanda (Kati = rug made of kangaroo or opossum skin; Tanda, a Tirari word meaning to spread out),[3] so that it is related to other legends of this area which explain the origin of lakes.

In another legend the kangaroo hunters are the dual heroes who institute circumcision. When they have finished skinning the

[1] Siebert, "Sagen und Sitten der Dieri und Nachbarstämme in Zentral-Australien," *Globus*, 97, 1910, 46.

[2] Strehlow, *A. & L.*, II. 11.

[3] Siebert, l.c., 46.

kangaroo they fasten the edges of the skin to the ground and raise it up in the middle, thus forming the sky-vault. Having done this, they said with satisfaction, "Now from this time people can walk upright and need not hide themselves for fear of the sky falling."[1] The heroes who separate the First Parents, Heaven and Earth (cf. the well-known Greek and Polynesian myths) are the same people who kill the kangaroo-father and introduce circumcision—all these motives meaning one and the same thing, the Victory of the Brother-Horde over the Jealous Sire and the state of society which followed that event.

However this may be, the interpretation must take that feature of these myths as a starting-point which it has in common with the former variant: again we have a kangaroo pursued by a hunter and killed as a part of an initiation ceremony. The youthful Oedipus tries, from the very minute of his birth, to "kill his father," but he can only succeed as an initiate who has conquered the infantile attitude within himself, who has become a man. Western Australian beliefs contain the retribution form of this myth: the father must kill the youth in the shape of a kangaroo and give the mother some kangaroo flesh before the youth can be born.[2] Moreover, this makes it possible to interpret the craving of the mother for kangaroo flesh, as a displacement upwards of the desire for intercourse with the kangaroo father. This is the reason of the child's birth, whilst the talking of the child in the mother's womb is paralleled by his pre-natal existence in animal shape in the west.

In the Arunta myth of "The Three Wild-Dog Men," it is the young men of the Wild-Dog totem who commit the parricidal act of killing the Old-Man Kangaroo, and the initiates are responsible for the same thing in the myth of the Pursuer. We think that this is only telling the same tale in other words. According to a Kaitish legend two men called Tumana arose in the country of the Luritja.[3] They heard Atnatu in the sky, and wanting to imitate him, they took a piece of bark, but that was not the right noise. At length one made of mulga wood was a success. Two wild dogs, living not far, heard the Tumana twirling it all day. They came and chased them, and then cut their heads off.[4] According to the Warramunga variant of the same theme

> A man named Murtu-Murtu came out of the earth in the Wingara and made a noise in the sacred ceremonies like the

[1] Howitt, *N. T.*, 649.

[2] Cf. A. R. Brown, "Three Tribes of Western Australia," *J. A. I.*, 1913, 168 If women eat a lot of kangaroo flesh they will bear children. R. Brown, "Description of the Natives of King George's Sound (Swan River Colony)," *J. R. G. S.*, I. 30.

[3] The name Tumana is given to the sound made by the swinging of the bull-roarer, and the two men had originally emanated from churinga (see below).

[4] Spencer and Gillen, *Nor. T.*, 426, 421.

murtu-murtu or bullroarer. His body was as round as a ball, his head had only a single tuft of hair on the top of it as if it had been shaved, and his feet had only toes and heels.[1] There lived two wild dogs who were very big and therefore called Wumtjilla. Their excrement produced a mass of red ochre. They began to perform sacred ceremonies and then stopped hearing the noise of the murtu-murtu. They sneaked up quietly and saw the man making the noise with his mouth, and then they rushed at him, biting pieces of flesh out which they threw about in all directions. As the flesh flew through the air it made a sound like that of the murtu-murtu and trees called nanantha (*Grevilla sp.*) sprang up where they fell on the earth. Out of these trees the natives now make their bullroarers. When the dogs had torn the body to pieces, they saw trees springing up all round. This made them angry, and they ran about biting the trees in the hope that they would thus be able to kill the muntalki—that is, the spirit of the murtu-murtu man which had gone into the trees.[2]

The next variant of the theme is found among the Manning, Hastings and Macleay tribes.

There were two brothers called Byama, each had a son and these boys were named Weerooimbrall. One day these two boys, who had voices just like the sound of a bullroarer, were left together in a place like the kackaroo ring of the keeparra ceremony. Thoorkook, a bad man, who had some animosity towards the brothers Byama, had some large and savage dogs, and when the little boys were alone these dogs came and killed them both. The two brothers Byama and their wives bewail the fate of the boys. Byama and his brother changed themselves into big strong kangaroos and killed all the wild dogs. Then they killed Thoorkook and changed him into "mopoke," who can only go about at night. The mothers of the two boys (the wives of the two Byama)

[1] The description tallies with that given by Strehlow of the Murramurra of the Arunta (Loritja Murrumurru—Dieri Murra-murra). The buzz of the bullroarer is the voice of the spirit Murramurra.

[2] Spencer and Gillen, *Nor. T.*, 434, 435, 493, 500. Murtu-murtu is the Murra-murra of the Dieri.—Howitt, *N. T.*, 475. Siebert, "Sagen und Sitten der Dieri und Nachbarstämme," *Globus*, 97, 1910, 44. We find the same word murramurra as the name of a bullroarer as far north as the Anula tribe.—Spencer and Gillen, ibid., 373, 501. Cf. the Binbinga wata-mura, ibid., 50. "Murramurra ist von hoher Gestalt hat einen spitzen Mund einen langen Zopf und nur einen Fuss." He cuts the women's breasts off (castration) if they don't bow on hearing him. Girls feel a prick in their stomachs when they hear him, and say "Sh! that is my husband." —Strehlow, IV. 41.

> were changed into curlews.[1] Once a chip from the tomahawk of the younger brother flew through the air, making a noise like the bullroarer and fell near the elder brother. He at once noticed that the noise made by the falling chip resembled the voice of the boys killed by Thoorkook's dogs. Then the elder brother made a bullroarer that gave out the voice of the little boys who had been killed. The two brothers then decided that all boys who should be born in the future must be shown this instrument to make them remember the boys who had lost their lives by Thoorkook's dogs.[2] At the Keepara ceremony some men personify Thoorkook's dogs coming to kill the boys.[3]

In all these legends[4] the Spirit of the Bullroarer, the First "Ancestor," is torn to pieces by the wild dogs, who seem to typify the Sons of the Horde. But we must not forget that the legend-cycle, as also the ritual of initiation is preserved in a form that has undergone a secondary rearrangement dictated by the feeling of retribution; originally it was the Father who was killed by the Sons and reborn in their own conscience, whilst afterwards this drama was enacted by the elder generation on the younger as a means of warning against the realization of their Oedipus complex. This makes it evident that all these legends and rites can be—like dreams that underlie the law of reversal—read both ways. In the last variant it is the boys, the initiates, the sons of Byame, who are torn to pieces by the dogs, which we can identify as the representatives of Byame's unconscious animosity against his sons, whilst the conscious part of his feelings is represented in the revenge he takes for their death. This part of the legend contains a surprising corroboration of our previous guesses as to the meaning underlying these myths. We have started with the supposition that the initiates in the myths given by Strehlow correspond to the wild dogs in Spencer and Gillen's Arunta myth. Now, in this last version Byame, in the shape of a big kangaroo (or rather "two Byames"—the dual is a sure sign that the legend is influenced by the concept of the Brother-Horde, although Byame is usually

[1] At night when curlews are heard screeching around the camp it is the mothers crying for their children.—R. W. Mathews, *Folklore of the Australian Aborigines*, 1899, 24. As to the curlew as Byama's wife, compare the part played by it in the sex-totem myths.

[2] Mathews, ibid., 23–25. Cf. Reik's remarks on similar Australian myths. Th. Reik, *Probleme der Religionspsychologie*, 1919, 247.

[3] R. H. Mathews, "The Keepara Ceremony of Initiation," *J. A. I.*, 1896, XXVI. 332.

[4] The legend of the dogs called "Longsharp teeth," littered by Byame's dog on the flight from the first bohrah, who have the bodies of dogs, heads of pigs, and the fierceness of devils, whom not even Byame dare go near, seems to be a variant of the same theme in Euahlayi tradition.—K. L. Parker, *Australian Legendary Tales*, 1897, 104, 105.

the representative of the Primeval Father), is the avenger and he vanquishes the wild dogs who have killed the initiates in the shape of a big kangaroo—and the initiates of our first legend fight and finally kill an "Old-Man Kangaroo."

We previously took no particular notice of the feature of the Warramunga legend that the excrements of the wild dogs produced a mass of red ochre; but when we find that the novices in the Keepara ceremony where the scene with Thoorkook's dogs is enacted are taken to a place called "excrement place," where they are shown the quartz crystal as excrement of Goign, and that afterwards they come to "urinating place" and see the bullroarer called "excrement eater,"[1] it is hardly possible to disclaim the common psychic and historic origin of all these traditions. Thus it seems that the wild dogs signify the castration-complex in connexion with the Oedipus attitude: primarily as a wish-fulfilment of the sons against the father, secondarily as the dreaded retribution for their unconscious tendencies. The fact that Australian lubras often suckle dingoes together with their own children may indicate the nature of the ontogenetic experience that led to the canine projection of this complex in Australian myth.[2] The myth connects the howl of the dogs with the sound of the bullroarer, but both the initiates and those who tear them to pieces are "dogs" in the sense of the complex. The initiates in the Kurbin-ai ceremony (who are called Kippu, cf. the Keepara above) make their bullroarers sound like the barking of dogs,[3] and the original representatives of the bullroarer made a buzzing sound with their mouths.[4] After this it will be no surprise to hear that in their secret languages the initiates call themselves "dogs" after circumcision,[5] here we have tangible proof for our identification of the Wild-Dog men and the "rukuta" (novices) in the myths.

Alcheringa heroes introduce circumcision.

If we regard initiation ceremonies, according to Reik's exposition, as the reflections of the primeval conflict for the mastery of the Horde between the Father and Sons, it will be easy to understand why the Alcheringa heroes are so often found as the originators of circumcision and subincision. Phylogenetically they represent the phase of evolution after the Murder of the Father in which the victorious brothers, actuated on the one hand by the fear of retribution and on the other by tender feelings towards the younger generation, institute the ceremony of initiation as a compromise. The boys are killed (but revived afterwards), something is done to their member (but

[1] R. H. Mathews, "The Keepara Ceremony," *J. A. I.*, XXVI. 329, 331.

[2] Cf. Róheim, *Spiegelzauber*, 1919, 155 n. 2.

[3] Howitt, l.c., 599.

[4] Cf. Reik, l.c., 244.

[5] Strehlow, l.c., IV. 26. The Binbinga call the Churinga a watamura, and according to this tradition it was first made by two men of the Wild-Dog totem. —Spencer and Gillen, *Nor. T.*, 50.

not castration). From a functional (and ontogenetical) point of view the heroes may be called representatives of the repression of castration-fear by the endopsychic Censor: it is they who teach the boys to undergo the ceremony of subincision or circumcision. According to the Yaurorka, the eastern Dieri and the Yantruwuntha, the first to be circumcised were two Mura-Muras, the usual dual heroes of Australian myth, called Kadri-pariwilpa-ulu.[1] They threw their boomerang at a pelican that was swimming about in Lake Perigundi. As they were wading into the water to secure their prey, the boomerang swept past them, almost striking one of them on its return. The boomerang fell into the water and one of the men dived for it but struck against the boomerang, which had become sharpened by its flight through the air. Thus it circumcised him, and on rising out of the water he saw to his great joy that he had now become a perfect man. He secretly informs the other one, who likewise dives and is likewise circumcised.[2] As their father was still merely a boy, they determined to circumcise him and they did this with a stone knife while he slept in the camp. The great loss of blood weakened him and as, notwithstanding the unhealed wound, he continued to have access to his wife, he got an inflammation and died. As soon as they had circumcised their father, they set out on their journey, everywhere circumcising youths and men. Coming to Kunauana ("Excrement-light")[3] they found a number of people who had collected to circumcise some young men by means of fire. They showed them the use of the stone knife, saying "Fire is death and the stone is life." They admonished the youths not to have access to women till their wounds healed, and were everywhere honoured as the benefactors of mankind.[4] In the first place the myth, which is evidently typical of a whole group of variants, is an infantile reversal of the real situation—instead of the fathei initi-

[1] Kadri in Yaurorka, or Kaiari, in Dieri, is "river course." Wilpa is the sky, Ulu the dual form: "both," Kadri-pariwilpa-ulu, is also a name of the Milky Way. Howitt, 645. Another version gives Kaiari (creek) and Kariwilpa-Jelu (sky: Jelu—"till")—as the names of the two heroes, and Gregory translates the names "one creek till up the sky."—J. W. Gregory, *The Dead Heart of Australia*, 1906, 229. But the former is probably right, as it conserves the usual dual ending (ulu), and as other dual heroes are also found in connexion with the Milky Way.—Howitt, 794. Besides this, we know that the Milky Way is found in connexion with initiation in other tribes. The two black spaces in the Milky Way are two old men who were speared at a Bora near the Taldora.—E. Palmer, "Notes on Some Australian Tribes," *J. A. I.*, XIII. 293 (see above).

[2] A water ceremony frequently forms part of the initiation ritual.—Howitt, l.c. 636. J. Fraser, *The Aborigines of New South Wales*, 1892, 14. B. Spencer, *N. T. N. T. A.*, 1914, 99. J. Mathew, *Two Representative Tribes of Queensland*, 1910, 104. That the heroes of the legend are made men in the water is evidently connected with the intra-uterine symbolic meaning of water and the element of re-birth contained in these ceremonies.

[3] An element of initiation ritual in the legend, cf. R. H. Mathews, l.c. *J. A. I.*, 1896, 329.

[4] Howitt, l.c., 645, 646.

ating his sons, it is the sons who initiate the father. But we must remember that the initiation ritual as such owes its origin to a similar reversal, the Elder Generation retaliates on the Younger for its own unconsciously aggressive tendencies against the Father. This double reversal gives us the original situation back again by means of a return of repressed elements; the originators of circumcision are the heroes who killed (and castrated) their father because he had intercourse with their mother.[1] It is only natural that those who have killed their father should prevent the repetition of the bloody deed against their own persons by instituting the puberty ceremonies. The legend regards the circumcision with the stone knife as a mitigation of a more savage and frequently deadly ritual performed with fire: which tallies well with our view that the initiation ritual as we have it at present originated in a compromise between the originally purely aggressive feelings of the elder generation and the feelings of love and tenderness which came afterwards in the course of evolution. This explains the origin of this mitigated attack on the genitalia which must have been outright murder of the youths.[2]

In the Karanguru and the Ngameni variant the heroes are characteristically called Malku-malku-ulu (the Two with the Pubic Tassel), and a kangaroo-hunt is substituted for the parricide which in this case (together with the creation of the sky-vault from the skin of the dead kangaroo) precedes the episode of circumcision in the water, thus justifying our conjectures as to the unconscious meaning of the previous myth. The dual heroes are also spirits of fertility, for their camps can be recognized by the luxuriant growth of the Moku, which is tabooed as their special food.[3] In the Urabunna and Kuyani legend the Yuri-ulu rise out of the earth and cut the foreskin off with their knife, when the men are preparing to circumcise the boys with fire, and sink back into the ground invisibly. In the astonished questions of the men, "Didst thou do this or thou?" we may recognize the Yuri-ulu as the personificators of an unconscious impulse, projections of the intention of the elder generation to mitigate the attack upon the boys into a mere symbol.[4]

[1] The secondary rearrangement of materials changes the course of events, and instead of intercourse, then circumcision and death, gives us circumcision and then intercourse, using the whole according to the tendency of rationalization as a precedent to enforce a rule of hygiene

[2] Th. Reik, l.c., 82, 89. Reik says that circumcision is not the mitigation of human sacrifice (murder), but only came to be connected with the simulated death of the novices (as punishment for their unconscious wish to kill their fathers), as it was the mitigation of castration, the talion-punishment for incestuous desire However, the legends show the crude, barbaric situation: a violent attack on the genitalia of the young by the jealous elders, a condensation of castration and murder in the same act. So, after all, the old interpretation of circumcision as a redemption of human sacrifice is right enough.

[3] Howitt, *N T.*, 646–50;

[4] Howitt, l.c., 650, 651.

The same movement is represented in Arunta tradition by Ulpmurintha, a great man of the "Little-Hawk" totem, who first performs the operation of circumcision with a stone knife instead of a fire-stick.[1] According to the variant given by Strehlow, circumcision was first introduced by Mangar-kunjer-kunja, the spirit of a lizard totem, but afterwards fell into disuse and had to be taught again by the Black Hawk and the Grey Hawk, who first circumcised each other with their stone knives and then the men of all the other totems. Some totems did not perform the rite at all, others, like the Podargus people, were doing it with the burning bark of the gum-tree, whilst the Echidna men castrated the boys so that they nearly all died in consequence.[2] The Hawk men told the others that if the ritual of circumcision were not performed on the boys these would become erintja, that is demons who would kill and eat man, woman and child,[3] and as the ritual is the means of sublimating the youth's Oedipus complex, we can see the truth of this admonition. Another Arunta variant coincides with Atkinson's views as to the mothers who might have been the means of the reconciliation between the Fathers and the Sons of the Horde.[4]

The southern Arunta tradition says that one day the men were as usual circumcising a boy with a fire-stick when an old woman rushed up, and telling the men that they were killing all the boys, showed how to use a sharp stone so that the fire-stick was discarded.[5] According to an Unmatjera tradition, a Crow man wanted to circumcise the people with his churinga lelira (sacred stone knife), but in the meantime two old Parenthie Lizard men came from the south and they both circumcised and subincised the men with their teeth.[6] Two Wild-Cat men are the heroes of the Warramunga myth. They initiated each other with their stone knives and then wandered about till they came to people who were crying for water. The younger brother cut the ground with his left hand and a great stream of water flowed out, and with it came a big snake which stood up so that its head reached the sky and ate every one up except the two wild cats. They go on and find out the means of making fire by twirling instead of rubbing two sticks together. Next they show the people how to

[1] Spencer and Gillen, *N. T.*, 394.

[2] A striking confirmation of the psycho-analytical theory that circumcision is a symbolic castration. The castration complex projected to the Echidna on account of his spines is the reason why he is called "bad" all over Australia. This is why the Echidna is an old woman who feeds on young men (castration complex and fear of the vagina), and why only an initiated man can deal with these animals.—Róheim, "Zwei Gruppen von Igelsagen," *Z. d. V. f. Vk.*, 1913, 411, 413.

[3] Strehlow, l.c., I. 8. Cf. Reik, op. cit., 77.

[4] Atkinson, *Primal Law*, 1903, 231, 232.

[5] Spencer and Gillen, *N. T.*, 401, 402.

[6] Id., *Nor. T.*, 399. Cf. 405.

circumcise with stone knives instead of with fire-sticks, and then they perform subincision on each other. They feel sorry and lose much blood, and both of them are at last swallowed by a snake in a water-hole.[1]

The invention of the twirling method of making fire that is attributed to the dual heroes of the stone knife is certainly to be interpreted as a hint at the libidinal (homoerotic) nature of the friendly current of feeling which softens the original tendency, castration and murder of the boys, to a mere symbolic rite. On the other hand, it also corresponds to the general tendency of Australian myth that represses the libidinal symbolism with regard to the representatives of the Father-Imago and allows it to become manifest in the representatives of the second generation, the Brothers, the Dual Heroes. It is more difficult to interpret the part played by the snake in this myth. The Kaitish have a myth, like the Arunta,

> of two Ullakepera men who introduce circumcision with a stone knife (thrown down from the sky by Atnatu). Creeks originate from the blood that flows from their subincision wounds. When they come to a water-hole near Aniania they see a big snake casting its skin, and as they are afraid of being bitten by it, they walk away and soon afterwards both are tired and sink into the earth.[2]

According to the Binbinga tradition two boys were circumcised at Akuralla.

> They went to an old woman and asked her for food.[3] She said, "I have no food for you!" So being angry, they tear off their pubic tassels, throw them at her and run away. After going a little way they make a fire, carrying a fire-stick with them. At Narulunka they make a water-hole. They go on and kill a female kangaroo, make a hole in the ground to cook the body and thus give rise to another pool of water. The snake Bobbi-bobbi hears the noise they make with their stones and sends flying-foxes to find out what they are doing. They kill the flying-foxes, but when they open the earth oven in which the foxes are being cooked, the foxes jump out and fly away screeching. The snake who is watching underground takes out one of his ribs, transforms it into a boomerang and throws it up on to the plain. They kill more flying-foxes. At last the snake drags them underground by means of the boomerang.[4]

[1] Spencer and Gillen, *Nor. T.*, 424, 426.
[2] Id., ibid., 345, 346.
[3] We shall see later on that food given or accepted between man and woman is equivalent to a marriage ceremony in Australian custom.
[4] Spencer and Gillen, *Nor. T.*, 436.

One of the two heroes is Paliarinji and the other Tjamerum, these being the names of the two moieties of the Binbinga tribe. The food asked from the old woman, the pubic tassels thrown at her, the fire made and the female kangaroo killed all mean the same thing: intercourse with the mother. The old woman refuses the request for food, and this non-attainment of the libidinal wish leads to a series of symbolic repetitions that mark the unconscious struggle between the libido and repression.[1] After the incest we should expect the struggle with the father as the other element of the Oedipus complex, and we get the episode of the killing and revival of the flying-foxes. Now the flying-fox is said by the Warramunga to have been the first man to knock his teeth out; this is a more symbolically repressed form of castration-ceremonies (as compared with subincision).[2] As he is sent by the Great Snake, this might mean a fight with the brother, a slightly altered form of the original complex.

In the Warramunga myth of the two Wild-Cat men we have a somewhat muddled account of the struggle with the monster: the great serpent destroys all the people and only the two Heroes escape, which amounts to the same thing as if the two Heroes were the dragon-slayers. Nor does the origin of the serpent from their own blood alter the interpretation given: it merely points to the aggressive aspect of the Father-Imago being in close connexion with the various symbolic forms of the castration-complex. The Anula variant of the myth tells us that one boy was a Roumburia (the equivalent of the Paliarinji) and the other Urtalia (Tjamerum). First they killed birds with their boomerangs, then a snake and then an euro. Then follows the episode of the flying-foxes[3] and then their being pulled underneath by the snake-rib boomerang just like the Binbinga tradition.[4] We are reminded by this episode of the Lake Eyre legend, which ascribes circumcision to their own boomerang that strikes the hunters when they dive for their prey. The snake (phallic symbol) taking out its own rib performs a symbolic castration and thus the origin of the fatal boomerang from this rib means, translated from the language of the unconscious into that of consciousness, that the Castration Fear of the youths is derived from their castration-wish against their Fathers.[5] It is the Boomerang (Castration-Dread) that leads to ultimate regression into the maternal womb symbolized

[1] Cf. S. Pfeifer, "Äusserungen infantil erotischer Triebe im Spiele," *Imago*, V., 1919, 243.

[2] Spencer and Gillen, *Nor. T.*, 427, 428.

[3] The snake Ulanji cut off the head of the flying-foxes in the Binbinga tradition. —Spencer and Gillen, *Nor. T.*, 438.

[4] Id., ibid., 437.

[5] They begin with an aggression against the Father-Imago. They throw the boomerang up into the sky and make a great hole in it.

by being dragged underground by the snake. Here we see the difficulty that hindered us in instantly reading the symbolic meaning of the serpent episode: it is a condensed, an ambisexual symbol meaning both the Father and the Mother, both the Phallos and the Vagina, but both genital organs appear in the aspect which they gain in the attitude of the psyche, which is characterized by the castration-complex.

The Anula tradition does not end here but goes on with a highly significant account of intra-uterine life as connected with the origins of totemism. The snake ate them but they remained alive in his stomach as he travelled along and at various places gave rise to mungai spots (totem-centres), Urtalia spirit individuals being left at some places and Roumburia ones at others.

At length the snake is taken ill and throws the boys out of his stomach.[1] In Binbinga tradition a man of the Dingo totem is the culture hero of the stone knife and it is the same person who introduces the twirling method of making fire.[2]

These various manifestations of the Oedipus complex have been discussed to demonstrate the wish-fulfilment attitude embodied in the Alcheringa tradition as compared with present totemic custom. This wish-fulfilment attitude is manifested most strikingly in the absence of the two fundamental totemic taboos. But both the absence or rather the deliberate breaking of the taboo and the wish-fulfilment attitude are equally characteristic of a certain "set apart" (*sacré*) aspect of native life, of the intichiuma ceremonies, and from this point of view we might regard the myths as projections of actual ritual into the dim past of the tribe.

Ritual and myth.

We have found that the Arunta, Loritja, Unmatjera and Kaitish Alcheringa heroes are reported to eat their own totemic animal or plant, and it is just in these tribes that we find the ceremonial eating of the totem as a feature of the Intichiuma ceremonies.[3] Further north the traditions never refer to totem ancestors as eating their own totem and the ceremonial eating is equally absent from their practice. It is certain that we have to do with a double series of causation: on the one hand tradition is an exaggerated projection of the tendencies embodied in ritual into the phylogenetic past; but on the other hand ritual itself is a reduced repetition of the tendencies that actually dominated the phylo- and ontogenetic past so that the traditions are history after all, but reflected through the double mirror of backward projection.[4]

[1] Spencer and Gillen, *Nor. T.*, 437.

[2] Id., ibid., 440.

[3] Id., ibid., 323. Strehlow, *A. & L.*, 1908 sq. Veröffentlichungen aus dem städtischen Völker-Museum, Frankfurt-am-Main.

[4] Both the ritual and the myth are survivals of past events which are re-acted and re-told: but, besides this, the ritual helps to mould and give shape to the myth.

The "magical omnipotence of thought" is equally characteristic of the traditions and of the ceremonies, the creative aspect of these beings is prominent and their principal occupation seems to be to produce things by intichiuma ceremonies. The Kangaroo-Rat man performs a totemic ceremony, after which he sends two younger bandicoot brothers to hunt the kangaroo-rat. They feast on it together. He goes on performing the ceremony and then eating his totem animal, till after the ceremony they only find one totemic animal and then none at all; [1] which shows the dire results of unbounded indulgence in wish-fulfilment, or rather, the original tendency of the ceremony which is an act of aggression on the totem animal.

Connexion between Alcheringa traditions and intichiuma ceremonies.

The tradition of the Wild-Cat man, Malbanka, contains the essential features of the sacred ceremony; it says that the Alcheringa hero was accustomed to perform these ceremonies day by day.[2] Another Wild-Cat man called Wontapare instructed the youths in various ceremonies: losing and stealing or giving tjurunga being an ever-recurring feature of these traditions.[3] Various ceremonies are performed by the Duck men, the way they imitated ducks and their other doings are described.[4] The Lizard People perform ceremonies [5] and the unmotivated episode that the Frog People strike their iwonba (small wands) against each other can only be understood as the rudimentary survival of ritual.[6] A woman shows her Nurtunja and sacred ceremonies to the Achilpa men and these perform an Engwura at Ooraminna.[7] They find a man and a woman of the Unjiamba totem and they tried to interfere with the woman but they could not because of their "quabara" (ceremonies). At Okirra kulitha they camped on the top of the range, performed quabara undattha and Ariltha on their young men.[8] Everybody seems to have Nurtunjas and sacred ceremonies,[9] the absence of such is sometimes stated as a peculiarity. The Achilpas repeatedly make Engwura and every night they hear the sound of bullroarers.[10] Another party of Alchipa men camps at Waterhouse Range for a short time and performs ceremonies,[11] and the same is repeated at Ningawarta.[12] They go on wandering, performing ceremonies everywhere and changing their language when they come to parts of the country inhabited by a different tribe.[13] They meet a party of women who are dancing all the way along and make quabara undattha at Mount Sonder.[14] They meet a Purula woman of the Arawa totem who had no Nurtunja, but was in possession of several

[1] Strehlow, *A. & L.*, I. 63, 64.
[2] Id., I. 51.
[3] Id., I., 56.
[4] Id., I., 75.
[5] Id., I. 80.
[6] Id., I., 81
[7] Spencer and Gillen, *N. T.*, 405.
[8] Id., ibid., 406.
[9] Id., ibid., 408.
[10] Id., ibid., 409.
[11] Id., ibid., 410.
[12] Id., ibid., 411.
[13] Id., ibid., 412, 413.
[14] Id., ibid., 415

wooden Churinga. They make quabara undattha and move on to Ariltha, where they change their language to the Ilpirra tongue.[1] In the western wall of Emily Gap there is a sacred cave which is called the Ilthura oknira or the great Ilthura at which the Alcheringa leader of the Witchetty grub men performed the ceremony for the increase of the grub on which he and his companions fed and where this ceremony is still performed.[2] Directly opposite to this, but low down on the eastern wall of the gap, is the sacred Ilkinia, a drawing on the rocks which is believed to have sprung up to mark the spot where the Alcheringa women painted themselves and stood peering and watching, while Intwailiuka and his men performed Intichiuma.[3] At Atnamala the men of the Grub totem cooked and ate many grubs and also made Intichiuma.[4] Wherever they stop they make Intichiuma and paint the sacred images on their bodies.[5] Three bandicoot women make quabara at various places till they are chased by a man of the Lizard totem.[6] The Echunpa People eat echunpa (big lizard) and at Irulchirtna they make quabara undattha carrying Churinga on their heads as shown during one of the Engwurra ceremonies, which represented one of those performed during this march. Here it was that some men of the Thippa-thippa (a bird) totem came and danced round them as they performed; the men were afterwards changed into birds which still hover over the Echunpa lizards and show the natives where they are found.[7] In the Loritja tribe the dog-chiefs call their young men together to perform ceremonies.[8]

The tradition of the Emu totem is nothing but a description of these ceremonies. The old man is an "Emu Father," the young ones imitate young emus and they all run away in the shape of emus to escape from an approaching bush-fire.[9] The Wild-Cat men perform the ceremony by running round their chief with a quivering movement of their body[10] Not only in sacred ceremonies do they excel but also in black magic; they make their enemies blind by spitting in their direction.[11] The Opossum men run in a circle round the Opossum chief, which seems to be the very essence of the ceremony.[12] The Lizard[13] and the Honey-ant people perform their own ceremonies[14] and so on. A Parenthie lizard man arose at Limpi, in the country of the Warramunga and made ceremonies there.[15] At Mirrinjungali the Wild-Cat men made some sacred sticks which they called thaburla, put them on their heads, painted their bodies and performed ceremonies.[16] A man of the Green Snake totem arose in the country of the Binbinga, and every time he performed

[1] Spencer and Gillen, *N. T.*, 416
[2] Id., ibid., 425.
[3] Id., ibid., 426.
[4] Id., ibid., 428.
[5] Id., ibid., 429. Cf. 430.
[6] Id., ibid., 433.
[7] Id., ibid., 440. Cf. 449.
[8] Strehlow, *A. & L.*, II. 16.
[9] Id., II. 18, 19.
[10] Id., II. 24.
[11] Id., II. 25, 26.
[12] Id., II. 28.
[13] Id., II. 39.
[14] Id., II. 40.
[15] Spencer and Gillen, *Nor. T.*, 423.
[16] Id., ibid., 424.

sacred ceremonies spirit children came out of his muscles, and as he changed his totem to other snakes he produced children of the new totem.[1] The Dingo men perform sacred ceremonies, and wherever they do so they leave spirit children behind who come out of their bodies.[2] The Wind man has a bullroarer, performs sacred ceremonies and leaves spirit children behind.[3] This continual performance of ceremonies is certainly connected with the continual eating of the totem animal. In actual life we only have a symbolic and ceremonial eating once a year, and a secondary relaxation of the taboo on other occasions: both represent the wish-fulfilment attitude as it manifests itself in a "dream-time" that is unhampered by hard reality.

When the Plum men made their intichiuma a curious phenomenon was witnessed—the Akakia trees shed their plums so quickly that it was just as if it was raining plums; the fruit run along the ground like a flood and the Ulpmerka would have been drowned in them if they had not quickly gone into the ground and so made their escape.[4] In the language of magic we might say that the "mana" gained by continual totem-eating manifests itself in the enhanced effectivity of these intichiumas of the Alcheringa: in the language of psychology we should say that there is a close connexion between the absence of inhibitions and the infantile attitude of wish-fulfilment by hallucination. Animals accommodate themselves to their environment by bodily modification. In his essay on hysteria Ferenczi has spoken of an autoplastic phase of human evolution.[5] This attitude characterizes the creative activity of the Alcheringa beings, which always take their own body as a starting-point and end in some modification of the landscape. The especial frequency with which the origin of creeks and floods is ascribed to these beings finds its explanation partly in the importance of water for the maintenance of native life[6] and partly in these episodes being a frequent feature of dreams.[7] For instance, the wanderings of the Honey-ant people are terminated by the following event:

Floods.

> When they came to Unapuna the local people resented their coming and at once drew forth floods of blood from their arms with the result that all strangers were drowned; their Churinga remaining behind, giving rise to an important honey-ant centre.[8] A group of Alcheringa men come to Ulir-ulira, which means the

[1] Spencer and Gillen, *Nor. T.*, 431. [2] Id., ibid., 441. [3] Id., ibid., 444.

[4] Id., *N. T.*, 404. [5] S. Ferenczi, *Hysterie und Pathoneurosen*, 1918.

[6] Cf. Haberlandt, Die Trinkwasserversorgung primitiver Völker, *Erg. Heft*, 174. *Petermanns Mitteilungen*, 1912.

[7] It is probable that with a people suffering considerably from thirst water will be even more frequent in dreams as a wish-fulfilment than it is in our climate.

[8] Spencer and Gillen, *N. T.*, 439.

> place where blood flowed like a creek and is a water-pool on the Todd Creek. The young men opened veins in their arms and gave draughts of blood to the old men who were very tired. Ever afterwards the water at this spot was tinted with a reddish colour, and it is so to the present day.[1]

At Ooraminna the Hakea men made the abmoara drink by steeping Hakea flowers in water. The water was held in their wooden vessels, and then opening veins in their arms they allowed the blood to flow into the vessels and mix with the abmoara, until the vessels overflowed to such an extent that the Ooraminna Creek became flooded and all the Erkincha men were drowned.[2] At Intatella-warika the Achilpa men found an old man of the Achilpa totem who, on seeing them approach, opened a vein in his arm, thus flooding the country and drowning the Achilpa men in blood; a large number of stones sprang up to mark the spot and still remain to show where the men went into the ground.[3] At Boggy water-hole on the Finke, a woman finds a number of Achilpa people making engwurra; she caused blood to flow from her sexual organs in great volume, directing it towards the people, who at once fled to a spot close by which is now marked by a number of stones which sprang up where they took refuge.[4] If we remember the urethral erotic meaning of a flood that we have discovered already in the myths of South-East Australia, it seems probable that the same interpretation holds good for these traditions.[5]

The urethral concept of creation is manifested more directly[6] in the Unmatjera tradition of the Lizard men. As they travelled along the elder lizard micturated and thus gave rise to equina, a whitish friable stone used by the natives for painting designs during the ceremonies.[7] As they travel on they continue to micturate, that is, to make equina.[8]

Multiplication by fission.

Another feature of these legends that recalls the infantile attitude and the mechanism of dreams is the narcissistic type of creation by fission of the personality (Abspaltungen).

> An Unkurta (Jew lizard) man lay on the ground, and when he looked he saw beside himself another little Unkurta who

[1] Spencer and Gillen, *N. T.*, 407. Cf. the "ball of blood" and the flood.—K. L. Parker, *More Australian Legendary Tales*, 1898, 84–9. [2] Id., ibid., 444.

[3] Spencer and Gillen, *N. T.*, 410. Blood given by the young men to the old (to strengthen them).—Spencer, *N.T.* 412, or by the old to the young (in initiation ritual), figures both in the Alcheringa and in actual custom.—Strehlow, I. 53.

[4] Id., ibid., 433.

[5] They are analogous to what Havelock Ellis calls vesical dreams.

[6] The blood-letting is also an integral part of the ritual: it is an over-determined action that can only be completely analysed in connexion with actual custom. (See Róheim, "Das Selbst," *Imago*, VII.)

[7] Spencer and Gillen, *Nor. T.*, 406. [8] Id., ibid., 407

> had come from him and said, " Hullo, that is all the same as me." Again and again he looked with the same result, and each time he said, " Hullo, that is all the same as me," until finally there were a large number of Unkurtas around him all of whom had sprung from his body. Then after a time he saw one die and said, " That is me dead—I will go and bury him in the ground." For a long time he remained quietly in the one spot and continually looked at himself until gradually he increased and became great in the flesh and grew into an oknirabata.[1] He meets a man of the nail-tailed wallaby (Iwuta) totem and tells him that if he lay down quietly, and went to sleep and woke up, he would see another Iwuta beside him all the same as himself and then another and another, and so on, until there were a great number of Iwutas, and he confers the same instruction to the Qualpa totem.[2]

Transformation is effected by mere will-power. Two beings came out of a small rock hole near Barrow Creek. The elder man was a Thungalla and the other an Umbitjana. The Thungalla looked at his shadow (illinja) and called himself Illinja. At first down grows all along his arms and hair on his head, and his eyes became big and stood out like those of the Titterai bird. The two men discussed matters and Umbitjana said to the Thungalla, " You and I sit down little birds," but Thungalla said, "No, we sit down blackfellows and we belong to the same country." [3] An old Opossum man meets another Opossum man called Illinja (that is his duplicate, shadow), and prevails upon him to lay aside some of the gum-tree seed that he was going to eat. In the middle of the night they got up and began to perform Intichiuma, and looking around he said, " Who is asleep there," for beside Illinja he saw another man who had arisen from the seed they had placed on one side. He looked at Illinja and said to him, " That man is all the same as you and me—why did he come up ? " [4] A Purula man splits in two, one half becoming Purula and the other Kumara.[5] The shape-shifting faculty is implicit in all the traditions even when not stated in so many words, just as the visual character of the dream expresses the variability and yet essential unity of endopsychical complexes in the form of outward shape-shifting. They naturally partake both of the shape and the behaviour of human beings and the animals they represent, but this is not more than the living Arunta does, especially in the ceremonies. From the native point of view it is more remarkable that they can change their totem [6] and even their

[1] Spencer and Gillen, *Nor. T.*, 400. [2] Id., ibid., 401. [3] Id., ibid., 409.

[4] Id., ibid., 412, 413. The Intichiuma ceremony is intended for the multiplication of the totem, and here results in the narcissistic creation of the totemite's double. Cf. infra.

[5] Id., ibid., 418. [6] Id., ibid., 430, 431.

nationality.[1] The psychological connexion between the dream-time traditions and real dreams is especially evident if we compare two recurring motives of the traditions with a very common dream experience that is rising (flying) and sinking.[2] A father who wishes to punish the sexual excesses of his daughters flies to the sky as a cloud and pours streams of water down upon them.[3]

Rising and sinking.

People rise to the sky on growing hills.[4] The Eagle-hawk men go up into the sky to hunt for wallaby.[5] Certain " Devil men " are said to have gone up into the sky at a place called Etuta.[6] Two Kurbaru men fly up into the air at Wontapara.[7] From Utiara the culture heroes fly up into the sky.[8] All these features certainly do not exceed the general similarity between dream and myth, but the closing sentence of these traditions which is peculiar to them seems to point to a more intimate connexion. When the kelupa snake ancestors finish their wanderings they go into a cave, roll themselves together and are turned into tjurunga.[9] The Wild-Cat man, Malbanka (with the big body), when he is tired by his long wanderings, sticks his tnatantja into the earth at the entrance of a cave, sends his wife and the young men who are exhausted into the cave where they simply fall down on the earth, Malbanka on top of them, and they are all turned into tjurunga.[10]

An Euro man had a churinga representing the lightning and he went down into the earth carrying this with him, and the lubras whose grass-seeds were their churinga went down on top of him and so formed a big oknanikilla.[11] Illinja strikes the rock with his churinga, making a hole into which both he and his companion went, thus forming a totem-centre.[12] Kulkumba finishes his wanderings by going into the ground.[13] The Unthippa women then entered the ground " and nothing more is known of them except that it is supposed that a great womanland exists far away to the east where they finally sat down." [14]

The Cormoran, the Crabs and the Fish sink into the depths of the earth and are turned into churinga.[15] The Snake ancestors throw themselves into two water-holes,[16] as serpents generally do, and are thought of as still living there.[17] The Opossum men go into a cave, throw themselves down on the ground and are turned into churinga.[18]

[1] On change of tongue, see above.

[2] Federn, "Über zwei typische Traum-Sensationen," *Jahrbuch*, VI. 1914. Mourly Vold, *Uber den Traum*, 1912, II. 797.

[3] Strehlow, *A. & L.*, II. 35.

[4] Id., ibid., 11.

[5] Spencer and Gillen, *Nor. T.*, 398.

[6] Id., ibid., 447. Cf. Strehlow, I. 50.

[7] Strehlow, V. 35.

[8] Spencer and Gillen, *N. T.*, 399.

[9] Strehlow, I. 50.

[10] Id., ibid., 54, 55.

[11] Spencer and Gillen, *Nor. T.*, 409.

[12] Id., ibid., 414.

[13] Id., ibid., 422, 442.

[14] Id., ibid., 442.

[15] Strehlow, I. 48.

[16] Id., I. 49.

[17] Id., I. 50.

[18] Id., I. 63.

In Strehlow's texts we see that these totem ancestors sink into the earth or go into the caves when they are tired, exhausted (borka). What does a present-day aboriginal do in a similar emergency? He lies down just as the Alcheringa people do at the termination of their wanderings and goes to sleep. It is true that the Alcheringa heroes end, instead of beginning, their dream-wanderings by going to sleep, but we know these displacements of motives to be a characteristic attribute of dream-work. At any rate, if the mythical heroes are still thought of as existing in a sleep-like state we may very well connect their wanderings with dreams. The Alcheringa heroes do more than merely lie down; they sink into the earth, or water-holes, or go into caves, and the places from where they disappear form totem-centres, that is, the places whence children are incarnated. "The souls of the totem-gods went into the earth and they are called iwopata, i.e. the inner hidden ones, the invisible ones. The eastern Arunta call them erintarinja. These souls of the totem-gods have a red body and live in great subterranean caves, therefore they are also called "rella ngantja" (hidden men). At night they emerge from their caves to visit the tjurunga-sticks and stones, which are regarded as their former bodies."[1] I think it can hardly be considered a too bold step in interpretation if we call a cave from which children are incarnated, and where the ancients exist with red bodies (like new-born infants), a symbolic representation of the uterus projected into environment, and the eternal life of the totem-ancestors a post-mortem repetition of the pre-natal life of the embryo.[2]

That this disappearance into a cave or into the earth is a sort of sleep (and not death) is emphasized by the fact that they often sink into the ground and reappear at another spot.[3] Psycho-analytical theory regards sleep itself as a partial regression into the position of the embryo. It is not surprising that the beginning of the race should be represented in unconscious mythical phantasy in ways similar to the beginning of the individual; we shall find ample proof in the course of our inquiry that these regressive features are also the ultimate source of the connexion between the Alcheringa heroes and dreams. But another side of our legends must be explained before we can finish our interpretation of the Alcheringa on these lines—namely, that the legends are made to account for all the prominent features of the landscape and to form a sort of mythical topography. When the Achilpa men crossed the Mount Sonder they saw a Bandicoot man with large wooden pitchis, and therefore they called it the place of pitchis.[4] A group of trees arises to mark the spot where a party of Alcheringa men stood.[5] At Alkniara

Cave as womb; return to embryonic life.

Mythical topography.

[1] Strehlow, *A. & L.*, I. 5.

[2] Cf. Róheim, "Primitive Man and Environment," *I. J. P. A.*, 1921, II. 163.

[3] Spencer and Gillen, *Nor. T.*, 415, 418, 432.

[4] Id., *N. T.*, 404, 415.

[5] Id., ibid., 432.

three women of the Bandicoot totem performed quabara undattha (down ceremonies) and introcision on each other; a great gully arising in the spot and in the middle of this a large stone to mark the exact place where after the performance the women went down into the ground.[1] The native will point out the exact spot where the Lizard men stood in the Alcheringa.[2] They killed a lot of Oruncha just at the entrance to the gorge and to the present day a great pile of jugged boulders marks the exact spot.[3] Clay-pans, that is a shallow depression capable of holding water for some time after a rainfall, arise to mark the spot where a circumcision ceremony was held in the Alcheringa. Inapertwa (cf. below) were transformed into human beings, and to the present day a fine group of gum-trees marks the spot where the operation was performed.[3] Curious-looking stones now regarded as sacred arise to mark the spot where the stone knives were spread out.[4] Turning their faces to the east, they look back upon the course whence they had come, and as soon as they had done this, two hills arose to mark the spots on which they had stood.[5] "As soon as the singing was heard they went on to the Apulla ground, a number of stones standing up on end now marking the spot where they stood up and waited."[6] Women mourn for a dead man; they are turned to stones, which still exist to mark the spot.[7] The Echidna falls down dead; a circular rock-hole appears to mark the spot.[8] All of them went into the earth carrying their Churinga and three stones arose to mark the spot where they went in.[9] "A large stone arises to mark the spot where a Wild-Cat man was buried."[10] A large number of stones standing up on end arose and still exist to mark the spot where the Ulpmerka danced.[11] At Apunga there was no water and the old men were very thirsty; they dug for water without finding any, and the holes which they dug out remain to the present day.[12] At a water-hole on the Jay Creek they erected their Kauaua and performed sacred ceremonies, a large rock-hole now marking the spot where the Kauaua stood.[13] A tall stone standing up above the ground represents the broken and still implanted end of a pole.[14] At a place near to Hanson Creek a number of Alcheringa men lay down to die and a large hill covered with big stones arose to mark the spot.[15] At Urichipma they paused and looked back to see their tracts and a row of stones arose to mark the spot.[16]

In Loritja legend the place where the Wallaby man went into the earth is marked by a spring of water; the other men who were with him were turned into white stones.[17] An Emu man and the Crow

[1] Spencer and Gillen, *Nor. T.*, 432.
[2] Id., *N. T.*, 391.
[3] Id., ibid., 391.
[4] Id., ibid., 397.
[5] Id., ibid., 397.
[6] Id., ibid., 398.
[7] Id., ibid., 398.
[8] Id., ibid., 400.
[9] Id., ibid., 400.
[10] Id., ibid., 403.
[11] Id., ibid., 407
[12] Id., ibid., 409.
[13] Id., ibid., 412.
[14] Id., ibid., 413.
[15] Id., ibid., 414, 415.
[16] Id., ibid., 415, 416.
[17] Strehlow, II. 28.

man are turned into rocks that are visible to the present day.[1] A place is called Mabakattji (vulva) in the Ilpirra language because an Emu man cohabited here with his wife. A place where Alcheringa people were turned to stone is called heap of stones[2] and so on. The import of these myths will be readily understood if we have recourse to the method of reversal applied in dreams and interpret the sentence "a stone arose to mark the spot" as an auto-symbolical reversal. It is not the stone that arose to mark the spot where an Alcheringa hero performed ceremonies, it is rather the ceremonies that are introduced at that particular point of the legend to mark the stone. The legend is a mythical attempt to keep in touch with environment by introjection, by interpreting the features of nature in analogy to the Unconscious of Man; or, expressing the same thing in a less finalistic way, we might speak of a projection of the father-complex into the land of the fathers—a fixation of the libido in the environment which precedes the realistic fixation of a people in the evolution of humanity.

But there is another important feature to be taken into account. Every Arunta individual is in a certain sense, as we shall see later on, a reincarnation of the Alcheringa ancestors. It is the members of the present generation who, according to myth, have lived in the Alcheringa and performed all those memorable deeds, and thus it is the actual Arunta who has contributed to the formation of the landscape. This is undoubtedly true "There is nothing either good or bad but thinking makes it so"—the stones "arose" when they were first perceived by the Ego in his infantile life. The explanation of the landscape by these legends is a mythical projection of the feeling of "déjà vu"[3] that sometimes arises from the similarity of a given situation to unconscious infantile fancies or dreams. The aggregation of the Subject to the Outer World is made possible by a sort of fictive precedent, but again this precedent is not quite a fiction as it really simply means that the Central Australian baby can feel at home in his environment as his fathers, with whom he is, in an unconscious apperception of racial and organic unity, one and the same being, felt at home before him.

The Inapertwa myth.

If we regard the Alcheringa myths as representations of an ontogenetic beginning with the tendency to an ultimate regression towards the fœtal state, it will not be difficult to interpret the mythical accounts of incomplete human beings which form such a characteristic feature of these traditions. According to the Yuin in South-East Australia, before there were men there were creatures somewhat like human beings but without members. Muraurai, the emu-wren, turned them into men and

[1] Strehlow, *A. & L.*, II. 33.

[2] Id., II. 37.

[3] For the psycho-analytic explanation of the phenomenon of "déjà vu," see Freud, *The Psycho-pathology of Everyday Life.* Ferenczi, *Ideges tünetek*, 1919, 84.

women by splitting their legs, separating the arms from the sides and slitting up their fingers and otherwise perfecting them.[1] In Victoria it is said that, at creation, a number of young men in an unfinished state were sitting on the ground in darkness when Pundyil, an old man, at the request of his daughter Karakarook, held up his hand to Gerer (the Sun), who then warmed the earth and made it open like a door.[2] According to a Dieri legend in the beginning the earth opened in the midst of Perigundi lake, and there came out one totem after another: the Crow, Shell-parakeet, Emu and so on. Being as yet incompletely formed and without members and sense-organs, they lay down in the sand-hills, and there by lying in the sunshine they were after a time invigorated and strengthened so that at last they stood up as Kana (human beings) and separated in all directions.[3] The Moon came out of the earth without a mother; when he had nearly reached the surface he heard the voice of a small hawk above his head; he wriggled further upwards through the layers of earth and he heard the voice of a crow—another pull and he appeared on the surface. He was dupu-dupu (lame, but here it means "formless person") and could only see a glimmer of a day-light. "He moved as an unformed mass to a flat plain, where he found a stone knife with which he separated his legs from the trunk and the latter from the head, divided legs, toes, arms, fingers from one another, and then made slits for the mouth, nose, eyes and ears;"[4] then he could get up, move about and see everything. According to the Yaurorka, the Mura-mura Paralina was hunting kangaroo when he met the incomplete beings. Going up to them he smoothed their bodies, stretched out their limbs, slit up their fingers and toes, formed their mouths, noses and eyes, stuck ears on them and blew into their ears in order that they might hear. Lastly, he perforated the body from the mouth downwards, projected a piece of hard clay through it with so much force that it passed through the body forming the fundament. Having thus produced mankind out of these beings he went about making men everywhere.[5] We shall see further on (in the chapter on conceptional totemism) that the circumstance that these incomplete beings are found in a kangaroo-hunt is not a purely accidental part of the legend.[6] Instead of incomplete human beings the next variant has an animal species.

The Dieri myth.

According to the Dieri the Mura-mura made a number of small black lizards,[7] and being pleased with them he promised they should have power over all creeping things. He then divided their feet into toes and fingers, and placing his fore-finger on the centre of the face created a nose, and so in like manner

[1] Howitt, *N. T.*, 1904, 485. [2] *J. A. I.*, 1878, 278. [3] Howitt, *N. T.*, 779, 780.
[4] O. Siebert, "Sagen und Sitten der Dieri," *Globus*, 97, 1910, 45.
[5] Howitt, *N. T.*, 780, 781.
[6] See also above, on the mythical theme of the kangaroo-hunt.
[7] These are still to be met with under dry bark.

afterwards eyes, mouth and ears. The Mura-mura then placed it in a standing position, but as it could not walk like this, its tail was cut off and the lizard walked erect.[1] For further variants of the legend we must go to the Central Australian tribes. In the early Alcheringa the country was covered with salt water. This was gradually withdrawn towards the north by the people of that country. At this time there dwelt in the western sky two beings who were Ungambikula, that is, "out of nothing," "self-existing,"[2] or "inkara, the deathless ones." In the Northern Macdonnell Ranges, there was a high mountain inhabited by two Kangaroo men. Near Finke George there was a great rock the cavity of which was inhabited by Duck men. As they found no food on the earth they used to go a-hunting in the Altjirra's celestial hunting-ground; on the hill-side there lived a number of incomplete beings[3] called "rella manerinja," because their members were grown together. Their eyes and ears were closed (manta), they had a small round opening instead of a mouth, fingers and toes were grown together (manerinja), the fists were closed and grown to their chests (innoputa, cf. Spencer inapertwa) and their legs were pulled up to their bodies. Besides this, these helpless beings were grown together in couples like the Siamese twins, and for this reason they were called "rella interinja" (an einander gewachsene Menschen). Some of them lived on the land and were divided into four marriage classes whilst others lived in the water and were divided into four other classes. Those who lived in the water had long hair and ate raw meat.[4] According to Spencer and Gillen's account, the Ungambikula came down from their home in the western sky armed with great stone knives and took hold of the Inapertwa one by one. First of all, the arms were released, then the fingers were added by making four clefts at the end of each arm, then legs and toes were added in the same way. The figure could now stand, and after this the nose was added and the nostrils bored with the fingers. A cut with the knife made the mouth, which was pulled open several times to make it flexible. A slit on each side separated the upper and lower eyelids, behind which the eyes were already present, and thus men and women were formed out of the Inapertwa.[5] According to Strehlow it was Magarkunjer-kunja, the "god" of the fly-eating lizard totem,[6]

[1] S. Gason, *The Dieyerie Tribe of Australian Aborigines*. Curr, *The Australian Race*, II. 47, 48. Brough-Smyth, *Aboriginals of Victoria*, I. 425. As to the lizard as sex-totem, see above and Spencer and Gillen, *N. T.*, 531, I, *Nor. T.*, 429. Mathews, *Ethnological Notes*, 144. Parker, *More Australian Legendary Tales*, 55, 56.

[2] Spencer and Gillen, *N. T.*, 388.

[3] According to Spencer and Gillen: "From their elevated dwelling-place they could see far away to the east a number of *Inapertwa* creatures, that is rudimentary human beings or incomplete men," p. 388.

[4] Strehlow, I. 35.

[5] Spencer and Gillen, *N. T.*, 389. Cf. *Horn Expedition*, IV. 184, 185.

[6] Spencer and Gillen's account tells us how the Ungambikula, after having performed their mission, transformed themselves into little lizards called amunga-quinia-quinia-fly, to snap up quickly.—Spencer and Gillen, *N. T.*, 309.

who with his stone knives cut the twins asunder, made incisions for eyes, ears, fingers, and circumcised them.[1] The clenched fists and the closed eyes, the gradual development of the organs and the general state of helplessness, together with the original salt water, do not allow a shade of doubt in the matter; the Inapertwa is the human embryo, who is originally grown together with another human being, perhaps his twin, but more generally and originally his mother. The mythical account of the phylogenetic past is an unconscious projection of ontogenesis, but it may be regarded as corresponding to facts in so far as the latter is but a shortened repetition of the former.

In the Alcheringa a spark of fire ascended into the sky at Urapuncha (the place of fire), and was borne by the north wind to Mount Hay. A great fire sprung up and by and by subsided, and from the ashes came out some Inapertwa creatures, the ancestors of the people of the Fire totem who were afterwards discovered by some Wild-Duck men.[2] The Loritja call these incomplete beings matu ngalulba; their eyes and ears were closed, arms and legs cleaved to the body. In this helpless state they were provided for by a Kurbaru (a small bird, *Cracticus nigrigularis Gould*) ancestor with grass-seed. According to the tradition of the western Loritja, they lived on a big plain south of Merina, where there is a big sea. From the north there came an Alcheringa ancestor called Namunaurkunjurkunju (the Mangarkunjerkunja of the Arunta), who cut openings for eyes, ears and mouth, divided their limbs and cleaved their fingers and toes.[3] The Unmatjera and Kaitish tribes have traditions dealing with incomplete human beings whom the former call immintera and who are similar to the Inapertwa of the Arunta. In the Alcheringa an old crow lived at Ungurla, one day he saw afar off a large number of immintera whom he determined to go and make into men and women. Accordingly he did so, separating their limbs, etc., with his bill.[4] According to another Kaitish tradition in the Alcheringa, there were no human beings, only indefinitely shaped creatures who sometimes are not called inter-intera but atna-thera-thera, that is beings with two anal openings. They had one on each wrist in the hollow between the ends of the ulna and radius. Two Ullakupera (Little-Hawk boys) came up from the other side of the Ilpirra country.[5] They started far away in the south and as they travelled along they transformed numbers of incomplete creatures into men and women, carving out the various parts of

[1] Strehlow, *A. & L.*, I. 6. Circumcision is dealt with as a separate episode in Spencer's account. He calls the stone knives used for both proceedings "lalira." Strehlow has the word "lélara" for the circumcision-knife, and "tula" for the other.

[2] Spencer and Gillen, *N. T.*, 445, 446.

[3] Strehlow, II. 4.

[4] Spencer and Gillen, *Nor. T.*, 152, 399.

[5] The same to whom Atnatu sent down the sacred stone knives to circumcise themselves with.

their bodies just as the ungambikula did amongst the Arunta.[1] In the Unmatjera tribe there is the tradition of the Idnimita (grub) totem:

> The Idnimita were, first of all, ignitha, small hairy caterpillars who walked about the Idnimita bushes eating the leaves. A big rain came which washed their hairs off and in this way they were changed into idnimita grubs and bored their way into the roots of the shrubs. Then there came a second rain, and with it a great wind which carried a little Idnimita grub from the sea country far away. When first it came down with the rain it had little spots, then it grew bigger and red in colour, then still bigger and white, and then it went down into the ground. When it was carried across by the wind it was only very little and was called atthithika. It came down to earth at India, which is now the central spot of the Idnimita totem. Like all other grubs it bored its way into the roots of the tree and there lay quiet in its irtnia, that is chrysalis case. After a time it came out of this and changed into an inmintera creature. Gradually he grew bigger and bigger. He could not see but felt his chin and said, "Hullo, my whiskers are growing." But he was stiff and could not undouble himself. Then an old crow came and said, "I think I will make him into a man," and setting to work with its bill, first of all made a slash across the creature's middle so that he could sit up; then cut across the elbow joints so that the arms could be straightened out; then freed the fingers, making first two cuts on the palm running one across the palm and the other around the base of the thumb. This done it cut the eyelids open, slashed across the face with its bill, up either side of the nose, thereby opening the two nostrils. Thus the crow transformed the imperfect creature into the first fully-formed man.[2]

It is noticeable that the legend has its well-marked geographical boundaries; it seems to be the universal mode of creation for all totems among the Loritja, Arunta,[3] Dieri; whilst the Unmatjera and Kaitish tribes have traditions relating to other totemic ancestors who originated directly in the form of human beings. A creek which runs on the north side of the Hart Range and flows across the Unmatjera country from north-east to south-west, marks the boundary between the groups of totemic ancestors who were first formed as inter-intera on the southern and those formed as men or ertwa on the northern side. Amongst the former are the ancestors of the following totems: Grub, Emu, Kangaroo, Crow, Water, Wild Cat, Galah Cockatoo.[4]

1 Spencer and Gillen, *Nor. T.*, 153.
2 Id., ibid., 156, 157.
3 But see Strehlow, *A. & L.*, I. 3.
4 Spencer and Gillen, *Nor. T.*, 153, 154.

Outside Australia we might find analogies in the creation myth of Central Borneo with its incomplete limbless first being;[1] perhaps also in the Torres Straits the two mothers of Sida who are grown together back to back so that Sida has to divide them with a cut.[2] However, leaving the question of ethnic affinities or migrations of mythical motives aside, the myth itself is certainly to be interpreted on the lines of ontogenetic evolution.

The incomplete human beings we have already recognized as representing the embryo; the lizard here plays an important rôle since we find it once as the being out of which man is to be developed, twice as the culture hero to whom this feat of development is attributed. Long ago Haeckel[3] showed that man has inherited his five fingers from amphibian ancestors, that his body betrays other signs of this descent. It seems, then, man has to reckon not only with his fœtal evolution but also with his pre-human stages.[4]

The totemic cult of the crocodile, with its explicative legends amongst the Fans, offers an interesting parallel and a striking confirmation of Freud's view on the origin of totemism. God Nzame, feeling lonely all alone, took some earth and made a formless being. This was a lizard. For five days he left it in a sort of incubation, after that he plunged it into the water, and after seven days it came out of the water as the first human being.[5] The identification of the lizard and the embryo corresponds to the Australian variants of the theme, whilst the plunging of the primary being into water, whence it comes out a man, makes the ontogenetic meaning of the myth absolutely certain. Instead of a totemic (i.e. clan) cult of the lizard, however, we have the great lizard, the crocodile, as one of the two major totems of the Fan people. In times long gone by the Fan dwelt on the borders of a great river and were subject to the rule of Ombure, the ruler of water and forest, the Giant Crocodile. Every day they had to give him a man and a woman for food, and every month a young girl as wife. As it was difficult to keep up supplies, they had to make war on their neighbours for slaves, and they were victorious as the powerful Ombure helped them. He spared the life of the chief's beautiful daughter, who was also exposed to him, but after nine months she gave birth to a child, who was called Ngurangurane, the Son of the Crocodile. He grew up to be a chief of the Fans and a powerful wizard. Aided by his mother, he made a beverage and

[1] Nieuwenhuis, *Quer durch Borneo*, 1904, I. 129–131. Cf. Schmidt, *Grundlinien*, 9. 26. According to a Hawaiian myth, when man was created he was jointless. Maui broke his legs at ankle, knee and hip, and then, tearing them and the arms from the body, destroyed the web.—W. D. Westervelt, *Legends of Maui*, 1910, 132.

[2] *Cambridge Expedition to Torres Straits*, V. 33.

[3] Haeckel, *Anthropogenie*, 1910, 620. Cf. ibid., 627 (lizard-ancestry).

[4] Cf. A. v. Gennep, " L'idée d'évolution dans les légendes des demi-civilisés," *Religions, Mœurs et Légendes*, IV. 139.

[5] R. P. H. Trilles, *Le Totémisme chez les Fân*, 1912, 263, 264.

intoxicated Ombure, whom, having secured with strong ropes, he compelled the Lightning, hitherto subject to his father, to come and kill. When he had killed his father (which he only managed to do through the magic help accorded to him by his mother), the Son of the Crocodile cut the corpse into pieces; he ate the brains and the heart, gave the best parts to the old men, the entrails to the women and children, but he took care that everybody should get a morsel so that they should not be afraid of the ghost of the murdered father. Ngurangurane, as he was not only the avenger of his race (that is of his mother's people) but also the son of the Crocodile, now ordered a great funeral to be celebrated. For thirty times thirty days the women cried after Ombure and sang songs in his praise for the same period. For thirty months the angry ghost of Ombure ran all along the village thirsting for vengeance, but as he found his own flesh everywhere (as everybody had taken part in the sacramental meal), he was compelled to desist. Ngurangurane then fashioned an enormous image of Ombure out of clay, and in the head of the image he put his father's bones. They recommenced the dances around the image, and killed two men and two women as sacrifices so that the blood dripped over the statue. The flesh was placed near the statue, the heads to the head, the feet to the feet, and so on. Everybody took his portion of the flesh and then they went home, and the Son of the Crocodile said: "This is what we shall do year by year, this is how we shall honour Ombure." And for this reason Ombure, under the mystic name of Ngan, is the Mwamayon (totem) of the sons of Ngurangurane.[1]

This is the Story of the Paternal Tyrant, of the Son who, favoured by his mother, achieves the feat of the Primeval Parricide, unites himself and his people with the Father in an anthropophagous totem-sacrament, and, prompted by his own ambivalent feelings, tries to expiate his sin (the father's ghost) in totemic ceremonies. The men and women that are sacrificed to Ombure represent, from the point of view of the unconscious, a symbolic repetition of the sinful deed as their blood unites them with Ombure's image and their flesh is consumed in the same way as Ombure's. The totemic cult is characterized exactly as Freud interpreted it, as a periodic repetition of the Primeval Parricide and Expiation. (The legend belongs to the Dragon-killer type and offers a valuable starting-point for the interpretation of the widely spread mythical motive.)

The Kaitish beings referred to above with two anal openings, remind us of the fact that the anus originated in the course of onto- and phylogenesis as the second opening of the body after the Coeloma.[2]

[1] Trilles, *Le Totémisme chez les Fân*, 184–202. Cf. Róheim, *Drachen und Drachenkaempfer*, 1912, for literature on this subject.

[2] Haeckel, *Anthropogenie*, 1910, 577.

It is, of course, easy to see that there can be no question of a direct survival of phylogenesis in myth, but as the embryo in its intra-uterine life gives a brief recapitulation of the development of the whole animal world, we might find here the most primitive psychological form of memory, the lowest strata of the Unconscious in their mythical projection. Whether the salt water that figures in these myths may be in any way connected with the fact that the basin of Central Australia was once covered with the sea is disputable;[1] at any rate, this salt water is a survival of the amniotic fluid and the opening of the earth at Lake Perigundi—a mythical version of the opening of the mother's womb. The intra-uterine water itself is a recapitulation of the age when animal life evolved in the salt water,[2] and similarly the various animal shapes of the inapertwa may well be interpreted as mythical reflections of the various phases of animal life through which the embryo passes. We have already found one pre-psychic root of totemism into which unconscious psychical contents are projected in the physical unity of man with his environment; here we find the second; from this point of view we define totemism as the psychical "engram" or rudiment of the various stages in the intra-uterine evolution of the embryo.

The omnipotence of the embryo and the origin of magical power.

Now we know that narcissistic omnipotence-phantasies such as are embodied in magical practices and beliefs are revivals of the real situation of the embryo who is omnipotent in the real sense of the word (Ferenczi), he is absolute master of his own world (in the womb) because the difference between Subject and Object, that is, the portion of the Universe which offers resistance to the wishes of the Subject, only begins to be experienced after birth. This gives us the key to the superiority of the magical powers of these Alcheringa heroes as compared with common mortals; they are all-powerful, since the impulses of the embryo never meet with the difficulties inherent in contact with an external world. It is this superior magic that descends from them to the human and animal members of the totem, just as the belief in magic is actually a partial survival of the embryonic and infantile psychical attitude.

The traditions of the Arunta tribe recognize four more or less distinct periods in the Alcheringa. In the first period men and women were created; in the second, the rite of circumcision by

[1] J. N. Gregory, *The Dead Heart of Australia*, 1906, 148. Cf. the legend about the canopy of vegetation that protected the country beneath from the direct ways of the sun (pp. 4, 222, 223). "Those who interpret the Kadimarkara legend by the light of a knowledge of tropical forests naturally see in it either a reminiscence of the time when the geographical conditions of Central Australia were different from those which prevail at present, or a reminiscence of the country whence the aborigines migrated to Australia" (p. 7).

[2] Cf. Gennep, *Mythes et Légendes d'Australie*, 1905, I., p. 2 (footnote), quotes R. Quinton, "L'eau de mer, constance du milieu marin originel, comme milieu vitale des cellules à travers la série animale," 1904.

means of a stone knife was introduced, in the third the rite of Ariltha or subincision was introduced, and in the fourth the present marriage system of the tribe was established.[1] Now this is the natural sequence of events in the life of an individual Arunta; birth, circumcision, subincision, marriage, and before birth naturally the intra-uterine life which we see in our legends.

The Alcheringa hero is not only the embryo but also the father.

But it would be quite beside the mark to think that even the unconscious meaning of these Alcheringa beings is exhausted by equating them with the embryo. The very names are sufficient to make this clear. We have an Alcheringa being of the tnunka totem called Katu-tankara, the immortal father.[2] Tradition mentions an Emu Father[3] and a Bat,[4] a Snake[5] and an Emu Father[6] amongst the Loritja. In the traditions of the tribes situated northwards from Central Australia the groups of Alcheringa heroes gradually disappear and their place is taken by single individuals in whom the idea of fatherhood is still more prominent. All the culture heroes who teach the natives the elements of their present social organization are evidently reflections of the part played by the father in the individual life; it is from him that the child learns the common arts of life as well as how to behave in accordance with tribal law.

If we analyse the legends with which we have just been dealing we find two actors on the scene—one is completed, the other completing. The being is generally completed by cleaving, rending asunder, and we know that the vulva is conceived as a slit, as a wound dealt to the woman by some instrument, which again symbolizes the penis. The bird's beak through which the transformation is effected is evidently a displacement upwards of the penis; the act itself a coitus which is again given in the legend at the wrong place, after and not before the existence of these embryonic beings. The father in his generative aspect is indeed a well-marked characteristic of these beings. A party of Wild-Cat men is spoken of who, on account of the abnormal development of their organs, were called Atnimma-la-truripa, that is Penis-standing-erect.[7] An old Murunda man had abnormally developed organs: they are represented by a stone from which evil magic can be made to emanate.[8] Others are mentioned as having exceeded even these heroes in the development of their male organs.[9] Even the embryo-people themselves are "fathers," as it is from them that the present animal and human race descends through a series of incarnations.

If we wish to do justice to the meaning of these beings with a single formula we are compelled to replace the psychic content by

[1] Spencer and Gillen, *N. T.*, 387, 388. [2] Strehlow, *A. & L.*, I. 8.
[3] Id., I. 42, III. 33. [4] Id., II. 44. [5] Id., II. 21.
[6] Id., II. 19. [7] Spencer and Gillen, *N. T.*, 405, 443.
[8] Id., *Nor T.*, 396. [9] Cf., id., *N. T.*, 446.

the psychic act, and to regard them as the mythical reflections of an unconscious mechanism. These beings originate in a phase of evolution which is one step beyond that of pure embryonic (narcissistic) omnipotence; the Reality Principle has left its mark on them in so far as the child does not vindicate this omnipotence for itself, but projects it on to the Father-Image. But the Father-Image is omnipotent through its embryonic attributes; the hero is a condensation of the power-ideal in its projective (father) and in its autistic (embryo) aspect.

It may be, although this cannot be affirmed with any degree of certainty, that the part played by the father in such myths represents an advance upon a still earlier stage of ideas. This may be regarded as probable if we remember that there is a general tendency in the unconscious mental attitude of the Australian race to attribute purely feminine functions to the male, and in connexion with this tendency we find the repression of sex. According to the Koko-warra the first aborigines were born from the dung of Anjir, a male being.[1] Some traditions of the North Australian aborigines might be taken as representative of this phase of mythic evolution:

The mother-beings in Alcheringa myths.

> In the far past times which the Waduman people call Jabulungu an old woman named Dodaduriman came up from the salt water following along which is now the Valley of the Daly River, which she made during her travels. As she journeyed on she made the grass, trees, rocks and country, in fact everything. She made the rocky bar in the Flora River that now serves as a crossing for the natives. On her back she carried a large pitchi as big as a boat, full of salt-water mussels, on which she fed. Finally she stopped at Idodban and there went down under the water. At the present day there is a spring at this spot which is always bubbling, and this is due to Dodaduriman's fire, which she keeps bubbling down below. Dodaduriman gave the natives their present marriage system and class-names.[2]
>
> The Kakadu traditions mention a woman called Ungulla Robunbun, who came from Palientoi, spoke the language of the Noenmil people and walked to Kraigpa, a place at the head of the Wildman Creek. Some of her children she carried on her shoulders, others on her hips and one or two of them walked. At Kraigpa she left one girl and one boy, and told them to speak the Quiratari language. Then she walked on to Koarnbo Creek, where she left a boy and a girl, and told them to speak Koarnbut, and so on. When she came to the Kakadu she told them she was a Kakadu like them, and taught

[1] W. E. Roth, *S. M. M.*, 15.

[2] Spencer, *N. T. N. T. A.*, 315.

> the lubras to wear an apron of paper bark, for she was completely clothed in sheets of paper bark.[1] She continues to wander about with her children and camps opposite to a camp of blackfellows. Although she was their "elder sister," they tried to approach her and have intercourse with her. She hit them all on their private parts and so killed them ; their bodies tumbled into a water-hole close by. Then she went to the camp where the woman and children had remained behind and drove them ahead into the water. The bones of all these natives are still there in the form of stones, with which also their spirit-parts are associated. After this she pulled out her vagina and threw it away, saying, "This belongs to the lubras." Then she threw her breasts away and a woman's fighting-stick, and said that also belonged to the lubras. A flat spear-thrower and a light reed-spear she said were for the men. Then she created the mosquitoes and with her remaining children went into the water-hole.[2]

Ungulla Robunbun seems to stand for a "culture wave" that started from the Noenmil people and ended with the introduction of the paper bark among the Kakadu. In her capacity of Mythical Mother she is a sort of duplicate of another Kakadu ancestress, Imberombera. We see castration and death of the men as the punishment for an attempted incest and as a starting-point for a series of reincarnations, but we see also the tearing asunder of the mother, which is evidently a motive that originated as the closing episode of the primeval Oedipus drama and is here applied by way of secondary transference to the death of the Mother.[3] Both she and Dodaduriman disappear in water-holes. The real mythical ancestress of the Kakadu tribe is Imberombera :

> She walked through the sea and landed at Wungaran. At Arakwurwain she met Wuraka, who came from the west, walking through the sea. His feet were at the bottom, but he was so tall that his head was above the water. Imberombera said to him, "Where are you going"; he said, "I am going straight through the bush to the rising sun." Wuraka carried his penis over his shoulder. At that time there were no blackfellows. Imberombera wanted Wuraka to go with her, but he was too tired and his penis was too heavy ; he sat down where he was and a great rock called Wuraka arose to mark the spot. Imberombera had a huge stomach in which she carried many children, and on her head she wore a bamboo-ring from which

[1] These paper-bark aprons are principally worn on the Melville and Bathhurst Islands.—Spencer, *N. T. N. T. A.*, 401.

[2] Id., ibid., 308, 309.

[3] But it may also be substituted for intercourse. Cf. Reik, "Oedipus und die Sphinx," *Imago*, VI.

> hung down numbers of dilly bags full of yams. At a place called Marpur, close to where she and Wuraka met, she left boy and girl spirit-children and told them to speak Iwaidja. They also planted many yams and told the children to eat them. She travels on, leaving spirit-children and planting yams everywhere, and thus becomes the ancestress of ten different tribes. She gave instructions as to food supplies and told them about the totems.[1]

This legend is remarkable, as it evidently contains the unconscious recognition of both the part played by the father Wuraka with the large penis, and the mother Imberombera with her huge stomach (of which the boat-sized trough of Dodaduriman is evidently but the symbolic equivalent) [2] in the procreation of children; only after having met with Wuraka does she begin to leave spirit-children behind, and through the children the series of reincarnations that constitute conceptional totemism is traced back the first children who are born as they ought to be from the Mother and not from the Father. We must leave the question undecided whether this is the more primitive form of the concept, and we must reserve for the next chapters the explanation of the meaning of such a phenomenon as children, be it even spirit-children, who are born from a father.

Summary.

The analysis of the Alcheringa myths has sharpened our insight into the necessarily complicated structure of a phenomenon that involves the greater part of the religious and social life of many primitive people such as totemism. The salient feature of these traditions is the dominance of the wish-fulfilment current of unconscious attitudes. The absence of the two fundamental totemic taboos, the alimentary and the matrimonial, is in itself sufficient to indicate that these traditions are genetically survivals of the early infantile period in human evolution, when the cultural repression of wishes was only very slightly operative. In connexion with mythical endophagy (a less symbolic form of the wish-fulfilment embodied in the totem-eating), we have met with slightly veiled mythical accounts of the Oedipus complex, and it seems that the two wish-fulfilments (eating the totem animal and totem endogamy) are, as supposed by Freud, only symbolic equivalents of primeval incest, in so far as the Father-Imago is projected into the totem animal and all the women of the clan are introjected into the Mother-Imago.

The Oedipus complex is only one, although the most important of the constituent elements of psychical infantilism. The Alcheringa

[1] Spencer, *N. T. N. T. A.*, 275–87.

[2] Another symbolic equivalent of the womb full of children is the bag full of yams: the planting of yams being everywhere mentioned in parallel to the leaving of spirit children.

traditions are regressive in a high degree; the general tendency is the projection of ontogenetic into phylogenetic beginnings. The conceptual reaction upon environment comes before motor reaction in the evolution of the individual, and therefore it is represented as having reigned undisputed in the golden age of the world. The Alcheringa ancestors are furnished with the attributes of omnipotence of thought; it is from them that the reduced quantity of omnipotence as manifested in totemic magic of the present day is derived. They create things partly by the mere manifestations of their will and partly on the lines of infantile (urethral-erotic and narcissistic) psycho-sexual attitudes.

The myths contain the elements of metamorphosis, levitation, sinking and floods that are typical of primitive forms of dream-life, and dreams are attributed by the natives to the appearance of the Alcheringa ancestors. They all finish their wanderings in "getting tired" and then going into the earth, which is symbolic of sleep as a return to the maternal womb. In their pristine forms as inapertwa creatures they are easily recognizable as mythical embryos, and as the fœtal evolution is a recapitulation of the phylogenetic history of the human species, the embryo creatures giving rise to the various totems would point to the feeling of unity of certain human clans with animal species being an endopsychical reflection of the pre-human phase of evolution. The Alcheringa heroes are beings of a composite type; they originate in the phase of human development in which the baby renounces its own claims to omnipotence, but only to reactivate them in the projection phase of "embryonic fathers."

Myths on the origin of totemism.

I shall now proceed to deal with the myths about the primeval origin of totemism. A. Lang denies the value of such myths, as they are evidently *post facto* explanations invented to account for the existence of certain institutions.[1] Other authorities are ready to regard certain myths as genuine traditions in so far as they accord with their own views as to the origin of the institutions in question. This is not very astonishing; since every institution is accounted for by a number of mutually contradictory myths, it is impossible to attribute the same historic value to each of them. All this is very true so long as we do not recognize the functions of the unconscious mechanism that are at the root of all psychical phenomena. Then we may take Lang's point of view as our starting-point and say: the desire to account for existing institutions operates just as do the conscious thoughts of the previous day which have not been brought to an end, the "day stimuli" in the origin of dreams; they are instrumental in the revival of unconscious contents.

There is no such thing as "inventing" myths; psychic life is governed by the same strict laws that obtain elsewhere. In

[1] A. Lang, *The Secret of the Totem*, 1905.

the myths that originate in the reaction of the Unconscious to existing institutions we see but a reflection of those unconscious mechanisms that led to the origin of these same institutions. The various myths that account for the origin of totemism are all true, but they represent various stages of psychic regression, that is more pristine and more recent forms of the mental attitudes which are condensed in the institution of totemism.

We have already mentioned the myths that account for totems as the animals most frequently consumed by the clan or the animals characteristic of the region inhabited by their human "brother," and we saw in these myths reflections of the wish-fulfilment side of the taboo or expressions of the biological bond which unites a tribe with its natural environment. The Dieri myth accounts for totemism as originally instituted to put a stop to incestuous marriages,[1] and a Kaitish myth (mentioned above) regards totemic cult as instituted to honour the memory of a dead father.[2] A myth of the aborigines of Western Victoria regards the introduction of totems (besides the two animal-named primary classes) as a consequence of exogamy.[3] There is no need to point out the facts to which these myths correspond ; and we shall also be able to understand what is meant when we learn that the Dual Heroes (who correspond to the two moieties) gave rise to the totem-centres (mungai spots) when travelling alive in the great Snake's stomach,[4] that is when passing through the various phases of evolution in intra-uterine life, just like the Dieri birth-legend[5] (opening of the earth at Lake Perigundi) with its embryo ancestors.

The Loritja account of the origin of totems is of considerable interest. The Tukutita (the eternal uncreated ones) arose at various places out of the earth. In the beginning they were in human shape, but then an evil being, a gigantic dog striped white and black called Tutururu (i.e. with white stripes along its head), came from the west and attacked the Tukutita, who took animal shapes to escape from the monster. Some of them were changed into kangaroos, others into emus, others into eagles, and so on. The Dual Heroes (called "the good ones") appear on the scene, drive the dog-demon back into the cavern of the west, whereupon the totem-ancestors regain their human form and only retain the faculty of assuming at will the semblance of the animals whose name they bore.[6] We have already shown that the wild dog symbolizes the castration complex[7] which is here made responsible for the projection

[1] Howitt, *N. T.*, 481. Curr, *Australian Race*, II. 48, 49.
[2] Spencer and Gillen, *Nor. T.*, 322.
[3] Dawson, *Australian Aborigines*, 1881, 26, 27.
[4] Spencer and Gillen, *Nor. T.* 437.
[5] Howitt, *N. T.*, 779, 780.
[6] Strehlow, *A. & L.*, I. 2, 3.
[7] Cf. the barking of dogs causes the Atnongara stones to leave the body of the medicine man.—Spencer and Gillen, *N. T.*, 525.

of the Father-Imago into the shape of animals, and thus totemism is represented as a neurotic substitute (Ersatzbildung) for the Father-complex. When the Brother Heroes succeed in repressing their own castration-dread, they drive the dreaded dog-demon back into the cave, that is into the womb as the representative of the most archaic elements of the Unconscious;[1] but totemism (the power of the ancestor to assume animal shape) remains as the rudiment of these social and psychic struggles in collective mentality. This interpretation of the myth is strikingly confirmed by the only exact parallel I know of: the Egyptian myth, according to which the Gods changed themselves into various animals through fear of Typhon.[2] We know enough of Typhon (Seth) if we remember that it was he who fought with his brother Osiris for the realm and for their sister, and who castrated Osiris and tore him into fourteen parts,[3] thus showing how both the Egyptian and the Loritja monster are personifications of the castration complex.

The Dieri legend of Mandra-mankana is of still greater interest, as it embodies not merely one phase but a considerable part of the history of the totemic complex:

> Mandra-mankana once came to the neighbourhood of the Lake Pandi. Two girls who saw him jeered at him, because his back was just the same as his front. He told their mother, who was his noa (that is legitimate wife), to send her two daughters to his camp the following night. They went and lay down, each on one side of their Ngaperi (father or father's brother). But they cheated him, and when he woke up he saw that his two "daughters" had crept away again. Through his songs he caused plants to grow, some with bitter and others with sweet fruit. The two girls found these plants, and delighted with the sweet ones they sprang from bush to bush. Behind a yellow bush lay Mandra-mankana in concealment. He pounced upon the girls, killed them and cut off their breasts. He came to a camp where young boys were playing and promised to invent a song to please them. But when he came to dance his new songs with the breasts of the girls dangling from his neck, the youth recognized their noas in the murdered girls and they broke the legs of the old Pinnaru. Then they split his head open, and at the same time all the people fell upon him and even the children struck him. Then they buried him, and laying his bag at the head of the grave, they went elsewhere. One day

[1] Freud tells us that the sensations experienced by the new-born in the act of birth are the prototypes to which neurotic fear is a regression.

[2] Plutarch, *De Iside et Osiride*, 72.

[3] Id., ibid., 36. According to another version it is the soul of Typhon himself that is distributed in the various holy animals (ch 73), which psychologically amounts exactly to the same thing.

a crow perched itself on the grave of Mandra-mankana. Three times it knocked with its beak, then the dead man woke up and came out of the grave. He followed the footprints of the people to the new camp, and concealed himself in the bushes where they were busy in the creek driving the fishes to catch them together. They had pulled up bushes and grass, and with these were driving the fish before them in heaps; Mandra-mankana kept himself concealed in the water and, opening his mouth, he sucked in the water, fish, grass and men. Those who saw the fate of their comrades ran away, and the Mura-mura Kanta yulkana (Grass-swallower), looking after them, gave each as he ran his totem name (the Grass-swallower is evidently a duplicate of Mandra-mankana, who swallows water, grass, fish and men). The Mura-mura came out of the water and vomited so that he threw out all his teeth, which are to be seen at Manatandri. Then he went a little farther, sat down and died.[1]

The absence of any difference between the front and the back view is really a remarkable sight in a human being, and we cannot quite account for it unless we know whether two back views or two front views are meant. In the former case we should have something like the limbless inapertwa creatures, in the latter the two male members might be meant to correspond to the two girls, the two primary divisions of the tribe. Anyhow, the father begins his mythical career by an attempted incest with his daughters, and the intichiuma he performs later to create plants appears as a substitute for the inhibited incestuous intercourse. He attains his end after all in another way, as killing is but a symbolical coitus.[2] When his incest becomes apparent the Younger Generation and the whole Horde unite to kill the Primeval Sire. But he revives after his death, that is in the Unconscious of his Sons and Followers.

The closing episode of the myth is slightly altered. Mandra-mankana swallows men and vomits his own teeth. Tooth-dreams often mean birth-dreams,[3] and we have good reason to suppose that the teeth vomited by the Mura-mura are in reality identical with the men he swallowed. Then the episode would conform to the well-known motive of the "Swallowed Hero," a myth of Death and Rebirth. But where have we to look for the rite that could serve as a starting-point for "Rebirth through a Male Being"? Only in the ritual of initiation where the rebirth of the novices through a representative of the Father-Imago stands for the social (homoerotic) sublimation of the Oedipus complex.[4] And here we are reminded of the fact that knocking out of teeth is a widely spread initiation

[1] Howitt, *N. T.*, 781–83; *J. A. I.*, 1904, 103.

[2] Breasts cut off are the feminine equivalents to castration.

[3] Freud, *The Interpretation of Dreams*, 1913, 235 sq.

[4] Cf. Reik, l.c., 59.

ceremony of the Australian Continent.[1] But it is those who escape from being swallowed, who are the first to bear totem names; this seems to indicate that the Oedipus complex must either be sublimated by the aid of the swallowing ritual or projected into the animal world as totemism, otherwise we must suppose that originally the Swallowing and Rebirth episode came first and the flight afterwards; in that case (which is not improbable) we should regard the initiation ritual as a *terminus a quo* for the origin of totemism.[2] After the institution of the initiation ritual clan-totemism originated as an outlet for the still unsublimated component of the Oedipus complex.

[1] Amongst the tribes who have circumcision we still find the evulsion of the teeth, although displaced from its original function as an initiation ceremony. Cf. Map 10, on Initiation Ceremonies.

[2] That is clan-totemism as distinguished from the proto-totemic complex.

CHAPTER V

CONCEPTIONAL TOTEMISM

THE question must be faced: How can sexual symbolism be valid in Australia when sexuality plays such a small part in the mentality of the aborigines that they do not even know that cohabitation has anything to do with conception? Evidence will be furnished that it is just this side of the question, the beliefs as to the origin of children, that contain the irrefutable proof of the general point of view here advanced, that gives me the right to regard all these beliefs and practices as the result of a compromise between the libido and repression.

The close connexion between the Alcheringa-myth, the beliefs as to conception, and the intichiuma ceremonies is well known. Myth, belief and ritual are the three different aspects of one system, and any explanation that is valid for one of these must hold good for all.

Ignorance and knowledge about conception.

Let us first see what the aboriginals believe as to the origin of children. Although sexual connexion as the cause of conception is not recognized by the Tully River blacks so far as they themselves are concerned, it is admitted as true for all animals; indeed, this idea confirms them in their belief of superiority over the brute creation.[1] Both the Arunta and Loritja know that sexual intercourse is responsible for conception as far as the animals are concerned, and even children are enlightened on this point.[2] On the other hand, the obvious conclusion from animal to human life is stoutly denied. The Central Australian tribes have no idea of procreation as being directly associated with sexual intercourse, and firmly believe that children can be born without this taking place.[3] In their first work Spencer and Gillen tell us that "we have amongst the Arunta, Luritcha and Ilpirra tribes, and probably also amongst others such as the Warramunga, the idea firmly held that the child is not the direct result of intercourse, that it may come without this, which merely, as it were, prepares the mother for the reception and birth of an already formed spirit-child who inhabits one of the local totem-centres."[4]

[1] W. E. Roth, S. M. M., *N. Q. E. Bull.*, 1903, 22.

[2] Strehlow, *A. & L.*, II. 52

[3] Spencer and Gillen, *Nor. T.*, 330.

[4] Id., *N. T.*, 265.

In his first report Strehlow affirmed that sexual intercourse had nothing to do with conception in the opinion of the Arunta,[1] but when asked by Leonhardi to inquire further into the matter he obtained the same results as Spencer and Gillen: without intercourse the womb remains closed (ilba worranta), and it is only cohabitation which opens the womb for the reception of the "ratapa."[2] The German missionary also tells us that the old men know the real facts well enough, but they take care not to enlighten the young men and women[3]—again in strong contrast with the fact that even the children are acquainted with the natural causation in so far as regards the animal world.

If an unbiased critic were to read these data for the first time, I dare say he would hesitate between saying that the Arunta do not know and that they deny the connexion between cohabitation and conception. Similarly among the Larrekiya and Wogait conception is not regarded as a direct result of cohabitation.[4] Amongst the Kakadu and other northern tribes Spencer again found "the absence of any necessary relation between sexual connexion and procreation."[5] The belief that procreation is not due to conception is universal among the northern tribes.[6] In the tribes north of the Ingarda many of the men believe that children result from sexual intercourse, whilst other men do not share this belief.[7]

Both Gennep and Frazer, who deny the knowledge,[8] and Schmidt and Lang,[9] who deny the ignorance of the Arunta, are in a difficult position. Psychologically, we know, however, that the word "knowledge" covers various mental attitudes, various degrees of recognition of a given concept. If we see, on the one hand, that the Arunta deny knowing anything of the matter and on the other that they have beliefs and rites that are only explicable on the assumption that such a knowledge exists somewhere and makes itself felt in their psychic system, we shall say that they are not conscious of their own instinctive knowledge of procreation,[10] and that the concepts that enter their consciousness are symbolic substitutes of a physiological account of the process of procreation.

[1] Strehlow, *A. & L.*, II. 52. [2] Id., III. xi. [3] Id., II. 52.

[4] H. Basedow, "Anthropological Notes on the Western Coastal Tribes of the Northern Territory of South Australia," *Trans. Roy. Soc. of South Australia*, XXXI. 1907, 4.

[5] Spencer, *N. T. N. T. A.*, 1914, 270.

[6] J. G. Frazer, "Beliefs and Customs of the Australian Aborigines," *Folk-Lore*, 1909, 350, 351; *Man*, 1909, 146.

[7] A. R. Brown, "Beliefs concerning Childbirth," *Man*, 1912, 180.

[8] A. v. Gennep, op. cit., LXI. 1905. Frazer, *T. and E.*, I. 157. Reitzenstein, "Kausalzusammenhang zwischen Geschlechtsverkehr und Empfängnis in Glaube und Brauch der Natur und Kulturvölker," *Z. E.*, 1909, 644. E. S. Hartland, *Primitive Paternity*, 1909, I. 11.

[9] A. Lang, *The Secret of the Totem*, 1905, 190. P. W. Schmidt, "Die Stellung der Aranda," *Z. E.*, 1908, 879.

[10] Carveth Read, "No Paternity," *J. R. A. I.*, 1918, XLVIII. 146.

Professor Gregory, without expressing his opinion in the language of psychology, comes fairly near to our views when he says: "The aboriginal idea that children have only a spirit-father and no human father may be a mere childish make-believe," and man's power of make-believe is so "strong that he does not realize his own imposture. And in the same way the people may believe that children are the result of a reincarnation of spirits and that a human father is quite unnecessary. But they are not sufficiently foolish to believe that, under normal circumstances, a tribe consisting only of women would have a prolific birth-rate." [1]

Conception through food.

There are various views current as to the origin of children; perhaps the simplest of these is that which attributes the birth of a child to something eaten by the mother. For instance, the Arunta say that if a woman eats a lot of the latjia she may soon afterwards be aware of the first signs of pregnancy, and in this case it is a latjia-ratapa that has entered her body—not through the mouth, but through the hips.[2] The usual doctrine as to the origin of children in this tribe is more elaborate; but at any rate the husband has to give the wife some meat, and this meat is in reality procured by the totem-ancestor, who has entered the woman and is about to be reborn by her.[3] According to the Wogait tribe, in the ordinary course of events, if a man, when out hunting, kills an animal or collects any other articles of diet, he gives it to his gin, who must eat it, believing that the respective object brings about the successful birth of a piccaninny.[4] The child is forbidden to eat the particular animal till it has teethed. Descent of the totem is in the direct patrilineal line.[5]

According to the Kakadu, when a man dies the spirit part (Yalmuru) keeps watch over the bones. After a time the Yalmuru, as it were divides into two parts, so that we have the original Yalmuru and a second spirit called Iwaiyu. When the Yalmuru desires to undergo reincarnation it takes the Iwaiyu and puts it in the form of a small frog, which lives under the sheathes of the leaves of the Pandanus tree, into some food such as fish or "sugar-bag" that the man is searching for. If it be, for example, fish, the Yalmuru goes into the water and drives the fish into the man's fishing-net. As soon as the man has caught the fish, out jumps the frog, unseen, of course, by the men. It is caught by the Yalmuru, and together the two spirits return into their camping-place. The food into which the Iwaiyu was placed will be the child's totem. Sometimes when

[1] J. W. Gregory, *The Dead Heart of Australia*, 1906, 196.

[2] Strehlow, II. 56.

[3] Id., II. 54.

[4] H. Basedow, "Anthropological Notes on the Western Coastal Tribes of the Northern Territory of South Australia," *Trans. Roy.*, XXXI. 1907, 4. See also William A. White, "Psycho-analytic Parallels." *The Psycho-analytic Review*, 1915, II. 187.

[5] Spencer, *N. T. N. T. A.*, 1914, 16.

an animal, such as a crocodile or fish, contains for a time the Iwaiyu, and the animal is speared, the child to which the Iwaiyu subsequently gives rise bears the mark of the spear wound.[1]

We again meet the frog, which in Europe is also a symbol of the womb,[2] in the beliefs of the Tully River blacks.[3] Here a woman begets children because she has been sitting over the fire on which she has roasted a particular species of black bream, which must have been given to her by the prospective father, or she has purposely gone a-hunting and caught a certain kind of bull frog.[4] The other elements of the Kakadu theory find their nearest equivalent in North-West Australia. In the Ingarda tribe, at the mouth of the Gascoyne River, the belief is that the child is the product of some food of which the mother has partaken just before her first sickness in pregnancy. A. R. Brown says: "My principal informant on this subject told me that his father had speared a small animal called bandaru. His mother ate the animal, with the result that she gave birth to my informant. He showed me the mark on his side where he had been speared by his father before being eaten by his mother. A little girl was pointed out to me as being the result of her mother having eaten a domestic cat,[5] and her brother was said to have been produced from a bustard."[6] A woman of the Buduna tribe said that native women nowadays bear half-caste children because they ate bread made of white flour.[7] The same theory has been reported by Stirling of the Arunta: the pale colour of a half-caste child was due to the fact that the woman had been eating flour.[8] In the Kariera, Namal and Injibandi tribes the conception of a child is believed to be due to the agency of a particular man who is not the father. This man is the wororu of the child when it is born. There were three different accounts of how a wororu produces conception. According to the first, the man gives some food to the woman; she eats this and becomes pregnant. According to the second, the man when he is out hunting kills an animal, preferably a kangaroo or emu, and when it is dying he tells the spirit of the dead animal to go into the woman and to be born as a child. In the third account, the hunter, after having killed the kangaroo or emu,

The duel with the father.

[1] Spencer, *N. T. N. T. A.*, 1914, 270, 271.

[2] Cf. Andree, *Votive und Weihegaben*, 1904, 129. Róheim, "Adalékok a magyar néphithez" (*Contributions to Hungarian Folk-Lore*), 1920, 219.

[3] In the Waduman and Mudburra tribes spirit-children live in the shape of little frogs.—Spencer, *N. T. N. T. A.*, 268.

[4] W. E. Roth, *S. M. M.*, 22.

[5] She was a Chinese half-caste.

[6] Brown, "Childbirth Beliefs," *Man*, 1912, 180. These animals are not the totems of the children who owe their origin to them.

[7] Brown, op. cit., 181.

[8] E. C. Stirling, "Anthropology," *Horn Expedition*, IV. 129. This is the common explanation of the existence of half-castes given universally by their mothers: "Too much me been eat em white man's flour." This explanation is accepted by old men without any further question. Spencer, *N. T. N. T. A.*, 1914, 25, 26.

takes a portion of the fat;[1] this changes into a spirit-baby and follows the man to his camp. When the man is asleep the spirit-baby comes to him, and he directs it to enter a certain woman, who thus becomes pregnant. In nearly every case the wororu is the father's brother (own or tribal). Again the conceptional animal is not the totem, for in a very large number of cases it is either the kangaroo or emu.[2]

These accounts contain two essential elements—an animal must be eaten by the mother, but that animal must be killed by the father (or his substitute, the wororu) to cause conception. Let us try the analysis of the former concept. To begin with, it will not be difficult to show that eating an animal which is here connected with conception is, on the other hand, also intimately bound up with the idea of sexual connexion. In King George's Sound it is believed that women give birth to children if they eat a lot of kangaroo flesh.[3] According to the Port Lincoln tribe, women give birth to children if they eat snakes.[4] Among some tribes visited by Eyre malformations of the body are attributed to the influence of the stars caused by the mother eating forbidden food during pregnancy;[5] and Gerstäcker reports, after information supplied by Moorhouse, that young girls believe that they will become pregnant if they eat food that is taboo to them on account of their age (or, rather, youth).[6] On the other hand, Strehlow tells us: "The custom still exists among the blacks for a man to offer meat to a woman or girl he wishes to seduce; her acceptance is taken as a sign of consent."[7] A Kurnai girl, if she fancied a young man, might send him a secret message, "Will you find me some food?" and this was understood as a proposal.[8] In the Encounter Bay tribe boys are considered "rambe" (sacred or holy) after initiation, and no female, not even their own sister, must accept any food from them until such time as they are allowed to ask for a wife.[9] Among the tribes around the Cairns district, in North Queensland, the acceptance

[1] When a man has killed another he preserves the fat to protect him against the blood-feud, because when the kindred of the dead man call him to account for the death he gives them the fat to eat, with the effect that they become pacified. —Howitt, *N. T.*, 449.

[2] Brown, l.c., 181. Id., "Three Tribes of Western Australia," *J. A. I.*, 1913, 168. Nobody may hunt over the country or any other local group without the permission of the owners. A single exception to this rule seems to have existed where a man was following a kangaroo or emu and it crossed the boundary; he was allowed to follow and kill it (p. 146).

[3] R. Brown, "Description of the Natives of King George's Sound," *J.R.G.S.*, I. 30.

[4] Wilhelmi, *Manners and Customs*, 1862, 15. C. W. Schnürrmann, *The Aboriginal Tribes of Port Lincoln in South Australia*. T. D. Woods, *The Native Tribes of South Australia*, 1879, 220.

[5] E. T. Eyre, *Journals of Expeditions into Central Australia*, 1845, II. 361.

[6] Gerstäcker, Reisen. IV. 1854, 367.

[7] Strehlow, I. 54.

[8] Fison and Howitt, *Kamilaroi and Kurnai*, 1880, 200.

[9] H. E. A. Meyer, *Manners and Customs of the Aborigines of the Encounter Bay Tribes*. Woods, *Native Tribes of South Australia*, 1879, 187.

of food from a man by a woman was not merely regarded as a marriage ceremony, but as the actual cause of conception.[1] If we thus find the acceptance of food connected with sexual union on the one hand,[2] with procreation on the other, it is difficult not to believe in the unconscious knowledge of the aboriginals, especially as the giver of the food is the husband or his substitute. Using the mechanism of displacement upwards and based upon oral eroticism, infantile sexual theories are found everywhere. These theories are the result of a compromise between the libidinal knowledge of the Unconscious and repression. Thus one of the most frequent of these theories is that which attributes the origin of the child to some food consumed by the mother. We have abundantly clear proofs of this displacement upward in Australian customs. In the northern and western Arunta and in the Ilpirra tribe, for the purpose of strengthening a delicate woman a part of the internal reproductive organs (called ertoacha) is taken from a male opossum, wallaby, euro or kangaroo. The woman lies on her back, and her husband, placing the ertoacha upon the mons veneris, " sings " over it for some time, after which the woman swallows it whole. In other cases the same part of the amimal is taken by the man and half-cooked, after which he coats it with grease, charms it by singing over it, and then presents it to his wife; she must swallow it whole without having any idea as to the nature of the object, which in this case is given for the purpose of promoting sexual desire. For the same purpose fluid material from the ertoacha may be squeezed into the vulva.[3] As giving food to a woman means having connexion with her, it is quite natural that the repression which is directed against the Oedipus complex should be also directed against certain symbolic manifestations of the same in which eating stands for intercourse. Amongst the Kakadu, up to such a time as a man is Kulori (that is, fully initiated), he may not give any of the foods to his mother that are prohibited to him. After having passed the ceremony, he takes the prohibited food to his father, and says, " Father, does my mother eat so and so? " The father says, " Give it to your mother." That is, after being aggregated to the society of men he may indulge in a symbolic equivalent of the forbidden deed, provided that his father, whose rights are violated by the proceeding, gives him permission to do so.[4]

But this is not all that can be said to explain certain particulars of these beliefs. We must remind the reader of the fact that the food is (*a*) in some cases the totem of the child, (*b*) eating forbidden food makes the girl pregnant. We shall hardly be astonished to see

[1] Frazer, *T. & E.*, I. 577.

[2] Among all the aboriginals the offer of food and sexual relations are closely associated.—R. Thurnwald, *Die Gemeinde der Bánaro*, 1921, 17.

[3] Spencer and Gillen, *N. T.*, 465.

[4] Spencer, *N. T. N. T. A.*, 1914, 347, 348.

pregnancy attributed to a breaking through of inhibitions and taboos, and we shall remind the reader of the Alcheringa, the epoch of wish-fulfilments, when eating the totem and endototemic incest prevailed. In the light of these facts the two cardinal taboos of totemism seem to express one and the same thing, not to commit incest either in reality or symbolically by eating the totem (transposition upwards). Freud has interpreted the eating of the totem simply as a sequence to the killing of the animal, and in this case the taboo of eating the totem is an inhibition of the symbolic repetition of primeval parricide and its sequel the anthrophagous meal. We see that this aspect of the question is not absent from these primitive sexual theories: the child often bears the mark of a pre-natal duel with the father. According to the Kagoro, a spirit may transmigrate into the body of a descendant; in fact, this is common, as proved by the likeness of children to their parents and grandparents, and this is lucky, for the ghost has returned and has no longer any power to frighten the relatives until the new body dies. Souls cannot take up their abode in animals, but those of beasts can enter into the bodies of children of their slayers, as is shown by the fact that more than one case has been known of a child being born with marks of wounds like those received by his father or mother when fighting with an animal or by the animal itself killed before the child's birth.[1] The pre-natal fight with the father and being eaten pre-natally by the mother in the shape of a snake means the unconscious Oedipus complex latent in every human being. The belief in reincarnation, the "other life," is often the projection of the other life latent in the unconscious psychic system of man, as when the Euahlayi say that quite young men often marry quite old women, and account for this by saying that these young men were on earth before, loved these same women, but died before their initiation and so could not marry until reincarnated.[2] The old woman is, of course, the representative of the Mother-Imago, and the other life is the period of infantile fixation to the Mother.[3] We can now take the pre-natal occurrence of this fight in a more literal sense; it refers again to the deepest strata of the unconscious rooted in intra-uterine life; the animal shape of the child previous to its birth is again a reminiscence of intra-uterine evolution through the various phases of animal life. From this point of view being "speared" by the father when in the mother's womb has a still more concrete meaning if we may substitute the penis for the spear, and remind the reader of the analogy with European folklore where intercourse with a pregnant mother quickens the birth of the child.[4]

[1] Tremearne, "Notes on some Nigerian Head-Hunters," *J. A. I.*, 1912, 159.

[2] K. L. Parker, *The Euahlayi Tribe*, 1905, 56.

[3] Cf. Reik, *Völkerpsychologisches. Zeitschrift für Psychoanalyse*, III. 180.

[4] Róheim, "Die Bedeutung des Uberschreitens," *I. Z. Pa.* 1920, 212.

The latest of those deep-searching analyses of the Unconscious of the individual that we owe to Freud contains also an explanation of the intra-uterine and re-birth phantasies. "The former has frequently arisen, as in our case, from the fixation to the father; the son wishes to be in the mother's body in order to replace her in coitus, to take her place with the father. The re-birth phantasy is usually a softening, as it were a euphemism, for the phantasy of incestuous relationship with the mother. The son wishes himself back in the situation in which he found himself in his mother's womb, the male thus identifying himself with his penis, regarding it as his representative. The two phantasies thus are seen to be complementary-formations, and, according to the male or female attitude adopted, give expression to the wish for sex-relations with either father or mother. The possibility must be admitted that in our patient's illness both phantasies and, accordingly, both incest wishes, are present." [1]

With the Australian beliefs this is certainly the case: the intra-uterine phantasy (being speared by the father) is followed by the re-birth phantasy (being eaten in the shape of a snake, that is penis, by the mother). The particular animal species with which the child is identified in his pre-natal career demands some explanation. Here we follow Reik's lead, who has shown that the customs of the couvade are to be attributed to a revival of the Oedipus complex in the form of retribution-fear, the husband dreading the punishment for his own unconscious Oedipus wishes that he felt against his own father, now that he, too, is about to become a father. The young husband was a rebel against his father in his youth; he fears that his son will be the same to him. His two enemies are thus identical from the standpoint of the Unconscious: the child is the grandfather back again and thirsting for revenge. In the four-class system child and grandfather belong to the same marriage-class, which is different from that of the father. Grandfather and child thus form one psychic unity: as indeed it is often believed that the grandfather is re-born in the child. That is why killing an animal at this period would injure the child as it is a symbolic aggressive act against the would-be-reborn grandfather.[2] The Arunta husband may eat meat, but he is not supposed to go out in search of large game. If he does so the spirit of the child which often accompanies him when he goes out into the bush, not only gives warning to any large game such as kangaroo or emu, but if the man attempts to throw a spear or boomerang this spirit will cause it to take a crooked course. The Unmatjera have the same belief,[3] and thus identify the infant-grandfather with the large game. "If a woman who is enceinte were to eat forbidden fish at such a time, the spirit of the

[1] Freud, *Sammlung kleiner Schriften zur Neurosenlehre*, 1918, IV. 693, 694.

[2] Reik, *Probleme der Religionspsychologie*, 1919, Die Couvade, 1.

[3] Spencer and Gillen, *Nor. T.*, 614.

unborn babe would go out of its mother's body and frighten the fish away." [1]

From the Unconscious point of view the infant itself is a "fish in the water." Although these spirit-children are invisible to human eyes, the old men know that they are present by the movements of the fish in the water.

We remind the reader that the kangaroo as father and the emu as mother have very definite symbolic meanings in the proto-totemic complex of the Australian tribes.

Thus the means by which a man procreates his own child appears in the light of a breaking through the cardinal taboos; he symbolically kills his own totem, that is, he either kills his kangaroo-father or has intercourse[2] with his emu-mother. Thus all children owe, in a twofold sense of the word, their birth to an unconscious (symbolic) realization of the Oedipus complex—from their own point of view in a fight with their own father and intercourse with their own mother, whilst from their father's point of view it is a revival of his own infantile Oedipus complex. When he procreates a child he again kills his father (who is identical with his child) and cohabits with his mother. This is why people are apt to undergo reincarnation if they have died uninitiated, that is, without sublimating their own Oedipus complex: [3] those who are initiated will not be reborn, as it is the incestuous-archaic type of the libido that is recognized as the real motor-agency of procreation.

Repression and the Oedipus complex.

The Alcheringa ancestors, the representatives of unbounded totemic wish-fulfilment, are the prototypes of all subsequent child-making and magic: children owe their origin and their totem to the breaking through of the very same taboos (eating the totem) which in after life they are most strictly enjoined to observe. Thus our explanation of these beliefs as symbolical representations of an unconscious knowledge has also furnished us with the principal reason of their repressed, that is merely symbolic, manifestation; the repression is like the greater part of the social structure of primitive man directed against the incestuous manifestation of the libido. The gradual disappearance of the libido in old age naturally makes the inhibitions that exist only as a counter-balance to the primary libidinal tendencies disappear; this is why, as Reik has explained, old men are allowed to eat anything; this is also why, in Arunta and Loritja tribes, only the old men "know" (that is, only they do not repress their knowledge) of the real connexion between cohabitation and procreation. Thus we are not obliged to qualify the denial of knowledge by the Arunta as a falsehood, and yet we are in the position to understand many of their beliefs and practices that evidently

[1] R. H. Matthews, *E. N.*, 53.

[2] Spearing = cohabitation.

[3] Parker, *Euahlayi Tribe*, 56.

involve the very knowledge of which they are not conscious. It is, therefore, not necessary to assume that the "Ambilyerikirra" ceremony has been borrowed by the Arunta from another tribe.[1] In the Urabunna tribe neither the husband nor the wife eats the echidna when the woman is pregnant; this is the only restriction in regard to the behaviour of the man.[2] We have already commented on the myth that tells us how an Echidna man of the Alcheringa castrated some of the youths who ought to have been subincised. By doing this the Echidna "spoilt" himself and all his totem kindred, so that they cannot rise up again except in the form of little animals covered with spines.[3] As a punishment for castrating the boys and thus depriving them of the faculty of procreation, the Echidna man loses his power of reincarnation: a punishment, that is, in full accordance with the "eye for eye" principle if we regard the incarnation-myth only as a symbolic account of procreation. Then we can also understand why the Echidna, who thus stands for the castration complex, should be tabooed to the father "in spe."

The Arunta account of childbirth.

Then again, we have the Arunta account of the childbirth, which, as Schmidt and Reitzenstein have pointed out,[4] is incomprehensible without supposing "knowledge" of some sort. A case out of real life will serve as a paradigm:

> Near to Arkororinja there is a totem-centre where a Ramaia (Big Lizard) ancestor went into the earth in the Alcheringa whilst his body was turned into a rock. Here lives a man called Urbula, with his wife Kaltia. One night the Lizard-ancestor leaves his rock and goes to the camp of Urbula to listen to the talk of the camp-mates. He hears that Kaltia is his class-mother. The same night Urbula dreams that an Altjiranga mitjina is approaching. (As this means the birth of a child, so it amounts to a statement that he dreams of his wife's pregnancy.) On the morrow Urbula gets up as usual, and goes hunting, but this time the iningukua (spirit-double) of the Alcheringa ancestor accompanies him.[5] The iningukua

[1] Cf. J. G. Frazer, "On Some Ceremonies of the Central Australian Tribes." *Austr. Assoc. Adv. of Science*, 1901, 322. (I received a copy of this paper through the kindness of Sir James Frazer.)

[2] Spencer and Gillen, *Nor. T.*, 614.

[3] Id., *N. T.*, 398, 399.

[4] W. Schmidt, "Die Stellung der Aranda," *Z. f. E.*, 1908, 885. Reitzenstein, *Z. E.*, 1909, 650. Spirit-children are supposed to have a strong predilection for fat women, and prefer to choose such as their mothers, even at the risk of being born into the wrong class (Spencer and Gillen, *N. T.*, 125), and in this their tastes agree with native ideas as to feminine beauty (N. W. Thomas, *The Natives of Australia*, 210).

[5] Cf., "When a spirit-individual goes into a woman there still remains the Arumburinga, which may be regarded as its double, and this may attend the woman's husband as he goes out hunting."—Spencer and Gillen, *N. T.*, 514. The Iningukua corresponds to the Arumburinga.

of the child has the same name as he has: it is a sort of spiritual double of the spirit-child.

In this belief we see a survival of the hunt as symbolic procreation with the identity of the hunted animal and the unborn child. After having speared an animal, for instance a kangaroo, the Urbula returns to the camp accompanied by the totem-ancestor. Kaltia, who is expecting her husband, sees at a distance two men coming, one of whom suddenly disappears. (Here again the totem-ancestor is a sort of double of the husband.) Urbula then gives his wife some meat: she eats it and feels sick afterwards. This meat has in reality been procured by the Altjiranga mitjina (it is thus he who has speared the kangaroo: identity of the "hunter and the hunted" [1]) and given as a present to the woman. When the totem-ancestor disappears, he is supposed to enter the woman's womb for a short time and cause her sickness; with the vomited food he comes out again. In the hunting and meat-offering we have one symbolic account of procreation that so far corresponds to the Ingarda, etc., theory: but to this is superadded a second account, giving the Arunta theory a more complicated aspect:

> Next day, when the woman passes at Arkororinja the rock into which the Altjiranga mitjina transformed himself, she sees a man standing there ornamented with a head-band who has a a stick and a "namatuna" in his hand. The Lizard-ancestor now throws the namatuna at Kaltia's hip and disappears into the earth: the namatuna goes into Kaltia, where it takes human form. The namatuna and the Lizard-ancestor are really identical; the same thing is told in two versions, in one of which the woman is replaced by a symbol—Mother-Earth—and in the other the man: bullroarer instead of ancestor. We have seen that the disappearance of the totem-ancestor is really supposed to be a disappearance into Kaltia's womb: thus we find our opinion strikingly corroborated, that the sinking into the earth by which the totem-ancestors end their career is a regression into the maternal womb. She comes home and tells her husband: "I went near the rock where I saw a man with a head-band standing before me. Although I saw him, I had nothing whatever to do with him. When I was preparing the seeds I felt something in my body." The husband answers: "You have conceived" (Njumereraka). After the woman has given birth to the child the grandfather of the infant, called Tjinnapuntu (Big-leg), Urbula's father,

[1] That is, to the intra-uterine phantasy of the child ("speared" by the father when in the mother's womb) we find another superadded phantasy of being identical with the father (grandfather who "spears" the mother). This condensation is characteristic of the ambisexual attitude in these Oedipus phantasies.

who, like the child and like the totem-ancestor who threw the namatuna, is a Paltara,[1] asks his son: "Where has the child been conceived?" Urbula answers: "He came along from Arkororinja." Then he asks his daughter-in-law: "Where did you see him for certain?" She answers: "Near the rock I felt something that made my legs stiff," and he says: "The youths shall be called Loatjira" (another word for Ramaia—"Big Lizard"), "the name of the totem-ancestor as he came to you in the camp of the palla."[2]

All our accounts of the childbirth-beliefs of the Arunta and their neighbours mention these childbirth-centres or symbolical wombs. The Rev. L. Schulze tells us that these natives believe that the souls of infants dwell in the foliage of trees, and that they are carried there by the good mountain-spirits "tuanjiralka and their wives melbata." The nearest tree to a woman when she feels the first pain of parturition she calls "ngirra," as they are under the impression that the "guruna" or soul has then entered from it into the child. Such a tree is left untouched, as they believe that whoever should happen to break off one single branch would become sick. But if the tree should be injured or broken down by winds or floods, that person would get ill whose ngirra the tree was.[3] This seems to be the exoteric account of an esoteric variant of the birth-belief, as the bullroarer spirits Tuanjiraka and Melbata are recognized as such.[4] At any rate, it is highly suggestive to find the bullroarer spirits, whose phallic nature we shall have occasion to demonstrate, made responsible for bringing the children into these symbolic wombs. The "ngirra" tree is the "ngarra" (eternal) tree of Strehlow,[5] the "nanja" tree of Spencer and Gillen. Both its quality as a haven of refuge and as an external soul are well brought out in this account. R. H. Mathews says: "It is a common belief amongst these natives that infants reside in rocky hills and in the dense foliage of the forest trees before they enter the bodies of women who give them birth."[6] The same author tells us that there are certain spots scattered up and down at short intervals in the territory of the Arranda, Chingalee and Wombaia which are traditionally haunted, some by one animal or object and some by another, from

[1] Cf. Strehlow, *A. & L.*, IV. 1913, 63. Husband Knuraia, wife Ngala, child Paltara; the husband's father having been a Paltara, and his mother a Kamara.

[2] Palla means a man of the same marriage-class, but a different age-grade from the husband. In this case the allusion is to the husband's grandfather, who would also be a Knuraia, and to whom only a Paltara totem-ancestor like the reborn child could appear. Cf. Strehlow, II. 54, 55; IV. 66.

[3] Louis Schulze, "The Aborigines of the Upper and Middle Finke River, Their Habits and Customs," 1891, *Trans. and Proc. Royal Soc. of S. A.*, XIV. 237.

[4] Cf. the "Märchen," published by Strehlow, op. cit., I. 102.

[5] Strehlow, op. cit., I. 5.

[6] R. H. Matthews, "Ethnological Notes on the Aboriginal Tribes of the Northern Territory," *Proc. and Trans. Geog. S. of Australasia*, XVI. 85.

which the children receive their totemic names instead of receiving them from the mother. When a woman first feels the movement of the fœtus in the womb, she reports to her friends that one night recently, when she and her husband were camped in the vicinity of a certain rock-hole, she dreamt that she saw a number of very tiny children [1] playing about and singing among the leaves of one of the trees close to the rock-hole. Her husband will also say that just before daylight he heard an infant coming down out of the tree, laughing as it came, and pulled his hair or his whiskers, asking him to find a mother for it, after which it vanished and was believed to have entered the woman's body. When the child is born it is given the totem belonging to the locality where the mother or father had the alleged dream. For example, if the spot be traditionally known to be hunted by wallaby spirits, the newly-born child would get the totem of the wallaby, quite irrespective of the totemic name of either the father or the husband.[2] In this account the child goes to the woman from the husband, which I should say is an effaced trace of the part he plays in procreation. As Strehlow gives the same account, only more fully, we shall use his version as a starting-point of the analysis. The whole account of Strehlow has two essential points, the throwing of the namatuna and the part played by the child's grandfather. We find an analogous theory as to conception caused by throwing in the Nimbalda tribe in South Australia. They believe that two old women called " Yammutu " live towards the east, a long way off; when rain comes they lie down on their backs with their legs open, and the water runs into their person and causes them to bear a lot of young blacks called Muree, who, as they grow up, start westward, always throwing a small waddy, called weetchu, before them till one of them meets a blackfellow with his lubra The Muree, being invisible, then walks in the blackfellow's tracks to make him or her look like the blackfellow,[3] and then throws the small waddy under the thumb nail or great toenail, and so enters into the woman's body. She is soon pregnant, and in due time gives birth to an ordinary child.[4] This account gives us the doubling of the birth as a motive of the supernatural birth theories in a characteristic manner. It is first the two mother-prototypes [5] who are impregnated

[1] Cf. Róheim, " Das Selbst," *Imago*, VII. 345. H. B. Wheatley, " Folklore of Shakespeare," *Folklore*, 1916, XXVI. 380.

[2] R. H. Mathew, " The Sociology of Arranda and Chingalee Tribe," *F. L.*, 1908, XIX. 102.

[3] As to the symbolic meaning of treading in somebody's footsteps, see Róheim, *Adalékok a magyar néphithez*, 1920 (*Contributions to Hungarian Folklore*), 259.

[4] H. O. Smith, *The Nimbalda Tribe.* G. Taplin, *F.L.*, etc., 1879, 88. Cf. " Women conceive invariably in consequence of the infant being conveyed by some unknown agency into the mother's womb from somewhere across the sea."—" Account Respecting Beliefs of Australian Aborigines," *Journal of American Folklore*, 1896 IX. 202.

[5] Cf. the two wives of Baiame, Daramulun, the two class system!

by the rain,[1] and they give birth to a swarm of baby-prototypes (" spirit-children " in Spencer's terminology). Their name Muree agrees with that used in some Australian languages for man and kangaroo.[2] These again appear in the shape of doubles—the continual doubling of motives leads to the doubling of persons—when they throw themselves into the woman's womb and are once more born, this time in the natural way.

As to the well-known sexual-symbolistic interpretation of this throwing, this is quite evident from the Arunta account, the denial of the woman of having had " anything to do " with the Alcheringa ancestor amounting to the avowal of an unconscious (that is symbolic) wish of cohabitation. What the small bullroarer, called namatuna, really is and what the throwing means has already been pointed out by P. W. Schmidt.[3] The namatuna is the namatwinna described by Spencer and Gillen. Armed with this smaller kind of bullroarer, the native goes into the bush accompanied by two or three friends. All night long the men keep up a low singing of Quabara songs, together with the chanting of amorous phrases of invitation addressed to the woman. In the morning he swings the namatwinna, and the sound of the humming is carried to the ears of the far-distant woman, and has the power of compelling affection and of causing her sooner or later to comply with the summons. The custom is not confined to the Arunta tribe, but exists also among the Ilpirra, Walparri, Kaitish and Warramunga tribes, all of whom use bullroarers, which are the equivalents of the namatwinna of the Arunta.[4]

It is evident that the use of the same instrument for procreation (by the Alcheringa ancestor) and for love magic (by the present-day aboriginal) is not a matter of mere chance. Strehlow states that the young man gets the namatwinna, which is the body of his iningukua (totem-ancestor), as guardian or spirit-double after his subincision. It is smeared with blood from the subincised penis, and only then handed to the young man, who uses it to compel the love of the girl he wants.[5] It is especially evident from this description that the small bullroarer gets its magic potency from the penis, that it is a sort of magical (symbolic) equivalent of the penis, and thus naturally the proper instrument for love-magic and for begetting a child.

But what does the part played by the grandfather mean ? To

[1] The soul of the dead is supposed to come back from the other world in the rain.—Strehlow, I. 15. At Pennefather River, Thunder can make lightning, men and women. At Cape Bedford, Thunder makes lightning by the rapid exposure of his penis. Roth, *Superstition*, 8. Thunder is a voice of a dead person who announces that he has returned to life.—Howitt, 785.

[2] Curr, *The Australian Race*, III. 119, and according to index.

[3] Schmidt, " Die Stellung der Aranda," *Z. E.*, 1908, 885.

[4] Spencer and Gillen, *N. T.*, 542. Cf. the " gin-busters," Roth, *S. M. M.*, 24.

[5] Strehlow, II. 81.

begin with, four- and eight-class systems (with paternal descent) are based on the return of the grandfather in the grandchild. Urbula's father is a Paltara, and so is his son; that is, Urbula is socially in the same relation to his father as to his son. That the son is a reborn "father's father" is indeed stated in so many words by the Arunta when they say that he is the rebirth of the Altjiranga mitjina, another "Big-Lizard." If such be the case, it is easy to see why the grandfather is the person to know all about the boy's "supernatural" origin[1] and later in life to conduct him to his arknanakaua.[2] The situation must now be considered from the mother's point of view. To her father-in-law she is strictly taboo; she is only allowed to talk to him in whispers.[3] All the members of the Paltara class to whom her husband's father and her own child belong are strictly taboo to her; having intercourse with them would be committing incest, from the native point of view. But so does the Alcheringa ancestor, with whom, as we have seen, she has symbolic (that is unconscious) intercourse; he is also a Paltara, again identical with the child and the husband's father. The husband's father again, as pointed out by Freud, is merely a revival of the woman's own Father-imago;[4] on that account he is avoided, as there is a strong tendency on the woman's part to realize her infantile Oedipus dream with him as partner.

Thus we have again found the Oedipus wish in its double form (intercourse with her own father and her own child) at the root of the symbolical description of the natural functions and repression, which is again directed against the manifestation of the unconscious tendencies that lie at the root of the whole birth-mythology. All these infantile sexual theories must be regarded as the outcome of a compromise between the archaic libido and repression; the degree of elaboration depends on the number of unconscious elements that find outlet in these theories. The libidinal tendencies that find expression in them may roughly be divided into two types: those of the Oedipus type, in which the genital impulse dominates, and those that are under the influence of the various erogenous zones. Repression is principally directed against the former, whilst the latter are utilized by the repressive tendencies as substitutes of the censored manifestations of the Oedipus attitude.

The cloaca-theory.

The sexual theory that takes its impulse from an anal-erotic constitution, the cloaca-theory, is described by Freud as ontogenetically the most primitive of these phantasies; he says that the theory of children originating from the food eaten by the mother is superadded to this in later years as the product of conscious reflection on these lines.[5] In this

[1] Spencer and Gillen, *N. T.*, 132.
[2] Strehlow, II. 81.
[3] Id., II. 91.
[4] Freud, *T. & T.*, 1919, 15.
[5] Freud, *Kleine Schriften zur Neurosenlehre*, II. 168.

case the most primitive of the widely spread Australian conception-beliefs corresponds to this second phase of ontogenetic evolution, although I think it would be dangerous to push the ontogenetic parallelism too far in this case. The speculations of the child are primarily connected with the problem of birth, those of the savage with conception, because among naked savages there can be no doubt of the part played by the womb and the vagina. On the other hand, there certainly are faint indications of the excremental theory, not in the beliefs as to the origin of actual children, but in anthropogonic legend.

> The Kokowara say that in the beginning Anjea was lying in the shadow of a thickly-leaved tree. He was a blackfellow with very large buttocks, but peculiar in that there was no sign of any orifice. Yalpan happened to be passing at that time, and, noticing this anomaly, made a cut in the usual place by means of a piece of quartz-crystal, with the result that the evacuations were expelled and spread over the surface of the ground. All blacks were thus originally born from Anjea's dung.[1]

Now Anjea is identical with a being who is responsible for the actual fabrication of children,[2] and the anthropogonic myth might represent an antiquated standpoint in these infantile theories as compared with the more advanced sexual theories that describe the origin of present-day children. The oral-erotic theory is also connected with the equation of children with excrement; food, the substance which is incorporated = seminal fluid (from the female point of view); fæces which leaves the body = child.

Anjea.

Anjea, originally made by thunder, is the individual who fashions the piccaninnies out of swamp-mud and inserts them in the bellies of the women. He is never seen, but can be heard laughing in the depths of the bush, amongst the rocks, down in the lagoons and along the mangrove swamps. When he is heard the blacks say, "Anjea, he laugh; he got him piccaninny." Women do not know when the infants are put inside them; they only feel them subsequently. They may be placed in position in the daytime, at night and during a dream. Before actually inserting these mud-babies in the women Anjea makes the boys travel in a roundabout way across the bush, their forms being already moulded into shape, whereas he causes

[1] W. E. Roth, *S. M. M.*, 15. The origin of humanity from the maggots that swarm out of the decomposing body of a pre-human giant (Kwasir, Panku, etc.) is a widely-spread cosmogonic myth; this is but a slightly modified form of this concept. A trace of this myth is to be found in the Dieri tribe.—Howitt, l.c., 800.

[2] At the Proserpine River the moon makes the first man and woman.—Roth, 61. According to the Euhalayi, Bahloo makes the children.—Parker, 56. In West Australia babies come from the moon.—A. R. Brown, "Beliefs concerning Childbirth in some Australian Tribes," *Man*, 1912, 182.

the girls to pass at a certain height over the path he instructs them to travel by. As each girl stretches her leg over the cross-piece she gets split in the fork, and is now completed. For cutting the posterior orifice in both sexes Anjea uses a piece of wood from the Acacia Rothii. Sometimes an accident befalls these infants before they get into their human mothers: they may catch one of their feet in a log, and so be born with various deformities. When the woman has plenty of room inside, twins are sent. Thunder can also make children out of swamp-mud, but creates them left-handed; these can thus be distinguished from Anjeas, who are all right-handed.[1] Why does Anjea laugh when he "got him piccaninny"? We do not know very much of the psychology of laughter, but at any rate we know that it is an act of psychical discharge, a "relief from restraint," as Bain puts it.[2] If we remember that laughter and comical effects—especially among primitive people—are very frequently associated with both adult and infantile sexuality, with the obscene, laughter may no doubt be regarded in this case as a symptom of relief from repression which has been circumvented by means of these symbolic beliefs. At Yappa kulimna, in the country of the Warramunga tribe, a laughing boy came out of the rocks. He played about all day with bits of bark. Later on some more laughing boys came from the country where the sun goes down. They played together with the bark and laughed loudly. At night they slept in the rock from where the first laughing boy had come out; in the daytime they laughed and played about. These Thaballa boys never died, and can be heard by any man of the "Laughing Boy" totem who goes near the rock. At the present day this place is in the charge of an old man, whose mother conceived him at the spot, and he performs the ceremonies imitating the laughing of the boys as he does so.[3] We shall see later on that Anjea is connected in more than one way with Central Australia; the only difference seems to be that, whilst in his case the laughter is projected to a representative of the father-imago, here it is the "spirit-child," the embryo about to be incarnated, that seems to find it excellent fun to be born into the world. But, as we have already remarked, the baby-spirits are in another sense of the word the "fathers" of the respective totems, and Anjea himself seems to indicate that one cannot preside over the baby department in Australia without conserving in one's own person some of the traits of babyhood.

[1] Roth, *S. M. M.*, 23. All fair-haired children were considered to be Tangaroas' (the god himself had sandy hair), whilst the dark-haired, which form the great majority, are Rogno's, whose hair was raven black.—W. W. Gill, *Myths and Songs from the South Pacific*, 1876, 1. The left-handed children, being, of course, the minority, correspond to the fair-haired ones. According to Strehlow, the iningukua sometimes enters personally into the woman after having thrown his namatuna at her, and in this case fair-haired children are born.—Strehlow, l.c., II. 56.

[2] Freud, *Der Witz*, 126.

[3] Spencer and Gillen, *Nor. T.*, 422.

Anjea (Anjir) was originally without a posterior orifice, and Yalpan cuts his back to make one just as he does with the babies he forms. In this respect he may be compared with the Atnatu of the Kaitish, whose name means "the one without an anus"; [1] with the Dieri Mandra-mankana (body hind-before), whose back was just the same as his front; [2] and with the Watchandie in the south-west. "A very long time ago there existed but one black man, and he was so unfortunate as to have no means for discharging the residuum of his food after his system had drawn from it all nourishment." [3]

These peculiarities have a double sense in the unconscious: they mean both the repression of anal eroticism as regards the father, the return of the repressed elements—for Atnatu, who has no anus, has a black face, and Anjea has exceedingly large buttocks from which he ultimately "breeds" all the blacks as his dung—and the survival of a certain phase in the development of the embryo prior to the origin of an anal orifice that is thus conserved in these double-faced embryo-father beings. The return of infantile elements corresponds to the return of the repressed and the "relief from restraint," whilst the laughing boys and the laughing Anjea as conceptional totems or spirits accord well with both theories. The swamp from which the babies are formed certainly contains an unconscious reference to the amniotic fluid of intra-uterine life; the mud may perhaps be connected with the excremental origin of the blacks in the Anjea anthropogonical myth.[4]

Other child-birth beliefs.

The belief in the origin of infants from water also forms a salient feature of the Proserpine River belief: here it is Kunya who makes the infants out of pandanus roots.[5] Kunya is a nature spirit most often dwelling in the ground, but he is also to be met with below the water-surface as well as in rocks and caves and in the quiet of the bush. When he inserts the infant into the mother he puts the Kuya or vital spirit into it.[6] As nature spirits are simply projections of human attitudes into nature, the similarity of the words Kunya and kuya is extremely suspicious and makes it probable that we have here (in one sense) merely the fission of the same attitude into its active and passive components. Kunya representing the active, kuya the passive side, or from another point of view, the Kunya is a condensation of the individual kuyas, the kuya of the community. What the kuya exactly means we shall try to explain later on.

The next instance of the babies' water-home is to be found in

[1] Spencer and Gillen, *N. T.*, 498.

[2] Howitt, *N. T.*, 781.

[3] A. Oldfield, "The Aborigines of Australia," *T. E. S.*, III. 259.

[4] The origin of the female genitalia from a wound corresponds also to well-known infantile theories.

[5] A ripe pandanus fruit was enclosed in the belly of the woman to produce her courses, according to the anthropogonic myth of the same tribes.—Roth, *Superstition* 16.

[6] Roth, *S. M. M.*, 23.

the beliefs of the Euhalayi. Here Bahloo, the moon, is a sort of patron of women. He it is who creates the girl babies, sometimes assisted by Wahn, the crow.[1] Bahloo's favourite spot for carrying on girl manufacturing is somewhere on the Culgoa. On one of the creeks there is to be seen when it is dry a hole in the ground. As water runs along the bed of this creek a stone gradually rises from the hole with the water, always keeping its top out of the water. This is the Goomarh or spirit stone of Bahloo. No one would dare to touch this stone where the baby girl's spirits are launched into space.[2] In the same neighbourhood is a clear water-hole, the rendezvous of the snakes of Bahloo, and should a man drink some of the water he sees hundreds of snakes.[3] A more explicit symbolism of childbirth than the stone which rises with the rising water can hardly be imagined, the water naturally representing the amniotic fluid and the stone the child. In Bahloo we have a mythical representative of the father, which is still more evident from the second water-hole inhabited by his mythical snakes (penis).

Death originates from the disobedience of the blacks to Bahloo, who refuse to carry his snakes (penis) over the water (mother's womb). Carrying the penis through the womb would mean passing into the mother (in the shape of the penis) and coming out again as a baby procreated by oneself, and this in truth would mean immortality. Bahloo says " that as the blacks refused to do what he asked them, they would just stay where they are put as the stone does under the water " (cf. above, the stone in the water as embryo), he having thrown a stone into the water which sinks, and a piece of bark which rises again, to show them the difference between death and immortality.[4] The same method to represent the fate of men, who are represented as his children, is employed by Nihancan (pieces of wood and other objects that float up again to the surface of the water; a pebble sinks for good), the culture-hero of the Arapho.[5] Nihancan himself is swallowed by a fish and cut out again alive;[6] he is cut to pieces and resuscitated.[7] Besides the father, there seems to be a representative of the mother-image in the Euahlayi birth-myth, for they say that the spirit-babies are

[1] Should Wahn attempt the business on his own account the result is direful. Women of his creating are always noisy and quarrelsome.—Parker, l.c., 50. (Of course, in imitation of the crows cawing.)

[2] The Goomarh and Minggah are stones and trees that serve as the receptacles of the external soul.—Parker, l.c., 22. Their complete identity with the nanja-tree and stones of Central Australia, as well as their unconscious origin, will be demonstrated below.

[3] Parker, l.c., 50. The boys were principally made by the wood-lizard, though Bahloo gave them assistance from time to time.

[4] K. L. Parker, *Australian Legendary Tales*, 1897, 8–10.

[5] Dorsey and Kroeber, *Traditions of the Arapho*, Field Columbian Museum, Anthr. Series V., 1903, 81.

[6] Id., l.c., 111.

[7] Id., ibid., 17, 81. On myths dealing with the origin of death, cf. Frazer, *F. O. T.*, I.

5. CONCEPTIONAL TOTEMISM

I. Belief in Supernatural Conception Existing Side by Side with but Independent of Totemism.
84, 85 (pp. 155, 196, 197), 150 (pp. 161, 164), 198 (p. 146), 199 (Roth: *S.M.M.*, 18, 22), 201 (p. 158), 201 (p. 160), 202 (p. 164), 204 (pp. 158, 176), 209 (pp. 158, 159), 234 (p. 146), 237 (p. 146), 249 (p. 146), 264 (p. 147), 326 (p. 155).

II. Supernatural Conception Connected with Patrilinear Totemism.
3 (p. 193), 7, 11, 21, 26, 27, 28, 31, 32, 35, 41, 42, 43, 46, 47, 49, 222, 319 (p. 193), 385 (R. H. Mathews: "Notes on some Native Tribes," *Journ. Roy. Soc. N.S.W.*, 1906, XL, 110.

III. Supernatural Conception Connected with Matrilinear Totemism.
12, 24, 25, 45 (p. 193), 75 (pp. 165, 167), 77 (pp. 165, 167).

IV. Pure Conceptional Totemism with Local Totemic Centres.
4 (p. 145), 13, 17, 18, 19, 20, 42 (pp. 145, 154), 43, 52 (pp. 152–154), 50 (p. 154), 51, 55, 56 (Sp. I, II, Strehlow: I), 386 (*Proc. Trans. Roy. Geog. S. Australasia*, XXII, 6).
Contradictions are not always easy to avoid; pure conceptional totemism is affirmed by R. H. Mathews for the Umbaia and Tjingilli, but according to Spencer and Gillen they conform to type II. They have been included in both catogories. The northern Tjingilli regard the spirit-child as a new being, not an ancestor reborn. R. H. Mathews: "Notes on the Aborigines of the Northern Territory," *Proc. and Trans. Royal Geog. Soc. of Australasia*, XXII, 16.

V. Intermediate Stage between II and IV.
48 (p. Sp. II, 175).

VI. Totem Centre.
42 (p. 154), 43, 48 (p. 154), 50 (pp. 152, 168), 51, 52 (pp. 152, 168), 55, 56 (pp. 152, 168), 152 (McDougall: "Manners, Customs and Legends of the Coombangree," *Science of Man*, 1901, IV, 46, 63), 386 (*Proc. Trans. Roy. Geog. Soc. Australasia*, I, XXII, 6).

VII. Supernatural Conception, amongst Tribes with Matrilinear Descent of Class.
261, 262, 263, 264, 265, 266, 267 (p. 193), 150 (Parker, 12).

VIII. Nanja Tree and Rock.
47 (p. 178), 48 (p. 173), 52 (p. 169), 56 (p. 169), 77 (p. 173), 150 (pp. 176, 177), 152 (McDougall: *Science of Man*, IV, 46, 63), 209 (p. 174), 229 (p. 184).

IX. Belief in Changing and Changeless Spirit Double.
18 (p. 185), 52, 56 (p. 170), 209 (p. 173).

[*Continued on p.* 163.

5. CONCEPTIONAL TOTEMISM—*contd.*

X. REINCARNATION.

1, 2, 4, 6, 12, 13, 17, 18, 19, 20, 21, 24, 26, 27, 28 (p. 193), 31, 32 (pp. 191, 192), 33, 34, 35, 38, 41, 42, 43, 44, 45, 46, 47, 48, 49, 50, 51, 52, 56 (pp. 152, 168), 65 (p. 192), 77 (p. 165), 222 (p. 193), 229 (pp. 183, 184), 385 (R. H. Mathews: "Notes on Some Native Tribes of Australia," *Journ. Roy. Soc. N.S.W.*, 1906, XL, 198).

XI. MORTUARY TOTEMS, TOTEMIC BURIAL CEREMONIES.

24 (p. 193), 31, 32, 35, 37, 87 (pp. 192–194), 90, 91, 95, 96, 119 (pp. 193, 194), 121, 122, 123, 214 (pp. 193, 194), 130 (Curr: III. 388), 152 (*Science of Man*, IV, 46, 63).

XII. ISLAND OTHER-WORLD, CONNECTED WITH A BELIEF IN REINCARNATION.

52, 56 (p. 198), 88 (p. 196), 87, 90, 91 (p. 194), 93 (pp. 193, 196), 95, 96 (pp. 193, 196), 119, 121, 122, 123, 124 (p. 194).

XIII. ISLAND OTHER-WORLD WITHOUT REINCARNATION, BUT FORMERLY PERHAPS CONNECTED WITH THAT BELIEF.

84, 85 (Angas I, 108), 89 (pp. 197, 198), 93 (p. 196), 111 (p. 205).

XIV. REINCARNATION OF AN ANIMAL SPECIES.

228 (p. 237).

XV. CONCEPTION THROUGH FOOD.

4 (p. 145), 6, 13, 17, 18 (p. 145), 19, 20 (p. 145), 52 (p. 145), 56 (p. 145), 84 (p. 147), 85 (p. 147), 198 (p. 146), 199 (pp. 146, 148), 232 (p. 146), 234 (p. 146), 237 (p. 146), 249 (p. 146), 264 (p. 146).

XVI. FOOD IN MARRIAGE RITES.

52, 56 (p. 184), 89 (p. 184), 108 (p. 184), 199 (p. 184).

XVII. FROG IN CONCEPTION THEORIES.

18 (p. 145), 24, 25 (p. 146), 198 (p. 146).

XVIII. PRENATAL DUEL.

4, 6, 13, 14, 18 (p. 145), 19, 20 (p. 145), 232, 234, 237, 249 (p. 146), 256 (p. 146).

XIX. CHANGE OF SEX IN SUCCESSIVE INCARNATIONS.

26 (p. 205), 27 (p. 205), 28 (p. 205), 31 (p. 205), 47 (p. 205), 75, 77 (p. 205), 76 (p. 205).

The Dieri are included in this list on the basis of Spencer, *Northern Territory*, 24, but as other authors do not mention this belief, or even positively state the absence of a belief in reincarnation, the case is open to doubt.

usually dispatched to Waddahgudjaelwon and sent by her to hang promiscuously on trees until some woman passes under where they are, then they will seize a mother and be incarnated.[1] Instead of symbolizing the father and the mother in the same fiction (a trace of this is represented, in so far as spirit-children are sent by Bahloo to Waddahgudjaelwon, as the spermatozoa by the father to the mother), two versions of the same theme are introduced, thus leading to the characteristic repetition of *motifs* which we so often find in these conception-beliefs.

According to the Cape Bedford blacks, the native spirits called Nguta-nguta or Talpan, who live in the dense woods or undergrowth, are they who send the babies along. These spirits have very long hair (a mythical exaggeration of the lanugo), big ears and two sets of eyes, one in front and the other behind,[2] i.e. they hear and see everything (the front and back view of the embryo-beings is identical); they are visible, however, to certain old men,[3] and disappear into the ground whenever anyone else comes near,[4] and are like human beings in that they have wives, children and spears.[5] They say that babies are made in that portion of the west where the sun sets, and in their original condition are full-grown, but in their passage into their maternal forms take the form of a curlew if a girl, of a pretty snake if a boy.[6] When once inside its human mother, baby takes its human shape again and nothing more is heard of that particular bird or snake. When at night the blacks hear the curlew, they will say, "Hullo, there's a baby somewhere about." In the case of a boy the woman will probably go out hunting, suddenly sing out that she sees the snake, and then run away; the whole party will join in looking to see where the serpent has gone, and turn over rocks, leaves and logs in their search. It cannot be found, and this is a sure sign that it has reached its destination, and the future mother knows that she is pregnant.

[1] K. L. Parker, *Australian Legendary Tales*, 1897, 50.

[2] The "devil-devil" is supposed to possess no nose, two blanks for eyes and two additional eyes at the back of the neck, by means of which he can see a very long distance. He usually camps in holes or caves.—H. Basedow, "Anthropological Notes on the Western Coastal Tribes of the Territory of South Australia." *Trans. of the R. S. of S. A.*, 1907, XXXI. 18.

[3] Amongst the Kia blacks it is the medicine man who tells the woman that she is about to be with child.—W. E. Roth, l.c., 22. In the Kakadu tribe there is a close association between Numereji (the primeval snake-ancestor) and the medicine men: they alone are supposed not only to be able to see him, but to have eyes that can withstand his glance.—Spencer and Gillen, *N. T.*, 295.

[4] We have seen this custom of the Altjiranga-mitjina, and also proved there what is meant by it: a regression into uterine life.

[5] The Iruntarinia (a spirit people formed out of the spirit doubles of living men and associated with the birth stones) spend the winter in underground caves, where are streams of running water and perpetual sunshine, the two great *desiderata* of the Arunta native.—Spencer and Gillen, *N. T.*, 513.

[6] The curlew and the snake would give another pair of conceptional sex-totems. —Roth, *S. M. M.*, 22.

Here it is the husband who asks for the baby " to be sent as a punishment when vexed with his wife."[1] There can be no doubt about the truth of the last sentence; it is certainly the husband who is responsible for the origin of the baby, as it is he who introduces his " snake " or " bird " into the woman. Here there is the tendency to form a series of birth myths that lead up to the real birth: for the first time the baby is made in the west where the sun sets—that is, the setting sun is assimilated as in the myth of Maui and Hine-nui-te-po to a human being disappearing into the maternal womb.[2]

The Arunta theory.

In the light of the foregoing an attempt can now be made to analyse the complicated birth mythology of the Central Australian tribes. We have already investigated these concepts in their simplest and more usual forms, recognizing behind the hunted animal and the eaten food the Oedipus complex and the oral erotic regression of the libido. We now shall come to the full-blown Arunta theory and try to solve the " Central Mystery ": the spirit-children and the whole system of Churingas and Nanjas. We may as well take the Central Australian birth theories in their geographical order and begin from the south with the Urabunna. In certain respects the beliefs of the Urabunna tribe, which inhabits the country to the south of the Arunta, bear the same relationship to those of the Arunta nation as do the beliefs of the Warramunga tribe in the far north.

In the Ularaka (the Alcheringa of the Arunta) there existed at first a comparatively small number of individuals who were half human and half animal or plant. These semi-human creatures were endowed with far greater powers than any living men or women possess. They could walk about either on the earth or beneath it, or could fly through the air. A great carpet-snake individual gave rise to the Carpet-snake group, two jew-lizards gave rise to the Jew-lizard group, one or two rain-creatures gave rise to the Rain group and so on. These semi-human ancestors wandered about all the country now occupied by the Urabunna tribe, performing sacred ceremonies, and when they did this they deposited in the ground or in some natural object such as a rock or water-pool which arose to mark the spot, a number of spirit-individuals called mai-aurli. After a time some of these became changed into men and women, who formed the first series of totem-groups. These mai-aurli who came out of the body of the totem-ancestors have ever since the Ularaka continually been undergoing reincarnation. Pigeon rocks are inhabited exclusively by pigeon spirit-children,

[1] Roth, *S. M. M.*, 23.

[2] W. D. Westervelt, *Legends of Maui*, 1910, 136. E. Schirren, *Die Wandersagen der Neuseeländer und der Mauimythos*, 1856, 33. L. Frobenius, *Die Weltanschauung der Naturvölker*, 1898, 183.

6. THE DISTRIBUTION OF CHURINGA

I. Churinga of the Arunta Type.
(Associated with spirit individuals kept in totemic ertnatulunga), 48, 50, 51, 52, 55, 56 (Sp. II, 212, 224, 257–74 Strehlow), 70, 71, 77 (Siebert, *Globus*, 97, 49 p. 412), 222 (Sp. II, 257–74), 229 (p. 184).

II. Churinga not Associated with Spirit Individuals but Nevertheless Connected in a Certain Degree with the Totems.
42, 43, 46, 47, 49 (Sp. II, 275–81).

III. Sacred Sticks Representing the Totem and Used in Intichiuma Ceremonies.
4, 6, 13, 17, 18, 19, 20 (Sp. III, 188, 277, 278).

IV. Bullroarers Resemble Churingas in Certain Respects. Stored away in Ertnatulunga.
21, 27 (Sp. III, 213).

V. Bullroarer causes Conception, Multiplies Animal Species, or Employed in Love Magic.
46 (p. 156), 47 (p. 156), 48 (p. 156), 51 (p. 156), 52 (p. 156), 54 (p. 156), 56 (p. 154), 75 (p. 412), 222 (p. 156).

VI. Sticks Connected with Childbirth Beliefs; Analogies to the Churinga.
18 (p. 179).

VII. Masculine and Feminine Churinga; Former Connected with Re-incarnation, the Latter Used as Amulet.
229 (*Z. E.*, 1907, 647).

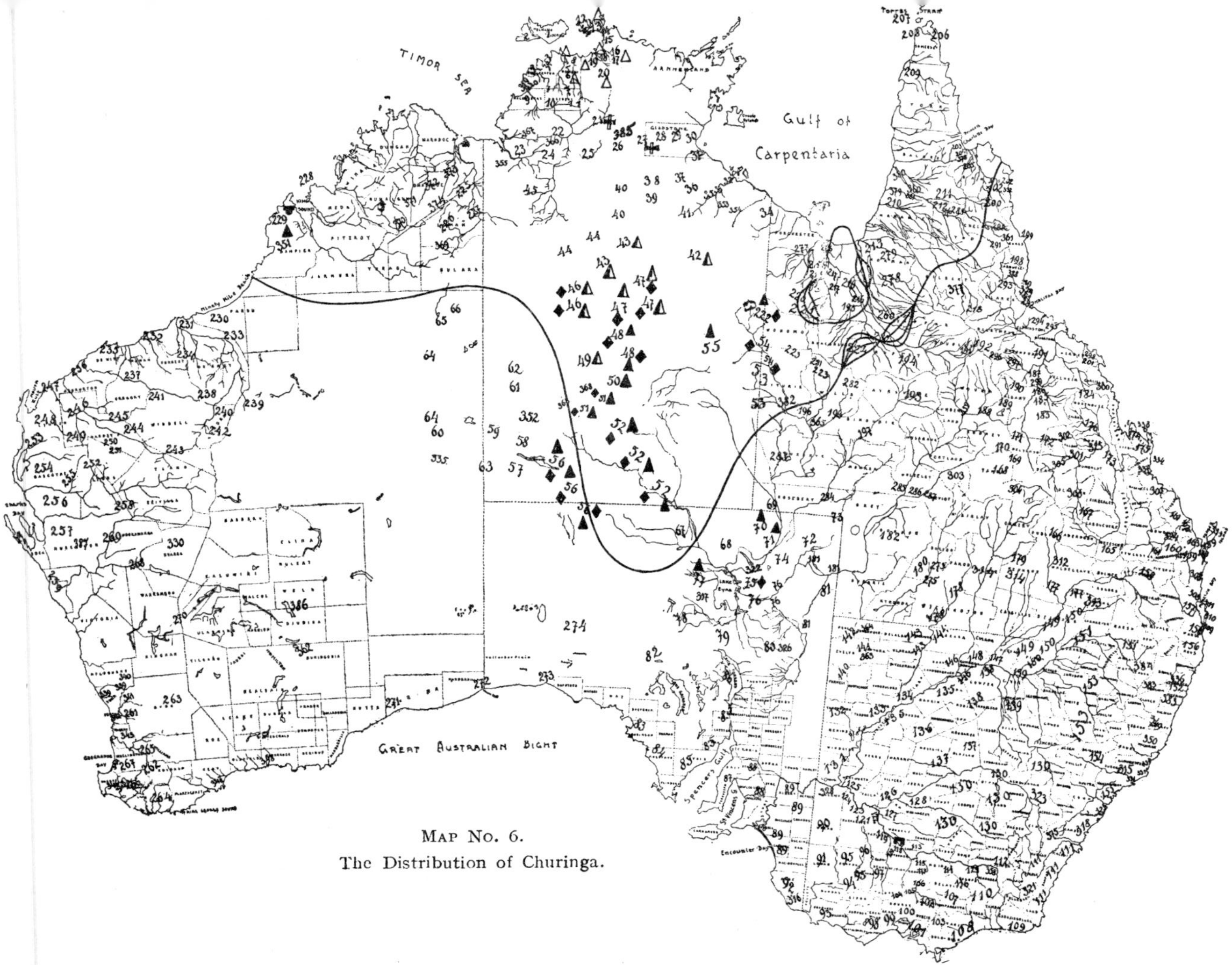

MAP No. 6.
The Distribution of Churinga.

but there is a water-pool where there are spirits belonging to the following totemic groups: Mosquito, Blow-fly, March-fly and Sand-fly.[1] The child belongs to the same totem moiety as its mother, but they believe that in each successive reincarnation the spirit-child changes its sex, moiety and totem. For instance, if a Kirarawa man of the Emu totem dies, his spirit goes back to the place at which it was left by the ancestor in the Ularaka. Here at the totem-centre it remains for some time, but sooner or later it is reincarnated. The spirit of the former Emu Kirarawa man will not go into a Kirarawa woman; if it were to do so it would either be born prematurely and die or cause the death of the mother. When undergoing reincarnation it can only enter the body of a Matthurie woman, who, of necessity, belongs to another totem, and thus at each reincarnation the individual changes its moiety and totem.[2]

The explanation of this belief is easy enough if we work on the hypothesis that the spirit is a symbolical representative of the spermatozoon. As a husband of a Matthurie woman can only be a Kirarawa man, "the spirit that goes into her" can only be a Kirarawa spirit, and as descent is through the mother, the child will be a Matthurie, thus changing its moiety with each generation. The totems are divided between the two moieties, so that a change of moiety means a change of the totem. But besides this they have also the belief that a spirit individual changes its sex at each successive reincarnation. If we start with a Kirarawa man; he is reincarnated as a Matthurie woman, and she again is reincarnated in the form of a Kirarawa man, and so on.[3] This complicated system is the result of a condensation of various unconscious attitudes. To begin with, it symbolizes the original bi-sexuality of all living beings: in another incarnation, in the totem-centre (that is in the womb), he who is now a man was a woman and vice versa. But there is still more in it. According to the two-class system, with female descent a man is allowed to marry his daughter, but not his mother.[4] In his post-mortem (and intra-uterine) life he attempts to realize this unconscious wish by changing from a Matthurie into a Kirarawa, but here again the ambivalency between desire and dread intervenes; as he is now a Kirarawa, there is nothing to

[1] Spencer and Gillen, *Nor. T.*, 145–47. Probably these various fly species originally formed one totem group.

[2] Unless she has had unlawful intercourse, in which case the death of mother or child is the punishment for her transgression.

[3] Spencer and Gillen, *Nor. T.*, 149. The Wonkangaru have the same system: they also have the inapertwa myth of the Arunta. The belief in a change of sex at each reincarnation is also found in the Dieri and Warramunga tribe (Spencer, *N. T. N. T. A.*, 1914, 24), as well as amongst the Mungarai, Yungman, Nullakun, and Mara.—Spencer, l.c., 267.

[4] Of course I am aware of the fact that a man is not really permitted to marry his daughter in the overwhelming majority of people who have a two-class system with female descent. But the class organization alone would be no obstacle.

hinder him from marrying his mother (after death), unless his sex be changed, when he is no more a Kirarawa man but a Kirarawa woman. Lastly, there is the change of the totem: the totem-centre is not the decisive point, a pigeon-spirit will be reincarnated in an Emu woman of the other moiety and the children will be Emu.

Further to the north we find the Arunta tribe; we must now grapple with the famous Churinga doctrine.

The ratapa and the Churinga.

After the Alcheringa ancestors had finished their wanderings they went back into the underground caves whence they had originally come. Here they continued to exist as rella ngantja—hidden men—whilst their bodies were turned into rocks, trees and bushes. In these rocks, trees and bushes the unborn children, the ratapa (derived from ratana: to come out, to originate) dwell, especially in the branches of the mistletoe that entwine themselves on some of these trees.[1] Not only the entire body, but also parts of the body are turned into tjurunga: for instance, an eagle-ancestor lost a long feather and this "tjurungeraka" and now constitutes a separate totem. The fat of a kangaroo ancestor "tjurungeraka" and so forth. Many of the altjiranga mitjina turned themselves into tjurunga and are now kept in the sacred storehouses; others dropped tjurunga in their wanderings and these turned into trees and rocks, from which again the ratapa emanate. The ratapa are completely formed boys and girls, with body and soul; their red colour is aptly compared by Strehlow to that of new-born Arunta infants.[2] When a woman goes near one of the localities—called knanakala[3]—where the metamorphosed body of the altjiranga mitjina dwells, one of the ratapa that has been on the look-out for her and recognizes her as his class-mother enters her body through the hips, causing her to feel pains in the inside. When the child is born it belongs to the totem of the altjiranga mitjina.[4]

The difference between this account and that given by Spencer and Gillen is really merely a matter of words.[5] The oknanikilla

[1] "The bronze mistletoe branches, with their orange-red flowers, are said to be the disappointed babies whose wailing in vain for mothers has wearied the spirits, who transform them into these bunches, the red flowers being formed from their baby blood."—Parker, *The Euahlayi Tribe*, 1905, 51. As to the mistletoe, see Frazer, *Balder the Beautiful*, 1913, II. 77–79.

[2] Strehlow, II. 51, 52.

[3] Knanakala, i.e. "von selbst entstanden d. h. Empfängnis-Platz."—Strehlow, I. 5.

[4] Strehlow, II. 52, 53. As to other groups ("the Arunta nation"), with this type of totemism, see Spencer and Gillen, *N. T.*, 152.

[5] It is futile to argue about the question whether we have to do with the belief in reincarnation or incarnation, as it is evidently the spirit-children who emanate from the body of the Alcheringa ancestors that are reincarnated. The Alcheringa ancestor continues to exist in his "eternal place," and yet is present in the actual native, who is the altjiranga mitjina, or rather his "Abspaltung," a part of his personality.

(knanakala of the western Arunta) is full of the spirit individuals of a certain totem; these are born into the woman.[1] When the spirit-child goes into the woman the Churinga is dropped. When the child is born the mother tells the father the position of the tree or rock near to which she supposed the child to have entered her, and he, together with one or two of the elder men, goes to the locality and searches for the Churinga. Either they actually find one, the paternal grandfather having provided himself with one for the occasion, or they make a wooden one from some hard-wood nearest to the Nanja tree, and carve on it some device peculiar to the totem.[2] Ever afterwards the Nanja tree or stone of the spirit is the Nanja of the child, and the Churinga is its Churinga nanja.

The Nanja tree or stone.

There is a definite relationship supposed to exist between an individual and his Nanja tree or stone. In one case a blackfellow earnestly requested a white man not to cut down a particular tree because it was his Nanja tree, and he was afraid that if it was cut down some evil would befall him. At the present time the special association between a man and his Nanja tree lies in the fact that every animal upon the tree is taboo to him. If an opossum or bird be in the tree it is sacred and must on no account be touched.[3] When the Alcheringa individuals went into the earth the Churinga remained behind and with it the spirit part: at the same time a Nanja rock or tree arose to mark the spot where the Alcheringa ancestor entered the earth. From that Nanja tree there issued another spirit, the Arumburinga of the Alcheringa individual; so that at each totem-centre we have a group of what is called the Iruntarinia, each of whom is either a spirit associated with a Churinga or else the Arumburinga of one of these spirits. The spirit of each Alcheringa individual is watched over by an Arumburinga.[4] These Iruntarinia (that is, the spirit-children, the Arumburinga) are aggregated in local totemic groups just as the living members of the tribe are. When a spirit individual goes into a woman there still remains the Arumburinga, which may be regarded as its double, and this may either dwell along with the Iruntarinia of whom it is of course one, or may follow the spirit which is within the woman, or it may attend the woman's husband when out hunting. Some men are especially popular with the Iruntarinia; two or three of the spirit people will often assist them by driving the prey towards them. A man's Arumburinga does not watch over him continuously, but only in a more or less general kind of way. For instance, if a man when out hunting with his eyes fixed on the prey suddenly happens to look down and see a

[1] Spencer and Gillen, *N. T.*, 124.

[2] Id., ibid., 132. The exact spot at which a Churinga was deposited was always marked by some natural object, and this is the spirit's Nanja where it frequently dwells.—Spencer and Gillen, *N. T.*, 124.

[3] Id., ibid., 133.

[4] Id., ibid., 513

snake just where he was about to tread, then he knows at once that his Arumburinga is with him and prompted him to look down suddenly. The Arumburinga spend most of their time at the Nanja tree or rock, but they frequently visit their human representative, making themselves visible to him if he has the gift of seeing spirits.[1] In addition to the medicine men who have the power of communicating with the Iruntarinia, there are others to whom this privilege is granted. Children who are born with their eyes open (alkna-buma) have this power when they arrive at maturity, provided that they grow up sedate, for the Iruntarinia much dislike scoffing, frivolous and chattering people. When all the mourning ceremonies have been carried out the Ulthana (ghost) is supposed to leave the grave and to return to its Nanja, where it rejoins and lives with its Arumburinga. This is exactly what it is not supposed to do according to Strehlow. After a time it gets itself another Churinga, with which it becomes associated just as it was before with the Alcheringa Churinga, and then after the lapse of some time, but not until the bones have crumbled away, it may once more be born in human form.[2]

The Iruntarinia.

In general appearance the Iruntarinia are supposed to represent human beings, but they are always youthful-looking, their faces without hair, their bodies thin and shadowy. They steal various objects such as fur-string, so that a man will awake in the morning and find that his spare string has disappeared. He looks around for tracks, but finds none, and at once concludes that the Iruntarinia have been visiting him. He must not be angry or else he would offend them; moreover, he feels that his Arumburinga, who has most likely taken the string, needed it for some special purpose and will return it safely when done with. Sooner or later he will awake to find it by his side.[3] Women are afraid to go out in the dark on account of the Iruntarinia, who might carry them away.[4] They have their totems just like the men, whose doubles they in reality are, though at the same time, unlike the men, they are endowed with the powers characteristic of Alcheringa individuals.[5] Spirit-land is the land of doubles, and it is the doubles of the natives that are projected into space and materialized in the Churinga.

In each Oknanikilla there is a spot called by the natives the Ertnatulunga. This is in reality a sacred storehouse, which usually has the form of a small cave or crevice in some unfrequented spot amongst the rough hills and ranges which abound in the area occupied by the tribe. The sacred Churinga are, in this cave, often carefully tied up in bundles, and in one or other of these storehouses every member of the tribe, men and women alike, is

[1] Spencer and Gillen, *N. T.*, 514. [2] Id., ibid., 515. [3] Id., ibid., 516.
[4] Id., ibid., 517. [5] Id., ibid., 518.

represented by his or her Churinga nanja. When a Churinga is found after the birth of a child it is handed over to the head-man of the local totem group and deposited by him in the Ertnatulunga.[1] The immediate surroundings of one of these Ertnatulunga is a kind of haven of refuge for wild animals; because any hunted animal which ran by instinct or chance towards the Ertnatulunga was taboo as soon as it came close, and safe from the spear of the pursuing native. Even the plants in the immediate vicinity of the spot are never touched or interfered with in any way.[2] The Arumburinga of the individual is supposed to be especially fond of paying visits to the storehouse in which the Churinga is kept; it is feared that if the Churinga be taken away the Arumburinga will follow it, and thus the individual will lose the guardianship of the spirit.[3]

The beliefs of the western groups differ in some details from those of the eastern Arunta, but only enough to be mutually illustrative. When the woman knows that a ratapa is in her, the paternal or maternal grandfather of the child (the woman's father! cf. ante) goes to a Mulga tree and carves a small tjurunga for the child with an opossum tooth, he engraves the totem mark in the wood, smears it with red ochre, and then puts it into the cave where the other tjurunga are kept. When the child is born it continually cries after its tjurunga. So the grandfather gets the tjurunga out of the cave; the women are told that the grandfather is looking for the tjurunga, or rather "papa" (wood, stick), that the child lost when it went into its mother. The tjurunga is wrapped in strings so that the women should not see it, and carried about in the pitchi that serves as a cradle to the child. "The child is so laid in it that his head comes to lie exactly over the tjurunga papa. It is believed that secret powers flow from the tjurunga to the body of the child; in consequence it gains rapidly and thrives." [4] When the child is bigger the papa is put back into the arknanakaua (ertnatulunga) to the other tjurunga. When the boy has been circumcised he gets a big tjurunga (bullroarer called nankara). This nankara represents the mythical body of his mother's totem-ancestor, his altjira who from this time onward is supposed to protect the rukuta in his wanderings. The women are told that the tjurunga nankara is the body of Tuanjiraka, the string by which it is swung is his pig-tail,

[1] Spencer and Gillen, *N. T.*, 133. [2] Id., ibid., 134. [3] Id., ibid., 138.

[4] Strehlow, II. 80. Besides his own totem every native is associated with his mother's totem called altjira. Although the children of one mother may belong to various totems by incarnation, yet they also have one totem in common, "which is regarded as their god, who nourishes and protects them just as a mother cherishes her child in its first years." This altjira appears in the dreams of the blacks, and warns their friends concerning them.—Strehlow, I. 57. It is a question of great interest whether this altjira has anything to do with the sky-god Altjira. If this should be proved we could understand the connexion on the supposition that both represent the maternal grandfather.

the buzzing sound, his voice. After the young man has been subincised he is called iliara instead of rukuta; he now gets a small tjurunga called namatuna that represents the body of his own totem-ancestor, his iningukua, who from henceforth again accompanies and protects him. As we have seen in the explanation of the conception myth, this tjurunga is smeared with blood from the subincised penis (of which it thus becomes a symbolic equivalent) and swung to attract the love of the chosen girl. When he is already a married man the grandfather leads the native to the arknanakaua, shows him the tjurunga of his totem ancestor, and says, "This you body are, nana (this) unta (you) iningukua (the same), do not take it to another place or you will feel pain." So long as this tjurunga is in safe custody the personal security of the individual is not in danger. This tjurunga represents the mystical bond between the individual and his totem-ancestor. In his nightly wanderings the iningukua convinces himself that the tjurunga is safe, but if it should have been stolen, lost, or shown to the women, the iningukua gets angry and pricks his human representative with the pointing sticks, so that he will get very ill or even die. If the tjurunga is being eaten by white ants, the iningukua appears in a dream and warns the man not to have connexion with foreign women.

If a man dies his tjurunga is taken out of the arknanakaua and hidden somewhere, as the sight of it would make his friends sad. After about two years the tjurunga is brought back to the arknanakaua. If it is lost or moulders away it is not renewed: this is regarded as a sign that the ghostly existence of the individual who was once connected with the tjurunga has come to an end. When after wandering about the soul is annihilated by lightning the tjurunga body also ceases to exist.[1] As to the meaning of the word, Strehlow translates tju as secret, hidden; runga as the personal, my own. Tjurunga—the personal mystery. The word is understood both as a substantive and as an adjective: ilia tjurunga = the emu cult. When the lizard totem-god was giving shape to the rella manerinja, he gave each of them a tjurunga and called it "the body which was bound up with it." When giving the Kangaroo-man a tjurunga, he said: "This is the body of a kangaroo; you are derived from this tjurunga." Strehlow says: "The tjurunga is regarded as the common body of mankind and his totem-ancestors; it connects the individual with his personal totem-ancestors and guarantees him the protection which the inigukua bestows, whilst the loss of the tjurunga entails the latter's revenge." The relation between a man and his tjurunga is expressed in the sentence, "Nana unta mburka nama" ("This you body are"). Every man thus has two bodies: a body of flesh and one of wood or

[1] Strehlow, *A. & L.*, II. 80, 81.

stone.[1] Women have also got tjurunga, but they are never allowed to see them.[2]

The mystery of the Nanja tree and the tjurunga must be solved together or not at all. There is a striking parallelism between them. The individual issues from the tjurunga: the protecting genius (arumburinga) from the Nanja. The individual gets one of the tjurungas (the nankara or Tuanyiraka one) at circumcision: the Alcheringa ancestors placed their foreskins in their Nanja trees.[3] Both the Churinga and the Nanja represent the body of the Alcheringa ancestors. Their body is subjected to a sort of splitting into tjurunga and Nanja. A grass-seed man of the Kaitish tribe feels that he has gone far enough; he puts his Churinga into the ground, thereby forming an oknanikilla. Then he walked by another track to the tree from which he had started and finally went into the ground there. That tree became his Nanja tree, where his spirit dwelt, though it continually paid visits to the Churinga in the oknanikilla.[4] On the other hand, the spirit associated with the Churinga haunts the Nanja, the ertnatulunga, which is in the immediate vicinity of the Nanja tree, is sacred and serves as a haven of refuge for animals.[5] As we have seen, the Kaitish tribe imagine the totem-ancestor as continually walking to and fro from the Churinga to the Nanja. They call the Nanja tree ai-il-pilla: periodically a man will visit his Nanja tree or rock and clear a small space around, moving away pieces of bark and rubbish which may have accumulated. This is what the Arunta call ertnatulunga, the Kaitish call it moama. The Urabunna call the Nanja spot Watthili. This is where the spirit-ancestors dwell on the hill-side, and anything on it is strictly tabooed to the men with whom it is connected. A man of the Snake totem has a water-hole for his Nanja, and he neither drinks water there nor eats any fish which may be caught in it.[6]

We have three starting-points from whence we may attempt the interpretation of the Nanja concept.

Nanja and Anjea.

Nanja is most probably the same word as Anjea. We have seen the birth theories associated with this spirit, but we did not mention that there was a duplicate of this belief intended to explain the origin of the soul, which may perhaps throw some light on the Central Australian state of affairs. On the Pennefather River the vital principles, the ngai and choi, are connected with the heart and the after-birth. The ngai talks to them and tells them when it is hungry or thirsty or wants to rest; it talks to them in their sleep and causes dreams—that is, it protects the individual like the Arumburinga, and appears in his dreams like the arumburinga and altjirra. Nobody has a ngai till his father dies,

[1] Strehlow, *A. & L.*, II. 76, 77. [2] Id., II. 78. [3] Spencer and Gillen, *Nor. T.*, 341.
[4] Id., ibid., 396. [5] Id., ibid., 448. [6] Id., ibid., 449.

the children inherit it from their father: a woman leaves hers to her younger sisters (Altjira—the mother's totem = Ngai—the parents' vital soul). When somebody is unconscious the ngai is separated from the body. The choi differs from the ngai principally in the fact that it is put into the body by Anjea as soon as he puts the baby into the mother's womb. That portion of the choi which Anjea originally puts into the baby remains in its afterbirth. Parallels to this part played by the afterbirth are found elsewhere. In the Yas, Murrumbudgee and Tumat countries the afterbirth is buried by the mother and then taken up and burnt ("delayed interment.") In New Zealand the placenta is called fenua = land: they suppose it to be the residence of the child, and if an offended priest procures it he can produce the death of mother and child by his incantations.[1]

The placenta is considered as something too sacred to be trifled with. As soon as thrown off from the uterus, it is carefully put away from the reach of animals; if eaten by any animal, that animal would certainly die.[2]

To return, however, to Mapoon. When the child is born into the earth the grandmother takes the afterbirth away and buries it in the sand, marking the situation by a number of twigs stuck in the ground more or less in the shape of a cone. Anjea comes along, recognizes the spot, and taking the choi, carries it to one of his haunts, where he places it and where it remains for years in a hole in the rocks, in a tree or in a lagoon. Three or four such haunts are known at Mapoon, one amongst the sand-stone-rocks, another amongst the rocks at Trokanguno, a third amongst the timber along the mangrove swamps at Lalla, and a fourth in one of the fresh-water lagoons. When Anjea actually makes the mud-baby which he inserts into the mother, he puts in it a bit of the choi of his father if a boy, of her father's sister if a girl; when he makes the next little child he puts another bit, and so on. These bits taken from the yet unchanged choi correspond to the spirit-children continually emanating from the unchanged Alcheringa spirit. When the navel-string is cut by the grandmother the different haunts of Anjea are called out, and the name mentioned at the moment of the breaking tells them whence the choi was brought. The child's own country, its "home" where it in the future will have the right to hunt and roam, is thus determined, not by the place of actual birth, but by the locality where its choi has been held captive, a place which may often be many miles away. Hence a baby is sometimes spoken of as a Ko (tree), Akworra (rock, stone), Ngo-i (fresh water) manu (obtained or received from) agamo

[1] G. Bennett, *Wanderings in New South Wales*, 1837, I. 127.

[2] M. Moorhouse, *South Australia, Papers ordered by the House of Commons*, 1844, 355.

(young infant).[1] The naming ceremony reminds us of the way the individual names are given in connexion with the totem in Central Australia, and the part played by the grandparents is similar in both cases. Among the Yaraikanna at Cape York, when the front tooth is knocked out at initiation, with each blow the name is mentioned of one of the countries owned by the lad's mother or by her father or other of her relatives. These names are given in order, and the country whose name is mentioned when the tooth breaks away is the land to which the child will belong.[2] The child is twice divided from his mother, once when passing from embryo to infant life (navel-string cut), once when passing from infant to adult life (tooth-pulling), and in both instances he receives a symbolic and sublimated substitute for the mother he loses in mother-earth. The totem evidently forms a part of this complex, for the ari or individual totem is determined by the resemblance to a natural object of the clot of blood formed when a tooth is knocked out at the initiation ceremony.[3] Not only the land, but the wife too, is a substitute for the mother. In the hinterland of Prince Charlotte Bay, when the tooth is being knocked out at the puberty ritual, the names of various eligible girls are called—the one which happens to be called when the tooth is actually knocked out being recognized as betrothed. Needless to say, the name of the favourite is always kept to the very last.[4]

Now, if we try to interpret the rite of putting the afterbirth under a mound, the natural suggestion will be to regard the rite as an "afterbirth," a repetition of birth, which is enacted by the mother, who in this ritual identifies herself with her own daughter. She puts the afterbirth back into the uterus, whence it has to be taken out again by Anjea, who carries it to one of his haunts and thence into the womb: thus we have two mythical births that come before that actual birth, giving us another example of the fission of an unconscious concept into a whole series which is so characteristic of these beliefs. Now, an Anjea spot is a Nanja spot: when he saw the pictures of the former, Spencer told W. E. Roth that they were strongly suggestive of the spots haunted by spirit-children in the Central Australian tribes.[5] The Nanja tree is an external soul, and we know the world-wide custom of burying the afterbirth or navel-string under a tree as the life-token of the

[1] Roth, *S. M. M.*, 18.

[2] Haddon, *Cambridge Expedition to Torres Straits*, V. 221.

[3] Id., l.c., V. 193.

[4] W. E. Roth, "Marriage Ceremonies and Infant Life," *B. N. Q. E.*, 10, 1908, 4.

[5] Roth, *S. M. M.*, 18. In Central Australia and Queensland we have mythical birthplaces, in New South Wales we have real ones. When a woman approaches the period of labour she is conducted to the locality which has been assigned by the elders as the place where that particular woman must give birth to her offspring. Certain spots are fixed by the elders for women to repair to in such cases.—R. H. Mathews, op. cit., 15.

child. We shall thus offer the hypothesis that the Nanja tree and rock are projections of the maternal womb, and if this is true their immediate vicinity, the totem centre and especially the Ertnatulunga, can be nothing else either.

The totem-centre as a symbolical uterus.

Since the Ertnatulunga is a cave in which the spirit ancestors and the children who are about to be incarnated lead their pre- and post-natal tjurunga-life, since the Iruntarinia, the spirit-doubles of existing aboriginals live in underground caves, since the totem-ancestors are supposed to live on with red bodies like an embryo in these places where they went down into the earth, there can hardly be any doubt that the Ertnatulunga, the first germ of a city of refuge,[1] the place where children are incarnated, is a symbolic womb. We know that for the neurotic the feeling of safety is originally and unconsciously associated with the idea of regression into the maternal womb, and thus we shall find it comprehensible that this idea originated out of the same unconscious complexes in the history of humanity. The Nanja spot and the Anjea haunt offer the two contrary sides of a medal that are so characteristic of the ambivalent totemic complex ; the former is the place where no man may hunt on account of its special magico-mystical connexion with his own person, the latter is the place where the individual has a special right to hunt, for exactly the same reason.

We remember that the first explanation we gave to totemism was that it might be regarded as the psychical survival of the animals' physical reaction to environment, and now we see that this phylogenetical repetition is effected through the means of an ontogenetic repetition ; the second environment met with by the individual in his post-natal life is psychically assimilated to the first environment that he has left behind himself in the maternal womb. The totem-centre, the germ at once of the temple and the altar in the evolution of humanity, is a symbolical uterus.

The spirit-stones of the Euahlayi.

The second starting-point for tackling our problem is the evident identity of the Euahlayi Goomarh and Minggah with the Arunta Nanja. The Minggah or spirit-haunted tree of an individual usually chosen from amongst the man's multiplex totems is both a source of danger to him and a help,[2] as the injury suffered by the tree evidently also injures the man. In a magician's Minggah the shadow-spirits he has stolen from his enemies are secreted, and there he often keeps his Yunbeai, that is, his animal familiar or individual totem.[3] Only the greatest

[1] Cf. Spencer and Gillen, *Nor. T.*, 267. [2] Parker, *The Euahlayi Tribe*, 1905, 21.

[3] Id., ibid., 29. The yunbeai is absolutely taboo like the Arunta totem, but the totem which is inherited from the mother may be eaten (Parker, 20), like the Arunta altjira, or maternal totem. It is the totem which warns people in their dreams exactly as the Arunta altjira does. Altjira (and the Loritja Tukura) have emu-feet (Strehlow, op. cit., I), and the Baiamai of the Euahlayi, whose lower extremities are deformed, is said to have hunted his mother-wife, the emu.

wirreenuns have stone Goomarh instead of Minggah,[1] just as stone Churingas are in a certain sense valued higher than wooden ones. And, last but not least, the Minggah and Goomarh are places of refuge in time of danger: no one save the wirreenun, whose spirit tree it was, would dare to touch the refuge.[2] The identity between Goomarh and Nanja being now completely established, we may remind the reader that Bahloo launches the spirit-children into existence from his Goomarh that rises with the water like the child coming out of the amniotic fluid in the maternal home.

Our interpretation gains additional force from these parallels; we will augment their number by a third. On the Goulburn River there are quite a number of dead trees, every one of them representing a member of an extinct tribe. The teeth are knocked out at initiation and given to the mother; it is she who hides them in the bark of a young gum tree. If the person to whom the tree is dedicated in this way dies, the bark is torn from the tree-trunk.[3] In the Pilbarra district the closing part of the initiation ceremony takes place as follows. After about a month, when the buckley (= young boy) has recovered, the elders take him to some bark creek, where, after further rites, the elders remove the foreskin that has been previously fastened in the buckley's hair and now dried; after raising the bark of a young tree they force the skin between the wood and the bark, the bark closing over it. They then express the hope that the youth may flourish like the green-tree.[4] Now this is exactly what the Alcheringa ancestors of the Arunta did with their foreskins; they hid them in their Nanja trees with whom their spirits were henceforth connected.[5] When the Kaitish knock out a tooth they throw it as far as possible in the direction of the Alcheringa camp of the mother.[6] Amongst the Gringai the youth's mother is the custodian of the tooth that is knocked out at initiation.[7] The Kamilaroi give the tooth to the lad's mother.[8] The tooth and the foreskin are substitutes for the lad and equivalent symbols; instead of the boy she loses at initiation she gets at least his tooth (foreskin), that is the infantile components of his libido which for ever must remain riveted to the mother, or, what is the same thing symbolically told, placed in a tree. Thus, from this point of view, we find

[1] Parker, *The Euahlayi Tribe*, 1905, 27. [2] Id., ibid., 36.

[3] Róheim, *Spiegelzauber*, 1919, 11, 12. R. Etheridge, "Geological and Ethnological Observations in the Valley of the Wollondilly River," *Records of the Australian Museum*, II, 1892–96, 49, 52, 54. Id., "The Dendroglyphs, or 'Carved Trees,' of New South Wales," *Memoirs of the Geological Survey of New South Wales*, Ethnological Series, No. 3.

[4] Withnell, *The Customs and Traditions of the Aboriginal Natives of N.W.A.*, 1901, 10.

[5] Spencer and Gillen, *Nor. T.*, 341.

[6] Id., ibid., 589. [7] Howitt, *N. T.*, 575.

[8] J. Fraser, *The Aborigines of New South Wales*, 1892, 14.

again the Nanja tree to be a symbol of the mother, or what amounts to the same thing, of the uterus.[1] The Erathipa is a sort of Nanja object. A plum-tree-boy went into the ground taking with him a store of Churinga, and the Erathipa stone arose to mark the spot and forms the centre of an Oknanikilla of the Plum-tree totem, the stone being the home of all the many spirit-individuals, one of whom was associated with each of the Churinga.[2] On one side of the stone there is a round hole, through which the spirit-children are supposed to be on the look-out for women who once may chance to pass near, and it is firmly believed that visiting the stone will result in conception. If a young woman has to pass near the stone and does not wish to have a child, she will carefully disguise her youth, distorting her face and walking with the aid of a stick. She will bend herself double, like a very old woman, the tones of whose voice she will imitate, saying: "Don't come to me; I am an old woman." Above the small round hole a black line is painted with charcoal, and this is always renewed by any man who happens to visit the spot. It is called Iknula, and a black line such as this painted above the eye of a newly born child which is supposed to prevent sickness. Erathipa means a child, but is a word seldom used according to Spencer, the usual expression being Ambaquerka.[3] The Erathipa stone arises where an Alcheringa ancestor goes into the earth; it forms part of an Oknanikilla; it may well be called a specialized form of Nanja rock. Erathipa is the ratapa of the western Arunta; this means, as we have seen, the embryo. The stone seems, then, to be a symbolical womb, and the hole through which the spirit-children look out for the women represents the vagina.

The erathipa.

A similar concept with reference to trees is found in the Warramunga tribe. Here the women are very careful not to strike the trunks of certain trees with an axe, because the blow might cause spirit-children to emanate. They imagine that the spirit is very minute, about the size of a small grain of sand, that it enters the navel and grows within her into the child.[4] It is easy to understand

[1] The "ernatulunga" are always small caves or crevices. In Western Australia "dumbu" means womb, "dumbun" a cave or cavern.—G. F. Moore, *Diary of an Early Settler in Western Australia, with a Vocabulary of the Language of the Aboriginals*, 1884, 25. In a myth of the Buandik tribe, Craitbul's sons are represented as living in a cave when they are escaping from their father's wrath. "After a time they began to get tired of the cave, being desolate, alone, and repentant of the evil thing they had done in stealing the kangaroos from Craitbul and the sorrow they had caused their mother by leaving home. One morning, as the boys were speaking about their mother, one of them said: 'It is raining.' The other replied: 'Yes, open your mouth and drink.' The water tasted like the milk from their mother's breast. They hurried out of the cave, and to their joy met their mother."—T. Smith, *The Booandik Tribe of South Australian Aborigines*, 1880, 15. The myth speaks for itself; life in the cave is intra-uterine life, followed by birth and by tasting the mother's milk.

[2] Spencer and Gillen, *N. T.*, 336.

[3] Id., ibid., 337, 338.

[4] Id., *Nor. T.*, 331.

this latter typically infantile sex-theory. The navel is substituted for the vagina, and the blow directed against the tree-trunk answers to the infantile sadistic concept of coitus. But if we investigate the matter somewhat further we come to the conclusion that these trees and stones are not simple symbols with one conscious and one unconscious content, but the results of a process of condensation. The Erathipa (ratapa) stone, at any rate, means both the womb and the child (embryo) in the womb. The same black line is painted above the eye of the new-born child, that is renewed by every man over the hole of the Erathipa stone, which gives the equations stone = child, hole = eye-hole. We know that by the mechanism of displacement upwards the eye is a frequent symbol of the vagina, and in this case the vagina in the stone is indeed the eye-hole through which the spirit-children look out into the world. In the first instance the black line means the black hair above the female genitalia, and in a secondary sense it stands for the eyebrows. The remedy used against sickness is a regressive libidinisation: the child is reminded of its intra-uterine life. A similar part is played by the tjurunga. We remember that the child is said to have lost something when it went into its mother, this is the tjurunga which the women call papa (= stick).[1]

Analogies to the Churinga.

In the Kakadu tribe, when it is quite evident that one of the spirit-children entered the woman, the father of the child first of all makes some string out of opossum-fur, which he puts into a little bag that is carried round his neck. Unless this be done the child will be born blind. Then he takes some of the sticky material that he procures from an orchid growing on the trunks of trees and smears this over a short stick, which he hands to the woman, saying: "You have a child." The stick is called Tjubulinjuboulu. It is enclosed in a dilly bag, specially made for it, and in this it is carried about by the woman, who must not part with it. I think we shall get at the truth if we take the words of the father who hands the stick to the woman in their literal sense: the stick in the bag is the child in the womb that has been "handed" to the woman by her husband. She sleeps with it under her head and may not talk at night-time. It is tightly tied up in a bag lest it should be lost, in which case the child would die in the womb and the father would be very angry and punish the woman. The stick remains in the bag and is carried about until the child is born, after which it is carefully kept until the child begins to walk. The father then takes it away from the woman and hands it to some relative such as his brother, telling him to carry it to some camp a long way off. The messenger ceremonially approaches the camp with the stick,

[1] Strehlow, *A. & L.*, II. 80.

where it is kept for a day or two. Then the messenger returns accompanied by some of the strangers. When they are a little distance away from the home camp where the mother and child are living, they halt for an hour or two and are then invited to come in; the mother brings the child up to them, having previously painted a white line across its forehead and lines of dots across its cheeks or nose. She herself is decorated in just the same way. The stick is given to the child, together with different kinds of dilly-bags, waist girdles, etc., brought by the visitors, to whom the relatives of the child give spears in exchange, etc. After this is over a general corroboree is held. As yet no name is given to the child, though the father knows what it is to be. Finally, he takes the stick, breaks it in pieces, and throws them into a waterpool.[1] The birth-stick of the child that serves as a medium of establishing relations of exchange and barter with a foreign tribe corresponds to the ngia-ngiampe custom of the Narrinyeri. When a man has a child born to him he preserves its umbilical cord by tying it up in the middle of a bush of feathers. This is called a kalduke. He then gives this to the father of a child or children belonging to another tribe, and those children are thenceforth ngia-ngiampe to the child from whom the kalduke was procured. The ngia-ngiampe mutually do not touch, speak or go near to each other, but when two individuals who are in this position with regard to each other have arrived at adult age, they become the agents through which their respective tribes carry barter.[2]

On the one hand it seems that the birth-stick is equivalent to the tjurunga, on the other hand it represents the total personality of the child just as the umbilical cord does. The papa-tjurunga is restituted to or rather stowed away in the arknanakaua after a certain time when the child grows, and the birth-stick is thrown away into a pool[3] (uterine symbol) when the child has learnt to walk. It seems that both represent the body of the individual only up to a certain stage of his ontogenesis. In the Kakadu and allied tribes the navel-string plays a very similar part to the birth-stick. The navel-string is dried and carried about in one of the small bags that the natives wear suspended from a string around the neck. When once the child can move about freely it is thrown into a waterpool, but up to that time it must be carefully preserved or else the child becomes ill and probably dies. Should the child die before it is thrown away it is burnt, but if it be burnt while the

[1] Spencer, *N. T. N. T. A.*, 328–330.

[2] Taplin, *The Narrinyeri Tribe*, 33. Teeth seem to serve a similar purpose. Robert Brothers, "Travelling Teeth: An Aboriginal Custom," *The Australasian Anthropological Journal*, 1896, 19. "The tooth travels for twenty years or so, and the man's life is then under the protection of these foreign tribes."

[3] The teeth that are knocked out are also frequently thrown into a pool of water. (They represent the person up to the age of initiation.)

child is alive the result is again serious illness and probably death. If the child dies while the mother is carrying the navel-string this is attributed to her having broken a taboo.[1] If we thus come to equate the papa-tjurunga with the navel-string, we shall not be surprised to find that it plays a part in Arunta custom that is very similar to that attributed to the navel-string in European folklore.[2] The tjurunga is wrapt in string, put into the child's pitchi; when " he cries for it the head of the child comes to lie upon the tjurunga, and this is supposed to make it grow quicker and to have soothing influence on its temper."[3] But if the tjurunga is, as we have just seen, in certain respects the equivalent of the navel-string, or as we remarked previously, of the afterbirth from which also the spirit of the child is supposed to have been taken, this cannot satisfy us, as we must put the question, What does the navel-string (afterbirth) that is thrown into the waterpool after a certain time represent? The answer is evident: it represents a period of ontogenesis, the psychical relationship between mother and child.

I think that the Idnimita (Grub) tradition of the Unmatjera tribe contains the key to the whole problem. These grubs were in the Alcheringa first hairy caterpillars who walked about on the Idnimita bushes eating the leaves. By and by they began to develop and the wind brought them down at India, the present central spot of the Grub totem. Like all the other grubs, it bored its way into the roots of the tree and there lay quiet in its irtnia, that is, chrysalis case. After a time it came out of this and changed into an inmintera (inapertwa creature). Gradually he grew bigger and bigger. He was stiff and could not undouble himself. An old crow came and made him into a man with a few slashes of his bill. When he was transformed from the first imperfect creature into a Grub man he lay down all day with his chrysalis case, out of which he had come by his side. This was his Churinga and was coloured red. From it there issued many Kurna or spirit-individuals, which later on gave rise to Idnimita men and women.[4] The answer to the question is clear enough: the tjurunga is the chrysalis case of man in a pre-natal stage of development; in a word, the fœtus, the embryo. The red tjurunga is the same thing as the red body of the totem-ancestors, as the red colour of the ratapa; the totem ancestors, who themselves are supernatural embryos, change into tjurunga. The omnipotence-phantasy of intra-uterine life is materialized in the magic power of the tjurunga. The tjurunga also unites the individual with his ancestor: the embryonic stage of development is common to both,

The churinga symbolizes the embryo.

[1] Spencer, *N. T. N. T. A.*, 325.

[2] Cf. Frazer, *The Magic Art*, 1911, I. 182–203. Id., *Balder the Beautiful*, 1913, II. 162, 163. Róheim, *Contributions to Hungarian Folklore*, 1920, 280.

[3] Strehlow, II. 80; IV. 3.

[4] Spencer and Gillen, *Nor. T.*, 156, 157.

and the embryo is physically the same person as the father. But we must give our meaning greater precision. The tjurunga is a symbol, a material substitute for the embryo, as it survives in the unconscious of the infantile adult.

The union between himself and his tjurunga is truly "sein eigener Geheimer," his most secret, most personal mystery; and this tjurunga can with full right be called his other body, the body he possessed in another, radically different state of existence. The tjurungas stored up in the erthalunga are embryos lying in their mother's womb. It is they who represent the continuity, the very essence of the tribe, or, as Durkheim puts it, of society; their loss may really be regarded as foreboding a dread calamity.

We find another theory of Frazer's justified; it approximates the truth as far as theories that do not take account of the unconscious elements of the psyche can: he thinks that the afterbirth which is treated as a sort of double of the child is the germ of the concept of an external soul.[1] This is very true, but the afterbirth again stands for the pre-natal stage in development when the child enjoyed the same safety in the maternal womb that is now regressively revived in the phantasies of hiding the essence of life in a soul-box or the like. When the grandfather brings the Churinga out of the arknanakaua, this is equivalent to bringing th^ nfant out of the womb, a mystical repetition of birth. If the child is said to lose the tjurunga when entering the uterus, this means that the state of double existence embodied in the tjurunga, a real body and a mystical body made up out of embryo reminiscences, does not exist; for the embryo the reality replaces the symbol—man is an embryo and hence he can have no tjurunga. When the papa-tjurunga is carried back to the ertnatulunga, this means that the period of infant life which is regarded as a sort of "marge" between fœtal and external life comes to an end.

Evidently the applicability of our theory here comes to an end too, for the nankara, which is the body of the maternal totem ancestor and is given to the boy at initiation, hardly fits in with the embryo concept. Tuanyirika, whom it is said to represent in the esoteric myth, is the bullroarer of the mysteries,[2] and deserves a separate treatise fully to understand his import. Here we must content ourselves with the remark that, with his one leg cut off,[3] Tuanyirika is the penis in the state of symbolic castration represented by circumcision. He represents another phase in the

[1] Frazer, *The Magic Art*, 1911, I. 201.

[2] R. Pettazzoni, "Mythologie Australienne du Rhombe," *Revue de l'Histoire des Religions*, 1912, LXV. 149.

[3] Strehlow, I. 102. The mother's totem is Altjira, Altjira is Baiamai, Baiamai is Daramulun's counterpart in the mysteries. Daramulun has one leg, like Tuanyiraka. On one-legged beings, cf. Schmidt, "Die Stellung der Aranda," *Z. f. E.*, 1908, 895. Id., *Ursprung der Gottesidee*, 1912, 374–376.

development of personality ; it is still the mother who is dominant, but in the person of her totem ancestor, her father. Next we come to the namatuna, which, as we have seen, is most evidently the symbol of the penis and stands for the child's own ancestor. But his own ancestor and he are one and the same person ; iningukua means " the same." Thus it is he himself who " threw " his mother with the namatuna before he was born and obtained the unconscious wish-fulfilment of his Oedipus attitude. It would fain seem to us that this second meaning of the tjurunga was there from the very first, only it had to be repressed exactly on account of the unconscious Oedipus complex it involves, and thus we get the second equation: tjurunga = child and tjurunga = penis. The tjurungas in the sacred caves = the penis in the vagina, and hence these spots are full of " spirit-children " that is spermatozoa. After subincision the repressed concept is permitted to manifest itself in symbolic fashion. The tjurunga bitten by white ants means intercourse with foreign women; evidently the dreaded vagina is symbolized by the white ant. Women also have tjurunga, but they are not allowed to see them : according to the sex theories of masculine children all persons have got a penis, only women's is invisible.[1] The tjurunga from which a man originates thus stands for his own father (the father-imago), the Alcheringa ancestor or rather his father's penis with which he " threw " his mother.

The bullroarer used in love-magic means the penis.

Although we are of the opinion that both meanings, embryo and penis, are condensed in all the variants of the tjurunga type, yet we would classify the small ones (namatuna) used for love-magic as pre-eminently penis symbols and the large ones, " the second bodies," as pre-eminently embryos. A striking, and as far as such proof is possible, conclusive, confirmation of our interpretation is contained in the beliefs of the Niol-niol. The middle-sized ones, the womat, are not important for our immediate purposes—at any rate they[2] have something to do with sexuality. The small ones are called Mandeken, the large ones are called Mirnbor. Now we come to the startling statement that " Mandeken ibaldien Mirnbor," the small tjurunga, is the father of the big one.[3] Philology helps us. Mandeken is the same word as the Loritja mantiki, mantiki is Loritja for the Arunta namatuna.[4] Thus the Mandeken would be the penis, and what is the Mirnbor ? The Mirnbor is decorated with an ornament that represents a duck wallowing in the mud for its food.[5] Mirnbor means a Duck-man, and the Njers, the souls of the dead, exist in the woods in the shape of "Duck-

[1] Cf. Freud, *Neurosenlehre*, III. 26.

[2] H. Klaatsch, " Schlussbericht über seine Reise nach Australien," *Z. E.*, 1907, 652.

[3] Klaatsch, l.c.

[4] Strehlow (note by Leonhardi), II. 82.

[5] Klaatsch, l.c., 651.

people." [1] After a time the Njer gets incarnated in the body of an animal, in this it develops to a Rai (= ratapa), a spirit-child that is capable of being incarnated in a woman.[2] If the small Mandeken is the penis, the large Mirnbor (= Duck wallowing in mud—souls of dead—unborn children in the womb) is the embryo, and thus "Mandeken ibaldien Mirnbor" means the penis is the father of the embryo. Every Niol-niol has a Mandeken and a Mirnbor, and these he keeps in a tree reserved for the purpose; or, as the Arunta would say, in his Nanja tree, and as we put it, in the uterus.[3]

Two types of churinga explained as symbols of the penis and the embryo.

The interpretation of the tjurunga as embryo is not without further consequences. The tendency to see one's own double has in psycho-analysis been always understood to be the result of the narcissistic stage of psychosexual evolution, or to put it shortly, an outcome of self-love. In his essay on narcissism,[4] Freud describes the various types of object-love on the basis of narcissism, one of which he says is the desire or love of the narcissistic individual for his own infantile personality.

In general appearance the Iruntarinia are supposed to resemble human beings, but they are always youthful-looking, their faces are without hair and their bodies are thin and shadowy.[5] What are the Iruntarinia? They are the Arumburinga issued from the individuals Nanja tree (maternal womb) and the tjurunga-spirits. The ultimate source of the narcissistic desire for the infantile personality is the desire for the return to the first stage in the evolution of personality: the "other body" of man is himself in the different condition of intra-uterine life.

Narcissism is characterized by an overestimation of the subject and an undervaluation or perfect negation of the object, both of these attitudes being comprehensible enough if we regard them as symptoms of regression towards a state of things in which the Ego is indeed almighty and the world non-existent.

The relation of these narcissistic doubles to each other is a question of special interest. There are two archetypes to be distinguished: (*a*) The Unchanged, (*b*) The Transformative. The former is represented by the Alcheringa-ancestor living on in his "eternal" (ngara) rock or tree, the latter by the spirit-individuals always on the look-out for fresh incarnations. In other words, the Arumburinga that issues from the Nanja tree is changeless and lives for

The changing and the unchanged spirit.

[1] Klaatsch, *Z. E.*, 1907, 650.

[2] Klaatsch, *Die Anfänge von Kunst und Religion in der Urmenschheit*, 1913, 35.

[3] Cf. on the ertnalunga as places of refuge, in the Mungarai tribe (Spencer, *N. T. N. T. A.*, 214), in the Kaitish (Spencer and Gillen, *Nor. T.*, 270).

[4] S. Freud, Zur Einführung des Narcissmus, *Jahrbuch*, 1914, VI.

[5] Spencer and Gillen, *N. T.*, 516.

ever; and the spirit part of the Alcheringa individual which also lives for ever, but from time to time undergoes reincarnation.[1] An important parallel to these ideas, together with the nescience of the relation of cohabitation and procreation, is (by nescience we mean, of course, the repression of conscious knowledge) found in the Kakadu tribe. After death the Yalmuru, that is the spirit part, keeps watch over the bones (benogra). After some time the Yalmuru, as it were, divides into two, so that we have the original Yalmuru and second spirit called Iwaiyu. The two are distinct and have somewhat the same relation to another as a man and his shadow, which to the native mind are very intimately associated.[2] For a long time they remain together, but when the Yalmuru desires to undergo reincarnation the two leave the Benogra or bones, which are always some distance out in the scrub, often miles away from a camp. They go forth together—the Iwaiyu leading, the Yalmuru behind. The Yalmuru takes the Iwaiyu and puts it in the form of a small frog into some food which the natives are searching for. When the man has secured the food, out jumps the frog, unseen, of course, by the men. It is caught by the Yalmuru, and the two spirits return to their camping-place.[3]

Here the doubling of motives begins again. Like their doubles the natives also return to their camp with the food quite unconscious of the fact that the Yalmuru and Iwaiyu have had anything to do with the matter. At night-time the two latter come back again to the camp and watch the men and women. The Iwaiyu is again in the form of a little frog. When all are asleep the two come up to the camp and enter the mia-mia where the man and his wife are sleeping. The Iwaiyu goes up and smells the man;[4] if it be not the "right" father he says "ngari koyada" (not this one). He tries another one, finds him right, and says "ngari papa" (this one is my father). Then he goes and smells the latter's lubra. The Iwaiyu gets into her hair, then feels her breasts and says, "these are my mother's breasts; this is my mother." Then he comes down and goes into the woman. The Yalmuru returns to the old camp. Every now and then he comes and looks at the woman, but does not speak. When it is evident that the woman is going to have a child, the Yalmuru comes up to the camp at night-time and tells the father that the child is there, tells him its name and also its totem. The case of Ungara illustrates

[1] Spencer and Gillen, *N. T.*, 515. [2] Cf. Strehlow, *A. & L.*, II. 82.

[3] The food in which the Iwaiyu was placed is the child's totem: the latter is thus always selected by the Yalmuru.—Spencer, *N. T. N. T. A.*, 271. Cf. above.

[4] The presence of the choi (birth-spirit) can be recognized by the nose. The smell of carbolic acid that was used to dress a wound was attributed by natives to the choi.—W. E. Roth, l.c., 18. On the Tully River, if a gin has connexion with a boy, the perspiration from under the armpit of the latter can be smelt on her.—W. E. Roth, l.c., 22. The close connexion of the olfactory nerves with the genital organs is a well-known fact.

the affair. When his father's brother died, his benogra or bones were left for some time in a tree not far from the camp at which he died, but later on they were carried more than twenty miles away and placed in a banyan tree overhanging a pool. Ungara, who had his wife Obaiya and one child with him, was once camped near this place. He threw his net into the water and then he left it there for some little time. He went into the water to drive the fish into the net. He did not know that the Yalmuru had already done this, and that the Iwaiyu was in one of the fishes. The net was so heavy that he called out to Obaiya to help him to lift it. While they were doing this the Iwaiyu jumped out and was caught by the Yalmuru, and then they both went back to the bones. Ungara and his wife carried the fish home at night, the Yalmuru and Iwaiyu came and the latter went into Obaiya. When the child is young the Yalmuru watches over it. If it strays away in camp and gets lost in the bush, the Yalmuru guides it back, and later on, when the child has grown into a man, the Yalmuru still helps it. In fact, a good deal depends on the Yalmuru, because if it be not vigilant some other hostile spirit may work evil magic against the individual associated with the Yalmurus Iwaiyu. Finally, when the individual becomes really old, the Yalmuru comes one night and whispers into his ear, "Iwaiyu, you look after a child, my back-bone and thighs are no good, and sore—you look after the Yereipunga (totem)." In other words, the Yalmuru is supposed to tell the Iwaiyu, that is the spirit within the man, that he is worn out and that the Iwaiyu must take on the part of providing for a new child being born, and must look after its totem. As the natives say, "The old Yalmuru is done for completely," "the Iwaiyu is the new Yalmuru."

The continuity of the germ-plasm.

Now let us hear Spencer's explanation of these concepts: "It is really rather like a very crude forerunner of the theory of the continuity of the germ-plasm. The old Yalmuru splits, as it were into two—one half, the Iwaiyu, persists, and the other finally disappears. In its turn the former becomes transformed into a Yalmuru, which again splits; one half remains, the other perishes, but there is an actual spiritual continuity from generation to generation."[1] This time we must say that "the plummets of Professor Spencer have indeed struck the very bottom"[2]: the possibility of this sort of "foreknowledge" being contained in the unbroken continuity of psychical unconscious and conscious life processes. But this meaning lies so very deep in the abyss of evolution that naturally we must

[1] Spencer, *N. T. N. T. A.*, 1914, 270–274.

[2] With regard to his conceptional theory of totemism, Frazer says: "After years of sounding, our plummets seem to touch bottom at last."—Frazer, "The Beginnings of Religion and Totemism among the Australian Aborigines," *T. & E.*, 1910, I. 161.

expect to find other "meanings" superposed on each other to obtain such a complicated phenomenon as a belief of this sort. The Yalmuru in this case is the father's father's brother's ghost, and if we regard the father's brother merely as the substitute for the father then we have the well-known concept of the child as the re-born grandfather in the Yalmuru-Iwaiyu relation. The protecting part played by the Yalmuru both with regard to the individual and to the Iwaiyu may be compared to the protection accorded by the mother's totem (Altjira) or his own iningukua. Indeed, there is a less far-reaching, although ultimately identical, prototype for the Iwaiyu splitting off from the Yalmuru than the splitting of the germ-plasm: it is the spermatozoa "splitting off" from the father at cohabitation. We know that the relation between father and child is eminently narcissistic, and this would accord well with the protecting part played by the Yalmuru and Arumburinga over the individual. A closer study of the myth makes it clear that the doings of the Yalmuru and Iwaiyu correspond exactly to those of father and child. The Yalmuru puts the Iwaiyu into a frog: that is, he puts the semen into the womb, and the proceeding continues with the mechanism of transposition upwards when the mother eats the food. Before the father has driven the fish into the net the Yalmuru has done the same, when the father returns to the camp with the fish the Yalmuru returns to his camp with the Iwaiyu. Yalmuru and Iwaiyu come to the woman at night;[1] it is naturally at night that the father, and in him the child, come to the mother, as representative of the Father-Imago. When a man gets old, the Yalmuru is a convenient medium for projecting the extremely unpleasant concept of impending death. The Censor represses this idea, and says that it is not the man whose backbones and thighs are no good, who is done for altogether, it is the Yalmuru. At the same time this negation contains as acknowledgment, the spirit within him, the Iwaiyu, is old, it is now a Father, a Yalmuru. The old man to whom this is told is really past the age of physical procreation, but he at least repeats his former achievements in the phantasy of his Iwaiyu becoming a new Yalmuru and begetting, like the old one, a new Iwaiyu-child.

If we follow the trend of Durkheim's ideas[2] we shall come to another equation that is, in reality only a more advanced form of the former: Changeless spirit = Society, Changeable one = the Individual. It is Society that protects the Individual against the dangers of the chase and foreign societies, or from a purely

[1] Cf., an evil being called Koin, who resembles the blacks themselves, makes his appearance mostly by night. In general, they think he precedes the coming of natives from distant parts.—Th. H. Braim, *History of New South Wales*, 1846, 248, 249. (Cf. the attacks of the foreign Yalmurus on the natives.)

[2] He does not state this view explicitly. Cf. Durkheim, op. cit., 394.

psychological point of view the feeling of belonging to a given society.

The social origin of what we call conscience is well brought out in these beliefs: if the tjurunga is lost the iningukua (arumburinga) gets angry and pricks the person allied to him with his pointing sticks so that he gets ill[1]; a mythical transcription of the "pangs of conscience." If we also remember that the Arumburinga is said to protect the individual when he, without knowing the reason why, defends himself against an impending danger, we shall be inclined to identify the Changeless Spirit under this aspect with the Ego, the Reality Principle, the connexion of which with the Father as representative of Society is well known. If this be the case, one of the narcissistic doubles would stand for the Ego (Reality Principle) and the other for the Libido; we should then be compelled to assign an Unconscious to the Ego besides the Unconscious of the Libido, as some psycho-analysts seem inclined to do. If questioned further as to the contents of this second unconscious we should say that it was made up out of the psychic residua of self-preservatory reflex actions. On the other hand, it is very possible that this second Unconscious is the Fore-conscious of psycho-analysis: the failure of repression as the limit between the Conscious and Unconscious seems to favour this theory.[2] Freud tells us that doubles of narcissistic origin are turned to account by the Fore-conscious to emphasize and represent the differences between an actual and an archaic stage in the evolution of the Ego,[3] and in this way the Iningukua ("The Same") might stand for a stage of greater fixation to the soil, although this naturally means to the soil as birthplace, as symbol of the uterus, thus leading us back to the iningukua as the projection of incestuous libido.

We may try to sum up the relation between the Unchanged and the Transforming spirit as follows. Like the germ-plasm, like life itself, the spirit is always the same and yet infinitely variable; like the species the Arumburinga is eternal, the individual ever new. Like the libido the spirit is eternally the same and like the libido it undergoes a series of continual changes. Like the Father the Arumburinga (Yalmuru) is relatively unchanged if we regard him from the viewpoint of the rapidly growing, that is changing, child. And lastly, like Society, the Senior spirit represents Continuity, the Junior stands for Individual Variability. As the Father and Society form the most important elements of an

[1] Strehlow, *A. & L.*, II. 81.

[2] An alternative theory would be that there are elements in the Unconscious that have never been repressed, as they have never reached the Threshold of Repression. These would be the "engrams" of reflex actions which form the germs of the development of the psyche.

[3] Freud, "Das Unheimliche," *Imago*, VI. 516.

environment that is principally differentiated from the individual in so far as it compels him to a series of adjustments (changes), the Senior spirit stands also for the Reality Principle as compared to the Pleasure Principle for the Fore-conscious versus the Unconscious (Libido). The two spirits correspond to the two constituent elements that are united in Narcissism; the Senior spirit is the Ego, it lives outside of the Individual, it means his relation to the outer world; the Junior is the Libido which lives in the Individual in the form of the Auto-erotic Libido that originates from and tends to regress to the Tjurunga, the Embryo.

Every native of the Arunta and allied tribes unites a double personality in his own self. He is a real human being, as he seems to be to the superficial onlooker, and at the same time he is a being semi-divine who lived on the earth in the mythical days of the Alcheringa, and has merely condescended to be re-born in our days of sober reality. For instance, we read in the wanderings of the Wild-Cat men: "One man, a Purula named Kuntitcharinia, was left behind, whose descendant is still living."[1] Close to a stone at the northern entrance of the gorge the great Alcheringa leader of the Witchetty Grub men sprang into existence. The stone has since been associated not only with the spirit of this dead leader but also with one or two men who have been regarded as his successive reincarnations, the last of whom was the father of the present Alatunja of the group.[2]

This double existence led by the aboriginals of Central Australia reminds us of a common conscious or unconscious infantile phantasy that has been called the family romance of neurotics. The child will often imagine that his parents are not his real blood relatives, that he is the offspring of kings, heroes or other great men, that his father and mother are only his foster parents; in a word, that he is by descent not what he seems to be, but something infinitely more elevated.[3] This phantasy is the first attempt of the individual to free himself from the original infantile attitude in which the child regards his father as the most powerful of men, his mother the most beautiful of women. When he realizes that his actual parents do not come up to his own high-pitched mark, he dethrones them in his own phantasy and creates new ones for himself in his day-dreams, who, however, are only the old ones under a new name.

The Arunta have worked out a similar theory which enables them to realize their unconscious infantilism and Oedipus complex in the stage of hallucinatory wish-fulfilment. Every Arunta has lived before this; that is, behind his conscious existence there is the realm of the intra-uterine, the infantile, the unconscious. It

[1] Spencer and Gillen, *N. T.*, 417. [2] Id., ibid., 425.
[3] Cf. O. Rank, *Der Mythus von der Geburt des Helden.* (Second edition, 1922.)

was he himself who performed those wonderful feats that are told of in the myths, enacted (perhaps by himself) in ritual; it was he himself who lived in the realm of unchecked wish-fulfilment in the days of yore before he knew repression, the outcome of the contact with a world of resistance. If he is one of those mythical heroes his father can naturally have had nothing to do with his procreation; the father is done away with altogether, his birth is entirely a matter between himself and his mother.

We saw that the throwing by which the Alcheringa ancestor incarnates himself in the woman is a symbolic coitus, and as the child is the ancestor, it is he himself who has had connexion with his mother, in another life, in the Unconscious, from which connexion he himself was born. The whole Arunta system is indeed nothing but an elaborate phantastic realization of an infantile wish common to all humanity: the Child wishes to be its own Father.

It has been remarked (A. Lang, P. W. Schmidt) that the Arunta cannot be primitive, since they have such an exceptionally complicated animistic philosophy and that their alleged nescience of procreation is merely an outcome of this system. We, too, are of the opinion that there is an intimate connexion between the nescience (as far as consciousness is concerned) and the system of animistic philosophy. It is well known that the impulse to scientific investigation and other psychical efforts of a higher order is, in a large degree, derived from a sublimation of the infantile sexual curiosity, and this sublimation can only take place if the uncensored manifestations of this curiosity are repressed by the psychic censor. Thus we come to the conclusion that the elaborate

The Arunta system an outcome of repression.

system of the Arunta is really derived from their energetic repression: it makes it possible for them to obtain a fulfilment of their Oedipus wishes in a sublimated form. We have repeatedly had occasion to point out that there is a tendency in all these beliefs towards the formation of a series through doubling and redoubling of one and the same motive, the repetition of which, through the unconscious contents embodied therein, affords a source of pleasure; whilst, on the other hand, the difference between imagination and reality is an obstacle to complete wish-fulfilment, and it is the partially unsatisfied libido which craves for repetitions.[1] This reincarnation myth is a series-formation on the largest possible scale, as it unites the whole tribe (down to its phylogenetic ancestry in animal-life) in a single chain of repeated incest phantasies.

Incarnation or reincarnation.

There has been some discussion between Strehlow and Spencer whether the beliefs may correctly be called reincarnation or incarnation. Providing that we do not call the continued swarming off of "spirit-individuals"

[1] Cf. Pfeiffer, "Ausserungen infantil-erotischer Triebe im Spiele," *Imago*, V. 255.

from the same parent stock (" archetypal idea ") a sort of reincarnation,[1] the question is whether the ghost of a dead man is actually re-born or not? This leads us to the problem of the relation between the idea of a post-mortem and a pre-natal world. When a man or woman dies there remains the spirit part or Ultana, which is supposed to haunt the burial-place and at night-time to come into the camp, or it may go back to its old Nanja rock or tree. When all the mourning ceremonies have been carried out the Ultana is supposed to leave the grave and to return to its Nanja, where it lives with its Arumburinga. After a time it gets itself another Churinga with which it becomes associated just as before with the Alcheringa Churinga, and then, after the lapse of some time, but not until the bones have crumbled away, it may be born again in human form.[2] The body is placed in a sitting position with the knees doubled up against the chin, and thus interred in a round hole in the ground; the earth being piled up on the body so as to form a low mound with a depression on the side which faces towards the dead persons' camping ground in the Alcheringa, that is the spot which he or she inhabited while in spirit form: the object of this is to allow an easy ingress and egress of the Ulthana which is supposed to spend part of the time (till the final mourning ceremony is over) at the grave, and part in company of its Arumburinga at the Nanja spot.[3] Amongst the Unmatjera and Kaitish, when the ceremony is over, the dead man's spirit is supposed to go away and remain in the Alcheringa spot, associating with those of his fellow tribesmen until such time as he once more undergoes reincarnation.[4] In the Warramunga tribe, when the ceremony of " breaking the bone " has been performed and the bone deposited in its last resting-place, the spirit of the dead person, which they describe as being about the size of a grain of sand (cf. above), goes back to its camping-place in the Wingara and remains there in company with the spirit parts of other members of his totem until such time as it undergoes reincarnation. The pit in which the bone is buried and covered over with a stone is called palpalla, as is also the totemic design drawn upon the ground representing the spot at which the totemic ancestor finally went into the earth.[5]

The ghost goes back to the totem-centre.

Among the Gnanji tribe the dead man is called kurti and the spirit moidna. While each man has a moidna the woman has none, and so when she is dead she is done with altogether.[6] The spirit of the dead man walks about, visiting his ancestral camping

[1] If we wish to be quite precise we should call this not, indeed, a reincarnation, but a continually repeated incarnation.

[2] Spencer and Gillen, *N. T.*, 514, 515.

[3] Id., ibid., 497.

[4] Id., *Nor. T.*, 508.

[5] Id., ibid., 542.

[6] Cf. the same belief in the Kwarranjee tribe (a part of the Chingalee nation):—R. H. Mathews, *Proc. Roy. Geog. Soc. Queensland*, 1907, XXII. 75, 76.

ground and undergoing reincarnation at some future time when the rains shall have fallen and washed and cleansed the bones.[1] In the coastal tribes, such as the Binbinga, Anula and Mara, the association of a dead man or ghost with his totem is emphasized in the ceremonies. At the final ceremony the local men sing sacred songs all of which are connected with the totem of the dead man. Early next morning they bring up a hollow log called lalanga, which is painted with a design of the dead man's totem.[2] The tribal fathers, but not the actual father,[3] and the tribal sons of the dead are painted with the design of the totem. Ceremonies relating to the ancestors of the totemic group are performed under the superintendence of the dead person's father. The hollow log that is marked with the design of the totem is afterwards placed by the side of a water-hole, where it is left untouched. In this way every individual of the tribe is thus, as it were, gathered finally into his totem. The spirit part which the Binbinga call kutulu goes back to its mungai spot and sooner or later undergoes reincarnation.[4] The hole, which is connected in the Arunta tribe with the idea of ingress and egress of the spirit, is also found in the graves of the Karkurera. A singular feature of the grave was that on the northern side of the mound a hole passing straight down to the body and only loosely covered at the surface with a few branches of mulga had been left open.[5] The hole being to the north, which in these tribes is usually the home of the spirits, seems to favour Spencer's suggestion as to its meaning. The hole in the grave corresponds to the hole in the Erathipa stone through

[1] Spencer and Gillen, *Nor. T.*, 546.

[2] Among the Eskimo of Behring Strait the totem mark is visible on a man's grave, or, instead of the totem, some animal which the father of the deceased excelled in hunting.—I. E. Nelson, *The Eskimo about Behring Strait*, XVIII, Rep., 1899, 311. When a child is born it is given the name of a deceased relative. The child then becomes the namesake and representative of the dead person at the feast of the dead.—Ibid., 289. We find here a sort of reincarnation-belief in conjunction with the grave-post symbolism of the totem, and the substitution (i.e. unconscious assimilation) of the totem, and the animal hunted by the father. But we also find another Australian custom, to be dealt with below, for " in case the child is born away from the village at a camp or tundra it is commonly given the name of the first object that catches its mother's eyes, such as a bush, or other plant, a mountain, lake, or other natural object."

[3] This exception points to a repression of the unconsciously felt connexion between the father and the totem.

[4] Spencer and Gillen, *Nor. T.*, 552–54, 173, 174. It seems probable that we ought to add the Leeanuwa, Larrekiya, Wogait, Wulna, Pongo-pongo, and Mulluk-mulluk to the list of tribes who believe in reincarnation. When a child is born it takes the name of some dead relative or friend of the same tribe.—W. G. Stretton, " Customs, Rites and Superstitions of the Aboriginal Tribes of the Gulf of Carpentaria," *Royal Geographical Soc. of Australia*, 1893, 230. " Every native believes in his reincarnation after death in the form of some living being which is always held in respect by him."—H. Basedow, *Trans. Roy. Soc. of S. A.*, XXXI, 1907, 8.

[5] H. Basedow, " Anthropological Notes made on the South Australian Government North-West Prospecting Expedition," *Trans. Roy. Soc. S. A.*, 1903, XXVIII, 34.

which the spirits peep out into this world, and both stand for the hole where the child must pass on its way out of the womb. The totemic design on the coffins find their next parallel in the so-called "mortuary totems" of the Wotjobaluks. The people of the Wotjo nation buried the dead with the head in a certain direction which is determined by his class and totem. The several directions are all fixed with reference to the rising sun.[1] The name of a man is changed when he dies, and this is what Howitt calls a mortuary totem. The man of the Sun totem who had been called "Sun" when alive, was spoken of as "behind the sun," which means a shadow cast behind the speaker by the sun. When a man of the Pelican totem died he would not be called Pelican, but Bark of the Mallee, and so on.[2] The tribes described by Mathews as observing the Dolgaritty ceremony have the same bisection (Krokitch-Gamutch) as the Wotjobaluk, and from them we can obtain further information as to the nature of the association between totemism and the directions observed at burial. Every clan has its own spirit-land, called miyur, a word signifying "home" or final resting-place, to which the shades of all its members depart after death. These miyurs are located in certain fixed directions from the territory of the tribe—like the Wotjo totems arranged with reference to the sun. Each clan has a number of totems, but as the clans are also named after animals, we would rather say that each totem

The "miyur" and the island other world.

[1] Howitt, *N. T.*, 64.

[2] Id., ibid., 124. Cf. the totemic death-rite of the Warramunga (Spencer and Gillen, *Nor. T.*, 168), Binbinga, Anula, Mara (Id., ibid., 173, 553), and of the Waduman tribe (Spencer, *N. T. N. T. A.*, 198). For the Larrekiya and Woolwanga, see also Eylmann, 237. For tribes No. 77, Spencer and Gillen, *Nor. T.*, 544, 146. For 56, Id., ibid., 146. For 52, Id., *N. T.*, 512; ibid., 123–27. For 51, Id., ibid., 157. For 50, Id., *Nor. T.*, 508, 512. For 48, Id., *N. T.*, 157; *Nor. T.*, 508, 512. For 222, Id., *Nor. T.*, 518. For 47, Id., *N. T.*, 157, 158; *Nor. T.*, 530, 542. For 46, Id., ibid., 515. For 44, Id., ibid., 146. For 43, Id., ibid., 515. For 42, id., ibid., 146. For 41, id., ibid., 546. For 49, id., ibid, 547. For 38, id., ibid., 547. For 35, id., ibid., 547, 554. For 34, id., ibid., 547. For 32, id., ibid., 554. For 31, id., ibid., 547. For 45, 12, 24, 26, 27, 28, Spencer, *N. T. N. T. A.*, 1914, 263–70. For 4, 6, 13, 17, 18, 19, 20, id., ibid., 270, 277. With reference to the data on "Supernatural conception connected with patrilinear totemism" and "Supernatural conception connected with matrilinear totemism" of Map 8, "Totemism and Descent," see Spencer, *N. T. N. T. A.*, and Spencer and Gillen, *Nor. T.* As to "Reincarnation," cf. for the tribes from 1 to 28 and 45, Spencer, op. cit., 264. For "Supernatural conception amongst tribes with matrilinear descent of class," cf. Daisy M. Bates, op. cit., *Victorian Geographical Journal*, XXIII, XXIV. 49, quoted by Frazer, *T. & E.*, I. 564. "Marriages are independent of personal totems, and a man whose oobaree is a kangaroo may marry a woman who is of his proper marrying class, and who may have the same totem, a different totem being bestowed on the children." These totems are always given from some circumstance connected with the birth of the child. A girl was called after a kangaroo which her father had killed, reminding us of the pre-natal duel between father and child found on the northern half of the Continent. These totems are classed among the individual totems by Frazer, and I have also included them under that heading on the map. We should need further information to determine their exact position in the totem world.

had a number of subtotems.[1] The children take their phratry, clan-totem, and miyur from their mother; everybody claims some animal (plant, object) as his own special totem, but all the totems of his fellow-clansmen are friends of his.[2] When a member of a clan dies the body is laid horizontally face upwards, with the head placed toward the part of the horizon which leads to the miyur of the clan. Each miyur has its fabled watering-place. The shades of Dyālup, Burt murnya and Burt wirrimal drink at Mūmbūl, Bial-bial water supplies Muiwillak, Wuran, Durrimurak and Burriwan. Wartwurt drinks at Bummir, etc. In some of these places there is clear spring water, in others ordinary water courses; some have greyish water, whilst others have sea-spray. When the men go out hunting and catch kangaroos, snakes, opossums and any other game, every animal is cooked with the head pointing to the miyur of its own clan. Even if dead animals are only temporarily laid on the ground while the hunters are resting, their heads are turned towards their respective miyurs. The spirits of the dead congregate in the miyurs of their respective clans during their disembodied state,[3] and from there they emerge and are born again in human shape when a favourable opportunity presents itself.[4]

A very similar distribution of other worlds between the totems, together with the special part played by water in each of these totem Elysiums, is reported from New Ireland. The souls of all the dead go to the water of their totem and sometimes live in great trees beside it. They can only leave the water at night, and then it is dangerous for living people of the other totem to go near them.[5] I think that the connexion of other-world and totem-centre, that is the place where the children are incarnated, may be regarded as the original state of affairs: we shall try to trace the chain of unconscious associations which evolved into the belief of a separate other-world for the whole tribe and also probably replaced the reincarnation myth.[6] If a woman who is pregnant were to eat forbidden fish the spirit of the unborn babe would go out of its mother's body and frighten the fish away. Although these spirit-children are invisible to human eyes, the old men know they are present by the movements of the fish.[7] The infant in the womb will not allow the fish in the water to be eaten, as it is regarded as identical with himself. In the Kakadu tribe, after the child is born and while it is young, the women must not drink out of a

[1] Mathews, *E. N.*, 85, 86.

[2] Id., 89. As to the miyurs in the Wimmera district, cf. ibid., 145, 146.

[3] Each local division of the Narrang-ga has its own spirit world in a separate direction.—Howitt, op. cit., 451.

[4] Mathews, op. cit., 91.

[5] A. Hahl, "Das mittlere Neumecklenburg," XCI. *Globus*, 1907, 313, 314.

[6] The customs of burying the body in the position of the embryo and the burial at the birthplace probably indicate the former extension of the totemistic reincarnation-area.

[7] Mathews, *E. N.*, 58.

deep water-hole; she must not break this rule or the child will die. Also she must not eat fish out of a deep water-hole. They believe that if the child were to see its mother drinking out of a deep water-hole its spirit would immediately leave its body, run to the water-hole and be drawn under and swallowed by a Numereji snake.[1] If, however, the mother breaks the rule, the father, mother and child, accompanied by a medicine man, go to the water-hole. The father gives the mother a little water in a bark basket. The spirit of the child is attracted, comes up, and the child is caught by the medicine man, who alone can see it. He immediately places it in the mother's head, from which it passes down into her breast and the child, who is at once put to the breast, drinks it in with its mother's milk. If the father finds out when the woman is away that she has been drinking at a deep water-hole, he will at once go to the latter with a medicine man, who catches the spirit and places it in the father, from whom it is supposed to pass into the mother and by way of her breast into the child.[2] The child leaves the womb for the deep water-hole, which is another womb, and is replaced in a water-basket, which again symbolizes the same thing.

The symbolic meaning of water and fish that is so evident for the pre-natal period of life gives us the key to interpret the meaning of the same symbols with reference to the post-mortem period. In the Minyung language dukkai means the dead, a dead man. In some dialects duggai, which is evidently the same word, means a kind of fish; in the Turrubul dialect it means man.[3] According to Westgarth, some of them think they become fishes after death, others think the soul inhabits whales.[4] They believe that the porpoises which drive large fish on shore are animated by the spirits of their fathers.[5] Thus the development from the miyur of each totem (which is an oknanikilla that is especially connected

[1] If a child is born dead this is often attributed by the Kakadu to Numereji, the snake who is supposed to have caused the iwaiyu to leave the mother's body while she was bathing. Women who are about to become mothers must not go into water while the wind blows, as the swish of the waves is due to Numereji. The spirit part of the child is frightened and leaves the mother's body, hastening back to its own camping-place. The natives say that when the body leaves the mother the spirit sometimes comes and looks at it, and at a later time may go inside the same woman again.—Spencer, *N. T. N. T. A.*, 326.

[2] Spencer, *N. T. N. T. A.*, 345, 346. How does it pass from the father to the mother? By way of the semen? Women when menstruating are not allowed to eat fish of any kind or go near the water at all because the men could not then fish successfully.—E. J. Eyre, *Journals of Expeditions into Central Australia*, 1845, II. 295.

[3] H. Livingstone, *Grammar and Vocabulary of the Minyung people* (*Wimmera*) joined to Threlkeld, *An Australian Language*, 1892, 24.

[4] W. Westgarth, *Australia Felix*, 1848, 138. The Dieri lay the body on a plant called kuya-mara (new fish).—Howitt, *N. T.*, 778. The Tangara preserve the body till a flood occurs, when the bones are pounded and cast into the waters as fish-seed. —Howitt, l.c., 450.

[5] L. Ph. Townsend, *Rambles and Observations in New South Wales*, 1849, 138.

with water) to the island other-world as the common resting-place of all the spirits of the tribe, is effected by the medium of the uterine symbolism of fish and water. The tribes whose territory adjoins those with the miyur beliefs in the country from Beaufort towards Hexham and Wickliffe, like those in the Wimmera district, have a spirit home which is called maioga or mungo. All the clans have the same maioga, which consists of an island a short distance off the coast of Victoria about half-way between Warrnambool and Portland. On the shores of the mainland facing the island there are some large rocks, into the base of one of which the ceaseless rolling of the billows has worn a cave-like recess which is believed in some way to be connected with Dhinmar, the spirit-isle. Every deceased person is laid with his head towards this island. His spirit then provides itself with a firebrand and proceeds to the shore where the rock is situated, where he divests himself of any clothing or trinkets he may be wearing on his body and disappears over the intervening sea to Dhinmar. The spirit of all the clans and phratries go to this island, which they occupy in common just as they did in their native hunting-grounds. There they remain until reincarnated.[1] These ideas are interwoven with those of another world in the sky. Collins tells us that after their decease some said they went on or beyond the great water, but the greater number said that they went up to the clouds. Bennil-long said they came from the clouds, and when they died they returned to the clouds. He seemed desirous to make it understood that they ascended in the shape of little children, first hovering in the tops of the branches of the trees; and mentioned something about eating, in that state, their favourite food, little fishes.[2] Their idea is that they will quit this world and enter the next in the form of little children, under which they would reappear in this.[3] At Port Lincoln they represent the soul as being so small that it might pass through a chink. After death the soul retires to an island as so small an atom as to be able to dispense with further nourishment of any kind. Some locate this island in the east, others in the west. On its journey to the island the soul is accompanied by a redbill, a kind of seabird notorious for its shrill, piercing voice audible during the night. They say that their souls will be reborn as white men. Probably the island is only the place of residence of the souls for a certain time, as they decidedly believe in a change of souls and assign this island to them as an intermediate place of residence.[4] Schürmann's account is exactly the same, even the expressions he uses. The soul is very small,

[1] Mathews, *E. N.*, 95.

[2] Collins, *An Account of the English Colony in New South Wales*, 1804, 355.

[3] Collins, op. cit., 356.

[4] Ch. Wilhelmi, "Manners and Customs of the Australian Natives," *Roy. Soc. Trans.*, 1862, 28–30.

so minute that it could pass through a crack or crevice, and when a man dies his soul, accompanied by a redbill, goes to an island in the east or west where it requires no food. They believe in the pre-existence of souls.[1] The souls of the Nauos go to an island in Spencer's Gulf, while the Parnkallas are supposed to take their departure to the island of the westward towards the Great Australian Bight.[2] The Narrinyeri say that when Nurundere left the world he dived under the ocean and as he descended he saw a great fire under the sea. He avoided this, and keeping away at last arrived at a land in the far west where he now resides. All the dead thus dive under the ocean, see the fire, but by avoiding it get to Nurundere.[3] The Buandik, who lived next to the Narrinyeri (to the east) believed that there were two spirits in mankind which they called Bo-ong. One went west and down into the sea: this one would return a white man; the other went up into cloud-land.[4] The return of the soul as a white man is evidently a recent improvement on the return of the soul as an aboriginal baby whose skin is white at birth as compared with that of the adult; it is important to note that the idea of re-birth is connected not with the cloud-land, but with the island (uterine other-world) myth. Perhaps we can also explain the curious feature of the fire under the water. If we regard the outward aspect of these myths, we shall be reminded of the sun's rays reflected on the ocean and the sun sinking into the western sea. But we know that in the Unconscious fire and water frequently in conjunction stand for urethral eroticism.[5] Indeed, we have met with something of the like in Australia; the legend of Nurundere pursuing and drowning his wives was evidently the mythical equivalent of a urethral-erotic dream.

Now we have a version of this myth as follows: When his two wives ran away from him, Nurundere crossed what is now called Lake Albert and went along the beach to Cape Jarvis. When he arrived there he saw the fugitives wading through the shallow water between the mainland and Nar-oong-owie—as Kangaroo Island was then called. Enraged at his wives he made

[1] C. W. Schürmann, *The Aboriginal Tribes of Port Lincoln in South Australia.* J. D. Woods, *The Native Tribes of South Australia*, 1879, 234, 235. Cf. Eylmann, *Die Eingeborenen der Kolonie Süd-australien*, 1908, 189. "Pindi: pit, den, ditch, grave, the habitation of souls before birth and after death." C. G. Teichelmann and C. W. Schürmann, *Outlines of a Grammar, Vocabulary and Phraseology of the Aboriginal Language of South Australia*, 1840, 39. Cf. the Kakadu word for earth-oven: peindi.—Spencer, *N. T. N. T. A.*, 27.

[2] G. F. Angas, *Savage Life and Scenes in Australia and New Zealand*, 1847, I. 108.

[3] Taplin, 58.

[4] Howitt, 434. The spirit is called bo-ong (the hereafter), ka-ngaro (up above). A fat kangaroo is said to be perfect, like a kangaroo of the clouds.—J. Smith, *The Booandik Tribe of South Australian Aborigines*, 1880, 28.

[5] Cf. H. Flournoy, "Dreams on the Symbolism of Water and Fire," *I. J. P. A.*, 1920, I. 245.

the water rise and drown them, when they were turned into two rocks that are visible to this day. After his wives were drowned Ngurundure walked into the water and dived out towards the island. There he tried to sleep, but as he could not sleep on account of the wailing of his drowning wives, he departed to his home in the sky where those who have kept the tribal laws go to join him. After death the spirit follows the footsteps of Nurundere over the island of Nar-oong-owie, and thence it is translated, as he was, to his home in the skies. The island is sacred to Nurundere and the spirits of the dead.[1]

These dreams, as we know, have a double meaning. They are urethral dreams and birth dreams, the death of the fugitives being "a representation by the contrary" of birth, which is also directly told in the language of myth in the person of the hero Wyungare, who escapes from the floodland and is translated into another land.[2] If the dead follow the very footsteps of Nurundere it is perhaps justifiable to interpret the fire under the water as a symptom of urethral eroticism, the reason why this unconscious component should appear in an eschatological myth lying in its second meaning of birth and re-birth. It is this myth of the Island of the Dead that has, among the western Arunta and Loritja, replaced the concept of the totem-centre as other-world. Far away to the north, surrounded by the sea, is a narrow long island, the Land of the Dead, the Place of Ghosts. On this island there are lime-wood trees with white bark (called ilumba, ilumba means to die); wild cats dotted white, bandicoots with white fur, lizards and snakes, white cockatoos and other birds are perched on the branches of the trees. White is the mourning colour of the Arunta. Pelicans swim about on the waters.[3] The souls of the dead are flimsy white images: they feed on lizards, snakes, rats and raw birds'-eggs, on grubs and berries and jelka (*Cyperus rotundus*). When a person is dead his ghost haunts the grave for some time after the mourning ceremonies are finished; it goes to the island and stops there till it rains on earth, when it longs for its relatives and comes back. It tells them: Be careful lest the same thing happen to you that befell me! "If the dead man had sons, the

[1] K. L. Parker, *More Australian Legendary Tales*, 1898–99, 100.

[2] Cf. O. Rank, "Symbolschichtung im mythischen Denken," *Psychoanalytische Beiträge zur Mythenforschung*, 1919. Id., *Der Mythus von der Geburt des Helden*, 1922.

[3] As to the white cockatoo and the pelican in the other-world, the myth of Western Victoria according to which Kuurokeetch (the Long-billed Cockatoo) was the first "great-great-grandfather,"and his wife was Kappatch (Banksian Cockatoo), see J. Dawson, *Australian Aborigines*, 1881, 26. The first name is also the name of the white cockatoo; it is the well-known phratry name, its pendant being the black cockatoo.—N. W. Thomas, *Kinship and Marriage Organizations*, 1906, 49. The sister-class of Kuurokeetch is the pelican.—Dawson, op. cit., 26. The first Kurnai marched across the country from the north-west with a bark-canoe on his head, in which was his wife Tuk (the musk-rat), he being Boran the Pelican.—Howitt, *N. T.*, 485.

spirit migrates into each of these for some time to promote their growth. If the children are full-grown, the spirit will dwell in the grandchildren for a time." After one or two years the ltana goes out of his sons or grandsons and goes back to the Isle of the Dead. He sees an ulambulamba (*Recurvirostra*) marching up and down the beach; he is frightened and flies from them. He comes to the western part of the island; there he sees one of the trees of the dead and looks at it, from everywhere asking: What sort of tree is this? He goes back to his own camp on the island and waits for rain. He sees a great black cloud mounting the western sky, and says to his friend amongst the ghosts, "You are the same as I am." They go and hunt together, catch a snake and eat it raw.[1] A second time the ghost leaves the Isle of the Dead and calls on his relatives on earth: they invite him to come and eat with them. He is horrified, and rushes back to the east of the island; other ghosts tell him to stop with them. But he wanders on: he sees a big black cloud on the sky and he goes to a raljuka tree. Suddenly the lightning strikes down just before him, "er macht eine abwehrende Geberde (ilbalama) bis ein weiterer Blitzstrahl sowohl den Baum zertrümmert als auch den Geist selber vernichtet."[2] The Loritja belief is exactly the same. The first time the soul departs it says to the mourners: "Why do you cry? I am alive. I have only gone for a short time, and soon I shall come back." But when it leaves its son, it says: "Now I shall not come back any more."[3] The whole myth, with its repeated comings and goings from the Isle of the Dead, reflects the ambivalent feelings of the living, who alternate between the wish to expel and to keep back the soul of the dead. The soul is continually horrified at the objects that remind it of its own death—that is, the living are horrified at what has happened. *Hodie mihi, cras tibi!* The second death that annihilates the memory-image of the dead is a repetition of the first; both are conditioned by the unconscious wishes of the living. It is thunder and lightning that kill the ghost, but it is also rain that brings him back to the earth. We saw that the Gnanji think the ghost will be reincarnated when it rains, and that the rain makes the two spirit-women bear the spirit-children, called Murree, who then incarnate themselves in human women, according to the South Australian belief. Just as the same motive is duplicated at birth, so it is at death; the soul is coming and going from Earth to the Isle of the Dead—that is,

[1] Feeding on small animals, eating food raw, etc., shows the survival of a primitive phase of culture; the island in the north is probably the place whence the Arunta migrated to Central Australia.—Cf. Róheim, "Primitive Man and Environment," *I. J. P. A.*, 1920. According to Eylmann, the western Arunta believe that the soul wanders to the north, where the dead live on the shores of a lake which is full of fish.—K. Eylmann, *Die Eingeborenen der Kolonie Südaustralien*, 1908, 189.

[2] Strehlow, *A. & L.*, I. 15, 16.

[3] Id., II. 7

from the Conscious to the Unconscious (Womb) till it is finally annihilated.

But if we compare this belief with that recorded by Spencer and Gillen it is not difficult to ascertain which represents the more primitive phase of evolution. To begin with, there is an evident survival of the reincarnation-belief in this myth: the years that the soul spends in the body of his son or grandson. Then there is the fact that the connexion of the ghost and the tjurunga survives amongst the western Arunta. When a man dies they take his tjurunga out of the arknanakaua, lest the sight should make his friends sad, but after about two years it is brought back again. "Should such a tjurunga break or get lost, it is not renewed. It is regarded as a sign that its existence, bound up with the tjurunga, is extinguished. Should the soul of the dead be destroyed by lightning the tjurunga body also ceases to exist after this accident."[1] And lastly, when a man is buried, his face is turned towards the tmara altjirealtja—that is, his mother's totem-centre—otherwise he could not reach the Isle of the Dead. "The body is placed in the side-chamber on its side, with its face towards the tmara altjira, so that no weight may oppress it and induce the ltana to injure its relations or remove itself quickly to the tmara altjira."[2]

According to Gillen's first account, when a native dies, his spirit is said to ascend to the home of the great Ulthaana (the emu-footed Altjira of Strehlow). This Ulthaana (same word as ghost) then throws it into the salt water, from which it is rescued by two benevolent but lesser Ulthaana, who perpetually reside on the seashore, apparently merely for the purpose of rescuing spirits who have been subjected to the inhospitable treatment of the great Ulthaana of the heavens (alkirra). Henceforth the rescued spirit of the dead man lives with the lesser Ulthaana.[3]

It is very remarkable to find this idea of one sky-spirit (hostile) and two earth-spirits (friendly) connected with eschatological beliefs in a reversed form amongst the coastal tribes. The Binbinga have two hostile sky-spirits, who can be heard singing when a man dies and who are prevented from killing the natives by a friendly spirit called Ulurkura, who lives in the woods. The Mara have the same belief.[4]

To return, however, to the body buried with its face towards the mother's totem-centre. If the man was put into the grave the other way round, he would sink down to the demons (erintja).[5] His mother's totem-centre is his mother's symbolic womb—that is,

[1] Strehlow, *A. & L.*, II. 81. [2] Louis Schulze, op. cit., 237.

[3] F. J. Gillen, "Notes on some Manners and Customs of the Aborigines," *Horn Expedition*, IV. 183.

[4] Spencer and Gillen, *Nor. T.*, 503, 504.

[5] Strehlow, II. 58. If he is turned the contrary way he goes to the demons, which is as much as to say that the demons are negative projects of the incestuous libido, where repression has turned pleasure into fear.

only if he is put in the right direction towards his mother's womb can he find the way to the uterine island other-world. It is quite evident that the island other-world is a second phase in the successive symbols, by which the same unconscious wish-fulfilment—death as a return into the mother's womb—is represented.

We are now in a position to try and sketch the probable evolution of these beliefs in worlds that differ from our own world. There is but one basis in actual experience from which a human being can project into space worlds that are different from the one we live in; previous to birth every human being lives in an environment radically different from the one we see every day, an environment where everything is far pleasanter than in this world—the mother's womb. As the repression of the Oedipus complex leads to a symbolic and projective account of birth, this original home is projected into the rocks and caves, glens and woods, pools and springs of environment. The "place from where the babies come" is the prototype of all other-worlds.

On the Daly River, Northern Territory, there is a hill called "alakyinga" in the Mulluk-mulluk language, and "verak yinda" in the dialect of the Hermite hill people. These words mean "place of children." The natives believe that the souls of future children, or perhaps the actual children, body and soul, are shut up there. They are under the care of one old man. He has to see that they do not escape and to supply them with water. This he does by means of an underground communication with the river about half a mile away. The range of which the hill in question is the last one runs right to the river. When a child is to be born, the old man sees to his business.[1] The old man who supplies the children in the hill with water (seminal fluid) through a subterranean passage (introitus vaginæ) is evidently a projection of the father-imago.

According to the Northern Chingalee it is always a new spirit-child that emanates from a rock or tree and is born as a man: the soul wanders to the north.[2] The next step would be the projection of this pre-natal state to the period after death as a narcissistic (return to the embryonic self) and incestuous (intercourse with mother in the womb) wish-fulfilment. This phase is represented by the eastern Arunta and others: the soul returns to the totem-centre. But as the tribal bonds in real life tend to replace those of the totem-group, the Unconscious meets these demands of the Reality-principle by

Totem-centre and other-world.

[1] Donald Mackillop, "Anthropological Notes on the Aboriginal Tribes of the Daly River," *Trans. R. S. S. Aust.*, XVII, 1893, 262.

[2] Mathews, *Proc. R. Geog. Soc. Queensland*, XXII, 1907, 75, 76, quoted by Strehlow, Leonhardi, l.c., II. 57. The return to the northern home of these tribes just as in the Arunta myth.

over-emphasizing the uterine symbolism of water and uniting all the souls in an island other-world.

Survivals of the totemistic complex in animistic beliefs.

Our view will evidently gain additional force if we are able to point out survivals of the totemistic birth beliefs in the other-world concepts. We remember the part played by the emu as a symbol of the mother, and that birth is attributed (in North-Western Australia) to the father having speared an emu. When the soul leaves the body it comes to a pathway; this divides into two roads, one of them is open and one is obstructed by brambles. The good soul takes the second road; this leads him towards an old and ugly, the other towards a young and fine woman. We know this road well—it is the *road of regression* that leads us through the tangled undergrowth of intrapsychic resistances to the mother-imago. He then jumps across a flaming chasm and also jumps over a rope held by two women to trip him. Now he is in Heaven and fed on heavenly diet. Finally, he is placed at a given post while some very fleet emus run past at a terrific pace; if he succeeds in driving his spear through one of the emus he is fit for introduction to Tha-tha-pulli. The shooting-stars are the spears of the departed thrown at the emu.[1] Cameron gives us a second account of these beliefs of the Wathi-Wathi with a slight variation of details. The moment the spirit leaves the body it is called Bo-oki, but afterwards the ghost of a dead man is called Boongarnitchie. The ghost having started on its road to the sky is met by another Boongarnitchie which directs it to the road for good men. After proceeding some distance he sees two roads running parallel and close together, one of which is swept clean, while the other is dirty. The spirit of a good man would choose the dirty road (regression to anal-eroticism), as it would know that the other is kept clean by bad spirits to allure him. He is next met by a woman who endeavours to seduce him, but escaping from her lures he soon meets two women holding a rope which they are twirling round like a skipping-rope. The woman who stands on the clear side of the road is blind and endeavours to trip the ghost, but keeping on the dirty road, and as far as possible from her, he avoids such mishap.

The blind woman seems to be a repetition of the seducer: she again represents actual intercourse, the talion-punishment (eye-vagina) being her blindness. Before the ghost has a place in the other-world assigned to him, Nurunduri carefully observes his eyes. If tears are flowing from one eye only it is a sign that he has only left one wife; if from both, two. If they cease to flow, he has left three, and according to the number he has left, Nurunduri

[1] A. L. P. Cameron, "Traditions and Folklore of the Aborigines of New South Wales," *Science of Man*, 1903, 46.

provides him with others.[1] We may compare this blind woman with Kui the Blind in Polynesia. Two lads go to the other-world in Tahiti in search of their departed father. Obedient to the charm of which they are possessed, the earth cleaves asunder and they find themselves in the land of Kui the Blind. She prepares food for herself which they steal; she comes out with her fish-hook and secures first merely a log and then one of the brothers. Fish for man is the usual Polynesian symbolism, but there is a special reason for employing it here. The boys say "Carefully secure thy fish before thou beest overtaken by a shark." She answers "For him that is caught by my hook there is no hope. Strong is my hook. Its name is Furnisher of Food for Immortals." The children are the fish in the womb of the mother, in this case in her negative aspect as the "dreadful mother." We shall see presently what the shark means. On seeing his brother caught, the other boy rushes in, seizes the fatal string of the fish-hook, snaps it asunder by sheer force and rescues his brother from her pitiless clutches. The brothers then enter the house of the now defenceless Kui, and discovering the stone-axe with which she is accustomed to dispatch her victims, slay her therewith. Her body is next chopped to pieces, her house pulled down and set on fire, and thus this foe of mankind is consumed.

As the "dreadful mother" is the reversed aspect of the beloved mother, this descent to the other-world is really birth, the snapping of the line being the cutting of the navel-string which frees the babe from the clutches of the mother's womb. It is not the mother who eats the children (cf. Hansel and Gretel), but the children whose first food consists of the mother. Children really steal food from their mother whilst in her womb, as in the legend, only it is not the mother who is blind but the children. This is perhaps a still deeper source of the "blind old woman" *motif* than that given above. She is blind from the point of view of the embryo, as she does not see him.

They come back to this world on the back of a shark, who turns out to be their grandfather: they find another old woman (a doubling of Kui the Blind), who has charge of their father's corpse; they kill her also and set her house on fire. The occurrence of so many "opposite aspects" is to be attributed to the fact that the myth is conceived from the standpoint of an inverted Oedipus complex, love for the father and enmity towards the mother being the dominant feelings. The myth begins by ascribing the father's death to the fact that their mother was enraged: Kui the Blind being thus a supernatural projection of the "dreadful mother."[2] We have a Mangaian version of the same myth: the god Tane

[1] Taplin, *Narrinyeri*, 61.

[2] W. W. Gill, *Myths and Songs from the South Pacific*, 1876, 250–55.

comes to the land of Kui the Blind, deludes her first with the food, then with the fish-hook, and at last lets himself be caught. She grabbed him tightly whilst demanding his name. He calmly said, " I am Tane." Kui instantly forgot her anger, and exclaimed, " Why, you are my own grandson, Tane; stay with me." Now there is no water in the land except in the coco-nuts (symbols of the womb), that are guarded by the giant lizard, the centipede, the beetle, and the mantis, who are called her children by Kui, and as she is Tane's grandmother we must say that these are, for Tane, the projections of the father-imago. He kills them all; and then slakes his thirst from the coco-nut (maternal womb). Now comes a duplicate episode with the same meaning. Tane throws (cf. the throwing of the tjurunga at conception) coco-nuts at the old woman's eyes; she cries out in agony (birth-pangs), but her eyesight is restored. That throwing something at her eyes and restoring her eyesight really means having intercourse with her and subsequently being born from her (she has her eyesight, she can see the child, the child has his eyesight; cf. the myth of the blind kangaroo-goddess) is quite evident from the sequel; Tane marries Kui's daughter Ina, that is a second edition of herself, and becomes her son.[1] In the third version of the myth it is Maui who visits the old woman; she is his grandmother and is herself called Ina the Blind.[2]

Returning to the Wathi-Wathi we find that the next obstruction is a deep and narrow pit extending between the two roads (the vagina), from which flames alternately rise and fall. Watching his opportunity, the good spirit leaps across in safety and is then met by two very old women, who take care of him till he becomes accustomed to his new abode. After a time, the deity, Tha-tha-pulli, comes with a host of spirits to see the new arrival and try his strength. A " nulla-nulla " is given by Tha-tha-pulli to one of the old women, who hands it to him. A number of emus are next driven past, at one of which the weapon is hurled and the emu stricken down.[3] When they see a shooting-star it is Tha-tha-pulli trying the strength of a new spirit.[4]

We arrive at an explanation by forming a composite picture of

[1] W. W. Gill, *Myths*, 111–114.

[2] Id., ibid., 65.

[3] We have seen above that Bahloo (the moon) partakes of the nature of both sexes. The Arunta say that " the moon is an unsexed male."—Louis Schulze, op. cit., 221. For while the crow only makes girls and the lizard boys, Bahloo lends a hand in making both. Spirits sit at the ends of the sky with ropes in their hands and will not let him pass, so when he wants to go to the earth and go on with the creation of baby-girls he has to sneak down past the spirits in the form of an emu. —K. L. Parker, *The Euahlayi Tribe*, 1905, 98. On the voyage to Kurrilwan, the home of their ancestor Byama, the Kamilaroi meet a tribe with emu-feet (genitalia), and it is said that if these succeed in touching a man's feet his feet will be transformed into those of an emu, that is sexual intercourse with them will make the wanderer one of their number.—R. H. Mathews, *Folklore*, 15.

[4] A. L. P. Cameron, " Notes of some Tribes of N.S.W.," *J. A. I.*, 1884, 364, 365.

the Kariera beliefs with those described by Cameron. As his father speared an emu (his mother) he was born. When he dies the scene is repeated with a slight modification : his father gives him the spear, and now it is his turn to "spear the emu." We have all reason to believe that the two old women and the emus both symbolize the mother-imago, the dual-number of the old women reminding us of Daramulun's two mother-wives of the two marriage-classes, and of the two women who give birth to the spirit-children in the Nimbalda myth.

The aborigines of Western Victoria believe every adult has a wraith or likeness of himself which is not visible to anyone but himself, and visible to him only before his premature death. If he is to die from the bite of a snake (narcissistic dread of castration) he sees his wraith in the sun, but in this case it appears to him in the form of an emu,[1] that is death is foreshadowed by the return of the narcissistic double into the mother's womb or, what amounts to the same thing, by an identification with the mother.[2] The two mothers also appear in the rejuvenated form as seen and desired by the infant. According to the Wide Bay blacks, the men of good character are allowed to enter the happy hunting-grounds at once, being ferried over the wide river which bounds it by two young women in a bark-canoe, one of whom subsequently becomes his wife.[3]

Another of these other-world myths may form the subject of discussion ; it will perhaps serve to bring out the part played by the father-imago in the unconscious origin of the other-world concepts. The myth is current among the natives occupying the south-east coast from Botany Bay to the Victorian boundary. There is a remarkable rock on the coast, the sloping of which is suggestive of having been worn by the feet of many persons. This has given rise to a legend among the natives that these marks were made in the rock by the feet of the spirits of many generations of natives sliding from the upper to the lower side of it.[4] It was from this rock that the shade of the native took its final departure from its present hunting-grounds, and this was accomplished in the following manner :

> A very long stem of a cabbage tree, imperceptible to human vision, reached from some unknown land across the sea to this rock. When a blackfellow died his soul went in the night

[1] Dawson, *Australian Aborigines*, 1881, 51.

[2] The sun itself is a mother-symbol—they call it "the feminine light"; the moon is the "masculine light."—Dawson, op. cit., 99.

[3] Curr, *The Australian Race*, 1886, III. 137.

[4] Cf. the leaping-place of the souls, passing through Backstairs Passage towards Kangaroo Island (see Eylmann, *Die Eingeborenen der Kolonie Südaustralien*, 1908, 189; and for parallels in Oceania, Gill, *Myths and Songs*, 1876, 159; Turner, *Samoa*, 257).

to the top of the rock, and standing there for a few moments looked out towards the sea, which is about two miles distant. Then he slid down the hollow grooves, and when he got to the lower side of the rock he could distinguish the end of a long pole on to which he jumped and walked away along it to the sea-coast and onward across the expanse of water. The pole continued over the sea;[1] following it along the ghost came to a place where flames of fire seemed to rise out of a depression in the water.[2] Bad men fell into the fire or the sea. After a while the end of the pole was reached at the other side of the sea. The traveller then continued along the track through the bush and after a time met a crow, who said, "You once frightened me," and thereupon threw a spear at him but missed him, and the man kept on his way, the crow calling him bad names and making a great noise. At another place he came to where a large native fig tree was growing, and two men were there. One of these men was standing on the ground and was some relative of the traveller; but the other man, who was up in the tree, was a vindictive person and would kill him if he got a chance. He gathers figs and squeezes them together to a quartz crystal, which has the effect of causing the figs to increase in size and weight. He then calls to the traveller to stand out in a clear space, but the soul walks into a scrubby place under the tree, and, being hungry, stoops down to pick some of the figs. The enemy in the tree then throws a bundle of figs that have been changed into a large stone at him but misses his mark. The soul now passes through a narrow rocky gorge (Symplegades!) with scrub growing on either side in which were some king-parrots of gigantic size who tried to bite him with their strong beaks, but he defended himself with his shield and succeeded in getting through the pass.[3] When he at last arrives at the happy hunting-grounds, an old dirty-looking blackfellow with a sore upon his body comes and asks, "Who came just now when the noise was made," and the other spirits say it is only the young people playing about. The hunting-grounds of this old man are separated from the other by a watercourse which he dare not pass.[4] If he were to see the new arrival he might point a bone at him. If the soul, however, is that of a greedy or troublesome fellow the crow's spear pierces him and the

[1] Cf., when the departing soul reaches the extreme edge of the cliff a large wave approaches the base, and at the same moment a gigantic Bua tree (*Beslaria taurifolia*) covered with fragrant blossoms springs up from Awaiki to receive the human spirits on its branches. There is a particular branch reserved for every tribe.—Gill, l.c., 160, 161.

[2] Cf. above, p. 197.

[3] Cf. the paroquet on the road to the other world.—Th. Williams, *Fiji and the Fijians*, 1858, I. 245.

[4] Cf. on water as a boundary of the spirit world.—Róheim, *Spiegelzauber*, 1919, 64.

> crow comes and picks mouthfuls of flesh out of him and knocks him about, after which he pulls out the spear and starts the man on the journey again. When he reaches the fig tree there is nobody to warn him of the danger, so he is stretched almost lifeless by the figs that are changed to stone. Bruised and bleeding from wounds he goes on. When he comes to the camp of his countrymen the people shout out to him that they do not want him there, and make signs for him to go on. When the scabby old man comes they tell him that a stranger has arrived, and he takes him away to his camp. The wounds made by the crow and the man in the fig tree never heal properly, and give the injured man a scabby and dirty appearance ever afterwards.[1]

We shall have to make a somewhat lengthy detour to get the key to this myth, and, speaking more generally, to the combat that awaits the soul on its journey to the other-world. Why is the soul of the dead considered dangerous, and especially so for those who are its nearest relatives? Freud reminds us of the unconscious feelings of enmity entertained by the relatives of the dead that, undergoing repression, are projected into the supposed feelings of the ghost, so that it is the mourner's own aggressive tendencies which turn upon him in the person of the vampire-dead.[2] Undoubtedly in the normal course of events the father becomes the prototype of all those who are dead.[3] It is against him that the feelings of resentment were first felt and first repressed, and the father's ghost is the vengeful demon *par excellence*. But there is another way by which the Australian rids himself of the contrition that follows the endopsychical acknowledgment of guilt—by projection to others. It is not he who is responsible for his father's death through the omnipotence of his unconscious wish; it is other men, preferably foreigners, who have caused the death of his beloved relative by their magic arts, and it is his duty as a loving son to identify himself with his father and revenge his death accordingly.[4]

When Ben-nil-long's wife died many spears were thrown and several men wounded. Ben-nil-long himself had a severe contest with Wil-le-mer-ing, whom he wounded on the thigh. Ben-nil-long had chosen the time for celebrating the funeral game in honour of his deceased wife when a whale feast had assembled a large number of natives together, among whom were several people from the north who spoke quite a different language. Ben-nil-long said repeatedly that he would not be satisfied until he had sacrificed

[1] R. H. Mathews, *Folklore of the Australian Aborigines*, 1899, 30–35.

[2] Freud, *T. & T.*, 1919, 102, 103.

[3] Cf. Roheim, *Spiegelzauber*, 1919, 226.

[4] Cf. id., ibid., 200.

someone to her ghost.[1] In Western Victoria a widower mourns for his wife three moons. Every second night he wails and recounts her good qualities and lacerates his forehead with his nails till the blood flows down his cheeks and covers his head and face with white clay. He must continue to mourn and wear the white clay for another nine months, unless he shall succeed in taking a human life in revenge for her death. If he cease wearing the clay before the expiry of three moons without taking a life, his deceased relatives say "He has told a lie," and they will attempt to kill him.[2] The reason why every death is attributed to the magical devices of unknown wizards is the fact that between all those who stand near to each other there is a certain amount of unconscious repressed ill-feeling, and the mourning ritual is essentially an expression of the pangs of remorse felt at having been responsible for the death.

That is why all contrary tendencies are repressed by a mechanism similar to that of the obsessional neurotic: the function of the continual howling and the continual praise of the dead is undoubtedly to inhibit the manifestation of the hostile feelings. Self-punishment is effected by the laceration and by the white paint laid on. These indicate a readiness to suffer at least a symbolic talion-punishment for having caused the death of the beloved: white, being the colour of the dead, shows that the mourner is dead and the ghost has its revenge. The symbol, however, is evidently not sufficient to give peace to the community and restore the equilibrium between the Conscious and the Unconscious. By wearing the colour of the dead the mourner represents the loving side of the ambivalent attitude (identification with the ghost); the second murder that he must commit in atonement for the first is the second part of a symptomatic double action which annuls the effects of the former, although at the same time it repeats the very deed which it expiates. If the atoning element of the symptomatic double action is not carried out, "he has told the relatives a lie" by putting on the mourning paint and indicating his identification with the deceased; they are then justified in regressing towards the original form in phylogenetic evolution, for which the whole ritual was merely a milder substitute,[3] and in taking his life.

The Barkunyj on the Darling River say that the ghost will not be appeased till the sorcerers' caul-fat is taken. When this is done the pipeclay worn on the head as a sign of mourning is removed.[4]

[1] Collins, *An Account of the English Colony in New South Wales*, 1804, 379.

[2] Dawson, *Australian Aborigines*, 1881, 66.

[3] The white clay is worn in mourning for the death of a chief till a person of a strange tribe is killed.—Dawson, l.c., 67. The dead promise not to haunt the tribe if sufficiently avenged.—R. Brough-Smyth, *The Aborigines of Victoria*, I. 107.

[4] E. M. Curr, *The Australian Race*, II. 199.

On the Pennefather River the avenger, who is usually one of the deceased sister's sons (instead of his own son), carries the fibula-bones wrapped in a bag and slung round his neck; besides this memento he identifies himself with the dead by eating little bits of his flesh. He is supposed to have lost the power of speech, a symptom that expresses the self-punishment for having caused his relative's death; he is as dumb as the corpse.[1] During all this loss of speech and eating of human flesh he has gradually discovered the murderer who doomed the deceased; now he regains his speech and makes a pointing-bone of the fibula he has been carrying about. If the pointing-bone does not take effect, the accused may have to stand the ordeal of having spears thrown at him, and this may lead to general fighting and trouble.[2] Eating the dead man's flesh and obtaining revenge for him are rites that have a parallel fore-conscious and a corresponding unconscious meaning. From the point of view of the former they are expressive of identification, from that of the latter both of them are outlets for pent-up animosity. The dead man is eaten, that is completely annihilated; another man is killed; the unconsciously committed murder is repeated in good earnest. The loss of speech is evidently an over-determined symptom, besides being a visible sign of the horror felt at having caused the death; and besides being expressive of identification with the dead, it also represents abstinence from the other oral function, eating. Fasting may be a form of self-punishment that is equivalent to dumbness, but, on the other hand, eating as such may represent the anthropophagous meal—such being the case, for instance, on the Lower Gulf Coast. The ritual is similar to that of the Pennefather River with slight variations. During the period of discovering the individual guilty of killing the deceased the nearer relatives, instead of losing their powers of speech, have to avoid eating red meats, e.g. opossum, bandicoot, etc.—such foods as iguana, etc., being permissible.[3] Evidently because the red meat is like the human flesh of the deceased, showing a case in which the original inhibition spreads beyond the limits of the action which it intends to repress.[4]

At Cape Bedford, when one's elder brother dies, the younger one prepares to spear the wife of the deceased, and pulls her about before the others because of the man's death; but one of the men gets hold of a spear and prevents him wounding the woman. Next day the wife of the dead man comes along crying, offering her head to all the men around to be struck; they strike her till she is covered with blood, after this they are no longer angry with

[1] Cf. Reik, "Die Bedeutung des Schweigens," *Imago*, V. 354.

[2] W. E. Roth, "Burial Ceremonies and Disposal of the Dead," *North Queensland Ethnography Bull.*, 9, 368, 369.

[3] Roth, l.c., 370.

[4] Thus it is not only prohibited to kill the father, but also the totem; not only to have intercourse with the mother, but also with all the women of the same clan.

her. If a woman dies the old men spear the husband in the leg, both being a sort of crying quits; they may have been jealous of each other, quarrelled with each other and the dead person may not have had the occasion in lifetime to settle accounts—now it is the mourners' duty to do this for him (or her).[1] When visitors come who have not seen the dead for a long time, although they used to be friendly with him, they protest against the possibility of his death being attributed to their agency: on the contrary, it is they who turn the tables of the usual projection—they throw spears at his own people, showing whom they consider responsible for his death.[2]

In the Bloomfield District, when the culprit is found, he denies having had any quarrel with the deceased, and tries to shift the blame on to somebody else; if he does not succeed in this he offers expiation by challenging his accusers to spear him. Should he come through the ordeal successfully, much depending upon his previous conduct and the influence of his powerful friends, his accusers will cling round his neck and make friends again, finally fixing the guilt generally upon the weakest tribe and its most friendless member. In this district someone must be killed for the death of every important male aboriginal.[3] Although there is a certain amount of repressed ill-will between all those who are closely related to each other, and hence the mourning ritual and the duty of revenge obtains for relations (and members of the same clan, tribe, etc.) of all sorts, it seems very probable that the repressed current of animosity is strongest between father and son. This may lead to an inhibition of the identification-tendency as in the case of the Dieri: the nearest relations eat of each other after death, but the father does not eat of his children nor the children of their sire.[4] The typical avenger is the son: it is he who, more than all others, is obliged to project his own repressed feelings into the person of the wizard. If once the unconscious hatred against the jealous sire is projected into the figure of an enemy ("It is not I who hated my father and thus caused his death, but X."), the feeling itself may become manifest in an altered form: "I do not hate the father (I love him), but X., whom I must kill to show that I am not responsible for my father's death." At this point there is a curious return of repressed elements, which shows that the enemy who must be killed after death is a duplicate of the father-imago, and the deed is a repetition of the very deed it is meant to expiate: the enemy is represented by his father-symbol, *by his totem*.

In the Belyando River tribe the culprit was determined by

[1] Roth, *Burial Ceremonies*, 380, 381. The meaning of the self-inflicted wounds as a form of self-accusation is clearly brought out in this ceremony.

[2] Id., ibid., 382.

[3] Id., ibid., 387.

[4] A. W. Howitt, *N. T.*, 1904, 449.

the following method: The ground which had been smoothed round the grave would be carefully examined, and if any animal, bird or reptile had passed over it, its track would be easily seen and the murder be assigned to some member of the tribe in whose dietary scale the animal, bird or reptile is included (these being subclasses with positive totems). If a brown or black snake had been there, some Wongoo would be declared to be the culprit; if a carpet-snake, an Obad; if a dog, a Banbey, and so on.[1]

The totem in the post-mortem inquest.

Amongst the Buandik, a man does not kill or use as food any of the animals of the same subdivision to which he belongs. These animals they call wingong (friends) or tumanang (their flesh), and they believe that the killing of his wingong will hasten a person's death. In the blood revenge arrangement these subdivisions bear a prominent part, and in cases of uncertain death the tuman of the slayer will appear at the inquest.[2]

The Australian ritual of eating the dead and obtaining revenge for them as a repetition of death is paralleled in a symbolic form by the custom of the Bini in Southern Nigeria, where on the first day of the burial ceremonies some families will make soup out of their totemic plant or animal with which to sacrifice to the feet of the dead man. The sacrificed portion is sometimes put to the lips of the members of the family and then thrown away.[3] On the other hand, we find the same thing in a symbolic but inhibited form in the Waduman tribe, for if a man of any totemic group dies the animal or plant is taboo to all members of that totemic group until after the performance of a special ceremony.[4]

If we inquire into the question of the duration of the soul's journey on the one hand and of the mourning ceremonies on the other, we shall find that everywhere, where information is forthcoming, the two periods correspond to each other.[5] It is not going too far to see a mythical reflection of the ritual in the belief, and thus the fight for the soul at the grave would be projected into the myth as a fight of the soul at the entrance of the other-world. Mourners and the soul are identified in a certain sense, and as the mourners or their

The fights of the soul on the road to the other-world are mythical reflections of the combats fought out by the mourners at the grave.

[1] J. Muirhead, *Belyando River.* Curr. III. 28. When a person dies the grave is swept, and according to the track they see next morning they determine the totem to which the murderer belonged.—K. L. Parker, *Euahlayi*, 89.

[2] Fison and Howitt, *Kamilaroi and Kurnai*, 149.

[3] Frazer, *T. & E.*, II. 588.

[4] Spencer, *N. T. N. T. A.*, 198.

[5] On the question of "delayed burial" and the journey of the soul to the other world, see Hertz, "Contribution à l'étude d'une représentation collective de la mort," *Année sociologique*, X. 1907. A van Gennep, *Les Rites de Passage*, 1909, 209. Negelein, "Die Reise der Seele ins Jenseits," *Zeitschrift des Vereins für Volkskunde*, XI. 161, 149, 263. N. W. Thomas, "Disposal of the Dead in Australia," *Folk Lore*, XIX. 388. G. Elliot Smith, "On the Significance of the Geographical Distribution of Mummification," *Manchester Memoirs*, 1915, LIX. No. 10.

representative have to obtain a victory in a combat before they can return to the world of normal human beings, the soul must conquer its principal enemy personified in the demon on the road before it can enter the other-world. Accounts must be squared, the law of talion must be observed. This is done for the soul by the mourners, but it has to be squared also against the soul on the Mythical Journey. The crow, who attacks the soul, says, "You once frightened me."[1] The soul of the Macateca Indian has to pass through the realm of the dogs, bulls, serpents and birds. He who has been friendly to the animals has nothing to fear from them, but if anybody has been wicked to them or has perhaps killed one, they will bite his feet and will not let him pass.[2] This retribution-fear is most probably rooted in the infantile Oedipus complex; everybody committed these unconscious sins against his father in infantile life: it is from that quarter that he has to dread retribution. Moreover, as everybody "killed his father" in the very act of obtaining revenge for him, everybody has good reason to dread his father's ghost.

If we remember the part played by the crow in cosmological legend, and as one of the phratric totems, we shall be inclined to say that the crow who attacks the man on the road is a representative of the father-imago. The next adventure the soul undergoes is at the fig tree: we see an enemy who attacks and a relative who protects the soul, which tallies with the ambivalent splitting of the paternal-imago in mourning ritual: there also we have the enemy who must be punished and the father whose soul is to be appeased (together with the relatives who help in the enterprise). The gigantic parrots that try to bite the soul evidently represent the castration-complex which can hardly be absent when the soul has just fought the father and is about to enter the maternal womb. Lastly, we have the dirty-looking old man, who represents the Father-Imago as embodied in Society; for those who have behaved ill towards Society, Society presents but an ill-aspect. That the dirty appearance of the old man is projected into him from the endopsychical dissatisfaction of the individual is evident from the fact that the ghosts who live with him have the same dirty aspect as himself.

All this certainly partakes of the nature of a conjecture, but that it is at least legitimate guesswork we are indulging in, is, I think, proved by the beliefs of the Lushei. The first man is said to have been Pupawla; he died before all those born after him. This Pupawla, the man who died first, shoots at those who died after him with a big pellet-bow, but at some he cannot shoot.[3]

[1] Mathews, 32.

[2] W. Bauer, "Aberglaube der Macateca Indianer," *Z. E.*, 1908, 858.

[3] Shakespeare, *The Lushei-Kuki Clans*, 1912, 62.

These are (*a*) the Hlamzuih, the first born who died shortly after birth and are buried without ceremony under the house,[1] the reason probably being that these children die before they can evolve an Oedipus complex; (*b*) Thangchuah, that is, those who have killed a man, elephant, bear, sambhur, barking-deer, wild boar, wild mithan, and by giving feasts in honour of the ancestor[2] (that is, conquering and appeasing the father); (*c*) he may not shoot at a man who had enjoyed three virgins or seven women who were not virgins,[3] erotic victories being evidently considered as good a title to the entry of the other-world as murder—both corresponding to one of the two main elements of the Oedipus complex. At any rate it is evident that the man who died first represents the father-imago, and thus if we see that the emus hunted in the other-world correspond to the pre-natal emu-hunt, we may say that the Fight with the Demon is a post-mortem projection of the pre-natal Duel with the Father.

The world after death is a repetition of the existence previous to life: the soul goes back to the womb whence it came.

To sum up: the evolution of the other-world in Australia is clearly traceable through the following stages: (*a*) Projection of the pre-natal environment into the actual environment gives rise to totem-centres as baby-caves. (*b*) Narcissistic regressive tendencies of old age are continued in an uterine regression after death. (*c*) There is a narcissistic tendency of a libidinal repression of the unbearable concept of total annihilation, and (*d*) the feelings felt by the father towards his father are revived in relation to his son: this leads to the idea that the children are the dead re-born and that ghosts go back to the totem-centre. (*e*) The double concept of a pre-natal post-mortem world splits into two; the form which projects the first into the future (ghost-land) long survives after the disappearance of the original (baby-land), although it conserves traces of its primitive origin.

[1] Shakespeare, *The Lushei-Kuki Clans*, 1912, 86.
[2] Id., ibid., 64, 88.
[3] Id., ibid., 62.

CHAPTER VI

INTICHIUMA CEREMONIES

WE have already pointed out that the mythical accounts of the Alcheringa, the beliefs intended to explain childbirth, and the intichiuma ceremonies are three aspects of the same complex. The totem-ancestors were closely connected with the Churinga ; it is from these Churinga that the spirit-children are supposed to emanate and the same Churinga are used in the ceremonies, the object of which is to make the totem-animal increase and multiply.

Intimate connexion between Alcheringa myth, childbirth belief, and intichiuma.

In connexion with the times at which the ceremonies are held, it may be said that while the exact time is fixed by the Alatunja in each case, the matter is largely dependent on the nature of the season. The Intichiuma are closely associated with the breeding of animals and the flowering of the plants with which each totem is respectively identified, and as the increase of the number of the totemic animal or plant is the object of the ceremony, it is most naturally held at a certain season. In Central Australia the seasons are limited, so far as the breeding of animals and the flowering of plants is concerned, to two—a dry one of uncertain and often great length, and a rainy one of short and often irregular occurrence.[1] The rainy season is followed by an increase in animal life and an exuberance of plant growth, which almost suddenly transforms what may have been a sterile waste into a land rich in various forms of animals, none of which has been seen perhaps since many months, and gay with the blossoms of endless flowering plants. In case of many of the totems it is just when there is promise of the approach of a good season that it is customary to hold the ceremony.[1] Neither the category of time nor that of space is a negligible quantity in trying to pierce the complicated strata of historic development that go to make up a ceremony of this sort. They are performed in the breeding season of nature, in places that we have recognized as symbolic equivalents of the maternal womb.

The Intichiuma ceremonies are performed at the breeding season of nature in places which must be interpreted as symbolic equivalents of the uterus.

When an Intichiuma is about to be performed the indispensable Churinga are brought out of the Ertnatulunga. The Intichiuma ground of the Honey-ant totem is situated in a depression in a rocky range at a considerable elevation above the surrounding plains, and

[1] Spencer and Gillen, *N. T.*, 169, 170.

all over the depression are blocks of stone standing up on end and leaning in all directions, each of which is associated with a Honey-ant man of the Alcheringa. On the east side of the pit there is a mulgy tree, which is the abode of the spirit of an Alcheringa man, whose duty it was to guard the sacred ground. In the centre of the pit there is a stone, which projects about eighteen inches above the ground and is the Nanja of an Alcheringa man who originated here and performed Intichiuma.[1]

The Intichiuma ceremony of the Kangaroo totem is performed at the Nanja stone of a great Alcheringa kangaroo.[2] When an Intichiuma (mbatjalkatjuma) is about to be performed the head man who has the charge of the ertnatulunga (arknanaua) or holy cavern orders a place to be swept clear near the arknanaua in the totem-centre, and has the Churinga brought out of the arknanaua and greased with fat and red ochre. The performers must either belong to the totem whose Intichiuma is about to be performed or at least it must be their altjirra (maternal totem).[3] Here the Intichiuma can only be performed in the totem-centre in the same spot where the spirit-children are incarnated.

In the Warramunga tribe, on the other hand, each totemic group has usually one great ancestor, who arose in some special spot and walked across the country making various natural features as he did so, and leaving behind him spirit-individuals who have since been reincarnated. The Intichiuma ceremony of the totem really consists in tracking these ancestors' paths and repeating one after the other ceremonies commemorative of what are called the mungai spots, the equivalent of the oknanikilla amongst the Arunta (totem-centres, that is places where the great ancestor left the spirit-children behind).[4] Any convenient place may be chosen by the Warramunga for the performance, but though this modification, this adjustment to the Reality Principle, seems to have obscured the original meaning of the rite, the unconscious meaning comes out again in the fact[5] that the original mungai spots are represented by highly conventionalized drawings, by concentric circles painted either on the ceremonial ground or on the body of the performers.[6]

The Intichiuma as such is a ceremony that is connected—in space, with a symbolic representation of the womb; in time, with the general breeding season of nature. We shall proceed to quote the account given by Oldfield of the Watchandie (Western Australia) ceremony called Caaro; we think there is sufficient evidence to prove this to be an instructive variant of the Central Australian Intichiuma.

The Caaro ceremony of the Watchandie.

[1] Spencer and Gillen, *N. T.*, 187.
[2] Id., ibid., 194.
[3] Strehlow, *A. & L.*, III. 2.
[4] Spencer and Gillen, *Nor. T.*, 297
[5] The ground-drawings are, except for a single case, absent in the Arunta tribe —Spencer and Gillen, *Nor. T.*, 737.
[6] Cf. G. Durkheim, *Les formes élémentaires de la vie religieuse*, 1912, 532, 533.

"Like the beasts of the field, the savage has but one time for copulation in a year—a season marked out by nature, and determined by the abundance of food and the comparative ease with which it is to be procured, as well as by the genial warmth of the season. The assemblage of these conditions is essential to the proper performance of this act in man and beast, and accordingly we find that spring has been accounted the season of love in all ages and climates.[1] About the middle of spring, when the yams are in perfection, when the young of all animals are abundant, and when eggs and other nutritious food are to be had, the Watchandies begin to think of holding their grand semi-religious Festival of Caaro, preparatory to the performance of the important duty of procreation. At the time of the first new moon after the yams are ripe the Watchandies begin to lay in a stock of all kinds of food sufficient to subsist upon during the continuance of the ceremonial. On the eve of the feast the women and the children retire from the company of the men, and henceforth, until the conclusion of the ceremony, the men are not permitted to look on a female. The men, thus left to themselves, rub their bodies with a mixture of charcoal ashes and wallaby fat, after which, having dug a large pit in the ground, they retire to rest. Early next morning they reassemble and proceed to decorate themselves with a mixture of ochre and emu-fat, dressing their hair with shavings and garlands. They dance round the pit they have dug, shouting, singing, and some few whistling (this they never do in their common corrobories), and thus they continue all night long, each in turn snatching a few moments for rest and gormandizing. Every figure of their dances, every gesture, the burden of all their songs, is calculated to inflame their passions. The pit is so dug and decorated with bushes as to represent the private parts of a female. As they dance they carry the spear before them to simulate priapus; every gesture is obscene and the character of the songs in vogue on such occasions may be understood from the following: Bool-lie (hair on female private parts), neera (none), bool-lie neera Bool-lie neera, Wadaga (private parts of female).[2] At the conclusion of the ceremony the men copulate with the women; then, to mark the scene of their orgies, they place sticks in the ground, which is a tabooed place, anyone looking on it will infallibly fall sick and die. For some time after the feast the men who have taken part wear shavings in their hair, to distinguish them as Caaro men."[3] The season is the same as

[1] On the evidence for a human or pre-human pairing season, see E. Westermarck, *The History of Human Marriage*, 1901, 25–38.

[2] The translation usually given in anthropological books that refer to this ritual, "Non fossa, non fossa, sed cunnus" (cf. *Globus*, XVIII. 230) seems to be erroneous; at any rate I cannot find "Bool-ie" in the sense of "fossa" in the vocabulary given by Oldfield. "Bool-ie" means hair on the female private part.—A. Oldfield, "The Aborigines of Australia," *T. of the E. S.*, III. 1865, 295.

[3] Oldfield, op. cit., 230, 231.

with the Intichiuma ceremonies, and the pit that represents the female genital organ corresponds exactly to the Ertnatulunga as a symbolic uterus. The whistling corresponds to the characteristic vibrating sounds produced at the Intichiuma, whilst the garlands and shavings in the hair of the men are the equivalents of the peculiar head-dresses made up of mulga-branches and fur-string in which the tjurunga are hidden at the Intichiuma.[1] The absence of the women, the tabooed character of the place, would accord with the general character of the Intichiuma,[2] whilst the closing feature of a general promiscuous intercourse is absent in the Intichiuma ritual. Unless, then, our parallel be a mistake, we shall expect to find some ritual survival of this feature.

Intichiuma as substitute for coitus in traditions.

In certain traditions we find magical and totemic ceremonies as a substitute for coitus. Intercourse is attempted by the hero but declined by the women, whereupon the hero straightway proceeds to perform magical ceremonies. An old man named Illipa came to a camp of Yelka (*Cyperus rotundus*) women and tried to cohabit with one of them. She resisted him; he struck her on the neck with his tomahawk and killed her (killing = coitus). The old man went back to his camp, where he made ceremonies of the Wild-Cat totem, and at last died there forming a big oknanikilla. The man was a Panunga and the women a Purula whom he might lawfully have married.[3]

A Dieri legend equally points to magical ceremonies as a substitute for intercourse between an old man and young girls; but in these cases it is the "daughters" (tribal) of the old man who frustrate his desire. He goes forth thinking of revenge, as his incestuous desires are not satisfied. Through his songs he causes plants to grow,[4] that is he performs a real Intichiuma.

These legends emphasize the fact that the totemic magic is the result of a compromise formation between the libido (as personified by the old men) and repression (represented by the resisting women) It seems also to indicate that the repression is directed primarily against the incestuous manifestation of the libido.[5] If we can point out certain seemingly unimportant but ever-recurring details in the complicated and elaborate structure of a variable ritual and find out the meaning of these details, we shall be probably very near to the unconscious meaning of the ritual itself.

[1] Strehlow, *A. & L.*, III. 3–5.

[2] An alternative hypothesis would be that the Caaro is an initiation. This view finds strong support in the last sentence of the account quoted above. We shall see that the two possibilities are not irreconcilable.

[3] Spencer and Gillen, *Nor. T.*, 395.

[4] Howitt, *N. T.*, 781.

[5] In the first legend the connexion would have been permissible according to tribal law; nevertheless it is an old man (Father) who desires a young woman (daughter). (Killing of the two girls as in the other variant.)

Such a common feature of all Intichiuma rites are the quivering and shaking movements of the performers. In the Honey-Ant ceremony the performer pauses every now and then to quiver.[1] In the water Intichiuma the head-man quivers his body and legs in the most extraordinary way, more even than is customary in other ceremonies, in many of which a quivering movement is a characteristic feature.[2] "As soon as all the preparations for the ceremony have been completed, one of the old men utters a loud long-drawn exclamation, waving his hollowed hand in front of his mouth, producing vibratory sounds. At this call the young men run up and perform rhythmical movements to the sounds 'wa-wa-wa-jai-jai-jai,' circling round the old man. The Arunta call the young men's performance warkuntama. In current Arunta 'wa' means 'yes,' but in this connexion means rather 'to make good;' 'jai' means 'move yourself, move your bodies in trembling movements, tremble.' The call is thus a request to the performer to play his part, but at the same time the young men express their applause by whirling round him." [3]

Quivering.

This quivering movement is absent from scarcely any of the Arunta or Loritja rituals as described by Strehlow.[4] In the Urabunna rain-intichiuma the performer rose from the ground to a stooping position, quivering his body and turning his head from side to side.[5] In an Arunta ceremony connected with the Unchalka-grub totem the performer quivers with his extended arms or wriggles in imitation of the grub.[6] In a ceremony of the Kaitish and Unmatjera the performers swayed their bodies, and wriggled backwards and forwards on their knees.[7] Fortunately, the legends give a clue to these movements. In the Nullakun tribe each of the Alcheringa (Musmus) ancestors is supposed to have had numbers of spirit-children who emanated from them when they shook their bodies during the performance of corrobories. It is these who are now constantly entering lubras and being born.[8] In the Mungarai tribe, whenever the ancestors stopped in their wanderings they performed ceremonies, and when doing so shook themselves, with the result that spirit-children (mall-mall), who, of course, belonged to the totem of the ancestor, emanated from their bodies. These spirit-children now go into the right lubras and are born as natives.[9] Warramunga tradition says that after coming up out of the earth the black snake made the creek now called Tennant Creek and travelled on to the Macdonnal Range, which indeed he also created. As he went along he made thuthu or sacred ceremonies (the representations of which are now performed by his descendents) and where he did so he left

[1] Spencer and Gillen, *N. T.*, 189.
[2] Id., ibid., 192.
[3] Strehlow, *A. & L.*, III. 4, 5.
[4] Id., ibid., III. 2 et passim.
[5] Spencer and Gillen, *Nor. T.*, 285.
[6] Id., ibid., 180; *N. T.*, 189.
[7] Id., *Nor. T.*, 186, 187; *N. T.*, 192.
[8] Spencer, *N. T. N. T. A.*, 267.
[9] Id., ibid., 266.

spirit-children behind him. When he performed the ceremonies he always shook himself, preparatory to going on to the next place, and this shaking was represented in the two next ceremonies which were associated with the small rockholes at the foot of the Macdonnal Range. This shaking of the body, which is very characteristic of these ceremonies, is done in imitation of an old ancestor who is reported to have always shaken himself when he performed sacred ceremonies. The spirit-individuals used to emanate from him just as the white down flies off from the bodies of the performers at the present day when they shake themselves.[1] We have recognized the spirit individuals as representative of the spermatozoa (seed), now we see that the white down, a characteristic feature of these ceremonies,[2] represents the same concept. If the white down is a "spirit-child" or spermatozoön, the wriggling which makes it fly off in all directions (spirit-children emanate) is a symbolic survival of the rhythmic movements of coitus.

This conclusion will be corroborated by examining two other constant elements of the Intichiuma ritual, rubbing and blood-letting. In the Intichiuma of the Witchetty-grub totem (Arunta) the stomachs of the men are rubbed with the Churinga uchaqua (represents the chrysalis stage from which the adult animal emerges) and the Churinga unchima (the egg).[3] Before the ceremony of the Hakea flower totem commences the pit is carefully swept clean by an old Hakea flower man, who then strokes the stone all over with his hands. After this the men sit around the stone (which represents a mass of Hakea flowers); by the side of it is the Nanja tree of an Alcheringa woman, and a considerable time is spent in singing chants, the burden of which is a reiterated invitation to the tree to flower much and to the blossoms to be full of honey. The stone is regarded as a Churinga and is forbidden to women, children and uninitiated men.[4] When the Intichiuma of the Manna totem is being performed the headman climbs on the top of a large boulder that represents Manna and discloses to view a Churinga that has been buried there ever since the Alcheringa, and is also supposed to represent a mass of Ilpirra. He rubs the boulder with the Churinga, after which he takes the smaller stones and with these rubs the same spot while the other men sit around and sing loudly, telling the dust produced by the rubbing of the stones to go and produce a plentiful supply of Manna on the mulga trees. Then with the twigs of the mulga he sweeps away the dust which has gathered on the surface of the stones, the idea being to cause it to settle on the mulga trees and so produce Ilpirra.[5]

Rubbing.

1 Spencer and Gillen, *Nor. T.*, 301. Spencer, *N. T. N. T. A.*, 266.

2 Totemic ceremonies are called "quabara undattha" = down ceremonies. *Nor. T.*, 179.

3 Spencer and Gillen, *N. T.*, 174, 175.

4 Id., ibid., 184, 185.

5 Id., ibid., 185, 186.

In the Honey-Ant ceremony a stone which has been taken out is rubbed over reverently with their hands by the old men and then rubbed over with the smaller stone, after which it is replaced in the ground.[1] In a kangaroo ceremony the stone is rubbed by the Alatunja and then examined by those present. The sides of the stone are worn smooth by constant rubbing.[2] They stroke the drawing of the snake on the back of the performers, an action which is supposed to please the Alcheringa snake on whose account the ceremony is performed.[3] In the Grass-seed ceremony the Alatunja takes two of the Churinga, red-ochres them and decorates them with lines and dots of down, the latter representing the grass-seed. When this is done he rubs them together so that the down flies off in all directions.[4] We know what the white down that flies about means and it seems that the rubbing is but a symbolic repetition of the friction produced by coitus.

The Yaroma is a hairy demon that eats the blackfellows. When one of the monsters is heard in the vicinity of camp during the evening the people keep silent and rub their genitalia with their hands and puff or spit in his direction.[5] The Churinga unites the individual not only with the totem ancestor but also with the totem-animal or plant itself, and gives him the power to multiply the animal and make it grow fat the same way as the ancestor did. "If the tjurunga is smeared with fat and red ochre, creative power emanates from it which has a powerful effect on the totem ; as the old men said, when the tjurunga is smeared, totem animals jump out of it."[6]

This reminds us of the erathipa stone that has to be rubbed for spirit-children to emanate from it. The fat used for greasing the stone is evidently symbolic of semen, and this explains the kangaroo fat laid aside by the hunter in North-West Australia, out of which spirit-children are said to emanate and incarnate themselves in the child in the womb of the hunter's wife as well as the magical value attached to fat all over Australia.[7] The tjurunga from which man originates is his father's body, the father being represented by his mythical projection in the Father-Imago, the Alcheringa ancestor, or more precisely by stone Churinga and rocks, a choice which may be attributed to the fact that hard substances are the best symbols of the penis in erection. Smearing the tjurunga with fat would then be a symbolical repetition of onanistic proceedings.[8] The close

[1] Spencer and Gillen, *N. T.*, 187.

[2] The stone represents the tail of an Alcheringa kangaroo.—Spencer and Gillen, *N. T.*, 200.

[3] Spencer and Gillen, *Nor. T.*, 300.

[4] Id., ibid., 292.

[5] Mathews, *E. N.*, 159.

[6] Strehlow, *A. & L.*, II. 76, 77.

[7] Cf. Róheim : *Imago*, VII. 20–22.

[8] According to a communication from Dr. Hollós, a patient of his in the lunatic asylum attributes creative force to the ritual of rubbing. He says : " When I rub myself, then Adam is born." Thus both the psychotic (dementia præcox) and the Australian native regress to an infantile form of the libidinal impulse, which they substitute for coitus, declaring that this will bring forth human or animal beings.

parallel which connects the Intichiuma ritual with the childbirth belief is well brought out by this rubbing rite. If a man wishes to make the ratapa emerge from the erathippa stone, all he has to do is to mutter an incantation to this effect and rub the stone with his hands. To cause a child to enter a woman a Kaitish man will take a Churinga and carry it to a special spot where there is a stone called "kwerka-punga" (child-stone), at the same time asking the "kurinah" or spirit of the child to go straight into the woman.[1] It is in full accordance with the ways of thinking of a primitive people to suppose that both humanity and the totem species will be multiplied by rubbing the mother's womb (child-stone) with the father's penis (Churinga).

The autoplastic character of Australian culture.

The poverty and extreme primitiveness of the material culture of the Central Australian natives is perhaps best emphasized by the fact that they have not yet completely attained the stage of evolution in worldly goods that clearly marks off Man from the Animal kingdom. Man accommodates himself to environment by acting on it. He does not grow fur to meet the requirements of a cold climate, but he uses the skin of animals; he has no claws for attacking other beasts, but weapons the materials of which are derived from environment itself. The Australian native has conserved the rudiments of a pre-human stage of development; his culture is autoplastic (to use a word coined by Ferenczi); in a certain degree he uses materials derived from his own body for practical, ornamental and ceremonial purposes. Strings used for various purposes are made of human hair.[2] Strings of animal or human hair are used for corroboree armlets.[3] Belts of human hair are used in North-Western Australia.[4] Hair strings used as charms against sickness are made of hair from the beard.[5] In the Arunta tribe a man's hair goes either to his brother-in-law or his wife's brother (tribal). A man receives hair: (*a*) From his actual mother-in-law (his principal supply); (*b*) from a son-in-law; (*c*) from his brother-in-law. In addition to this he will sometimes receive hair-string in return for a favour rendered.[6] Human blood is required as gum to fix the down on the bodies of the performers during the ceremonies.[7] Blood may be given by young men to old men with a view of strengthening the latter.[8] When very thirsty and no water is procurable men will either drink their own blood, obtained by cutting open a vein in the arm, or else they will exchange blood with another man. Sometimes under the same

1 Spencer and Gillen, *N. T.*, 338. Id., *Nor. T.*, 271.

2 Spencer, *N. T. N. T. A.*, 411.

3 H. Basedow, "Notes on the Natives of Bathurst Island," *J. A. I.*, 1913, 297.

4 A. R. Brown, "Three Tribes," *J. A. I.*, 1913, 167.

5 A. J. Peggs, "Notes on the Aborigines of Roebuck Bay, Western Australia," *Folk-Lore*, XIV. 365.

6 Spencer and Gillen, *N. T.*, 465, 466.

7 Spencer, *N. T. N. T. A.*, 144.

8 Spencer and Gillen, *N. T.*, 461.

conditions they will sprinkle blood over one another's heads with the idea of thereby cooling each other. But it is very natural that this poverty of external resources should go hand in hand with a corresponding autoerotic fixation of the libido which is demonstrated by the still greater ceremonial use of portions of their own body, or objects unconsciously equated with such portions.

The drawing of blood from the body is of very frequent occurrence in all tribes in connexion with the performance of ceremonies. Its most common use is to fasten the down used for drawing designs either on the man's body or some implement. For this purpose it is either taken from the arm or from the subincised urethra. It is astonishing what an enormous amount of blood is used for decorative purposes by these savages, one of whom will think nothing of bleeding himself perhaps twice a day for a week or two in succession.[1] We are here concerned primarily with the meaning of blood-letting in intichiuma and analogous rites, and we only intend to mention the other variants of the custom in so far as the parallels will prove indispensable to our purpose.

Blood-letting.

When the Kalkadun of the Selwyn Ranges make rain the feather down of the emu is stuck with blood over the whole face, neck and chest, back and front, down to the waist, including the upper limbs as far as the wrists.[2] In the Dieri tribe, when they wish to make rain, all the men huddle together; an old man takes a sharp flint and bleeds two men who are especially inspired by the Murramurra inside the arm below the elbow on one of the leading arteries, the blood being made to flow on the men sitting around, during which the two men throw handfuls of down, some of which adheres to the blood, the rest floating in the air. The blood symbolizes the rain and the down the clouds.[3] In the rain Intichiuma of the Kaitish tribe small pieces of white down are thrown about at intervals. The white down represents the clouds and throwing it about will make the rain fall.[4] In the Intichiuma of the Emu totem, several of the men, the Alatunja and his two sons amongst them, each opened a vein in their arms and allowed the blood to stream out until the surface of a patch of ground occupying a space of about three square yards was saturated with it. The blood was allowed to dry, and in this way a hard and hardly permeable surface was prepared on which it was possible to paint a design. The sacred design of the Emu totem was then outlined on the ground.[5] In the Hawk ceremony the men let blood flow into their shields, in the Dove Intichiuma the blood flows on to a stone Churinga.[6] In the Water-hen ceremony the blood flows into a crevice in the rocks.[7]

[1] Spencer and Gillen, *Nor. T.*, 596.

[2] Roth, *S. M. M.*, 10.

[3] Curr, II. 66, 67 (Gason). Cf. Eylmann, *Die Eingeborenen der Kolonie Südaustralien*, 1908, 209.

[4] Spencer and Gillen, *N. T.*, 179.

[5] Strehlow, *A. & L*, III. 43.

[6] Id., ibid., III. 43, 46.

[7] Id., ibid., III. 56.

In the Lizard ceremony the old men let their blood flow on dry leaves in a crevice,[1] in the Snake Intichiuma it drips into a shield.[2] In the Intichiuma of the Hakea flower totem the old leader asks one of the young men to open a vein in his arms, which he does and allows the blood to sprinkle freely over the stone while the other men continue "singing" the Unjiamba tree and asking it to flower much. The blood flows until the stone is completely covered, the flowing of blood being supposed to represent the preparation of Abmoara, a very favourite beverage of the natives,[3] made by steeping the flower in water. As soon as the stone is covered with blood the ceremony is complete. The stone is regarded as a Churinga and the spot is ekirinja to the uninitiated.[4] That the reference to the Abmoara drink is merely a rationalization of the real purpose of the rite adapted to the special requirements of a Hakea flower ceremony is self-evident.

A meaning that is applicable not only to one totem but very probably holds good for all, is given in the various kangaroo ceremonies. In the ceremony of the ara (*Macropus rufus* Desm), "the old men open a vein of the upper arm, allowing the blood to flow into a plate; the blood is then poured out on to a place with hard earth where in prehistoric times an ara altjirangamitjina rested or where he is said to have become a tjurunga. This blood, poured forth on the earth, makes the kangaroos in the earth grow and come out of the ground." [5]

In the cult of the aranga (grey kangaroo, *Macropus robustus* Gould), "the old men open a vein in the arm and allow the blood to flow on to a rock where in prehistoric times an aranga-altjirangamitjina rested or tjurungeraka. By this means many grey kangaroos came forth from the earth." [6]

In the Intichiuma of the Kangaroo totem at Undiara the same element of the ritual is found as follows: "When the painting is done a certain number of young men, two or three Panunga and Bultara and five or six Purula and Kumara, go on to the top of the ledge. The former sit down at the left and the latter at the right side, and then they open veins in their arms and allow the blood to spurt out over the edge of the ceremonial stone on the top of which they are seated.

[1] Strehlow, *A. & L.*, III. 67. [2] Id., ibid., III. 71. Cf. 80, 87, 89.

[3] Curiously enough the same term (Abmoara) is used to express the mutual relationship existing between a young man and the old man under whose charge he has been placed during the Engwura ceremony.—Spencer and Gillen, *N. T.*, 645.

[4] Id., ibid., 185.

[5] Strehlow, *A. & L.*, III. 13. "These kangaroo ceremonies, as we may call them, are usually performed at some rock or stone specially sacred to this particular animal and believed by the natives to have imprisoned within it, or at any rate in its near neighbourhood, a number of kangaroo spirits, who are only awaiting the due performance of the ancient ceremonies to set them free from their prison and again go forth and become once more embodied."—H. Pitts, *Children of Wild Australia*, 1917, 50, 51.

[6] Strehlow, *A. & L.*, III. 14.

While this is taking place the men below watch the performers and sing chants referring to the increase of the numbers of kangaroos which the ceremony is supposed to ensure."[1] The members of each totem claim to have the power of increasing the number of the animal or plant, and in this respect the tradition connected with Undiara, the great centre of the Kangaroo totem, is of especial interest. In the Alcheringa a special kangaroo was killed by kangaroo men,[2] and its body brought to Undiara and deposited in a cave close by the water-hole. The rocky ledge arose to mark the spot, and into this entered its spirit part and also the spirit parts of many other kangaroo animals (not men) who came subsequently and went down into the earth here. The rock is, in fact, the Nanja stone of the kangaroo animals, and to them this particular rock has just the same relationship as the water-hole close by has to the men. The one is full of spirit kangaroo animals, just as the other is full of spirit men and women.

The purpose of the Intichiuma ceremony at the present day—so say the natives—is by means of pouring out the blood of kangaroo men upon the rock to drive out in all directions the spirits of the kangaroo animals and so to increase the number of the animals. The spirit kangaroo enters the kangaroo animal in just the same way as the spirit-child enters the Kangaroo woman.[3]

If we add to this the fact that though we have no imitation of human coitus in the Central Australian ritual that could be said to correspond to the Watchandie Caaro scene, yet the intercourse of the kangaroos is imitated in the kangaroo Intichiuma of the Loritja,[4] we shall be in a position to draw three inferences of the very greatest importance. (*a*) That the pouring out of blood is a symbolical effusion of semen. (*b*) That the childbirth beliefs and the Intichiuma ritual have one common root in the Unconscious. (*c*) That the ritual must originally, like the belief, have had to do with the multiplication of human beings whence it has been projected into nature.

We remember that Frazer has shown in connexion with initiation ceremonies and the bullroarer that the "same processes which had been formerly directed to the multiplication of the species were now directed also, on the principle of sympathetic magic, to promote the fertility of the earth." We think we can show that the same evolution has taken place in the case of the Intichiuma ceremonies if we substitute "the fertility of the totem animal" for "the fertility of the earth."[5] We shall attempt to show the common root to which both initiation and Intichiuma ceremonies must be traced back,[6] and at any rate it is obvious that the bullroarer (the instrument

1 Spencer and Gillen, *N. T.*, 201.
2 Cf. the tradition.—Id., ibid., 198, 199.
3 Id., ibid., 206, 207.
4 Strehlow, *A. & L.*, III. Part ii. p. 2.
5 J. G. Frazer, "On some ceremonies of the Central Australian tribes," *Austr. Ass. Adv. of Science*, 1901, V. 321.
6 Cf. below.

of the initiation ceremonies) is a special kind of tjurunga (the instrument of Intichiuma ceremonies).

We shall begin by examining further proofs obtainable for the first of these three inferences.

Whenever there is a bad season for iguanas some of the natives proceed "to make them." Each old man sings a song and pierces his ear while doing so, telling "the male and female iguanas to come together and increase."[1] The ear is evidently a displacement upwards for other parts of the body: when the Dieri wish to make a species of frog called tidnamara they pierce their own body to the right and left of the navel with a pointed bone. When they want to "make" snakes they pierce first the right and left arm and then the scrotum; when they "make" black swans they pierce the scrotum first with an emu and then with a kangaroo bone.[2] If they want to make the wild fowl lay eggs they pierce their scrotum with the bone of a leg of a kangaroo several times and sing a song "too obscene to be translated." After this they are generally laid up for two or three weeks, unable to walk.[3] The Urabunna make snakes by piercing the skin of each arm with three or four bones.[4] In the Wonkgongaru tribe the headman of each totemic group paints himself all over with ochre and, taking little pointed bones, goes into a pool of water. He pierces his scrotum and the skin around the navel with the bones and sits down in the water; the blood from the wounds goes into the water and gives rise to fish.[5] The part played by blood from the masculine genital organ makes the meaning of blood in these rites doubly clear. We know that there is a close connexion between hate and love, and we find blood from the vulva or from the subincised urethra playing an important part in various magical means of destroying enemies.[6] Blood drawn from the penis is used to smear the namatuna or "gin-buster."[7] Blood is given to both men and women to strengthen them when they are ill. When given to a man it is drawn from the labia minora, when to a woman from the subincised urethra.[8] When blood is drawn from

[1] Gason, Curr, II. 68, 69.

[2] O. Siebert, "Sagen und Sitten der Dieri," *Globus*, 97, 55.

[3] Gason, Curr, II. 68. See also K. Eylmann, *Die Eingeborenen der Kolonie Südaustralien*, 1908, 207, 208.

[4] Spencer and Gillen, *Nor. T.*, 286.

[5] Id., ibid., 287, 288. The Wiimbaio have the negative aspect of the same complex. They were afraid of blood falling into lakes or rivers lest the fish should be destroyed.—Howitt, l.c., 399.

[6] Strehlow, *A. & L.*, IV. 2, 33, 37, 38.

[7] Strehlow, *A. & L.*, II. 81.

[8] Spencer and Gillen, *Nor. T.*, 464. The man draws a quantity of blood from the subincised urethra, and she drinks part of it, while he rubs the remainder over her body, adding afterwards a coating of red ochre and grease. In all cases where a man or woman falls ill the first thing to be done is to rub red ochre over the body, which may possibly be regarded in the light of a substitute for blood, just as sometimes a ceremonial object may be rubbed over with red ochre instead of blood. This would throw a new light on the smearing of the tjurunga with fat (cf. above, pp. 219, 220) and red ochre.

a woman it is always taken from the labia minora.[1] The son-in-law in the Kaitish tribe will give his father-in-law, when ill, blood from his arms, the daughter-in-law will give some from her labia minora.[2] But this is certainly not the only meaning contained in the ritual. Other aspects of the blood-letting rite must be taken into account before we can say that we have laid bare all the strata that go to make up this over-determined ritual. There is a close parallelism between legend and ritual, the latter being a dramatization of the former. We remember that blood-letting played an equally great part in the Alcheringa myths, the blood that flowed from the veins of these mythical heroes usually giving rise to a flood. This is in the first instance simply a new proof of the wish-fulfilment character of these myths, the actor in the ritual trying to identify himself with the Father who had so much semen that it was sufficient to flood the whole country.

Going further back towards the infantile background of these concepts, and remembering that blood is a substitute for water in the arid desert of Central Australia, we shall not be far amiss if we regard it also as an equivalent to " making water " and interpret the flood episode in the myth as an urethral erotic fancy and the ritual as a dramatization of the same, especially if we remember that blood taken from the urethra plays an important part in magic. When we are speaking of the sexual determinants in the magical value of blood we must not forget its connexion with the sado-masochistic complex : the pain felt is projected into nature with the same consequences as if it were lust. Moreover, there is a special sort of blood prominent in savage fancy, which may with full biological truth be connected with multiplication : the menstrual flow. At the time of the menstrual period women are strictly taboo,[3] and the horror of the menstrual blood is extended to women's blood in general. Men had a peculiar dread of contact with the blood of a woman, and for this reason the ornamental scars on women were cut by those of her own sex. They have a great aversion to pass under a rail or a leaning tree : they said it was owing to the fear that the blood of a woman might have been upon the wood and that some might fall upon the person passing underneath.[4] The explanation seems at first sight somewhat farfetched unless we regard it as a displaced form of the castration complex : passing under the leaning tree would be symbolic of having connexion. Women are never allowed to witness the drawing of blood for decorative purposes ; indeed, the feeling with regard to women seeing men's blood is such that when a quarrel takes place and blood is shed in the presence of women it is usual for the man whose blood is first

[1] Spencer and Gillen, *Nor. T.*, 599. [2] Id., ibid., 600.
[3] Roth, *S. M. M.*, 24. Spencer and Gillen, *N. T.*, 466 ; *Nor. T.*, 601.
[4] J. Mathew, *Two Representative Tribes of Queensland*, 1910, 177, 178.

shed to perform a ceremony connected with his own or his father's or mother's totem by way of reconciliation.[1] Woman gives birth when she ceases to bleed, but only in the period of life when she has her bleedings, and as mythical representations go by negatives, the rock is likely to give birth when a bleeding is produced. Death by a flood is merely a reversal of the typical birth- (and urethral) dream, birth in a flood. We see this fully corroborated in our material: the Alcheringa heroes die in a flood of blood and they are reborn in another flood of the same nature. But as the blood is the blood of a man, we come to the seemingly curious conclusion that the Central Australian native at least in one of the strata of the Unconscious regards himself as not merely engendered by, but also born from the representative of the father.[2]

This reminds us of a category of dreams and the unconscious attitudes involved in them that has been analysed by Silberer. The dreamer sees himself and others as spermatozoa, represented by various small objects, such as seeds, but also by mythical beings, small angels; he passes in the dream from the father's penis into the mother's body, symbolized by another country and so on.[3] We may compare this with the spirit-children, the down, the dust and the blood that emanate from the body of the Alcheringa ancestor (Father-Imago) or with the blood that flows to the rock (uterine symbol) from the vein of the totem headman. Anyhow in these phantasies of existence as a spermatozoön we clearly have the features of what is called a "Vaterleibs-phantasie," which I would interpret as the repression of the usual uterine phantasy to which the phantasy of existence prior to the uterine life as a spermatozoön in the father's body is substituted. Silberer surmises that as the uterine phantasy of a male is really the wish to have intercourse with the mother, this second variant of pre-natal phantasies must be founded on the homoerotic variant of the Oedipus complex.[4] Now it is at any rate remarkable that similar rites of blood-letting between men are found in Australia, the fore-conscious determinant of the rite being always that of magico-mystical union between two parties. We know that the function of the initiation ritual is a social sublimation of the Oedipus complex and that this is facilitated by an appeal to the auto- and homoerotic components of the libido. These components are to be utilized as the unconscious sensual basis of good-fellowship between those of the same sex and as mitigators of heteroerotic rivalry.

[1] Spencer and Gillen, *N. T.*, 463.

[2] Cf. H. Silberer, "Spermatozoönträume," *Jahrbuch*, IV. 141.

[3] The conscious denial of fatherhood is, of course, followed by a corresponding return of repressed elements: by birth-beliefs, in which the origin of life is attributed to the Father alone. Cf. "Notwithstanding this, they believe that the daughter emanates from the father solely, being only nurtured by her mother."—A. L. P. Cameron, l.c., *J. A. I.*, 1884, 352.

[4] H. Silberer, "Zur Frage der Spermatozoënträume," *Jahrbuch*, IV. 708.

The kuntamara ceremony of the Warramunga is a case in point. The kuntamara is a repetition of subincision so as to make the cut more complete. It is the regular custom for the newly initiated youth and the older men to gather together and for every man to cut himself or be cut by someone else. After the performance of a sacred ceremony on the corroboree ground, all the men gathered together in the bed of the creek where the youths were camped and performed the kuntamara. Each man took a sharp flake of stone and cut himself till the blood flowed freely, the newly initiated youths following their example. The object of the custom is said to be that of assisting the boys in their recovery to strengthen the bond amongst the men and to make the youths grow up into " good " blackfellows. When it was all over, the Thakomara youth first of all touched the head of his actual father with a little of the blood from himself and then, taking a green twig, stroked the head of a very old Thakomara man who was his kankwia or grandfather.[1] After the ceremony of Karaweliwonkana or circumcision the Dieri perform the ceremony called Wilyaru. A young man, without previous warning, is led out of the camp by some old men who are in the relation of Neyi (elder brother) to him, and not of near but of distant relationship. On the following morning the men, except his father and elder brother (actual) surround him and direct him to close his eyes. One of the men then binds the arms of another old man tightly with string, and with a sharp piece of flint lances the vein about an inch from the elbow, causing a stream of blood to flow over the young man until he is covered with it and the old man is becoming exhausted. Another old man takes his place, and so on until the young man becomes quite stiff from the quantity of blood adhering to him. The reason given for this practice is that it infuses courage into the young man and also shows him that the sight of blood is nothing, so that should he receive a wound in warfare he may account it as a matter of no moment. The next stage in the ceremony is that the young man lies down on his face, when one or two of the other young men cut from three to twelve gashes on the nape of his neck with a sharp piece of flint. These, when healed into raised scars, denote that the person wearing them has passed through the Wilyaru ceremony.[2] We know that the Wilyaru ceremony is also performed in the Urabunna tribe, and a myth that turns on the fight with the Primeval Sire (the eagle-hawk) is told to explain its origin.[3]

The cuts which are made on the body of the Wilyaru men are supposed to represent the marks on the back and on the neck of the bell-bird,[4] who defeated the Eagle-hawk. On the other hand, when

[1] Spencer and Gillen, *Nor. T.*, 359–361.

[2] Howitt, *N. T.*, 658, 659. Curr, *The Australian Race*, II. 58, 59 (Gason).

[3] Spencer and Gillen, *N. T.*, 640, above p. 53.

[4] Id., *Nor. T.*, 454.

the novice is painted during the ceremony he is supposed to resemble the Eagle-hawk.[1]

There are two points of importance to be noted here. (*a*) The blood-letting is a sort of sequel to another ceremony. (*b*) It is brought into mythical connexion with a legend that explains how a great man-devouring bird, who, as we have shown above, evidently symbolizes the Father as a Monster, was vanquished. A Yerkla-Mining variant says that Budera, who vanquished the bird, marked his own sons with their class mark:[2] it seems as if the marks were a punishment dictated by the Retaliation Fear of Budera, and intended to prevent them doing by him as he did by the bird. The Port Lincoln tribe has three man-making ceremonies that form a series: (1) The Warrara (at fifteen); (2) the Pardnappa (at sixteen or seventeen); and (3) the Wilyalkinyi (at eighteen). In the first ceremony one of the men opens a vein, causing the blood to run on the Warrara's head, face and shoulders, and also in a few drops into his mouth; in the second ceremony the youth undergoes circumcision;[3] and in the third ceremony, the name of which, Wilyal-kinyi, proves it to be a variant of the Wilyara, several men open veins in their lower arms while the young men are raised to swallow the first drops of the blood. They are then told to kneel on their hands and knees so as to give a horizontal position to their backs, which are covered with blood. As soon as this is sufficiently coagulated one of the men marks with his thumb the places where the incisions are to be made, namely, one on the middle of the neck and two rows from the shoulders down to the hips. These are named Manka, and are ever after held in such veneration that it would be deemed a great profanation to allude to them in the presence of women.[4] The details of these rites furnish the key to their meaning. In the Kunta Mara ceremony the elders repeat the subincision they performed on the youths on their own person, that is they confess to being guilty of the same unconscious sins for which they inflicted the same punishment on the youths. The youths also repeat the ceremony, and henceforth the common guilt (of Unconscious Rebellion against the Sire) is to unite the two contracting parties (Old and Young), and by uniting them to their elders make the young into "good" blackfellows.

The sequel of the rite clearly indicates against whom the youth committed the original rebellion in the course of phylogenesis, and with whom the union of a blood covenant must be cemented, for he touches the head of his own father with a little of the blood drawn from his subincision wound. In the Dieri ritual there is no such return of the repressed elements; the rite is carried out by the "elder

[1] Spencer and Gillen, *N. T.*, 641.
[2] Howitt, *N. T.*, 666.
[3] Id., ibid., 668, 669. Schürmann, *The Aborigines of Port Lincoln*. Woods, *Native Tribes of South Australia*, 1879, 226, 234.
[4] Howitt, *N. T.*, 670.

brothers" as representatives of the Father-Imago, but the actual father is conspicuous by his absence. Then the old men bleed themselves till they are exhausted and the blood that flows on the young man is said to infuse courage into him. Very naturally so; we should say the young man must gain courage when he sees the old men doing the very same thing to themselves which he, although he dares not confess as much to his own consciousness, would himself like to do. The next phase of the ceremony clearly shows that it is he who has been allowing free play for his aggressive impulses against the old men; he is punished for what has happened by the Wilyaru gashes. It is the same in the Port Lincoln ceremony: first the men are bled and then the youths are circumcised and scarred.

We must not forget, however, that the blood that flows from the scars and the veins is but a substitute for the blood that flows from the penis (semen), and the union between the Elders and the Youths is one not only of mutually confessed guilt, but also an ambivalent over-compensation for original aggressiveness, one of mutually confessed homoerotic feelings. This explains the belief that partaking of blood together prevents the possibility of treachery. If, for example, an Alice Springs party wanted to go on an avenging expedition to the Burt country, and they had with them in camp a man of that locality, he would be forced to drink blood with them and then he could not warn his friends of the danger impending.[1] The men taking part in an Atninga avenging party of the Arunta tribe assembled together and after each one had been touched with the girdle made from the hair of the man they were about to avenge, they draw blood from their urethras and sprinkle it over one another. Sometimes blood is drawn from the arm and drunk for the same purpose.[2] The avenging party is an effort of the Unconscious to project the guilt for the death out of the tribal boundaries; it is when thus identifying themselves with the dead that the cutting as self-inflicted punishment is performed, which, together with the homoerotic tendency apparent in the sprinkling of urethral blood, cements the new union of common guilt and common over-compensation. The sham fight (as an outlet for the traces of animosity) and the blood-drinking at a reconciliation-meeting are cases to the point.[3]

The same rite is also found as a sign of renewed friendship. Two friends who had not met for a long time sat down by the fire facing each other, until the younger or inferior rose, banged herself on the head with a stick and made blood run, then banged her friend, and there was a mingling of blood, a sign of renewed friendship.[4]

The blood that the elders let flow on the rock which symbolizes

[1] Spencer and Gillen, *Nor. T.*, 461.
[2] Id., ibid., 598.
[3] Id., *N. T.*, 462.
[4] A. J. Peggs, "Notes on the Aborigines of Roebuck Bay," *Folk-Lore*, XIV. 336.

the dead ancestor is the sign of self-punishment for having caused his death, but also the sign of being willing to undergo this punishment, that is, being willing to make their peace with him. This peace-making is effected by utilizing the homoerotic current of feeling; the father is made to take the place of the mother when by letting their own blood (semen) flow on him " spirit-animals " are called into existence. When the performers of the ritual run round the elder man who represents the Alcheringa ancestor and ask him to wriggle his body well, or when they wriggle together with him, they are—in the Unconscious—identifying themselves with the Father in the moment of cohabitation. When they rub the Churinga or the boulder they are performing onanistic manipulations with their own and the father's penis.

The Intichiuma ritual is a symbolic repetition of collective and mutual onanistic actions between the elder and the younger members of the Horde, these actions in their turn being caused by, and indicative of, an extreme reaction against the Oedipus complex. In all these rites that are symbolic of multiplication the feminine element is vigorously repressed, and were it not for the faint return of the repressed elements in the uterine symbolism of the sacred cave, we would be at a loss to find its traces. But in the very act of flying from the Oedipus complex rebellious youth finds a satisfactory outlet for its unconscious wishes in identifying itself in the symbolic intercourse indicated in the ceremony with the Father, the Son copulates with the same female organ (Ertnatulunga cave) with whom the Father copulates, and it is from this never-exhausted source of infantile libidinal impulses that the Intichiuma derives those magic qualities that enable it to assure the supernatural propagation of the species.[1]

However, before we finish with the Blood rite we must follow the indications already gathered of a still deeper meaning underlying these ceremonies. The Union with the Father (totem) is effected in a symbolic repetition of the Great Rebellion. We have called attention to the fact that in the blood-letting ritual of initiation, both the Elders and the novices undergo a self-inflicted punishment for unconsciously killing the Father, or, in the secondary, retribution-formation, the Son.

The Dieri have a curious custom that is an excellent illustration of the mechanism of these rites. Should a child meet with any accident all its relatives immediately get struck on the head with a stick or boomerang, until the blood flows down their faces ; such a surgical operation being presumed to ease the child's pain.[2] Naturally the explanation of the rite is that the relatives must be made to suffer for their unconscious ill-will against the child, that they, in a word, are responsible for the accident.

[1] As symbolized by the totem animal.

[2] Gason, Curr, op. cit., II. 69.

When somebody dies among the Narrinyeri a great lamentation and wailing is made by all the relations and friends of the dead man. They all beat and cut themselves and make violent demonstrations of grief. All the relatives are careful to be present, and not to be wanting in proper signs of sorrow, lest they should be suspected of complicity in causing the death.[1] By complicity ill-will is meant; the cutting is the self-inflicted punishment. It is interesting to note that we have also clear indications of the nature and origin of those repressed feelings that call for this cutting punishment in mourning ritual. The "Gammona" of the deceased, that is the men who may lawfully marry his daughters, must not only never mention his name, but they neither attend the actual burial nor do they take any part in the subsequent mourning ceremonies which are carried on at the grave. It is their duty to cut themselves on the shoulder when a man who is their Ikuntera (father-in-law) dies. If a son-in-law does not well and faithfully perform this cutting rite then some Ikuntera will punish him by giving away his special wife to appease the Ulthana of the dead father-in-law.[2] We know that the relations between a man and his father-in-law are what may be called "strained" in the normal Australian tribe. They avoid each other, the younger man may not eat of any animal that has been killed by his father-in-law, whilst on the other hand, he is supposed to send food to the elder.[3] This avoidance evidently indicates that there is something "repressed" between them; the food-presents seem to show that the younger man has something to expiate with regard to the elder. It is not difficult to guess what this is: he has taken away a daughter, to cohabit with whom was one of the jealously guarded privileges of the Sire in the Primeval Horde. The ghost of the dead father-in-law (a substitute for the father) is angry with him for usurping this privilege; unless he offers expiation by the cutting rite, he is apt to loose his "Unawa," the cause of the strained relations (indicated by his absence at the mourning rite) between them. The repressed feeling is originally and primarily the animosity arising out of sexual jealousy; it is the Son who must cut himself as expiation for having desired the Mother and killed the Father.[4] Similarly among the Unmatjera and Kaitish tribes the cutting is done by the gammona.[5] In the Tongaranka tribe before the grave is filled in, the nearest male relation present stands over the grave and receives several blows with the edge of a boomerang; the blood being allowed to flow on the corpse.[6]

[1] Taplin, *The Narrinyeri*, 1879, 20.

[2] Spencer and Gillen, *N. T.*, 500.

[3] Spencer and Gillen, *Nor. T.*, 610.

[4] Of course there is always a great amount of repressed animosity between near relations, the greater the love the more is this animosity repressed, finding its natural outlet here in the cutting rite.—Cf. Spencer and Gillen, *N. T.*, 509. Howitt, *N. T.*, 453. Curr, I. 272, 348.

[5] Spencer and Gillen, *Nor. T.*, 507.

[6] Howitt, *N. T.*, 451.

In Victoria, when the male mourners assemble, the first who arrives seizes the tomahawk and endeavours to maim himself with it—aiming a blow usually at the head—but the relative of the deceased whose duty it is to see that all the rites are fulfilled wrenches it from him.[1] When a chief dies his assembled friends wail and lacerate their foreheads.[2] Just as the Son inflicts self-punishment for the Father, the Daughter does it for the mother. At the death of an old Euahlayi woman, the daughter took a sharp stone which was beside her and hit it against her head till the blood gushed out. They took the stone from her.[3] At Roebuck Bay when the father and mother wept for their dead baby, they howled and finally banged their heads together until the blood ran, which blood was allowed to drip on the dead child lying on the ground.[4] The same has been observed at the Vasse River in Western Australia—the blood is allowed to flow all over the corpse of the deceased.[5]

Now we see that the totemic Intichiuma is really a repetition of the totem-father's mourning feast; the union between the youths and the elders is effected by the avowal of the common guilt in having murdered the Primeval Sire. Moreover, as the players in the Intichiuma drama actually represent the Alcheringa ancestors, drawing blood from their own veins is a symbolic repetition of the same deed (rebellion against the father) that it is supposed to expiate. The symbolic repetition is also a reduced, a neurotically inhibited repetition, for the rebellion against the father is reacted under the guise of a self-punishment for this very deed. This reduced repetition is a survival of a more primitive form of the Intichiuma than we have to do with at present; from the point of view of the unconscious meaning of actual ritual, the blood that flows on the Alcheringa father's grave represents the homoerotic current of feeling the renewal of the blood-covenant[6] which will enable the totemite to ensure the multiplication of the totem animal. But why the animal? Why not the human members of the clan? Was this always the case, and, if not, what is the reason that the real and original meaning of the Intichiuma, the propagation of the human species, has been obscured under the mask of this projection?

We shall try to answer these questions. To begin with we must draw attention to the fact that there is an exact parallelism between legend and ritual and that legend is the prototype of the actual

[1] Brough-Smyth, op. cit., I. 101.
[2] Dawson, op. cit., 64, 66.
[3] Parker, *The Euahlayi Tribe*, 1905, 88.
[4] A. J. Peggs, "Notes on the Aborigines of Roebuck Bay, Western Australia," *Folk-Lore*, XIV. 336.
[5] G. Grey, *Journals of Two Expeditions*, 1841, II. 330.
[6] On the other hand, the blood falling on the dead in the mourning rite is equally a means of communion with him, and as the prototype of communion is coitus (or at least libidinal contact) it may also be interpreted as an attempt to make him reincarnate himself in his descendants, to make spirit-children jump out of the grave as the spirit kangaroos do when the blood is poured on the Nanja rock.

rite. The quivering movement may serve various purposes in the resetting of the ritual; it may be imitation of the rain-ancestors in producing rain,[1] or of snake-ancestors in multiplying snakes.[2] In all cases the sacred ceremonies are avowedly imitations of those performed by the ancestors. But where the ancestors performed sacred ceremonies they left spirit-children behind; when they quivered (the same quivering being invariably reproduced in the ritual), spirit-children used to emanate from them.[3] This clearly indicates that in the prehistoric period of phylogenesis and in the deepest infantile strata of the Unconscious there is a period that precedes that of projection into the animal world; these rites must once have had a purely human meaning; we shall suppose that this meaning must for some reason or other have undergone repression with subsequent projection into environment.

The anthropic origin of the intichiuma.

We have other survivals of this phase of evolution besides the legend. When the Tjingilli wish to make both young men and women grow strong and well-favoured the men perform, at intervals of time, a long series of ceremonies, called collectively wantju, dealing with the various totems. There is a special reference to the young men or women in them, but they are performed solely with the idea and object of increasing the growth of the younger members of the tribe, who are not of course allowed either to see or to take any part in them.[4] The "anthropic totems," hitherto regarded as a freak of Central Australian conceptionalism, may be considered as another rudiment of this "pre-totemic" phase of totemic evolution. In the Warramunga we have the totems "laughing boy" and "full-grown man." They are regarded in all essential characters as strictly equivalent to any other totemic group. They have their mungai spots where their ancestors left spirit-children behind in the early days, and the ceremonies performed in connexion with them are in no way to be distinguished from those of the other totems in conjunction with which they are carried out.[5] The Loritja have the ceremonies representing mythical women and "circumcised youths."[6] The Arunta have the "worra = uncircumcised youth" ceremony.[7] Two other ceremonies of theirs are of special importance in this connexion, that of ilba-mara, the "fruitful womb," and that of the ratapa or "spirit-child" totem. The former describes how a mythical woman of the Alcheringa gave birth to a child, cried at the absence of her husband and painted herself red when she expected him to return, then turned away when he did come, and ends by indicating how she will get chastised for it.[8]

[1] Spencer and Gillen, *Nor. T.*, 285.
[2] Id., ibid., 301.
[3] Cf. above, p. 218.
[4] Spencer and Gillen, *Nor T.* 476.
[5] Id., ibid., 207, 208.
[6] Strehlow, *A. & L.*, III. Part 2, 1911, 45–54.
[7] Id., ibid. III. Part 1, 1910, 124
[8] Id., ibid., III. 119.

Although the purpose of the ceremony is not given, it can hardly be any other than what the name indicates, to make the womb fruitful by describing the ups and downs of married life, threatening the women with the punishment if they prove recalcitrant to the wishes of their husbands. The ratapa cult describes the wanderings of a mythical ancestor and two ratapa who always remained in this state;[1] it is performed when they want the ratapa to come out of the trees and rocks and go into the women.[2] This we suppose to be the original uncensored form of the Intichiuma ceremony; by ministering to the "fore-pleasure" in onanistic movements and phantasies it really makes the spirit-children emanate and incarnate themselves.

Proceeding from the centre of Australia to the north-west and west we seem to get less and less elaborate, more primitive forms of the same complexes. We have interpreted the Central Australian Churinga as a penis.

At Nannine in Western Australia actual imitations of a penis and a vulva have been found. "They represented the greatest treasure of the tribe and were prepared from a mass, which could not be more closely identified, of string and animal hair smeared with a reddish dye." "These objects cannot be said to be very successful imitations of the originals. On the other hand, very realistic imitations of the *membrum virile* have been found in the Kimberley District." "They are made from red sandstone and represent the life-sized male member, in its flaccid as well as in the erect state. On the under surface the vulva is very clearly represented."[3]

Mjöberg promises to explain the use of these objects that are kept strictly secret—like the tjurunga—at some future occasion; meanwhile we should not wonder if they were ultimately connected with the ceremonies of the baby totem.

West Australia is the home of the tarlow ceremonies, the exact equivalent of the Central Australian Intichiuma. When rain is badly wanted by the Ngaluma, the rain-maker and his apprentice (generally his son) proceed to the piece of ground especially set apart for the ceremony of rain-making. He builds a heap of stone or sand two or three feet high and replaces his "millia gurlee," that is "Potent" or "Live Stone," on the top of it. This stone is generally handed down for generations and is of a striking appearance; it might be taken for a vulva symbol. The rain-maker walks and dances for hours round the stone-heap chanting incantations; when he is utterly exhausted his assistant takes his place. Water is sprinkled on the stone and huge fires are lighted. A tarlow is generally a large heap of stones (rarely a simple one) to which certain of the blacks proceed to perform the ceremony of "willing" that

[1] Strehlow, *A. & L.*, III. 122. [2] Id., ibid., III. 8.

[3] E. Mjöberg, "Phalluskult unter den Ureinwehnern Australians," *Anthropos*, 1913, 555, 556.

scanty articles of food may become more plentiful than they are.[1] In Western Australia a totem (tarlow) does not regulate marriage. A tarlow is a stone or a pile of stones set apart as a hallowed spot dedicated to the ceremony of "willing" that certain things such as children, birds, animals, reptiles, insects, frogs, grass-seed be made to multiply and increase: each living thing having a separate tarlow, all of which belong to the head of the family as master of the craft and descend from father to son." [2]

A. R. Brown says: "In several tribes I found totemic groups that claimed babies as their totem, and performed totemic ceremonies the avowed object of which was to provide a plentiful supply of children. I found one such totemic group in each of the following tribes—Baiong, Targari, Ngaluma, Kariera, Namal and two in the Injibandi tribe. One such group in the Injibandi tribe performs its ceremony at a spot in the Fortescue River where there is a small cave. According to a legend, in times long ago the men and women once left the camp to go hunting, and left all the babies in the camp in the charge of one man. After the others had been gone some time the babies began to cry. This made the man in charge of them very angry; so he took them to the cave and put them inside, and lit a big fire of spinifex grass at the entrance and so smothered them all. An essential part of the totemic ceremony consists in lighting a fire at the entrance of the cave.

"There is a very interesting totemic group in the Kariera tribe. The group has a number of edible objects for totems and also 'whirlwind,' 'baby,' and 'sexual desire.' A man who belonged to this group told me that when it was decided to attempt to produce an increase of children the men and women of the totemic group first proceeded to Kalbana and performed the ceremony for the increase of sexual desire which seems to have consisted of setting fire to the bark of a tree. Only after this they moved to Pilgun and performed the ceremony of the baby totem." [3]

Fire in Intichiuma ritual.

Fire plays a similar part in the Kangaroo Intichiuma of the Mara tribe. Layers of grass are put over kangaroo dung. The whole is then set on fire and the men, taking green bushes, light them at the fire and scatter the embers about in all directions.[4] Fire is one of the best-known symbols of the libido. According to an Arunta tradition fire was contained in the penis of an euro man.[5] In a Kakadu myth the lubras hide fire in their vulvas,[6] and it is indeed hardly astonishing

[1] E. Clement, "Ethnological Notes on the Western Australian Aborigines," *Int. Arch. f. Ethn.*, XVI. 1904, 5, 6.

[2] J. G. Withnell, "Marriage Rites and Relationships," *Science of Man*, 1903, VI. 42.

[3] A. R. Brown, "Beliefs Concerning Childbirth in some Australian Tribes," *Man*, 1912, 181, 182.

[4] Spencer and Gillen, *Nor. T.*, 312.

[5] Id., ibid., 446.

[6] Spencer, *N. T. N. T. A.*, 305.

to find that the ritual to promote sexual desire should consist in setting the bark of a tree on fire. According to the belief of the Wogait the evil spirit makes a big fire from which he takes an infant, and places it at night in the womb of a lubra, who must then give birth to the child.[1]

We have noticed the reversal technique in the relation of Intichiuma ritual to Alcheringa tradition. In the Alcheringa myth the hero dies in a flood of blood, in ritual the totem animal is born by flooding the Nanja stone with blood. Myth represents the reversal, ritual the restitution,[2] of the original motive. Instead of saying that the babies die we should say that they are born when "fire is lighted" at the entrance of the cave (maternal womb). The babies are not put into a cave, they come out of it; and it is not when left alone by the adults that they cry, but on the contrary when they are not alone any more but introduced into the outer world (after their birth). On the whole, it seems a justifiable hypothesis to assume that in Western Australia a very primitive phase in the evolution of the Intichiuma has been conserved. We have here a ritual that tends to procreate babies, like love magic in general, by reduced, that is, symbolic equivalents of intercourse. This gives us a hint as to the fore-pleasure character of a ritual that looks like a "compromise" between the libido and the repression. In the Caaro festival this is clearly indicated; first the dance around the pit (uterus) and then the actual intercourse. On the whole, I hardly think we are beside the mark if we call the Watchandie ceremony an Intichiuma of the baby totem.

As to the origin of repression in this case, we have had ample proof of its intimate connexion with the Oedipus complex.

The projection of these complexes to various animal species represents a latter phase in the evolution of the ritual. The same transformation has begun to operate in the evolution of the child-birth beliefs. According to the North-West Australian beliefs the spirit of the animal speared by the man is reborn in his wife. The Ewenyoon who inhabit the adjacent Buccaneer Islands believe that if a man kills a dugong the spirit of the dugong enters into the man and dwells therein. After a time the man can release it and it materializes itself in a young dugong.[3] Here again the original belief was the incarnation of an animal spirit in a human being, the re-birth as an animal being a latter development. In the Larrekiya tribe the women are not allowed to be present when a dugong is killed as the dugong is said to have been a lubra before

Transference of child-birth beliefs from human to animal species; an analogy to the evolution of the Intichiuma.

[1] H. Basedow, "Anthropological Notes on the Western Coastal Tribes of the Northern Territory of South Australia," *Trans. Roy. Soc. S. A.*, XXXI. 1907, 5.

[2] Second reversal.

[3] W. H. Bird, "Ethnographical Notes about the Buccaneer Islanders," *Anthropos*. 1911, 278.

it was transformed into an animal. When it is killed it wails and whines pitifully like a human being, and the female animal is said to carry her own young, like a lubra carries an infant.[1] But probably, as belief is a less serious matter from the point of view of the psychic censor than action as embodied in ritual, the latter has undergone a more thorough transformation in its avowed purpose than the child-birth beliefs. At the same time, however, ritual has conserved rudiments hoary with age—unchanged survivals of the pre-human phase in the history of the genus Homo.

Rites performed at fixed seasons.

We have as yet paid no attention to the fact that these rites are performed at a fixed season. In the Australian tropics the year is divided into two seasons—a long season of rainless heat, when man and beast can hardly procure the life-minimum of food, when everybody seems to be dying for a drop of water, and a shorter season of sudden rainfall when the showers change the aspect of the landscape as if by magic. The desert of yesterday is a blank sheet of water, everything begins to blossom, it is the breeding season of nature. When the oppressive stress of the heat and want is the greatest everything is suddenly changed as if it were by a stroke of magic. Like the migrating birds, the native seems to feel the impending change in advance and to meet nature half-way by imitating it. His magic is truly a prelude to nature's magic, and the explanation of it is that he himself is an integral part of nature ; nowadays he responds to the changing rhythm of nature by ritual, that is, reduced action; formerly he changed with changing nature—he also, like everything around him, had a breeding season.[2] In our opinion the Intichiuma ritual is a survival of the breeding season and we shall now proceed to note the points of similarity between them.

" All these bower birds have the habit of erecting other structures besides the breeding nest and of decorating them in a peculiar manner. These are the so-called arcades, dance-huts or mating-temples which the birds erect wherein to woo one another in a variety of pantomimic movements. The building of these arcades takes place long before mating ; both sexes share in it, but the males pre-eminently. According to the species, there is every kind of combination in the joint work. The saw-billed bower bird (*scenopo etes dentirostris*) clears spots under high trees free from all dead leaves and thoroughly cleans the ground. When the place has been arranged, the bird perches itself on a branch and sings its peculiar song. This bird is one of the cleverest imitators imaginable. It imitates the note of all the other birds which live in its proximity. It does even more than this : it chirps like a grasshopper, croaks

[1] H. Basedow, " Anthropological Notes on the Western Coastal Tribes," *Trans. Roy. S. A.*, XXXI. 1907, 4.

[2] Cf. Westermarck, *History of Human Marriage*, 1901, 29.

like a frog and imitates in a most artistic way the whirring of a large cricket caught by a bird. From time to time it hops down from its branch to arrange the leaves on its playground. After weeks of patient observation, a change was visible in November. The mates had found each other and were sitting together on the top-most branches of the trees." [1]

In Australia, the lyre-bird (*menura superba*) forms small round hillocks and the *m. alberti* scratches for itself shallow holes, or, as they are called by the natives, corroborying places, where it is believed both sexes assemble. I think the Intichiuma ground swept clean by the natives is a survival of these play-houses in which we should also see the pre-human prototype of all sacred and social buildings from the "Men's House" to Church and Parliament. The imitation of all nature around him by the breeding bird seems to be a consequence of an enhanced biological unity between all nature at the common breeding season, and thus it is understandable that the biological unity projected into totemism should find its ritual expression in the animal-imitation of the Intichiuma.

Playhouse and intichiuma ground. Biological origin of imitation in ritual.

The next point of comparison lies in the dancing exhibitions of rutting animals. "The black-cock holds his tail up and spreads it out like a fan, he lifts up his head and neck with all the feathers erect and stretches his wings from the body. Then he takes a few jumps in different directions, sometimes in a circle, and presses the under part of his beak so hard against the ground that the chin feathers are rubbed off." [2] "In antelopes the mock battles often consist of a series of movements of attack and retreat. The males of the pala antelopes conduct these mock combats by means of dancing and bounding movements. The South African springboks appear to excite the females by means of extraordinarily high jumps, often two metres high, while at the same time they display their beautiful white manes. This display recalls some of the waltz-like dances of birds." [3]

In the Intichiuma a performer will rise from the ground to a stooping position and begin to move another performer forwards and backwards.[4] The first day of the Muraian consisted of a Fire, a Wallaby and a Turtle ceremony. The performance opened with a fire ceremony. The performers were led out of and round the wurley in single file by an old man, who stationed himself beside the ground, clanging his sticks and shouting, while the men danced for a short time. The dancing was very vigorous, the men often running round and round with exaggerated knee action and arms extended. Then

[1] Hesse-Doflein, *Tierbau und Tierleben*, 1910, II. 458. Cf. Fountain and Ward, *Rambles of an Australian Naturalist*, 1907, 255.

[2] Darwin, *Descent of Man*, 2nd Edition, II. 50.

[3] Hesse-Doflein, II. 466.

[4] Spencer and Gillen, *Nor. T.*,

they knelt down, swaying their bodies from side to side and moving their hands as if they were working fire-sticks. "The performance of the Turtle ceremony came to an end with all the performers prancing about with their arms extended and yelling." [1] It is especially the seemingly meaningless movement expressive of pure pleasure in muscular discharge, the prancing about with its characteristic high knee action, that reminds one of the dances in the animal world. It is well known since Darwin that the development of the vocal faculties is closely connected with the breeding season. The male birds endeavour to charm or excite their mates by love notes, songs and antics. "Like the birds, the males of mammals, we notice, feel the impulse to vocal display in the breeding season."[2]

These vocal displays tally strikingly with the description given by Strehlow, but in the Intichiuma ritual the young males alone take the place formerly occupied by them in company with the females; probably in early times only the females of the Horde formed the audience, the alteration being due to repression, the effects of which we have already studied and shall continue to see at work in this connexion. Strehlow says: "As soon as all the preparations for the performance are completed, the old men who are to form a part of the audience sit down and the actors arrive. They occupy the ditch which serves as a stage. One of the old men then makes a long-drawn sound (raiankama = to breathe in Arunta) as the signal for the young men to rush to the scene of action and to run in a circle round this old man shouting wa-wa-jai-jai meanwhile." [3] The tjurunga-songs consist of a sort of recitative, the words being given without regard to their normal accentuation.[4] Possibly these songs go back to a root which is earlier than human language, to the vocal display of the rutting season in which accentuation was determined by other laws than those which exist at present.

An important aspect of the ritual has hitherto not been mentioned: I refer to the ornaments. During the ordinary dancing festivals or Altherta the principal feature of the decoration is usually a more or less elaborate head-dress. This is made by first of all bunching the hair on the top of the head and then surrounding it with small twigs so as to form a helmet-like structure of the desired shape.[5] The top of the helmet is often further decorated with a bunch of eagle-hawk feathers, or a semi-circular structure made of grass stalks bound round with a hair string and with a tuft of tail-tips at each end, fixed through the helmet.[6]

The head-dress and other ornaments in the Intichiuma ritual.

[1] Spencer, *N. T. N. T. A.*, 150, 151.

[2] Hesse-Doflein, op. cit., II. 444.

[3] The call of the young men is said to mean "play your part well, bring your body into vibration."—Strehlow, *A. & L.*, III. 5.

[4] Id., ibid., 6.

[5] Spencer and Gillen, *N. T.*, 619.

[6] Id., ibid., 621, 622.

On the latter there is always some design drawn in down, and the design almost always includes a band passing across the bridge of the nose and enclosing the eyes. The down is affixed as usual by means of human blood.[1] In the totemic down ceremonies as in the ordinary dances special attention is almost always paid to the head-dress. The hair is tied up, and the helmet is made out of twigs or grass stalks wound round with human hair strings. In the case of one of the emu performances it forms a slightly tapering column about five feet in height, the end being ornamented with a tuft of emu feathers. Owing to the flexibility of the column the end droops somewhat and moves about as the performer walks, imitating well the continuous up and down movement of the emu's head while the bird walks aimlessly about.[2] In connexion with some of the ceremonies flat slabs of wood, shaped like large Churinga, may be carried on the head.[3] In many of the Arunta ceremonies real Churinga are used as head decorations, but they are always ornamented with birds' down and never with pipe-clay, and with only very rare exceptions bear incised patterns.[4] Other head-dresses are flat discs made of grass stalk.[5]

Another form of head-dress is worn in a ceremony of the Plum-tree totem. It consists of a central mass of grass stalks, bound round as usual with human hair string and then ornamented with alternate lines of red and white down. For the time being the head-dress, which is really a "Nurtunja," is symbolic of a plum tree. As soon as the ceremony is over it is normally taken to pieces.[6] A Nurtunja is a structure made up of from one to twenty spears; round these grass stalks are bound, and then rings of down are added, and a few Churinga will be suspended at intervals; occasionally from the top end of a large Nurtunja a small one will hang pendent, at other times it may be in the form of a cross or it may be **T**-shaped. At times it may have the appearance of a torpedo resting on the head or it may be in the form of a huge helmet firmly attached to the head and of various shapes, according to what it is supposed to represent. This form differs from all the others in the fact that one end of the Nurtunja is actually continuous with the head-dress instead of being, as in all other cases, a structure independent of the head-dress and affixed after the completion of this.[7] Both the Nurtunja and the Waninga[8] seem to be merely developments of the fundamental-concept that is embodied in the head-dress or helmet.[9] What the head-dress really is may perhaps be guessed from a negative

[1] Spencer and Gillen, *N. T.*, 622.
[2] Id., ibid., 625; *Nor. T.*, 723.
[3] Id., ibid., 724.
[4] Id., ibid., 725.
[5] Id., ibid., 725.
[6] Id., ibid., 726.
[7] Id., *N. T.*, 627.
[8] Cf. id., ibid., 225, 628.
[9] It may also be evolved from a mask which does not make much difference. On the distribution see W. Foy, "Fadenstern und Fadenkreuz," *Ethnologica*, 1913, II. 67.

testimonial; it is something that women have not got, this being the most conspicuous difference between a woman's corroborie decorations and the usual ones.[1] The connexion of the head-dress with the Churinga as a procreation-symbol accords well with the idea that it is a distinctively masculine attribute. "A head-decoration or 'tonka' is made for the performer in the following way: mulga twigs are placed upright on his head and are fastened on with his hair; the twigs are covered with a cushion bound round with yarn and then ornamented with down, the whole forming a kind of pointed hat. Frequently a long wooden tjurunga is also placed in the performer's hair and so a connexion is made with his altjiranga mitjina. Creative powers proceed from this tjurunga to its wearer."[2] The Nurtunja and the Waninga have also conserved some traces of having been originally connected with the sexual sphere. The Nurtunja is embraced by the initiates before undergoing subincision.[3] According to Basedow nobody was allowed to see the Waningi before initiation. The sight of the Waningi may be considered an introduction to manhood.[4] Amongst the Niol-Niol the act of circumcision itself is called Waninga, and Klaatsch saw frames through which they put their heads (in the south-west) at certain dances that were strictly forbidden to women. Curiously enough, these are not sacred decorations, the association with the act of circumcision being only kept up by the identity of the terms.[5]

When we see that the aboriginals have certain more or less mystic decorations made for the ceremonies and discarded when this season is over, we shall be tempted to draw a parallel between these ceremonial decorations and the secondary sexual characters that the animals develop for, and discard after, the rutting season. If we accept the view that these ornaments are a sequel of the secondary sex-characteristics, we shall be able to understand the truth in the assertion of the natives that the ornaments represent a part of the body of their semi-human and half-animal ancestors. Strehlow says there are various ornaments which the performers wear suspended on their head or in their hands, e.g. kanturanga (arches), various forms of tnatantja (spears), which are fixed to the head or held in their hands, or necklaces made of human hair. All these objects represent parts of the altjiranga mitjina. The same applies also to the Wonninga; this too represents a part of the body of the Alcheringa ancestor—his ear, leg, etc. These Wonninga are usually

[1] Spencer and Gillen, *Nor. T.*, 720.
[2] Strehlow, *A. & L.*, III. 1910, 2, 3.
[3] Spencer and Gillen, *N. T.*, 254.
[4] Basedow, op. cit., XXVIII. 22–23. Basedow supposes the "Faden-kreuz" to be originally symbolic of a human figure in dancing posture ("Archiv für Anthropologie," *N. S.*, VII. 219. Cf. also Foy, "Fadenstern," *Ethnologica*, 1913, II. 106), which would lead us to the conclusion that a man acting in a ceremonial dance wore the symbol of a dancer on his head.
[5] H. Klaatsch, "Schlussbericht," *Z. E.*, 1907, 654, 655.

worn on the heads of the performers, but they are also employed at the initiation ceremonies, where, however, they are held in the hand by the performers.[1]

The origin of the secondary sexual characters of animals cannot be said to be quite clear. At any rate they stand in close connexion to the primary ones, as they are absent in castrated male animals.[2] Hesse inclines to the view that they are "Überschussbildungen aus den Ersparnissen bei der Bildung der Geschlechtsprodukte,[3] the male giving less energy out in the sexual act than the female. If this is true, then these crests, manes and all sorts of ornaments of the rutting season may be described as the physiological pre-formations of certain unconscious mechanisms that we are well acquainted with, or rather the displacement upwards is a "psychical" survival, a reduced repetition of the biological process manifested in these secondary sex-characters. The helmet of the ceremonies is a Churinga transposed upwards and the Churinga itself a symbolical penis. That is why we see a return of the repressed elements when the Churinga, which radiates its creative faculties on the wearer, is put into the head-dress, and that is why even the latter developments of this head-dress have conserved traces of their ancient connexion with the male organ of generation.

Displacement upwards explained as psychical survival of the biological process which leads to the formation of secondary sex-characters.

Among animals the rutting season is also the season of battle among the males. Numerous instances of fierce fights among birds have been recorded. The polygamous ruff, for example, is notorious for his extreme pugnacity, and in the spring the males congregate day after day at a particular spot where the females prepare to lay their eggs. Here they fight like game-cocks, seizing each other with their beaks and striking with their wings. Among the polygamous mammals we find the adult males separated from the rest of the herd during the greater part of the year. At the pairing season all the old males attempt to secure large harems. They drive the females together and chase away the other males. In this way small hordes are formed where an old male possesses a large number of females; only very young, sexually unripe, males are allowed in the horde. Whilst the fighting among the old males is often extremely fierce, the fight between the old and young males does not usually seem very serious; it appears as if the young male was simply testing his strength and withdraws as soon as he recognizes his inferiority.[4]

It is easy to see that the period of the Great Revolution, the Victory of the Sons over the Sire, can only have been a rutting

[1] Strehlow, *Die totemistischen Kulte*, 1910, 3.

[2] Hesse-Doflein, op. cit., I. 498.

[3] Id., ibid., I. 496. Which is about as much as to say that they are phalloi coming out at the wrong place.

[4] Hesse-Doflein, op. cit., II. 450, 462, 465, 474. Darwin, op. cit., II. 46.

season. Probably the youths were suffered in the horde all the year round, and only expelled whilst the rutting season lasted; the dichotomy of the tribe between initiated and non-initiated, between eagle-hawk and crow, having its first germ in this annually repeated expulsion, but once the pubescent males succeeded in uniting their growing forces and killing or driving off the Leader of the Horde, an event that can only have taken place in the Season of Rut, we shall expect to find traces of it in the Intichiuma ritual.

Eating the totem as an Intichiuma rite.

We shall take up our investigation at the point where we broke off and try to explain the origin of the animal projection in the alleged purpose of the ritual. The blood-letting of the elders [1] and performers is an acknowledgment of and a self-punishment for having caused the death of the Alcheringa ancestor. By the blood-letting, however, they also engender the animal from the stone and thus in a certain sense of the word they become the fathers of their own fathers. In the case of the Kangaroo totem of Undiara, after the men have allowed the blood to pour out of their arms over the stone ledge, they descend, and after rubbing themselves all over with red ochre return to the main camp. All the younger men then go out hunting kangaroo, which, when caught, they bring in to the older men who have stayed in camp. The old men of the totem, the Alatunja being in the middle of them, eat a little and then anoint the bodies of those who took part in the ceremony with fat from the kangaroo, after which the meat is distributed to all the men assembled. The men of the totem then paint their bodies with the totem design or Ilkinia in imitation of the painting on the rock at Undiara and that night is spent in singing about the doings of the Alcheringa kangaroo people and animals. Next day the ceremony is repeated. After this the animal is eaten of very sparingly by the Kangaroo men, and they must on no account touch the choice bits.[2] Painting the totem design on their body and singing the totemic chants is a clear sign of identification: we shall conclude that this absolute identification must be a reaction-formation after a period of absolute, though unconscious rebellion.[3] Both the young and old man have previously done just what is prohibited for a Kangaroo man to do: they have hunted the kangaroo and they have eaten it. The elder and the younger generation have acted seemingly in absolute harmony: we find that both have given free vent to their repressed wishes. For have not the young men hunted the kangaroo, the symbol of the father? And have not the Elders eaten of the animal, which to them also is, in a primary sense, a Father-symbol,

[1] Spencer and Gillen, *N. T.*, 204, 205.

[2] According to legend, the great Alcheringa kangaroo buried under the rock was killed by kangaroo men.—Spencer and Gillen, *N. T.*, 198.

[3] The same mechanism of rebellion and identification is found in the mourning ceremonies.

but which they have also procreated by letting their own blood drip on the rock, and which therefore, from the retribution point of view of the Father, means the Son? We now see what the eating of the totem means in all these ceremonies: it is the necessary preliminary step for the rite of magical procreations, just as breaking through the inner inhibitions, the endopsychic taboo must precede the free flow of the libido that is necessary for actual procreation.

The two types of totem eating in intichiuma ritual.

There are two principal types of totem-eating in connexion with the Intichiuma ceremonies. In one type the eating is an integral part of the multiplication rite; in the other it has become split off and has developed into a second ritual that follows the Intichiuma in two or three months. Before they go forth to produce the Grey Kangaroo the men eat a little grey kangaroo flesh and smear their body with the fat of the animal. They let their blood flow on the rock and some time afterwards, at the "Freigabe" (liberation) of the totem, they again eat a little of the cooked kangaroo flesh.[1] The Arunta name for the ritual called "Freigabe" (liberation) by Strehlow is tmaltakal-tailalajinama, to prepare something, to make it ready for use.[2] In the Red Kangaroo ceremony the elder men and those who play the part of the kangaroo ancestor eat some kangaroo flesh and rub their bodies with the fat in the camp of the young men; then they proceed to the Intichiuma ground, perform the blood-letting ceremony and make red kangaroos jump out of the rock. About two months after the ceremony, it is repeated as an intitjiuma,[3] and after the performance the chief actor eats some kangaroo flesh in the shade. Then he sends the young men out to hunt the kangaroo; they bring the animals to the elders, who distribute them.[4] Again in the Wallaby cult we have the eating both in the multiplication ceremony and in the subsequent liberation ritual.[5] In the Opossum and in the Grey Wallaby cult the totem is only eaten at the second ceremony.[6] In the Tjilpa (Dasyurus spec) ritual some flesh is eaten by the actor after the ceremony,[7] and the same obtains at the Emu [8] and the Owl ceremony.[9]

At the Duck ceremony eating takes place before the ritual,[10] as is also the case at the Lizard ceremony, where we again find the ceremonial blood-letting,[11] and at the Varanus Gould Lizard ceremony, where clashing stones against each other is substituted for it.[12] In the Snake ritual the flesh is eaten in the young men's camp before

1 Strehlow, *A. & L.*, III. 14.
2 Id., ibid., III. 7.
3 As to the difference and the connection between the mbatjalkatjuma (this is what Spencer and Gillen call an intichiuma) and the intitjiuma see below.
4 Strehlow, *A. & L.*, III. 13.
5 Id., ibid., III. 19. The multiplication is achieved by blood-letting.
6 Id., ibid., III. 23, 25. In the liberation ritual it is always eaten.
7 Id., ibid., III. 29.
8 Id., ibid., III. 36.
9 Id., ibid., III. 50.
10 Id., ibid., III. 59.
11 Id., ibid., III. 67.
12 Id., ibid., III. 68.

the dramatic ceremony takes place, then there is blood-letting and repetition of the rite as a liberation ceremony.[1] The proceeding at the Grub ceremony [2] is exactly the same. In the eastern part of the Arunta tribe, however, the ceremony of eating the totem before the Intichiuma seems to be absent, unless Spencer and Gillen's observations are inaccurate on this point, and the meaning of the ceremonial eating seems to be developing from its multiplicatory to the "taking off the taboo" aspect. After the performance of the Intichiuma the Witchetty Grub is taboo to the members of the totem, by whom it must on no account be eaten until it is abundant and fully grown, any infringement of the rule being supposed to result in an undoing of the effect of the ceremony resulting in the grub supply being very small.[3] Evidently there is a sort of contrast that jars on the feeling of the aboriginals in first multiplying the animal and then helping to reduce the supply. This indicates that the aggressive tendency underlies the multiplication ritual; originally they wish to kill the totem (eat the father), and this is over-compensated in the conscious desire to multiply it.

This sort of altruistic attitude naturally presupposes a certain stage of not quite primitive development, and if we remember that the multiplication ritual is merely the reduced survival of actual intercourse in the first instance, of onanistic movements that serve to stimulate the fore-pleasure in the second instance, we may infer the unconscious meaning of the inhibition: those who have produced the totem-animal ought not to eat it, just as they ought not to devour their own children.

The men of the Purula and Kumara classes and those of the Panunga and Bulthara who are not members of the totem, and did not take part in the ceremony, may eat it at any time, but it must always be brought into the camp to be cooked. It must, on no account, be eaten like other food out in the bush, or else the men of the totem would be angry and the grub would vanish.

When, after the Intichiuma, the grub becomes plentiful and fully grown, the Witchetty-Grub men, women and children go out daily and collect large supplies, which they bring into the camp, cook and store away in pitchis, whilst those who do not belong to the totem are out collecting. The supply of grubs only lasts a very short time, the animals appearing after rain; when the grubs grow less plentiful the store of cooked material is taken to the men's camp, where, acting as usual under instructions from the Alatunja, all the men assemble. Those who do not belong to the totem place their stores before those who do, and the Alatunja

[1] Strehlow, *A. & L.*, III. 71.

[2] Id., ibid., 80. Cf. another grub ceremony (p. 84), honey-ant ceremony (p. 89), and the bee ceremony (p. 91).

[3] Spencer and Gillen, *N. T.*, 203.

then takes one pitchi and, with the help of the other men of the totem, grinds up the contents between stones. Then he and the same men all take and eat a little, and when this has been done he hands back what remains to the other people. Then he takes one pitchi from his own store, and, after grinding up the contents, he and the men of the totem once more eat a little, and then pass the bulk of what remains over to those who do not belong to the totem. After this ceremony the Witchetty-Grub people eat very sparingly of the grub: we remember that they were absolutely forbidden to do so after the Intichiuma. They are not absolutely forbidden to eat it now, but must only eat sparingly; for, were they to eat too much, then the power of successfully performing the Intichiuma would depart from them and there would be very few grubs. On the other hand, it is equally important for them and especially for the Alatunja to eat a little; eating none would have the same effect as eating too freely.[1]

The totem-eating partakes here both of the character of a ceremony of first-fruits and of a rite intended to multiply the totem. The proceeding is very similar to what takes place in the case of the Kaitish "Ilkitnainga" (Intichiuma) of the Grass-seed totem. The Ulqua (Alatunja) is an old Thungalla man, and when he decides that the time has come to perform the ceremony he goes to the Ertnatulunga, clears the ground all around it, and then takes out the Churinga, greases them well and sings over them. Then he takes two of the Churinga, red-ochres them and decorates them with lines and dots of down, the latter representing the grass-seed. When this is done he rubs them together so that the down flies off in all directions.

We know that the down flying about really means the emanation of spirit-children, that is spermatozoa, which follows naturally after the rubbing of the Churinga, that is onanistic proceedings with the male member. Then for days the old Thungalla man walks about by himself in the bush "singing" the grass-seed and carrying one of the Churinga with him. At night-time he hides the Churinga in the bush, returns to his camp and sleeps on one side of the fire with his lubra on the other; the two having no intercourse whatever. During all this time, from the period at which he first visits the Ertnatulunga to the close, he is supposed to be so full of Churinga—that is of the magic power derived from these—that not only would it be iturka for him to have any intercourse with her, but such would result in making the grass-seed no good and in causing his body to swell up when he tasted any of it.

This part of the ritual reminds us of the mythical episodes in which the Intichiuma appeared as a substitute for intercourse: here we see that the man who is stock full of Churinga, that is

[1] Spencer and Gillen, *N. T.*, 204.

sublimated symbolical sexual potency, may not break through the very inhibition to which the sublimation owes its origin. The word iturka that is applied to such a transgression shows us the nature and origin of this check on sexual activity: iturka is a man who has access to a woman of a forbidden group, that is who commits incest.[1] The unsublimated form would sap the roots of projection which lie in the inhibition: if he procreated human beings, naturally there would be no need for him to procreate the grass-seed. When the seed begins to grow he still goes on "singing" to make it grow more, and at length, when it is fully grown, he brings his Churinga to his camp hidden in bark. Then he and his lubra go out and gather a store of seed and, bringing it back to the camp, the woman there grinds it up with stones; the Thungalla man himself takes some to the men's camp and grinds it there, and the Panunga men catch the meal in their hands as it falls off the edge of the grinding-stone. One of the Panunga (who of course belongs to the Mulyanuka, the other moiety) puts a little of the seed to the Thungalla's mouth, and he blows it away in all directions—the idea of this being to make the grass grow plentifully everywhere. After that he leaves the seed with the Mulyanuka, saying when he does so, "You eat the grass-seed in plenty: it is very good and grows in my country." When he returns to his camp he gives some of the seed to his wife, telling her to eat it and to tell the other women to do the same, unless they belong to the Grass-seed totem. The lubra makes four cakes of the grass-seed, and at sundown the Thungalla returns to the men's camp with these. One he gives to the Panunga, one to the Uknaria, one to the Bulthara, and the fourth he tells his lubra to send to the Appungerta (his sons-in-law to whom he is taboo). A Purula woman gives him some seed, which he takes to his own camp and hands over to his lubra to make into another cake; of this he eats a little and gives the rest to the Umbitjana men, who are his fathers, saying, "I am glad to give you this."

These men belong to his own moiety of the tribe, but unless they belong to the totem the seed is not tabooed to them. Then he tells his own lubra to instruct the women to gather seed in plenty, the greater part of which is carried to the Mulyanuka, the smaller part gathered by his own lubra and the women of her subclass being brought to him. After a time the Mulyanuka men once more come up to him bringing a little seed with them, but leaving the greater part of it in their own camp. In exchange for this which he eats they receive from the Thungalla the supply which the women have brought him, and then he tells them that all is now over and that they may eat freely. He himself and the men of the totem only eat very sparingly. If a man of his own totemic group eats too much of his own totem, he will be, as the natives say, "boned"

[1] Spencer and Gillen, *N. T.*, 750.

by the men who belong to the other moiety of the tribe, for the simple reason that if he eats too much of his totem then he will lose the power of performing Intichiuma and so of increasing his totem.[1]

These two parallel rites seem to help us a considerable way onwards in the understanding of the meaning of the totem-eating. We have noted one case in which the man would lose his power to multiply the animal if he were to lie with his lubra at such a time. The same would follow if he were to eat too much of his totem, that is if all inhibitions would disappear. We have also explained why he would lose his Churinga power by having intercourse with his own wife at such a time, for it would amount to committing incest and thus to breaking through all inhibitions: if there is no inhibition it follows that there is no sublimation of sexual potency, no projection into the animal world, and hence no Churinga power. The same is the case if he eats his own totem like any other food; then it ceases to be a totem, a symbol, something which is fraught with the ambivalent attitude of wish and dread, and hence again the ritual loses its meaning as an act of compromise between contrary psychical tendencies. If there is no libido or no repression to check its direct manifestation, then again there can be no projection, no multiplication of the totem species. In the former case (intercourse with his wife when the ceremonies are going on) the repression is directed against incest. Now, as we have seen in the chapters on the origin of children and the Alcheringa myth, this is just what totem-eating symbolizes: eating the totem means eating the murdered father and (in the displacement upwards) having intercourse with the mother. The totem must be eaten, that is the actor must indicate that he is guilty of the incestuous impulse; and it may only be eaten sparingly, that is repression must come into play, as it is only the interaction of these two contrary tendencies that can produce a successful Intichiuma. This interaction results in the splitting up of the ritual into a whole series: first he only takes some seed into his mouth, next he eats a little and then he eats more, although still sparingly. The second phase of the rite clearly indicates the original external conflict that gave rise to this psychic situation of libido and repression; he begins to eat of the totem (to commit incest with the mother), but after eating a very little desists, and says to his tribal fathers, " I am glad to give you this," that is he willingly renounces his infantile Oedipus wishes.

The general character of the rite and its taking place after the Intichiuma prove that it is meant as a liberation ceremony, although at the same time it is necessary for the multiplication of the totem. The liberation is twofold: it begins by eating the totem and giving it free for the non-totemites, especially those of the other moiety,

[1] Spencer and Gillen, *Nor. T.*, 291–94.

and continues by partially liberating it even for the members of the totem. The progress of the rite indicates the headway made by libido against repression without going so far as totally to break through the latter. For the strangers, those of the other moiety, where repression is but slightly operative (but not totally absent: they may not eat the seed without first bringing it into the camp and showing it to the totem head-man, etc.) the "liberation" sets in at the beginning of the rite, and sets in completely, for the members of the totem, where the play of the conflicting tendencies of libido and repression is specially prominent with regard to that particular symbol, only at the end and only in a certain degree.

In the Waduman tribe the different totemic groups perform ceremonies for the increase of the totemic animal or plant. These ceremonies are called Tjutju and are the equivalents of the Intichiuma of the Arunta tribe. When performing the ceremony the men of the group paint and dance, the others watching them. After the ceremony of any particular totemic group has been performed, the men of all other groups go out and gather some of the animal or plant. If, for example, it be "Eramalgo," the latter, after being brought into the camp, is taken to the Eramalgo head-man, the men saying, "Here is Eramalgo." He replies, "Give it, I eat." It is handed to him, and he puts it in a pitchi, mixes it with water, eats a little himself, and hands it over to the other men, saying, "I have finished." After this they may all eat it. So in the same way a Flying-fox man will eat a little of the animal and hand the rest over to the other men who do not belong to the totem.[1] The Mudburra natives also perform the Tjutju[2] ceremonies to increase the animal or plant. After securing the latter the men who do not belong to the totem group bring it up to the head-man and hand it to him, the old man saying, "Give it, I eat." He takes a little and then hands it back, saying "I have finished."

In the case of the Arunta Kangaroo totem (Undiara) we have the eating of kangaroo and anointing the body with kangaroo fat as an integral element of the Intichiuma, and the repetition of the eating on the following day evidently as a liberation ceremony. In the Irriakura totem (bulb of a Cyperaceous plant) the members of the totem do not eat the totem for some time after the Intichiuma (repression after the wish-fulfilment in the rite). Those who do not belong to the totem bring a quantity of it to the men's camp, where it is handed over to the Alatunja and the other men of the totem, who rub some of the tubers between their hands, thus getting rid of the husks, and then, putting the tubers in their mouths, blow them out again in all directions. After this the Irriakura people

[1] Spencer, *N. T. N. T. A.*, 198.

[2] The Warramunga word for sacred ceremonies. Spencer and Gillen, *Nor. T.*, 301, 302, 308.

may eat sparingly.[1] In an analogous rite of the Worgaia it is just after the spitting (or throwing about) that the members of the totem may not eat any more of the animal. Before performing the yam ceremonies the head-man takes a Churinga, wraps it up in bark, and leaves it on the ceremonial ground at a spot where yams grow. When these ceremonies are over the men of the other moiety of the tribe ask him to go and walk about in the bush and " sing " the yams as they want them to grow. Accordingly, he takes the Churinga and, carrying it under his armpit, goes out into the bush every day for about two weeks. At length, when he sees the plants growing well, he tells the men of the other moiety to go out and gather some. They do so, and, leaving their main supply in their own camps, bring a little up to the head-man of the totem, asking him to make them grow large and sweet. He bites a small one and throws the pieces out in all directions, an action which is supposed to produce the desired effect.[2] The throwing of the Worgaia rite is a substitute for the blowing about of the Arunta rite, and both are clearly multiplicatory ceremonies. This multiplicatory element of the rite is organically connected with the eating ritual, and seems to point to a period previous to the development of the " liberation " meaning of the totem-eating when it primarily stood for multiplication. After the symbolical incest (contained in the eating of the totem) as a multiplication rite has been once committed, the path is set free for its repetition, and hence the secondary meaning of the totem-eating as a liberation ritual.

In the Idnimita (grub of a large longicorn beetle) totem the grub must not be eaten after the Intichiuma by the members of the totem until it becomes plentiful, after which those men who do not belong to the totem collect it and bring it into the men's camp, where the store is placed before the Alatunja and men of the totem, who then eat some of the smaller ones and hand back the remainder to the men who do not belong to the totem. After this men of the totem may eat sparingly of the grub. In the Bandicoot totem the animal is not eaten after Intichiuma until it is plentiful. When it is, those who do not belong to the totem go out in search of one, which, when caught, is brought into the men's camp; there they put some of the fat from the animal into the mouths of the Bandicoot men and also rub it over their own bodies. After this the Bandicoot man may eat a little of the animal.[3]

As we have pointed out before, the symbolical totem-eating in the Intichiuma is the result of a compromise between the Oedipus attitude and repression; if there is no rebellion against the father (that is no eating the totem) there can be no intercourse whatever, as every intercourse is the repetition of the original incest and hence

[1] Spencer and Gillen, *N. T.*, 205.
[2] Id., *Nor. T.*, 296.
[3] Id., *N. T.*, 205, 206.

no symbolical intercourse, no Intichiuma. If, on the other hand, one eats too much of the totem, this means the complete absence of repression. In this case (*a*) a symbolical coitus would again be impossible, as a symbol is determined by the two contrary currents of repression and libido, that is we should have courting-dances and coitus, the propagation of the human species and no ritual, no multiplication of the totem-animal. (*b*) Eating too much of the totem would mean unchecked rebellion against the father (symbolized by eating), the complete victory of the aggressive tendencies leading to the dying out of the animal.

In the Kaitish tribe a man does not eat his own totem except ceremonially, for if he were to do so freely he would be "boned" by men of the other moiety because such conduct would prevent him from successfully performing Intichiuma. He eats a little just at the time of the Intichiuma, when it is essential especially for the head-man of the tribe to do this. If, for example, an Emu man comes into the country of a Grass-seed group, before eating the seed he will take what he has gathered to the head-man of the Grass-seed group and ask his permission to eat it. The totems are somewhat more clearly divided between the groups than in the Arunta, and when any animal is killed, if a man of the totem is in camp, it is taken to him by men of the other moiety. He eats a very little and then hands it back to the other men to eat.[1]

It is of interest to study the further progress of repression in the Warramunga tribe. If the men of the Snake totem should eat of the snake it would cause their death and at the same time prevent the animal from multiplying (the multiplication of the animal being the symbol of human multiplication). Here the eating of the totem is absent, but indications of its former existence have survived in the liberation ceremony. When the snake appears after the ceremony the men of the other moiety go out and bring one in to the head-man and say to him, "Do you want to eat this?" He replies, "No, I have made it for you: suppose I were to eat it, then it might go away; all of you go and eat it." In the same way a kulpu (honey or sugar bag) is brought to a man of that totem, after he has made Intichiuma, but he declines to eat it, and tells the others that he has made it for them, and they can go out and collect and eat it.[2] The original form of the totem-eating rite seems to be that found among the Western Arunta. Here the members of the totem clan are in the "Son-Attitude" with regard to the Totem-Father. It is before they can successfully multiply the animal, that is commit totemic incest, that they must kill and devour the father, and this act of rebellion is committed by the head-man of the totem—as if they wished to indicate its unconscious sources—in the camp of the young men. However, this phase of

[1] Spencer and Gillen, *Nor. T.*, 323, 324.

[2] Id., ibid., 308, 309.

life is not merely that of rebellion, but viewed from the other (and secondary) side of ambivalency also that of peace-making, of union with the father as indicated in many elements of the initiation ritual.[1] From this point of view the totem-eating is a Communion with the father: it is only when the members of the clan have united themselves with the totem, by eating its flesh and by anointing their bodies with its fat, that they can undertake to multiply it; it is only when they themselves have become fathers that they can successfully undertake procreation. And again, as they are now the fathers (the impersonators of the Alcheringa ancestors!), what is the procreation that they perform in the ceremonies? Evidently a symbolical repetition of the father's intercourse with the mother, a projection of incest into the animal world.[2]

The ritual of "setting free" the totem appears in the sequence of the ceremony as a reduplication of the first eating, and at the same time the "mbatjalkatiuma" is repeated as an "intitjiuma."[3] Probably what comes first in the ceremony also comes first in the course of evolution; the formation of an elaborate ceremony being due to the splitting off (Abspaltung) and gradual independent development of the elements of the original rite.

After the member of the totem clan has conquered the father in the first totem-eating, he proceeds, in the procreative element of the Intichiuma ritual, to turn the tables, to reverse the relations between himself and his totem animal; now it is he who becomes the (magical) father of the animal. At the same time his own attitude undergoes a change, and with growing years it is the Father-Attitude of the Oedipus complex that unconsciously dominates his own doings. It is not the father that he wishes to devour, but the rebellious son, and after having made the kangaroos by blood-letting (or an analogous symbolic coitus rite), he eats the kangaroo, the son he has procreated. We must not forget that the ritual is always performed by old men; this is the reason why the totem-eating after the Intichiuma has survived far more generally than the totem-eating before the multiplication.

In its double aspect the ritual represents the whole ontogenetic development of the Father-Son conflict and by performing it in ritual it leads to a partial catharsis, a partial abreaction of this conflict, and hence the members of the totem are permitted after the liberation ritual to eat sparingly of their totem. However, the ritual contains not only the permission for the members of the clan to eat the animal, but also for members of other totem-clans, and in this shape it can only have developed at a period when there

[1] Some of these we have mentioned when dealing with the blood-letting rite.

[2] We must not forget that they are the same person as the Alcheringa-ancestor, who magically procreated them by having symbolical intercourse with their own mother.

[3] Cf. below the explanation of these terms.—Strehlow, *A. & L.*, III. 13.

were already various clans united in one tribe. The head-man of the totem gives the men of other totems permission freely to eat and use the animal; more than that, he says that he has "made" the animal for them. That is, the union of the clans is made possible by a mutual respect shown to each other's compulsion-neurotic complexes, and these inhibitions are sublimated into an "altruistic," a "social" attitude.

This sublimation seems originally not to have been an affair between one totem and the rest of the totems, for in the Intichiuma these are largely replaced by the two primary divisions. The ceremonial period is truly a regression in tribal history towards the time of the "Alcheringa," as it has conserved the state of things that existed after the first division of the Original Horde. In the Witchetty Grub Intichiuma those men who belong to the other moiety of the tribe, that is to the Purula and Kumara, are about forty or fifty yards away sitting down in perfect silence, and at the same distance further back the Panunga and Bulthara women are standing with the Purula and Kumara women sitting down amongst them. The first-named women (that is those of the moiety to whom the ceremony belongs) are painted with the totem Ilkinia of red and white lines, the second are painted with lines of white faintly tinged with red.[1] At the conclusion of the ceremony, when the decorations are removed, the Alatunja says, "Our Intichiuma is finished; the Mulyanuka must have these things or else our Intichiuma would not be successful and some harm would come to us." They all say, "Yes, yes certainly," and the Alatunja calls to the Mulyanuka (i.e. men of the other moiety of the tribe), who are at the men's camp, to come up, and the things are divided amongst them.[2] The Intichiuma of the Hakea Flower totem is performed at a place called Ilyaba by men of the Bulthara and Panunga classes.[3] In the Kangaroo Intichiuma the Panunga and Bulthara men sit on the left hand, looking towards the stone, whilst the Purula and Kumara men sit on the right.[4] We must remind the reader that the Arunta totems are not divided between the classes, that the ceremonies are inherited by individuals, and that the "Mulyanuka" are always the men of the moiety to whom the possessor of the ceremony does not belong. Anyhow, it is remarkable that the "inner circle" of initiates and the "outer circle" of the uninitiated should be determined by classes in a totemic ceremony. However, we find exactly the same state of things in the north-west.

The part played by the dual organization in the Intichiuma ritual.

If kangaroos should become scarce in a season of drought the head of the family under whose charge the Kangaroo tarlow may be at the time (let us say a Ballieri) proceeds with other Ballieri

[1] Spencer and Gillen, *N. T.*, 176.
[2] Id., ibid., 178.
[3] Id., ibid., 184.
[4] Id., ibid., 201.

men to the tarlow and performs the Intichiuma (" willing ") there. Should the head-man of a tarlow die, if he is a Caiemurra, his child being Burong, the tarlow would be henceforth under the care of the Burong family, if a Ballieri his tarlows succeed to the care of the Baniker family, etc. Both men and women may inherit the control of the tarlow and one tribal family (that is class) may have charge of several tarlows at the same time.[1] In the Warramunga group of tribes the totems are divided between moieties. The totemic ceremonies proper are divided into two groups—one associated with the Uluuru moiety of the tribe and the other with the Kingilli.[2] In every case the men of the Kingilli moiety were requested to perform their ceremonies by Uluuru men. For instance, the head-man of an Ant totem who is a Thakomara was asked by Thapungarti men to perform, and when consenting to do so he asked the latter to decorate him, he in return subsequently made them a present of honey bag. This special offering of food to the men who decorate the others is called litjingara.[3]

A feature which is common to all the Kingilli ceremonies, and distinguishes any one of them at once from all those of the Uluuru, is that every performer in a Kingilli ceremony carries on either thigh what is called a tjintilli.[4] These tjintilli are also worn in the Intichiuma ceremonies of the Gnanji tribe,[5] whilst in the Binbinga tribe it appears in initiation ritual. The first time the novice sees a sacred totemic dance (immediately previous to circumcision) the men dance with tjintilli, which are here bunches of leafy twigs tied round the ankles.[6] The Warramunga tjintilli (conspicuous by its absence in Uluuru ceremonies) consist of a central stick about a yard long, to which are attached a number of leafy, green gum-twigs. The free end of the stick is passed on either side through the waist girdle, and the tjintilli is held in the middle by the hand and pressed down on the thigh when the performer dances and runs about with the usual high-knee action.

We do not know enough of these ceremonial objects to be able to ascertain their meaning with certainty; at any rate, we must note their connexion with the initiation ritual and the fact that a Lizard man is said to have made the first—the lizard, as we have seen, being all over Australia the originator of the difference between the sexes. If we then provisionally assume that the tjintilli represents the male member, we shall find an interesting parallel to its use

[1] C. Clement, " Ethnographical Notes on the Western Australian Aborigines." *Int. Arch. f. Ethn.*, XVI. 1904, 5. Cf. the distribution of the totems (or rather of the multiplication ceremonies) between the two primary classes (one pair of the four-class system on each side).—A. R. Brown, " Three Tribes of Western Australia," *J. A. I.*, 1913, 172.

[2] Spencer and Gillen, *Nor. T.*, 194.

[3] Id., ibid., 197, 98.

[4] Id., ibid., 198, cf. 213.

[5] Id., ibid., 366.

[6] Id., ibid., 198, 199.

amongst the Kingilli and absence in the Uluuru moiety in the closing act of the ceremonies.

The concluding act of the ceremonies.

A very characteristic feature in connexion with all the Kingilli ceremonies is the nature of their concluding act. In the Arunta, one or two men from amongst the audience walk up to and lay hands on the performers' shoulders;[1] in the Kaitish and Unmatjera the heads of the performers are pressed down; and in the Warramunga the head-dress which is invariably worn in connexion with Kingilli ceremonies is roughly knocked off by an Uluuru man. In each instance the performers run in on to the ground where the audience is standing. One man, always a member of the Uluuru moiety, stands by himself in the very centre of the ground, and the performer finally circles round and round, quite close to him, with his body bent and the usual high-knee action, while all the time he stares up into his face. The man does not take the slightest notice of the performer until, all of a sudden, the former lifts his right arm and, with what is often a smart, rough blow, knocks the helmet flying.[2] We have inferred the origin of these ceremonial head-dresses as derivatives of the secondary sexual characters: if the helmet is a penis that has been transposed upwards, knocking off the helmet would be a symbolical castration. The tjintilli worn by the Kingilli men only and the termination of all Kingilli ceremonies by a symbolical castration inflicted by the members of the other moiety[3] seem to correspond to each other, but it is only in the light of Atkinson's views on the evolution of society that we can get any clue to the origin of the dual organization and to the origin of these rites.

It is perhaps permissible to read the origin of the Two-Class System out of the Eagle-hawk and Crow myths; the bi-partition of the tribe was then an act of compromise after the great primeval conflict between the Son and the Sire. Half of the women are marriageable for Crow (Son), half for Eagle-hawk (Father), and the conflict of the two generations comes to a peaceful end. The ending of the ceremonies has conserved various stages of this conflict in various tribes: in the Warramunga the Uluuru men kill and castrate their Kingilli fathers, the wearers of the phallos (helm and tjintilli); in the Kaitish and Unmatjera the heads are pressed down, which is a half-peaceful and half-aggressive finish of the performance; whilst the hugging in the Arunta indicates the completely peaceful settling of all disputes.

We have already seen that the origin of the Intichiuma ceremonies

[1] A sort of hugging. Cf. Strehlow, *A. & L.*, III. 5.

[2] Spencer and Gillen, *Nor. T.*, 205, 206.

[3] In the Uluuru performances there is no running round and round a Kingilli man, but the performers come on to the ground and run round a few green boughs which have been placed in the centre, and immediately sit down on them.—Spencer and Gillen, *Nor. T.*, 206, 207.

in their present shape, with the repression of the feminine element and the homoerotic onanism represented by the rubbing of the Churinga, must be attributed to the phase of evolution that followed the victory of a group of brothers over the Primeval Sire, and the ritual is also prompted by the intention to strengthen the feeling of unity between these victorious brothers on the one hand, and (by allowing for a partial abreaction of the Oedipus complex) to prevent the repetition of their victorious rebellion by the next generation. The same phase of phylogenesis also accounts for the origin of the two-phratry system: the Group of Brothers "goes by halves" with the men of the next generation as regards the women, and thus forestalls the next rebellion.[1] We again find the parallelism of eating and intercourse so often observed in Australian ritual. In actual custom, a man will exchange his daughter for a woman of the opposite marriageable class of the other moiety; in the ritual he gives the animals, magically procreated by himself, as food to the men of the other moiety, in exchange for other animals magically procreated by them. A man thus "makes" both his daughter and the totem-animal for the men of the other moiety, and thus it seems as if the altruism of the alimentary side of life was merely the result of transposition upwards of the taboo aspect of the Oedipus complex. On the other hand, however, this taboo itself has its roots in a real conflict between the Father and the Son-group, and we may perhaps surmise that this conflict had a realistic beside an erotic side: that it was fought not merely for the women but also for the better hunting-grounds and the food animals. The choice between these two solutions is a *quæstio facti*, the decision of which lies not with social anthropology but with the study of animal behaviour.

Intichiuma and initiation.

Thus the primary division of the tribe may be regarded as the outcome of a phase of evolution in which the victorious group of brothers prevented the continuation of a series of inter-tribal revolts by institutions of a compromisory character, that met desire half-way and yet kept the inhibition up in a reduced form. We must remember that we have (following Reik) regarded the same phase of evolution and the same conflict as responsible for the rise of the initiation ritual. On the

[1] This is, of course, only a hint at the way in which I think we can explain the origin of the dual system without having recourse to the theory of design (Frazer), or to the theory of fusion (Rivers), which leaves the regularity of the two classes unexplained. Three-class systems are nearly unknown, but there is no reason to suppose that three people might not have formed a coalition just as well as two. The three divisions of the Iwaidji, which function for marriage purposes as if they were two, may very well be due to the fact of an alien element having joined a tribe with the two-class system. If the Jealous Sire of the original horde kept his wife and daughter for himself, but consented to an arrangement by which his sons might marry his sisters (their paternal aunts), we should get a two-class system with female descent.

social side these institutions are represented by the primary (totemic) division, on the ritual and social side by the puberty ceremonies. In the initiation ritual the Group of Elders are represented as vanquishing their would-be revolutionary sons, the primeval punishment of castration is re-acted symbolically and the first inhibitions are inculcated. The whole mechanism of the ritual is dictated by the fear of retribution ; the old men repeat the infantile rebellion against their own Elders in a symbolically reduced form on the next generation. But it is not only the Strife that is re-acted but also the Covenant that put an end to animosity, and the ritual contains not only the repression of the Oedipus attitude but also its homoerotic sublimation.

Intichiuma and mbatjalkatiuma.

In the course of our investigations we have had occasion to prove that nearly all these remarks apply to the Intichiuma ceremonies as well, so that it would not surprise us if we could make use of the initiation ritual and the dual organization to determine the phase of evolution to which the present form of the Intichiuma should be attributed. To begin with, we shall learn from a competent observer that the ceremonies we have been dealing with are not called Intichiuma at all, that being the designation of a different, though evidently closely related, series of ceremonies. " In the puberty ceremonies there are a whole series of performances which resemble very closely those of the ritual acts, but are not intended to affect the increase or prosperity of the particular totem ; they are only intended to show those who are entering or who have entered the ranks of manhood how these actions should be carried out—hence with reference to this purpose these ceremonies are called Intitjiuma, i.e. to initiate, to show how something is done. If, however, these ceremonies are carried out on the totem-places where the original altjiranga mitjina had its home, and with the object of causing the totem to increase and prosper, these actions are called mbatjalkatiuma, i.e. producing, fructifying, improving the condition." [1]

Before circumcision the novices are shown three Intitjiuma—(*a*) the Red Kangaroo ceremony, because a Red Kangaroo ancestor circumcised many youths in the Alcheringa ; (*b*) the Hawk ceremony, as the Hawk-man re-introduced circumcision that had already fallen into oblivion ; (*c*) the Bat ceremony, as many Bat people instructed others in the ceremonies in the Alcheringa.[2] Besides these there are also other Intitjiumas that vary according to the occasion and the decision of the old men.[3] It seems that these

[1] Strehlow, *A. & L.*, III. 1, 2.

[2] These three introducers of circumcision probably represent three distinct waves, all belonging to the large family of tribes who were in possession of this ceremony. The Manning, Hastings and Macleay tribes have a myth, in which the initiation hero Byama appears as a kangaroo.—R. H. Mathews, *F A. A.* 1899, 23.,

[3] Strehlow, *A. & L.*, IV. 19.

ceremonies correspond to the "down ceremonies" of Spencer and Gillen (Quabara undattha), who use the term Intichiuma for the same thing that Strehlow calls mbatjalkatiuma. "It is astonishing how large a part of a native's life is occupied with the performance of these ceremonies, the enacting of which extends sometimes over the whole of two or three months, during which time one or more will be performed daily. They are often, though by no means always, associated with the performance of ceremonies attendant upon initiation of young men, or are connected with Intichiuma, and so far as general features are concerned there is a wonderful agreement between them in all the northern and central tribes." [1] The Quabara which are performed at the initiation ceremonies vary according to the locality in which they are performed and the men who are taking the leading part in them. If, for example, the old man who is presiding belongs to the Emu totem, then the Quabara will to a large extent deal with incidents concerned with ancestral Emu men, but the totem of the novice has no influence whatever on the nature of the particular Quabara performed.[2] The body of the performer is decorated with ochre and lines of birds' down which were supposed to be arranged in just the same way as they had been on the body of the Alcheringa ancestor.

In a Kangaroo performance, for instance, we find a ball of fur-string, that represents the scrotum of the kangaroo, hung from the waist of the performer. When all was ready, he came hopping leisurely out from behind the men's brake, where he had been decorated, lying down every now and then on his side to rest as a kangaroo does. For about ten minutes he went through the characteristic movements of the animal, acting the part very cleverly, while the men who sat round the novice sang of the wanderings of the kangaroo in the Alcheringa. He was told about the doings of the kangaroo ancestor, about his death and about the final transformation of his spirit part into a Churinga. This spirit, the old men told him, went at a later time into a woman, and was born again as a Purula man whose name was, of course, Unburtcha (like the ancestors), and who was a Kangaroo man just as his ancestor was. He was told that the old men know all about these matters and decide [3] who has to come to life again as a man or woman.[4] In the ceremony of the Rat totem the particular Rat-man or Man-rat (the identity of the human individual being sunk in that of the object) with which he was associated and from which he is supposed to have originated, to whom the ceremony referred, is supposed to have travelled from a place called Pulkira to Walyira, where he died and where his spirit remained associated with the Churinga.[5]

[1] Spencer and Gillen, *N. T.*, 177, 178.

[2] Id., ibid., 226.

[3] The exclusive knowledge and right of decision of the old men in these matters seems to be a psychical substitute for their lost or waning sexual powers.

[4] Id., ibid., 228, 229.

[5] Id., ibid., 231.

The Waninga carried in this ceremony represented the body of a rat; the main part was supposed to be the trunk of the animal, the point end the tail, and the handle end the head, so that when in use it was carried downwards. The cross-bars represented the limbs. The other two men were decorated to represent two little night-hawks. They approached from the south side to the novice, making a circuit and walking with their backs turned to the circumcision ground until they got opposite to the novice, who has been blindfolded all this time. The bandage is now taken from his eyes and he sees the two little Hawk-men, with legs wide apart and hands grasping the ends of a stick, come along towards the audience, sliding and quivering as they did so. They were followed by the Waninga carriers, who were also quivering and bending the Waninga towards the novice. The ceremony ended by the novice embracing the Waninga.[1]

When we remember the sexual significance of the Waninga on the one hand and the usual termination of an Intichiuma ritual on the other hand (embracing the performer), we shall be inclined to see an element of homoerotic sublimation that is in accordance with a certain phase both of the Intichiuma and the initiation ceremony in the closing act of this Quabara—all the more so as we know the sexual significance of another Intichiuma feature of this Quabara, the quivering in a Kangaroo ceremony in which the men imitated the movements of young and old kangaroos. When preparing for the ceremony the bodies were first of all rubbed over with red ochre, then two young men opened their veins and allowed the blood to flow out in a stream over the heads and bodies of those who were about to take part in the ceremony.[2] Each man carried on his head and also between his teeth a small mass of wooden shavings saturated with blood.[3] The men stood in the path with their legs wide apart, one behind the other, shifting their heads from side to side and making the twigs quiver. When the novice is told to look up, the man who represented a young kangaroo begins to frisk about and pretends to rush at the other performers, finally darting between the legs of each man and emerging at the western end of the column.[4]

We have met with this latter feature in the Kangaroo Intichiuma of the Loritja, where it is said to represent a " game " played by the Alcheringa kangaroos, although it is evidently an imitation of the act of copulation.[5] The rubbing with red ochre may be compared to the rubbing of the Churinga, whilst the blood-letting is found both here and in the Intichiuma in identical form as a sublimation of homoerotic tendencies. In the Engwura, which is the concluding

[1] Spencer and Gillen, *N. T.*, 233, 234.
[2] Id., ibid., 234.
[3] Id., ibid., 235.
[4] Id., ibid., 236.
[5] Strehlow, III, Part ii, 2.

part of the initiation ceremony and which lasted (as observed by Spencer and Gillen) from September to January, there was a constant succession of these Quabara ceremonies.[1] The ceremonies performed at an Engwura depend upon the men who are present; that is, if at one Engwura special totems are better represented than others, then the ceremonies connected with them will preponderate.[2] Indeed, the main object of the Engwura seems to be the handing down of the traditional knowledge referring to the totems and Churingas to the younger generation.[3] When the totem-eating of the Alcheringa is represented[4] two men imitate the Eaglehawk,[5] and even the Churinga appear in some of these ceremonies,[6] not to mention the Waninga, Nurtunja, etc. An " Ulpmerka " head-dress with churingas fastened on represents a special form of Nurtunja.[7] In a ceremony of the Fish totem the opening and closing of the fish's gills is imitated.[8] In a ceremony of the Irriakura totem the Bulb-man is represented gathering bulbs, tufts of feathers representing the growing bulbs.[9] Alcheringa ancestors of the Plum-tree totem are represented as continually eating plums.[10]

Evidently it is not easy to determine the difference (except in the intention of the ceremony) between the Quabara (Intitjiuma: Strehlow) and the Intichiuma (Mbatjalkatiuma: Strehlow), especially when in the Engwura the Churinga also come into prominence. It is evident that there is a connexion between the " Quabara " and the " Intichiuma " type of totemic ceremony, and as the former are principally performed at initiation, especially at the Engwura, the same remark holds good with regard to initiation and Intichiuma. We have already commented upon the part played by the primary moieties in the Intichiuma rites, and we may compare this with the following remark of Spencer and Gillen: " The division of the tribe into two moieties, which stands out so clearly on the occasion of a ceremony such as the Engwura, points to the fact of the original division of the tribe into two halves, each of which was again divided into two."[11] We shall not be surprised to find the moieties coming out clearly in the initiation ritual, as according to our theory both institutions represent the original settling of affairs between the fathers and the sons.

The same phase of social evolution is also represented in both groups of totemic ceremonies; in the Warramunga the series of totemic ceremonies (Quabara) are intimately associated with and performed at certain times as Intichiuma ceremonies.[12] Even here, however, there is a difference between the cere-

[1] Spencer and Gillen, *Nor. T.*, 178.
[2] Id., *N. T.*, 279.
[3] Id., ibid., 280.
[4] Id., ibid., 295.
[5] Id., ibid., 296.
[6] Id., ibid., 298, 304.
[7] Id., ibid., 310, 313.
[8] Id., ibid., 307.
[9] Id., ibid., 318, 319.
[10] Id., ibid., 320.
[11] Id., ibid., 277.
[12] Id., *Nor. T.*, 193.

monies of the Quabara type (called Thuthu) and those of the Intichiuma type (called Thalamintha).[1] The Thalamintha series, here also, is performed with the intention of multiplying the animal,[2] whilst the Thuthu are performed at initiation.[3] Now, it is very remarkable that the Thalamintha of the present day are said to be performed in imitation of the Thuthu of the Alcheringa ancestors. When the ancestor used to perform Thuthu the spirit-individuals used to emanate from him just as the white down flies off the Thalamintha performers at the present day.[4] Wherever the Alcheringa ancestors went they performed Thuthu and left spirit-children behind.[5] This remarkable relation between the two ceremonial types may perhaps also be illustrated by a custom of the Tjingilli. To make both young men and women grow strong and well-favoured, the men perform at intervals of time a long series of ceremonies called wantju dealing with the various totems. There is no special reference to the young men or women in them, but they are performed solely with the object of increasing the growth of the younger members of the tribes.[6] Increasing the growth of youngsters is perhaps only a slight alteration for making babies be born, and the Thuthu, which are the mythical prototypes of the Thalamintha, served this purpose.

Nowadays the Thuthu and the corresponding Quabara are performed as anthropic ceremonies, that is in connexion with puberty rites, whilst the Thalamintha-intichiuma type has undergone a projection into the animal world. In this later form of ceremony we may distinguish a procreative and an imitative element. The former is represented by the rites of rubbing, blood-letting, quivering and throwing (to be dealt with below), all of them symbolical of intercourse, the latter, as we shall see, consists in the imitation of the life of the animal and of the methods employed to secure it as food. The former part of the ritual represents the Pleasure Principle pure and unalloyed, whilst in the latter, as we shall see, the Reality Principle also plays a considerable part. If we compare the two types of totem ceremonies with one another we shall find that the procreative element is only to be found in vestiges in the Quabara rites, whilst both series correspond entirely as regards the imitative element. Moreover, the former series can be performed anywhere (preferably, of course, on the initiation ground), whilst the latter is restricted to the totem-centre (Arunta) or at least to a drawing representing it (Warramunga), that is to an environmental repetition of the uterus.

We have ample reason for supposing both elements to have formed part of an original rite, and we can easily see why the procreative

[1] Spencer and Gillen, *Nor. T.*, 297.
[2] Id., ibid., 308.
[3] Id., ibid., 351.
[4] Id., ibid., 301.
[5] Id., ibid., 302.
[6] Id., ibid., 476.

(libidinal) element had to undergo repression in the first instance and survived in the second.

In the Intichiuma the ritual is directed towards the animal world, in the Quabara it is performed in connexion with the human members of the clan; projection or repression are alternative methods by which the psychic censor obscures the original meaning of the ritual. As a common starting-point for the two sets of totemic rites, we must postulate a ritual that contained both the imitative and the libidinal element (as the Intichiuma), that was performed in connexion with initiation ceremonies (like the Quabara), at the rutting season (like the Intichiuma), and where the object of the rite was to make human spirit-children incarnate themselves (like the Thuthu rites of the Alcheringa and the ceremonies of the Baby totems). We can now also understand why the difference between the two series is far less evident among the Warramunga than the Arunta. The Warramunga Intichiuma (Thalamintha) is chiefly a ceremony that represents the wanderings of the ancestors, the magical (procreative) element being much less prominent than amongst the Arunta, that is we find repression superadded to projection—which makes it easily interchangeable with the Thuthu ceremonies.

It has not escaped the notice of Spencer and Gillen that ceremonies of the imitative type are widespread—indeed, perhaps a universal feature of the Australian initiation ritual. " We meet with descriptions of performances in which different animals are represented, but except in the case of the Arunta tribe no indication of the meaning and significance of these performances has been forthcoming beyond the fact that they are associated with the totems. In the Arunta and Ilpirra tribes they are not only intimately associated with the totemic system, but have a very definite meaning. Whether they have similar significance in other tribes we have as yet no definite evidence to show, but it is at all events worthy of note that whilst the actual initiation rite varies from tribe to tribe (knocking out of teeth, circumcision, etc.), in all, or nearly all, an important part of the ceremony consists in showing to the novices certain dances, the important and common feature of which is that they represent the actions of special totemic animals.

" In the Arunta tribe . . . it looks much as if all they were intended to represent were the behaviour of certain animals, but in reality they have a much deeper meaning, for each performer represents an ancestral individual who lived in the Alcheringa . . . as a descendant or transformation of the animal the name of which he bore."[1] As we have been able to show that there is a close connexion between the " Down ceremonies " and the Intichiuma in the Central Australian area, it is to be presumed that a study of

[1] Spencer and Gillen, *Nor. T.*, 227, 228.

these animal-dances in the initiation ritual will throw further light on the relation between that rite and Intichiuma.

In the Melville and Bathurst Island initiation ritual ceremonies connected with the totems Kangaroo, Cockatoo, Crocodile, Lizard, etc., are performed.[1] Next morning they are shown first a Crocodile ceremony. Two men, imitating the movements of a crocodile, sprawl on the ground and crawl about.[2] In the Kakadu tribe initiation ceremonies are a complicated affair, consisting of five distinct rites that mark the various phases in the life of a native from childhood to manhood. In the Yam ritual we find an old man playing an important part who is supposed to represent a great old kangaroo ancestor called Munamera, and we find men imitating the sound made by the kangaroo.[3] Next we have the Ober ceremony. A log of wood is supposed to represent the old ancestral Kangaroo-man or Man-kangaroo watching the ceremony. Sixteen men were decorated, two of them representing fish-men, whilst the rest were rush-tailed wallabies. Two men performed a dance, during which they were supposed to be imitating the movements of native companions.[4] In another performance the men imitate kangaroos and smash a wurley to bits. It has not been possible to ascertain the exact meaning of this ceremony, but in some way it is associated with a group of ancestors who were led by a very big old Kangaroo-man called Jeru Ober (Ober is the name of the ceremony). The wurley belonged to him and he used to rest in it during the day just as an old Man-kangaroo now rests in the shade of a tree or bush during the heat of the day. He told the others to kill white cockatoos and make head-dresses. Then he made the ceremonial ground and the hollow trumpet and showed them how to perform the ceremony. The kangaroo then said, "We are like blackfellows now, we will go under ground or the natives will see us." So they all went down excepting the Jeru Ober, who remained up for some time till he, too, went into the earth a short distance away by the side of a big paper bark tree. The original ceremonial ground was at a place called Kupperi, between the East and South Alligator Rivers.[5] This shows a connexion between the totemic dances of initiation and the typical Alcheringa-ancestor legend just like the state of things in the Central tribes.

Another important Ober ceremony is associated with three snakes. The ground is "sung" to make it slippery so that the performers could dance well, and the snake is sung also. One man represented a male snake called Ngabadaua (a vicious animal of whom the natives are very much afraid) and two non-venomous

[1] Spencer, *N. T. N. T. A.*, 118.
[2] Id., ibid., 119.
[3] Id., ibid., 127.
[4] Id., ibid., 136.
[5] Only men who have been through the Ober ceremony may go there; women and children must not go anywhere near.—Id., ibid., 139.

snakes called Kuljoanjo[1] and Jeluabi. The first-named snake has a sacred or ceremonial name unknown to the women.[2] A mythical episode, how Ngabadaua killed the other snakes, is represented, and a general quivering and swaying of the performers' bodies is going on.[3] The ceremonies of the third stage, the Jungoan, are all associated with the totemic groups.[4] Kangaroos and emus are represented; at last one of the old men knocks the performers' helmets off, and this is an indication that they have been killed by the men in pursuit of them.[5] The Jungoan simply consist of the performance of a series of ceremonies which are strongly reminiscent of those performed by southern (central) tribes such as the Tjingilli, Warramunga and Arunta.[6] The next phase of the initiation rite is the Yam ceremony. The various articles of food that have hitherto been taboo to the novice (the Kulori yam, the Jabiru bird, the flying-fox, the quail, the barrammada, the mullet, the lily) are "sung."[7] The concluding ceremony of the series, the Muraian, may be compared to the Engwura of the Arunta. Here we have a fire, a wallaby, and a turtle ceremony on the first day.[8] Then there was a kangaroo and turkey ceremony. The Kangaroo men had curious bands running slantwise down their chest and backs and along their legs, which designs represented the backbone of the kangaroo.[9] The Muraian themselves are objects such as sacred sticks and stones which are as intensely "kumali" as the Churinga of the Arunta and equally intimately associated with the totems. These are all Muraian sticks and stones, and the most sacred of them, the Muraian itself, is produced at a certain phase of the ceremony. The man carrying it tumbled down on the ground and was followed by the others, and they all wriggled and rolled about in the most grotesque fashion. The Muraian was in the form of a slighty curved slab of wood with the representation of a head at one end and two little projections at each side, representing limbs. It was supposed to be a turtle, to which it certainly showed a considerable resemblance quite enough to be recognizable; the rolling about of the men was supposed to be an imitation of the movements of the animal itself.[10] This Muraian was found a very long time ago by an old ancestor called Kulbaran. He saw something strange in the form of a turtle moving about in the water, caught it and discovered that it was Muraian, or rather the turtle told him so. The turtle then described

[1] Cf. the restrictions as to eating the Kuljoanjo.—Spencer, *N. T. N. T. A.*, 1914, 347.

[2] Id., ibid., 140.

[3] Id., ibid., 142, 143.

[4] Id., ibid., 144.

[5] This confirms our view as to the inimical meaning of the helmet knocked off in the Warramunga rites.

[6] Spencer, *N. T. N. T. A.*, 146.

[7] Id., ibid., 148, 149.

[8] Id., ibid., 350.

[9] Id., ibid., 151. The portable ornaments were probably substitutes of the articles they represented, and the designs substitutes of the ornaments. The series would be: Human backbone → kangaroo backbone → Nurtunja → design.

[10] Id., ibid., 187.

the ceremonies and taught Kulbaran how to perform them and how to make the sacred sticks and stones. He also told him that the old men might eat the Muraian animals, but that the young men must not do so.[1] Then he showed him the whole series of dances and the stones that were representative of the various totems.[2] When all the sticks and stones had been brought on to the ground they were arranged in a circle and the men danced round and round them with their arms alternately extended and drawn back while they yelled " Brau, brau," that is " Give, give." It was, as the natives said, a request, in fact a demand, to the sacred representatives of the various animals and plants to provide them with these same animals and plants that form their food supply,[3] so that the Muraian serves both as a finale, a sort of supreme initiation, and as an Intichiuma ceremony,[4] the multiplication of the animals being here again brought into connexion with a sort of Churinga.[5] The Mungarai have the usual totemic animal dances in connexion with initiation and they here have a special name, warwirran, which corresponds to the quabara of the Arunta.[6] We may compare the Gnamulla who expound the mystery of " tarlow," that is Intichiuma, at initiation [7] to the Kakadu, where the same totemic rite serves as initiation and Intichiuma. Animal dances at initiation have also been observed on the Buccaneer Islands.[8] Various animals (kangaroo, emu) are represented at the Kabi and Wakka initiation ceremonies.[9] In the initiation ceremonies of the Coast Murring tribes we have the magical dances and images of the porcupine and the brown snake.[10] The totemistic element comes out more clearly in a number of performances. Whenever possible the men who represented animals were of those totems, and all the animals which were represented in the performances were the totem animals of the tribe. Thus when it is a kangaroo hunt it is a Kangaroo-man who performs and the Wild-Dog men hunt him.[11]

In the case of the dances performed by the natives on the right bank of the Murray towards Lake Alexandrina, we do not know whether they belong to the initiation ceremony, are ordinary corroborees, or perhaps Intichiumas. They are performed at water-holes, and this seems to indicate a magical intention for the frog dance, which consisted of men pointed and armed with wirris, squatting on the ground and then leaping along one after the other

[1] Spencer, *N. T. N. T. A.*, 189, 190.
[2] Id., ibid., 189.
[3] Id., ibid., 187.
[4] Id., ibid., 191.
[5] Cf. Map 6, p. 166, " Distribution of Churinga." For the data see Spencer and Gillen, *N. T.* and *Nor. T.*, and Spencer, *N. T. N. T. A.*, chapters on ceremonial objects and Intichiuma ceremonies.
[6] Spencer, *N. T. N. T. A.*, 165, 166.
[7] E. Clement, " Ethnographical Notes on the Western Australian Aborigines," *I. A. E.*, 1904, XVI. 10.
[8] W. H. Bird, " Ethnographical Notes about the Buccaneer Islanders," *Anthropos*, 1911, 175.
[9] Mathew, *Two Tribes*, 101.
[10] Howitt, *N. T.*, 523.
[11] Id., ibid., 545.

in circles imitating the actions and movements of a frog. In another dance they go through the performance of hunting an emu, one man imitating the voice of the bird.[1] Of the Yuin totem dances, some consisted of a magic dance to the name of the totem. Others were prefaced by pantomimic representations of the totem animal, bird or reptile. Thus there was a dance to the word Yiraikapin, the dog's tooth, referring to the "ravenous tooth which devours everything." It commenced with the lifelike howling of a dingo in the forest, answered by other dogs on the other side. Then it came nearer, till a man ran into the firelight on all fours, with a bush stuck in his belt behind to represent a dingo's tail. Others followed, till half a score were running round the fire, smelling each other, snarling, snapping and scratching the ground; in fact, representing the actions of wild dogs, until the medicine man leading them sprang to his feet, clapped his hands, vociferating in measured tones "Yiraikapin." While he danced the others followed him, dancing round him, and the usual totem dance was made. Then there was the crow dance, in which men with leaves round their heads cawed like those birds; and then danced the owl dance, in which they imitated the hooting of the owl; the lyre-bird dance, and that of the stone plover. Finally, there was a rock wallaby pantomime.[2] In the Port Jackson initiation ceremonies we find men disguised as dingoes and kangaroos.[3]

In the Chepara tribe the men pretend that it is stormy and raining, making noises to represent the wind. Then a number of the men hop about and croak like frogs. There are pantomimes representing the flying-foxes on the branches of the trees, bees flying about, curlews and many other creatures. There are no totems in this tribe, and Howitt is inclined to see survivals of a totemic system in these dances.[4]

In the Kurnai initiation these animal dances are represented by an "opossum game" and a kangaroo hunt.[5] At the Kamilaroi Bora the old men taught novices all the native games, to sing the songs of the tribe, and to dance certain corroborees which neither the gins nor the uninitiated are permitted to learn (? Intichiuma). The men and boys cut grasses and reeds and tied them up to resemble kangaroo-tails, then sticking them in their belts while they danced a corroboree imitating kangaroos. There was a legend to explain these tails. Baiamai and his two sons were out hunting one day and caught two kangaroos and cut their tails off. The next Bora they went to Baiamai's sons danced with these; this custom has been followed by the tribes at all Boras ever since.[6] The episode of

[1] G. F. Angas, *Savage Life and Scenes in Australia*, 1847, I. 63.
[2] Howitt, *N. T.*, 546, 547.
[3] Id., ibid., 568.
[4] Id., ibid., 581, 582.
[5] Id., ibid., 631, 635.
[6] R. H. Mathews, "The Bora, or Initiation Ceremonies of the Kamilaroi Tribe," *J. A. I.*, 1894, 425.

the cut-off tail seems to suggest that the pantomime has something to do with the castration complex, and a closely parallel version contains a corroboration of this hint.

In the Wiradhuri rite we find that Thoorkook's dogs as they come to kill the boys are personified by the men.[1] We have already dealt with the myth of Thoorkook's dogs, who personify the castration complex and are killed by the brothers Baiamai in the shape of kangaroos.[2] In the Wonggoa ceremony the performances consist for the most part of imitating animals or of scenes from the daily life of the people. Some of the animals selected are totems of those present, whilst others are connected with various myths and superstitions.[3] There is a performance to imitate the rolling of distant thunder,[4] an opossum hunt; then there are mimic plays of the locust, native companion, kangaroo, porcupine and other animals.[5] In the Multyerra ceremony kangaroos and native companions are imitated.[6]

Whilst the kangaroo scene of the Kamilaroi rite perhaps represents the castration of the kangaroo father and the annexation of his tail (penis) by his kangaroo sons, and the Thoorkook episode represents a more advanced form of the same complex, that is, the retribution on the son for his castration wishes,[7] some representations contain clear allusion to the death of the Primeval Sire at the hands of his sons. The novices are brought to a place where one of the old men who conduct the ceremonies is lying on his back in mortal agony. Some men go round and round him, imitating crows, from time to time picking with their beaks at the penis of the dying man, who groans loudly.[8]

In the Dolgarrity ceremony the novices are brought within view of a kangaroo, wallaby or other animal lying dead upon the ground. Several men are walking about it, imitating eagle-hawks and making the peculiar whistling call of that bird. Upon being disturbed they run along swaying their arms up and down to represent the flapping of wings of these large birds, which enables them to raise their heavy bodies from the ground when they commence to fly away from their prey. Sometimes this performance is varied by the men representing crows instead of eagle-hawks. In such cases the action and cry of the crow is mimicked.[9]

[1] R. H. Mathews, "The Bŭrbŭng of the Wirathuri Tribes," *J. A. I.*, 1896, 332.

[2] Id., *F. A. A.*, 23. At any rate we find Baiamai imitating the animal he has killed, or even changing into it in another myth, which shows the mechanism that led to the origin of totemism.

[3] Id., *E. N.*, 113.

[4] Id., ibid., 113, 117.

[5] Id., ibid., 117.

[6] R. H. Mathews, *Die Multyerra Initiations Zeremonie*, 1904, 81. (Separate reprint from *Mitt. d. Anthr. Ges. in Wien*, XXXIV.)

[7] The paternal animosity being, however, projected into the Wild-Dog demon, leaving for Byama, the manifest representative of the father-imago, the role of avenger.

[8] Mathews, ibid., 81.

[9] Mathews, *E. N.*, 131.

Now it can be no mere chance that the crow and the eagle-hawk are the eponymous animals of the primary divisions, the proto-totems of a whole stock. We have connected the origin of this primary division with the victory of the Brother Horde over the Father and the subsequent compromise between the brothers and the next generation, and it seems that the same episode is represented in these scenes of the initiation ritual. We have noticed the part this original bisection plays in the Intichiuma ceremonies, and indeed this has been noticed in conjunction with an analogous state of things at the initiation ceremonies by H. Webster, who, however, attributes this state of things to a later phase of development.[1] Anyhow, we have seen that one moiety makes Intichiuma for the other, i.e. produces food for the other, just as the men of the moiety do not engender their own daughters for themselves, but for the men of the other moiety.[2]

This is exactly paralleled in initiation; the men of the other moiety from whom the youth obtains his wife, are also those who initiate him, this pointing to the real reason underlying the repressed hostility of initiation ritual: the men who "kill" him and subsequently permit him to be born again are those from whom he is about to take their daughter or sister away as his wife.

From the viewpoint of the Conscious and the friendly current of Ambivalency the remarks of Howitt may be quoted. "Calling the classes for convenience A and B, then it may be said that it is the men of A class who initiate the youths of class B, and vice versa. A class cannot initiate its own young men, but both classes co-operate in this ceremony." "The reason of this seems to be that it is only when a youth is admitted to the rights and privileges of manhood that he can obtain a wife. As his wife comes to him from the other moiety, it is the men of the other moiety who must be satisfied that he is, in fact, able to take his place as provider for and the protector of the woman, their sister, who is to be his wife. In this connexion one can therefore see why it is that the future wife's brother, who is also his sister's husband, is the guardian of the youth in the ceremonies."[3]

If we argue that the animal dances of initiation have the same root in the past of the race as those of Intichiuma, it is for us to

[1] H. Webster, "Totem Clans and Secret Associations in Australia and Melanesia," *J. A. I.*, 1911, 484, 485.

[2] Cf. "They also called incestuous anyone who killed or ate any portion of a person of the same class as himself, e.g. a Maramara who killed or ate a Maramara." (The two classes are Maramara and Pikala, each with an insect for its totem.)—Brown, *Melanesians and Polynesians*, 1910, 28. Any breach of class relationships was regarded as incest (p. 253). "A person who had committed incest (kuou) would be horribly tormented and killed by his own friends, who would say that they were killing themselves in the action which they were taking."—Id., 411. "Killing themselves" evidently means punishing themselves for their own unconscious desires.

[3] Id., op. cit., 608; cf. 640.

show how they got into their present ritual "ensemble." This leads us to a question of general import: the connexion between initiation and Intichiuma already abundantly indicated as regards the Arunta tribe. To begin with, no Intichiuma is complete without the Churingas, which, from the general point of view, are a specialized form of bullroarers, whilst from the Arunta point of view the bullroarer is a species of Churinga. The bullroarer, at any rate, which is thrown at a woman by the Alcheringa ancestor, which is used for love-magic, smeared with blood from the subincised penis, is the central mystery,[1] the very symbol of initiation ritual. Now, this same object is in use for magical purposes analogous to those of the Intichiuma, more especially as a rain-charm. The headquarters of the Dugong clan at Mabuiag was at Dabungai, and it was at the kwod (ertnatulunga) there, close to the seashore, that the magical ceremony took place which had for its object the constraining of the dugong to come towards the island to be caught, and Dabungai is the area where the dugong is the most abundant, as it faces the reefs, which are the great feeding-grounds of the dugong. The first dugong of the season obtained by a Dangal man was put on "medicine" plants. Several men hoisted the dugong up by its tail in such a manner as to indicate to the dugong of the sea the way from the reefs to the island. The men of the clan paint themselves to resemble the dugong and use a wooden model of a dugong to attract it.[2]

Similar rites of the Torres Straits Islanders.

This rite is like a Central Australian Intichiuma in nearly every detail; it partakes also of the nature of a "liberation ceremony," as the first dugong of the season that has been employed in the ceremonies is afterwards given to the Turtle men. The first turtle caught during the turtle-breeding season was handed over to the men of the Turtle clan. It was not taken to the village, but to the kwod of the clan, where it was smeared all over with red ochre, when it was known as Parma surlal. The clansmen painted themselves with a red mark across the chest and another across the abdomen, evidently to represent the anterior and the posterior margin of the plastron or under-shell of the turtle. They wore cassowary feather head-dresses, and danced round the turtle whirling bullroarers and shaking rattles. The meaning underlying this Intichiuma rite is made particularly evident by the next detail. A length of a creeper was cut off and slightly sharpened at one end; this was inserted in the cloaca of the turtle and pushed up and down

[1] In the Warramunga tribe the men show their penes to the novices, spreading them out and stretching them as far as possible, saying: "You must not talk about what we tell you; you must not say that you have seen our penes. Sit down quietly; never go and talk close to your kaballa (elder sister)."—Spencer and Gillen, *Nor. T.*, 350. The penis is shown here just like the bullroarer is in other tribes.

[2] Haddon, *Cambridge Expedition to Torres Straits*, V. 183.

several times. This was an act of pantomimic magic to make him (that is all the turtle) proper fast (fast = copulation)—in other words, to ensure a good surlal turtle season, just as the Loritja will imitate the copulation of the kangaroos in the Kangaroo Intichiuma.[1]

The bullroarer is a materalized symbol of the fructifying powers; it is swung when the lad is about to enter on the duties of manhood and when the animals are about to be made to breed.[2] At Muralug[3] the actual initiation ceremony consisted mainly in showing the lads a bullroarer and in instructing them how to use it. The Kiwai ceremony shows us the connexion between Intichiuma and initiation in a striking fashion, for here we have initiation at a fixed season of the year, a season which, in the light of our previous remarks, may with ease be identified as the pairing season of our pre-human ancestors. At Jam in Kiwai there were two initiation ceremonies. At the first a madubu (bullroarer) is shown to the youths, in a tabooed and fenced-in part of the bush, who are shown how to use it. Each youth receives one and the whirling of the bullroarer ensures a good crop of yams, sweet potatoes and bananas. According to one account the bullroarer is swung and shown to the youths when yams are planted in the season: a fence is made in the bush and the women and boys are kept out of the way as long as the ceremonies last. The second initiation ceremony takes place during the rainy season. The youths are again taken to the bush and this time the orara is shown to them. This is a wooden image of a nude woman which was described as "god belong moguru"; a smaller form of it is known umuruburu—this is usually a thin flat board cut into the shape of a human being. These effigies are supposed to ensure a good supply of sago. When food is scarce or of poor quality, if for instance a sago palm is split and the pith found to be "no good," the men "make moguru" (the name of the second initiation rite) and "put medicine along moguru for kaikai" (food). During the Moguru ceremonies the men are decorated and wear a head-dress made of cuscus skin. Women and uninitiated boys may not see any of these sacred emblems nor the head-dresses. Between the Moguru ceremony and the yam harvest the men make pan-pipes, and every young man carries and plays one.

Yam ceremonies.

At the mouth of the Fly River the bullroarer is called burumamaramu, "the mother of yams." The old men swing it and show it to the young men when the yams are ready for digging. An idol used at the initiation ceremony is called Uvio Moguru; he makes everything grow—that is (*a*) the

[1] Cf. Strehlow, *A. & L.*, III, Part II, p. 2.

[2] Cf. J. G. Frazer, "On Some Ceremonies of the Central Australian Tribes," *Australasian Association for the Advancement of Science*, 1901, 320.

[3] Haddon, V. 217. See below for the discussion of the connexion between the Torres Strait and Central Australian Rites.

lad's penis (erection), (*b*) the vegetation—and they bring him presents of food when the planting season comes. Kurumi and Uruparu are human effigies that are shown to the lads at initiation, and when first seen the youths have fire showered over them and fire-sticks thrust at them. Should a man have made a new garden, he provides himself with these figures before eating from it, and the effigies are shown to the young man. The initiation ceremony always takes place before harvest.[1] The intimate connexion between initiation and harvest is certainly an argument in favour of our theory, nor is the whole ritual without its pre-agricultural parallel in Australia.

The fire ritual reminds us of the Engwura and similar initiation rites,[2] whilst the Melville Island initiation affords still closer parallels. The ritual is closely associated with what is known as a Yam ceremony. This special form of yam, which is eaten, but does not form such an important article of food as certain other yams, is called Kolamna. It is covered with a number of little roots which look like very strong hairs. These are called itjimma, the same name being applied to the hair on the arms and legs.[3] On the first day of the ceremony the men collected together early in the morning and after much singing and yelling they went into the bush to collect yams. These men have very much better beards than most of the northern tribes, and a prominent feature of the ceremony was the treatment of the beard. During the first part of the ceremony it was smeared with a white liquid that exudes from the bark of the milk-wood tree.[4] The first performer opened the ceremony and sang about the salt water, then another began and sang about his house and so on, till all the men were singing of rain, sea, oats, trees, grass, and in fact of everything they could think of. Often a man would come to the end of one "song" and while thinking of something else to sing kept up a cry of Ha-ha-ha-er-er-er, the former on the higher, the latter on a lower note. The yams were in a little side pool with logs placed on the pitchis to prevent them from floating away. They were inspected and then suddenly several old men seized the novitiate (Watjinyerti), plunged into the water with him and rushed backwards and forwards, some having hold of his legs and others of his arms. In this helpless state he was dragged backwards and forwards several times, for the most part completely immersed in the water. When they released him they turned their attention to the boys, who were made to lie down in the side pool. First of all each of them had his head put into a bark pitchi along with a few yams, and then, in this uncomfortable position he was held under the water, which was very muddy, for quite half a minute. As the yams had "whiskers,"

[1] Haddon, *Cambridge Expedition*, V. 218, 219.
[2] Cf. above.
[3] Spencer, *N. T. N. T. A.*, 92, 93.
[4] Id., ibid., 99.

their close association with the heads of the boys was supposed to be efficacious in stimulating the growth of the hair on the faces of the latter. The boys were then made to stand up. In order to assist further in the growth, each one had his chin rubbed hard with a hairy yam and then forcibly bitten by any older man who chose to do so.[1] The pubic hairs, including those on the upper and lower lip of the novice, were plucked out by the men, who were walking round the fire striking their buttocks and singing fiercely at intervals. At the end of about an hour the men went to the fire and drew out lighted sticks which they threw away, first facing the north and then the south. Taking small boughs, the men approached the fire and then beat it down from above, the idea of this being to cleanse it of all evil influence—if this were not done they believe the evil would go inside them, and they would break out all over in sores.[2] Then one old man, who took the lead and was always in front in the processions, walked slowly round and round the fire singing of the yams and the grass. At last the yams were taken out of the fire, skinned and sliced up. This was done on the ceremonial ground, and while it was in progress one man walked round and round striking sticks together while the others chanted. The men sung, time after time, " Yams, you are our fathers." The natives said that as a result of the performance of the ceremony all kinds of yams would grow plentifully, not only the kolamma, but more especially other kinds, which as articles of diet are more useful to them than the kolamma, which is very hot and needs special preparation. They evidently regard the kolamma, probably because it has to be specially treated before being safe to eat, as a superior kind of yam endowed with properties such as ordinary yams do not possess. If a boy sees this ceremony, and afterwards does not do what he is told by the old men, he becomes very ill and dies.[3]

This ceremonial slicing up of the yams, after which men and women are rubbed all over with them,[4] as an Intichiuma and initiation rite, not only proves the close and original connexion of these two rites, but also gives us an important cue to the meaning of both.

We know that the initiation ritual is an occasion for letting out all repressed animosity that exists on the part of the elders against their younger fellow tribesmen. This feature of the ceremonies is represented by the biting in which the old men can indulge to their hearts' content. In the Warramunga tribe there is the painful operation of " punthan " for the novice to undergo, when his scalp and chin are bitten so as to make his hair grow.[5] Although this is not the alleged purpose of the head-biting in the Melville ritual,

[1] Spencer, *N. T. N. T. A.*, 99.
[2] Id., ibid., 101.
[3] Id., ibid., 102, 103.
[4] Id., ibid., 103.
[5] Spencer and Gillen, *Nor. T.*, 352.

yet it is the purpose, as we have seen, of the whole yam ceremony. The curious ambivalent attitude with regard to hair seems to indicate that it has here the same symbolic value as in the unconscious, in neurotic symptoms and in dream-life: that it stands for the penis and sexual potency. The ceremony avowedly wishes to make the hair grow and yet plucks both the youth's and the elder's hair out, which looks very much like a symbolic castration as a punishment for the "growing of the hair" (penis in erection).

When the old men reached the water in the Melville ceremony the yams were put in the water—the roots or "whiskers" had been carefully preserved—and were "sung." Then an extraordinary ceremony took place: most of the men began to pluck their beards and whiskers out. Some did it for themselves, some allowed others to do it for them, and not a single man seemed to flinch in the slightest degree during the performance of what must have been at all events a decidedly uncomfortable operation. When it was over the hair was placed in the pitchis together with the sliced yams and their whiskers; all was left in the water for the night. Afterwards the yams were taken out and the hair left behind. In camp everyone partook of the yams, and all were supposed to begin eating at the same time.[1]

The first part of this ceremony belongs to the category of rites, in which the old men inflict the same symbolic chastisement on themselves that they have been visiting on the youths, and by this self-punishment avow their complicity in a common guilt.[2] What is the guilt that is punished by this symbolic castration rite? We get the answer to this question when we take the second part of the ceremony into account, in which the men's whiskers and the yam's whiskers, and consequently the men and the yams, are identified. Now, the yams are eaten at the end of the ceremony, and this seems to be a repetition of the very sin they are about to expiate by plucking their hairs out—that of unconscious parricide. This interpretation is fully borne out by the ceremonial song, for the yams that are cut up and eaten are expressly stated to be "our fathers."

That the yam should be multiplied by destroying it seems to be a curious case of ambivalency, comprehensible, however, if we take the deeper meaning of the rite into account. If—like with the Central Australian tribes who have the incarnation doctrine—every intercourse is regarded as an act of incest, then intercourse cannot be accomplished without first killing and devouring the father. Multiplying the yams is a magical, a projected symbolic form of copulation; hence a symbolic father must be killed if it is to prove successful. As the yams are their fathers and the whole

[1] Spencer, *N. T. N. T. A.*, 108, 110.

[2] Cf. Reik, "Pubertätsriten," *Probleme der Religionspsychologie*, 1919. 159.

tribe is identical with the yams ("whiskers"!), they put a whole generation of fathers[1] in the place of the one father whom they kill, and on the other hand they provide for the next generation of "yams" by procreating them. Hence the yam-eating ceremony is, in certain respects, the counterpart of the chin-biting; there the youths are punished, and here we see the reason why: the youths have eaten their fathers.[2]

As Intichiuma is a magical coitus, it is natural that only the initiated men take part in it, and as the positive component of the initiation ritual, incestuous libido, undergoes repression, it can only manifest itself in the multiplication of animals or plants instead of human beings—that is, in an Intichiuma.

The initiation ceremony of the Dieri, the second phase of which is also an Intichiuma, is another case to the point. First there is the Karaweli wonkana or circumcision, when the boy gets a new name that is derived from the legend of his Mura-mura. Howitt is right in remarking that this connects the Dieri tribes with those of the Alcheringa—reincarnation area as represented by the Arunta,[3] and this connexion is all the more significant as the Dieri are also the tribe that has, if we go towards the south, the last, although somewhat modified, forms of the Intichiuma rite.

The second degree of initiation is the Wilyaroo, the blood-letting rite mentioned above. After the incisions have been made on the young man a bullroarer is given to him, which he is instructed to whirl when hunting so that the tribe may reap a good harvest of reptiles, snakes and other game; every night until his wounds are healed he must come within hearing and twirl it, so as to inform his parents that he is alive, that they are to send him some food; in the meanwhile he must look upon no woman.[4] If a woman were to see a bullroarer that had been used at the ceremonies and knew the secret of it, the Dieri tribe would ever afterwards be without snakes, lizards and such other food,[5] that is projection (the existence of snakes, lizards, etc., being due to the fact that they exist as symbols of the libido) is not possible when repression ceases (women are permitted to take part in the ritual). When the bullroarer is handed to the young Wilyaru he becomes inspired by the Mura-mura of this ceremony so that he has the power to cause a good harvest of snakes and other reptiles by whirling it round his head when out in search of game.[6] Again we see exactly the same psychical sequence in the rite as in the Melville ceremony. First the youth

[1] Themselves, their own generation.

[2] The biting is a reduced talion-punishment. "We shall eat you for daring to eat your fathers."

[3] Curr, op. cit., II. 57. Howitt, *N. T.*, 657, 658.

[4] Curr., op. cit., II. 59.

[5] Howitt, *N. T.*, 660.

[6] Id., ibid. As to the connexion of bullroarer, snakes and vegetation-magic in one ceremony, cf. the snake-dance of the Pueblos.—Frazer, *T. & E.*, III. 230.

and the elders identify themselves with each other by a mutual abreaction of their repressed animosity (old men bite the youngster's head; the people eat the yams who are their fathers; mutual cutting at the Dieri Wiljaroo), and then when the young man is possessed by his Alcheringa ancestor (Mura-mura), that is when his psychical attitude has undergone the change from Son to Father, then he can multiply the tribe, at the same time projecting the incestuous elements of his libido into the magical rite of eating and multiplying the totem.

Food taboos at initiation.

Australian initiation rites contain, at the same time, another important parallel to the Intichiuma; they imply the liberation from a number of food taboos which, although of course not totemic in the ethnological sense of the word, may nevertheless be compared to the totemic taboos in so far as the inhibition of the alimentary process is in both cases transposed upwards from an inhibition of the sexual functions. For instance, we remember that the emu is a symbol of the mother-imago. In the Euahlayi tribe, when a boy after his first Borah killed his first emu, whether it was his totem or not, his father made him lie on the bird (symbolic of coitus with the mother by permission of the father) before it was cooked. Afterwards a wizard and the father rubbed the fat on the boy's joints and put a piece of flesh in his mouth. The boy chewed it, making a noise as if he did so from fright and disgust; finally he dropped the meat from his mouth, making a blowing noise through his lips of "Ooh ooh!" After that he could eat the flesh.[1]

In the Kakadu tribe there is the kulori (yam) ceremony at the fourth grade of initiation, the equivalent of the kolamma ceremony of the Melville Islanders. The lubras are instructed to go out into the bush and collect quantities of kulori. The latter is a special kind of yam, potato-shaped, that they secure by digging down from two to six feet in the ground. It is what the natives call "hot," and before being eaten it has to be treated in a special way—just like the kolamma. When they decide to hold a kulori ceremony the old men take the youths and they are made to lie on the ground flat on their back. Then slices of kulori are taken and spread out all over the body of each youth. Everyone, men, women and children, come round and watch what is being done. After a short time they remove the slices and lift each youth up by the arm. Each youth is then given a little bit, a part of which he chews and the rest he hands on to his mother's elder sisters and to his younger brothers and sisters. They must all chew it, and then, putting their heads close together, they must spit it into a small hole in the ground, which is then covered up. After the "yam communion" the youths are called Kulori men and led to a special hut that the

[1] Parker, *Euahlayi*, 24.

women are not allowed to see. Every day six men station themselves close around the hut and sing refrains, each one associated with an article of food which until now has been taboo to the young men. Some of the foods are "sung" on one day, others on other days, and as each one is "sung" the taboo on that particular kind of food to which it refers is removed.

The list of foods begins with the kulori yam (whence the ceremony takes its name) and goes on through the Jabiru bird, the flying-fox, the quail, the barramada, the mullet and the lily. After the singing the men go out searching for food, and if they capture any of those referred to, they must bring it into camp. If, for example, a man catches a barramada, he brings it up to an old man, who rubs him all over with red ochre, and takes a wristlet off; he then is free to eat the fish, and so on with all the others.[1]

If we leave out the important detail that the animals brought in for the first time by the younger men (for the first time in the season or for the first time after the initiation rite?) have been produced by the magical ceremonies and songs of the elders, the structure of the rite corresponds exactly to that of the Intichiuma rite. We have the totemic communion, the songs in the absence of the women, the bringing in of the first animal caught and the liberation ceremony in both cases. The second degree of initiation, the Ober, is also followed by a liberation ceremony. Before a man for the first time after he has seen the Ober eats any food, such as fish or kangaroo, one of the old men must take a little bit of the flesh and rub it under his armpit. Then he hands it to the other man, who smells it, puts it in his mouth and then spits it out again. In the case of the sugar bag an old man smears some of it over his whiskers and it is sucked off by the youths, who are then free to eat it.[2] In the Yamba ceremony (first degree), when five days have passed a series of little ceremonies is enacted. One old man goes out and catches a fish called Bararil. Returning to the camp, the old man goes to the youth and throws the fish at him so as to hit his thigh. This ceremony removes the taboo from the fish, which henceforth the youth may catch and eat.[3] The ceremonies are not all performed on the same day, but according to the caprice of the old men. Another old man will go and spear a cat-fish and with its jaw make a slight cut on the youth's arm, saying, "You eat cat-fish." These ceremonies go on till all the taboos are removed, and on each occasion the old man cuts off one of the youth's waistbands till there are none left.[4] In the Bunurong tribe freeing the boy of the forbidden animals is all that seems to have been done

[1] Spencer, *N. T. N. T. A.*, 146–49.
[2] Id., ibid., 144.
[3] In a Wongaibon legend two boys by a ruse make their uncle throw a piece of fat emu to them, henceforth they are allowed to eat it.—Mathews, *E. N.*, 158.
[4] Spencer, *N. T. N. T. A.*, 132.

by way of an initiation ceremony.[1] In the Wurrunjerri tribe from time to time the young man was made free of the forbidden food by having a piece of the cooked meat given him to eat by one of the old men.[2]

In the Kurnai Jeraeil the youth becomes free of the flesh of the forbidden animals by one of the old men suddenly and unexpectedly smearing some of the cooked fat over his face.[3]

The kangaroo, being however one of the usual father-symbols, a more elaborate ceremony is needed before the boys are made free to eat it. The name of the ceremony is "Seeing the ghosts"; the men imitate the ghosts hunting a kangaroo and at last tell the youths who had been carefully shrouded in their blankets that "the ghosts had caught a kangaroo." The noise now ceased and the head-man, holding his throwing-stick pointing to the sky, tells them to look up; and their blankets being thrown off, he pointed three times successively to the sky, to the horizon and to the meat on the log, saying "Look there!" each time. The novices were now seated on the log, each one having a pile of meat beside him. The head-man gave some of this to them and the rest was eaten by the other men.[4] In this way the youths were made for ever free of the flesh of the kangaroo. This ceremony is a most important one, for if it is not carried out the youth is never lawfully able to eat the flesh of the male kangaroo, as the necessary qualification can only be acquired by eating the flesh in common with all the men who are present at the Jeraeil.[5] This kangaroo communion seems to liberate the boys of the kangaroo by an avowal of the common unconscious guilt of parricide by the whole tribe; even the ghosts, the representatives of past generations, participate in it; or rather it is they, the fathers themselves, who have killed the kangaroo (father) so that the youths may do the same, as they are merely repeating the proceedings of a dim past.

So far the parallelism between Intichiuma and initiation rites involves the common instrument used for both (bullroarer) the positive (multiplying magic) as well as the negative (food taboo) and liberation aspect of the ceremony. We have taken the Caaro feast of the Watchandie with its pit representing the female, the spears representing the male genital organ, for a ceremony of the baby totem, although, as we remarked, it may also have acted as an initiation rite.

A parallel is found in the Multyerra ritual of the Kurnu tribe. Some old men dig a number of small holes into the earth, and each old man sits down at one of the holes and lets his member hang into the hole whilst the novices are told carefully to observe the

[1] Howitt, *N. T.*, 612, 613.
[2] Id., ibid., 611.
[3] Id., ibid., 633.
[4] Id., ibid., 635.
[5] Id., ibid., 636.

men.[1] It can hardly be doubted that the holes are meant to represent the vagina, and it is on the whole remarkable to what a degree the usually repressed elements of sexuality are openly represented in these rites. Indeed, we find exactly the same elements represented here as in the Intichiuma, but the attitude of the psychic censor to the libido is utterly different. There the representation is symbolic, the result of a compromise between libido and repression, and therefore magically and projectively effective. Here the old men attempt to bring the same elements into consciousness, to replace unconscious repression by conscious condemnation, whilst on the other hand these ceremonies afford an open outlet to the infantile components of sexuality: projection is replaced by the affirmation that this is the very thing they are not to do or they do not want to do. Thus we may compare the pantomimic representation of masturbation[2] with the rubbing of the Churinga or the representation of pederasty[3] to those of the cohabitation of animals and equally to the rubbing of the Churinga.[4] The latter is also represented in initiation by other parallels which we call magical, that is projective; for instance, when the novices are rubbed with the yams,[5] or when fat is rubbed on their private parts to make them grow strong.[6] Further on we shall find anal erotic rites as an element of the Intichiuma ceremonies, and at initiation we find the novices gesticulating in an indecent manner, complying to the necessities of nature in view of everyone[7] picking up filth in their baskets[8] and even eating human ordure.[9]

If we wish to go to the roots of this parallel we shall have to go back to our interpretation of the Intichiuma rites. We have had reason to suppose that these were a survival of the rutting season, although, as this rutting season must of necessity have been the time of the year when the fight between the old and young males for mastery broke out, it was equally evident that the piece of archaic sexuality conserved in these ceremonies was dominated by the Oedipus complex.

In the case of the initiation rites it is the same thing—only we have to go the other way round. These rites represent pre-eminently the Oedipus complex, but as the outbreak of this fight must have taken place at the rutting season, the ritual has also conserved traces of this pre-human state of development. In the animal world we see the young males forming separate herds that frequently dwell on the peripheries of the Cyclopean horde,[10] and only try to reunite

[1] R. H. Mathews, *Multyerra*, 81.
[2] Id., " The Bora of the Kamilaroi Tribe," *J. A. I.*, 1894.
[3] Id., ibid., *J. A. I.*, 1894, 124.
[4] As the father's penis.
[5] Spencer, *N. T. N. T. A.*, 103.
[6] Id., ibid., 120.
[7] Mathews, *E. N.*, 124.
[8] Howitt, *N. T.*, 612.
[9] Mathews, *E. N.*, 112. Howitt, *N. T.*, 549.
[10] Lang-Atkinson, *Social Origins and Primal Law*, 1903, 219.

with the parent stock at the rutting season,[1] when they are either driven off again or succeed in conquering the Leader of the Horde. It is evident that those hordes composed exclusively of young males are the animal prototypes of the age grades, of the societies of young men, as we find them in savage tribes, just as the initiation rite is a repetition of the attempts made by those young males to attain sexual maturity. But we also know that it is not a direct repetition that we have before us—the repetition is enacted from the point of view of the retribution fear of a generation of fathers ; it is a reversal rather than a repetition. As the rites originated from the attempts made by the young males to get back to the women, they begin to-day by the old men seizing the boys and dragging them away from their mothers and sisters. The names of the ceremonies "of the bush"[2] and "leafy"[3] refer to this isolation of the novice from the usual camping-place of the tribe. If we remember that beside the Intichiuma ceremonies these are the only other occasions when a separate sacred enclosure and head-ornaments such as masks and helmets are recorded in the life of these lowest of savages, it seems tempting to assume a common origin for both these features and both occasions in the playground and the secondary sexual characters of the breeding season. But we must not forget that rites are not the survivals of a static but rather of a dynamic prototype, not of a state of things at a certain period but of a section out of the Curve of Evolution.

Animal prototype of age grades.

If we want to be quite precise we shall say, not that these rites contain the survival of the rutting season, but what survives in them is rather the process that led to the disappearance of the rutting season. We see repression at work. Whilst the ceremonial dances and combats of the rutting season were meant for the females as spectators, the present ceremonies are chiefly the affair of the men, although the women and children still appear as spectators.[4] In this connexion an acute observation of Spencer and Gillen is of extreme importance ; they tell us that tradition points to a time when women had more to do with ceremonial matters than at present.[5] Now it is exactly this repression that leads to the substitution of a fictive aim in place of a realistic one ; the animal in the rutting period is by a reflex-action attracting the attention of the women : a movement-series which continues in a realistic phase becomes inhibited, and a "magical idea," the multiplication of the animal species, replaces the original action, which has thus inherited its magical from a real efficacity.

There seems to me to be a more than casual connexion between

[1] Hesse-Doflein, op. cit., II. 464.
[2] Howitt, *N. T.*, 518. [3] Id., ibid., 617.
[4] Cf., for instance, Spencer and Gillen, *Nor. T.*, 183, 186.
[5] Spencer and Gillen, *Nor. T.*, 195, 196.

the disappearance of the rutting season and the psychical phenomenon we call repression. In the Animal World we have a period devoted exclusively to the Ego, the Anoestrum, and one devoted nearly exclusively to the Libido (Oestrum). In man there is no period devoted exclusively to the Ego; the Libido is always present, but the necessary self-defence of the Ego that manifests itself, in the animal world, in keeping a period reserved to itself, survives as a function of the human psyche known to us as repression. Biologists regard it as a well-known fact that the disappearance of a separate rutting season is conditioned by an advance in the general conditions of life (better food supply, protection for the young all the year round, domestication), so that we might suppose that outward circumstances, such as cultural advance with hordes that migrated to a more favourable climate, or the invention of superior weapons, improved the conditions of life and food supply, leading to the disappearance of the rutting season or rather to a fusion and blending of the two separate seasons of animal life into one; the non-sexual period leaving repression behind as a rudiment of its previous separate existence.

In favour of this view we might refer to the state of things in Central Australia: the Intichiuma ceremonies which may be regarded as a ceremonial atavism of the rutting phase of development are more marked towards the centre of the Continent where the climatic conditions are far worse than on the seashore.[1] On the other hand, the period of material advance was in a great measure conditioned by social advance, by the victory of the Brothers over the Father, in the additional force which lay in Union. The disappearance of the primitive form of the Primeval Horde (the Cyclopean family) led by a single male and of the rutting season cannot have followed each other in a very large span of time: thus Repression bears the marks of the period of its origin imprinted on it to our own days. It is primarily directed against the most archaic form of sexuality that we call in its unconscious and mythical survivals the Oedipus complex. Indeed, I should not be surprised if subsequent investigation would lead us to the further conclusion that the Reality Principle as such is rooted in the Anoestrum, the Pleasure Principle in the Oestrum period of animal life. On the other hand, we have identified the Pleasure Principle with the intra-uterine, the Reality Principle with the extra-uterine period of life, which seems to contain a contradiction, as the former (in some lower organisms) corresponds to the purely nutritive phase to the Anoestrum, the latter to the Oestrum;[2] but in more developed organisms the two fundamental principles are not divided in this way: the longer

The origin of repression, of the pleasure and reality principle.

[1] Cf. J. G. Frazer, *T. & E.*, I. 115 (quoting a letter from Professor Spencer).

[2] Hesse-Doflein, l.c., 489; II. 471.

duration of extra-uterine life makes it impossible for it to be a purely sexual affair and creates a state of things in which the self-preservatory instinct dominates; whilst, on the other hand, the intra-uterine phase may be identified with a state of pure nutrition, but in no case with the Reality Principle, which is essentially characterized by the necessity of adaptation to environment. The nutrition of this phase is pure pleasure, and contains equally the germs of both sexual and nutritive pleasure in itself.

The ceremonial dance and the ordinary corroboree.

It can be often observed with social phenomena that when once they have lost their original function and acquired a new secondary one the original function will provoke a copy of the social phenomenon into existence, which, although later in origin than the primary phenomenon, has yet conserved its original setting in the one detail that the original function or aim of the action is retained. The dances of the rutting season were originally meant for the women as spectators; they were exhibitions given by the male members of the horde to attract the attention and the fore-pleasure of the females. At the disappearance of the rutting season, when repression set in, the dances acquired the character of a rite, a ceremony, that is they acquired a fictive, a "magical" purpose, that was the symbolical representative of their original aim. Instead of trying to please the women as onlookers and then going on to multiply the human species, the rite aims at multiplying the totem, its magical efficacity being the survival of a primary, very real efficacity. But the original aim of the ceremonial dance still survives in another set of dances, the ordinary corroborees, where the men perform in a way not unlike that of the ceremonial dance and the women are the onlookers. In this case the fore-pleasure has developed into an independent action, the dance has lost all trace of its original connexion with the rutting season, and except in one case also all conscious connexion with procreation. This one case, as we shall proceed to show, may be regarded as a link between the ceremonial and the profane sides of the dance.

In the eastern and north-eastern parts of the Arunta, and in the Kaitish, Iliaura and Warramunga tribes, considerable license is allowed on certain occasions when a large number of men and women are gathered together to perform certain corroborees. When an important corroboree is held it occupies perhaps ten days or a fortnight, and during that time the men, and especially the elder ones, spend the day in camp preparing decorations to be used during the evening. Every day two or three women are told off to attend at the corroboree-ground, and with the exception of men who stand to them in the relation of actual father, brother or son, they are for the time being common property of all the men present on the corroboree-ground. In the Arunta tribe a man goes to another who is actually or tribally his son-in-law and says to the latter, "You will take my Unawa (wife) into the bush and bring in with you some undattha altertha" (down used for decorating during ordinary corroborees). The son-in-law then goes away, followed by the woman who has been previously told what to do by the husband. The woman is actually the man's mother-in-law, that is one to whom under ordinary circumstances he may not even speak or go near, much less one with whom he may have anything like marital relations. There are perhaps two or three women on the grounds for this purpose.[1] It is the duty of every man at different times to send his wife to the ground, and the first man who has access to her is the very one to whom, under normal conditions, she is most strictly taboo, that is her son-in-law.[2] The natives say that the presence of these women during the preparations and the sexual indulgence which was a practice of the Alcheringa prevents anything from going wrong with the performance; it makes it impossible for the head decorations, for example, to become loose and disordered during the performance. In the evening the women are painted with red ochre by the men, and then they return to the main camp to summon the women and children to the corroboree.[3]

The first thing to be noted is that sexual license during the corroboree is said to have been a practice of the Alcheringa, that is the phase of phylogenetic development represented by the Intichiuma ceremonies. The rutting season, the period of sexual license, is the prototype of the corroboree as well as of the Intichiuma, and the intercourse at this occasion clearly shows us both what we may regard as the archaic form of the libido and against which type of coitus the repression is directed. It is this repression which ultimately causes the disappearance of cohabitation in its uncensored form and is also responsible for its magical sublimation. It is the intercourse with the mother-in-law, who again is nothing but a repetition of the mother in flesh, the real mother. Even in this case where there is no animal projection as in the real Intichiuma the coitus is not a matter of pure pleasure: it is done with a "magical" aim to assist the performance; this proves it to be one of the many offsprings of the interaction between libido and repression. The magical aim, again, is a case of functional reversal; it is not the intercourse that magically assists the performance; on the contrary, it is the performance as an act of fore-pleasure that magically assists copulation. When the magical effects of the copulation come to be specified there is a return of repressed elements and the real meaning appears; the copulation prevents the head-dress, which we have shown to be an upward transposition of the penis, from becoming loose, that is it causes erection. Strehlow says

[1] Spencer and Gillen, *N. T.*, 96, 97.

[2] Id., *Nor. T.*, 99.

[3] Id., *N. T.*, 97.

that the Wuljankura dance has wandered from the east to the western Arunta and Loritja, and in certain respects it is a parallel to the above-mentioned rite and corroboree.

To begin with, we find here the indisputable proof that we were right in calling the idea of the natives that copulation assists the proper performance of the ceremony a reversal. "This performance," says Strehlow, "is carried out by the women with the assistance of the men, with the object of exciting in the women erotic desire for strange men." [1]

In the western tribes the dance is not a corroboree: it presents all the aspects of a real Intichiuma ceremony—indeed, an Intichiuma ceremony of a remarkably primitive, unrepressed type. To begin with, women, as well as men, participate in the performance: it is performed in imitation of the Alknarintja (Miniera) women of the Alcheringa, whose wanderings and doings are related in the song and re-acted in the performance. Wuljankura means the women that are greased with fat, and they begin by smearing their body all over with fat and red ochre. (Cf. above, p. 219, on the greasing of the Churinga.) The Alknarintja women felt so homesick that their body quivered with the strength of emotion (quivering acted). They met a man with a wonninga on his head who keeps swinging a lighted torch and begins to quiver all over. This ends the performance. The interpretation of the quivering as the rhythmic movements of coition and of the fire as a symbol of the libido is confirmed by what follows: there is a general exchange of women, so that the function of the ceremony, "to cause desire for other men's wives," is really accomplished.

In this ceremony the southern Loritja and the eastern and southern Arunta even allow a man to have intercourse with his own mother-in-law.[2] If we acknowledge that there is good reason to suppose a common origin for both the "ceremonial" and the "profane" dance, we shall not be surprised to note that the imitation of nature and animals plays as large a part in the latter as in the former.[3]

It seems probable that the common rutting period of all nature gives special emphasis to the biological unity which envelops all that is living in a certain geographical area, and evokes a series of circular reaction by which man responds to the stimuli of environment. On the Tully River the programme consists of dances pertaining to and imitative of the various animals—flying-fox, cockatoo—and portions of these animals, especially the heads, are utilized for purposes of ornament.[4] The Euahlayi represent various birds—cranes, pelicans, black swans and ducks—the

[1] Strehlow, *A. & L.*, IV. 94.

[2] Id., ibid., IV. 94–97.

[3] Cf. below as to imitation in the Intichiuma.

[4] W. E. Roth, "Games, Sports and Amusements," *N. Queensland Bulletin*, No. 4, 1902, 23.

peculiarities of which are well imitated.[1] Spencer tells us of the northern tribes that when they are not performing sacred ceremonies the evenings are always occupied with corroborees, which may be witnessed by everyone. These corroborees deal with some particular incidents such as a buffalo hunt, a crocodile securing its prey, or the putting out of a lugge to sea. The actions of the crocodile and the buffalo are imitated in a very realistic manner.[2] Carnegie describes an emu corroboree, where everybody in his turn stalked solemnly along with the right arm raised, with elbow bent, wrist and hand horizontal, and poked backwards and forwards to represent the emu's neck and head. The mallee hen is represented building her nest, and so on: all the more common animals are mimicked.[3]

The subject of animal imitation will call for our attention below in connexion with its function as an Intichiuma. We have analysed certain elements of what has been called the magical in contradistinction to the dramatic part of the Intichiuma, where we found that the rubbing and the rhythmic movements are survivals of onanistic and fore-pleasure actions, whilst the blood-letting is both an act of aggression and of self-punishment for having caused the death of the Primeval Sire and an effusion of semen by which the totem animal is multiplied. The same double aspect corresponding to the two fundamental tendencies involved in the Oedipus complex is implicitly contained in the ceremonial eating of the totem: it means both the killing of the father and totemic incest with the mother.

Resume the analysis of the Intichiuma.

The part played by the two moieties, who "make" their respective totem animals for the men of the other moiety to eat exactly in the same fashion as they procreate their own daughters for the men of the other moiety to marry, has compelled us to set the analysis of the Intichiuma ritual aside for the time being, and we have tried to determine the interrelation between the Intichiuma on the one hand and other social and ceremonial aspects of the life of an Australian tribe such as the Two-Class System, Initiation Rites and the Animal Dances on the other. Our immediate business was not to deal with these latter institutions; they were only made use of to aid us in determining the phases of development that have left their traces in the Intichiuma.

We now resume our analysis of the procreative as distinguished from the imitative elements of the Intichiuma. We shall have to deal with a ceremony that we may call "Striking the rock." The purpose of the totemic ceremonies of the Kariera tribe is said to be

[1] K. L. Parker, *The Euahlayi Tribe*, 1905, 130.
[2] Spencer, *N. T. N. T. A.*, 32, 33.
[3] W. Carnegie, *Spinifex and Sand*, 1898, 332, 333.

to increass the supply of the animal plant or other object with which it is connected. Thus the purpose of the Mungu or White Ant ceremony (insects eaten by the aborigines) is to make these animals multiply. At many of these totemic ceremonial grounds there is either a single boulder or a heap of small stones, and these play a part in the ceremony connected with the place. In some cases it would seem that the stone or heap is struck with clubs or with stones held in the hand.[1] Withnell says that they hammer the cairn or boulder (tarlow) with other round stones and go through many speeches.[2] In the Kangaroo "willing" ceremony the tarlow is beaten with spears, stones and clubs.[3] In the Emu ceremony of the Arunta the old men knock stones that represent emu eggs against each other.[4] Stones are also knocked against each other in the ceremony of the brown-rock dove,[5] the owl,[6] the raven,[7] the Melopsittacus undulatus Shaw,[8] the big lizard,[9] the frog,[10] and the red locust.[11] In the Witchetty-Grub Intichiuma the head-man begins singing and taps the stone (which represents the adult animal) Maegwa with his small wooden trough (Apmara), while all the other men tap it with their twigs, chanting songs as they do so, the burden of which is an invitation to the animal to lay eggs. When this has gone on for a short time they tap the smaller stones, which are Churinga unchima, that is they represent the eggs of the Maegwa. The Alatunja then takes one of the smaller stones and strikes each man in the stomach with it, saying, "You have eaten much food." When this has been done, the stone is dropped and the Alatunja strikes the stomach of each man with his forehead.[12]

Striking the rock.

In the Urabunna country there is a hill called Coppertop, which is supposed to represent an old jew-lizard in the act of standing up to throw boomerangs. The Kadni men can make the lizards increase by simply knocking pieces of stone off the face of the rock and throwing them about in various directions.[13] In the Mara country there is a large heavy stone representing a big honeybag, which was carried about by the old ancestor of that totem and left there on the spot where he finally went into the ground. The Murungun and Mumbali men who form the half of the tribe to which the Honey totem belongs can increase the number of the bees, and therefore of the honey supply, by striking powder off the stone

[1] A. B. Brown, "Three Tribes of Western Australia," *J. A. I.*, 1913, 160.

[2] I. G. Withnell, "Marriage Rites and Ceremonies," *Science of Man*, 1903, 42. Id., *The Customs and Traditions of the Aboriginal Natives of North-Western Australia*, 1901, 5, 6.

[3] E. Clement, op. cit., XVI, 1904, 5:

[4] Strehlow, *A. & L.*, III. 1910, 36.

[5] Id., ibid., 47.

[6] Id., ibid., 50.

[7] Id., ibid., 52.

[8] Id., ibid., 54.

[9] Id., ibid., 68.

[10] Id., ibid., 75.

[11] Id., ibid., 93.

[12] Spencer and Gillen, *N. T.*, 172.

[13] Spencer and Gillen, *Nor. T.*, 288.

and blowing it in all directions; this scattered powder gives rise to bees.[1]

To understand this ritual we must begin by taking it in its simplest form: a rock, which, as we know, represents the ancestor, is struck with a club at the ceremony held in his honour. We shall not be surprised at finding the repressed feeling of enmity betray itself in such a characteristic manner in a ceremony which is professedly dictated by the feelings of the deepest piety, and we shall immediately correlate the ritual with that of blood-letting (with which it seems to alternate), where we found that the lancing of the veins was a self-punishment inflicted for having caused the death of the ancestor. There is a formal difference between the two rites; the blood-letting is a secondary form, a reaction formation, the blow that is struck at the rock is a direct repetition of the sinful deed. But the self-punishment form is not without its parallels.

The spirit of rebellion.

When the head-man of the Witchetty-Grub totem strikes the stomachs of the men with the Witchetty Churinga stones, he seems to be retaliating on them for having (just before) struck the rock, and when he tells them that they have eaten much food, although they have eaten nothing since the very beginning of the ceremony, giving everything caught to the old men,[2] he seems to be reproaching them for some undutiful conduct or wishes towards the elders. We have found the next parallel to the blood-letting rite in the behaviour of the tribes in cases of death, and explained blood-letting at the Nanja rock where the animal ancestor died and went into the ground as a periodical repetition of the blood-letting at the grave as an act of mourning.

That we have not been led astray by a mere coincidence seems to be proved by the fact that striking the rock—which is the petrified body of the ancestor—is equally paralleled by the rites of mourning. The Lower Murray tribes mummify the body. When a friend or anybody belonging to the same tribe sees one of these bodies thus set up for the first time, he approaches it and commences by abusing the deceased for dying. They tell him there is plenty of food, and he should have been contented to remain; after looking at the body intently for some time he throws his spear and his wirri at it, exclaiming, "Why did you die? Take this for dying."[3] Although the conscious motivation of this ritual is given in terms of love and piety, yet the action that follows it, together with the abuse, cannot be mistaken for other than an outlet of a repressed inimical attitude. At the Herbert River a shallow grave is dug with pointed sticks close to the water, and the father or brother of the

Parallel features in mourning rites.

[1] Spencer and Gillen, *Nor. T.*, 312. [2] Id., *N. T.*, 171.
[3] G. F. Angas, *Savage Life and Scenes in Australia*, 1847, I. 96.

deceased if a man, or the husband if a woman, beats the body with a club, often so violently as to break the bones. The legs are generally broken to prevent the ghost from wandering at night, and the beating is given in order so to frighten the spirit that it would be unlikely to haunt the camp, whilst stones are put in the body to prevent it from going far afield.[1] It is as if the deed, this killing of him who is killed already, were to show the projection behind the accusation levelled at other blacks of having caused the death by their evil magic;[2] it is they themselves who are responsible for the decease by the mana of their unconscious wishes and by giving the corpse a thrashing they are repeating their unconscious sin in good earnest. This gives us the key to the meaning of the striking of the rock: the members of the totem clan are repeating their primeval sin of having killed the totem father at the very festival held in his honour.

This attitude of open rebellion becomes apparent in the Wollunqua ceremony. Amongst the Warramunga tribe the snake totems are of considerable importance, the great majority of individuals of the Uluuru moiety belonging either to the Wollunqua, Thalaualla (black snake) or Tjudia (deaf adder) totems, but at the same time the Wollunqua is undoubtedly the most important, and is regarded as the great father of all snakes. The Wollunqua is regarded as a sort of dominant totem; its magical powers are greater than those of other totems.[3] The Wollunqua is not a species but an individual, only it lives in a water-hole in a lonely valley of the Murchison Range, and there is always the fear that it may take it into its head to come out of its hiding-place and do some damage.[4] As with other totems, the ceremonies consisted in acting the wanderings of the Alcheringa ancestor: the men run to the ground, shake themselves in imitation of the snake, and finally assist in an Uluuru ceremony; their head-dresses are knocked off by a Kingilli man, and that ends the ceremony of the first day.[5] On the fourth day of the ceremonies the Kingilli men spend the whole day in building, out of sandy earth, a mound called Mini-imbura. On the mound there was a double band of sand, which indicated the body of the Wollunqua and was finally covered with dots of red down, the rest of the surface of the mound was one mass of little dots of white down. The mound itself was emblematic of the sand-hill, by the side of which the snake stood up and looked around.[6] In the evening the Uluuru men (that is the man of the same moiety to which the Wollunqua belongs) urged on by the Kingilli, fiercely attacked the

The Wollunqua.

[1] Howitt, *N. T.*, 474.

[2] "No one is believed by the tribes of the Herbert River to die from any cause but the magic of some one of a neighbouring tribe."—Howitt, *N. T.*, 474.

[3] Spencer and Gillen, *Nor. T.*, 248.

[4] Id., ibid., 227.

[5] Id., ibid., 229.

[6] Id., ibid., 234.

mound with spears, boomerangs, clubs and spear-throwers, until in a few minutes it was hacked to pieces and all that remained was a rough heap of sandy earth. This ceremony is associated with the idea of persuading, or almost forcing, the Wollunqua to remain quietly in his home under the water-hole at Thapauerlu and not to harm any of the natives. They say that when he sees the mound with his representation drawn upon it, he is gratified and wriggles with pleasure. The savage attack upon the mound is associated with the idea of driving him down; taken together, the ceremony indicates their belief that at the same time they can both please and coerce the mythic beast.

It is evident that the belief of being able to do something is but a reflection of the wish to do something, and as such the outcome of an ambivalent attitude towards their dominant totem, the father of all the snakes, whom they seemingly strive to please in the ceremony, which, however, ends in a savage attack on his person. The knocking of the Nanja rock, the thrashing of the corpse and the attack on the Wollunqua mound are all links in the same chain: repetitions of the Primeval Rebellion against the Leader of the Horde. In some of the instances mentioned above, however, we find another element that calls for explanation: small bits of stone are struck off the rock and thrown about in various directions.

If the rock is the totem-ancestor, this looks very much like a rite where the body of a giant animal is torn asunder, and the bits rent from it are supposed to develop into new animals. Amongst the rocky gorges in the Murchison Range there are spots especially associated in tradition with the euro. Just above the water-hole called Thapauerlu, which is the home of the great Wollunqua snake, there is a smaller one with a curious large pot-hole by its side. Here in the Alcheringa a wild dog caught and killed an old euro and made the rocky pool while swinging its body round and round as the two animals fought fiercely. In the pot-hole are numbers of round, water-worn stones which represent different parts of the body of the euro. Still higher up on the hill-sides there are little groups of similar stones carefully covered up with little heaps of rocky debris. Any old man passing by will take the stones out, renew the red ochre with which they are covered, and rub them well. The rubbing may be done at any time by an old man irrespective of the totemic group he may belong to, and is supposed to increase the number of euros, who are believed to emanate from the stones. The larger stones represent the "old men" euros, next in size are those which represent the female euros, and the still smaller ones stand for the little animals. Near one of the hills the recent dropping of an old euro were observed, and the natives said that the animal had only lately come out of one of the stones.[1] The small stones that correspond to the various parts of the euro's body prove that the contest must have ended by the dog rending his adversary into pieces, and indeed we have had occasion to observe the wild dog as the animal that castrates its adversaries or that tears them into pieces in a considerable number of myths. Tearing to pieces and castration amount to the same thing, and we have called the wild dog a personification of the castration complex.

It is one of the curious contradictions so well known in all products of the Unconscious that the multiplication of euros should be attempted[2] from the body of a castrated animal, but we can at least try to guess how this can be explained. We know that the category of time, the sequence of events, is a matter of no importance with the Unconscious, and perhaps we can understand the myth and ritual if we put first the multiplication and then the castration. We have also tried to show that the reason why the procreative energies are projected from the human species to the animal world in these rites is that cultural advance inhibits the manifestations of the archaic (incestuous) elements of the libido through repression. The multiplication of animals is then a sublimated incest, and the punishment for incest is the usual talion-punishment, castration. On the other hand, by the light of our previous investigation, the myth may also be read without having recourse to this reversal of the sequence of elements, and then we should say: before man can proceed to procreation, the Euro Father, who represents the Jealous Sire of the Primeval Horde, must be conquered and castrated or torn to pieces. This connexion between the combat and the parts of the euro's body is evident; it follows especially if we take the legend in connexion with the Kaitish myth of the two Opossum men, who did not feed on opossum but on grass-seed. One of them had the habit of eating too much of it. Once, however, he noticed that another man just like himself and his comrade had arisen from the grass-seed put aside by him. He looked at his comrade and said: "That man is all the same as you and me; why did he come up?" Then he took a churinga and struck the man on the back so that he died. Then they cut him in pieces, throwing the intestines in one direction, the head, heart, liver, lungs, etc., in others.[3] Here we have perhaps the most primitive variant of what I would call the myth of the death and dismemberment of the Food-Man which we find amongst agricultural tribes as an explanation of the origin of cultivation. In this connexion the way the Wonkanguru make rain is of special interest: it serves to prove that the death

[1] Spencer and Gillen, *Nor. T.*, 310.
[2] By the ritual of rubbing explained above, p. 219.
[3] Spencer and Gillen, *Nor. T.*, 414.

of the animal, which in the Intichiuma ritual comes before multiplication, is really the death of a man. They dig a hole and the rain-makers put a certain stone, called talarapalku, i.e. body of rain (= cloud) in a pitchi in the hole. Then the stone is struck and its pieces are set up at the ends of the trough: "kana-jeri," i.e. like a human being.[1] Another native said that the rain-stone was smashed on the chest of a man, both cases showing that the smashing of a stone (= killing an animal) to produce rain (= to multiply animals) is a substitute for killing a man before proceeding to multiply the human species.[2]

The chase of the giant animal.

If we wish to prove the plausibility of these suggestions we shall again have to go somewhat far afield and draw comparisons with myths that explain the origin of certain actually existing animal-species and with those that explain the rite of initiation. The myths tell us how an enormous animal was chased in the days of yore, and sometimes they account for certain features of the landscape, sometimes for the origin of certain animal species.

A great warrior of ancient times, named That-tyu-kul, was camped at Swan Hill on the Murray River. His two sons told him that they had seen a monstrous cod-fish in a big water-hole, and he set out in pursuit. He kept throwing spears at the fish, but it swam on to the end of the water-hole and commenced forming a channel by tearing up the ground, and in this manner compelled the water to flow after it and bear it away from its enemy till at last he lost sight of it in a large hole.[3] The Willandra Creek is supposed to be the track of a giant kangaroo flying from two "Bookomuri" pursuers, and the origin of the Merowie Creek is attributed to a similar event.[4] The Narrinyerri tell us how Wyungare and Nepelle (or according to another version Punggane) chased the giant kangaroo and the giant fish.[5] Once upon a time it is said that Nurundure and Nepelle together pursued an enormous fish in Lake Alexandrina, near Tippin.[6] Nepelle caught it, then Nurundure tore it in pieces and threw the fragments into the water, and each piece became a fish, and thus ponde, tarke, tukkeri and

[1] O. Siebert, "Sitten und Sagen der Dieri und Nachbarstämme," *Globus*, 97, 56. Here we find that the stone that is broken to pieces is a substitute for a man torn to pieces, and the Nanja rock is called the body of the Alcheringa ancestor. Cf. the mourning custom of smashing the skull to pieces, breaking the bones.—Spencer, *N. T. N. T. A.*, 255.

[2] The youth must have taken the life of a man before he can be initiated or marry.—A. C. Haddon, *Migrations of Culture in British New Guinea*, 1920, 15.

[3] R. H. Mathews, *E. N.*, 1905, 82.

[4] A. L. P. Cameron, *J. A. I.*, 1884, 369.

[5] Taplin, 55, 56. Cf. R. Brough-Smyth, *The Aborigines of Victoria*, 1878, I. 425. Pungarre creates fish.

[6] According to another version, Nurundure and his sons drove this great fish down the Darling and Murray to a place called Piltungk, at the Lake Alexandrina, and there obtained assistance from Nepelle to catch it.—Taplin, *Narrinyeri Tribe*, 1878, 56.

pommere, different kinds of fish, had their origin.[1] This way of multiplying animals would perhaps, if we had more material from South Australia, appear to be the regular thing for a South Australian Alcheringa being to do; before his ascent to the sky-land it is related that Wyungare took a gigantic kangaroo and tore it into pieces and scattered the fragments through the scrub, which became the comparatively small kangaroos which now exist.[2] Pundjil is said to have found a single kangaroo, emu and other animals on earth; he caught them, cut them up, and by some mysterious power made each piece into a new kangaroo, etc., and hence the country was filled with all these animals.[3] The same method was adopted by Pundjil when he wished to disperse humanity all over the earth. He cut men, women and children into little bits, but these bits continue to live like worms and they are taken up by the whirlwind and blown about the world so that they give rise to human beings everywhere.[4] A Port Lincoln myth tells us of a giant kangaroo called Kupirri, said to have been of such enormous size that he swallowed each and all who attempted to kill him. His aspect alone filled the natives with such fright that they flung the spear-thrower as well as the spear, which caused the latter to lose all effect. At last Pilla (the opossum) and Idnya (the wild cat) discovered his track in the Ranges running north of Port Lincoln. They came up to him at Mount Nilawo, and finding the beast asleep, they immediately attacked it, but their spears became blunted.[5] Nevertheless, they managed to kill the Kupirri, and they found several of their swallowed comrades in his belly, whom they restored to life again.[6]

Tearing to pieces and initiation ritual.

When we started on our investigation of the tearing or cutting into bits in creation myth and initiation ritual, we could not even know how close the connexion would prove to be between the two. The personage who cuts the kangaroo into bits is Wyungarre, the same who, as we have seen above, was a kaingani, that is an initiate from the very beginning, and who breaks through the cardinal taboo of the initiates in absconding with the two emu wives of the All-Father. A taboo must be broken through before an Intichiuma can be successful, and both running away with the emu women and eating the totem is a form of breaking through the taboo. Both represent totemic incest with the mother, the prototype of all "magical"

[1] Taplin, *Narrinyeri Tribe*, 1878, 56.
[2] Id., ibid., 57.
[3] Th. H. Braim, *History of New South Wales*, 1846, 244, 245.
[4] Brough-Smyth, I., 427, 428. According to the Koko-warra of Princess Charlotte Bay, iguanas were multiplied by cutting one into innumerable pieces and strewing them about in all directions. This is why they are so plentiful at present.—Roth, *S. M. M.*, 1903, 12.
[5] The motive of the ineffectually hurled missile is also contained in the version recorded by Mathews (above).
[6] Ch. Wilhelmi, *Manners and Customs of the Australian Natives*, 1862, 33.

procreation. The two heroes of our last myth are the well-known Dual Heroes, the representatives of the brother clan. But who is the giant kangaroo? On the Upper Hunter River the word Buba (father) is used to designate an old kangaroo, the father of the whole race of kangaroos whose thigh-bone is preserved (four feet long and eight inches round) and carried about by the members of the kangaroo clan.[1] If we remember that Kupirri, the giant kangaroo, in other variants of the legend, is said to give rise to the whole race of kangaroos by being torn into bits, then we may say that the myth represents the united attack of the Brothers on the Father (who is, from the infantile point of view, a giant) and the way they tear the semi-human Sire into pieces.

We shall hardly be going amiss if we guess that the brothers ate the pieces of flesh rent from the body of the Sire in a sacrificial meal (the prototype of totem-eating), after which they proceeded to multiply humanity[2] by having intercourse with their mothers and sisters. But by tearing the father into pieces they also multiplied him in another way, for now there was a whole generation of fathers, as they themselves had succeeded to his dignity instead of the original father whose flesh they had eaten and with whom, accordingly, they had become identical. We know that this is the state of things reflected in the initiation ceremonies, and we have already shown that Buba (the kangaroo father) is also the name of the bullroarer.[3] Now where do we find the ritual prototype of men being swallowed by a monster and restored to life again? As we know very well, in the ceremonies of initiation.

One of the many performances shown to the novices at the McIvor River initiation is called the Black Palm. Certain of the old men cover the eyes of the novices, and in the meantime a large black-palm leaf is brought from the neighbouring scrub and stuck upright in the centre of the circular area. The novices are now turned round and allowed to see it when it is shaken about and subsequently torn to pieces, the central figures stamping the ground with their knees and the chorus shouting and stamping. The novices are told by the old men that they have made the plant grow where they saw it, and they believe them.[4] However, it is not only the plant but the novices themselves who are torn to pieces, at least according to the exoteric myth that accompanies the ritual. According to what they say to the uninitiated, there is a being called Thuremlin, who takes the youth to a distance, kills him, and in some instances cuts him up, after which he restores

[1] Honery, " Wailwun; Australian Languages and Traditions," *J. A. I.*, VII. 250.

[2] On the identity of the words for man and kangaroo, see above, p. 47.

[3] Cf. above, p. 48.

[4] W. E. Roth, " On Certain Initiation Ceremonies," *N. Q. E. Bulletin* 12, 1909, 173.

him to life and knocks out a tooth.[1] Women and children think that the noise made by the bullroarer is the voice of a spirit called Katajina, who lives in an ant-hill and comes out to eat the boy.[2]

According to the Wiradthuri, Daramulun pretended to Baiamai that he always killed the boys, cut them up and burned them to ashes. Then he formed the ashes into human beings and restored them to life: new beings, but each with a tooth missing.[3] If we remember that all these various accounts that refer to the initiation spirit, cutting up the boys and doing something with them, evidently a symbolic castration, are told to account for a ritual that turns on the fear of retaliation, we shall suppose that the spirit is only doing to the boys what they wish to do to him or what the Younger Generation really did to him in the days of yore.

According to the Loritja, the Maiutu knocks the boy's head off when the boy is looking up towards the sky, then he runs after the boy's head and sticks it on again. The first thing the youth does when he has come to life again is to deal the Maiutu (here we have a plurality of bullroarer spirits) a deadly wound with a spear,[4] which seems an ill recompense for having brought him to life again, but is a natural reaction for having been killed by the bullroarer spirit. The spirit evidently knows what it is about; this single return of the repressed elements shows that the death of the boy is the punishment of a would-be murderer.

Now we must recall the myths that tell us how the spirit of the bullroarer ended, and we shall see that it was originally the band of young men who tore the spirit into pieces, and that the actual bullroarer who retaliates on them is merely a reincarnation of their original victim. The original bullroarer was made by the two men called Tumana: two wild dogs who heard it, chased them and cut the men's heads off, just as Maiutu cuts the youth's head off. The Tumanas, however, made the down fly about from their Churingas when they swung them, and trees sprang up wherever the down fell, from which the bullroarers of to-day are made.[5]

In the Warramunga variant of this Kaitish myth the bullroarer man is called Murtu-murtu. Two wild dogs rush at him, biting pieces of flesh, which they throw in all directions. As the flesh flew through the air it made a sound like that of the Murtu-murtu, and trees called nanantha sprang up where they fell on the earth, out of which the bullroarers of the present day are made. When the dogs had torn the body to pieces they looked round and saw trees springing up all round. This made them angry and they ran about biting the trees in the hope that they would thus be

[1] A. L. P. Cameron, "Notes on some Tribes of New South Wales," *J. A. I.*, 1884, 358.
[2] Spencer and Gillen, *Nor. T.*, 366, 367.
[3] R. H. Mathews, "The Bŭrbŭng of the Wiradthuri Tribes," *J. R. A. I.*, XXV. 297.
[4] Strehlow, *A. & L.*, II. 48, 49.
[5] Spencer and Gillen, *Nor. T.*, 421, 499, 500.

able to kill the spirit of the bullroarer which had gone into the trees.[1] In the secret language of the initiates, the Arunta novices are called rukuta, that is wild dogs,[2] so that we cannot doubt their identity with the bullroarer's murderers. After the initiates have torn the Spirit of Initiation, the Father, to pieces,[3] these pieces of flesh or down (which is equal to semen) give rise to a fresh vegetation, like the chips of stone flying off the kangaroo's petrified body engender a new generation of kangaroos in the Intichiuma.

The Mungarai have a detailed tradition on the origin of the sacred sticks of initiation. We shall now make use of it to prove that our interpretation of the legend of Kupirri, the giant kangaroo, colligates the facts.

> In the far-away times which they call Kurnallan (Alcheringa) there existed a very big man named Kunapippi. He existed before there were any of the present-day blackfellows and is reported to have had many dilly-bags. In these bags he carried a lot of spirit-children, who were all of them boys. For some time he sang out like the men do now when they perform sacred ceremonies, quivering his head in front of his mouth so as to make the sound called Tjungulamma. He had at first been underground, but he came out and made a camp with a raised bank all around it. In the middle of the camp he put the boys on the grass. He possessed several of the sacred sticks called, like himself, kunapippi. He had made them and was the first to have any. Then he made forehead bands for the boys and decorated them in just the same way as the natives now decorate the youths during the initiation ceremony. He divided the youths into the two primary moieties, and afterwards told them their subclass and totem names. Kunapippi himself belonged to no special class or totem group ; he belonged to everything and was a very big man with a very big foot. After he had given the boys their subclasses, he gave them their totem names ; before, however, he actually did this he showed them all the different ceremonies, telling them to which totemic group each of them belonged. These special ceremonies are called Tjon.[4] He began to perform them at sundown and kept them up all night, making Tjungulamma continuously.[5] After this, Kunapippi performed the ceremonies of circumcision and showed them

[1] Spencer and Gillen, *Nor. T.*, 434, 435, 493, 500. Cf. the death of the bullroarer spirit.—Parker, op. cit., 67.

[2] Strehlow, *A. & L.*, IV. 26.

[3] The bullroarer is the great-grandfather, the ancestor (Wehntwin).

[4] These may be the equivalents of the Arunta Intichiuma ; another series called warwiran are said to correspond to the quabara.—Spencer, *N. T. N. T. A.*, 166. The Anula call these ceremonies kunapippi (Spencer and Gillen, *Nor. T.*, 223), which points to a close connexion with the Mungarai.

[5] Spencer, *N. T. N. T. A.*, 215.

how to conduct the operations. Then other natives came from a distinct part, and when Kunapippi saw that they had no class and totem names, he did not let them come near the ceremonial ground. He divided them between the two classes, gave each man his proper subclass and totem and told them which was the right woman for each man to marry. Tradition relates, without giving any reason for it, that Kunapippi then killed and ate all of them except two, who managed to escape. Later on he disgorged all their bones, and when after a time the two men came back, they found nothing but these, because Kunapippi had eaten all the flesh. The two men hastened back to their own country, and meeting with a number of their own people, told them what had happened. The men all armed themselves with stone tomahawks and crept quietly up towards the camp where Kunapippi was sitting down with his boys. They came up silently, and making a sudden rush, one man hit him on the back and another on the side with an axe. After he had been thus wounded, a man ran up, hit him on the back of the neck and killed him. Before this he had eaten two of his own boys, but they cut him open and rescued them alive. Kunapippi's boys then mixed with the strangers and instructed them in all things relating to totems, classes and initiation ceremonies.[1]

If the legend were not slightly veiled by the technique of a "doublette" episode, we should here have a nearly verbatim report on the origin of initiation ceremonies and human society in general. The way Kunapippi introduces initiation and other ceremonies is told twice over; once it relates to the tribe, once to foreigners. The Censor only allows the return of the repressed elements in the second, projective variant, for here without any apparent reason tradition says that Kunapippi killed and ate the boys except two. These two, who afterwards come with other men and kill Kunapippi, the big man, are evidently the Dual Heroes and representatives of the brothers who kill the Father and after their victory introduce initiation (third repetition in the legend). Here we have the clear proof that the Conflict is only rationalized as a conflict between two tribes, for the Dual Heroes are clearly identical with the two of Kunapippi's own boys whom he swallows but who come to life again when he is cut open. This swallowing episode is the regular thing in an initiation legend, and connects Kunapippi, the big man, with Kupirri, the giant kangaroo. Both swallow and disgorge people, both are conquered

[1] Spencer, *N. T. N. T. A.*, 1914, 214–17. They also made different corroborees and showed them to the men, and they told them how to conduct the ceremonies of circumcision and subincision. Finally, they secured the sacred sticks belonging to Kunapippi, and have kept and used them ever since.

by two heroes, and the cutting open of Kunapippi evidently corresponds to the tearing to pieces of the giant animal. Kunapippi, the giant, who existed before the present-day blacks,[1] is clearly the Jealous Sire of the semi-human Horde. He kills all the young men,[2] and at last succumbs to their united efforts, and this is the origin of the two-class system, initiation rites, totemism, and Intichiuma ceremonies. We may then conclude that when the Nanja rock is hit and the bits of stone that fly off from it are thrown about, we have a ceremonial repetition of Primeval Parricide of the way the brothers rent the Father's body to pieces, which serves to multiply the animal (= human) species (*a*) as it opens the path to incestuous intercourse, (*b*) as it substitutes a number of fathers for the one father.

Throwing and scattering in ritual.

Another of the motor elements of our ritual is still insufficiently explained, namely, the throwing. The Kakadu legend tells us how Imberombera scattered yams and spirit-children about wherever she went. When she came to Imbinjairi she threw the seeds of the bamboo in all directions, and also left children behind.[3] For the purpose of securing a downfall of rain, the Gnanji use the crystals called bi-oka. These are sent down to them at their request by a great rain-man who lives far away in the north. They pulverize the crystals and throw the powder in all directions, requesting the rain to come as they do so and bring the fish with it.[4] In the Anula tribe dugongs are a favourite article of food. In the Mungaia (= Alcheringa) times, one jumped out at a place on the Limmen River. The black-fellows, armed with spears, gave chase in a canoe, wanting to kill and eat it. At present a large tree represents the natives and a big stone the dugong, while close down by the sea a number of small white stones (visible at low tide) represent a mob of dugong, which the animal wanted to join but could not. Numbers of dugongs now emanate from these rocks without the help of the natives, but if they desire to bring them out, the dugong men can do so by singing and throwing sticks at the rocks. Similarly a legend relates how a crocodile arose at a place called Yalko. He wandered about, making what is now Batten Creek and the water-holes along its course, leaving spirit-children at different spots as he did so. His excreta gave rise to deposits of pipeclay, now used

[1] His underground life is the pre-natal life in the womb, his big foot a big penis. Australian initiation spirits are either lame or have some other abnormality on the leg.

[2] The foreign men come without women; this may be a survival of the separate herd of young males driven off from the main herd and living on its boundaries, but ever ready to come back and attack the leader of the herd. Cf. also the theories of Rivers on the migrations of tribes which consisted mostly of men.—W. H. R. Rivers, *H. M. S.*, 1914, II. 295, 296. Perhaps the Primeval Conflict was the most primitive form and reason of migrations.

[3] Spencer, *N. T. N. T A.*, 277.

[4] Spencer and Gillen, *Nor. T.*, 311.

for decorations during ceremonies. If the Crocodile men who alone can perform the ceremony want to increase their numbers, all they have to do is to go to the edge of the water-hole, "sing" the rock, and taking mangrove sticks, which grow all around by the water's edge, break these up into small pieces and throw them at the rock.[1] When dealing with the beliefs on the origin of children, we saw what throwing a tjurunga at a woman by the Alcheringa ancestor really represented: it is symbolic of intercourse, perhaps more precisely of the ejaculation (throwing out) of the semen.

When we hear that spirit kangaroos emanate from the rock in the blood-letting rite and incarnate themselves in female kangaroos, or when dugongs emanate from the dugong rock, at which sticks are thrown, we have to do with exactly the same symbolism. In the rite the rock is an ambisexual symbol that represents both the father and the mother,[2] and when a stick is thrown at it, then the actual members of the totem are procreating the animal species by means of a symbolic incest, just as in the case of the birth of human children it is the Son himself who, as Alcheringa ancestor, has intercourse with his own mother, and thus replaces his own father. This explanation also serves to point out why the same rite that represents the death of the Father at the same time symbolizes copulation: because the father's death must precede all copulation as all copulating is from the point of view of the Unconscious a repetition of incest with the mother. If we remember the polyphyletic origin and constitution of the libido, moreover that all secretions and excretions of the body fall, in a certain sense, under the category of multiplication by division, we shall expect to find that these archaic types of eroticism have also been as active in the building up of our rites as the genital erotic components of the libido.

When the Dieri wish to make rain, all the men huddle together and an old man takes a sharp flint and bleeds two men from one of the chief arteries; the blood being made to flow on the men sitting around, during which the two men throw handfuls of down, some of which adheres to the blood, the rest floating in the air. The ritual is a case of mimetic magic, for the blood is supposed to symbolize the rain and the down the clouds.[3] If they wish to multiply the fish called paru, they pulverize gypsum (called paru-mada-fish stone) and throw the dust into the water.[4] The rain Intichiuma of the Kaitish tribe is conducted by the head-man of the water-totem. He goes to a place called Anira, where in the Alcheringa two old men sat down and drew water from their

[1] Spencer and Gillen, *Nor. T.*, 313.

[2] Cf. above on Alcheringa myth of children emanating from a male ancestor's body, p. 227.

[3] Gason-Curr, II. 66, 67.

[4] Siebert, l.c., *Globus*, 97, 55.

whiskers,[1] the latter being now represented by two stones. The head-man keeps throwing small pieces of white down, which is supposed to represent clouds, in various directions, so as to make the rain fall.[2] As the rite is always professedly a repetition of the myth, we must suppose that the throwing is a repetition of the way the Alcheringa men drew rain from their whiskers: that which is thrown or separated must originally be a part of the human body. The Dieri have throwing and blood-letting as co-ordinated rites: and we get some inkling as to the unconscious erotic meaning of the rain charm when we read that it is accompanied by a taboo on intercourse,[3] which is usual with rites that represent sublimated forms of coitus. But what phase in the evolution of the libido is represented by throwing?

Although this repetition of the cruel battle fought in the Primeval Horde seems a sufficient explanation, not only for the striking of the rock, but also for making bits of stone fly off it, yet we shall immediately proceed to prove that we have here a typical case of the over-determination of psychic contents so well known in the analysis of dreams and in neurotic patients.

The whole action falls under the general law of Ambivalency; if I wish to augment something and tear it into bits, I am really annihilating that which I professedly intend to multiply. We have seen the same attitude manifest itself in the ritual of totem-eating and characterized it as typical of the position taken by the infantile psyche towards the Father-Imago. Again, from the point of view of Consciousness and Logic, the rite is to be explained equally well; if we tear anything to pieces we really multiply it in a certain sense, we get more units. This experience was not inaccessible to the savage; for instance, when distributing some larger game between the hunters, he would get so many pieces of kangaroo. If this experience, which has its roots in everyday life, serves as a given material for the operation of the unconscious mechanism of day-dreaming, these will probably take the shape of wishing that each piece of kangaroo should become a whole kangaroo again, and that the act of consuming the animal and thus lessening the food supply should, on the contrary, have the effect of augmenting it.[4] Similar concepts may, therefore, originate without a revival of the "engrams" made by the Primeval Combat: for instance, when we read that the origin of mountains is accounted for by a single original mountain torn to pieces by fire.[5] However, in

[1] Spencer and Gillen, *Nor. T.*, 294.

[2] Id., ibid., 295.

[3] Id., ibid., 295.

[4] Cf. the belief that the animals killed will be reborn if the bones are not broken.—J. G. Frazer, *Spirits of the Corn and the Wild*, 1912, II. 256.

[5] Th. H. Braim, *History of New South Wales*, 1846, 245. But as Pundjil is said to have made the animals in the same way, it is very well possible that the mountain origin of legend is modelled on the former.

our case, where the rock from which chips are knocked off by a member of the totem is expressly stated to be the body of the Alcheringa father, this cannot be said to make the former explanation superfluous; both are accordingly correct and complementary to each other—one from the point of view of the Unconscious, the other as a rationalization that must have occurred to the natives themselves from the point of view of Consciousness.

As we have to do with rites that principally turn on the subject of the food-supply, we shall not be surprised to see the part played by oral-eroticism in the ritual. In the Grass-seed Intichiuma of the Kaitish tribe, one of the Panunga (a man of the opposite moiety) puts a little of the seed up to the Thungalla man's mouth and he blows it away in all directions, the idea of this being to make the grass grow plentifully everywhere.[1] The transition between blowing and throwing is represented by a parallel rite in the Yam Intichiuma of the Worgaia tribe; the other men bring some yam to the head of the Yam totem asking him to make them grow large and sweet. He bites a small one and throws the pieces out in all directions, an action which produces the desired effect.[2]

A snake in the Alcheringa is said to have made rain (Anula tribe) by spitting up into the sky.[3] In the Mara tribe the men of the moiety to which the honey-bag belongs can increase the number of bees, and therefore the honey supply, by striking powder off the stone and blowing it about in all directions; this scattered powder gives rise to bees.[4] In the same way as spitting and blowing as a means of magical multiplication stand for the oral-erotic phase in the evolution of the libido, other rites represent the libidinal feelings that evolve from the complementary part of alimentary functions—I mean anal eroticism.

Legends of rending to pieces. Anal components of the Libido.

We recall the Anula legend of the crocodile leaving spirit-children and its excrements at various spots of its wanderings.[5] The Dieri perform the Minkani ceremony in order to obtain a plentiful crop of lizards and carpet-snakes. The Mura-mura Minkani is hidden in his cave deep in a sand-hill. His remains seem to be those of one of the fossil animals called Kadimarkara by the Dieri. The men dig down till damp earth is reached and also what they call the excrement of the Mura-mura. Then two men stand over it and the vein of the arm of each being opened, the blood is allowed to fall on the Mura-mura. The Minkani song is now sung and the men, in a state of frenzy, strike at each other with weapons until they reach the camp. Here the women rush forward and stop the fighting. The men who are connected with this special Mura-mura from their

[1] Spencer and Gillen, *Nor. T.*, 293.
[2] Id., ibid., 296.
[3] Id., ibid., 314 (Anula tribe).
[4] Id., ibid., 312.
[5] Id., ibid., 312.

mother's side collect the blood dropping from the wounds and scatter it, mixed with "excrement" from this Minkani's cave, over the sand-hills, so that they bring forth the young woma and kapiri hidden in them.[1] We know what the blood-letting on the ancestor's body means, and the state of frenzied fighting that follows is evidently a ceremonial revival of the awful Primeval Conflict between the men of the Horde. Naturally it is the women that put an end to it; the sadistic and anal-erotic phase of the infantile erotic organization identifies the substance which fructifies the sand-hills and the cave-womb both with blood and with excrements.

The Wonkgongaru ceremony of the louse totem replaces the excrements with dirt. At a sand-bank which was associated with lice ancestors in the Alcheringa, there is an ordinary "louse tree" and a "crab-louse tree." They take some dirt from the sand-bank, rub it on to the two trees and throw it about in all directions, and a plentiful crop of lice is the result.[2] When it is desired to increase the number of kangaroos at any special place in some other spot among the Mara tribe, men of that locality go to some other spot where kangaroo is abundant and ask the men of the moiety to which the kangaroo belongs to allow them to send kangaroos into their country. Permission being granted, the men go out to the sandy ridges and collect a certain grass of which the kangaroo is very fond and which also belongs to the same moiety. They then get some kangaroo dung and wrap it up in the grass. After making a cleared space, on the ground upon which grass is then strewn, the dung is placed on this, and on the dung another layer of grass. The whole is then set on fire and the men taking green bushes, scatter the embers in all directions. These embers are supposed to go to the country of the men who are performing the rite. While this is in progress they keep saying to the kangaroo, "There are plenty of you here; there are none along our country; you go there."[3] What happens is perfectly in accordance with infantile birth theories; new kangaroos spring up from the dung of kangaroos.

The complexes represented by the burning and scattered embers can, however, only be guessed at: in our opinion they stand for urethral eroticism, that is so often found in conjunction with the anal component.[4] Burning as a substitute for throwing is found in another case. The Urabunna natives make lizards by throwing pieces of the lizard-rock in various directions. As the Wonkangaru have no Lizard man amongst them, they must invoke the aid of

[1] Howitt, *N. T.*, 798. Cf. the Tirari tribe has a stone called "the heart of the snake," used in the making of the carpet-snake (Woma).—Gregory, *Dead Heart*, 80.

[2] Spencer and Gillen, *Nor. T.*, 288.

[3] Id., ibid., 312, 313.

[4] Cf. A. Bálint, *Imago*, however, 1923, ix. 424, on purely anal origin of fire symbolism.

the Urabunna when they want a fresh supply of lizards. In this case the Urabunna lizard man goes to the lizard tree, strips off some of its bark (which represents the lizards' skin) and sends it to the Wonkangaru men, who burn it in their own country to secure a supply of the animal.[1] We have found this same rite in the Cariera Intichiuma for the increase of sexual desire which is performed by a group that has (beside edible objects) the whirlwind, sexual desire and the baby for its totems. As to the connexion of the former with the two latter Brown has well pointed out that the reason of the combination is the belief that women can be impregnated by the whirlwind.[2] But in this case the whirlwind simply takes the place of the flatus,[3] so that we again have the burning rite in conjunction with anal-erotic complexes. It is evident that the principle of multiplication by division is applicable to the various components of the auto-erotic libido; the original being who is divided into pieces is man himself; he however projects the infantile components of his narcissistic libido into his excreta and secreta whereby these gain a new personality forming, nevertheless, a fragment of the original one. Mathews says: "Human ordure has also a place in their mythology as well as in their most important ceremonies. It is supposed to possess many virtues, among which may be mentioned the power of speech to personify the individual who deposited it."[4] Stones and rocks play a considerable part in all the variants of Intichiuma rites, and we may compare this to the way children play with pebbles and marbles, which has been demonstrated to be a substitute for playing with the excrements.[5] According to the Kabi and Wakka, a magician is a man who is full of magic stones (kundir-bongan) and these magic stones confer an extraordinary degree of vitality on the man who possesses them. These magicians, with crystals in their body, would lie down on the margin of Dkakkan's (Rainbow) water-hole. He was taken down by Dkakkan into his domain, and a grand exchange was effected. The man imparts stone-crystals to Dkakkan and Dkakkan gives him rope in exchange. The man is laid to rest again on the edge of the water-hole, and when he wakes up he is "manngurngur," that is "full of life."[6] This connexion of stones with vitality reminds us of the "millia gurlee," that is "Potent" or "Live-Stone," of

[1] Spencer and Gillen, *Nor. T.*, 288.

[2] A. R. Brown, "Beliefs concerning Childbirth," *Man*, 1912, 182.

[3] Cf. Jones, "The Madonna's Conception through the Ear," *Essays in Applied Psycho-Analysis*, 1923.

[4] Mathews, *E. N.*, 136. As to the reason why excrement should be credited with all magical virtues, more especially with that of speech, see Róheim, "Das Selbst," *Imago*, VII. 160, 161.

[5] See Ferenczi, "Ontogenie des Geldinteresses," *I. Z. Pa.*, 1914, 507.

[6] Mathews, *Two Representative Tribes*, 171, 172.

the rain-maker used in the Rain Intichiuma by the North-Western tribes.[1]

On the other hand, there cannot be the slightest doubt as to the anal-erotic meaning of these crystals that are exchanged between man and a supernatural being; we have other versions where the would-be magician gets a new set of bowels from the spirits in exchange for his own. All his intestines are cut out of the medicine man when he gets atnongara stones (kundir) put in his body instead.[2] But on the other hand the principle of multiplication by division applies equally well to the genital process; at procreation the semen is divided from man to give life to a new being and at birth the child is divided from woman. Last but not least we know that the lowest organisms multiply by division, a process that has only been supplanted by sexual multiplication in the course of evolution. Ultimately, then, the magical rites of the Intichiuma represent a regression to the very Sources of Life.

In the Mara tribe all the magician's internal organs are taken out and replaced by those of one of the spirits.[3] The boglia in Western Australia has got a quartz crystal in his stomach, and this is the embodiment of all his power; the crystal itself is called boglia and after the magician's death it passes on into his son's stomach.[4] On the other hand, we are told that the human body is the only, and the anus the favourite, source of boollia.[5] In South Australia the mundie, a crystal believed by the natives to be an excrement of the Deity, is used at initiation and held sacred.[6] This is probably one of the sources of the magical value attributed to hard substances, and helps us to understand why rocks and stones play such an important part in the multiplication ceremonies.

The hard substance also corresponds to the male organ in the state of erection; at least the churinga thrown at the woman, the stone thrown at the rock, is certainly the penis, and the dust that is rubbed off when two churingas are rubbed against each other most probably the semen. When a chip of stone is struck off a large rock and gives rise to spirit-animals (embryos) of the totem-species, the process probably symbolizes birth—the chip of stone representing the child, the rock, the mother.

Evolution of the Intichiuma.

We shall now try and determine the principal phases in the evolution of the Intichiuma as far as such an attempt may be warranted by our investigations. The germ of the present ritual is represented by the survival of those movements of the rutting season that served to introduce and promote sexual activity (fore-pleasure). The

[1] E. Clement, l.c., *Internationales Archiv für Ethnographie*, 1904, XVI. 6.

[2] Spencer and Gillen, *Nor. T.*, 480.

[3] Spencer and Gillen, *Nor. T.*, 488.

[4] Monsig. D. Rudesindo Salvado, *Memorie storiche dell' Australia*, 1851, 299.

[5] Oldfield, "Aborigines of Australia," *Transactions of the E. S.*, III. 235.

[6] G. F. Angas, *Savage Life and Scenes in Australia and New Zealand*, 1847, II. 224

common rutting season of all nature in the tropics serves as a psychical starting-point for the feeling of identification with a natural species: this is the prototype of projection which is regressively revived when the Father-Imago is projected into an animal species. In the second phase Intichiuma is still identical with rut: but the conflict between the Old and Young Males, the Father and Son for the women of the Horde is already beginning to leave its traces in the ceremonies. The third layer represents what we should call the beginning of human and the end of semi-human evolution. With the victory of the Brothers over the Father and the improvement of the general conditions of life, the rutting-season disappears and repression appears: the period of Anoestrum in animal life corresponding with the function of repression in Man, while the ever-present libido is, of course, represented in the animal world only in the rutting season. But as the libido in this transformation period is still an infantile, an archaic libido, exogamy does not exist. It does seem, however, probable that the exogamic tendency is much older than what we are accustomed to call the origin of the Oedipus conflict. We see it at work, and in conflict with the regressive tendency of endogamy, in the lower organisms. The conflict of the Jealous Sire and the Young Males only served to establish the repression of the endogamic and the dominance of the exogamic impulse out of which civilization was ultimately evolved. When the young males killed the Lord of the Herd it is probable that this inherent exogamic tendency would soon manifest itself so far that each member of the victorious party chose other "mothers" of the group in preference to his own, but these others mothers were of course only substitutes for their real mothers. This choice of substitutes led to what we call "tribal" mothers, fathers, etc.—in a word, to the classificatory system of relationships.

The young males, instead of searching for their mates amongst other herds, still try to get at their mothers and sisters; it follows that repression is first and foremost directed against the Oedipus complex—indeed, that the latter is in the main identical with the repressed. In the rutting season the ceremonies presupposed women as onlookers, repression gives independent existence to the initial phase of the movement-series and substitutes a symbolic for a real aim. The ceremony is chiefly an affair of the men, but repressed incestuous libido returns, the ceremonial ground becomes a symbol of the maternal womb. This third phase is represented by the ceremonies of the "sexual desire" and baby totems, and also the Caaro festival. In the fourth phase Intichiuma evolves with the new institutions of initiation and the two-phratry system. The repression of the Oedipus complex leads to a projection of the rites into the animal world, and the ceremonies of the baby-totem type begin to disappear. The magical multiplication of the totem animal forms part of the instruction given to novices in the initiation rite as a sort of substitute for their incestuous desires which they are henceforth held to relinquish. The animal dance with woman as audience reappears afterwards as revival of the original type, but without the procreative element. The conflict between libido and repression and the character of the whole rite as a compromise is manifest in the act of the totem-eating: this symbolical repetition of incest forms, like other analogous proceedings (blood-letting, etc.) an integral part of the rite, yet it must only be done in a very moderate way: the taboo must be broken through, the food "liberated" by the old men before the other members of the totemic moiety may eat it. Later on the aspect of this liberation ceremony changes, the animal is liberated for the men of the other moiety to consume, neurotic inhibitions[1] are sublimated into social feeling (altruism), and the libido is beginning to be sublimated into economical effort. The fifth phase of evolution is one both of disintegration and integration. The original totemic moieties split into the present totemic clans, and these unite to form what we call a tribe. Every totem clan has its own Intichiuma and legend to correspond; the animal is liberated for the members of other totems.

So far we have only discovered the part played by the libido in the evolution of the Intichiuma, but at first sight it must be evident that the economic aspect of these rites which has hitherto alone been taken into consideration by anthropologists cannot be neglected nor explained merely by a later sublimation of libidinal energies into economic effort. This in itself is an evident fact, but it only means that the economic side of the rite has in course of evolution gained a surplus, additional emphasis, from libidinal sources; it cannot mean that the instinct of Self-Preservation is not as primitive and as important as that of the Maintenance of the Species.

We shall now proceed to show that these rites have a double aspect, a composite character, from the very origin, and to determine the part played by the Reality Principle in their evolution.

The imitative element in Intichiuma.

We have observed that an Intichiuma consists of two elements —the procreative rite whereby animal embryos are supposed to emanate from the rock, and the imitative or dramatic, which consists in acting the animal or animal ancestor. The initiated men learn the churinga songs by heart, and these songs contain either episodes of the wanderings of the altjiranga mitjina or they describe the life of the totem-animal, so that Strehlow is inclined to attribute a certain import-

[1] Themselves derived from the social conflict of the father and son.

ance to them on account of the natural history embodied in them.[1] While the men are singing churinga songs that refer to the kangaroo ancestor, the performer hops about like a kangaroo.[2] The performer in the Wallaby ceremony imitates the wallaby ancestor by killing wallabies,[3] and the churinga song tells us how the wallaby father ran with his tail hanging behind.[4] The sounds made by the kangaroo-rats are imitated in the ceremony of that totem;[5] the opossum song tells us how the Old Man opossum stamps the damp earth.[6] The sounds made by bats are imitated.[7] In the Emu ceremony we have an extremely realistic copy of the way these birds go to their drinking-places.[8] They imitate the call of the itoa (*Otis australis* Gray).[9] The two performers in the eagle ceremony sit on a shield that represents the nest of the eagle-ancestor and cry like young eagles.[10] In the Duck ceremony the performers imitate ducks.[11] In the lizard ceremony a man does as if he were catching lizards.[12] Men imitate the movements and the buzz of bees,[13] and flies.[14] In the Witchetty-Grub ceremony a long narrow wurley represents the chrysalis case from which the fully developed insect emerges. In the wurley the men sing of the animal in its various stages, and when they come out of it they sing of the insect emerging from its case.[15] Various parts of the emu's body are represented in the Emu intichiuma.[16] The performers, who are decorated with emu feathers, represented ancestors of the Emu totem, imitated the aimless gazing about of the emu, each man holding a bunch of twigs in his hands, the Churinga on the head with its tuft of feathers being intended to represent the long neck and small head of the bird.[17] In the water ceremony they scream in imitation of the spur-winged plover.[18] Rain is imitated by pouring water in the Kaitish Rain Intichiuma.[19] The Warramunga ceremony to increase the number of white cockatoos consisted in imitating the cry of the cockatoo with tedious monotony; all night long the headman held in his hand a conventional representation of the bird, and when his voice failed his son took up the call and relieved the old man.[20] Decorations in the Ant ceremony represent ants.[21] In the case of the White Cockatoo and Eagle-hawk totems, the performers marched out imitating the cry of the bird.[22] A man who represents a snake ancestor in a Loritja Intichiuma glides on his knees, quivers, and imitates the sound made by the snake.[23] The duck performers

[1] Strehlow, *A. & L.*, III. 5. [2] Id., III. 11. [3] Id., III. 15.
[4] Id., III. 17. [5] Id., III. 20. [6] Id., III. 22.
[7] Id., III. 31. [8] Id., III. 34. [9] Id., III. 36.
[10] Id., III. 37. [11] Id., III. 56. [12] Id., III. 65.
[13] Id., III. 90. [14] Id., III. 94.
[15] Spencer and Gillen, *N. T.*, 176. [16] Id., ibid., 179.
[17] Id., ibid., 181, 183. [18] Id., ibid., 193. [19] Id., *Nor. T.*, 295.
[20] Id., ibid., 310. [21] Id., ibid., 201. [22] Id., ibid., 217.
[23] Strehlow, *A. & L.*, III. 2, 30.

imitate the duck's cry.[1] In the Emu ceremony one of the performers imitates the way an emu goes to drink: he bends his head slowly down, looking round him on both sides, and then slowly slides down on to his knees. One performer whistles like a young emu carrying out the movements of drinking.[2] The Dog performers run on all fours like dogs.[3] "Um padi (Raupen) hervorzu bringen färbt man sich, wie die Raupe gefärbt ist und geht mit einer Mulde in die Emufedern oder Fett vom Emu getan ist herum."[4] At the kangaroo tarlow they hop about in imitation of kangaroos and drink kangaroo-fashion from wooden troughs placed on the ground.[5] In the evening there is a corroboree, the boomerangs are rattled together and a kangaroo bone is moved rapidly up and down on the incisions of the throwing-stick. Should food-seed become less plentiful another tarlow set apart for the "willing" of these is visited by the head of the "family" (subclass) under whose care it is: say a Caiemurra. In this case wooden bowls for winnowing the grass-seeds and stone mills with the grinding-stone play a prominent part. The ground around the tarlow is beaten flat with stones and sprinkled with water, and the women go through the performance of winnowing and grinding whilst songs are sung and dances are performed. The tarlow for the willing of fish is visited with fishing-nets; these and a poisonous plant called "kuraru," with which they stupefy fish by placing it in the pool, are largely displayed. At the emu tarlow the walk and run of the emu are imitated, and emu feathers are largely worn on this occasion.[6] Whatever is used in gathering or procuring the thing to be willed is carried with them; if it is grass-seed they take wooden scoops, if kangaroo spears, if turkey nets.[7]

If we try to explain these rites we must begin by distinguishing the three principal types of imitation met in them: (*a*) The animal and its movements are imitated (met with everywhere); (*b*) Imitating the Alcheringa ancestors who are identical with the totem-animals (chiefly characteristic of Central tribes, but probably coexistent with (*a*) in many cases, as a second explanation given to the same rite); and (*c*) Rites that we shall call labour imitation—that is they mimic the hunting, fishing, grinding, etc., whatever they will have to do with the animal when it is abundant (North-West and perhaps Dieri). Before proceeding further, I am compelled to give the merest outlines of a theory, very simple in itself, which I shall attempt to establish elsewhere. According to

[1] Strehlow, *A. & L.*, III. 2, 21.
[2] Id., III. 2, 16.
[3] Id., III. 2, 14.
[4] Siebert, *Globus*, 97, 55.
[5] Clement, "Ethnographical Notes on the Western Australian Aborigines," *Int. Arch. für Ethn.*, 1904, XVI. 6.
[6] Clement, l.c., XVI. 7.
[7] J. G. Withnell, "Marriage Rites and Relationships," *Science of Man*, 1903, VI. 46.

7. INTICHIUMA CEREMONIES.

I. Imitative Rites.

47, 48 (p. 306), 52, 56 (p. 306), 235 (p. 307).

II. Procreative Rites.

(*a*) Quivering.

4, 6, 8, 16, 17, 18, 19 (Sp. III, 138), 27, 28 (p. 218), 47, 48, 50 (p. 218), 52, 56 (p. 218), 77 (p. 218).

(*b*) Bleeding.

48 (p. 222), 52, 56 (pp. 222, 223), 69, 70, 71 (p. 298), 73, 74 (p. 298), 75 (p. 225), 76 (pp. 225, 299), 77 (p. 225), 85 (p. 298), 223 (p. 222).

(*c*) Throwing.

4, 6, 13, 17, 18, 19, 20 (p. 297), 31 (p. 286), 32 (p. 297) 48 (pp. 290, 299), 75 (G. Horne and G. Aiston: *Savage Life in Central Australia*, 1924, 134), 76 (p. 298), 77 (p. 286), 222 (Roth: *S.M.M.* 1c).

(*d*) Striking.

31 (pp. 286, 300), 32 (p. 297), 52 (p. 286), 69, 70, 71, 73, 74 (p. 300), 76 (p. 300), 77 (pp. 286, 301), 85 (p. 300), 232 (p. 286), 235 (p. 286).

(*e*) Rubbing.

12 (Sp. III, 213), 52 (p. 219), 56 (p. 219).

(*f*) Fire in the Multiplication Ritual.

77, 237 (p. 301).

III. Connected with the Ceremonial Eating of the Totem.

24, 45 (p. 250), 48, 50 (p. 247), 51 (Sp. I, 211), 52, 56 (p. 244–246). 222 (p. 251).

IV. Survival of Anthropic Intichiuma in Custom.

43 (p. 234), 47 (p. 234), 52, 56 (p. 234), 232, 234, 235, 237, 253, 255 (pp. 235, 236), 259 (p. 215), 330 (p. 235).

V. Survival of Anthropic Intichiuma in Legend.

27, 28 (Sp. III, 266, 267), 48 (p. 217), 76 (p. 217).

VI. Use of Churinga in Intichiuma.

4, 6, 13, 17, 18, 19, 20, 48, 50, 52, 55, 56 (p. 266).

VII. Intichiuma in Connection with Initiation Ceremonies.

1 (p. 264), 4, 6, 13, 17, 18, 19, 20 (pp. 265, 266), 41, 42, 43, 44, 46, 47, 48, 49, 50, 51, 52, 55, 56 (pp. 259–264), 222 (Sp. II, 308, 309), 259 (p. 217).

VIII. Survivals of Intichiuma in Legend.

85 (p. 292), 89 (p. 291), 97 (p. 292), 119 (p. 291), 124, 125 (p. 291), 204 (p. 292).

IX. Survivals of Intichiuma in Ritual.

2 (Basedow: *J.R.A.I.*, 1913, 308), 89, 103 (H. 400), 198, 201 (Roth: *Superstition*, 20), 274 (H. 450), 333 (H. 400).

X. Animal Dances Performed at Initiation.

1, 2 (Sp. III, 107), 4, 6 (Sp. III, 132), 12 (Sp. III, 107), 13, 15, 16, 17, 18, 19, 20 (Sp. III, 138, p. 265), 27 (Sp. III, 165, 176), 41, 42, 43, 44, 46, 47, 48, 49, 50, 51, 52, 55, 56 (p. 258), 89 (p. 266), 90, 91, 94, 95, 96 (p. 268), 102, 106 (p. 268), 108 (p. 267), 111 (p. 267), 114, 115, 116, 117, 119 (p. 268), 121, 122, 123, 124 (p. 268), 129, 130 (p. 268), 146 (p. 268), 150 (K. L. Parker: *Euahlayi*, 81), 153, 156 (p. 267), 159, 160 (p. 266), 200 (Roth: *Initiation*, 177), 202 (Roth: *Initiation*, 170), 204, 205 (Roth: *Initiation*, 179), 206, 209 (p. 293), 222 (p. 258), 327 (p. 267), 358 (R. H. Mathews: *Mitt. d. Anthr. Ges. in Wien*, XXXVIII, 1908, 19).

XI. Liberation Performed as a Totemic Ceremony.

24, 45 (p. 250), 47 (p. 254), 48 (p. 256), 52, 56 (p. 258), 222 (p. 258).

XII. Liberation in Initiation Ritual.

4, 6, 13, 15, 16, 17, 18, 19, 20 (Sp. III, 132, p. 264), 35 (Sp. II, 613), 47 (Sp. II, 612, 613), 98, 99, 100, 101, 102, 103, 104, 105, 106, 107 (H. 609–12), 108 (H. 633), 137 (p. 268), 153 (H. 595), 156 (H. 583), 157 (H. 597), 158 (H. 607), 171 (H. 608), 189 (C. III, 20), 198 (Roth: *Initiation*, 178), 200 (Roth: *Initiation*, 177), 204, 205 (Roth: ibid., 180), 231 (C. I, 289), 235 (C. I, 297, *Journal*, 1913, 174), 302 (C. III, 64), 337 (Roth: *Initiation*, 185), 358 (R. H. Mathews: "Initiations-ceremonie des Birdhawalstammes," *Mi. d. Anthr. Ges. Wien*, 1908, XXXVIII. 19).

XIII. Intichiuma Performed at Totem Centre or Representation of Centre in the Ceremony.

47, 48, 50, 51, 52, 55, 56 (pp. 214, 258), 232, 235, 236 (p. 235).

XIV. Terminations of Ceremonies.

(*a*) Hugging.

52, 56 (p. 256).

(*b*) Pressing the head of the performer down.

43 (p. 256), 48, 50 (p. 256).

(*c*) Knocking the head-dress off.

18 (p. 256), 47 (p. 256).

XV. INTICHIUMA CEREMONIES OF UNCERTAIN TYPE.

150 (Parker, 81), 369 (Carnegie: *Spinifex and Sand*, 334).

XVI. TYPOLOGY OF INTICHIUMA RITES.

(*a*) Dieri type: absence of totem-eating, procreative aspect prominent. 67, 68, 69, 70, 71, 72, 73, 74, 75, 76, 77.

(*b*) Arunta type: liberation, totem-eating, procreative and imitative element, use of churinga. 48, 50, 51, 52, 55, 56, 222.

(*c*) Warramunga type: historical element dominant, absence of churingas and totem-eating.
41, 42, 43, 44, 46, 47, 49.

(*d*) Coastal type: slight development of rite, contains both procreative and historical element.
27, 28, 31, 32, 35.

(*e*) Kakadu type: connected with initiation ceremony, use of churinga.
2, 4, 6, 13, 18, 19, 20.

(*f*) Waduman type: totem-eating and liberation. 24, 25, 45.

(*g*) Western type: procreative anthropic ceremonies.
230–59, 330.

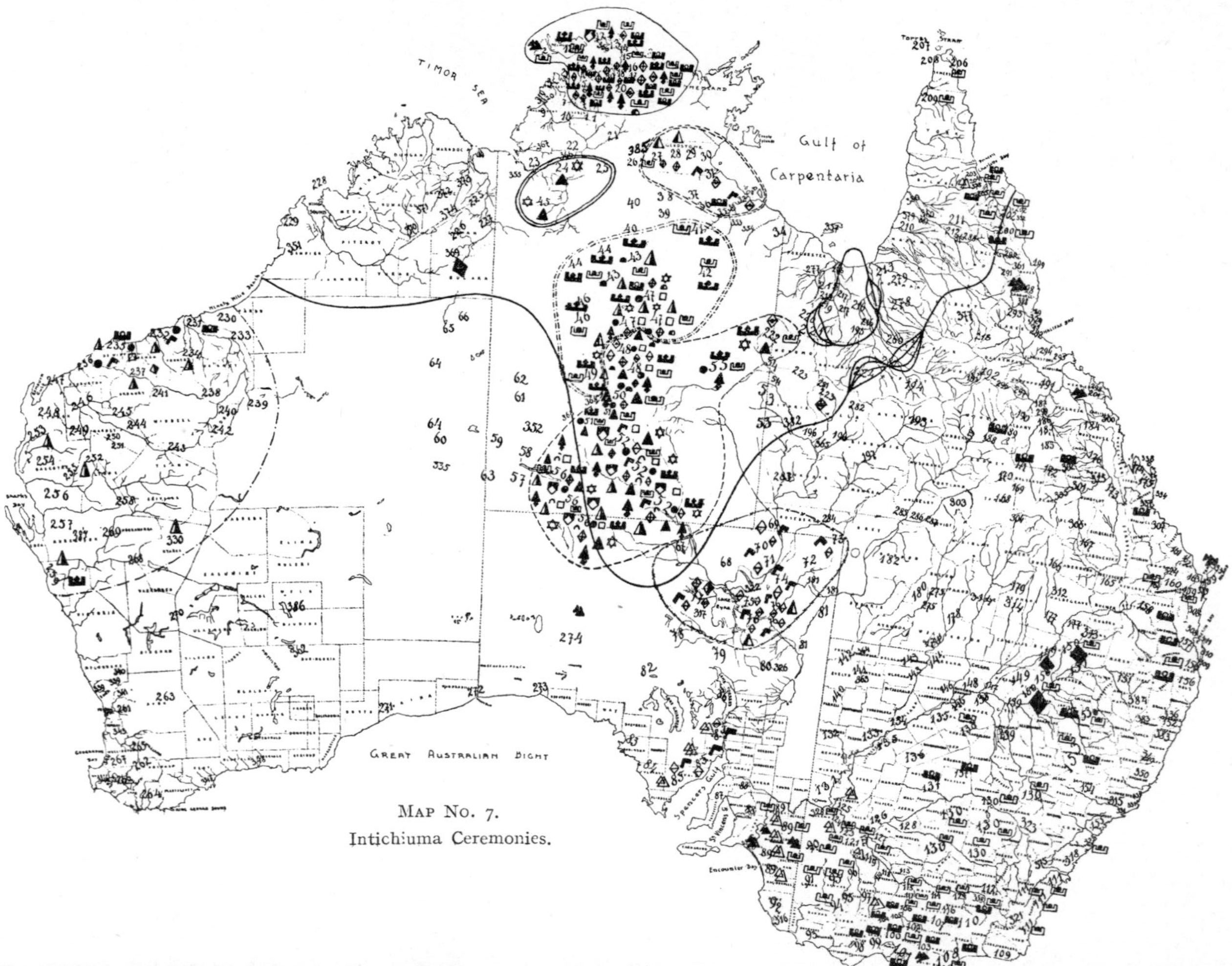

Map No. 7.
Intichiuma Ceremonies.

this theory all our movements consist of three phases—the initial, the realistic, and the final phase—which make up what I call a movement series.[1] The first and last of these phases are reduced copies of the middle, realistic or "full" phase and their function is to bridge over the gulf from repose to action and back again from action to repose. When either through the interference of the psychic censor or from external difficulties these motor series become inhibited, the initial stage tends to split off from the original series and gain a sort of independence with a fictive aim: this marks the transition from mere motor discharge to magic rite, such as is the case, for instance, in the evolution of the fore-pleasure movements of the rutting season to magical rites of the Intichiuma. We must not forget that the rutting season is the rainy season, when everything begins to flourish as with a stroke of magic, when there is enhanced sexual activity and also nourishment in plenty. We know that the arid desert of Central Australia, where the contrast between the two seasons is the greatest, is the proper home of the Intichiuma; it is here that climatic conditions are worse, the adaptation to environment made the most difficult; it is also here that repression has been the least successful, and here that we have to deal with a return of repressed elements on a large scale.

The difficulties presented by environment play the same part on the side of the Reality Principle as repression does towards the libido: the inhibition of wish-fulfilments of the self-preservatory kind augments the necessity of hallucinatory substitutes; there are mere unperfected movement-series tending to abreaction. In the same way as the approach of the rutting season cannot come without transition, but is marked by a number of rites that are reduced copies of copulation, so the approach of the "feeding season" is announced by rites that imitate the very animal that will be hunted, etc. In both cases the magical efficacy of these rites is a projected survival of their realistic efficacy; they are efficacious in the sense that they prepare Man himself to act.[2] We shall thus say that the procreative element of the Intichiuma rite is split off in this way from the movement series pertaining to copulation (fore-pleasure), and the imitative is split off from that dealing with the procuring of food. In the strict sense, however, this only applies to type (*c*) of our imitative rites, whilst types (*a*) and (*b*) are of composite nature, concerned both with Hunger and the Libido. Imitative circular reaction as such is the motor expression of the biological unity with environment.[3] Thus unity

[1] Cf. the views of Avenarius, *Kritik der reinen Erfahrung*, 1907.

[2] That is, they are the links between a state of repose and a state of action (realistic phase of the movement series).

[3] Cf. Ankermann, "Ausdrucks und Spieltätigkeit als Grundlage des Totemismus," *Anthropos*, X, XI, p. 586.

is always existing, and existing especially in the rutting period, and as such it must precede even the feeling of this unity. When man is craving for nourishment of a particular kind, say kangaroo, he will identify himself with that nourishment and imitate it; the power of desire changes him into a kangaroo.[1]

In this craving the necessity of nourishment, however, is inextricably blended with oral-erotic elements, and we must not forget that eating the kangaroo is not a simple alimentary process for the totemite, but symbolic of totemic incest. If we remember that multiplication by imitation, wishing to create copies of one's own self, or what amounts to the same thing, identifying oneself with the copies one wishes to create, is a proceeding that characterizes the narcissistic phase of ontogenesis,[2] we shall readily understand the intermediate position occupied by our type (*a*) between the Libido and the Ego (Reality Principle). Type (*b*) represents a further well-known development on the same line; here narcissism is at the same time an identification with the Father-Imago, which identification in its turn serves to fulfil the incest wish in a symbolic and hallucinatory fashion. It is probable that the part played by the Reality Principle in these rites has been there and has been largely unchanged from the very beginning; it has only been blended with various phases in the evolution of the libido—thus oral-erotic, anal-erotic, incestuous, narcissistic—in the course of time.

[1] Cf. Freud, *Group Psychology and the Analysis of its Ego*, 1922, on the problem of identification.

[2] G. Róheim, *Spiegelzauber*, 1919, 113, on narcissistic creation myths.

CHAPTER VII

HISTORY AND DEVELOPMENT OF AUSTRALIAN TOTEMISM. SUMMARY AND CONCLUSIONS

If we attempt to reconstruct the evolution of totemism as it is found in Australia we must not confound the ethnological side of our work with the psychological conclusions to be drawn from the affinities between groups of tribes who have certain forms of the totemic complex. A true insight into these connexions cannot, however, be gained without a psychological understanding of the social and religious phenemona that we use as means of classification.

We begin with the ethnological part of our work and shall state our position briefly as follows: Australia has been peopled by two consecutive immigrations; the first wave is represented by the tribes of the south and south-east, with their negative form of totemism; the second by those of the north, centre and west, with their positive form. From a psychological point of view the chief difference between these two waves lies in the relative position of the libido to repression, the first wave being characterized by a successful repression of the Oedipus complex, the second by the return of repressed elements.

Totemism and history of Australian culture.

In trying to ascertain something of the history as distinguished from the psychology of these tribes, we are avowedly going beyond the legitimate limits of our investigation. These problems are perhaps the most difficult ones in the realm of anthropology, and they have always attracted both those who are not aware of the difficulties and those who are and yet feel strong enough to deal with them. Now it is evident that if such questions are to be solved, it is only by a complete analysis of the physical anthropology, language, culture, social organization and religious institutions of these peoples that we can hope to get satisfactory results. This lies quite beyond the scope of our book and there is no *a priori* reason for supposing that totemism and allied phenomena are the most reliable starting-points for these investigations. We are thus fully aware of the conjectural nature of all we have to say on this subject, and are prepared to modify or withdraw these suggestions if subsequent research by more competent investigators proves that our guesses have missed the mark. Throughout this book we have been led by one assumption: myths are records of the past, both of onto- and phylogenesis. If we can show the traces of biological events in myths it would be illogical to deny the possibility that they are also records of a less remote past—that they represent history as well as evolution. Indeed, the analysis of dreams has sufficiently shown that we must regularly expect a high degree of condensation in the latent content of all psychic phenomena, so that we shall expect the same myth to contain records both of a remote and of a more recent past. Although I think we have shown it to be fairly probable that the inapertwa myth is a projection of the human embryo into racial history, this does not say that the same myth may not contain the memory of the advance of a certain tribe from sociological conditions which were regarded as infantile when compared with other social forms under the influence of immigrant tribes.[1] Indeed, when we remember that this myth is limited to definite tribes and even definite totem clans we shall be compelled to suppose that historical events are responsible for this peculiar distribution.[2] And if we have found that the Alcheringa myths of the Central tribes are safe guides into the prehistoric dawn of humanity, it would be unscientific and unwise to ignore the evidence which they may afford as to more recent events in the history of the race. Indeed, Spencer and Gillen interpreted the myths which they recorded, as historical evidence.

Myths contain records both of the biological and historical past.

It is not without interest to note that, according to tradition, the Emu men who introduced the division of the classes now in use lived away to the north, because the adoption of the distinctive names for the eight groups thus created is at the present time taking place in the Arunta tribe, and as a matter of actual fact these names did originate in the north and are now slowly spreading southwards through the tribe.[3] Strehlow calls our attention to another remarkable fact.

Northern origin of the Arunta.

In the traditions of the Arunta tribe all benefactors of mankind come from the north, while every social movement which is regarded as immoral is said to have spread from the south.[4] Thus the Echidna

[1] Cf. W. H. R. Rivers, "The Sociological Significance of Myth," *Folk-Lore*, 1912, 330, 331. P. W. Schmidt, *Anthropos*, III. 623. Id., "Die Stellung der Aranda," *Z. E.*, 1908, 880.

[2] Cf. also Róheim, "Zwei Sagengruppen vom Igel," *Zeitschrift des Vereins für Volkskunde*, 1913, 414.

[3] Spencer and Gillen, *N. T.*, 422.

[4] There are exceptions to this rule; or, perhaps, it does not apply to the tribes who live to the north of the Arunta. Two Parenthie lizards who introduce circumcision and subincision in the Unmatjera tribe came from the south.—Spencer and Gillen, *Nor. T.* 405. This probably refers to back-waves of culture which spread in the contrary direction, perhaps to the influence exercised by the Arunta on their

man who is called " kunna " (bad), as well as the Emu people, came from the south, and it was especially amongst the Emu men that a total disregard of the exogamic classes was observable, so that a man would even marry his " maia " (mother, mother's sister), and a father would marry his own daughter, after the death of his wife. Corruption spread towards the north, so that the marriage regulations of Mangarkunjerkunja (a lizard culture hero) fell into disuse and had to be re-introduced by a hero of the Kangaroo-Rat totem who was called Katutankara (the immortal father), who came from Anjatjiringi in the north.[1] We have other positive evidence of the correctness of the tradition of the Emu men. The marriages mentioned in the myth still occur amongst the southern Loritja, where a widower will marry his own daughter or his " jaku," a grade of relationship which includes " father's brother's wife," " mother " and " mother's sister." [2] Mangarkunjerkunja, who introduced the fire-borer and the stone knife, came from the north.[3] " All the narratives of Central Australia . . . give an account of beings coming from the north who introduced certain elements of the material and magico-religious culture and modified the social institutions." [4] Moreover, we have already noticed a sure test of the northern origin of the Arunta tribe ; the land of ghosts lies to the north, and the land of the dead, as is well known, is usually the land of the ancestors.[5] To this we may add the fact that there seems to be a specially close connexion between the Arunta and one of the coastal tribes investigated by Spencer : the Kakadu. Although there are important differences between these two groups of tribes, we cannot ignore the points of contact, especially as both the Kakadu and the Arunta group of tribes may have been modified by culture-contact or intermixture in the course of their migrations.[6] The Kakadu as well as the Port Essington tribe have the custom of giving a stick to a woman when enceinte ; this stick represents the child and is (as shown above) the same thing as the wooden Churinga (called papa) of the Arunta infant.[7] The Muraian sticks and stones are in a certain degree the

The Arunta and Kakadu.

northern neighbours. See the distribution of Intichiuma ceremonies on the map, which shows how some northern tribes have adopted the Arunta type of ceremonies. For a legend which may contain a trace of this northerly movement, as it asserts the southern origin of the Arunta, see J. W. Gregory, *The Dead Heart of Australia*, 1906, 226, 227.

[1] Strehlow, *A. & L.*, I. 8.

[2] Id., ibid., IV. 83, 102.

[3] Id., ibid., I. 6.

[4] Rivers, op. cit., *Folk-Lore*, 1912, 329.

[5] Cf. E. Schirren, *Die Wandersagen der Neuseeländer und der Mauimythos*, 1856, 90. W. J. Perry, " The Orientation of the Dead in Indonesia," *J. R. A. I.*, XLIV, 1914. Id., " Myths of Origin and the Home of the Dead," *Folk-Lore*, XXVI, 1915. Claus, " Die Wangómwia," *Z. E.*, 1910, 491.

[6] The Kakadu are probably modified by intermixture with the real aboriginal population of Australia, which seems to have left traces of its existence especially among the coastal tribes of the north and south.

[7] Spencer, *N. T. N. T. A.*, 1914, 328, 329. Strehlow, II. 80. (Above, p. 179).

equivalents of the Arunta Churinga,[1] whilst the ceremony itself corresponds to the Engwura of the Arunta.[2] But we have evidence which is far more important than these parallels; for it is only in the Arunta and Kakadu tribes that totems depend purely on the childbirth beliefs,[3] and only these two groups of the tribes have the belief in the existence of a Changing and a Changeless Spirit.[4] If we regard the area occupied by the Central Tribes as a separate territory, then we shall notice that the Arunta and Kakadu with pure conceptional totemism are situated on the outskirts of the area; they are divided by nations like the Anula and Warramunga who have conceptional totemism combined with paternal descent of the totem. We shall thus legitimately infer: (*a*) That the great immigration of the Central tribes must have taken place in many (at least two) separate waves. (*b*) That the tribes with conceptional totems and paternal descent came after those with pure conceptional totems and drove a wedge between them. (*c*) That the Kakadu and Arunta were once closely connected—in other words, that the Arunta were one of the coastal tribes of North Australia.[5]

The Torres Straits and Central Australia.

Having thus far traced the path of Arunta migration from the north, we are tempted to go into closer details on the connexion between them and the Torres Strait Islanders. Certain similarities in magico-religious institutions have already been noticed by A. C. Haddon and W. Foy,[6] and the whole question has been dealt with in an admirable article by Father W. Schmidt.[7] Indeed, it would be sufficient to refer to this paper if it were not for the fact that, although we agree with the learned Father in claiming a connexion between the Torres Strait Islanders and Central Australia, we venture to differ from him in the psychological interpretation of this historical connexion, and we think it possible to follow the traces of a prehistoric movement further north to New Guinea.

The kwod and the Ertnatulunga.

In the western islands open spaces called kwods are permanently set apart for ceremonial purposes.[8] They are more nearly related to the clubhouses (Männerhaus) of New Guinea and Melanesia[9] than to the ertnatulunga of Central Australia.[10] The main feature which they have in common with the latter seems to be that both contain magical objects of stone which are regarded as the materialization of the forces inherent in the totem-clan. "The unique features of the totem-cult

[1] Spencer, *N. T. N. T. A.*, 225.
[2] Id., ibid., 152.
[3] Id., ibid., 180.
[4] Id., ibid., 270.
[5] See maps on conceptional totemism and intichiuma ceremonies.
[6] *Reports of the Cambridge Anthropological Expedition*, V. 373. *Archiv für Rel. Wiss.*, X. 135.
[7] P. W. Schmidt, "Die Stellung der Aranda," *Z. E.*, 1908, 806.
[8] Haddon, l.c., V. 365.
[9] Id., ibid., 3.
[10] Schmidt, "Aranda," *Z. E.*, 1908, 900.

of Yam were the representation of the augud in a definite image, each of which was lodged in its own house and the presence of a stone beneath each effigy in which resided the life of augud" [1] (totem). It has been pointed out by W. Schmidt that this "materialization of the totem" (Haddon) is the same thing as the Central Australian Churinga.[2] The two magical crescents of Kwoiam have already been compared with Churinga by A. C. Haddon,[3] and perhaps the crescent-shaped paraphernalia mentioned by Klaatsch,[4] and the crescent-shaped Intichiuma decorations of Central Australia [5] are links of the same chain. Some of the kwods present greater similarity to the Ertnatulunga than others. The sacred island of Pulu, associated as it was with initiation and death ceremonies and with some of the exploits of Kwoiam, contained no more sacred spot than the cave of Augudalkula. No woman might approach the place; its custody was entrusted to the oldest and most influential men of Mabuiag the tumaiawai-mabaegal, that is the "watching-men" or "watchers." Here in the depths of the thickest bush that grows in Pulu, amidst rocky scenery whose very grotesqueness is mysterious, were stored the heads of those who were slain in war.[6] It is also in this direction that the most illuminating parallel between these two regions has been found.[7] "When it is determined that a woman hitherto childless is pregnant her husband collects food, which is cooked and eaten by the whole community including the expectant parents.[8] Meanwhile one of the husband's brothers has a peculiar ornament called 'bid' prepared for his sister-in-law.[9] "The 'bid' represents the fœtus, as is shown by the names of its constituent parts, which are those of the limbs and organs of the body. This ornament is worn by the pregnant woman so that the 'gamu' (body) is immediately over the pit of the stomach, the strings representing the arms and legs being tied at the back of the body respectively, while the fringe hanging down in front reaches to about the level of the knees." [10]

The "bid" and the Churinga.

Here we find ethnological research confirming the results obtained through the psycho-analytical investigation of Central Australian evidence in a most striking manner; after having come to the conclusion that the Churinga is the embryo we find that, in an ethnologically connected territory, an emblematic representation of

[1] Haddon, *Cambridge Expedition*, V. 377.
[2] Schmidt, l.c., 900.
[3] Haddon, l.c., V. 373.
[4] Klaatsch, "Schlussbericht über seine Reise nach Australian," *Z. E.*, 1907, 638.
[5] Strehlow, *A. & L.*, I. Plate V.
[6] Haddon, l.c., V. 368.
[7] Schmidt, *Z. E.*, 1908, 900.
[8] Father Schmidt is inclined to connect this with conception by food in Central Australia.
[9] The "wororu" in North-West Australia (cf. above, p. 146) is also the husband's brother.
[10] Seligmann, "Birth and Childhood Customs," *Cambridge Expedition*, V. 194.

the embryo figures in birth customs, that is the contents of the symbol which is unconscious in Central Australia is fully conscious in these islands.

Father Schmidt thinks that this parallel is evidence for the secondary, derived nature of Central Australian beliefs which are based on a misunderstanding. Quite apart from the unpsychological terminology in which he expresses this idea, there are other objections to this view. It contains the implicit assumption that because the Torres Straits are geographically nearer to the starting-point of these migrations than the Macdonnell Ranges, the forms of ritual and belief found in these islands must explain the evolution of those of the Arunta and not the other way round. Proximity to the cradle of the race is no proof of primitivity; if it were, we should have to regard the Chinese, for instance, as more primitive than the Lapps and Ostyaks, as these have certainly migrated from the south-east to the inhospitable regions at present occupied by them. Besides, we must not forget that we have succeeded in comprehending the "Arunta system" as a perfectly harmonious whole in itself. Naturally it has a past, a psychic history, but it cannot be treated as if it were the broken-down remains of another system. The relation of the "bid" to the Churinga is one which we know very well from analytic practice and theory. The Churinga is a real symbol, with a repressed, i.e. an unconscious meaning; the "bid" represents the phase which we call the return of repressed elements. Of course, the "bid" might also represent the primary unrepressed phase in the evolution of the symbol, and then we should say that repression took place in the space of time which elapsed between Torres Straits and the Macdonnell Ranges, which would be the view Father Schmidt takes, only stated in a more psychological language. But we shall see further on that certain phenomena in the cultural areas north of Australia are only explicable if we regard the return of repressed elements as the general psychological key to these cultures.

In Australia we needed analysis to show that the Churinga is an embryo; here this connexion is perfectly evident to those who practice the custom. This explains why the magico-religious importance of the Churinga is so much greater than that of the "bid." In a compulsion neurosis we always find that the symptoms are determined by the repressed elements, and it is more than probable that a similar root will always be found at the bottom of religious symptoms. If analysis lifts the latent content of the complexes into consciousness the symptoms gradually disappear, and this explains why the "bid" plays such a small part in religious life in comparison with the Churinga.

We shall find that this is not an isolated case but generally characteristic of the psychological relations existing between these two cultures. We have found that the Churingas are symbols of the child, the fœtus and the penis. In the Torres Straits we find that a fruit resembling the penis is pressed against the abdomen of the pregnant woman who wishes to have a male child.[1] It is but a short step from the idea of influencing the sex of a child to that of causing pregnancy, indeed we have sufficient evidence from other parts of the world of the custom of making a woman pregnant through dolls (artificial children) and through wooden or stone phalloi.[2]

Zogo, augud and Churinga.

As we are discussing childbirth beliefs we may as well continue the survey by recalling the parallel between the inapertwa myth and the two mothers of Sida who are separated by him.[3] We shall turn to the analysis of such ideas as are contained in the words "zogo" and "augud" to show that they present a marked resemblance to the category of "Churinga" objects and festivals in Central Australia. "The word Churinga is used either as a substantive, when it implies a sacred emblem, or as a qualifying term, when it implies sacred or secret." Aritna Churinga is the secret name.[4] The man who has a Churinga will feel superior to the man who has none in case of a fight.[5] "The burden of these stanzas or verses is either a prayer to save them from some disease (as 'Headache quiet become') or a prayer for tjurunga or food substance or some such object."[6] "Their tjurunga, corroborees, are mostly animal tjurunga (feats); thus at an Emu tjurunga they imitate exactly an emu in all its movements."[7] "The well-known festivals or dances of the natives are called by them tjurunga and ildada." "One of them owns the emu, the other the fish tjurunga,"[8] Certain magical practices and implements are called "zogo" in the Torres Islands. Thus we have "zogo" for rain, wind, wild plums, coco-nuts, bananas, tobacco, for a good harvest, for garden produce, for yam, for turtle, for dugong, for fish, for mosquitoes, for terns' eggs.[9] These "zogo," which are used for increasing the food supply, might with full right be called Intichiuma ceremonies if they were connected with certain totem clans. Haddon tells us that there was a recollection of a time when the zogo had been equivalent to the western augud or true totems. In the Eastern Islands the word agud (augud) occurs seldom, but it was stated to be the "big name of the zogo."[10] One

[1] Seligmann, *Cambridge Expedition*, V. 196.

[2] Cf. Frazer, *The Magic Art*, 1911, I. 70–74. Cf. W. E. Roth, "Games, Sports and Amusements," *North Queensland Ethnography*, Bull. 4, 1902, 13. S. Eitrem, *Opferritus und Voropfer der Griechen und Römer*, 1915, 305.

[3] Haddon, *Cambridge Expedition*, V. 32.

[4] Spencer and Gillen, *N. T.*, 139.

[5] Strehlow, *A. & L.*, II. 79. "Spose we no got augud, how we fight?"—Haddon, l.c., V. 372. The Tikowina (bullroarer) is a sort of war-charm worn round the neck of the warrior.—Howitt, l.c., 499.

[6] L. Schulze, "The Aborigines of the Upper and Middle Finke River," *Trans. and Proc. Royal Society of S.A.*, 1891, 220.

[7] Schulze, ibid., 221.

[8] Id., ibid., 242.

[9] Haddon, op. cit., VI. 192.

[10] Id., op. cit., VI. 245.

of the most important zogos was called nam zogo and was represented by two turtles made of turtle shell. The nam zogo were used not only to help men catch turtles but also to prevent them from doing so; to kill men and also to make them better.[1] This nam zogo was called agud, that is totem.[2] The information on zogo is summed up by Haddon as follows: "From the foregoing enumeration it is evident that rain, wind, a concrete object or a shrine can be a zogo; a zogo can be impersonal or personal; it belonged in a general way to particular groups of natives, but it was the particular property of certain individuals, the zogo le, who alone knew the ceremonies connected with it and therefore the rites were confined to them; the 'making' of the zogo was usually more or less secret, and in no case might women be present; the zogo was always treated with great respect, and sacrilege was punished either by human or spiritual means. I do not know how the word can be better translated than by the term 'sacred.' A zogo may therefore be a sacred object or place, the rite was sacred as were the words that were uttered." [3]

Taken in conjunction with the probability that zogos were evolved from or represent a special aspect of agud, that is totems, we cannot deny that every word in the above description might apply just as well to the Central Australian churinga, and especially to their function at the Intichiuma ceremonies. The zogo le (Eastern Islanders) employ a foreign language, probably an archaic form of the western language, and thus can only guess at the meaning of the words and songs.[4] "Associated with the western origin of the zogo mer is the fact that so many of the natural and worked stones in the Murray Islands are of foreign origin, and there can be but little doubt that the majority of these must have come from the Western Islands." [5]

Zogo and Intichiuma.

The same connexion between the totemic multiplication of the food supply and sacred stones is well known as one of the salient features of the magico-religious institutions of Central Australia. The rain-making zogo is invariably associated with the stone images called doiom. These rudely carved images are said to represent a man and each man was supposed to possess one of them.[6] The Loritja call their kuntanka—the equivalents of the Arunta Churinga—the image of the body.[7] The Nauamareb zogo for garden produce is a somewhat pyriform boulder of granite.[8] The Sewereat u zogo shrine consists of two or three large clam shells

[1] Haddon, *Cambridge Expedition*, VI. 51.
[2] Id., op. cit., VI. 245.
[3] Id., op. cit., VI. 245.
[4] Id., ibid., VI. 243. "Chanting songs of which they do not know the meaning."—Spencer and Gillen, *Nor. T.*, XVI. However the meaning is comprehensible to the old men.—Strehlow, *A. & L.*, III. p. vi.
[5] Haddon, l.c., VI. 243.
[6] Id., ibid., VI. 194–196. Every man has a churinga.
[7] Strehlow, *A. & L.*, II. 82.
[8] Id., ibid., 210.

on a block of volcanic ash under a zom tree.[1] The turtle zogo is of especial interest. When a turtle was caught at Mer it was placed on its back on the beach and a number of men carrying bullroarers walked three times round it, counter clock-wise. When the head-man had finished going round the turtle, he chewed some red earth and inserted a piece of the stem of the gaurgaur creeper into the cloaca of the turtle, pushed the stick backwards and forwards, and then he spat on the undershell of the turtle so as to make four red spots one on each flapper. One version states that this ceremony was performed over every turtle caught, but a second statement which connects it with the first turtle of the season is perhaps nearer the truth.[2] This seems to afford conclusive evidence for deriving the zogo, at least the original ones, from totemic ceremonies of the Intichiuma type, as this same ceremony occurs at Mabuiag as an "Intichiuma" of the turtle totem. The first turtle caught during the turtle breeding season was handed over to the men of the Surlal clan. It was not taken to the village but to the kwod of the clan, and was there smeared all over with red ochre and was then called parma surlal (parma = red ochre). The Arunta will bring the first kangaroo of the season to the ertnatulunga; the red ochre is smeared on the Churinga and not on the animal. The clansmen painted themselves with a red mark across the chest and across the abdomen, evidently to represent the anterior and posterior margin of the undershell of the turtle. They wore cassowary-feather head-dresses and danced round the turtle whirling bullroarers. A length of the gawai creeper was cut off and slightly sharpened at one end; this was inserted in the cloaca of the turtle and pushed up and down several times. This was an act of pantomimic magic "to make him proper fast," in other words to insure a good surlal season. The turtle was then given to the Dangal (dugong) men who ate it.[3]

The turtle and dugong ceremonies. Survival of totem-eating and liberation.

It is evident that the two rites are identical, showing that the zogo rites were originally Intichiumas which lost their totemic character in migrating from the western to the eastern islands. We have shown how the "liberation" ceremony developed out of the multiplication aspect of totem-eating and how again repression succeeded in obliterating the traces of totem-eating in the Liberation ceremony.[4]

[1] Strehlow, *A. & L.*, 206. [2] Id., ibid., 213, 124. [3] Haddon, l.c., V. 183, 184.

[4] W. Schmidt assumes a contrary development from the taboo to the eating. —*Z. E.*, 1908, 875, 876. But as we have proved the primitivity of totem-eating from the Alcheringa traditions, there is no way to get beyond this evidence. Besides this the psychological analysis shows that there is an unconscious but very close connexion between totem-eating and the multiplication ritual. As first pointed out by Freud in *Totem and Taboo*, a taboo is always a repressed wish; before repression began to operate it is probable that the wish was realized, so that a period of totem-eating (as a symbolical equivalent of anthropophagy) must have preceded the period of non-eating.

In the Murray Island custom the Turtle and Dugong men stand in the same relationship to each other as the men of the two moieties in Central Australian Intichiuma rites; they exchange the products of their magical arts. A very similar ceremony was performed at the headquarters of the Dugong clan. These headquarters were situated opposite to the extensive reefs of the north which are the great feeding-grounds of the dugong, and consequently this is the area where they are most abundant. A wooden model of the dugong is used in these ceremonies to attract the animal. The coitus of the animal is only imitated in the negative aspect of the rite; if a member of the dugong clan wished to send the animal away [1] he would take the penis of the dugong and pass an arrow through it. The dugong used in the ceremony was given to the men of the turtle clan.[2] This does not only point to the existence of a dual organization—there is no need to prove this from survivals as it is the actual state of affairs in the Western Isles—but also to a special connexion between the dual organization and Intichiuma ceremonies. This ceremonial aspect of the dual organization still survives in the two divisions of the Malu cult with their specific magical functions. The members of the fraternity are divided into the Beizam le and Zagareb le. The Beizam have the exclusive right to practise certain forms of divination, whilst the Zagareb alone possess the power of making rain and of drum-beating, and the prerogative of certain forms of malignant and curative magic.[3]

The dual organization.

We have already noted the fact that the dual organization is especially prominent in the ceremonial life of the Arunta and other Central tribes. The fact that the same phenomenon is met with in the Torres Islands seems to me to afford some evidence against a theory which would explain this connexion as the result of culture mixture between a people who had society organized on a dual basis and between those who introduced the Intichiuma ceremonies to Australia. At any rate, if we are to explain this fact with the aid of the fusion theory we must suppose this fusion to have taken place before the immigrants arrived in Australia, as we find it amongst the Torres Straits Islanders. But there is a still more remarkable fact about this dual organization which seems definitely to prove that these islanders are connected with the Arunta. The clans in Mabuiag were formerly grouped into two divisions which were called respectively the "Children or People of the Great" and the "Children of the Little Totem." The totems of the first group are all land animals, the crocodile forming the only exception, which,

[1] Cf. the zogo's to make people insane or hungry, to cause constipation (Haddon, VI. 232, 233), to avert sickness (ibid., 236). After the zogo had become disassociated from totemism (Oedipus complex), they might be turned to various magical purposes besides multiplication.

[2] Haddon, *Cambridge Expedition*, V. 183.

[3] Id., l.c., VI. 174, 175.

however, is classified as a land animal on account of its four legs. The second group has all marine animals as totems. "They all belong to the water; they are all friends." This probably indicates that two groups formerly occupied separate localities, those of the Little Totem being nearer to the coast, and those of the big-totem dwelling inland.[1]

In the Arunta account of creation we find the inapertwa creatures arranged in two groups. One of them lived on the hill-side and was divided into the four classes of Purula, Kamara, Ngala and Mbitjana; these were called the Alarinja or Land people. The four other classes, Pananka, Paltara, Knuraia and Bangata, were called Water people, because they lived in the water. They had long hair and consumed raw meat.[2] The territorial division of the two classes still exists amongst the Warramunga between Kingilli and Uluuru.[3]

It is only fair to point out that these facts speak rather in favour of the theory of Dr. Rivers, who explains the dual system by a fusion of two distinct tribes, than for the theory of fission which we have put forward in this book. If Mangarkunjerkunja tells land-dwellers to marry water-dwellers,[4] this looks quite like a connubium between two originally foreign people. The Mono people have a couple of totems for each clan. One of these is always a bird and this one is called "tua," that is grandfather; the other is a marine animal and this totem is called "tete," grandmother.[5] This would indicate that the contrast between land-dwellers and water-dwellers was the same thing as the distinction between the bush-people and the Coast people,[6] and would point (*a*) to the possibility that the "Children of the Little Totem," marine animals, represent later immigrants, and (*b*) to the composite character of the Arunta as well as to the possibility that this composite character originated before their immigration to Australia. The two people here referred to as land-dwellers and water-dwellers need not be the kava plus dual people on the one hand and the betel people on the other.[7] Similar fusions of "land-dwellers" and "water-dwellers" probably took place more than once in the ethnic history of Oceania and Australia. But the fact that the two moieties may preserve the traces of a racial fusion does not modify or weaken our view that the original basis of the Dual Organization is the contrast between Father and Son, and that this is a universal phase in the evolution of humanity. The new

[1] Haddon, l.c., V. 172, 173.

[2] Strehlow, *A. & L.*, I. 3, 6. Cf. Schmidt, *Anthropos*, 1908, 623. Id., "Sociologische und religiös ethische Gruppierung der Australier," *Z. E.*, 1907.

[3] Spencer and Gillen, *Nor. T.*, 28, 29.

[4] Strehlow, *A. & L.*, I. 6.

[5] G. C. Wheeler, "Sketch of the Totemism and Religion of the People of the Islands in Bougainville Straits," *Archiv für Religionswissenschaft*, 1912, XV. 6, 29. Cf. Id., "Totemismus in Buin," *Z. E.*, 1914, 41; and Rivers, *History of Melanesian Society*, II. 1914, 342.

[6] Rivers, op. cit., II. 304.

[7] Id., ibid., II. 306, 307.

contrast overlayed the old, whilst the previous existence of a dichotomy must have facilitated the assimilation of an alien element: a native who migrates from one tribe to the other in Australia is immediately incorporated into one of the marriage classes.

Myths of petrified culture heroes and the Alcheringa.

These analogies which have hitherto been shown to exist between Central Australia and the Torres Straits both as regards the child-birth beliefs (Churinga) and the Intichiuma ceremonies (dual organization) make it probable that the third link in the chain, the Alcheringa myths, will also be found to exist in some more or less modified form on these islands. The frequent connexion between these myths and rocks and stones, as well as the petrification of the principal heroes, again points to Central Australia—a fact which has been noticed and duly emphasized by W. Foy.[1] The story of Adi, the first man, and his two wives, who were caught by the rising tide and converted into rocks,[2] conforms rather to the South Australian type than to the Alcheringa traditions; it may also be unconnected with these and of purely local origin. But then we have a Dogai, a widow,[3] and other actors who simply turn to stone at the end of their earthly career; this is very similar to the behaviour of Central Australian totem-ancestors.[4] Myths which tell us that the dugong, formerly a human being, was transformed into its present shape, present a certain similarity in North Australia, Torres Straits and New Guinea.[5] It seems also very probable that the existence of totemic traditions like those found in Central Australia must have served as a favourable background for the evolution of such more individualized totem-heroes and their cult as we actually find in the Torres Straits. We shall find it instructive from our point of view to examine the mythic cycle of at least one of these heroes. We mean Sida, the bestower of vegetable food. He comes from New Guinea—doubtless a historical reminiscence of the origin of cultivation. He travels through all the islands, continually having connexion with women and planting trees at the same time. One of the women is called Sokoli; at present she is represented by an ovoid stone in a cleft in a lava stream on the beach. Her companion Maimri is another rock close by. He has connexion with a girl from whom blood flows in great quantity; he erects a shrine and zogo at the spot and plants a tree fern. He spills semen on the ground in the act of intercourse—whereupon coco-nut palms spring up.[6] He travels from island to island in search of women, and as he throws the food-

[1] W. Foy, "Melanesien," *Archiv für Religionswissenschaft*, X. 135.

[2] Haddon, op. cit., V. 17. [3] Id., V. 20, 27. [4] Cf. Id., VI. 11–13.

[5] H. Basedow, "Anthropological Notes on the Western Coastal Tribes of the Northern Territory of South Australia," *Transactions of the Royal Society of South Australia*, 1907, XXXI. 5. Larrekiya, Haddon, op. cit., V. 38.40. H. H. Romilly, *From My Verandah in New Guinea*, 1889, 133, 134. Cf. also, on dugong ceremonies, Schmidt, *Z. E.*, 1908, 900.

[6] Haddon, VI. 21, 22.

plants out of his basket these give rise to the vegetation of those islands.[1]

Besides this we have the legends in which the death of a human being accounts for or gives rise to general fertility.[2] Now if we remember the mechanism which underlies the traditions and cults of Central Australia, we shall find very evident similarities. There is a constant connexion between the death of the totem-ancestor and the multiplication of the species; bits of his (symbolic) body are thrown about, thus magically procreating animals, besides which human beings are also procreated when the Churinga which represents the ancestor is thrown at a woman. In analysing Central Australian myths we have found that the actions which lead to human and animal multiplication are unconscious, symbolic equivalents of coitus; here we find the open statement that it was coitus which made the food-plants grow. The state of things will not surprise us after the comparison of the "bid" to the Churinga; in both cases we have come to the conclusion that our interpretations of Central Australian data are strikingly confirmed by what we find in these islands and in both cases it is Australia which has conserved the repressed and Torres Straits which possesses the unrepressed forms. What is quite conscious in the north is merely symbolic in the south. However, like every other tribe on earth, the Torres Islanders have a history, and it is probable that these and other similarities with Australia have not all equal historical value. We have assumed that the migrations of the ancestors of the Central Australians took place from the north to the south, but we always have to reckon with back-waves in this case, with the influence exercised on the islanders at a later period by the inhabitants of the mainland. The representative of such a recent movement is evidently Kwoiam, the berserker-hero of Mabuiag, whose magical emblems (augud) have already been compared to the Churinga. His head was frequently said to be like that of an Australian ("all same belong Mainland"). He was also said to have straight hair, or "hair like a mainlander." Psychologically also, the Mabuiag people recognized an affinity between Kwoiam and the Australian; like them he had a "wild throat and a half wild heart." One informant said, "that mainlanders fight all the time just like Kwoiam." He always fought with the characteristically Australian weapon, a javelin hurled by a throwing-stick—a weapon which his adversaries never used. Indeed, all he did was "mainland fashion"; he, his mother and his wadwam always kept to themselves and were like mainlanders.[3] The natives of Cape York Peninsula also talked about Kwoiam.[4] The cult of Kwoiam centred

Evidence of a back-wave of culture: Australian influence in the Torres Straits.

[1] Haddon, l.c., V. 28, 29.
[2] Id., V. 35, 36, 37.
[3] Id., V. 81.
[4] Id., V. 82.

round his cairn; however, no remains were found on investigation and it seems that the islanders had the custom of erecting a cairn independently of the grave.[1] The head of his unfortunate mother is still to be seen at Mabuiag as a large ovoid boulder. A long double row of stones represents the heads taken by Kwoiam.[2] A short distance up the hill are some rocks, from out of a cleft in which a perennial stream flows. One day Kwoiam was thirsty and he drove his spear into the rock; water gushed forth and has never ceased to flow. Only old and important men were permitted to drink from the pool which it forms; those who broke this taboo would become prematurely grey.[3] Kwoiam belonged to all the totems,[4] and similar "dominant totems" have already been noted by us in Australia.[5] Another peculiarly Australian institution are the sex-totems.[6] In the Western Islands we find that there is a vestige of totemism in the belief in "lamar ebur" or ghost animals. Usually it is the eponymous animals of a group with an animal name that appear at the death of a male member. The remarkable thing, however, is that we have separate ghost animals for the men and different ones for the women. Women are represented by flying animals, bats and birds. "This looks suspiciously like what has been termed a sex-totem."[7] To these remarks of Dr. Haddon we shall only add that the bat is usually regarded as the typical representative of the sex-totem complex in Australia; he teaches the natives to make fire which amounts to the same thing. Here again we find that Eguon, a giant bat, is said to have introduced fire to Mowat.[8]

Central Australia and New Guinea. Intichiuma elements in initiation rites.

If the ancestors of the Central Tribes, or at least of one of the races which have contributed to the formation of these tribes, came from the North and touched the Torres Straits in their wanderings, we shall expect to find some traces of their migrations in New Guinea. We have traced the origin of the Intichiuma ceremonies back to a primeval pairing season and that of the Initiation ceremonies to the fight between the old and young males for the possession of women. This fight must have been the prelude to the act of copulation with our brute ancestors, as this is actually the case amongst various species of mammals. This is why we find a close connexion between Initiation and Intichiuma ceremonies, the latter often appearing as the closing phase of the

[1] Haddon, l.c., V. 368. [2] Id., ibid., V. 82. [3] Id., ibid., V. 82. [4] Id., ibdi., V. 367.

[5] Cf. above, p. 288, 295; Parker, *Euahlayi*, 7; Spencer, *N. T. N. T. A.*, 215.

[6] These need not be the result of a secondary influence from Australia; they may be vestiges of the migration which we shall call the (*b*) wave, and which seems to have developed sex-totemism.

[7] Haddon, l.c., VI. 257.

[8] Beardmore, "The Natives of Mowat, Daudai, New Guinea," *J. A. I.*, XIX. 462. Haddon, l.c., V. 17. The bat is also the Prometheus of the Pennefather tribe. —Roth, *S. M. M.*, 1903, 110

former.[1] Amongst various people the closing phase of the Initiation ceremony is a sexual orgy; this must have been repressed on account of its incestuous contents at an early period in the evolution of the Central Australian tribes, and a series of symbolic representations which we call Intichiuma must have developed out of this repression. Amongst the Dieri tribe the boy gets a bullroarer after initiation; he is told to twirl this when hunting so that the tribe may reap a good harvest of reptiles, snakes and other game.[2] The Kaitish abstain from killing a certain species of snake which they think makes the yams grow.[3]

Further north we come to the Melville Islands; here we find an intimate connexion between initiation and yams. The yams are the "fathers," the Initiation ceremony is a Yam ceremony, an Intichiuma to make the yams grow.[4] At Kiwai each youth receives a bullroarer at initiation; by whirling it he ensures a good crop of yams, sweet potatoes and bananas. A wooden image of a nude woman, shown to the boys at the Moguru (Initiation) ceremony in the rainy season, ensures a good supply of sago. If the food supply is insufficient a Moguru ceremony is held.[5] At the mouth of the Fly River in New Guinea the bullroarer is called the mother of yams.[6] There are two main elements in the Moguru: the first forms part of the initiation and is concerned chiefly with fighting; the other includes sexual excesses to ensure the productivity of food-plants, especially the sago.[7] Segera of Sumai was a man of the Sago totem. He desires to be revenged for the death of his son which is ascribed to sorcery, and spoils all the sago of the district by his magic. Many people die in consequence. He goes around the country planting one sago shoot after the other, one in each garden. He tells the people that when he dies they are to cut him up and place pieces of his flesh in their gardens, but his head was to be buried in his own garden.

I have put forward the hypothesis that the exaggerated craving for revenge exhibited by savages is merely a veil behind which they hide their bad consciences. It is they themselves who most fervently, though unconsciously, have wished to kill their comrade, and hence they show an all too great zeal in searching for the culprit in a foreign tribe. When they do find him and kill him they are really repeating the murderous deed which they intend to expiate.[8] Thus

[1] Cf. the Engwura of the Arunta, the Muraian of the Kakadu.

[2] Gason-Curr, II. 59.

[3] Eylmann, *Die Eingeborenen der Kolonie Südaustralien*, 1908. 224.

[4] Spencer and Gillen, *N. T.*, 97.

[5] Haddon, l.c., V. 218.

[6] Chalmers, *J. A. I.*, XXXIII., 1903, 113, 116, 118.

[7] A. C. Haddon, *Migrations of Cultures in British New Guinea*, 1920, 4, quoting Landtmann, "Papuan Magic in the Building of Houses," *Acta Arboensis Humaniora*, I, Abo. 1920. Id., "The Folk-tales of Kiwai Papuans," *Acta Soc. Sc. Fennicae*, 1917, 339, 344. See also the sexual elements of the moguru ceremonies at Goaribari (Haddon, ibid., 7), and at Torobina (ibid., 22).

[8] Róheim, *Spiegelzauber*, 1919, 198.

we should explain Segera, the avenger of his son's death, as a reaction-formation; originally it was he who killed his son. When he spoils the sago, he is repeating the same deed; for we have had occasion to observe in connexion with the Sida legend that the food-plant is the son of the vegetation-hero sprung from the intercourse between the foreign hero and the women of the island. We have shown how the zogo charms, originally pure Intichiuma rites for the multiplication of food-plants and animals, have, after becoming disconnected from the Oedipus complex, produced offshoots in which the purpose of the rite is not the multiplication of an animal, but the exact contrary. Here we have the same development: the Sago-man who plants sago is also the man who spoils it. In these aberrant variants we again have the representatives of a more original type; destruction of the totem (father) was the primary tendency of the rite for which afterwards multiplication was substituted. The type of the Oedipus complex which we have here is the one which is fashioned by the fear of retribution: it is the father who kills the son out of fear of his successor. This phase is also represented in the Intichiuma ceremonies, when the old men eat the kangaroo which they have procreated from the rock. In the sequel, however, we can restore the original version; the death of the father Segera at the hands of the son is the prelude to new life in vegetation. To this day it is thought that the sago planted by a Sago-man flourishes better than any other sago, and, arguing from Australian analogies, we shall say that originally it was the Sago-man who, in totemic incest, procreated first the young sagos and then "magically made" the sago palm. There is also a Sago Intichiuma, of which, however, no details are known.[1] In the Hood Peninsula there is a girls' maturity festival called "kapa." Besides being a maturity ceremony for girls it may be regarded as a "special development of one disassociated phase of an Initiation ceremony."[2] We can make an important observation in this connexion: the analogies to the Intichiuma ceremonies are to be found in the magical rites for the multiplication of the food-plants.[3] After the cult of the yam and the sago[4] the next example is the cult of the mango tree. There is a Mango ceremony, "oilobo," connected with the initiation rite of the Mailu. Mango saplings with creepers attached to them are

The sago Intichiuma.

[1] Frazer, *T. & E.*, II. 31, 32.

[2] A. C. Haddon, *Migrations of Cultures in British New Guinea*, 1920, 11.

[3] This fact has been emphasized by P. W. Schmidt, "Die Stellung der Aranda," *Z. E.*, 1908, 870, who also shows that plant-totemism was introduced by the Central and Northern tribes to Australia. The psychological explanation of this fact would probably lead us very far afield.

[4] Another element of this phallic complex is the serpent, which is thought to influence the growth of the food-plants among the Kaitish. According to a Kai legend the various sorts of yam grow from the cut-up body of a serpent.—Keysser, *Aus dem Leben der Kaileute*. Neuhauss, *Deutsch Neu Guinea*, 1911, III. 180-85.

brought from the bush. There is a ceremonial eating of the betel nut, accompanied by the Betel-nut incantation, in which are mentioned two legendary men, Alcheringa beings, who lived at Maivaro in Milne Bay, and were the first to introduce betel nut into the country; the song makes the nut plentiful. Then there is the ceremonial cutting of the saplings into small pieces. Here we have animal fertility again brought into close connexion with the food plants, for these pieces of the mango sapling are wrapped into mats with the creepers, and they form a charm which ensures an abundance of pig.[1] Here we have the ceremonial eating of the object which ought to be multiplied, a reference to mythical beings of the past, and probably also the concept of multiplication by division (cutting the mango to pieces), which are all prominent features of the Intichiuma ceremonies. The connexion between the Walaga feast (Mango cult) and Initiation ceremonies is proved by the fact that the Mango cult is the only occasion at which bullroarers are swung at Awaima and Taupota.[2] Another prominent feature of the festival is the ceremonial platform, the planks at the edge of which are usually made of the wood of the tree called Dabedabe.[3]

The death of the giant boar.

We should need a separate investigation on the subject of ceremonial platforms; at any rate, they form a feature of Australian, Papuan and Melanesian initiation ceremonies, and are either degenerate survivals or the incipient stages of the men's house ("Männerhaus").[4] As the killing of pigs is a very prominent feature of the feast, we shall be tempted to connect it with the myth on the death of a giant boar, in which platforms play a part that can only be explained with reference to a ceremony.

An enormous pig used to make fearful inroads in the gardens, besides devouring men and women, so that all the inhabitants of Wamira (Goodenough Bay) had to leave the village. Only one woman who was big with child remained alive; she hid in a hollow tree.[5] When her child attains full manhood[6] he begins to inquire

[1] Haddon, *Migrations*, 29, 30, quoting Malinowski, "The Natives of Mailu," *Trans. Roy. Soc. S. Australia*, 1915, XXXIX. 494.

[2] Seligmann, *The Melanesians of British New Guinea*, 1912, 592.

[3] Id., l.c.

[4] See W. Foy, "Baumstumpfs-Symbole und Zeremonial-platformen in Ozeanien," *Ethnologica*, II. 231.

[5] Seligmann, l.c., 414. Or in a hole in the earth.—A. Kerr, *Papuan Fairy Tales*, 1910, 121.

[6] "The men's house (darimo) suggests the idea of a gigantic pig."—Haddon, *Migrations*, 3. "Greedy monster desiring lives of young men, bought off with pigs" (ibid., 5). "At the terminal feast, each boy stands on a dead pig" (p. 13). "The initiation of the boys begins with eating wild pigs and ends with eating domesticated pigs" (p. 19). "A human victim, a cassowary, and a pig sacrificed when the war canoe is complete" (p. 24). "Each boy stands on the pig presented by his mother" (p. 32). The men at the initiation ceremony "wear huge head-dresses of feathers and frames of pigs' teeth over their faces." Formerly a man was

about the pig ogre. He builds a series of long and high platforms, stacking each of them full of spears. When the pig ogre attacks him he keeps jumping from one platform to the other and retreats before the animal, showering spears on him all the while. The boar demolishes all the platforms; when it comes to the last the young man kills him with a huge spear. The body floats on a raft to the place "where people are mourning." The exiles return and all feast on the boar's flesh; the boy who killed him becomes chief.[1]

The child who, when he attains full manhood, kills the boar-ogre is doing very much the same thing as the novices do at initiation. They stand on a dead pig or in other cases they must kill a man before being admitted to full manhood. The pig is a symbolic substitute for the man; and the novice suffers the talion-punishment when he is devoured by the pig-monster, or, with another modification of the same motive, the monster is hungry for pigs instead of youngsters. We know that initiation is the repetition of the primeval conflict between the Father and the Son, and we shall not be surprised if the boar who is killed by the young man proves to be a representative of the Father-Imago. The platforms would be the ceremonial platforms of initiation, and we should thus get back to the primitive root of that ceremony when it was not the boar who slew (and revived) the boy, but the boy who slew the boar. ("The boy stands on a dead pig.") But in the original setting the boar must have been not only an enemy who is slain, but also the father who is mourned, as the body drifts to the country where people are mourning. Then comes the cannibalistic communion; the corpse of the semi-brutal leader of the herd is devoured by his people and the first rebel becomes chief.

If we connect this pig-eating with the Walaga feast, we are avowedly making use of a conjecture, but this conjecture is soon verified by comparing the myth of Dabedabe. Dabedabe is the name of a tree which is used in constructing the ceremonial platforms of the feast; this reminds us of our Australian initiation spirits, who, after their death, are turned into trees out of which the bullroarer is made. A sow gives birth to a litter of pigs and one man child. The boy is brought up in the village but the old sow comes after him and takes care of him. One day when he is bigger he hears his mother crying for food, and he resolves to make a garden so that he might grow food to give her.[2] Dabedabe's foster-father wishes to provide food for the men

Dabedabe.

cut up for the boys to eat, now a wild pig is substituted (p. 34). Wild pigs killed at burial feast (p. 35). We intend to devote a separate paper to the ceremonial use of pigs in Oceania. Cf. Rivers, *Melanesian Society*, 1914, II, in the index.

[1] Seligmann, l.c., 414, 415. Ker, l.c., 121–27. Twins kill boar ogre. J. Meier, *Mythen u. Erzählungen der Küstenbewohner der Gazellehalbinsel*, 1909, 25.

[2] There seems to be an intimate connexion between cultivation and the only domesticated animal, the pig. The identification of the pig and the mango is very prominent in the Walaga ceremony.

who help Dabedabe in his gardening work. He kills Dabedabe's mother, the old sow. When Dabedabe hears this he says that he must leave them, as they have eaten his mother. He tells them they are not to throw one bone of the pig away; he makes a bundle of all the bones, slings it on his shoulder and wanders from village to village. He wishes to abide at Quamana, but the people would not suffer him, as his body was full of sores. He lives in a cave with a child, who tells him that the people are going to hold a Walaga feast and eat men who will be cut up for the feast. Hearing this, he goes down to the river, and opening the bag which contained his mother's bones, he flings some of the bones with his full might at a stone. They become men; he tells them to go and cut poles for him. Then he takes the rest of the bones, throws them at a stone, and they become a great number of pigs. He makes his men carry his pigs with the help of the poles to the place where the feast is given, and persuades the people to accept the pigs instead of the men they are about to eat. "From that day until now men are spared and pigs are slain when a feast is made, and at Quamana as also at Bou (the home of Dabedabe) are abundance of pigs to this day." [1]

The legend looks as if it was complementary to the other myth on the death of the wild boar. In the former version we have got a boar-father and a human mother: here the reverse is the case. The parent who appears in the guise of an animal must be the one in regard to whom the censor deems it expedient to throw a symbolic veil over the latent import of the action; in one case it is the death of the totem-father (killing the boar), in the other it is the incest with the totem-mother that is emphasized. We must suppose that Dabedabe actually did eat of the old sow in the original setting of the tale, and eating represents coitus transposed upwards. In the Anula ceremony dugongs and crocodiles are multiplied by throwing sticks at the rock,[2] which we have recognized as the symbol of the maternal womb (throwing is coitus); here the motive is reversed and the mother's bones are thrown at the rock.[3] Evidently this is an Intichiuma of pigs, hence the clause of the legend which says that the myth explains the abundance of pigs at Quamana and Bou to this day. This Intichiuma consisted in multiplying pigs by

[1] Ker, l.c. 13–18. Dabedabe is the wild ginger (ibid. 22). Perhaps the belief of the Kuni that ginger causes miscarriage may be connected with this myth. Eschlimann, "L'enfant chez les Kuni," *Anthropos*, 1911, 261. Then Dabedabe would stand for the incest complex, and the belief would refer to incest as causing barrenness. In another version the bones are washed instead of being thrown at a stone near the river (Seligmann, 416). "Ever since then pigs have been eaten instead of men at the walaga."

[2] Spencer and Gillen, *Nor. T.*, 313.

[3] There is a widespread belief amongst savages that the bones, if not consumed, will ensure the rebirth of the animal.—Frazer, *Spirits of the Corn and of the Wild*, 1912, II. 256, 259.

having symbolic intercourse with the mother (eating her and throwing her bones at the rock), but it must have passed through a phase in which it was not pigs but men who were procreated in this fashion. As it is, first men and then pigs are created in this manner in the myth. If we attempt to condense these two myths we shall get the story of a hero who killed his boar-father, mourned for him, and proceeded to multiply the species in incestuous intercourse after his death.[1]

The Walaga feast (continued).

We shall now return to the present Walaga feast and see whether our conclusions are confirmed by it. The feast takes its name from a big dancing platform (walaga) which is built specially for the occasion; Walaga is also the name of a dance performed in single file by both sexes upon saplings placed round the outer edge of the dancing platform. The head-man of one of the more powerful clans of the community becomes taniwaga, that is master of the ceremonies. Eight to twenty men are chosen from his own community as his assistants. The taniwaga selects a wild mango tree from the jungle and his assistants clear a circle round the tree. From the time that this is done the taniwaga and the men who have cleared the ground around the tree are sternly differentiated from all others, being in the highest degree vivivireina, i.e. set apart or "holy." They may not wash or drink water, they may not eat boiled food, nor may they eat the fruit of any mango tree. These fasting men who are the coadjutors of the taniwaga live by themselves in a separate house, where all the rubbish and fragments of their food is stored in baskets, whence it may not be removed till after the end of the ceremony. About the same number of women of the clan of the taniwaga begin to fast on the same day as the men. They avoid the opposite sex, abstain from water, boiled food, and the fruit of the mango tree. However, they do not have a separate house of their own and their rubbish is not stored up. Before the posts of the platform are stepped down, the medicine men perform a ceremony to extract the spirit of any dead man who might happen to be present in the post, so that it should not be injured by the erection of the post. When the platform is ready it is time to cut down the mango tree which has been previously selected. Great care is taken to prevent any chips of the tree from falling on the ground when the tree is cut, which is done with a special stone adze. A procession is formed which brings in the mango tree, whilst others bring the pigs for the feast. As the men passed a house they speared the wall

[1] Cf. the pig in the totemic system of the Trobriand Islands.—Seligmann, l.c., 679, 681. Certain of the Marshall Bennett Islanders would not eat pigs of a yellowish-brown colour because this was the colour of man (ibid., 681). In the myth of Dabedabe, the man claims the "brown one" of the pigs littered by the old sow because it is a man, the mythical hero.

with the branches they had been waving and left them stuck in the walls. They said that the particular house speared indicated some connexion between the head of the family or clan living in the house and the pigs in the procession. One of the mango poles is placed in the centre of the platform and one in the house of each of two chief men. The men and women who had fasted since the mango pole had been selected danced round the platform charging the evil spirits to keep away from the people. At daylight the pigs are killed, being speared as slowly as possible so that the maximum amount of squealing takes place; their cries are now said to be heard by the mango tree, and it is absolutely necessary that they should cry loudly for some time before dying. If the mangoes do not hear the pigs squealing they will not be fruitful. The food is distributed between the guests in a ceremonial manner; one of the head-men climbed the mango pole in the centre of the platform and chanted what sounded like a prayer. The next day the mango is taken down from the platform, wrapped in new sleeping-mats, and carried by the fasting men to their sleeping-house, where it is hung from the roof. The feast is ended, but the men still abstain from mango, pigs, eels and water—to break the fast would entail the risk of breaking out in sores. After an interval of about twenty-two months the mango was again brought. Some informants said this was done when the house which contained the mango began to rot, while according to others the mango would speak to the taniwaga in his dreams, saying to him, " Let me smell smoking pig's fat, so your pigs will be healthy and your crops will grow." Follows a repetition of the festival. The taniwaga and the fasting men go to the house in which they slept before the mango was cut, decked in the dancing costumes they wore when they cut the mango, and they hand out all the rubbish which has been collected in the house. Then come the mats with the mango leaves and chips, and finally the mango tree wrapped in its mat; as these things are handed out the men present rush up and, wiping the dust off them, smear it over their bodies. They bring the mango back to the platform. Now, the man who climbed the mango pole on the former occasion takes a number of young green mangoes from a basket, and cutting them into pieces, places them with his own hands in the mouths of the fasting men, or he places fragments in the hands of the fasting men, who chew the mango small and spit the fragments in the direction of the setting sun. This is done, according to certain informants, in order that " the sun should carry the mango bits over the whole country and everyone should know." A part of the tree is then broken off and burnt with the refuse, and the ashes are perhaps mixed into the food given to the pigs. The tree is exhibited at intervals and a part of it is burnt at each exhibition; a new Walaga can only take place when the old mango tree is completely consumed by fire. This is how the feast is conducted at Bartle Bay.[1] The description of the Walaga feast at Diwari contains additional details. Objects belonging to certain dead men are hung on the mango pole.[2] When fewer pigs are brought than "one mango" (five pigs are called one mango), the people bringing them carried branches of trees and pieces of sticks with a wisp of grass tied to the end, and with these speared the house of the man to whom the pigs are given. These sticks and branches, which are called Dabedabe, were afterwards collected from the houses.[3] The mango leaves and the property of the dead men which were suspended from the pole were burnt in the fire, over which the pigs were singed whole.[4] It seems that the Walaga is regarded as a sort of finale for all death feasts, the idea being that the spirits of the dead should be gratified by knowing that all duties have been performed. If not, sickness, death and failure of the crops would be sure to follow. There is a constant identification of pigs and mango; five pigs are called "a mango," and a young mango is cut and carried in procession with the pigs as they are brought in.[5] The mango tree must hear the cries, smell the burning fat, and know that blood has been poured out. Otherwise the crops will fail, the fruit trees will be barren, the pigs will not be productive, and even women will fail to bear children. Before Dabedabe substituted pigs for men human victims were offered at the festival. After he died his spirit can be passed by ceremonies and incantations into the mango tree selected for the Walaga feast.[6]

The great feast as a mortuary ceremony.

We had best start with a seemingly insignificant detail. When the posts are erected there is some fear of injuring the spirits of the dead and the medicine men are called in to neutralize the danger. If we go back to a phase in the development of the ceremony which came before the medicine men were introduced, we shall come to the conclusion that the original intention of the ceremony is the very thing they seem to be so anxious to avoid: to injure the spirits of the dead. We know that it is a wellnigh universal method in dealing with dangerous ghosts to drive a stake into them. The platform may originally have been a burial-mound to prevent the dead from returning, the dance round the platform would be a funeral dance, and the fasting men would be the mourners who punish themselves with fasting for their sins in having "wished" and thereby magically caused the death of a man. If a ghost is dangerous it must have good reason for being what it is, and this reason can only be that it thirsts for revenge on its murderers. The posts of the platform are so many

[1] Seligmann, l.c., 588–99. [2] Newton, apud Seligmann, ibid., 602.
[3] Id., ibid., 603. [4] Id., ibid., 604, 605. [5] Seligmann, 651, 652.
[6] Haddon, *Migrations*, 30, 31. Besides Seligmann, Haddon uses another author who is inaccessible to me, and from whom these details are taken (Stone Wigg, *The Papuans*, 1912).

stakes in the body of the dead ;[1] a dead man's things are consumed by fire with the mango pole, and indeed the mango itself is no other than Dabedabe, the culture-hero who first substituted pigs for men in the Walaga festival. The ritual thus permits us to add a detail which is missing in the myth ; Dabedabe was evidently killed for his pains by ungrateful humanity. The rite compels us to assume it, for is not the wild mango tree which represents him cut and slowly consumed by the flames ? Pig and mango are identical symbols—they mean the same thing—and Dabedabe after all was the son of a sow just like the pigs who are slaughtered for this feast as his representatives. The identity of pigs with men is not quite lost in the ceremony, for the men who bring in the pigs throw their spears at the house of the head-man of the clan, and they say that this indicates a connexion between the head of the clan and the slaughtered pigs. There is another obscure ceremony which may be mentioned. The taniwaga rolls over in the house when he hears the pig squealing. Is he imitating the agonies of the animal ? When fewer pigs are brought than one mango the house of the man to whom the pigs are brought is speared : the man is a substitute for the missing pig. We must not forget that pigs have been substituted for men ; and the taniwaga who rolls over, the head of the clan whose house is speared, seem to show that they have been substituted for a head-man, a chief, a representative of the Father-Imago. Now we are fathoming the reason why the beneficent Dabedabe had probably to suffer death at the hands of his worshippers ; the son of the sow killed his father, the wild boar, or rather he is identical with the nameless hero who performs this feat in the legend. This would give meaning to another obscure detail ; the spears which are hurled at the house of the head-man are called Dabedabe, which means that Dabedabe is the man who killed the chief and succeeded to his glorious but dangerous post. We have also had the temerity to accuse Dabedabe of having committed another sin of similar nature, and, disregarding the denial of the legend, we said that he too must have eaten the flesh of his sow-mother, that is committed totemic incest. The ceremony strictly prohibits the fasters from eating mango and pig (Dabedabe refuses to eat of the sow), and if they do not observe this taboo they will break out into sores. Now Dabedabe is full of sores when he comes to Quamana, which shows us that, in an earlier form of the myth, he had actually broken the taboo and eaten the flesh of the sow, his mother. He is one of those Alcheringa ancestors who ate their own totem and lived with the women of the same totem, and the fact that he substitutes pigs for men only means that he represents a phase of social evolution in which the Oedipus complex

[1] " It is obligatory to kill a man when a new long house is built."—Haddon, *Migrations*, 23.

was gradually being projected from human beings to domesticated animals. At every Intichiuma the death of the totem-ancestor is commemorated and repeated in the death of the totem-animal; at the walaga the pigs who are the brethren of Dabedabe are slaughtered, the mango into which his soul has migrated is cut into pieces. Perhaps the platform is a burial platform, then the mango pole on it would correspond to the corpse. The custom of smearing the body of the mourners with the exudations of the desiccating corpse is one of the features of delayed burial, and we find that at the repetition of the feast the taniwaga and his coadjutors actually smear their bodies with the dust of the mango tree. That these fasting men are mourners is affirmed by the identity of the taboos they have to observe with those to which the "gariauna," the men who take part in the mourning ceremony, are subjected.[1] The fast is also observed by the men who perform the Intichiuma ceremonies; it is the inhibition aspect of the cannibal meal (eating the father or mother) and is projected from human flesh to that of the totem-animal (or the pig) and then to food in general.[2] Dances are often performed at funerals in an ambivalent attitude of pleasing and imitating the dead and of driving them away by a show of vigorous action, and here the dance of the fasting men is said to drive the evil spirits away. After death there comes the multiplication of the species, the Father was the obstacle between the sons and the women of the Horde. We know that the pig is a substitute for the Father-Imago, and thus we can explain why the squeal of the dying animals, the agony cry of the dread leader of the Horde,[3] should fertilize first the women and in a latter phase of evolution the sows, mango trees and crops.

The mango feast and Intichiuma.

In this multiplication-phase of the rite[4] we find certain details with which we are acquainted from Central Australia. The mango is cut into pieces (multiplication by division), bits of it are put into the mouths of the fasting men, who may not eat mango (the usual Australian way for terminating a taboo period), and they spit these fragments about towards the setting sun. In the Arunta tribe one of the Panunga puts a little of the seed up to a Thungalla's mouth and he blows it away in all directions, the idea of this being to make the grass grow plentifully everywhere,"[5] just as the sun is expected to carry the bits of the mango over the whole country.[6] We shall come to the

[1] Seligmann, l.c., 611. Taboo of water, boiled food and pigs.

[2] Cf. Róheim, *Imago*, IX. 93.

[3] Cf. Reik, *Probleme der Religionspsychologie*, 1919, 253.

[4] The care which is taken of all the rubbish as well as the water taboo points to an anal-erotic element in the multiplication ceremony.

[5] Spencer and Gillen, *Nor. T.*, 293.

[6] "That everyone should know" (Seligmann, 598) is probably a rationalizing addition. The original meaning must have been, "and mangoes should grow everywhere."

conclusion that what we have called the liberation-phase in the evolution of the Intichiuma has left its traces in New Guinea (cutting sago sapling and mango palm to pieces, removal of taboo and multiplication), and that, taken in conjunction with other facts, its presence is probably one of the traces left by the ancestors of the Central Tribes in their migrations. We ought to know more of the unexplored regions of New Guinea and perhaps also of Australia than we do to be able to hazard more than guesses as to the nature of the cultural connexion between these two neighbouring continents (or islands). At any rate, we cannot deal adequately at present with this problem, but must turn to another aspect of the question which is very characteristic of Central Australian culture and totemism. I mean the prominent part played by stone objects, natural and artificial, in the magico-religious concepts of these people. When Dabedabe dashes his mother's bones to a rock, men and pigs come into existence just like the ratapas who emanate from the Nanja rock, which is also struck when the totem-animal must be multiplied. The Churingas lie and the Alcheringa ancestors live in a cave—in the Ertnatulunga. Now it is a remarkable coincidence that Dabedabe, too, is recorded to have lived in a cave, and that he has a child in his company there whose origin is not mentioned in our myth. Caves play a considerable part in the traditions of New Guinea and Torres Straits which deal with the days of old, and we may perhaps compare the Ertnatulunga, the final resting-place of the Alcheringa ancestors, from where the children are supposed to emanate, with these mythical caves. "In the old days men lived not in houses, but dwelt in caves and holes in the ground."[1] We hear of an old woman who lives in a cave with a rock door, which opens when the magic words are pronounced, "O rock, be cleft."[2] According to Wagawaga traditions, in ancient times everybody lived in a cave "inside great stone,"[3] that is in a place very similar to those in which the unborn babies are still supposed to dwell in Central Australia. According to the opinion of the Kai, all the animals came out of caves, and it is dangerous for men to approach these caves.[4] "Miloal was the name of the first man who lived at Saibai. He lived in a hole in the ground."[5]

Stone culture, Ertnatulunga caves, stones in magic, petrified culture heroes.

Hand in hand with the myths on cave-dwelling ancestors and on stones giving birth to human beings (see infra, p. 370) we have the magical importance of stones, legends of petrifaction and of culture heroes who erected stone monuments or introduced a stone cult. There

[1] Ker, *Papuan Fairy Tales*, 1910, 135. [2] Seligmann, l.c., 399.
[3] Seligmann, l.c., 388.
[4] Keysser, *Aus dem Leben der Kaileute*. Neuhauss, *Deutsch New Guinea*, III. 160.
[5] Haddon, V. 27.

is a legendary old woman called Irado connected with the Turtle Zogo (Intichiuma) legend. She was not born of a woman but grew out of the earth at a place called Zuz-giri, a rocky piece of ground between Werbadu and Terker. She seems to be the personification of a special kind of yam called ketai, perhaps the "mother ketai," the original tuber which is believed to be everlasting and which keeps on producing new tubers for ever if not injured in any way. When Irado arrived at Kop she settled down there, eventually turning herself into the stone that stands behind that village.[1]

Aigeres is a stone rudely carved and said to represent a woman. Every evening she called out to the zogo stones on the surrounding gardens and scoffed at them for having dark earth and not red earth like hers. Beside her was a small clam shell which contained a pebble; these were her basket and her food. She ensured good crops of yams.[2] If we recall the fact that some of these stone zogo have definite legends associated with them which represent them as petrified mythical beings, we shall find the similarity to the Alcheringa ancestors who are turned to stone and who after their death survive as Churingas, and multiply food, animals and plants. We may safely assume that the "impersonal" stones which were kept in the Murray Island gardens to make the yams grow or any other sort of food to be fruitful were once "personal" ones,[3] that is that they represented petrified ancestors whose legend had been forgotten while the practical side of the matter, the ritual, still survived.

The Koitapu tribe in New Guinea respected two small round stones from the river bed as powerful spirits which produced rain and abundant crops.[4] Wararovuna is a stone totem, pieces of which were chipped off and boiled, the water being drunk to give strength in war.[5] All over the Kai country we find rocks, the existence of which is a puzzle to the natives. These are regarded as petrified spirits or human beings.[6] The Kai have tales of a bygone generation of human beings, the Nemu, who may perhaps be called demi-gods. They lived on earth before the present species of mortals came into being, and their power far exceeded that possessed by any man on earth. They are the culture heroes who invented all the customs that are observed to-day. At their death they were transformed into animals or into the great boulders which testify the greatness of bygone days. They all perished in a great flood.[7] The tales which relate their doings are not merely told for pleasure,

[1] Haddon, l.c., VI. 52. [2] Id., VI. 212. [3] Id., VI. 212.

[4] H. H. Romilly, *From the Verandah in New Guinea*, 1889, 76.

[5] Seligmann, op. cit., 454. Both the augud and the Churinga (Spencer and Gillen, *N. T.*, 135) are war medicines. There is an incised stone called "garuboi," after the serpent, which is a sort of "dominant totem" of the Massim.—Seligmann, ibid., 466.

[6] Keysser, *Aus dem Leben der Kaileute*. Neuhauss, 154. [7] Id., 156.

it is thought that they will be pleased by hearing the record of their deeds and make the food-plants grow,[1] just as the wanderings of the Alcheringa ancestors (who are also transformed into rocks and animals and also perish in floods) are related and acted at the Intichiuma ceremonies.

The stone culture of Indonesia and Central Australia.

If we follow these tracks where they lead us we shall be rather surprised to see that we have arrived at Indonesia, and we shall be forced to assume a historical connexion of some sort between the inhabitants of Central and Northern Australia on the one hand, and the stone-using immigrants of Indonesia on the other.[2]

Stone culture and sky beings.

The Arunta value the stone Churinga higher than the wooden ones, because it is the totem-ancestors themselves who were usually turned into stone Churinga, whilst those who were instructed by them in the ceremonies are represented by the wooden ones.[3] All the narratives of Central Australia " . . . give an account of beings coming from the north, who introduced certain elements of the material and magico-religious culture and modified the social institutions." [4] We may also add that these beings are usually represented as having introduced stone implements and are closely connected with the sky world. Coming down from their home in the western sky the Ungambikula (self-existing) introduce the stone knife and transform the inapertwa creatures into real human beings.[5] If not from the sky then all the culture heroes who bring the stone knife are said to come from the North.[6] According to a Kaitish tradition the stone knife was thrown down by the sky-being Atnatu.[7] The Binbinga and Mara believe in sky beings who have knives (evidently stone knives) instead of arms, and the fact that these beings are represented as hostile to the natives perhaps only reflects the attitude of the aboriginals towards the culture wave which must have been characterized by the use of stone for practical and magical purposes.[8]

According to the Dieri and allied tribes, the stone knife was introduced by two heroes who were called River-bed of the Sky, that is Milky Way.[9] Moreover, there seems to be a very close

[1] Neuhauss, 161.

[2] Cf. W. J. Perry, *The Megalithic Culture of Indonesia*, 1918.

[3] Strehlow, *A. & L.*, II. 79. Spencer and Gillen think that there is no difference between stone and wooden Churingas, the greater magical value is only a sign of greater antiquity.—Spencer and Gillen, *N. T.*, 142 ; *Nor. T.*, 277. Cf. Eylmann, l.c., 193. However, as all totem groups are said originally to have had stone ones (Spencer and Gillen, *N. T.*, 152), these are evidently the real ancient type. In some groups, especially in the southern part of the tribe, stone ones may be absent and only wooden ones found, which again indicates the northern origin and the southern limits of the stone culture wave.—Id., ibid., 152.

[4] Rivers, " Sociological Significance of Myth," *F.-L.*, 1912, 329.

[5] Spencer and Gillen, *N. T.*, 388, 389.

[6] Strehlow, *A. & L.*, I. 6, 8, 9.

[7] Spencer and Gillen, *Nor. T.*, 345.

[8] Id., ibid., 501.

[9] W. W. Howitt and Otto Siebert, " Legends of the Dieri and Kindred Tribes of Central Australia," *J. A. I.*, 1904, 100.

8. TOTEMISM AND DESCENT.

I. Two-Class System and Male Descent.
115 (H. 127).

II. Four-Class System and Male Descent.
7 (Sp. III, 179), 158, 163, 332 (H. 116–18, 333), 230, 231, 232, 234, 235, 236, 237, 238, 239, 240, 241, 242, 243, 244, 245, 246, 247, 248, 249, 250, 251, 252, 253, 254, 255, 256, 257, 258, 259 (Brown: "Three Tribes of Western Australia," *J.R.A.I.*, 1913, 147; Id.: "The Distribution of Native Tribes in Western Australia," *Man*, 1912, 143).

III. Four-Class System and Direct Male Descent; Former Two-Class System and Male Descent.
28, 31, 32 (Sp. II, 179, Sp. III, 60).

IV. Localized (Animal Named) Moieties with Male Descent of Totem.
47 (Sp. II, 26), 98, 99, 100, 101, 102, 103, 104, 105, 106, 107 (H. 126–29), 110, 114, 116, 117 (R. H. Mathews: E.S., 99).

V. Eight-Class System and Male Descent.
21, 27 (Sp. III, 179), 35, 41, 42 (Sp. II, 169, 171), 43, 46, 49, 222 (Sp. II, 161–66).

VI. Local Organization and Male Descent.
87 (H. 130), 89 (H. 131), 108 (H. 135, 146), 111 (H. 133), 272 (H. 129).

VII. Local Organization and Female Descent.
1, 2, 12 (Sp. III, 179).

VIII. Two-Class System and Female Descent.
67, 71, 74, 75, 77, 78, 81 (H. 91, Sp. II, 148), 92, 93, 95 (H. 121), 90, 94, 96, 119 (Mathews, 89), 109, 110, 112, 121, 122, 123, 124, 125, 126, 127, 128, 132, 133, 135, 140, 141, 143, 321, 328 (H. 96–109. A. R. Brown: "Notes on the Social Organization of Australian Tribes," *J.R.A.I.*, 1918, XLVIII, 248–50).

IX. Four-Class System and Female Descent.
113, 130, 137 (H. 107, 108), 138 (Mathews, 6), 152, 153, 154 (H. 104, 105, Mathews 12), 151, 165, 171, 173, 174, 177, 179 (H. 109, 111), 180 (H. 113), 183, 185, 186, 187, 188, 189, 190, 191 (H. 113), 193, 196, 204, 210, 223, 224, 280 (Roth: *Nomenclature*, 103, E.S. 57, 58), 297, 299 (H. 113).

X. Matrilinear Descent of Totem Coexistent with Patrilinear Descent of Class.
24, 25, 45 (Sp. III, 179).

XI. Patrilinear Descent of Totem Coexistent with Matrilinear Descent of Class.
131 (C. Richards: "The Marran' Waree' Tribes or Nation," *Science of Man*, 1903, 165).

XII. Double System: Patri- and Matrilinear Totems.
76 (Siebert: "Sagen und Sitten der Dieri und Nachbarstämme," *Globus*, 97, 48).

XIII. Mother's Totem Respected in Addition to own Totem. The Latter is either Inherited from the Father or Dependent on the Locality of Incarnation.
31, 32, 41 (Sp. II, 173), 35 (Sp. II, 171), 46, 47 (Sp. II, 166), 52, 56 (p. 415), 222 (Sp. II, 166).

XIV. Conceptional Totemism.
4, 6, 13, 17, 18, 19, 20 (Sp. III, 277), 48, 50, 51, 52, 55, 56 (Sp. I, II, Strehlow), 261, 262, 263, 264, 265, 266, 267, 344, 345, 346 (D. M. Bates: "The Marriage Laws and some Customs of the West Australian Aborigines," *Victorian Geographical Journal*, XXIII, XXIV, 1905–1906, 47. Frazer: *Totemism and Exogamy*, I, 563, 564).

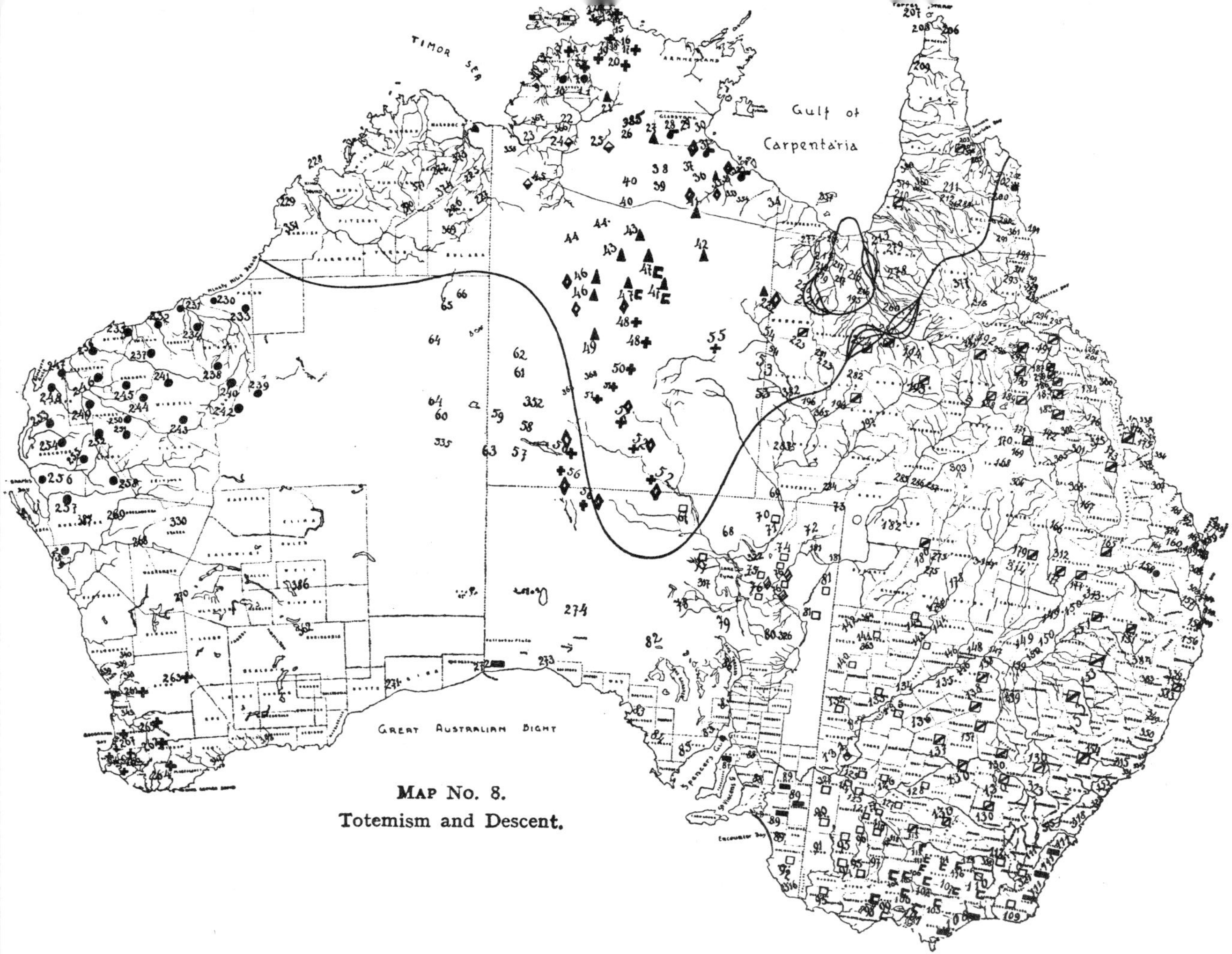

Map No. 8.
Totemism and Descent.

association between the stone knife and the stone Churinga. According to a legend of the Ngameni and Karanguru, both the stone knife (used for circumcision) and the Wolkadara (Churinga) [1] were brought from Antiritcha in the McDonnel Ranges.[2] The stone knives used by the ancestors for circumcising the boys are also Churinga.[3] Now, it is a remarkable fact that recent research has demonstrated a close association between mythical sky beings and the practical as well as magical use of stone in a part of the world which lies opposite to North-West Australia and which has certainly influenced New Guinea—especially the western half of that island—in Indonesia.[4] We shall now proceed to examine whether there are any other resemblances between what may be called the Churinga culture wave of Australia and this region. If we find that such analogies can be demonstrated we shall have to face the question how far they are to be accounted for by the general similarity of human nature, by the laws of the Unconscious which we owe to the genius of Freud, and how far they are to be regarded as proofs of culture contact or common origin between these two regions.

Analogies to the churinga in Indonesia.

In Belu small stones, called voho matan, which have cylindrical or elliptical forms, or are shaped like the human body, are supposed to be the residence of spiritual beings. When such a stone has been obtained through a dream revelation the priest chooses a spot where it shall be placed and a rectangular structure of stones is erected with a flat stone on the top on which the voho matan (holy eye) is placed.[5] The rain-maker of the Gnamulla in North-West Australia builds a heap of stones or sand two or three feet high, and places his "millia gurlee," that is "Potent or Live-Stone," on the top of it. This stone is generally handed down for generations.[6] "In an interior Lundu house at one end were collected the relics of the tribe. These consisted of several round-looking stones, two deers' heads and other trumpery. The stones turn black if the tribe is to be beaten in war and red if they were to be victorious; anyone touching them would be sure to die, if lost the tribe would be ruined." [7] The greatest misfortune which a totem clan can suffer is to lose the Churinga which are kept in custody in the holy cave. The Kenyahs have a number of large spherical stones in the house. When a household removes and

[1] Cf. Siebert, "Sagen und Sitten der Dieri," *Globus*, 97, 49.

[2] Howitt and Siebert, "Legends of the Dieri," *J. A. I.*, 1904, 108.

[3] Spencer and Gillen, *Nor. T.*, 275.

[4] W. J. Perry, *The Megalithic Culture of Indonesia*, 1918, 160, 181.

[5] Gryzen, "Mededeelingen omtrent Belu of Midden Timor," *Verh. Bat. Gen.*, LIV, 1904, 75, 76, cited according to Perry, *Megalithic Culture*, 57; and Krujt, *Het Animisme in den Indischen Archipel*, 1904, 207.

[6] Clement, "Ethnographical Notes on the Western Australian Aborigines," *Int. Arch. f. Ethn.*, 1904, XVI. 6.

[7] H. Ling-Roth, *The Natives of Sarawak and British North Borneo*, 1896, I. 232.

builds a new home for itself these stones are carried to the new site.[1] The Keisar Islanders will fetch a small stone of remarkable appearance from the grave a few days after the burial—as long as this stone is in the hands of the family it keeps them in connexion with the soul of the dead man ; the soul sometimes visits the stone and chooses it as its temporary abode. There is usually a hole in the roof of the house to permit free entry for the soul in case it should feel tempted to pay a visit to his stone. The loss of the stone would be fatal ; the " nitu " (soul) would not come any more.[2] In Wetar small carved wooden images called " jene," which represent human beings in the doubled-up position in which the dead are interred, and which is so characteristic of the human embryo, are regarded as embodiments of the soul. The soul is first lured into a stone which is put on its grave and thence it is transferred to the carved image.[3] On the island of Leti these stones are made use of in another way. When they go on voyages they desire to be accompanied by the ancestral ghosts, and as it would be inconvenient to carry the images along with them they incorporate the souls in small flat stones which they take along so that they are accompanied by the petrified ghosts of their ancestors.[4] If we suppose that the Arunta have reached their present home through a long series of migrations then this custom will throw new light on the development and origin of their Churingas. The ancestors of the Arunta carried such small stones along on their wanderings when they were compelled to leave the bodies of their ancestors behind, and they buried these stones in caves because they had a dim memory of a time when their ancestors were buried in caves. Several incised stones shaped like Churingas have been found in New South Wales and can be seen in the Sydney Museum. They are obsolete now among the New South Wales aboriginals, but it is said that they were collected from old round graves of the dead,[5] and the Whites called them

[1] Hose and McDougall, *The Pagan Tribes of Borneo*, 1912, II. 16.

[2] J. G. F. Riedel, *De Sluik en Kroeshaarige Rassen tusschen Selebes en Papua*, 1886, 421. Cf. 394.

[3] H. Berkusky, " Totengeister und Ahnenkultus in Indonesien," *Archiv für Religionswissenschaft*, 1915, 314, citing Jacobsen, *Reise in der Inselwelt des Bandameeres*, 120.

[4] Baron Van Hoevell, " Leti Eilanden," *Tijdschrift voor Indische Taal Land en Volkenkunde*, XXXIII, 1889, 206. The Tasmanians seem also to have been acquainted with the idea of symbolizing absent persons by stones. Backhouse writes : " One day we noticed a woman arranging stones ; they were flat, oval, about two inches wide, and marked in various directions with black and red stripes. These we learned represented absent friends, and one larger than the rest a corpulent woman on Flinders Island known as Mother Brown." W. J. Sollas, *Ancient Hunters*, 1911, 77. H. Ling-Roth, *The Aborigines of Tasmania*, 57. J. Backhouse, *Narrative of a Visit to the Australian Colonies*, 1843, 104.

[5] Andrew Lang, *The Secret of the Totem*, 1905, 77. Articles on these stone objects have been contributed by W. R. Harper and Graham Officer, *Proceedings Linnæan Soc., New South Wales*, 1898, XXIII, XXVI (quoted by A. Lang). Cf., " In parts of New South Wales curious-looking stones marked with scratches and

"grave-stones." The custom is recorded from Perth, West Australia, that after death women carry small bundles of leaves and sticks with them. These bundles are placed at night beside a fire made for that purpose, and they are said to attract the ghost and thus keep it from visiting the huts of the living.[1] A bundle which attracts a ghost looks like a substitute for the corpse, and indeed it seems that we have a local variant of the well-known Australian custom of women carrying the corpse of the deceased relative wrapped in a bundle. Afterwards the bundle becomes a substitute for the corpse, and a stone or stick may acquire the same meaning and develop into a full-blown Churinga.

The Churinga in the Ertnatulunga is the corpse in the grave. We must only stick to the ipsissima verba of the natives to see that we have not been misled by a tendency to speculate on ethnic origins. They tell us that the Churingas are the transformed bodies of their Alcheringa ancestors,[2] the body of the ancestors whose reincarnations they are;[3] and if we interpret the word "transformation" in a historical and psychological sense we can understand how the belief in Churingas was developed. It seems probable that the ancestors of the Arunta practised cave burial in their original home, but that this practice was dropped for some reason in the course of their migrations and only survived in the storing away of "ancestral bodies" made of wood and stone in caves. In the extreme north-east of Australia the Gudan natives (Cape York Peninsula) sometimes buried the dead in the clefts of the rocks.[4]

Cave burial.

The Ewenyoon expose their dead on platforms, cremate them and put the ashes in a niche beneath a large rock.[5] Cave burial is recorded in Western New Guinea[6] in conjunction with the custom of re-burial and the custom of erecting stone circles round the grave.[7] The natives of Adie (small island opposite to the western coast of New Guinea) have a tradition that they originated from a colossal tree-trunk which was drifted by the sea from the west and on which the earth grew till it developed into the island of Adie.[8] The myth can only be interpreted as the record of the eastern migrations which started from Indonesia. Here we find that cave-burial is recorded amongst the Benguet Lepanto Igorot,[9] amongst

of the shape of a banana were put upon the graves just above the head of the corpse; one sort is said to have been used for men, another for women."—N. W. Thomas, *Natives of Australia*, 1906, 199.

[1] Curr, op. cit., I. 330.
[2] Strehlow, *A. & L.*, II. 76.
[3] Id., II. 81.
[4] Dr. Creed, *J. A. I.*, VII, 1877, 268.
[5] W. H. Bird, "Ethnographical Notes about the Buccaneer Islanders," *Anthropos*, 1911, 178.
[6] O. Finsch, *New Guinea und seine Bewohner*, 1865, 76, 82, 87.
[7] Id., ibid., 92.
[8] Finsch, l.c., 93.
[9] Perry, *Megalithic Culture*, 22. F. H. Sawyer, *The Inhabitants of the Philippines*, 1900, 259.

9. THE DISPOSAL OF THE DEAD

I. PLATFORM BURIAL AND ANOINTING.

3 (Sp. III, 250, C. I, 255), 24 (Sp. III, 249), 26, 28 (Sp. III, 253), 27 (Sp. III, 251), 31, 32, 34, 35 (Sp. II, 547), 37 (Sp. III, 253), 38, 39 (Sp. II, 547), 41 (Sp. III, 245), 43 (Sp. II, 506, 515), 45 (Sp. III, 249), 46, 47, 48, 49, 50 (Sp. II, 506, 515), 53, 54 (Roth: *Burial*, 396), 61, 62 (Strehlow: IV, 26), 89 (Taplin: 20), 108 (H. 459), 139 (J.A.J. VII, 253), 149 (H. 467), 157 (H. 469, Roth: *Burial*, 401), 163 (H. 470), 171, 174, 175 (H. 471, Roth: *Burial*, 397), 177 (H. 467, 468), 179 (H. 467), 184 (Roth: *Burial*, 397), 189 (C. III, 20), 192 (H. 474), 198 (Roth: *Burial*, 388), 209 (Roth: *Burial*, 368), 210 (Roth: *Burial*, 370), 222 (Roth: *Burial*, 396, Sp. II, 506–15), 228 (*Anthropos*, 1911, 177), 232 (Brown: *J.R.A.I.*, 1913, 169), 300 (Roth: *Burial*, 397), 304 (C. III, 79), 312 (H. 467, 468), 334, 337 (Roth: *Burial*, 397), 338 (Roth: *Burial*, 398), 368 (Strehlow: IV, 26).

II. BODY OR RELICS CARRIED ABOUT.

14 (C. I, 272), 87 (H. 450), 89 (Taplin: 20), 93 (H. 456), 157 (Leichhardt: *Briefe*, 1881, 132), 158 (H. 469), 174, 175, 184 (Roth: *Burial*, 397), 198, 200 (Roth: *Burial*, 387, 388), 203, 204, 205 (Roth: *Burial*, 371), 209 (Roth: *Burial*, 368), 210 (Roth: *Burial*, 370), 300 (Roth: *Burial*, 397), 308 (Leichhardt: l.c., 1881, 132), 302 (C. III, 64), 334, 337 (Roth: *Burial*, 397), 389 (*J.A.I.*, XIII, 298).

III. EARTH BURIAL.

(*a*) Extended and other positions.

3 (C. I, 255), 4, 6, 13, 17, 18, 19, 20 (Sp. III, 241), 69, 70, 71, 73, 74, 76, 81 (H. 448, *Globus*, XCVII, 56), 82 (H. 450), 97 (H. 458), 100 (H. 458), 111 (H. 462), 121, 124, 125, 126 (H. 452, Cameron: *Journal*, 1884, 363), 130 (H. 466), 132 (H. 451), 136, 137 (Cameron: *Journal*, 1884, 363), 153 (H. 466), 158 (H. 469), 163 (H. 470), 174, 175 (Roth: *Burial*, 397), 177 (H. 467), 192 (H. 474), 196 (Roth: *Burial*, 394), 198 (Roth: *Burial*, 388), 209, 210 (Roth: *Burial*, 368–70), 307 (C. III, 122), 312 (H. 467), 328 (H. 452), 329 (H. 474), 334, 337 (Roth: *Burial*, 397).

(*b*) Doubled up and sitting.

1, 2 (Sp. III, 230), 42 (Sp. II, 545), 95 (H. 453), 115 (E. M. Curr: *Recollections of Squatting in Victoria*, 1883, 286), 156 (H. 469), 224 (Roth: *Burial*, 395), 232 (Brown: *Journal*, 1913, 169), 261 (C. I, 339), 262 (C. I, 348), 321 (H. 461), 351 (*Folk-Lore*, XIV, 337), 366 (D. W. Carnegie: *Spinifex and Sand*, 1898, 36).

(*c*) Side-chamber.

52, 56, 65 (pp. 192, 353, Strehlow: IV, 16, 25), 110 (H. 460), 321 (H. 462, Fraser, 81).

(*d*) Buried at birth-place.

14 (C. I, 272), 232 (Brown: *Journal*, 1913, 169).

IV. CREMATION.

93 (H. 456, Angas, I, 96), 100 (H. 443), 163 (H. 470), 198 (Roth: *Burial*, 388), 327 (H. 463).

V. CANOE IN BURIAL RITES.

327 (H. 463).

VI. FLIGHT.

56 (Strehlow, IV; Teil, II, 1915, 25), 271 (C. I, 396), 272 (C. I, 404, H. 450), 334 (H. 471).

VII. BURIAL-MOUND.

1, 2 (Sp. III, 230), 4, 6, 10, 13, 17, 18, 19, 20 (Sp. III, 241; Basedow: *Trans. Roy. Soc. S.A.*, XXXI, 7), 47 (p. 354), 67, 70, 71, 72, 73, 74, 75, 76, 80, 81 (p. 353), 83, 84, 85 (p. 353), 88, 95, 110, 130, 135, 153 (pp. 352, 353), 196 (p. 354), 261 (C. I, 339), 284, 285, 286 (p. 353).

VIII. CAVE BURIAL.

203, 204, 205 (Roth: *Burial*, 384), 206 (p. 341), 228 (p. 341), 232 (Brown: *Journal*, 1913, 169).

IX. MEGALITHS.

75 (p. 355), 335, 336 (p. 354).

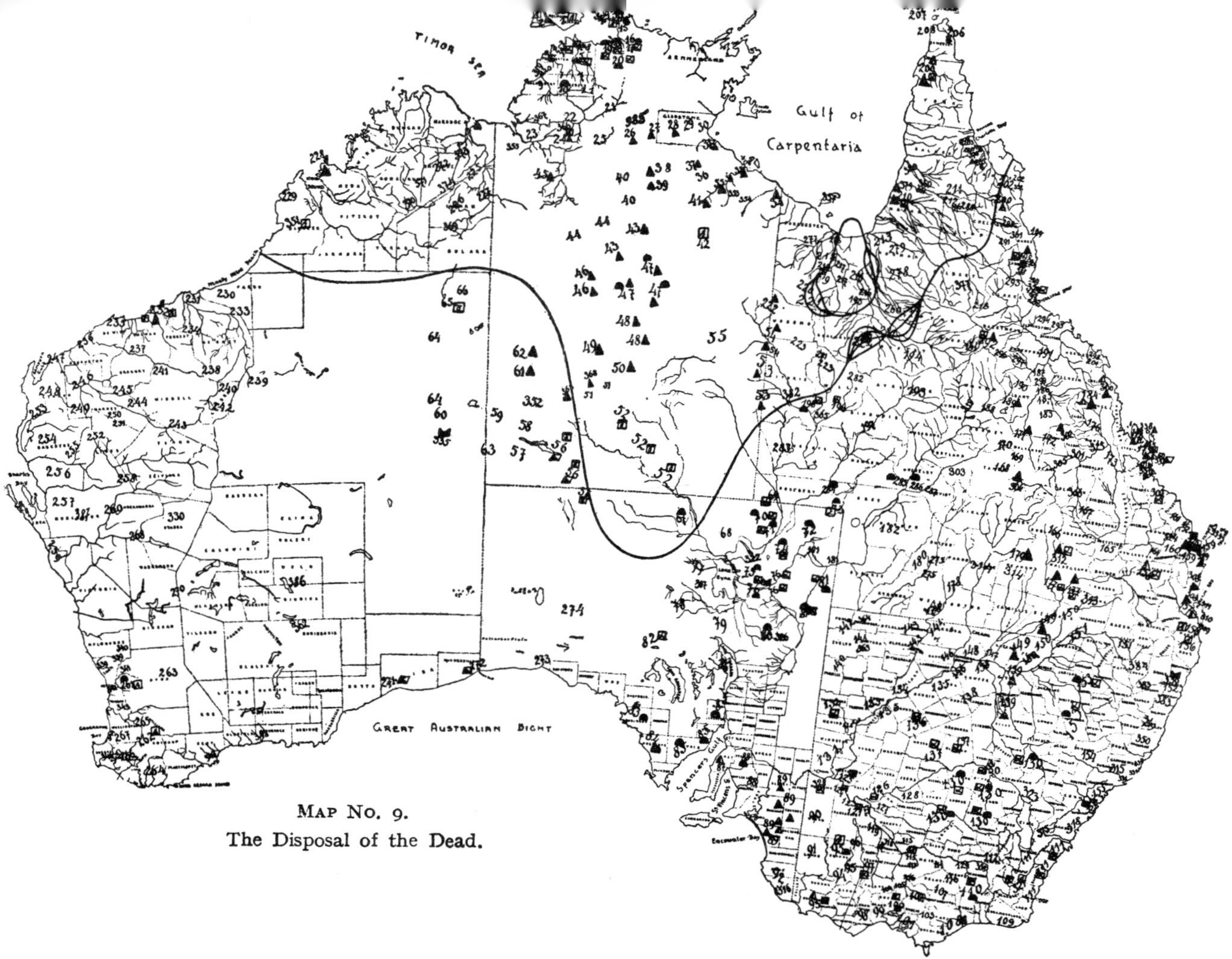

Map No. 9.

The Disposal of the Dead.

the Ifugao of Luzon,[1] in Central Celebes,[2] and amongst the Kabui Naga.[3]

Another remarkable link between Indonesia and Central Australia are the stories of floods and petrifaction. It is time to call attention to a very marked feature of Central Australian traditions; the Alcheringa ancestors who go into the ground are dead, and if tradition says that "stones arose to mark the spot," this must be taken literally; it is as much as to say that stones were erected on their graves.

The Alcheringa ancestors are dead men, their Nanja stones are the stones on their graves.

We are told about an Eagle-hawk ancestor who died and went into the ground. Before he died he made a large Nurtunja or sacred pole, which he placed on his head; it went right through his body and a big stone called Eagle-hawk Nurtunja arose to mark the spot.[4] A Crow ancestor died at Ungwurla, and a big black stone marks the spot.[5] When the two Parenthie lizards died two great stones arose to mark the spot, and on the top of each of these there is a hole in which are placed a number of round Churinga stones, representing the eggs which the lizards used to carry about in a cavity on the top of their heads.[6] The ancestor of the Laughing Boy totem is killed by the sky falling down and a great pile of stones arose to mark the spot.[7] When the local people resented the doings of the Honey Ant people they opened the veins in their arms, making such a flood that the whole party was drowned, and a black hill covered with black stones arose where the wanderers perished, and their Churinga are now in the storehouse of the local group.[8] For a similar reason the Ooraminna Creek became flooded and all the Erkincha men were drowned, a stone arising at the spot where these men perished.[9] We think that the stones did not arise of their own accord originally, but were erected as memorial columns by the survivors. Of course, we do not mean the actual rocks which have been scattered about the country by natural forces and under which there is no one buried. When applied to these, then the legend is indeed a reversal as we have explained above; it is located at a certain part of the landscape so as to facilitate psychic adjustment to environment; it is the myth which marks the stone and not the other way round.

[1] Perry, *Megalithic Culture*. Beyer, "Origin Myth among the Mountain Peoples of the Philippines," *Philippine Journal of Science*, VIII, 1913, 237.

[2] Id., 23. Grubauer, *Unter Kopjägern in Zentral Celebes*, 1913, 200.

[3] Id., 23. Hodson, *The Naga Tribes of Manipur*, 1911, 14.

[4] Spencer and Gillen, *Nor. T.*, 399.

[5] Id., ibid., 400.

[6] Id., ibid., 408.

[7] Id., ibid., 423. Cf. 424, 433, 434.

[8] Id., *N. T.*, 438. Cf. 439.

[9] Id., ibid., 444. Charec, an "Alcheringa being," who is regarded as the ancestor of the Woolwonga tribe by the Larrakia dies, and after death his body turned into a large stone on the banks of a creek, and anybody who touches this stone is bound to die shortly.—P. Foelsche, *The Larrakia Tribe*. Curr, I. 253, 254.

If this reversal was brought about by the fact that an immigrant people was trying to explain the features of a new environment, we shall assume that these immigrants had in their former home both the custom of burying their dead in caves and also—a variant of that custom—of putting stones on the earth grave. This would make it natural for them to speak of their ancestors as having " gone down into the earth," and to try and explain the rocks they saw by supposing somebody buried under them. But, and this is the great question, why did tradition obliterate the detail that the stones were piled up over the body of the ancestor by human hands, which would have been more in keeping with the actual customs of the " ancestors of the Alcheringa ancestors " ? An important detail forgotten means that it has become repressed for some reason, and we have to go considerably out of our way to get at the reason of this repression.

The punishment tales in Indonesia.

Perry has tabulated a group of Indonesian traditions which he calls " punishment tales." The heroes of these tales end either by petrifaction or by a flood, and we shall now have to investigate whether there is any other connexion between them and the Alcheringa ancestors. In ten of these tales the offence for which people are punished by petrifaction or drowning is that they are said to have " laughed at animals " ; in six, the reason is that they are guilty of incest or adultery.[1] If we do not take the mysterious injunction about " laughing at animals " too literally, we shall perhaps fathom the meaning of these traditions. To laugh at something means to disregard it, and in this case it would not be disregarding the animal which is such a great sin, but disregarding the animal taboo. Now, from certain beliefs found in Indonesia Perry comes to the conclusion that the stone culture introduced into these islands was totemic, so that the animal taboos would be totemic taboos.[2] But what are the two cardinal taboos of totemism ? Not to kill the totem animal, who represents the father, and not to marry a woman of the same totem, for this would be equivalent to committing incest and marrying the mother. The two offences of the punishment tales thus appear to mean one and the same thing ; committing incest and laughing at animals both mean breaking through the totemic taboo, only in one case the sin is expressed in a direct manner, in the other we have a roundabout statement. The punishment for these offences is death, and the heroes of the Indonesian traditions must suffer this punishment in two ways. Either they are drowned in a flood—in which case, as we have pointed out in dealing with the

[1] W. J. Perry, *The Megalithic Culture of Indonesia*, 1918, 124–134. E. H. Gomes, *Seventeen Years Among the Sea Dyaks of Borneo*, 1911, 205–207. J. Warneck, *Die Religion der Batak*, 1909, 86. Perry and Gomes also record a few cases in which the breach of hospitality is the reason of petrification.

[2] Perry, op. cit., 155–160.

Central Australian traditions, there is a wish-fulfilment discernible behind the punishment (flood = amniotic fluid, return into the maternal womb = incest)—or they are petrified. We think that they would not be petrified if there were no human hands to move the stones, indeed, by saying they were petrified we are simply using another word for stoned. But we must defer this point for further consideration till we see any reason to suppose that the same punishments are suffered by the ancestors of the Central Australians for the same offences. We remember that these ancestors are constantly represented as having lived with women of the same totem and eaten their totem animals, and there were certain signs in tradition that a neurotic feeling of anxiety was coming up in the footsteps of this primary stage of wish-fulfilment. However, the dominant attitude of Central Australian mythology is to find wish-fulfilment quite natural on the part of the Alcheringa ancestors, and if there is any reason why they should die, it is rather because they are an obstacle to the wish-fulfilment of the next generation than for " moral " reasons.

These are far more emphasized in the Indonesian tradition. The relation between the two groups seems to be that the Australians represent the more primitive offshoots of the same parent stem. In both cases we have mythical ancestors who commit incest, must die for it, whilst the death they suffer is nearly identical. But in Indonesia the attitude of the storyteller is more like one who resents the contents of his tale, whilst in Australia the " criminal " is glorified by apotheosis. As in many cases, we see here how further development is likely to call repressed elements to the surface; here the original, but originally purely selfishly inimical attitude of the primitive horde towards the hero of the tale, which is repressed by the desire to exalt the dead father to a deity, comes to the surface under the thin veneer of moral reprobation. We shall now have to discuss the original and unconscious meaning of petrifaction.

The heap of stones.

A myth of the Philippine mountain people tells us about a man called Ango who went a-hunting. He killed a fine boar, but broke his spear in the process. He went to a stream and began to mend the weapon. The croaking of the frogs attracting his notice, he began to imitate them and told them that it would be better if they would stop their noise and help him. After this he continued his course up the torrent, but noticed that a multitude of little stones began to follow him. Surprised, he began to quicken his steps, and looking back he saw bigger stones joining in the pursuit. When he arrived at his potato patch he was quite exhausted, whereupon the stones overtook him and became attached to his finger. His wife and children tried to stop the petrification, but it was all of no avail, for first his feet, then his body up to his hips, and then the chest and head turned to stone. To this day the petrified forms of Ango and his wife and children are to be seen on the peak of Binaci.[1] At Bulili there is a female image representing a woman who committed adultery with her husband's brother; that is, incest. She was beaten for this and during the punishment she was turned into stone.[2] This leads us to suppose that it was probably human hands who moved the stones in the case of Ango, that the stones were hurled at him, and his retreating and dying figure was buried beneath a heap of stones. That the sin of "laughing at animals" is connected with totemism seems to be corroborated by this tradition; for what he really does is simply to perform a totemic rite in imitating animals. A latter age which "laughed" at something it had left behind has left its imprint on the tradition, for it interpreted a totem rite as pure mockery.[3]

At one spot on the Buccaneer Island there is a large rock on the top of which there are a number of small stones. The natives say that an evil spirit troubled the camp at one time, that they co-operated and chased him all over the island till they cornered him on this rock, where they exterminated him with stones.[4]

If we wish to explain who this "evil spirit" was, we must inquire into the probable antiquity and the magico-religious survivals of the custom of hurling stones at an enemy or object of chase. It is a well-known fact that monkeys are in the habit of using stones they find for breaking hard fruits and as missiles to hurl at their aggressors.[5] Basedow tells us that amongst the Aluridja in Central Australia a fair amount of hunting is done with the simple aid of stones and sticks which they hurl at the smaller game. In the making and use of implements and weapons these tribes were particularly primitive, apparently more so than the natives of any other part of Australia.[6] The extremely archaic character of the hurled stone as a weapon is also made probable by the fact that it is pre-eminently used by spirits and magicians against man and by man in dealing with the spirit-world, and we know very well that spirit world is extremely conservative and usually lags behind

[1] Perry, *Megalithic Culture*, 124, 125. Beyer, *Philippine Journal of Science*, VIII. 90. [2] Perry, l.c., 125.

[3] The infantile parallel to this is the case of children who often imitate their teachers and parents in derision, thus allowing the aggressive tendency to crop up behind what is apparently an act of identification.

[4] W. H. Bird, "Ethnographical Notes on the Buccaneer Islanders," *Anthropos*, 1911, 178. On one of the hills on the island there is a cairn of stones seemingly thrown on a heap; it is said to have been built by the wagtail. Perhaps this is a trace of a lost bird-cannibal myth of the South Australian type.

[5] Darwin, *Descent of Man*, I. 75. Cf. L. Noiré, *Das Werkzeug*, 1880, 387. Noiré seems rather to underrate the mental capacities of apes when he denies that their intention in throwing is to hit the object of their wrath.

[6] H. Basedow, "Anthropological Notes made on the South Australian Government North-West Prospecting Expedition," *Trans. R. Soc. S. A.*, XXVIII, 1904, 28.

the times in technical achievements. The natives of the Yas Tumut and Murrumbudgee believe that they can kill an invisible foe by throwing the magical quartz-crystal in the direction where he is supposed to be.[1] The contents of the bag of a Kabi magician, would be a few pebbles, bits of glass, bones, etc. This artillery is enough to kill at any distance. A blackfellow gets a stitch in his side, and immediately he believes that an enemy has cast a pebble at him from behind a tree.[2] Magical stone-throwing causes death among the Kamilaroi.[3] Sometimes there is a further modification; instead of throwing the stone it suffices to ground some powder off it and strew it on the victim. In the districts north of the Boulia, i.e. the Upper Georgina River, Upper Leichardt River and Selwyn Ranges, and at Cloncurry, a white powder somewhat the appearance of very fine ashes is placed in close proximity to the place where the victim sleeps with the object of killing him. The Maitakudi call this powder "mau-ar." In order that the performer should not injure himself by contact he sprinkles it where required from out of a mussel shell.[4] Amongst the Kaitish, Warramunga and northern tribes generally a very potent form of evil magic called mauia is supposed to be associated with certain little stones. Each little stone is wrapped up in fold after fold of paper bark or string. When it is used among the southern tribes the usual plan is to powder a little off on the top of a spear and then to drop it very quietly on the victim's body when he is asleep.[5] The Bakerewe believe that their wizards can "throw" a disease at a whole district.[6] The "pains" which are "shot" into their victims seem to be quartz crystals and other stones.[7] At Gelaria a spirit called "labuni" throws a stone or human tooth at its victim.[8] The same archaic artillery is also used by man in his combats against the spirit-world. In South Australia a species of black fly catcher is regarded as an evil spirit. Whenever they see it they pelt it with sticks and stones, though they are afraid to touch or destroy it.[9] In Western Hungary a stone is thrown towards the owl because its hooting is thought not merely to presage, but also to cause death.[10] Similarly in New Britain they pelt the owl, which

[1] G. Bennett, *Wanderings in N.S. Wales*, 1834, I. 191.

[2] Mathew, *Eagle-hawk and Crow*, 1899, 144. Curr, III. 164.

[3] Ridley, "Report on Australian Languages and Traditions," *J. A. I.*, 1872, II. 272.

[4] W. E. Roth, *S. M. M.*, 1903, 32.

[5] Spencer and Gillen, *Nor. T.*, 466, 467.

[6] E. Hurel, "Religion et Vie domestique des Bakerewe," *Anthropos*, 1911, 87.

[7] A. L. Kroeber, "The Religion of the Indians of California Univ. Cal. (*Publ. Am. Arch. Ethn.*, IV. No. 16), 1907, 329, 333, 349. E. Sapir, "Religious Ideas of the Takelma Indians," *Journ. Am. F.-L.*, 1907, 40–42. Dixon, "Notes on the Achomawi and Atsugewi Indians of Northern California," *American Anthropologist*, 1908, 218, 219.

[8] Seligmann, op. cit., 640-42.

[9] G. F. Angas, *Savage Life and Scenes in Australia and New Zealand*, 1847, I. 96.

[10] Róheim, "Adalékok a Magyar Néphithez" (*Contributions to Hungarian Folk-Lore*), 1913, 11.

they regard as a death omen, with stones.[1] The same method is employed against other birds of evil omen,[2] whilst to throw a stone over the roof of a sick man means causing his death by magic.[3] If we accept these and similar data as indicating the antiquity of the hurled stone as a weapon of mankind, and take it in conjunction with the use made of the same by the anthropoid apes, we shall go on to assume that the first battles of man were fought by this method, or at least that throwing stones in a blind fury with or without taking aim must have been a habit of our Pithecoid ancestors in which they indulged before making a rush for their foe.

We are sufficiently acquainted with the life of the higher mammals to know that among them there is hardly any other occasion for open battle than the repeated attempts of the young males to dispossess the old ones from the leadership of the herd and the mastery over the females. Moreover, we know that the ultimate victory of the pubescent males over the Paternal Tyrant must have been obtained through sheer force of numbers. Their number was legion, the Old Male stood alone, and although still more than a match for any one of his sons in a single-handed fight, he could not resist their combined attack. They probably lacked courage to rush at him, for the first one who came to clutching distance was sure to pay with his life for his temerity, but they could form a circle round him and bruise and exhaust him by hurling stones at him without coming to close quarters. The "mana" (hypnotic influence) of the Old Male held them at bay and created a taboo-area round him.[4] Their ambivalent attitude towards him would prompt them to rush at him and yet they would feel inhibited in doing so. The result would be an act of compromise: they kept their distance and only approached him by means of an object which had, through introjection, become part of their own selves, i.e. by hurling a stone at him.[5]

The hero of the Indonesian tales is pelted to death for having committed incest, and this is just the sin of the leader of the herd in the eyes of those who envy him his power to commit the sin and accuse him of selfishness for committing it quite alone. In the Intichiuma ceremonies it is the rock which represents the body of an Alcheringa ancestor that is pelted with stones, and the Alcheringa ancestor represents the Fathers of the Primeval Horde in the days before the laws of exogamy came into existence.

It is by a transference from the Sire to the criminal who committed the first Regicide that the legal survival of stoning criminals

[1] Kleintitschen, *Die Küstenbewohner der Gazellehalbinsel*, 1906, 344.
[2] Parkisson, *Dreissig Jahre in der Südsee*, 1907, 119.
[3] Id., ibid., 118.
[4] Cf. S. Freud, *Group Psychology and the Analysis of the Ego*, 1922, 96.
[5] Cf. R. Hirzel, "Die Strafe der Steinigung," *Abh. d. sächs, Ges. d. Wiss*, XXVII. 225.

to death can be explained. In Dabaiba it was ordained that a priest who has offended "shall eyther be stoned to death or burned."[1] It looks like a repetition of the primeval murder which must have occurred at the season of love and battle, when we read that the Athenians used to stone two victims as vicarious sacrifices, one for the men and one for the women, at the yearly festival of the Thargelia in May.[2] At Tenedos a calf was dressed in boots to represent the young bull Dionysos. He was sacrificed to the "cannibal Dionysos," evidently as the substitute for a youth who represented the god in former days. The priest who slew the animal had to fly for his life to the sea and he was pelted with stones all the way.[3] If we examine the mythic and ritual complex which clusters around Dionysos we shall find that the god himself is said to have been driven into the sea by Lykurgos who uses the same axe, the bouplex which is employed in the slaughter of the human calf. The young boy who is sacrificed to the cannibal god is Dionysos himself, who in the shape of a bull is rent asunder by the Titans, and these Titans, whose habitual weapons are the rocks and stones they hurl at their adversaries,[4] are the initiates of the mysteries, because the latter are said to be painted white in commemoration of the white paint used by the Titans when they attacked the bull Dionysos.[5] Both the calf who is killed by the priest and the priest who flies to the sea are representatives of the god, and if the latter is stoned then we may guess that the god had to suffer the same lot at the hands of his savage adversaries. But if these are the prototypes of the initiates, who again stand for the rebellious group of brothers in the primeval horde, we again come to the conclusion that stones must have been hurled by them in their rebellion against the paternal tyrant. This bit of ethnological speculation in which we have been indulging with the aid of psycho-analysis must, if correct, permit us to make a forecast. The initiation ceremonies are, as we know very well, a reversed repetition of the Primeval Conflict. Fear of retribution prompts the Elders to turn the tables on youth; instead of permitting themselves to be unmanned and killed by the next generation they circumcise the boys and kill them in a fictive or symbolical manner. If, then, stones were frequently hurled at the Old Male in the primeval conflict, we shall expect to see them projected back at the initiates.

It is a remarkable fact which needs closer investigation from an ethnological point of view that there are two "central mysteries" in Australian initiation rites; besides the bullroarer we have also

[1] F. B. Jevons, *An Introduction to the History of Religion*, 1911, 73, 74, quoting Hakluyt, *Historie of the West-Indies* Decade, VII. 10.

[2] J. G. Frazer, *The Scapegoat*, 1911, 254.

[3] M. P. Nilsson, *Griechische Feste von religiöser Bedeutung*, 1906, 308.

[4] Eitrem, *Opferritus und Voropfer der Griechen und Römer*, 1915, 283.

[5] Weniger, "Feralis exercitus," *A R. W.*, IX. 212.

the quartz crystal. We do not know whether this was perhaps the initiation symbol of a population that occupied these territories before the bullroarer was introduced or whether on the contrary it was carried by one special wave of the stone-using immigrants to regions in which the bullroarer held undisputed sway. However, that may be, and it matters little for our present purpose which of the two possibilities be corroborated by investigation, it seems certain that these stone initiations have survived in a pure form in the special initiation rite of the medicine man. That this rite is derived from a puberty initiation is made probable by the fact that it is based on the scheme of death and rebirth and also as the vocation of shaman is often chosen at puberty.[1] An Euahlayi boy who belongs to the Iguana totem and wishes to be initiated as a shaman first sees his totem animal, the iguana. The animal crawled all over him, but he was not frightened, as he knew it would not hurt him. Then however came the snake, the hereditary enemy of his totem animal. Next came a huge figure to him, having in his hand a yam stick. The figure drove this into the boy's head, pulled it out through his back, and in the hole thus made he placed a " Gubberah " or sacred stone, with the help of which the boy would work his magic in the future.[2] The interpretation of this personal vision, which must, however, be made up of traditional elements, seems easy enough. The boy is unconsciously travelling backwards in the history of his tribe. First he sees the protective aspect of the totem concept. Then comes the hereditary enemy of his totem (father) imago, or rather, his own hereditary enmity towards the father, which has been buried in the course of time by the belief in the totemic protector. Now he begins to be frightened, and the next phase is the attack he has to suffer from a huge human figure—the father as he was before the age of animal projection. The weapons used in this attack are the primeval weapons of mankind—the stick and the stone.

The Arunta medicine men are initiated in a very similar way. The man leaves the camp quite alone until he comes to the mouth of a cave. At the break of day one of the Iruntarinia (spirit doubles of the Alcheringa ancestors) comes to the mouth of the cave, and finding the man asleep throws an invisible lance at him, which pierces the neck from behind. A second lance thrown by the Iruntarinia pierces from head to ear and the victim falls dead, and is at once carried into the depths of the cave where the Iruntarinia live. Here the Iruntarinia removes all the internal organs and supplies him with a completely new set, also implanting in his body a supply of magic Atnongara stones, which he in his turn is able to

[1] Cf. on these initiations, Hubert et Mauss, " L'origine des pouvoirs magiques dans les sociétés australiennes," *Mélanges d'Histoire des Religions*, 1909, 131.

[2] K. L. Parker, *The Euahlayi Tribe*, 1905, 26

project into the body of a patient.[1] Besides showing that a spirit closely connected with the dead and with the totem is responsible for introducing these stones into the body of the neophyte, this account furnishes us with additional proof for connecting the Ertnatulunga cave with the grave. Naturally the cave of the Iruntarinia can only be a specific variant of the cave in which the Altjiranga mitjina (or the Churinga which represent them) reside. Now, murrokun is the name of a mysterious bone obtained by the magicians of the Awakabal. Three of these sleep on the grave of a recently interred corpse; during their sleep in the night the dead person inserts a bone into each man. The bones remain in the flesh of the doctors without any inconvenience to them until they wish to project it into any person, thereby causing the death of their victim.[2] The chief difference is that in one case we have a grave which is only a fictive grave tenanted by an " Alcheringa ancestor," whilst amongst the Awabakal it is a ghost with whom the candidates for the bone were probably personally acquainted. At any rate if the initiate is " stoned " we shall think it very probable that this is only a just act of retribution. He must have stoned the spirit of initiation, the All-Father.

Indeed the bullroarer is a stone giant Sosom, who swallows the youths of the Tugeri at initiation,[3] and the Unmatjera say that Tuanyirika, the initiation spirit, dwells in a rock.[4]

Stone and half-stone supreme beings.

Besides these we find mythical or supreme beings in the regions we are concerned with who exist in a half-petrified condition, and who evidently are so similar to each other that a historical connexion, however remote, must be supposed to lie at the bottom of their evolution. The Tontemboan of Minahassa tell us that their sun-lord Kerito was half human and half stone, just like the " God-man " Maror, whose flesh was half human and half stone.[5] The Kai have got a primeval being, the Malengfung, who was in the world even before the Nemu (the Alcheringa ancestors) although he is himself sometimes called a Nemu. He is a typical otiose high-god, he does not interfere in the destinies of mankind, only when there is an earthquake; this is caused by Malengfung rolling over. His dwelling-place is the horizon. One day he will rise from his couch at the eastern sky and break through heaven, which will then crash down on the earth and set an end to all manifestations of life. This Malengfung is a peculiar being; his front half is like that of a human being and his face is human, but his back view presents the aspect of a gigantic rock all grown over with moss. He created a giant called " the old Panggu," who is

[1] Spencer and Gillen, *N. T.*, 523–525.

[2] L. E. Threlkeld, *An Australian Language as spoken by the Awabakal*, 1892, 48.

[3] Haddon, *Migrations of Cultures in British New Guinea*, 1920, 21. *Z. E.*, 1907, 392. A stone effigy is used at the initiation ceremony of Mawata (Haddon, ibid., 4).

[4] Spencer and Gillen, *Nor. T.*, 498.

[5] Perry, l.c., 91.

evidently a duplicate of Malengfung. His body is also a rock, only the part of his face beneath his forehead is human, whilst his cranium is again made of stone. His head is the support of the blue vault; he may not move lest the sky should crash down.[1] These respectable personages have many relatives both to the East (in Melanesia) and to the South (in Australia). Ndengei in Fiji is a serpent, at least the head and part of the body are those of a serpent, whilst the rest of his body is of stone.[2] A saying of the Arunta and Loritja is only comprehensible if we interpret it as the half-forgotten survival of this stone giant who supported the vaults of heaven. They say that the sky rests on pillars which they call "stone-leg," at the same time they are afraid of the sky falling down and crushing everybody.[3] The Euahlayi believe that Baiamai and his wife Birrahngooloo cannot move from their place in the sky camp, for the lower part of their body is crystallized whilst the upper part is human.[4] If we read about Boyma seated on a throne of crystal with beautiful pillars of crystal on each side,[5] we may be sure that we have to do with the same crude aboriginal idea of a semi-petrified deity, only in a transcription adapted to a European taste. As to the unconscious origin of the idea of a half-petrified ancestor, this seems to lie in the fundamental ambivalency of the attitude of the youthful rebels towards the Father-Imago; it is as much as to say that they were half inclined to petrify, that is to kill him, but that there was also a tendency in them to let him live. This is confirmed by the fact that we have to do with otiose high-gods, beings who, as we shall see elsewhere, really represent the Father who has been killed and translated to the sky vault after his death. In this case we shall re-interpret the block of stone out of which the human figure is thought to rise; it is the stone which is rolled on the grave to keep the ghost down, out of which, however, he rises by what may be called a return of repressed elements.

Grave mounds.

The custom of raising various structures of earth, wood or stone over the grave really belongs to those universal modes of behaviour and concepts which are the common property and heritage of mankind. The Kamilaroi on the Namoi and Barwon bury the dead in the ground in a hole deep enough for them to be put upright on their feet, and to have an empty space above them which is covered in with wood so that

[1] Keysser, 155. Neuhauss, *Deutsch Neu Guinea*, III.

[2] Th. Williams, *Fiji and the Fijians*, 1858, I. 217.

[3] Strehlow, *A. & L.*, I. 2.

[4] K. L. Parker, *The Euahlayi Tribe*, 1905, 7. This crystallized woman is closely connected with floods, thus once more confirming the parallel between floods and petrifaction. These floods are started by a flood-ball of blood rolling down the mountains (ibid., 8), just like the Arunta cause a flood by opening a vein in their arms. The connexion of the flood with amniotic fluid explains its association with a representative of the Mother-Imago. Birrahngooloo is claimed as the mother of all.—Parker, ibid., 7.

[5] Howitt, *N. T.*, 502.

nothing may touch the head of the deceased. The earth is carefully pressed down over the wooden roof of his tomb and a mound is raised over it. They are very careful about keeping these mounds in their cemeteries in order and decorum.[1] In the country of the Barcoo and Diamantina deltas a large stack of wood is placed on the grave.[2] The tribes in the district of Adelaide, Gawler, Gumerache, dug a hole about three feet deep, deposited the body and covered it up first with earth and sand and then if convenient with stones. At the head of the grave a crescent of earth or stones was erected.[3] The Wotjobaluk put logs on the grave to prevent the dogs interfering with it.[4] The Theddora believed that the dead do not always remain in the grave, but come out at times. This accounts for their graves being dug like cylindrical pits with a side chamber in which the corpse was placed blocked in with pieces of wood. An account of a burial by a member of this tribe reads as follows: " We were at the Snowy River and one of the old men died. We dug a hole in the river bank and as we were putting him into it we thought that he moved. We were all much frightened and all fell back except old Nukong, who stood forward and said, ' What are you doing that for? What are you trying to frighten us for? ' We rammed up the hole with wood and stones and earth and went away."[5] This account brings out one important fact which cannot appear in the mere description of the grave—that the wood and stones piled up on the corpse are meant to protect the living from the ghost. The usual explanation given is that the log is a protection not for the living, but for the corpse—to prevent the wild dogs from getting at it.[6] Large mounds (three or four feet high, seven feet long) composed of sticks, stones and earth, have been observed on the Barwon River.[7] Small tumuli are erected by the tribes who live northwards from the sea-coast of South Australia.[8] The Dieri have long mounds on their graves.[9] Eylmann describes a double grave mound of the Arunta.[10] The earth is piled over the body so as to make a low mound with a depression on one side; this being the side which faces the Alcheringa place of the dead man,

[1] W. Ridley, " Report on Australian Languages and Traditions," *J. A. I.*, II. 271. Cf. Macdonald, " The Aborigines of the Page and the Isis," *J. A. I.*, VII. 255.

[2] Howitt, *N. T.*, 449.

[3] Id., 451. Cf. W. Wyatt, *Some Account of the Manners and Superstitions of the Adelaide and Encounter Bay Aboriginal Tribes*. J. D. Woods, *Native Tribes of South Australia*, 1879, 165, who only mentions branches and tree-bark on the graves.

[4] Howitt, *N. T.*, 452.

[5] Howitt, *N. T.*, 460, 461.

[6] F. Bonney, " On some Customs of the River Darling Natives talking the Weyneubulckoo Language, especially Bungyarlee and Parkungi," *J. A. I.*, XIII, 135, 136. Logs also used by the Wiradjuri.—Howitt, l.c. 466. Parker, *Euahlayi*, 88.

[7] R. Oberländer, Die Eingeborenen der australischen Kolonie Victoria," *Globus* IV. 282.

[8] G. F. Angas, *Savage Life*, 1847, I. 86.

[9] Gason in Curr, *The Australian Race*, II. 63.

[10] Eylmann, *Die Eing. der Kolonie S.A.*, 233.

or according to another account his mother's Alcheringa place.[1] In the Boulia District the body is laid horizontally with the head pointing towards the North, which is considered the orthodox position.[2] The depth of the grave varies with the nature of the soil. The corpse is covered with logs placed longitudinally, then with a layer placed transversely to be followed by a filling in of earth and soil: on top of all this are placed heavy logs and bushes, and perhaps some heavy stones, all closely interlaced and reaching to a height of three or four feet.

In the Pitta-Pitta language a grave is called mur-ra kambo, stick-stone.[3] The burial customs of the Warramunga seem to indicate that there has been a change in the disposal of the dead and an older ceremony has left its rudimentary survivals which are incompatible with the present structure of the ritual. They have the " delayed burial " type, exposing the body in a tree for a certain period and then burying it inconspicuously in an ant-hill.[4] But an important part of the mourning ceremonies is not concerned with the tree or ant-hill which really contains the corpse; there is a small mound of earth called kakiti placed on the spot where the dead man had actually died. The body is lifted on a bier by the Adelaide tribe and the ground upon which the man died is dug up by his wives with their long sticks. A little heap of earth is thus formed, supposed to contain the " wingko " or breath that has left the body and is set free by the digging.[5] It is here that the ground is smoothed down and that the tracks of the animal which represents the murderer are sought for;[6] a ceremony which is performed at the grave or grave mound itself amongst the Southern tribes.

The burial mound seems to be especially developed in West Australia. The Whajook tribe raised a mound in a half-circle around the grave, into which they stuck green boughs and the weapons, tools, ornaments of the deceased.[7] Mounds of stones placed due East to West have been described by Grey at Hanover Bay;[8] Giles mentions several mounds of stones at Rawlinson Range placed at even distances apart and paths cleared between them. There

[1] Spencer and Gillen, *N. T.*, 497. Schulze, *Trans. and Proc. R. S. S. A.*, XIV. 238. The same type of burial mound is described by Basedow, " Anthropological Notes made on the South Australian Government North-West Prospecting Expedition, *Trans. Roy. Soc. S. A.*, 1904, XXVIII. 35.

[2] Cf. above, pp. 198, 312 on spirit-land in the north and northern origin of Central tribes.

[3] W. E. Roth, " Burial Ceremonies and Disposal of the Dead." *N. Q. E. Bull.*, 9, 394.

[4] Spencer and Gillen, *Nor. T.*, 532.

[5] W. Wyatt, op. cit. 164. J. D. Woods, op. cit.

[6] Cf. Spencer and Gillen, *Nor. T.*, 519, 526.

[7] Curr, I. 339. Semi-circular mounds are also reported from the Kukatha. Ch. Provis, *The Kukatha Tribe*. G. Taplin, *F.-L.*, etc., 1879, 95.

[8] G. Grey, *Journal of two Expeditions to North-West and Western Australia*, 1841, I. 227. Cf. on cairns in Queensland, Hamlyn-Harris, " Mummification," *Memoirs of the Queensland Museum*, 1912, I. 12.

was also a large piece of rock in the centre of most of these heaps. He adds, "I have concluded that these are small kinds of teocallis and that on the bare rock mentioned the natives perform their rites of human butchery."[1] These are probably not burial mounds, at least not at present, but parallels to the tarlows of the North-west, and thus connected with the Intichiuma ceremonies. Three huge pillar stones or rocks have been observed in an elevated position on a mountain range in New South Wales, and the natives say that when they see these three stones in a time of drought and wish formerly for one, two or three days of rain, the rain will certainly come.[2] The blacks at Clarence River mark the burial-places by placing stones in a circle and a large upright slab in the centre.[3] Stone circles from ten to one hundred feet in diameter are reported from Victoria and Cooper's Creek, with another row of stones forming an inner circle.[4] We may distinguish two types of these burial mounds besides those resulting from a combination of the two.[5] (*a*) Earth mounds, (*b*) Stone heaps or large slabs of stone. The differences may either be due to local circumstances or to definite cultural influences. At any rate, we see that not much evidence as to the meaning or intention of putting a huge stone on the grave is forthcoming from Australia.

The prevalent opinion of ethnologists, however, seems to be that the stone is put on the grave to prevent the dangerous ghost from returning and haunting the camp of its former fellows. Thus we find a mound piled over the corpse of the Arabian hero Antar to "prevent his mighty soul from breaking through."[6] In Modern Hellas we find the idea that the heavier the heap of stones piled over the body the surer will the soul of the criminal sink right down to Hell.[7] We have noticed the case of the Theddora above; they pile earth and stones on the grave out of fear of the ghost. If we are right in supposing that the young males of the Horde originally hurled stones and rocks at their solitary but still formidable foe, it would seem very probable that they continued to do so when he was already half or quite dead and thus a pile of stones would be raised above the wriggling body. The tales which speak of the gradual petrification of evil-doers may well contain a memory of this struggle. When they had at last made sure of their victory they would probably with united efforts drag a large boulder or slab of stone to the scene, and with an intention that must have been the direct contrary of

The interpretation of the burial mound.

[1] E. Giles, *Geographic Travels in Central Australia*, 1875, 171.

[2] J. Fraser, *The Aborigines of New South Wales*, 1892, 68.

[3] G. F. Angas, *Savage Life and Scenes*, 1847, II. 280.

[4] J. Fraser, l.c., 68.

[5] Large stone on burial mound (Blackman's Bay, Tasmania).—Oldfield, "The Aborigines of Australia, *Trans. Ethn. Soc.*, III. 248.

[6] A. Bastian, *Der Papua des dunklen Inselreichs*, 1885, 40.

[7] B. Schmidt, in *Neue Jahrbücher*, vol. 147, 1893.

the pious Roman's wish ("Sit tibi terra levis"), covered the body of the murdered father with it, to make assurance doubly sure.

Stone heaps.

The question of stone heaps has often been discussed in ethnology and folklore, but none of the rival theories which hold the field offers sufficient explanation of the regularity with which the cairn is associated with the memory of murder committed at a particular spot. In Sweden they point out a place where two men murdered each other and every passer-by stops to add his contribution to the heap of sticks and stones.[1] Norse saga tells us how Hrafnkell Freysgodi had a pile of stones heaped up over the body of the murdered Einarr.[2] In Pomerania and West Prussia every passer-by must cast a stick or stone at the place where a suicide is buried. Piles of sticks or stones are accumulated on these graves.[3] In Brandenburg they call the places where somebody has met death by violence (suicide, murder or accident) "dead man," and the place is regarded as haunted whether the body has actually been buried there or not. Everybody who passes throws a stick to the pile which keeps growing in dimensions. This pile of sticks, which is a sort of grave mound, is called the "dead man."[4] Stones are cast at the graves of murderers in Senegambia.[5] It was a custom of the bushmen to place heaps of stones over their graves and each passer-by considered it was his duty to add to the heap. In the Hantam there is a narrow defile between two mountains called The Murderer's Pass on account of several colonists having been killed there by bushmen. Near the same spot were six large piles of stones or cairns which had been raised to commemorate a bloody conflict between two tribes.[6] Besides the common graves covered with heaps of stones larger heaps are also found in the country, and if the Namaquas are asked what these are they say that Heije Eibib, their great father, is below the heap.[7] On the other hand, the same author tells us that the bushmen are of the opinion that the devil is interred under these cairns and the stones are piled up in heaps to hinder his resurrection.[8] It seems very probable that "the devil" refers to the legendary antagonists of Heitsi-Eibib (Ga Gorib), or perhaps even to that hero himself. It was the custom of the Akamba to pick up sticks or stones at the side of the road, a place where something bad or

[1] Liebrecht, *Zur Volkskunde*, 1879, 272.

[2] Kahle, "Uber Steinhaufen, insbesondere auf Island," *Z. d. V. f. Vk.*, 1902, 92.

[3] A. Treichel, "Reisig und Steinhäufung bei Ermordeten oder Selbstmördern," *Z. f. E.*, 1888, XX. 569. Frazer, *Scapegoat*, 17.

[4] Kahle, l.c., 209, 210.

[5] Waitz, *Anthropologie der Naturvölker*, II. 195. Frazer, *Scapegoat*, 16.

[6] G. W. Stow, *The Native Races of South Africa*, 1095, 128. Stow and Kidd, *The Essential Kafir*, 1904, 249, think the mound of stones was originally erected against the wild animals.

[7] Hahn, *Tsuni-Goam*, 1881, 52.

[8] Th. Hahn, "Die Buschmanner," *Globus*, XVIII. 141. Frazer, *Scapegoat*, 16.

unlucky had been seen; for instance, if a man saw some human excrement near the side of the road he would throw a stick or stone on it, and the next passer-by would do likewise, and so on till quite a heap accumulated. The same custom prevailed among the Masai and great cairns of stone may be seen at places on the road between Kinobop Plateau and Naivasha.[1]

On the Zambesi the making of these heaps of stones was supposed to have originated in a rape having been committed at that spot, and everyone passing would pick up a stone, spit on it, and throw it on the heap; or if a young woman jilted a man, he would start a heap, spitting on the stones, believing that all passers, by spitting on the stones and throwing them on the heap, would cause her to want lovers and be jilted.[2] In Sweden and the island of Oesel cairns are heaped up on scenes of clandestine or illicit love, and in Oesel, when a man has lost his cattle, he will go to such a spot and say: "I bring thee wood; let me soon find my lost cattle," at the same time flinging a stick or stone at the cairn.[3] In the Sahara it is again the connexion with murder which is prominent; the heaps are called "nza," from the plaintive wails of the soul of the victim of a bloody deed.[4] The eastern tribes of North America have many cairns as burial mounds, and tradition always connects these with the memory of some awful event that happened at that place. The Hudson Bay Indians will throw a stone at the grave to protect themselves against ill-luck, and the Pueblo believe that by throwing stones on the corpse they are driving the evil spirit out.[5] In the south-west of West Australia the natives throw rushes and branches upon certain sacred spots to mollify the spirits that haunt them.[6] The Cowarrwel blacks who lived near the mountains west of Port Macquarie used to sew up the body in tree bark and then suspend it from a tree ten feet from the ground and close to one of their paths; each black in passing throws a piece of wood beneath the corpse, and the body is burnt as soon as the pile is large enough.[7] In Queensland the burial mound is composed of earth and logs, and out of respect for the dead every passer-by throws a branch on the mound.[8]

[1] C. W. Hobley, *Ethnology of Akamba and other East African Tribes*, 1910, 101.

[2] H. W. Garbutt, "Native Witchcraft and Superstition in South Africa," *Journ. Anthr. Inst.*, 1909, 532.

[3] J. B. Holzmayer, "Osiliana," *Verh. d. gel. Estn. Ges. zu Dorpat*, VII, 1872, 73. Liebrecht, *Zur Volkskunde*, 1879, 274. Frazer, *Scapegoat*, 14.

[4] Doutté, *Magie at Religion dans l'Afrique du Nord*, 1909, 425.

[5] Th. Preuss, *Die Begräbnisarten der Amerikaner und Nordostasiaten*, 1894, 293.

[6] Mathew, *Two Tribes*, 168, quoting D. M. Bates.

[7] Breton, *Excursions in New South Wales, Western Australia and Van Diemen's Land*, 1833, 228, 229. Here we have another case of a burial custom which has lost its original meaning through an immigrant custom. Originally the heap was piled over the body before burial, and this was displaced by exposure and cremation.

[8] H. G. Schneider, *Missionsarbeit der Brüdergemeinde in Australien*, 1882, 42.

If we start from the hypothetical assumption that all humanity passed through a state of society which resembled that still found amongst the higher mammals, especially the anthropoid apes, when the Law of Love was the Law of Battle between the young males and the old Leader of the Horde, and if we also assume that the young males would hurl stones at their formidable adversary, we shall come to the conclusion that every death, and especially every violent death, re-excites the unconscious but very powerful impressions left on the psyche of mankind by the first murder and revives the whole scene in the symptomatic reaction-formation of ritual. Just as the Father was stoned by the rebels of the Horde, the dead man must be stoned after his death and the murder committed is continually repeated in the archaic form which characterized the first murder. There is a remarkable ambivalency both as to the object and the meaning of the whole rite. The person who is stoned after his death may be both a criminal, especially a murderer and an ancestor ("the father" hero-god of the Hottentots), or a saint. The stones are thrown as an act of aggressiveness to keep the spirit down, to protect oneself from harm and as an act of homage, a sacrifice. From the point of view of the brother-clan the Lord of the Horde must have appeared to be a criminal who drove the brother-clan from their camp and kept all the women to himself, yet at the same time he was the beloved father of their childhood; as soon as remorse for the bloody deed got the upper hand the deed itself was re-interpreted as an act of worship.

The primeval murder and death rites.

Other objects which are less and less like the original weapon of the semi-ape become substituted for the stone and the rite may even be looked upon as a sort of communion; by throwing at the god, man is not showing his rebellious attitude towards these supernatural beings, but establishing a mystic communion between them and himself.[1]

Twelve miles to the east of Alice Springs there is a special heap of stones. Here in the Alcheringa there lived two men of the Eagle-hawk totem who one day ate a large number of Eagle-hawk men, women and children. They vomited the beings they had devoured, and these are now represented by the heaps of stones called ulkutha. These stones are full of evil magic, and for the purpose of keeping it from coming out, they must be covered with sticks and hidden from view. At the present time any native passing by must throw a stick on to the heap and so help to keep the evil magic down and prevent it from issuing forth.[2] These dead are of considerable interest from our point of view. Their death is caused by the sin of the Eagle-hawk, the cannibal father of the primeval horde. The

[1] Hartland, *Legend of Perseus*, II. 96.
[2] Spencer and Gillen, *Nor. T.*, 472.

sin seems to be aggravated by his devouring people of his own totem, which is a symbolic equivalent of totemic incest. Another similar heap is found in the Urabunna tribe and is connected with the wanderings of a rat-ancestor who was always having intercourse with uninitiated girls. As a punishment for forbidden cohabitation his penis broke off, he died, and two stones arose to mark the spot. These stones are so full of evil magic that only old men dare go near the place. Every now and again a very old man will go near and throw stones and bushes in order to keep the evil magic down.[1]

These two Central Australian variants of the stone-heap contain interesting confirmation of our views as to the relative position of the usual Alcheringa myth and the Indonesian Punishment Tales. In Australia the ancestor who has been committing symbolic incest is rewarded by subsequent apotheosis, in Indonesia he is stoned.

In the cases mentioned above he is evidently punished: the inimical attitude of the Horde towards the Leader breaks through just as in Indonesia (his sin is an aggravated form of totem-eating or prohibited sexual intercourse). Yet these evil-doers are Alcheringa ancestors like all others and they participate in the usual form of apotheosis, a stone arising to mark the spot of their death.

Another important phase in the evolution of the rite is the idea of retribution. The first crime of humanity survives under the guise of a legal execution of criminals,[2] and the murderer who is stoned after his death suffers his punishment as the representative of a host of primeval parricides. It is this which explains why the ritual should be applied to localities where anything which revolts the feeling of propriety and especially illicit love has taken place; for was not illicit love the very object of "man's first disobedience"? We have come to similar conclusions in connexion with the ritual of pelting the priest who sacrificed the calf which represented Dionysos with stones, and the myth which explained the origin of cairns in Greek antiquity seems to have belonged to the same category.

The word for cairn is ἕρμα, and everybody who passes by must throw stones at these milestones. Hermes is "he who dwells in the stone heap," the genius of these milestones.[3]

Hermes, "of the stone heap."

Hermes was tried by the gods for the murder of Argos; all the gods flung stones at him as a means of freeing themselves from the pollution contracted by bloodshed; the stones thus thrown made a great heap and the custom of rearing such heaps at the wayside images of Hermes continued ever afterwards.[4] Perhaps we have got a parallel to this myth in the story of Kaineus, who sinks into the earth under a heap of stones and pine trees

[1] Spencer and Gillen, *Nor. T.*, 472.

[2] R. Hirzel, "Die Strafe der Steinigung," *Abh. d. sachs Ges. s. Wiss*, XXVIII. 228

[3] Nilsson, *Griechische Feste von religiöser Bedeutung*, 1906, 389.

[4] Frazer, *Scapegoat*, 24.

hurled at him by his foes the Kentaurs. For this Kaineus is the son of a certain Elatos, "he of the pine tree," and he is buried beneath pine trees.[1] Now Hermes is the son of Zeus, who is sent by his father to kill the many-eyed Argos and rid his beloved Io of her unwelcome custody, and who fulfils the command of his divine father by hurling a stone at the watchful monster. It seems that the gods are this time at least unjust, for although they are throwing stones at a murderer who killed his victim with the same missile, are they not punishing at the same time a dutiful son? Now, we are not so sure of this. For, like all the goddesses prosecuted by the wrath of Hera, Io seems but to be a younger edition of the queen of gods. They both appear as cows and Zeus has intercourse with Io in the shape of a bull. If Io is the same person as Hera we begin to feel suspicious about the identity of Argos. His many eyes were interpreted in antiquity as the many orbs of a star-spangled heaven, which makes him look like a cruder form of the Heaven god Zeus. Moreover, there are two disconnected items of this mythic cycle which gain in importance when joined together. Zeus is introduced to the scene of his amours with Io as a bull, and Argos is reported to have killed a giant bull which devastated the country and to have worn a bull's hide ever afterwards.[2] A man in a bull's hide is a bull, the fit guardian of the cow Io, and to all appearances identical with the bull whom he has killed, with Zeus. Thus we come back to a prehistoric form of the myth in which the bull Argos-Zeus was murdered by a stone which his son Hermes hurled at him. After this great achievement Hermes took possession of Io, who was first a woman, and when the myth was taken up by pastoral society, a cow. Argos was guilty of the same sin as Hermes; he, too, had killed a bull, the representative of the Father-Imago. They suffered the same punishment, to be wounded to death by a stone or buried under a heap of stones. Greek myth mitigated the punishment of Hermes; he was pelted with stones and not killed, for was he not one of the immortals? But, as we have seen, that originally he is the dead man under the cairn, we must regard his immortality as a secondary development, perhaps as the ambivalent over-compensation of his death. As a dead man he is a leader of souls to the other-world and as the hero-god of a pastoral stage of society he affords fertility to the herds.

It is also worth while noticing that the archaic rite of stoning survives, especially in connexion with the equally ancient crime of parricide. Plato says that if any man had murdered his father or mother, brother, sister or child, he should be put to death and his body should be cast forth naked at a cross-roads outside the city.

[1] Eitrem, l.c., 287. Roscher's *Lexikon on Kaineus.*

[2] See the articles on Hermes, Io and Argos in Roscher's *Lexikon*, and Roscher, *Hermes der Windgott*, 1878.

There the magistrates as the representatives of the city should assemble, each carrying in his hand a stone, which he was to cast at the head of the corpse by way of purifying the city from the pollution contracted by the crime.[1] When the gods fling stones at Hermes they are said to free themselves from the pollution of bloodshed.[2] In doing so they seem to be avowing the very crime which they openly disclaim; the contagious character of the crime of parricide lies in the fact that it corresponds to the unconscious wishes of the whole town, of the whole community of gods. The stones hurled at the criminal prove this, for they are a mimetic repetition of the very crime for which he is condemned. "Stoning was the mode adopted of killing, first the animal and afterwards the plant totem, because by means of it the whole community could share jointly and equally the responsibility of killing the god." [3] The responsibility for killing the father was originally really shares in equal measure by the whole community of brothers, and the stones were used as they were the only weapons that were to be had in that stage of evolution. But by the time the totem or the god became substituted for the father the stones were transformed into mere symbols of the original sin of mankind.

Stoning the parricide.

We are now in a position to go a step further backwards in the history of the Intichiuma rites. The Alcheringa ancestor represents the Jealous Sire (or his rebellious son) who was buried under a pile of stones hurled at him, and a huge rock was finally rolled over his body. When the Arunta or the Gnamulla strikes the Nanja rock with the small stone, he is repeating this primeval scene, for the Nanja rock is the body of the ancestor. If this is the case, then what can the stone be with which he is struck? Naturally the original stone which dealt him his death blow.

We must risk the danger of wandering too far from our original subject and hazard a few remarks on the psychology of repression and the return of repressed elements in mourning customs. All mourning customs are, as has been pointed out by Freud, characterized by a strong but unconscious repressed feeling of guilt in having caused the death of the deceased by their own ill wishes. This is what leads to the transformation of the dead into a vengeful demon; if he thirsts for the blood of his surviving relatives it is because they must feel that he has good reason to do so.[4] This is why they are continually searching for the magician who caused the death by his malevolence; the great efforts which they make to project this concept into space, beyond the boundaries of the tribe, prove that they have great

Repression and its consequences in death rites.

[1] Frazer, *Scapegoat*, 24, 25. Plato, *Laws*, IX. 12. [2] Frazer, l.c., 24.
[3] F. B. Jevons, *An Introduction to the History of Religion*, 1911, 255.
[4] Freud, *T. & T.*, 107, 108.

difficulty in ridding the depths of their psychic constitution of it.[1] We would even go one step further and try to find the phylogenetic behind this more functional explanation of the guilty conscience of the savage. To primitive man every death is the result of a murder, because the first death which left an ineffacable conflict impressed on his " mneme " was actually and really a murder, the death of the father who was killed by his own sons. The dead man is an object of respect as a representative of the ancestor, but at the same time an object of fear for those who unconsciously know that they are not exempt from the common guilt of bloodshed. It is a general custom of primitive man to avoid mentioning the name of the dead,[2] and yet at the same time weeks are spent in wailing over him at his grave.[3] The former taboo is avowedly intended to avoid thinking of the dead, the latter equally openly aims at rescuing his memory from oblivion. In analytic psychology we are accustomed to speak of repression, by which we mean an effort of the censor to prevent unpleasant or dangerous complexes from rising into consciousness, whilst this function is often circumvented by what we call a return of repressed elements. The further back we go in the evolution of culture the more we shall find that our metaphoric expressions become crude realities; by rolling a stone or piling a heap on the corpse primitive man is attempting to repress or rather to press the dead man and death down in good earnest. His attempt is successful in the realm of realities, the corpse cannot rise and shake off the heavy boulder which weighs on his chest. But it is otherwise with the soul, which is mere fiction and hence more powerful than flesh and bone. It rises from the tomb of oblivion to which it is consigned by a guilty conscience and takes possession of the very object which was put there to keep it out of sight. The log or stone which is a means of defence against the ghost becomes a memorial column, the ghost

[1] G. Róheim, *Spiegelzauber*, 1919, 197.

[2] Frazer, *Taboo and the Peril of the Soul*, 1911, 349–75. Reference can be made for this well-known custom to J. D. Lang, W. W. Dobie Breton, G. Grey, etc.

[3] J. Fraser, *The Aborigines of New South Wales*, 1892, 79. " The loud wailing which is raised at a death is repeated every day for a whole moon." Howitt, *N. T.*, 451. " For weeks and months they bemoan their deaths, especially at even-time." Wilhelmi, op. cit., 40. Taplin, *The Narrinyeri*, 1878, 20. F. Bonney, *On some Customs of the Aboriginals of the River Darling*, XIII. 135. Howitt, op. cit., 451, 452, 459, 465, 466. K. L. Parker, *The Euahlayi Tribe*, 1905, 85, 87, 134. Spencer and Gillen, *N. T.*, 504, 509; *Nor. T.*, 515–17, 521, 522. Eylmann, op. cit., 242. A. J. Peggs, " Notes on the Aborigines of Roebuck Bay," *Folk-Lore*, 1903, 336–38. H. Basedow, " Anthropological Notes made on the South Australian Government North-West Prospecting Expedition," *Trans. R. S. S. A.*, 1904, XXVIII. 53. Clement, op. cit., 8. A. Oldfield, " The Aborigines of Australia," *Trans. Ethn. Soc.*, III. 245. Rudesindo Salvado, *Memorie storiche dell' Australia*, 1851, 299, 358, 361. (Deeds of dead are sung at grave.) W. E. Roth, " Burial and Disposal of the Dead," *Bulletin of North Queensland Ethnography*, IX. 371. (The mourners alternately sleep and cry over the grave.) Le Souëf, *Wild Life in Australia*, 238 (Fitzroy River, Queensland).

inhabits the rock or stone and exacts the homage of the survivors in its new temple and abode. As the process of identification proceeds further we see the first efforts to give a human aspect to the rock or stone and the return of repressed elements is complete when, instead of the frail body the sight of which they intended to avoid, we get a carved image of the ancestor.[1] The Melville Island grave posts, which apparently indicate a latter cultural wave from Indonesia,[2] represent crude attempts in imitating the human form.[3] In Nikunau the gods and goddesses were represented by sandstone slabs or pillars, an erect pillar representing a god, one laid down on the ground standing for a goddess.[4] If the stone which was originally placed upon his body came to be identified with the ancestor[5] the cult of the stone phalli would develop through a return of repressed elements. The stone would not only be shaped in a human form, thereby indicating its identity with the dead man, but it would also be unconsciously identified with the male member, thereby showing the sexual origin of the conflict which lead to the death and subsequent apotheosis of the father-god. Prehistoric carved representations of animals, possibly of animals as embodiments of ancestors, have been found in New Guinea of a markedly phallic character, and probably connected with these was a stone slab showing the spiral incised ornamentation which is so characteristic of the Churinga.[6]

Phallic gravestones.

The worship of phallic stones is associated with that of a natural grotto in the Ladrone Islands,[7] an exact counterpart to the Churinga in the Ertnatulunga. Other cases show more clearly that the phallus is the phallus of the dead father. In the Leti, Moa, Lakor, and Babar groups the sun-god and ancestor Upulero is represented by an image which consists of a head placed upon a wooden post. This seems to indicate the memory of a time when the skull of the murdered father was worshipped; and beneath the image we find the wooden representation of a phallus. The grave of Kikilai, the hero-god of Keisar, shows an image sitting at the foot of a post and on either side of the image is a wooden phallus. In Sumba human figures, male and female, with huge genitalia are carved upon the

[1] Cf. R. Thurnwald, *Forschungen auf den Salamo-Inseln*, 1912, I. 190.

[2] F. Gräbner, "Kulturgeschichte der Melville Insel," *Ethnologica*, 1913, II. 12.

[3] B. Spencer, *N. T. N. T. A.*, 1914, 231.

[4] Turner, *Samoa*, 296.

[5] Cf. the stone images representing ancestors in the Ingiet secret society; they are probably connected with totemism, as has been shown by Rivers, *H. M. S.*, II. 517. Stones are erected to ancestors and to "God."—Kenneth R. Dundas, "The Wawanga," *J. A. I.*, 1913, 31.

[6] R. Etheridge, "Ancient Stone Implements from the Yodda Valley Goldfield, North-East British New Guinea," *Records of the Australian Museum*, VII. 26, 27. Cf. Spencer and Gillen, *N. T.*, 633. Id., *Nor. T.*, 698.

[7] W. W. Gill, *Myths and Songs from the South Pacific*, 1875, 33.

10. INITIATION CEREMONIES

I. Finger-Joints Mutilated.

3, 5, 10, 111, 155, 156, 157, 159, 163, 192, 206, 207, 223, 229 (Stokes: *Discoveries*, 1846, 92, p. 437), 292, 308, 315, 318, 319, 320, 327, 333, 336, 359, 360 (p. 443). R. Pöch: *St. an Ein. v.N.-S. u. an aust. Schädeln*, 1915, 34. P. Etheridge: "Notes made at Copmanhurst, Clarence R.," *Records of the Aust. Mus.*, V, 272.

II. Avulsion of Teeth.

(*a*) Initiation rite.

76 (H. 655), 97 (H. 613), 110 (H. 565), 111 (H. 515, 517), 112 (H. 563), 113, 119, 120, 121, 122, 123, 124, 125, 126, 127, 128 (H. 577), 131 (R. W. Holden: *The Maroura Tribe* in Taplin: *F.L.*, etc., 27), 132 (H. 675), 135 (C. II, 198), 137 (H. 589), 139 (*J.A.I.*, VII, 252), 150 (Parker, 74), 153 (H. 595), 154 (H. 590), 156 (H. 578), 159 (Mathew: *Two Tribes*, 108), 194 (C. II, 342), 195 (C. II, 332), 199, 200, 203, 204, 205, 208, 211 (Roth: *Decoration, Deformation and Clothing Bull.*, XV, 30–32), 216 (C.) II, 332), 229 (Stokes: *Discoveries in Australia*, 1846, 92), 268 (C. I, 377), 275 (C. II, 37), 285, 286, 287 (C. III, 379), 288 (C. II, 396), 290 (C. II, 403), 292 C. II, 425), 296 (C. II, 465), 297 (C. II, 475), 315, 318, 321 (H. 563), 322 (C. II, 18), 327 (G. B. Barton: *History of N.S.W.*, 1889, I, 284, H. 567), 331 (H. 571), 350 (H. 576), 351 (Stokes: l.c., 89, 92), 364 (C. II, 159).

(*b*) Unconnected with initiation.

31, 32, 35 (Sp. II, 596), 41, 43 (Sp. II, 594), 47 (Sp. II, 592), 48 (Sp. I, 453), 51, 52 (Sp. I, 259, 450), 53, 54 (Roth: *Bull.*, XV, 30–32), 196 (Roth: *E.S.*, 111), 197, 210, 213, 279, 284 (Roth: *Bull.*, XV, 30–32), 285, 286, 287 (C. II, 378), 379, 380 (Roth: *Bull.*, XV, 30–32).

III. Circumcision (without Subincision).

7, 9, 10, 11, 21, 28 (Sp. III, 90, 91), 87 (H. 671), 140, 141, 142 (H. 675), 237 (Brown: *J.A.I.*, 1913, 167), 275 (C. II, 38), 258, 269 (C. I, 306), 284 (C. II, 371), 319 (Sp. III, 90, 91), 351 (*F.L.*, XIV, 345), 385 (R. H. Mathews: "Notes on the Aborigines of the Northern Territory," *Proc. and Trans. of the Royal Geog. Soc.*, XXII, 16), 387 (Oldfield: 252).

IV. Subincision.

22, 23, 24, 25, 26, 27, 29, 31, 32, 34, 35, 36, 37, 38 (Sp. III, 90, 91, Sp. II, 364, 369), 42, 43, 46, 47, 49 (Sp. II, 348), 45 (Sp. III, 90, 91), 48, 50 (Sp. II, 337, 347), 51, 52, 56 (Sp. I, 251, Strehlow, IV), 53 (Roth: *Ethnological Studies*, 177), 54 (Roth: *E.S.*, 170–77), 75 (Sp. II, 335), 76 (H. 662), 77 (Sp. II, 333), 85 (H. 669), 196, 197 (Roth: *E.S.*, 177–79), 215, 217, 219, 220, 221, 222 (Roth: *E.S.*, 177–79), 223, 224 (Roth: *E.S.*, 170–77), 268 (C. I, 277), 272 (H. 664), 273 (H. 667), 276, 277, 281 (Roth: *E.S.*, 177–79): 280 (Roth: *E.S.*, 170–77), 281 (C. II, 346), 282 (C. II, 361), 283 (H. 667, C. II, 366), 322 (C. II, 18), 353, 354 (Sp. III, 90, 91), 357 (Roth: *E.S.*, 177), 364 (C. II, 159), 365 (Roth: *E.S.*, 168), 382 (C. II, 35), 386 (R. H. Mathews: l.c., XXII, 7).

V. Scarification.

1, 2 (Sp. III, 43), 3 (Sp. III, 154), 76 (H. 658), 75, 77 (Sp. II, 335), 85 (H. 670), 100, 102, 106, 107, 110, 114, 115, 116, 117 (Mathews: *E.N.*, 119), 198 (Roth: *Initiation*, 177), 253 (C. I, 303), 259 (Oldfield: 252), 261 (C. I, 338), 272 (H. 666), 358 (R. H. Mathews: *Mitt. d. anthr. Ges. in Wien*, 1908, XXXVIII, 19).

VI. Ligatures.

94, 95 (H. 615), 96 (H. 614), 100, 102, 106, 107, 110, 114, 115, 116, 117 (Mathews: *E.N.*, 108), 231 (C. I, 291), 232 (Brown: *J.R.A.I.*, 1913, 167), 235 (Brown: ibid., 174).

VII. Perforation of the Septum.

18 (Sp. III, 330), 47, 48 (Sp. II, 615), 50, 51, 52 (Sp. I, 459), 100, 108, 111, 156, 157 (H. 626, 740, 741; Fison and Howitt: 191), 200 (Roth: *Initiation*, 177), 199, 200, 202, 203, 204, 205, 209, 211 (Roth: "Decoration," *Bull.*, XV, 29), 256 (C. I, 306), 257 (C. I, 307), 259 (Oldfield: 252), 261 (C. I, 338), 303, 304 (C. III. 73, 79), 315 (*Austr. Anthr. Journ.*, 1896, 180), 331 (H. 740, 741).

VIII. Depilation and Red-Ochre Paint.

1, 2 (Sp. III, 108), 88, 89 (H. 673, 674, Moriarty: in Taplin, *F.L.*, 53; Angas: *Savage Life*, I, 58), 90, 91 (Mathews: *E.N.*, 130), 92, 93, 94, 95 (H. 615), 94, 95, 96 (Mathews: *E.N.*, 130), 97 (H. 613), 98, 99, 100, 101, 102, 103, 105, 106, 107, 110, 114, 115, 116, 117 (Mathews: *E.N.*, 130), 131 (H. 675, Holden in Taplin: *F.L.*, 27), 159, 160 (H. 610, Mathew: *Two Tribes*, 101), 314 (C. III, 273), 328 (Mathews: *E.N.*, 130).

IX. Ceremonial Combat.

76 (H. 656), 88 (H. 673), 156 (H. 580), 157 (H. 598), 163 (H. 605), 200 (Roth: *Initiation,* 177), 202 (Roth: *Initiation,* 177), 337 (Roth: *Initiation,* 185).

X. Head-Biting.

1 (Sp. III, 99), 50 (Sp. II, 341), 52 (Sp. I, 251), 56 (Strehlow: IV, 58).

XI. Absence of Mutilations.

1, 2, 3, 4, 6, 8, 12, 15, 16, 17, 18, 19, 20 (Sp. II, 92), 200, 202, 204 205 (Roth: *Initiation,* 169–83), 253 (C. I, 303), 256 (C. I, 306) 257, 259, 261 (C. I, 302–38), 264 (C. I, 386), 337 (Roth: *Initiation* 187).

XII. Absence of Bull-Roarer, Use of Bamboo Trumpets.

1, 2, 4, 8, 17, 18, 19 (Sp. III, 92).

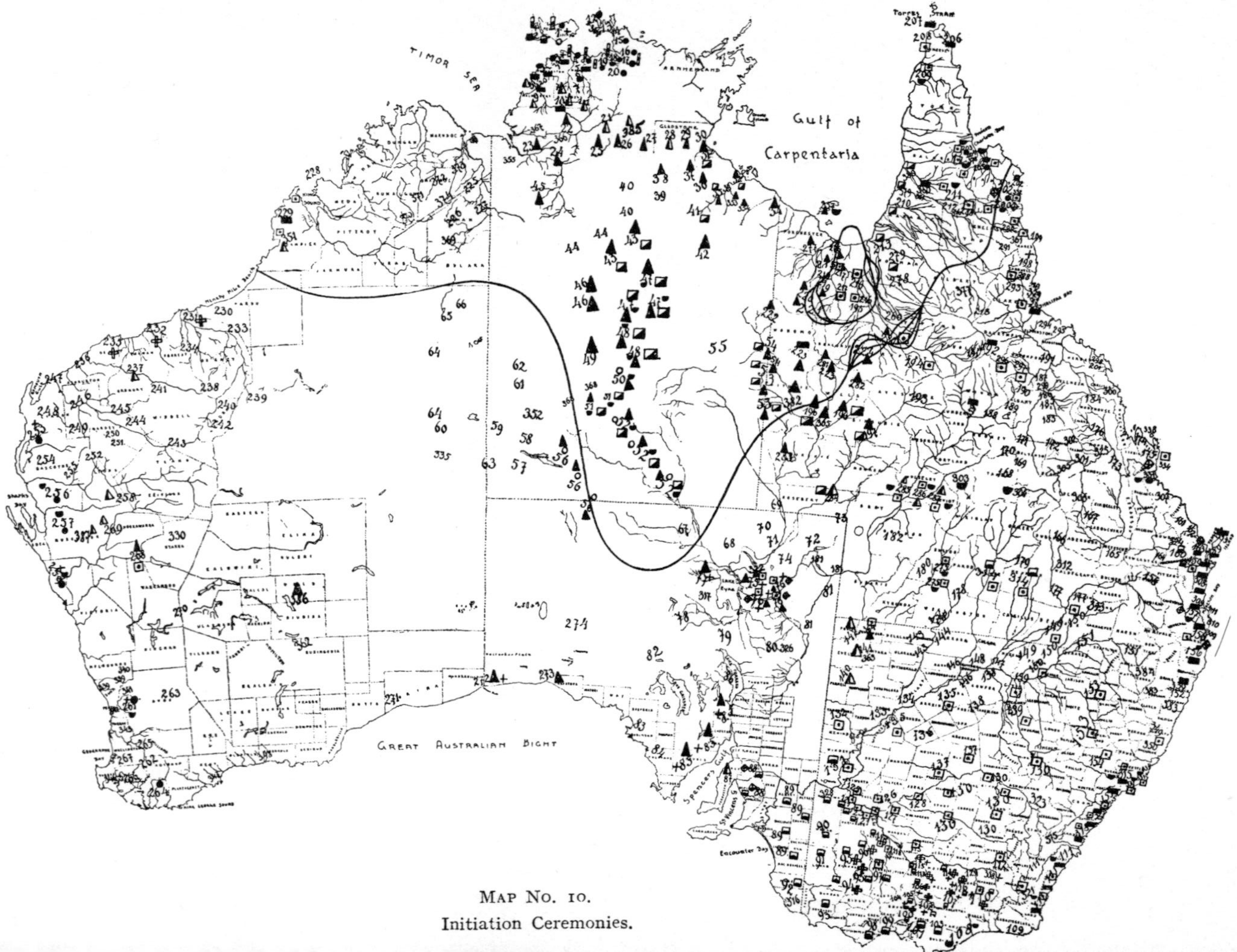

Map No. 10.
Initiation Ceremonies.

menhirs at the head and foot of the dolmen graves.[1] In many cases these phallic images are not purely ornamental; they are thought to import fertility to the country, the cattle and especially the women. We may say that the worship of phallic gravestones is a reaction-formation against the wish to castrate the Jealous Sire who selfishly keeps all the women for himself. When the survivors and murderers begin to worship his virile member which their phantasy projects into the pillar or boulder raised above his grave, they are bowing their heads before their worst antagonist, and when they form the idea that the women of the horde are made pregnant by the dead father they are probably giving way to the Oedipus wishes of the women and at the same time rendering the very thing for which they raised their rebellion to their dead father. The battle was waged for the women, and by supposing that it is the ancestor who gives them plenty of children, food-animals and plants they are fully acknowledging the claims of the dead man against whom they waged war whilst he was alive. The custom of women resorting to the graves to get pregnant, the idea that pregnancy is afforded by certain rocks or stones as well as the use of stones to fertilize the gardens or procure an abundance of animals, are all branches of the same stem.

Rocks and small stones.

We may conveniently distinguish between the worship of the large boulder which is regarded as the equivalent of the tombstone or cairn and that of small stones which is derived from the weapons used in the primeval strife. Now we remember that the conscious meaning of throwing small sticks and stones at the boulders is to make the unborn spirits of the totem animal emanate from them. We find the rite of throwing objects at graves or deities both with the intention of obtaining and with that of preventing the birth of a child. The latter is the case amongst the Baganda.[2]

People in the earlier times were, like the Arunta, uncertain as to the real cause of pregnancy and thought it was possible to conceive without any intercourse with the male sex. Hence, when they passed a place where either a suicide had been burnt or a child born in the wrong way had been buried, they were careful to throw grass or sticks on such a spot, for by doing so they could prevent the ghost of the dead from entering into them and being reborn.[3] On the

[1] Perry, *Megalithic Culture*, 108. On phallic gravestones in Palestine, see, for instance, P. Thomsen, *Palästina und seine Kultur in fünf Jahrtausenden*, 1909.

[2] Roscoe, *The Baganda*, 1911, 46, 47.

[3] Young married couples pay visits to the graves of the ancestors begging them to give them children.—L. Frobenius, *Und Afrika Sprach*, 1913, III. 129, 172. The Dravidian races of India worship Dulha Deo, the bridegroom godling, at marriage. He is said to have been an unfortunate bridegroom who was turned to stone for breaking a taboo.—W. Crooke, *The Popular Religion and Folk-Lore of Northern India*, 1896, I. 119-122. An Anglo-Saxon custom directed women who had miscarried to go to the barrow of a deceased man and step thrice over it.—

other hand, in Japan women who desire children will go to a sacred stone on the Holy Hill of Nikko and throw pebbles at it. If they succeed in hitting it their wish is granted. Women were also in the habit of flinging stones at the knees (phallic symbol) of a seated statue of Buddha for the same purpose.[1] Throwing stones at a god is symbolic of procreation because stoning the nearly superhuman leader of the horde was the unavoidable preliminary for procreation on the part of the young males and hence the magical power of the smaller stones which are the weapons of the first rebellion. On the other hand, there is a whole class of beliefs that identify a man with the weapon which has dealt him the mortal wound,[2] and in certain cases the soul of the murdered man is supposed to incarnate himself in the murderer or in the weapon which dealt the death-blow.[3] This would explain how the ancestral ghost becomes associated with small stones and how the fecundating power of the father continues to emanate from these symbols.

The stone age and the age of wood and bone.

It can hardly be ascertained with any degree of certainty how man came to the phase of culture usually known as the stone age; for it is certain that the use, especially the dominant use, of stone in culture must have been preceded by another age which we can fitly call the age of wood and bone. Von den Steinen describes what relatively small part stone implements play in the life of the Bakairi as compared with wood and bone.[4] " In tropical regions at least, wood, bamboo, bone and shell can provide all that is needful for the hunter, and the use of stone by the pygmy (of New Guinea) is practically confined to the application, for certain purposes, of hammer-stones and of flakes and splinters such as may be obtained with a minimum of labour and skill. They do not make, and probably they never made, the stone axe-heads, knives and arrow-heads which are characteristic of many advanced Stone-Age peoples ancient and modern, and they do not even get so far as to chip stone into implements comparable with those of the men of the European Paleolithic Age. The pygmies

E. S. Hartland, *The Legend of Perseus*, 1894, I. 165, quoting O. Cockayne, *Leechdoms, Wortcunning and Starcraft of Early England*, 1864–66, III. 66. On the symbolic meaning of stepping over, see G. Róheim, " Die Bedeutung des Ueberschreitens," *I. Z. Pa.*, VI. 1920, 242. J. G. Frazer, *Adonis, Attis, Osiris*, 1907, 70; " Sons of God," 73; " Reincarnation of the Dead," 81; " Sacred Stocks and Stones among the Semites." Id., " Women fertilized by stones," *F.-L.*, XXIX. 254. At Carnac the young girls who wanted a husband undressed completely and went and rubbed their navels against a menhir specially devoted to this usage. In Eure et Loir they turned up their skirts, and in the evening rubbed their stomachs against a projection of the Pierre de Chantecoq, which was also called Mère aux Cailles. P. Sebillot, " The worship of stones in France," *American Anthropologist*, IV. 1902, 82.

[1] Hartland, *The Legend of Perseus*, 1895, II. 197.

[2] J. G. Frazer, *The Magic Art*, 1911, I. 201–4.

[3] R. Salvado, op. cit., 1851, 299. A. Oldfield, " On the Aborigines of Australia," *Trans. Ethn. Soc.*, 1865, III. 240.

[4] K. Von den Steinen, *Unter den Naturvölkern Zentralbrasiliens*, 1897, 196.

are in an 'age' of wood, bone and shell, and if some of them, such as the Andamanese, make use of iron, it is only a borrowed material, foreign to their own culture." [1]

Ceremonial use of stone contributed a large share to evolution of stone ages. Originated in various centres independently and spread from these in prehistoric migrations.

Now it is very probable that the increased use of stones, which was perhaps first of a more ceremonial nature, was developed independently by mankind in various centres, and from these centres it must have spread over large connected areas, probably whole continents. For Oceania this centre from which the stone-using immigrants started on their migrations must have been Indonesia and at a remoter period the south-eastern parts of the Asiatic Continent. From Indonesia these migrations extended to Melanesia and Polynesia on the one hand and to New Guinea and Australia on the other.

We do not think that there was only one wave of migration of stone culture, and we should be cautious in ascribing the whole influence of stone culture to the people who must be regarded as the builders of megalithic monuments. These may represent a relatively ancient or a relatively modern stratum of the stone-using race; further research will perhaps be in a position to settle that question. We rather intend to indulge in a little speculation as to the origin of stone culture, meaning by origin not the area in which it first developed, but the psychical reasons for its development. It is fairly certain that in the Central Australian tribes we have the representatives of one of the most primitive of these stone-using migrations.

The Central Australians represent man as he must have been at the beginning of the Stone Age.

It would not make much difference in this respect even if we could prove the "disappearance of useful arts" [2] for the wandering ancestors of the present natives; we should then say that their protracted migrations and unfavourable surroundings had thrown them back to a stage of development which they had once held but which may have been a little surpassed by their ancestors. On the other hand, it is far more probable that in their isolation they have conserved in a relatively unchanged form the state of things which once existed amongst the ancestors of the stone-using Indonesian tribes. The latter have cultivation of the soil, terraced irrigation and other signs of a relatively high culture, their environment has been much more favourable, and more important still, they have been in contact with

[1] C. G. Rawling, *The Land of the New Guinea Pygmies*, 1913, 273, 274. Cf., "In other words, the rudimentary stage of culture through which these tribes have passed, and in some cases are still passing, may be more accurately described as a wood and bone age, than as an age of stone."

[2] W. H. R. Rivers, "The Disappearance of Useful Arts," *Festkrift tillegnad Edward Westermarck*, 1912, 109.

India and China at a period when the ancestors of the Central Australians were already cut off from the rest of mankind on the parched deserts of their present home.[1] Therefore the use of stone amongst them in all probability presents features which explain the use of stone in general. We may with a certain amount of exaggeration speak of a ceremonial stone culture in Central Australia, for the ceremonial importance of stone is extremely prominent.

We have found reasons to reduce this ceremonial aspect to what has usually been called in ethnology the cult of the dead, but what in taking account of the results obtained by psycho-analysis in penetrating to the lowest depths of the Unconscious should be called the cult of the murdered father, or the reaction-formation against the Oedipus complex. It seems probable that the semi-human ancestors (we are near to the home of the *Pithecanthropus erectus* Dubois) both of the Central Australians and the Indonesians had the type of organization which has been called the Cyclopean family. The young males would unite in a band against the strongest of old males who lorded it over the women at the commencement of every rutting season. They would probably make use of stone missiles in the fight, thereby gaining all they could from superior number and risking as little as possible from inferior force. The Old Male who had continually been committing incest would be buried under a heap of stones with perhaps an additional larger stone on the top. The record of these events would be preserved in the tales of the petrification in Indonesia as well as in the Central Australian traditions which regularly relate how a heap of stones arose to mark the spot where the ancestor sunk into the earth. Long before these representatives of the Stone Age (if we may already call them such at this period) started on their migrations, a reaction formation must have set in, and the purely aggressive attitude towards the Sultan of the Horde must have been superseded by veneration. The cairn was the dwelling of the ancestor or the ancestor himself, at any rate an object of worship. When they were compelled to leave their original homes, compelled by more powerful invaders or by a natural catastrophe, they probably carried stones from these cairns along with them, with the idea and feeling that the fate of the individual and of the whole community was closely bound to these stones as the connecting links between them and their ancestors. The stone which originally was perhaps regarded as a magical weapon, for in the hand of the Titans of the Horde it had sufficient "mana" to subdue God-Father himself, was now identified with the ancestor and regarded as his second self.

The real mechanism of procreation was repressed—relegated to

[1] W. Schmidt, "Soziologische und religiös-ethische Gruppierung der Australier," *Z. E.*, 1909, 349, is inclined to derive the Intichiuma ceremonies from agriculture, which, to me at least, seems to be a direct reversal of the real lines of evolution.

the unconscious—because coitus in general was equated with incest against which repression as such was originally directed. But the theories which were resorted to in explanation of the origin of children contained a huge return of just these repressed elements. The tribe had taken the women from the exclusive possession of the Old Male in reality, his ghost now came to haunt them and vindicate his rights; he possessed them all; he alone was reborn from them all in fiction. It was his sperma (the pre-existing spirit-children) which filled rock and stone (his dead body), the stone Churinga penetrated into women and reappeared there as an embryo.

Similar motives must have been at the background of the other great stone-using migrations. All through Oceania stone circles and monuments are associated with burial, human sacrifice and cannibalism, which is very natural if they originated in the murder and burial of the Paternal Tyrant whose flesh was devoured in the first act of communion by his successors.[1] When a wave of these people left their original home, it would either continue to develop the tombstone idea, which had become its principal seat of worship in its original home (megalith), or it would regard the natural rocks of its new environment as the transformed bodies of superhuman ancestors (Central Australia). It might of course do both, and it is probable that the primitive forms of cairns and the stone on the grave were added to the earth-mound of the people whom they found in possession by the same immigrants who brought the cult of stone, or rather of petrified ancestors, with them into Australia. Wherever the descendants of those hordes went who had started by the aid of natural stones on the path of civilization, from the prehuman savagery of the Oedipus complex, stone must have played a prominent part in their psychic life. After grinding them or knocking them against large ones in ritual (see the Intichiuma ceremonies), they would gradually acquire the art of moulding them into new shapes for practical purposes.

Ritual origin of stone-work.

But we are forgetting an important aspect of these rites. Death is generally unconsciously regarded by mankind as a return into the mother's womb. This is the origin of the other-world and the cave or pit in the earth into which the dead man, or his substitute the Churinga, is placed; it is as we have shown above, a symbol of the matrix. The Churinga in the Ertnatulunga is the penis (embryo) in the womb, and by

The grave as a symbol of the uterus.

[1] Speiser, *Südsee, Urwald, Kannibalen*, 1913, 71, 207. (Head of ancestor buried under stone, skulls placed on stone.) C. G. Seligmann, *The Melanesians of British New Guinea*, 1912, 464–66, 556. B. Thomson, *The Fijians*, 1908, 146. T. Macmillan Brown, *Maori and Polynesian*, 1907, 5, 118, 258. T. B. Stair, *Old Samoa*, 1897, 228. W. W. Gill, *Myths and Songs from the South Pacific*, 1876, 305. W. Ellis, *Polynesian Researches*, 1830, II. 191. Scoresby Routledge, "The Bird Cult of Easter Island," *Folk-Lore*, 1916, 337. W. H. R. Rivers, *H. M. S.*, II. 427.

extending the range of comparison beyond the limits of Australia we have only added some results of historical importance to this psychical (unconscious) equation. The womb in which the penis lies is originally a grave and the stone penis is the member or rather the whole person of a dead man. It is again repression which explains the necessity of projecting the womb into environment; the cave is regarded as the entrance of the uterus because the incestuous desires regarding the maternal uterus must be repressed.

The Siara call the ghosts of those who have died by violence fiu; they all wander to Tanga, where they dwell in two huge rocks called maleu. The souls of unborn children whose mothers died in childbirth transform themselves into spirits who are continually craving for sexual intercourse with human beings and especially haunt those who have had connexion with members of the same totem. They dwell in stones and in caves in the rocks.[1] The sexual appetite of these unlucky spirits must be regarded as a yearning for the mother they have lost, and if these spirits attempt to cohabit with human maidens they are seeking substitutes for their mother. Thus we may say that they are symbolic of the incest-libido and this is why it is especially those who have broken through the taboo of totemic exogamy who succumb to their temptations.

That the cave and the rock as dwelling-places of unborn infants arise out of a repression of incest phantasies and the necessity of a substitute for the mother's womb, is made fairly evident by these beliefs.

Now, in Central Australia children as well as totem-animals regularly emanate from the Nanja rock, and we shall show that this represents an earlier phase of belief which is only present in mythical survivals amongst the people who live to the north and west of Australia, and who, as we are trying to show, were originally in a culture contact of some sort with the ancestors of the Central Australians.

Stone in anthropogonic myth.

The Western Arunta say that the first couple originated out of two stones which were thrown down from the sky by the spirit Arbmaburinga or Altierry. They think this heavenly creator is a great strong old man who lives at a place called Jirilla far away to the north.[2] Here again we may take association between sky beings, the north, and stone culture as a starting-point for further investigation, only that this time the stone has a special function in myth as the material from which mankind originates. A stone falling from heaven also occurs on the Western Islands of Torres Straits. The Mabuiag people were camping in Pulu. Boys and girls were fond of continually twirling round the beach with extended arms, a game which was

[1] Parkinson, *Dreissig Jahre in der Südsee*, 1907, 308, 309.
[2] Eylmann, l.c., 184.

prohibited by their parents. A great stone fell from heaven and crushed every man, woman and child in the island excepting two sweethearts who fled to Mabuaig, and by biting a piece of the kowai tree that grew there stopped the stone.[1] The pair of lovers became the progenitors of the present population.[2]

A second variant presents an additional detail of importance. Here it is not the original couple rescued from the stone that appear as the progenitors of mankind but the woman has twins who marry each other, and the sister again has twins who are again husband and wife, and this goes on for generations till there are plenty of people.[3] These traditions evidently relate to both the extermination and the multiplication of mankind.

The conflict which lies behind this ambivalent attitude has its root in the disobedience of the younger generation to a taboo imposed upon them by the parents. Instead of originating out of stone they are all crushed by a stone, and yet the myth continues to relate the origin of mankind from a surviving pair who correspond to the stone-born pair of the Arunta. This can only be understood with reference to our views on the development of the cairn and the Nanja rock. The Nanja rock from which men are born represents the body of an ancestor who has been stoned and identified with the stones which cover his corpse. Our myth deals with the same motive in the shape of retaliation; to be crushed under stones is the punishment with which parents threaten their disobedient children. In the original setting it was the children who stoned the parent who stood in their way, after which they commenced to multiply mankind. The incest which follows ought to be found at the beginning of the myth as the reason both of the conflict between parents and children and of the repression which leads to the substitution of a stone for the mother's womb.

Another reversal of these myths is recorded from the Torres Straits. A Virgin of Sumaiut gave birth to a stone which was reverenced as a god. The Moon was regarded as the father of this stone.[4] We shall find that the connexion between incest and stone origin is such a frequent feature of myth in Indonesia and Oceania that the cases in which it is absent may with full right be attributed to a repression of the incest-complex. A man of Luang

[1] In a Mindanao tradition magic lines are used to put a stop to the petrifaction. —Beyer, "Origin Myths among the Mountain Peoples of the Philippines." *Journal of Science*, 1913, VIII. 97. Perry, 124.

[2] Haddon, *Cambridge Expedition*, V. 22.

[3] Id., ibid., V. 22.

[4] Cf. id., V. 23. The Tsalisen in Formosa say that their ancestors came from the moon. There is a spherical stone in the house of the chief which represents the moon.—J. W. Davidson, *The Island of Formosa*, 1903, 574. Perry, op. cit., 78. According to the Proserpine River natives the moon made the first man and woman—the former out of the stone used for making tomahawks, the latter out of the box tree.—W. E. Roth, *S. M. M.*, 1903, 16. Stones representing sun and moon have been observed at Mau (near Efate) and Anaiteum.—Rivers, op. cit., II. 426.

Sermata fished up a stone in his net, and at the end of nine months the stone burst and out came a boy. He married the man's daughter, his foster sister, and they were the ancestors of the Patumeral (red-stones) clan.[1]

The Tontemboan of Minahassa say that a rock stuck out of the sea in the east. The stone became heated by the sun and sweated, and out of this sweat Lumimut, the ancestress of the Tontemboan was born. Lumimut conceives from the west wind, and afterwards marries her son Toar. The Tontemboan are descended from this union.[2]

In the Toumpakewa version a youth is born of the foam and he finds a little girl crying in a heap of stones. The girl was sweated out of a stone to which her navel string was still attached. This was Lumimut who had been produced by the friction[3] (coitus) of two stones. The origin-myth of the Makassars relates how the Prince of Daha (in Java) urinated into a hollow stone. The urine is drunk up by a sow, who conceives. Incestuous marriages occur among the descendants of the sow.[4] In other variants it is the seminal fluid of Batara Guru[5] or of Smara Wrediman which drops on a stone.[6] In the Marshall Islands we find Lejman having intercourse with her son Edao, and from them descends the human race. Lejman means Rock Woman.[7]

Other myths record that the ancestral pair, whose marriage gave rise for instance to the Taiyal in Formosa, came out of the same rock —that is they were brother and sister.[8] The origin myth of the Lamgang from a cave or of the Chowte from a hole in the earth, which was covered by a stone belong to the same group.[9] The repression of the father, so evident in the Central Australian beliefs, indicates the presence of the Oedipus complex in the Unconscious. Quat, the ancestor of the people of Alo Sepere,[10] was born from a woman who was a stone without a father. Amongst his various exploits are his battles with the ogre Quasavara, whom he finally conquers. Quasavara's head knocked against the sky and he fell back upon the earth. There he lay upon his face and turned into stone. Sacrifices for valour are offered at that stone which is said

[1] Bastian, *Indonesien*, 1884, II. 62. Perry, 67.

[2] Schwartz u. Adriani, *Tontemboansche Teksten*, 1907, I. 406; II. 377, 379, 389–94, 744. N. Graafland, *De Minahassa*, 1898, I. 211, quoted by Schmidt, " Grundlinien der Vergleichung der Religionen und Mythologien der austronesischen Völker," *Denkschriften d. Kais. Ak. d. Wiss.*, 1910, LIII, 57–9. Cf. Perry, 77, 78. Wilken, *De Verspreide Geschriften*, 1912, III. 182.

[3] Perry, l.c., 77, 78.

[4] Van Eerde, " De Kalang legende op Lombok," *Tijdschrift*, XLV. 1902, 36–40.

[5] Id., ibid., 43–5.

[6] Id., ibid., 46–7.

[7] Schmidt, *Grundlinien*, 111. Erdland, *Marschall Insulaner*, 1914, 309, 310.

[8] Perry, l.c., 77. Other variants from Formosa (ibid., 78).

[9] J. Shakespeare, *The Lushei Kuki Clans*, 1912, 150, 151.

[10] Codrington, *The Melanesians*, 1891, 155.

to be Quasavara.[1] This Quat is one of the brothers Tagaro; in Leper's Island (Tagaro-mbiti), Tagaro the little is the spirit who corresponds to him, and all the stones that are accounted as sacred are connected with this Tagaro.[2]

Tangaloa leads us on to Polynesia. According to one variant of the Polynesian cosmogony all things originated from the intercourse of Tangaroa with his daughter Hine.[3] A Maori variant has Tangaroa as the father, Papa the Earth as the mother and their son Tane (man), who wishes to have intercourse with his mother. In his search for his mother he marries various women, quite evidently her mythical equivalents. One of these is the "Mountain-maid," born from the rusty water of the mountains.[4] Papa means not only earth but also rock in Tahiti, Te Papa-raharaha was the Mother of all things, the rock-foundation of all lands.[5]

Another link in the chain of evidence is the Samoan version. All things are created by the mere word of Taggaloa telling the rock to "open itself in fissure," so that as we may well say everything comes out of the womb of the rock.[6] It is possible that these traditions are connected with another group of Indonesian myths. These tell us how a hero (like Moses) struck a rock and made water flow out of it. It is perhaps not too bold to remind the reader that we interpreted the flood in which the petrified heroes of Central Australia perish as reversal of the waters at birth, and here we have water instead of a child coming out of the rock. Lumawig is the supreme being of the Bontoc Igorrot. In the early days the lower lands around Bontoc were covered with water. Lumawig saw Fa-tang'-a and his sister Fu'kan on Mount Porkis, north of Bontoc. Lumawig goes away to fetch fire for them as all fires are extinguished, but when he returns Fu'kan was heavy with child. Soon the child was born and the water subsided in Bontoc. Here the connexion between the birth of a child and the water is made quite evident. The fire episode looks suspicious; it seems that Lumawig is off for the fire of sexual desire and that his rival Fa-tang'-a only succeeds in having intercourse with Fu'kan in his absence. The myth goes on to tell us that Lumawig also married a girl called Fu'kan who is called a "namesake" of the mother of the Bontoc pueblo.[7] But a few lines below we hear that Fa-tang'-a was Lumawig's brother-in-law,

Water struck from a rock.

[1] Codrington, *The Melanesians*, 1891, 156–66. [2] Id., ibid., 170.

[3] Domeny de Rienzi, *Ozeanien*, 1839, II. 460. Waitz-Gerland, *Anthropologie der Naturvölker*, II. 1872, 264. He is symbolized by a hollow stone.—Turner, *Samoa*, 53.

[4] E. Shortland, *Maori Religion and Mythology*, 1882, 20.

[5] Tregear, *Maori Polynesian Comparative Dictionary*, 315.

[6] A. Bastian, *Die samoanische Schöpfungs Sage*, 1894, 30 (according to Pratt). Cf. J. B. Stair, *Old Samoa*, 1897, 213. Papa taoto, "reclining rock," then "sitting rock," etc.

[7] A. J. Jenks, *The Bontoc Igorot*, 1905, 201.

that is the brother of his wife Fu'kan.[1] Evidently we must suppose a less modified version in which Lumawig was either the father or the brother of Fa-tang'-a and both were rivals in their incestuous desire for Fu'kan. Fa-tang'-a keeps taunting Lumawig; he tells him that he cannot supply them with water. Lumawig thrusts his spear in the side of the mountain and as Fa-tang'-a turns to drink he is thrust into the mountain. Fa-tang'-a is turned into a rock, and the water passes through him to this day.[2] Dori is a Toradja mythical hero who struck a rock with his spear to make water flow out of it. He married not his sister but his cousin, and both were turned to stone and worshipped after their death.[3] To the variants of this theme which have been noted by Perry and Frazer [4] from Indonesia we may add one from Torres Straits, thus coming a step nearer to Central Australia.

One day when Kwoiam was thirsty he drove his spear into a rock and water rushed forth and has never ceased to flow.[5]

Central Australia and Indonesia rock-born children and nations originating from rocks.

In assuming a historical connexion between the ceremonial use of stone in Central Australia and the same phenomenon in Indonesia (as well as its offshoots in Melanesia and Polynesia), we have expressed no opinion as to the nature of that connexion. Dealing with the traditions of floods and petrified ancestors in both areas, we have attributed the seemingly primitive character of the Indonesian material (as compared to Central Australia), not to a primary but rather to a "tertiary" state of things. The secondary phase is found in Australia; we see repression at work, for petrification which originally must have represented an inimical attitude towards the hero (stoning) appears under the guise of apotheosis. In Indonesia we have a return of repressed elements which seems regularly to follow cultural advance; the hero is stoned to death for having committed incest (broken the totemic taboo). The stone-origin myths contain definite proof that this way of regarding the relative position of the two areas is correct. We cannot possibly imagine a people proceeding from the belief in the origin of ancestors from stone to the idea that this is still the case with all children, whilst if we suppose them to have overcome the belief that "all children are born from rocks," this will naturally survive in a myth which does not affirm this for the present day but declares that this was the state of things (= the belief) in the days of their ancestors.

Stone-origin myths have been recorded from other areas and have probably originated from the same motives in various centres.

[1] Jenks, *The Bentoc Igorot*, 1905, 202.

[2] Id., ibid., An Ifugao variant quoted by Perry (66, 67) conclusively shows that the man who turns the other into a rock (Lumawig) is the brother of his victim.

[3] Perry, l.c., 69.

[4] Frazer, *F. O. T.*, II. 463.

[5] Haddon, *Cambridge Expedition*, V. 82.

Water flows out of the rock from which Mithras is born—the same Mithras who, according to an Armenian version, commits incest with his mother.[1] There are many variants: the stone appears as the symbolic substitute for a woman; fully formed children (ratapa) are taken out of rocks.

Pouring blood on the stone.

According to the Kabyls the wild buffalo Itherther and the cow Thamuath, who both emerged from a dark place under the earth, were the first living beings. They have intercourse; a young bull and a cow are born. The young bull desires to cohabit with the mother and sister and drives the old buffalo out of the herd. The old buffalo rushes away to the rocky country near Häithar. One day he sees a stone with a depression in it. He thinks of the cow and fecundates the stone with his semen. It is from this stone that all the wild animals are born. The Kabyls still point out the stone and sacrifices are made to it for luck in hunting, since it is the mother of wild animals. Rock-drawings representing buffaloes and men are found among the rocks. In one of the rocks there is a cave which is much venerated by the Kabyls. Sacrifices are brought to the cave for rain and crops and by women for children.[2] It is needless to make any comments on this myth; it shows the connexion between the Oedipus complex, stone-origin myths and the beliefs concerning childbirth in an absolutely irrefutable way. Women who sacrifice for children at the cave are really having intercourse with the murdered Bull-Father, whilst the prayer for rain and crops is a parallel to the Intichiuma ritual.[3]

[1] Cf. R. Eisler, *Kuba-Kybele Philologus*, LXVIII. 135. (Cf. ibid., 123, petrifaction from illicit intercourse.) Id., *Weltenmantel u. Himmelszelt*, 1910, II. 411.

[2] L. Frobenius, *Volksmärchen der Kabylen*, 1921, I. 64–69.

[3] *Proof of the Indonesian Origin of Central Australians.*—This book was completely finished, typed and the last chapter delivered in the form of a lecture (October 1921) to the Hungarian Psycho-analytical Society, when Dr. Radó called my attention to a new publication by Dubois which seems destined to play a similar part in scientific speculations on the development of mankind as his previous finding—the Pithecanthropus erectus. In the Wadjak District of Java two human skeletons were found by van Rietschoten and Dubois which prove the existence in the Pleistocene of a human sub-race (called by Dubois Homo-wadjakensis) which must have resembled the present inhabitants of Australia in all their characteristic features. The only important difference seems to be that these Proto-Australians had a larger skull-capacity and a greater bulk than their present-day representatives, so that Dubois calls the Proto-Australians an "optimal" form of the race, which attained its highest development under the favourable conditions of food-supply found in Java and degenerated when compelled to migrate to the arid deserts of Central Australia. In the light afforded by Paläo-anthropology our comparison between Punishment Tales and Alcheringa traditions, as well as our "Indonesian" explanation of the Churinga, receives a striking confirmation. It is now definitely certain that Indonesia was inhabited by a Pre-Malayan, Proto-Australian population (E. Dubois, "The Proto-Australian Man of Wadjak, Java," *Proceedings R.A. of Amsterdam*, XXIII. No. 7) which was perhaps partly assimilated by the Mongolian immigrants and partly driven off in small hordes eastwards by these people, who had better weapons and a higher degree of organization. The megalith-builders probably only represented the last of a series of migrations, and we must either assume that the Proto-Australians adopted the elements of stone culture from these

The Long Pokun people who form a branch of the Kayan group place stones on separate posts outside the houses. As a rule these stones are simply rounded boulders which the natives believe have the power of increasing in size with age. Fowls' or pigs' blood is smeared on the stones on ceremonial occasions.[1] At Beloe in Timor there is a stone in the centre of the rice field which represents the "soul of the rice." Before sowing the rice a pig and a fowl are sacrificed on the stone. They strew rice on the stone or sacrifice an egg, and the blood smeared on it, as well as the egg and rice, is supposed to invigorate the soul-stuff of the rock.[2] In Burma the wild Bghai tribes hold certain stones in great reverence as possessing superhuman powers. Hogs and fowls are offered and the blood poured on the stone.[3] Anointing a stone with oil is probably a latter substitute for smearing it with blood. In the Kei Islands everybody keeps a black stone at the head of his sleeping-place, which he anoints before he goes out to war.[4] The Malagasies offer sacrifices especially at the headstones of tombs. These are rude undressed slabs of blue granite and basalt which are anointed with blood and the fat of the animal sacrifice. Other stones are anointed by women who wish to obtain children.[5] We know that the ritual of pouring blood over a stone which represents the body of an ancestor is a prominent feature of Intichiuma rites. We have also explained how the blood which flows from the veins of the totemites to the ancestor serves both as an expiation of the primeval sin of parricide,[6] and as a symbolical effusion of the seminal fluid by which human and animal life originates from the stone; this as an ambisexual symbol represents the vagina in these cases. In Central Australia we have the blood of a human being in Indonesia and elsewhere we have animal sacrifice. In Fiji the Nanga is a large stone alignment which is called the "bed" of the ancestors. The most impressive scene of the initiation ritual is when the boys have

immigrants (cf. W. Perry, *The Megalithic Culture of Indonesia*, 1918, 180), or, more probably, that they possessed a primitive and eolithic culture of their own, and in especial that they made use of unworked stones as projectile weapons. We should be inclined to suppose that certain elements of the "stone-culture-complex" do not properly belong to the immigrants at all, but must be assigned to this earlier population; whilst others may perhaps embody the impression made on them by the advance of another people with a higher (neolithic) form of stone culture. However this may be, it seems safe to continue the comparison of certain elements of the Intichiuma with Indonesian rites.

[1] A. C. Haddon, *Head Hunters*, 361. The round spherical stones are called Batu tuloi. They are perpetual possessions of a family; they grow gradually larger, and move spontaneously when danger threatens the house. When a household removes, these stones are carried ceremonially to the new site.—Hose and McDougall, *Pagan Tribes of Borneo*, 1912, II. 16.

[2] Kruijt, l.c., 209.

[3] Forbes, *British Burma and its People*, 1878, 295.

[4] J. G. Frazer, *F. O. T.*, II. 74. Riedel, l.c., 223.

[5] Frazer, l.c., II. 75.

[6] "De Acosta describes the practice when at a funeral human beings were sacrificed to the dead to be their slaves in the other world; the victims' blood was smeared on the corpse from ear to ear."—Hartland, *Legend of Perseus*, II. 241.

to crawl through a row of naked bodies of dead men smeared with blood and with protruding entrails. When they have got through this ordeal the "dead" men jump up and all run away to the sea; the blood and entrails were only those of the sacred pigs who are kept and fattened for this occasion.[1] The sacred character of these pigs makes them suspicious; they seem to be merely substitutes for the men who may have been killed in real earnest at an earlier phase in the evolution of the rite. The youths took the kingdom of heaven by violence, they were regarded as initiated, as men, when they had killed their venerable elders, feasted on their bodies and appropriated all the women.[2] The respect paid to the huge pigs in the precincts would then only be transferred to them from the elders; it is the elders who were first respected and then killed outright,[3] afterwards the pigs which were to be killed came to be regarded as sacrosanct before their time to die had arrived. Hose and McDougall tell us that there is reason to suppose that the custom of sacrificing pigs and fowls arose through the substitution of them for human beings in various rites. The people themselves admitted this of many rites in which pigs and fowls are now substituted, but they still mention cases in which there was a relapse into the original human sacrifice. Killing a human being was regarded as equivalent to killing a pig, only much finer.[4] The blood of pigs is sprinkled on men as well as on altar posts.[5] In Australia the blood of men is sprinkled on a rock altar which represents the body of an ancestor. The mechanism which differentiates these rites from each other and from their one primeval pattern is that of substitution in its varying aspects. Originally the blood of man had to flow before the male could get access to the female. Then this pouring of blood was repeated in a neurotic manner in the spirit of self-punishment; the mourners inflict deep wounds on their head, arms, etc., and the blood is due to the corpse. This is also the phase of development reached by the Intichiuma rites. An ancestor transformed into a rock, that is a corpse buried under a stone, is periodically reanimated by the blood of the survivors, but as the body lies in the grave like the penis (or embryo) in the mother's womb, this flowing blood is not merely a self-punishment but also a wish-fulfilment. They are repeating the very thing for which they intend to punish themselves, when their blood flows towards the womb (rock, grave) from which their ancestors emerged and to which they return; this is a repetition of the first revolt by having intercourse with the mothers of their

[1] B. Thomson, *The Fijians*, 1908, 152–55.

[2] The Nanga ends in a scene of general license, when all taboos on incestuous intercourse are disregarded.

[3] Cf. a Fijian king sacrificed by his son.—Williams, *Fiji and the Fijians*, 1858, I. 192.

[4] Hose and McDougall, *The Pagan Tribes of Borneo*, 1912, II. 105

[5] Id., ibid., 107.

fathers. It is from this intercourse that first the children of the tribe and then the animals of the totem are procreated. But here the complicated mechanism of projections and substitutions sets in.

The living men, as we know, do not fecundate the women of their own tribe; instead of this they multiply animals. By this fictive self-denial they are giving the very thing back to the ghost of the dead father for which they killed him when he was alive. It is now his turn to step in, as the men do not generate their own children (coitus has nothing to do with procreation); it is the ancestor who performs this office by entering the woman and being reborn through her. The ghost has thus got back all that the living antagonist lost. Like the Sultan of the Cyclopean Horde, the Alcheringa ancestor procreates all the young people of his clan quite alone and has access to all the women; for the real coitus is a matter of no importance—it does not count. Rebellion was victorious in reality but the old state of things triumphed in fiction. This covenant was only possible above the stone which covered the body of their dreaded foe; after having settled accounts in reality the victors had to settle accounts in their own conscience, and here the reaction-formation triumphed and they showed themselves magnanimous to the utmost degree.

This is the prototype of all blood covenants and has been transferred to the initiation ceremonies as well as to the rites of blood-brotherhood. By substituting the blood of a slaughtered domestic animal the people of Indonesia developed the new rite of smearing the blood of pigs on rocks; again the "human" element might crop up behind the rock and the blood of the animal might be sprinkled on a human being; the animal may be a vicarious sacrifice for a sick man,[1] killed at the ritual of blood-brotherhood[2] and so on. We are not concerned here with all the possible variations, but it is remarkable how our opinion that the incest complex lies at the root and is the reason for all these substitutions is confirmed by what we find in Indonesia.

A legend which explains the origin and introduction of Islam to Indonesia, but which is probably much earlier and can be referred to another movement of migrating peoples, explains the prohibition to eat pork by the fact that those who observed this prohibition descended from an incestuous union and that their ancestress was a sow.[3] The incestuous union of a brother and sister (survivors of a flood) from whom the Maram originated is permitted on the condition that none of their descendants should eat the flesh of the pig. The ancestress of this couple was a sow.[4] In a Toradja origin myth the sacrifice of a pig and a fowl is the atone-

[1] Hose and McDougall, II. 31. [2] Id., ibid., II. 66.

[3] J. C. van Eerde, "De Kalang-legende op Lombok," *Tijdschrift voor Indische Taal Land en Volkenkunde*, 1902, XLV. 42.

[4] Hodson, *The Naga Tribes of Manipur*, 1911, 13, 14.

ment demanded by the gods for incest;[1] at the Fijian Nanga the initiation of the boys (circumcision) ends in a general orgy at which not even the nearest relationship (brother and sister) is regarded as a bar to the general licence. The extent of licence is indicated by the expressive phrase of an old chief, "While it lasts we are just like pigs."[2] If a pig is killed instead of a man we must say that the man for whom he dies ought to have died in atonement for the general sin of the community in attempting or desiring to kill the father, and as this desire forms a component of the incest complex, the death of a pig is regarded as an atonement for the Oedipus complex just because it is a repetition thereof. The blood of the dead pig poured on the stone and fecundating the rice-field is the seminal fluid of the dying father whose incestuous intercourse with the stone grave as mother is regarded as the universal source of fertility.

Thus in extending the limits of comparison beyond Australia, and in attempting to indicate the probable direction of the migrations of the Paläo-Central Australians, we come to conclusions which confirm those arrived at by a purely psycho-analytical treatment of Central Australian traditions, whilst at the same time they lay additional stress on certain aspects of these questions. Rock, stone and cave played an important part in the burial ceremonies of these migrating tribes at a period when they had not yet adopted or developed their present method of platform, tree and earth burial. The Intichiuma ceremonies which to-day are performed at a mythical tomb were performed at a real one in the days before these tombs had to be left behind. In the course of these migrations the stones taken from the ancient cairns came to be identified with the ancestors, and they served as a link to perpetuate the memory of a primeval mourning ceremony.

As to mourning ceremonies in general we may state that the longer they last the greater must have been the impression created by the event (the decease) which first gave rise to them. The "delayed burial" with the re-burial of the bones after a certain period shows that the psychical conflict provoked by a decease takes longer in settling than is the case with those tribes who practise simple earth burial. The death wail of a noted warrior or a tribal leader lasts immeasurably longer than those of a stillborn infant or a decrepit old man whose social importance was next to nothing. But the Intichiuma ceremonies last for ever; they will only be ended with the tribes who practise them. It seems just to argue that the events which gave rise to them and which must have happened in the prehistoric age of these tribes must have been of such tremendous importance that the impression they created will

Intichiuma as mourning rites for the murdered father. Death the road to immortality.

[1] Perry, op. cit., 98.

[2] Thomson, *The Fijians*, 157.

never be washed away. Such an event would be the recurring battles between the males of the horde, with their triumphs and periods of awe-struck horror which mark the upward path from a semi-bestial to a primitive human state of society. One powerful Leader of the Horde after another must have been weighed down beneath the boulders hurled upon him and consequently mourned for by his rebellious sons before that which was a grim reality in the beginning was softened down to a rite. For every father killed there was more of grief and less of triumph than for his predecessor; repression grew in force till first the killing, then the orgy which followed were projected into the animal world, and the Great Rebellion only survived in an ever-repeated mourning ceremony.

Now that they were dead the omnigamous Sultans got all they wanted, all the women of the tribe. Now that they were dead they became immortal indeed, for who could kill a ghost? This is the way to Olympian honours; only a dead man can grow into a god. There is a tendency for popular heroes to emulate this primeval career to divinity in all ages, but the mould is already given by the semi-bestial hero, the physically powerful father of the first tragedy. His death and apotheosis lie at the root both of ghost-worship and the cult of the gods. In the former case the old complex is revived by each death. For if primitive man thinks that murder, meaning magical murder, is the only possible reason for death, we should like to go even a step further than Freud, who taught us to regard mourning rites as an endopsychical recognition of the ill-wishes which lie repressed in the Unconscious of primitive man. These ill-wishes are not only like deeds; they are derived from deeds of a similar order; for savage man is not so far removed as we are from the age in which murder was really the cause of every death. Or if not of every death we must assume that the deaths of the less significant members of the horde did not create such deep and lasting impressions in the mind of the survivors as the tragic death of the Sire. The death-concept of primitive mankind was moulded on this prototype, hence to them death was always a murder. The death ceremonies of an ordinary mortal are reduced copies of this original, whilst the gods represent the murdered father more in the abstract, more functionally as the Oedipus complex immanent in every man, as the foundation of all that is repressed in us, and thus finds an outlet in religious sublimation.

The fact that the Intichiuma ceremonies can be traced back to the behaviour of the horde after the tragic death of the Leader and Father is one which involves various consequences of considerable importance. These reflex actions called forth by the after impression of what had happened became conventionalized into a mourning ritual and this ritual is being repeated ever since. But it is repeated over an empty grave—a Cenotaph, the original lying many hundreds of miles away at the place whence the ancestors started on their voyage. The chance finding of fossil bones of huge extinct animals[1] permitted the original meaning of the ceremonies to be revived with peculiar distinctness in certain cases. The object of the Minkani ceremonies of the Dieri, Yaurorka, Yantruwunta, Marula, Yelyuendi, Karanguru and Ngameni tribes is to obtain a plentiful crop of Woma and Kapiri. The Mura-Mura himself is hidden (that is buried) in his cave, deep in the sandhill. To judge from the description given, his remains seem to be those of the fossil animals or reptiles which are found in the deltas of the rivers emptying themselves into Lake Eyre and which the Dieri call Kadimarkara. The men dig down very carefully till, as the Dieri say, the " elbow " of the Mura-Mura is uncovered.[2] Moreover as animals are, in the present time, re-created every year through the Intichiuma ceremonies; it is natural to suppose that this was the way they first came into existence. However, a remarkable feature of these ceremonies is that they are closely connected with, and take place immediately after the death of, a great man of the totem.

The Unmatjera believe that a man named Amulia sprang into existence at a place close to where Unkurta died coming out of one of his Churinga. He made the first ceremony of Intichiuma connected with the Unkurta totem, and this resulted in the formation of Unkurta lizards which did not previously exist. In the same way a Wallaby man made the first wallabies. A Qualpa man made Intichiuma after the death of the first great Qualpa man and thus created the long-tailed rats. An Iwuta man arose after the death of the first great Iwuta man and, making Intichiuma, created thereby the first nail-tailed wallabies.[3] Another universal feature of these ceremonies is what has been called their commemorative or historic aspect.[4] They are perfect dramas; the deeds and the death of the hero are recorded—we have the protagonist, the chorus and the audience.[5] Just as our Central Australians act the part of the Alcheringa ancestors, the Torres Islanders perform at funeral ceremonies, appearing as the ghosts of recently deceased men.[6] Ridgeway has collected the cases in which the life and death of the dead man is acted at the grave and traced the origin of the drama to these mourning ceremonies.[7] The Intichiuma ceremonies conform to this type in its most archaic form; for instead of recording the

[1] Cf. Gregory, *The Dead Heart of Australia*, 1906, 231.

[2] A. W. Howitt, *N. T.*, 798. Howitt and Siebert, " Legends of the Dieri," *Journal*, 1904, 124, 125. For an explanation of the details of the ceremony see above.

[3] Spencer and Gillen, *Nor. T.*, 442.

[4] Cf. Durkheim, *Les Formes Elémentaires de la Vie Religieuse*, 1912.

[5] See especially the descriptions given by Strehlow.

[6] Haddon, op. cit., V. 253.

[7] Ridgeway, *The Drama and Dramatic Dances of Non-European Races*, 1915, 340–344. Id., *The Origin of Tragedy*, 1910 (on intichiuma ceremonies).

deeds of the recently dead they go back to the mythic age, which is evidently identical with the period when mankind was becoming what it actually is, when it was toiling upwards on the steep path which leads from a simian to a savage state of society through a long series of tragic battles fought out between the old and the young males of the Horde.

The Intichiuma ceremonies as mourning rites and the origin of totemism in metempsychosis.

The views opened up here compel us to reconsider a theory of totemism which we owe to the famous Dutch ethnologist Wilken, and which has received the approval of the " Father of Anthropology " himself.[1] If the principal totemic ceremony of our Central tribes is demonstrated to be the offshoot of a mourning rite, the theory which derives totemism from a belief in metempsychosis gains very much in probability. We get still nearer to our point if we compare the views put forward by W. H. R. Rivers in his great work on Melanesian Society. In several parts of Melanesia—he tells us—there is a belief that after death a man becomes an animal, or part of one, or is embodied in one. This belief is very general in the Solomon Islands. Sharks are believed to be the abode of ghosts in Florida, Ysabel, and Savo ; ghosts also abide in eels, crocodiles, lizards, and the frigate bird. Again in Ulawa we hear of a case in which a man announced that after his death he would be in the banana : " The animals or plants into which the dead are believed to have entered are regarded as sacred and are not killed or eaten, but we do not know whether there is the association of sacred animals with social groups which is required to connect them with totemism. In the Shortland Islands, however, we find beliefs and practices which furnish intermediate links between typical totemism and the embodiment of ghosts in animals. In these islands the bones of the dead obtained from the ashes after cremation are thrown into rivers or the sea, and each clan has its appointed place where it was once believed . . . that the bones are devoured by the fish, lizards, shark or other kind of animal which is the totem of the clan. Apparently, the practice is based on the idea that the dead are by this rite incorporated into the bodies of these totem animals." [2] Dr. Rivers also shows that a connexion is demonstrable between the varieties of animals which form the totems and burial practices. This is most evident in the case of marine animals and the custom of throwing the body into the sea, but it seems that cremation which dissolves the body into air is also connected with bird totems,[3] and we add as a conjecture that the form of totemism corresponding to the sitting-interment rite

[1] E. B. Tylor, " Remarks on Totemism, with special reference to some modern theories respecting it," *J. A. I.*, XXVIII. 146. G. A. Wilken, *De Verspreide Geschriften*, 1912, III. 86, 87 ; *Het Animisme bij den Volken van den Indischen Archipel*, 1884–85, IV. 110, 186.

[2] Rivers, *H. M. S.*, II. 361, 362.

[3] Id., ibid., II. 342, 343.

is the one in which large land-animals predominate. People who believe in their incarnation in animals or plants after death cannot possibly transmit this belief in an unaltered form in a new environment. If the belief in incarnation is to persist in a new home, it is inevitable that the vehicle of incarnation should be an animal or plant of this new home. "We have evidence even now that a Melanesian chief will tell his people not to eat a plant into which he intends to enter after death."[1] If the germs out of which totemism was developed are to be attributed to an immigration of the Kava people into Melanesia, we should have to search for the custom or belief in Polynesia which can explain this peculiar habit of Melanesian chiefs.[2] But again the Polynesians must have come to their present home from Indonesia, and as we are attempting to reconstruct a state of things and the origin of beliefs which must have long antedated these assumed migrations; and as, moreover, we have also found reasons to connect the ancestors of the Central Australian tribes with which we are dealing with Indonesia, it will perhaps be legitimate to argue from Indonesian beliefs as to the process that led from mortuary to totemic ceremonies and to assume that this process must also lie at the root of the belief in metempsychosis.

The ghost-animal haunts the grave in the phantasy of the murderer.

The Bahau believe that the ton luwa, the ghost, can in the space of time that it spends at the grave before passing on to the other world transform itself into a deer or a grey monkey; therefore, the Bahau will only eat these animals when compelled to do so by hunger. As the Malays refrain from pork, the Bahau imagine that their souls are transformed into swine after death.[3] "The people of Miri who are Mohammedan Malanaus, claim to be related to the large deer, Cervus equinus, and some of them to the Muntjac deer also. Now these people live in a country in which deer of all kinds abound, and they always make a clearing in the jungle around the tomb. On such a clearing grass grows up rapidly, so the spot attracts the deer as a grazing ground; it seems not improbable that it is through frequently seeing deer about the tombs that the people have come to entertain the belief that their dead relatives become deer, or that they are in some other way closely related to the deer." The Bakongs, another group of Malanaus, hold a similar belief with regard to the bear-cat (Artictis) and the various species of Paradoxurus; in this case the origin of the belief is admitted by them to be the fact that, on going to their graveyards, they often see one of these beasts coming out of a tomb. "These tombs are roughly

[1] Rivers, *H. M. S.*, II. 363.

[2] Dr. Rivers presupposed the same state of things which exists at present (telling children not to eat an animal), at the time of the migration. But this leaves us completely in the dark as to how such a state of things arose. Why are the children told?

[3] A. W. Nieuwenhuis, *Quer duch Borneo*, 1904, I. 105.

constructed wooden coffins raised only a few feet from the ground, and it is probable that these carnivores make their way into them, in the first place to devour the corpse, and that they make use of them as lairs."[1] Certain tutelary animals are connected with "kramat" (holy) places at Malacca Pindah. It was reported that the tigers were in the habit of "wailing" at the private burial place of a certain family.[2] We have various stories of "ghost tigers" (also a white-ghost elephant) associated with the shrines (tombs) of local heroes as the guardians of the shrine.[3]

If we picture to ourselves the psychical situation of the victorious brother-clan assembled round the cairn, which they had piled up in triumph and yet trembling from what might follow after their victory, we may very well understand the exact moment in which the projection of the Father-Imago into an animal took place.

The conscience-stricken murderer sees the image of the man he has killed in every tree of the forest, he hears his voice in the rustling boughs and, at least so popular belief will have it, he is compelled by irresistible force within him always to return to the scene of his crime. These parricides at the dawn of human evolution must have been subject to these emotions in an enhanced measure, for was not their victim their beloved father, the very source of their being? Their attitude towards him was ambivalent, a compound of hatred and love; after hate had obtained free play in the bloody deed it was but natural that love should get the upper hand in the mourning period. They now felt a lively desire to resuscitate their powerful leader as a help in the struggle for life against other species, although his desire was not unmingled with a very natural dread of what he would do to his murderers if he came back again. At any rate, they were expecting his return, and so it was very natural that they should identify the wild beasts of the jungle or desert who come to haunt his grave with his now thrice sacred person.

Watching for the murderer's totem-animal in Australia.

The totem-animal at the grave is still watched for in Central Australia. The Warramunga remove the camp to a considerable distance from the scene, since everybody was afraid of meeting either with the spirit of the dead man or with that of the man who had brought about the death by evil magic. This spirit would probably come to visit the grave in the form of an animal.[4] The burial mound and the smooth ground around it are carefully examined to see if there be any tracks visible which might give the clue to the identity of the murderer of the dead man. If a snake track were visible this would be regarded as a sure sign that a man of the Snake totem was the

[1] Hose and McDougall, *Pagan Tribes*, 1902, II. 81.

[2] W. Skeat, *Malay Magic*, 1900, 674.

[3] Skeat, l.c., 163.

[4] Spencer and Gillen, *Nor. T.*, 519.

culprit, and then the task would only be to find out which particular Snake man was guilty.[1]

Now, in the Primeval Horde or Cyclopean family there could be no such thing as a mortuary inquest. There was no question of guilt, for everybody was guilty, and it must have taken many generations to repress this will of parricide as well as the consciousness of guilt, and relegate both to the Unconscious. When this had come to pass it would become necessary to project this unconscious complex of guilt into one fictive man: this was the imaginary person who had really done the deed which they all desired to do. He appeared in the guise of his totem-animal, thereby indicating that the sin he had committed was a sin against the totem (= the father), and also that after he had done the deed it was time for him to identify himself with his totem, to appear in the guise of the father-animal. Now the animal which haunted the grave was not the father but rather his mortal enemy the parricidal son, the man who had killed the father. But, we must ask, what was the reason which made them see anything particular in the animal which visited the grave? The very fact that they had killed the father and were expecting his return with anxious suspense, amid dread and desire. The animal thus symbolizes both the returning father and the reason why he returns to haunt the grave of the murderous son. This latter aspect of the animal at the grave only became specially developed in the mortuary inquest, but it must have been immanent in the earlier forms. We often notice that the rite or object which symbolizes the punishment for anything condemned by the Censor but desired by the Unconscious, at the same time from the standpoint of the latter, contains a wish-fulfilment, a repetition of the very deed which it punishes. An acute remark of Hose and McDougall helps us in this connexion; the animals which gather round the grave were probably originally carrion-eaters who were attracted by the smell of the putrefying corpse.[2] In other words they were doing the same thing as the

[1] Spencer and Gillen, *Nor. T.*, 526.

[2] Hose and McDougall, l.c., II. 81. Cf. In New Ireland the two prominent secret societies are the "sikim" and the "kipkipto." A "sikim" is "a blackish cricket, exactly like the German meadow-cricket (*Gryllus campestris*), except that it is rather larger. It is also called a "koh na pare." The purpose of the two societies is to protect the corpses from these insects, but as their principal ceremony consists rather in an imitation of, than in a magical effort at, counteracting the doings of the insects, we must conclude that this is a reversal, and that the secret society goes back ultimately to the members of the brother-horde, who, after killing the father, devoured his flesh and adopted the cricket, a corpse-eater, for their patron-animal. The ceremony begins outdoors. The "sikim" people crack their whips to imitate the shrill noise made by the cricket. Then they unite indoors for their meal, the principal ingredient being the bones of the dead with a shred of flesh still clinging to them here and there.

The "kipkipto" are a brother society; the only difference seems to be that instead of gnawing the bones they drink the juice of the putrefying corpse. After the trance the "sikim" is restored to his senses by eating warm food, which is

mourners—the murderous brothers—devouring the dead father; this originally represents the wish of complete annihilation of the object which is devoured; it is also in a secondary (but still very primitive) phase the sign of identification with the object that has been consumed.[1] The beast that feeds on the corpse is thus naturally identified with the father. Eating the corpse was originally an inimical action towards the dead man; the totem animal, by devouring the corpse, must have been thought to be retaliating on the dead man for having, in his day, killed and eaten the totem animal, that is the symbol of the father.

In this connexion another fact becomes important, especially from a purely ethnological point of view. The totem animals of the two primary moieties which were probably already formed when the ancestors of a large group of south-eastern tribes invaded Australia were Eagle-hawk and Crow, that is carrion-eating birds of prey. There are, as we have pointed out, survivals of the part played by these birds, especially the Eagle-hawk, amongst tribes which have not got this two-class system, and the nature of these survivals indicates two possibilities. We must either assume that they are traces of a primitive Eagle-hawk-Crow population which has been assimilated by the immigrants, or that these immigrants themselves had the Eagle-hawk-Crow organization or at least the cult of the Eagle-hawk in the dim past, and thus were related to the group of people who came before them.

The original phratric totems would have been conserved by the first but modified through other influences in the second wave of immigrant tribes, and only survived in their myths and religious beliefs. The Eagle-hawk appears in two aspects in these myths. He is either the father as the divine creator and lawgiver or a cannibal monster. Amongst the Arunta the taboo of the Eagle-hawk is directly explained by the carrion-eating habits of the bird. On general grounds it is much more likely that the bird which symbolized their own ancestors should have become tabooed by these tribes than one which represented an alien race. Moreover, if we follow the cult of the hawk outside Australia we are again led back to Indonesia, which we have assumed was the original home of these tribes. Just as a Central Australian magician will imitate

strictly taboo to him in his cricket stage of existence.—P. G. Peekel, *Religion und Zauberei auf dem mittleren Neu-Mecklenburg*, 1910, 78–80).

The reason for the last taboo may perhaps be that the germs of the rite go back to a time which antedates the use of fire and warm food; we seem to have found the ritual in transit from anthropophagy and totem-eating. A further development might well be imagined, in which the "sikim" would drop eating corpses and sacramentally consume their patron-animal. Rivers thinks that the secret societies are developed out of the totemic groups of the immigrants.—Rivers, *H. M. S.*, 1914, II. 222.

[1] Cf. K. Abraham, "Untersuchungen über die früheste prägenitale Entwickungsstufe der Libido, *I. Z. Pa.*, IV. 71.

the Eagle-hawk,[1] the maidelaig of Mabuiag will compare himself and his pupil to the fish-eagle and its egg, and point out that the pupil was then in the egg stage, but would some day become as fierce an eagle as himself.[2] At Menapi (Goodenough Bay, New Guinea) the fish-hawk is looked upon as the chief of birds,[3] and called " our master," which looks like a translation of the title of the Eagle-hawk-Bunjil, who is called " our father " by the Kulin.[4] This bird, which feeds on carrion, is the bird totem of the Aurana clan, the strongest clan in Goodenough Bay. As they hold the highest position among the clans of this part of the coast, it is with a certain pride that a man will say, " I am of the Aurana." [5]

The hawk is the patron bird of one of the Banks Island societies which is organized on a gerontocratic basis, as it excludes young men.[6] " Bunjil " (Eagle-hawk) is also an honorific title applied to important old men by the Kurnai,[7] or if the word does not originally mean the eagle-hawk, we should say that the latter is called " the old man." The Vihunuvagi clan has as " major totem " the eagle called " vihunuvagi," from whom they trace their origin.[8] The sacred animal of the whole Navatusila people in Fiji is the " nganivatu," the fish-hawk, which may be eaten by none of the members of the tribe.[9] More important still, we habitually find birds of prey, eagle and hawk, as the totems of the dual divisions in Melanesia,[10] which corresponds exactly to Eagle-hawk and Crow in Australia.

The cult of hawks, however, is specially prominent in Borneo—Bali Flaki, the white-headed carrion-hawk (*Haliaster intermedius*), occupies an important place in the Kenyah pantheon. It is the principal omen bird observed during the preparation for and the conduct of war.[11] Without favourable omens from the hawks the Kenyahs will not set out on any expedition, and even when they have secured them they are anxiously on the look-out for further guidance. If one of a party dies on the journey they will stop for a whole day for fear of offending Bali Flaki. If a hawk should scream just when they are about to attack their foes it indicates the death of one of the elder men.[12] When a new house is built a wooden image of Bali Flaki with wings extended is put up before it. Offerings of food are put on the shelf before the image; it gets bits of flesh and is smeared with pig's blood. The women, although they are not allowed to participate in the public cult of the omen hawk, have small wooden images of the hawk with a few feathers of the bird stuck in it to protect them against evil spirits. The Kenyahs

[1] See Map 1.
[2] Haddon, V. 322.
[3] Cf. Ker, *Papuan Fairy Tales*, 1910, 57, 63.
[4] Howitt, l.c., 492.
[5] Seligmann, op. cit., 419.
[6] Rivers, *H M. S.*, I. 119.
[7] Howitt, *N. T.*, 738.
[8] Rivers, l.c., I. 245
[9] Id., ibid., 280.
[10] Id., ibid., II. 501.
[11] Hose and McDougall, *Pagan Tribes*, II. 15, 51.
[12] Id., II. 55.

naturally will not kill a hawk.[1] The Klemantans say that Bali Flaki is the messenger of their Supreme Being, "Bali Utong." If a hawk circles over their heads some of the party will fall sick and die on the journey.[2] The Singalang Burong of the Iban is more anthropomorphic than Bali Flaki, for he is believed to inhabit a house like the Ibans themselves. He is the king of all the omen birds, and a feast was given in his honour once a year. He used to be present at these feasts himself in person, looking just like an Iban. At the end of the feast he would go out, take off his coat, and fly away in the form of a white-headed hawk.[3] Singalang Burong probably means "bird-chief." He manifests himself in the white and brown hawks which are known by his name. He is also the god of war and head-taking, and a feast is celebrated in his honour when a head is taken. He is represented by a carved bird erected on the top of a pole with its beak pointing towards the enemy's country so that he may "peck at the eyes of the enemy."[4]

The Kayan have the large brown-headed hawk as their patron and omen-bird. Like the Bali Flaki of the Kenyah, Laki Neho is regarded as a deputy and messenger of Laki Tenangan. This supreme being is an old man with long white hair who speaks Kayan. Somewhat nearer, on a tree-top beside the river, is the house of Laki Neho. They are both seen in dreams. Although Laki Neho is really the brown hawk, all large hawks (including the white-headed hawk of the Kenyahs) are identified with him, as it is not possible to distinguish them when flying at a distance.[5] We must either assume that the respect paid to hawks originated in the dim past and was inherited by these Malay immigrants from the people who inhabited Indonesia before them, and who were also the ancestors of the Australians, or we must suppose that it was brought by them from their ancient home to Indonesia and transmitted to that part of the dark-skinned population of these islands which helped to people Australia.[6] In discussing the varieties of totemism in Melanesia, Rivers comes to the conclusion that one of the branches of the immigrant Kava people brought a type of totemism with them in which birds occupied a specially prominent position.[7]

He connects the development of bird totemism with cremation,[8]

[1] Hose and McDougall, *Pagan Tribes*, II. 56, 57. The hawk is also appealed to for purposes of black magic both by the Kenyahs (ibid., II. 56) and the Sebops (ibid., 118), a practice which again has parallels in New Guinea. Zahn, *Die Jabim*. Neuhauss, *Deutsch Neu Guinea*, 1911, III. 336. Cf. also Nieuwenhuis, *Die Wurzeln des Animismus*, 1917, 40.

[2] Hose and McDougall, II. 79.

[3] Hose and McDougall, II. 86.

[4] E. H. Gomes, *Seventeen Years among the Sea Dyaks of Borneo*, 1911, 196; cf. 227, 284.

[5] Hose and McDougall, II. 74, 75

[6] The tribe which inhabited the district of Antananarivo in Madagascar had the hawk for its symbol.—Gennep, *Tabou et Totémisme à Madagascar*, 1904, 261.

[7] Rivers, *H. M. S.*, II. 339.

[8] Cremation is found in Borneo (in connexion with delayed interment), and attributed to Hindu influence.—Hose and McDougall, II. 50, 230.

but perhaps these birds of prey became connected with the dead at a phase of development when other disposal customs were practised. In platform-burial there would be ample opportunity for the hawks to act as scavengers. Going back one step further to the primitive root out of which platform burial was developed by some races, we come to the custom of simply leaving the dead where he was and shifting the camp.[1] We must imagine that flight pure and simple was also the first reaction of the ancestors of the tribes we are dealing with at the sight of a corpse. After a time they would recover from their first shock so far as to return to the scene of their ghastly deed. Then they would come back to stone the corpse a second time as they had stoned the man when he was alive, and from a rationalistic point of view they might then invent the explanation that the log or cairn on the corpse was meant to protect him from the carrion-eating animals. But the hawk will by this time have had its share of the prey and become imbued with the essence of the old man, the murdered father. The state of things which followed upon the death was certainly one of anxious suspense, and at such a time man is particularly liable to regard everything that happens as an omen of things he is expecting. Thus the hawks would come to be messengers of the murdered father and birds of omen.[2] Being a plurality, the birds which haunted the grave would naturally represent first the warlike element of the tribe, the band of brothers, but, for the reasons already put forward, they would in time come to be identified with the Father, the Supreme Being. These birds, or other carrion-eating animals, shared another custom of the brothers which we see reasons for projecting back into the abyss of the dim past. After they had killed the Sire they proceeded to annihilate him completely, at the same time identifying themselves with him; they devoured the flesh and either left the bones or used them for other purposes. We have shown that the Intichiuma is an anthropic ceremony which has been transferred to the animal world, so it will not surprise us if we come to the conclusion that the custom of eating the murdered father survives in the rite of killing and eating the totem as an essential part of the Intichiuma. As to this detail of the original rite, or rather of the wild scenes which were softened down and conventionalized into ritual in the course of ages, we shall attempt to get some information from the present customs of this kind. Anthropophagy is a universal practice of these tribes. In the Mara tribe the dead are regularly eaten. Both men and women participate

The cannibal communion. Devouring the paternal tyrant.

[1] C. G. Seligmann, *The Veddas*, 1911, 122. E. Palmer, *The Cloncurry River*. Curr, II. 332. A. R. Brown, "Description of the Natives of King George's Sound," *J. R. G. S.*, I. 46.

[2] In Australia the omen-giving animal is usually the totem; in Borneo, as in Rome, the omen cult is called "beburong," i e. "birding."

in the feast, although the latter are not allowed to witness the preparations made.[1] In the Binbinga tribe the women are not allowed to touch the flesh which is eaten by the men alone.[2]

We may connect this with another specific cannibal taboo found in the Dieri tribe. All relatives eat of the flesh of the dead man excepting the father, who does not eat his children and the children who do not eat their Sire.[3] We know that all taboos are repressions —a thing forbidden is almost always something that was practised in bygone times—but which has been repressed on account of a conscious or unconscious meaning attaching to the act. If the sons are not allowed to eat the father, it is probable that they regularly eat him " in the Alcheringa " ; if women may not eat human flesh they probably always used to eat it once upon a time and there is a specific reason why they are forbidden to do so.

The feeling of the uncanny is, as has been shown by Freud, the result of an effort made by the Conscious against the recognition of the once familiar ;[4] if women practised corpse-eating in the infancy of the race and dropped this custom later on, we should expect to find occasional relapses on their part qualified as magical, that is, as uncanny practices by the community. This association is just what we find in various parts of the world, for instance amongst the southern Massim in New Guinea—a witch, a "parauma" is a woman who eats corpses.[5] Now we have assumed that when the young males had killed their Sire to be able to satisfy their craving for the women, one of the phases of the repression of the Oedipus complex which followed made them ignore their own part in procreating and attribute the birth of children to the fact that the dead father had entered the woman and had been reborn through her, thus vindicating after death the privileges which were his in his lifetime. "If, as seems probable, the animals or plants which influence expectant mothers were once believed to represent or embody dead ancestors, there is suggested the possibility that the Kava people may have brought with them the belief, not merely incarnation in animal form but also in reincarnation after a time in human form. According to this hypothesis the incarnation in animal form would be only a stage towards the process of reincarnation."[6]

If our whole idea as to the anthropic origin of the Intichiuma and the conceptional totemism with which it is connected is not a mistake we shall be able to guess how this reincarnation took place. In Central Australia a child is conceived when a woman eats of the totem animal or plant, or rather the food which was eaten by the woman when she first noticed being pregnant becomes the child's

[1] Spencer, *N. T. N. T. A.*, 1914, 253, 254.
[2] Spencer and Gillen, *Nor. T.*, 548.
[3] Howitt, *N. T* . 751.
[4] J. Freud, " Das Unheimliche," *Imago*, V. 5–6.
[5] Seligmann, op. cit., 551.
[6] Rivers, l.c., II 369

totem. Eating the totem is also a custom of the Alcheringa, but in the case of the Wild-Dog totem we have Alcheringa ancestors who did not only eat wild dogs but actually devoured Wild-Dog men.[1] In the Banks Islands, where the belief in animals influencing the birth of children is also found, we are told that the child who in after life eats of this animal which had procreated it would in a certain sense be eating itself. It seemed that the act would be regarded as a kind of cannibalism.[2] If an act is regarded as a kind of cannibalism it is probable enough that it is derived from cannibalism.

We thus come to the conclusion that there was a time in the prehistoric evolution of the Central Australian tribes when the women were supposed to conceive, not from eating the totem, but from eating human flesh. They probably partook of the festive meal and ate of the flesh of the murdered father. From the point of view of the Unconscious this was equivalent to having intercourse with him, as eating is a transposition upwards of the sexual act.

We have explained the idea of metempsychosis in connexion with the animals that haunt the vicinity of the grave. However, we always need two factors to form a specific belief, an outward stimulus and something which lies ready in the Unconscious to meet it half-way. But we have also explained totemism as a consequence of Haeckel's biogenetic law—ontogenesis a recapitulation of phylogenesis. The embryo in the womb is really an animal in an evolutionary sense, and hence the belief in the identity of human beings with various natural species. When man dies he is put into the grave, into the womb of Mother-Earth, and hence he is re-transformed into an embryo, an animal. But it is only his bones which are given up to the Earth; his flesh is really and materially put back into the inside of a woman or rather of many women.[3] In this connexion we shall recall a custom of the western Solomon Islands which has already been quoted.

Each clan has a special place where the bones of the dead members of the clan are disposed of. In many cases the bones were given to the big fish known as Samoi, which was one of the "tete" totems, but the place where the bones were put was usually in the sea or in rivers,[4] that is the bones were usually devoured by marine animals. Now, as Rivers has pointed out, the "tua" totems are nearly all birds and the "tete" totems aquatic animals, so that this is as much as to say that the bones are swallowed by the "tete" totems. "Tua" means grandfather, "tete" grandmother, and thus the

[1] Spencer and Gillen, *N. T.*, 435.

[2] W. H. R. Rivers, "Totemism in Polynesia and Melanesia," *J. A. I.*, 1909, 174.

[3] "The corpse of a very young child was roasted whole and eaten by very old women only."—W. E. Roth. *Ethn. Bul.* IX. 1907, 402.

[4] G. C. Wheeler, "Sketch of the Totemism and Religion of the People of the Islands in the Bougainville Straits," *A. R. W.*, XV. 26.

dead man gets back into the inside of his ancestress. The women were women before they were symbolized by fish, the murdered father was devoured by the women of the horde. It is also quite in keeping with these views if the fish which swallows the bones is supposed to convey them to a submarine or island other-world,[1] for we know very well that the concept of another world is only the post-mortem projection of a pre-natal existence in the womb. The only answer as to the destiny of the dead which Hagen could elicit from the "wild" Kubu of Muara Bahar was, "If somebody dies he returns thither whence he came."[2] Thus the return of the dead into the body of a woman was a reality before it became a symbol. The taboo against women eating human flesh is really a repression of the Oedipus complex; they are not to eat the flesh of their fathers, i.e. not to have intercourse with him. When this taboo came into force the positive aspect of the rite would still survive in the eating of the totem and in the belief that totem-eating resulted in conception. The taboo on "red meat" to be observed after death by the near relatives of the deceased is half-way between the taboo on eating human flesh and tabooing an animal species, as the animals with "red meat" are those whose flesh resembles human flesh.[3] Survivals of eating the corpse as a means of inducing pregnancy are still found in fairy tales, saga, and popular custom. In a Slavonic tale a daughter who is courted by her father becomes pregnant through swallowing the gratings of bones dug up from the churchyard.[4] The phase of totem-eating is the stage of development in which we actually find some Central tribes, but we have also seen instances of the next step in repression, the taboo against eating the totem animal. An Intichiuma is a magical ceremony for the multiplication of an animal species. We have traced the development of the ceremony to a time which was before the age of animal projection, when the intention of the ceremony was the multiplication of the human species; and the means by which the end was attained were not "magical" at all, but those foreseen for this purpose by nature. However, this seems a contradiction to the death-rite theory which we have just been expounding. The solution of this apparent contradiction must be sought in a feature of mourning rites which has so far only been touched upon.

Mourning and Intichiuma.

In Fiji there is a mourning custom which offers the strongest possible contrast to the bitter lamentation for the dead that

[1] Cf. Rivers, *H. M. S.*, II. 343.

[2] Hagen, *Die Orang Kubu*, 1908, 144.

[3] W. E. Roth, "Burial Ceremonies and Disposal of the Dead," *N. Q. E. Bul.*, IX. 370.

[4] Krauss, *Sagen und Märchen der Südslaven*, 1883–4, I. 195. Quoted by E. S. Hartland, *The Legend of Perseus*, 1894, I. 86, 87. Cf. ibid., 97, 123–4, 144, 162–3. Eating the corpse of a child causes conception in the Tibetan national epic—J. J. Schmidt, *Die Thaten Bogda Gesser Chans*, 1839, 80, 81.

characterizes these rites. Companies gather together to entertain the friends of the dead with comic games, in which decency is not always regarded, for the purpose of helping them to forget their grief.[1] At Yap, the women perform obscene dances before the corpse.[2] In New Ireland the erotic dances were chiefly performed at festivals held in honour of the dead.[3] In the mourning ceremonies of the Kobeua in South America masked dancers representing various animal-demons appear on the scene. But all the "animals" united in a phallic dance, the intention of which was to multiply men, animals, plants, the whole living nature.[4] If we can rely on Eylmann's informant, there seems to be a case recorded on the Daly River of promiscuous intercourse as an element of mourning ceremonies.[5]

Orgiastic elements in mourning rites.

The ritual of the Aru Islands contains a characteristic survival of these orgies in connexion with death rites. When the mourning period of the widow comes to an end she is permitted to marry again. The entire village is assembled on the coast—the men hold a wooden penis in their hands and the women the "kodu," an object made of sago leaves and stalks, which represents the vagina. All symbols of mourning are discarded and they jump round the fire like lunatics. The "kodu" are given to the men by the women, whereupon the former insert the wooden penis into them and imitate the act of cohabitation so as to induce the widow to coitus in her second marriage.[6] We may give various functional explanations for the phenomenon that mankind is inclined to unite mourning with sexuality,[7] but behind these functional explanations we shall look for a genetic or historical explanation, an organization of society in which such a state of things was inevitable, in which it must have originated. Arguing from Atkinson's theory of "Primeval Law" we can quite see how the young males could only have access to the women of the herd after the violent death of their venerable Sire, who would not let them touch his harem as long as he was alive. The Season of Rut was also the Season of Battle and Death, year by year as they felt the sexual impulse manifesting itself in them, again and again the young males would band together to attempt the deed they had failed to accomplish a season hence. Every failure would demand losses on the side of the attacking party. At last they would succeed, and a period of awe-struck panic at what they had done would ensue. They were paralysed by their victory; this was the prototype of all mourning rites and of "tabooed

1 Th. Williams, *Fiji and the Fijians*, 1858, I. 198.
2 W. Müller, *Ergebnisse der Südsee Expedition*, 1908–1910. *Jap*, 1917, I. 269.
3 R. Parkinson, *Dreissig Jahre in der Südsee*, 1907, 276, 277.
4 Th. Koch-Grünberg, *Zwei Jahre unter den Indianern*, 1910, 132–138.
5 K. Eylmann, *Die Eingeborenen der Kolonie Südaustralien*, 1908, 263.
6 Riedel, *De sluik en kroeshaarige rassen tusschen Selebes en Papua*, 268.
7 Cf. Róheim, *Spiegelzauber*, 1919, 105.

periods," "rest days," in general.[1] But at the same time the dreaded foe who jealously guarded all the females of the horde was no more; what more natural than that they should make a rush for the women. It was now their rutting season with a vengeance and they were multiplying their own species in incestuous intercourse with their mothers and sisters. Comparatively few traces of these primeval orgies have survived till our days, and the fact that the connexion between the death of the totem ancestor (repeated in eating the totem animal) and the idea of multiplication has survived so manifestly in our Intichiuma rites, is only due to the long isolation of the tribes who practised them from the rest of mankind and to the projection of the whole complex from the human clan to the animal species.

Amongst the Bungyarlee and Barkungi on the Darling we find traces of a still earlier phase in which the multiplications of animals was connected, not with totem-eating, but with its prototype, the cannibal meal. The piece of flesh cut from the dead body is taken to the camp, cut into small pieces and distributed among relatives and friends of the deceased. Some use it for purposes of evil magic; others suck it to get strength and courage, or throw it into the river to bring a flood and fish when both are wanted.[2] Originally the Intichiuma was a mourning ceremony, when the Leader of the Horde had been killed and eaten and the young males had access to the women. Then the second phase becomes repressed and symbolic; after the cannibal meal there is no coitus, but fish are multiplied, and in the third phase totem-eating replaces anthropophagy. But the Intichiuma are also closely connected with Initiation ceremonies.

Mourning rites and Initiation ceremonies.

Certain similarities between mourning rites and Initiation ceremonies have frequently been observed by ethnologists, but we have no satisfactory theory to explain this similarity. The Kamilaroi hold their Bora on Baiamais ground always near a place where blackfellows are buried.[3] The Nanga where the youths of Fiji are circumcised and initiated is regarded as the "bed" of the dead ancestors.[4] "The central mystery" of Initiation ceremonies is nearly always an object which is traditionally connected with ancestral spirits. The "Ngosa" or bullroarer is called "grandfather" by the Kai,[5] and the same name is applied to the same object by the Kurnai.[6] Balum means a ghost, an ancestor as well as the bullroarer.[7]

[1] Cf. H. Webster, *Rest Days*, 1916, Chapter II.

[2] F. Bonney, "On some Customs of the Aboriginals of the River Darling," *J. A. I.*, XIII. 135.

[3] W. Ridley, "Report on Australian Languages and Traditions," *J. A. I.*, II. 1872, 269.

[4] Thomson, *The Fijians*, 1908, 147.

[5] Ch. Keysser, *Aus dem Leben der Kaileute*. Neuhauss, *Deutsch Neu Guinea*, III. 36.

[6] Howitt, *N. T.*, 638.

[7] Neuhauss, op cit., III. 410–14.

The principal bullroarers or balums represent eminent ancestors of the village. The peculiar characteristics of the dead man, such as a highly pitched voice, malformations, etc., are reproduced on the bullroarers, which are passed on from one generation to the next.[1] There is reason to believe that the bullroarer as such represents a dead man, so that we should have to postulate a similar origin for the " Schwirrholz " of the mysteries as for the stone Churinga; both are substitutes for the corpse carved out of wood or stone, but at any rate more durable and less obvious materials than human flesh and bone. The Minangkabau of Sumatra carve their bullroarers out of bones of brave men.[2] We have drawn attention to the giant thigh-bone of the father of all kangaroos carried about by the Kangaroo totem of the Wailwun tribe.[3] It is no more than a guess, but one which falls into line with many facts, if we say that human and animal corpses or bones were exhibited originally to the novices, and that a wooden " rhombos " was substituted when repression made it necessary to throw a veil over the original meaning of these mysteries. The fact that the bullroarer itself represents a dead man is evident enough if we compare the Australian myths which explains the origin of this thrice holy symbol. The bullroarer spirit Gayandi was transformed into a large piggiebillah-like animal (that is, killed), but he still haunts the Borah grounds.[4] The Wiradthuri say that Baiamai destroyed the disobedient deputy Dhurramoolan and put his voice into the trees of the forest.[5] The Kaitish relate that the Tumana, the spirits of the bullroarer, were killed by wild dogs. Murtu-murtu, the bullroarer spirit of the Warramunga, was a man who was torn to pieces by the wild dogs. The trees out of which the present bullroarers are made grow where his flesh touched the earth. The view which commends itself to us is that the Initiation ceremony is a mourning rite for the murdered father. When the Brother Horde had obtained its decisive victory, the shock they felt in consequence of their deed must have led to the first social crisis, the phylogenetic fixation of a taboo-period, which is since then repeated in every mourning ceremony. Like mourners[6] the initiates are painted white,[7] thereby identifying themselves with the murdered father, the dead man. Both are

[1] Neuhauss, *Deutsch Neu Guinea*, III. 410, 411.

[2] Th. Reik, *Probleme der Religionspsychologie*, 1919, 242; who, however, does not give his authority.

[3] Honery, " Wailwun," *J. A. I.*, VII. 249.

[4] K. L. Parker, *The Euahlayi*, 1905, 67.

[5] R. H. Mathews, " The Bŭrbŭng of the Wiradthuri Tribes," *J. R. A. I.*, XXV. 295.

[6] Frazer, *J. A. I.*, XV. E. S. Hartland, *Ritual and Belief*, 1914, 235. The Philosophy of Mourning Clothes. L. Weniger, " Feralis Exercitus," *Archiv f. Religionswissenschaft*, X. 69, 229. R. Brown, op. cit., I. 40, 46.

[7] H. Schurtz, *Altersklassen u. Männerbünde*, 1902, 101. Weniger, op. cit., IX. 242. G. Tessmann, *Die Pangwe*, 1913, II. 50 J. Macdonald, " Superstition, Manners, Customs, and Religions of South African Tribes," *J. A. I.*, 1889, XIX. 268.

subject to privations,[1] which must be interpreted as the punishment for what they have done or intended to do. The taboo of speech applies to both,[2] as a fixation of an involuntary inhibition which must have been one of the outward signs of the psychic shock wrought on them by the dire event. The relation between the two most important ceremonies of primitive man becomes still more evident when we recall the fact that even the most specific symptoms of initiation ceremonies, mutilations like tooth-expulsion, cutting a finger joint, scarification and circumcision, find their exact equivalents in mourning ceremonies.[3] Technical details are of great importance, for it is only in these two rites that we find marked trees,[4] mounds[5] and platforms. The obvious explanation of this parallelism seems to be that the nucleus of Initiation ceremonies is a mourning rite for the murdered father. The victorious brothers experienced a shock at what they had done; they felt an unconscious dread of the time when their sons would deal with them as they had dealt with the Sire. Their straightforward aggressivity would be repulsed by this first inhibition; in the moment they had done the deed they themselves were transformed into fathers; their feelings on the subject of their revolution were undergoing a rapid change. This was the first victorious Opposition Party "changing colours" for those of the Government Party, the first oppressed who were growing into oppressors. "Changing colours" must be interpreted in a literal sense—the white paint of their bodies is an effort to imitate the pallor of the corpse. Then they played a part which was that of judge and criminal at the same time. The mutilations they inflicted on themselves were the visible signs that the aggressive impulse had been blocked and was turning against its own author. The mound

The starting-point of initiation ceremonies is a mourning rite for the murdered Sire of the Cyclopean Family.

[1] Westermarch, *The Origin and Development of the Moral Ideas*, 1908, II. 302. Frazer, *J. A. I.*, XV. 94.

[2] As to initiation, see Spencer, *N. T. N. T. A.*, 168. Roth, *Ethnological Studies*, 177.

[3] Waitz-Gerland, *Anthropologie der Naturvölker*, III. 196, VI. 403. Spencer and Gillen, *N. T.*, 510. Fraser, *Aborigines of N. S. W.*, 1892, 44.

[4] R. Etheridge, "The Dendroglyphs, or Carved Trees of N.S. Wales," *Mem. Geol. Survey, N.S.W. Ethonol. Series*, No. 3.

[5] The characteristic feature of the Bunan Bora and Dora types of south-eastern initiation ceremonies is the circular mound.—Howitt, *N. T.*, 519, 541, 564, 582, 584. These earth mounds often represent human or animal beings, especially the supreme beings, Baiamai, Daramulun, in a reclining position (P. W. Schmidt, op. cit., 360, 361). As we have found various reasons for identifying these supreme beings with the leaders of the Cyclopean family murdered by their sons and worshipped after their death, we may say that we have here a representation of Baiamais burial mound, for we are already acquainted with the return of repressed elements which transforms the mound which ought to blot out the corpse from human view into a likeness of the very object it was intended to obliterate. The mythical serpent-ancestor of the Wollunqua totem is represented by an earth mound, and a fierce attack upon the mound is made with the idea of coercing the ancestor.—Spencer and Gillen, *Nor. T.*, 238.

raised over the dead body, the platform on which it is placed, the fire to keep it warm (originally to annihilate it),[1] the tree which represents a man—all these elements of Initiation rites represent the survival of an ancient mourning ritual which has been transformed into an initiation into manhood.

Just as telling the deeds of the dead man is an important element of mourning rites, initiation rites would not be complete without the mythical lore of the tribe. The knowledge imparted to youths on this occasion refers to the mythic events as things that were done in bygone days by the gods or ancestors of the tribe who inhabited the earth at that time, and were, to all appearances, simply human beings. Only when their days on earth are spent are we told that they were translated into the skies or transformed into animals, an euphemism for the straightforward statement that they died, or rather that they were murdered by their rebellious offspring. Baiamai, the god of the initiation rites, ascends to the sky or leaves for an island far beyond the sea, and ever since then all the dead follow his footsteps. In other words, he is the first man who died who showed the path to the other-world where he still continues to exist in a semi-petrified state. The Initiation ceremonies are really his obsequies, the mourning rite in honour of the murdered father, and it is now that the boys hear about "Mungan-ngaua," "Our Father," and the things he did and said when he was living amongst men. The Dakka always killed their king at the harvest season (the equivalent of the rutting season projected to the Earth-Mother in an agricultural community), and as soon as he is dead preparations are made for the circumcision festival. It is only when the festival is terminated that the new king commences to rule. The Dakka say that the blood spilt at circumcision flows towards the dead king; and if the new king were already in office, he would die on account of this blood.[2] The circumcision of the youth appears to be a sacrifice offered to the ghost of a murdered king. It is true that the ordinary mourning ceremony lacks the dramatic details which are characteristic of Australian initiation rites, but then we must not forget that the latter commemorate a death of far greater importance or rather a series of deaths which opened the way for civilization. In the mourning ceremony at the grave of the murdered father the rebellious Titans repeated the deed they had done as well as the battle which preceded it. When they mutilated themselves they were playing the part both of father and son, and it is only when they repeated this ceremony on the next generation that it became again an action in which subject and

[1] On the sacred fire of initiation ceremonies see J. G. Frazer. On some ceremonies of the Central Australian tribes.—*Australasian Association for the Advancement of Science*, 1901, 318, 319. Howitt, op. cit., 525, 537, 573, 615.

[2] Frobenius, l.c., III. 141, 255.

11. CLASS ORGANIZATIONS ACCORDING TO N. W. THOMAS

I. MURI, KUBI, KUMBO, IPAI.

II. KURBO, MARO, WOMBO, WIRO.

III. PARANG, BUNDA, WOMBO, BALGOIN, THEIRWAIN.

IV. KARILBURA, MUNAL, KURPAL, KUIALLA.

V. WONGO, KUBARU, BUNBURI, KOORGILLA.

VI. KARAVANGI, CHIKUN, KURONGON, KURKILLA.

VII. WANDI, WALAR, JORRO, KUTCHAL.

VIII. RANYA, RARA, LOORA, AWUNGA.

IX. JIMMILINGO, BADINGO, MARINGO, YOUINGO.

X. MURUNGUN, MUMBALI, PURDAL, KUIAL.

XI. AWUKARIA, ROUMBURIA, URTALIA, WIALIA.

XII. (INCLUDES ALL EIGHT-CLASS SYSTEMS.)

XIII. PANUNGA, BULTHARA, PURULA, KUMARA.
(*a*) Deringara, Gubilla, Koomara, Belthara.
(*b*) Burong, Ballieri, Banaka, Kymerra.

XIV. TONDARUP, DIDARUK, BALLARUK, NAGANOK.

XV. LANGENAM, NAMEGOR, PACKWICKY, PAMARUNG.

XVI. KARI, WAUI, WILTU, WITHUTHU.

XVII. ADJUMBITJI, APPULARAN, APPUNGERTI, AUINMITJI.

See N. W. Thomas: *Kinship Organizations and Group Marriage in Australia*, 1906, Chapter IV. Map II is reproduced here with a slight modification in the north following Spencer, *Northern Territory*, 1914, 55. For further details on this important question see F. Gräbner: "Wanderung und Entwickelung sozialer Systemem in Australien," *Globus*, XC, 181–91, with a map on p. 183.

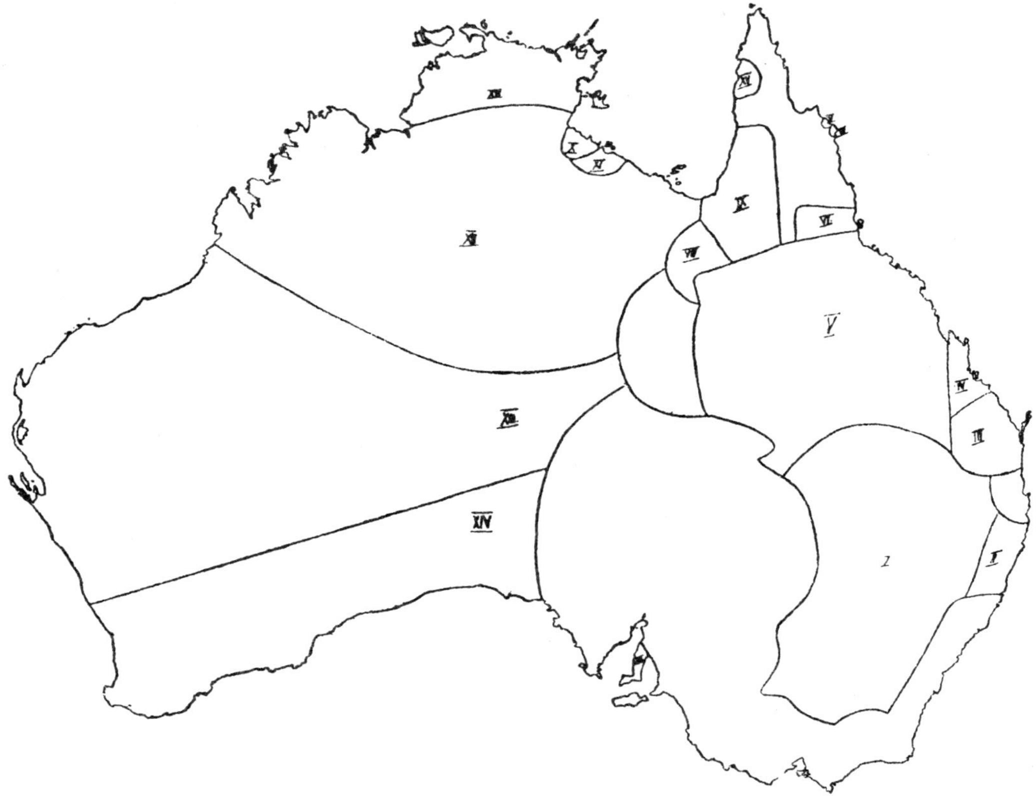

MAP No. 11.

Class Organizations according to N. W. Thomas (supplemented by B. Spencer's *Native Tribes of Northern Territory*, 1914).

object, initiators and initiates were separated. To say that the stone-knife was introduced by sky beings is equivalent to saying that it was introduced by the dead, a ceremony performed in honour of the dead. Or, we can refer to the Urabunna legend of the Yuri-ulu, " the Two living ones," who rise out of the earth invisibly and cut the foreskin with their stone knives.[1] Somebody who rises out of the earth, looks very much as if he was coming out of his grave, and the adjective " living " seems in this connexion to be an ambivalent euphemism to cover the contrary meaning. These first ceremonies which were held at the grave of the father and immediately after the first parricide were puberty rites and ceremonies of initiation into manhood in *optima forma*. As long as the young males had not killed their father, felt the loss and the self-caused shock after the deed, and at the end of this " period de marge " had access to their mothers and sisters, they were not men in any sense of the word. For we must not forget that these battles took place at the rutting season, and that they ended in a general orgy which still survives in their late descendants. From a genetic point of view we must regard the murder and the rut as the original elements; the inhibition represented by mourning was only interposed between them when the impressions made on living matter, the engrams of many futile revolutions, were beginning to make themselves felt, and instead of continuing the fight against each other and being punished by their brothers for what they had done to their father, they began to punish themselves. At this stage of evolution an intermediary period would be evolved in which they acted as if the father who did not let them have access to the women was still alive, and therefore they did not rush upon their sisters as they were wont to do. This period was spent in neurotic actions at the grave of the man whom they had killed, and this was the prototype of both mourning and initiation rites. The central mystery of these rites was the corpse itself; it was only when the sons of these victorious brothers grew up and when, as Reik has pointed out they were afraid of the next generation, that the mourning rite was repeated but the murder left out, and that the necessity of a substitute for the corpse began to make itself felt. This must have happened at about the same epoch when the ancestors of the Central Australians were for some unknown reason compelled to start upon their migrations from their ancient home. The further they wandered from the scene of their first rebellion the less chance there was of showing the real grave, the real corpse, or at least the bones to the next generation. Society was hitherto a scene of permanent revolutions or of violent measures to obviate this danger, but for the wandering tribes need was pressing and the old males began to make a compromise; they could permit the young ones, who became

[1] Howitt and Siebert, " Legends of the Dieri," *J. A. I.*, 1904, 109.

indispensable helpmates in the many needs of the journey, to have access to some of the women on condition that they underwent a ceremony of contrition (mourning) for the unconscious parricidal impulse that was within them. But as we have said, there was no corpse to appear before the awe-struck eyes; wood and stone, bull-roarer and Churinga had to do duty instead.

At the Kurnai Jeraeil the cryptic phrase used for the central mystery, that is the exhibition of the bullroarer to the novices, is "showing the grandfather."[1] Perhaps the burial ceremony of the Binbinga, Anula and Mara, who put the body in a coffin ornamented with the totemic design, perform ceremonies after death which relate to the ancestors of the dead man's totem group and introduce any newly initiated boy who happens to be present to sit round the parcel of bones with the men,[2] may represent a fair copy of the original undifferentiated rite, which was a mourning Intichiuma and initiation at the same time. The "Central mystery" revealed to the neophyte was the parcel of bones, which were replaced in the course of time by "grandfathers" of wood and stone.

It is perhaps not without significance that the spiral and concentric ornaments which are so characteristic of Central Australian bullroarers and Churingas (the zigzag lines of West Australia seem to be a local modification of the spiral type) can be traced to New Guinea, and that, as pointed out by Haddon, the development of spiral ornaments from the representation of the human face is still traceable in this island.[3] The bullroarer which represented a dead man had a human face or figure on its surface, and the growth of conventionalization in this case may be traced to the obliterating work of repression. The reversal which characterizes this second phase in the development of Initiation ceremonies was carried through along the whole line. It was not the father who was killed in good earnest and revived afterwards as a ghost in the imagination of his sons, his murderers; it was the youths who were killed (in imagination) and revived (in sober reality) by the old men. When the brothers had killed the Jealous Sire, the women undoubtedly felt sorrow at his death and mourned for him. Now they continued their mourning, but the object had suffered a displacement; they mourn for Youth killed by the Aged Men. Assuming that we have not been going totally wrong, we shall regard the following conclusions as established:—

Summary.

(*a*) The Ancestors of the Central Australian tribes came from the north and the north-west; they must be regarded as immigrants into Australia.

[1] Howitt, *N. T.*, 628.

[2] Spencer and Gillen, *Nor. T.*, 173, 552, 553.

[3] Haddon, *The Decorative Art of British New Guinea*, 1894. Spencer and Gillen, *N. T.*, 634, 635. The Tikowina (bullroarer) of the Herbert River tribes is about a foot long, brought gradually to a point at the bottom, whilst the top is cut in the rude representation of a man's face with mouth and eyes. All over the front it is painted red and black with human blood and clay.—Howitt, *N. T.*, 499.

(*b*) They brought a religion with them in which the worship of stones played an important part. There must have been two principal migrations—the first with Churinga and local conceptional totemism, represented by the Arunta and Kakadu; the second with patrilineal conceptional totemism represented by the Warramunga and allied tribes.

(*c*) There is reason to assume a prehistoric contact between these immigrants and the people who have been called the "stone-using immigrants" of Indonesia by W. J. Perry.

(*d*) In both areas the introduction of the Stone Age is attributed to sky beings. In both areas ancestors are petrified and these myths are developed out of the incest complex. Australian traditions clearly point to an age (the Alcheringa) in which the ancestors raised cairns over their dead. The legends of petrifaction are connected with floods in both areas. In Australia, every child is born from a rock, in Indonesia (and Oceania) birth from a rock is a cosmological or anthropogonical motive. This proves that the ancestors of the Central Australians had a common stone culture with the ancestors of the "stone-using immigrants"; but it also proves that they have conserved a much more primitive variant or phase of this culture, for the myth which says that the first men were born out of rocks is a trace of a period when it was generally believed that men are born from rocks. In both areas the rock from which children are born is the stone under which the ancestor is buried, and the belief which explains the birth of children not from real coitus between the mother and the father but from a symbolic coitus between the woman and an ancestor represents a return of the Oedipus complex.

(*e*) The rock or the cairn is piled up over the corpse of the ancestor to keep him from getting up again; but by a return of repressed elements it becomes identified with the very ancestor against whom it was erected. Small stones from the grave are used in Indonesia as symbols of the body on voyages; hence migrating tribes must have developed the belief in the Churinga as a substitute for the corpse.

(*f*) The consequences, from the standpoint of social psychology, of the ethnological connexion established in this way. are as follows: The Intichiuma are developed out of the death rites of the murdered father. The animal which haunted the grave and ate the corpse was regarded as identical with the dead father; the "immortal" Alcheringa-being as hero or god is a dead man. Behind totem-eating we find the devouring of the Jealous Sire; there must have been a period when conception was regarded as the result of the women eating, not the totem but the flesh of the dead man. The mourning period for the dead father is the common root of initiation, intichiuma and mourning ceremonies.

(*g*) The ethnological connexion between Australia and Indonesia involves a striking confirmation of Freud's views as to the origin of totemism. We have analysed the totemic institutions and beliefs of the Central Australian tribes and found that they are reaction-formations against the Oedipus complex. Perry has been led by purely ethnological considerations to ascribe the introduction of totemism to Indonesia (and hence probably to Oceania in general), to a people who practised incestuous unions although the traditions contain evidence of the disapproval of these unions. This apparent contradiction cannot be solved by ethnology alone; it is only through psycho-analytical research that we can understand the disapproval as well as the totemic taboos as the result of the conflict between libido and repression. We may add that both the "stone-using immigrants" of Indonesia and the Central Australians are characteristic examples of the "Stone Age" in religious evolution, and we shall feel that the probability of a prehistoric contact between these two areas is not to be underrated.

The stone-totemism of Central Australia and the complexity of Australian culture.

From an ethnological point of view we must treat these immigrants as an unknown quantity. We shall now proceed to examine how far this ascription of the magico-religious complex which consisted in the threefold unity of Alcheringa myths, Intichiuma rites, and Conceptional totemism to a separate culture cycle or wave coincides with the results obtained by authors who have dealt with other sides of Australian culture.[1] In sociology the characteristic feature of the area in question is paternal descent and the existence of four- and eight-class systems, whilst the area of negative totemism is occupied by tribes with maternal descent and two- or four-class systems[2] (cf. Maps 2, 4, 5, 6, 7, 8, 9, 10, 11). The characteristic burial customs of this area are those which conform to the type of delayed burial and involve the use of platforms or trees as temporary resting-places of the corpse as well as a sort of mummification,[3]

[1] The cultural and historical connexion between stone churingas, conceptional totemism, and Intichiuma ceremonies has been emphasized by P. W. Schmidt in various articles (see especially, "Die Stellung der Aranda," *Z. E.*, 1908), but without accounting for the psychological nature of this connexion.

[2] Gräbner, "Kulturkreise in Oceanien," *Z. f. E.*, 1905, 30. Id., "Wanderung und Entwickelung socialer Systeme in Australien." *Globus*, 90, 183. N. W. Thomas, *Kinship Organizations and Group Marriage in Australia*, 1906.

[3] On the distribution of platform-burial in Australia, see Gräbner, "Kultur kreise," *Z. E.*, 1905, 30. Id., "Wanderung," *Globus*, 90, 223, 224. G. Elliot Smith, *The Migrations of Early Culture*, 1915. N. W. Thomas, "The Disposal of the Dead in Australia," *F.-L.*, 1908, 406.

The question of burial customs is not so simple, and shows the complicated mechanism of the clash of culture as well as the variability of a custom from purely evolutionary causes. As we have seen from the study of the Alcheringa legends, the Central tribes must have practised burials in caves or under cairns in the prehistoric age of the Alcheringa, so that they may very well have developed the custom of carrying the corpse about in the course of their migrations. (Rivers, *H. M. S.*, II. 278: "According to this view, the practice of preservation would be a feature of culture of the same order as the use of the canoe in the funeral rites. It would

12. CULTURE AREAS ACCORDING TO F. GRÄBNER (WITH MODIFICATIONS AND ADDITIONS FOLLOWING N. W. THOMAS, B. SPENCER, W. E. ROTH, ETC.)

Tribes with paternal descent (" Western Papuan ").
Tribes with maternal descent (" Eastern Papuan "). (White on map).
Class paternal, totem maternal.
Local organization.
Absence of spear-thrower.
Absence of shield.

I. Platform-Burial.

II. Stone-Headed Spear.

III. Daggers and Knives.

IV. Bark-Girdle.

V. Traces of Two-Class System in " Western Papuan " Area.

VI. Clubs.

VII. Spear-Thrower.

? Descent unknown or uncertain.

Cf. F. Gräbner: " Kulturkreise in Ozeanien," *Zeitschrift für Ethn.*, 1905, pp. 30, 31. N. W. Thomas: " Kulturkreise in Australien," ibid., p. 762. B. Spencer: *Northern Territory*, 1914. W. E. Roth: " Social and Individual Nomenclature," *North Queensland Ethnography Bull.*, XVIII, 102, 103. Idem: *Ethnological Studies*, 57.

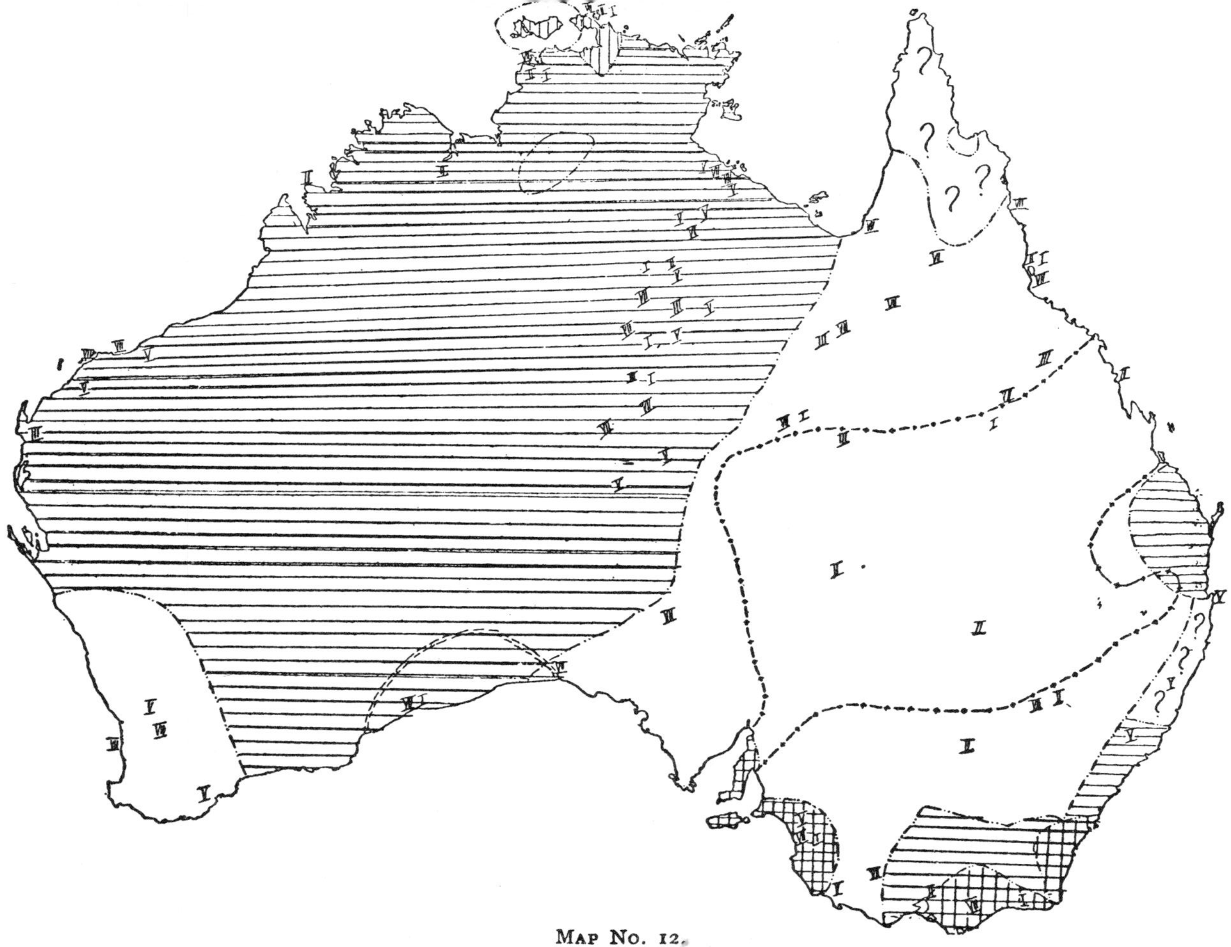

MAP No. 12.

Culture Areas according to F. Gräbner (with modifications and additions following N. W. Thomas, B. Spencer, W. E. Roth, etc.).

whilst simple earth burial immediately after death seems to be the original mode of disposal of the dead in the south-eastern area (*see* Map 9). Another question which seems to divide the Australian aboriginals into two principal sections is that of initiation ceremonies. The remarks of H. Webster on this subject are so very much in accordance with our own views that we cannot do better than quote them in full: " Over the wide expanse of the Australian Continent two great types of Initiation rites prevail. There are the Bora ceremonies of the tribes occupying the eastern coast and the interior westward throughout the greater portion of Victoria, New South Wales and Queensland, and what we may for convenience call the Apulla ceremonies of the Central and Western tribes which range over half the Continent." " A line drawn from Cape Jervis at St. Vincent's Gulf, South Australia, and continued in a north-easterly direction through New South Wales, and then northerly through Queensland to the Gulf of Carpentaria, separates the tribes that practise circumcision and subincision from those that do not. East of this line Bora ceremonies in which the principal rite is either evulsion of teeth or depilation prevail. Between this and a second line which begins at Port Augusta at the head of Spencer Gulf, South Australia, and then continues in a northerly direction until it joins the first line at Longreach, Queensland, is the area occupied by the tribes which practise circumcision alone. The ceremonies of these tribes may be described as a mixture of Bora and Apulla rites. Extending in a westward direction from this second line is the large area occupied by tribes which possess the Apulla rites and practise both circumcision and subincision. Beyond a line drawn from Cape Arid on the Great Australian Bight to North-West Cape on Plymouth Gulf, neither of these rites has been observed." [1] " On the theory that the Tasmanians, now extinct, were the remnants of a Nigritic race which once peopled Australia, it is possible, as Mr. H. L. Roth suggests, that an invading race may have adopted some of the customs of the earlier inhabitants." [2] " Initiation ceremonies among other customs may have been so borrowed or at least modified by contact with aboriginal inhabitants. On this hypothesis the South-Eastern Australian tribes representing the first invaders ought to possess the most archaic customs,[3] and these ought, of all the

be a consequence of the fact of migration, and not a necessary indication of the original nature of an immigrant culture.") But on the other hand, the custom of platform-disposal may have existed in the original home of the Central tribes. The paths by which this custom was transmitted to the south involve other questions, which have not been solved by Gräbner (l.c.), as platforms outside the central area are by no means confined to the " bara " tribes. The Arunta and the tribes of the extreme north have platforms, a fact which may be interpreted in various ways.

[1] H. Webster, *Primitive Secret Societies*, 1908, 191.

[2] Cf. H. Ling Roth, *The Aborigines of Tasmania*, 1899, 227, 228. Ibid., 116, on teeth-evulsion.

[3] We shall be compelled to investigate the legitimacy of this view and similar conclusions below.

Australian Initiation ceremonies, show most likeness to those of the Tasmanians.[1] "Circumcision, practised by the people of the south and east coast of New Guinea, may have been introduced by an invading race which came from that direction. Subincision is undoubtedly a native Australian development, for its like is not to be found outside the Continent (cf. Map 10 and p. 445).[2] In material culture the absence of the spear-thrower in the matrilinear area, as well as other features enumerated by Gräbner (but requiring more detailed investigation), might be mentioned.[3] The most important link in the chain of evidence has been furnished by the linguistic researches of Father Schmidt. He shows that the great dichotomy of the Australian race is quite evident in the classification of languages. The South Australian languages coincide with the matrilinear two-class area, whilst the immigrants who introduced the specific forms of totemism which we have been dealing with into Australia spoke languages which belong to another linguistic family and must be described as Neo-Australian. A glance at the maps[4] will show that the cultural area of Central Australian influence extends, especially to the West, far beyond the tribes speaking these Neo-Australian languages. Indeed, it is quite evident that the Western tribes must have originated out of the interaction of the immigrants and the tribes they found in possession; immigrant influence has been strong enough to modify the culture but not the language. Father Schmidt also points out that science will probably be able, in the future, to demonstrate the further links which connect these northern languages with the Papua of New Guinea, as well as with the Dravida of India or rather the "Pre-Dravidian" population of Indonesia.[5]

Anthropologists on the origin of the Australian race.

It is at this point that the results derived from many branches of research seem to join hands. For all that we have said of the two principal sections of the present population of Australia from the point of view of (*a*) Religious belief, (*b*) Sociology, (*c*) Linguistics agrees remarkably with the views of anthropologists on the origin of the Australian race. Flower and Lydekker think that the physical characteristics of the Australians can be best accounted for by regarding them as a cross between a low form of Caucasian Melanochroi and a frizzly haired population represented by the Tasmanians.[6]

[1] Webster, *Primitive Secret Societies*, 1908, 193.

[2] Webster, l.c., 194.

[3] Gräbner, "Kulturkreise in Ozeanien," *Z. E.*, 1905, 30. Id., "Kulturkreise in Australien," ibid., 765. Luschan, "Das Wurfholz in Neu Holland und Ozeanien," *Bastian Festschrift*, 1896. P. W. Schmidt, *Anthropos*, 1912, 230, 251.

[4] The boundary-line of Neo-Australian languages is indicated on all our maps according to P. W. Schmidt in the *Anthropos*. (VI. 1911).

[5] P. W. Schmidt, "Die Gliederung der australischen Sprachen," *Anthropos*, 1912, 250; ibid., 1917–18, 437. (Cf. recent views of the same author in Buschan, *Illustrierte Völkerkunde*, 1923, II. 11.)

[6] W. H. Flower and H. Lydekker, *An Introduction to the Study of Mammals, Living and Extinct*, 1891, 748, quoted by Howitt, *N. T.*, 31.

As to the connexion with the Dravidas, an idea which keeps re-occurring in anthropological literature, notwithstanding the seemingly far-fetched, and at any rate far from proven aspect of such a hypothesis, certain arguments which have been brought forward in this connexion seem to deserve consideration. If the linguistic affinity is more than a dream, the coincidence of two weapons which cannot be said to form the general property of primitive man, namely the spear-thrower and the boomerang, deserves consideration.[1] Of course, this could only be a connexion as between two widely divergent branches of a common and very ancient parent stock.[2] This parent stock could be no other than the wavy-haired, brown-skinned, aboriginal population of Indonesia, represented at present by such broken-down and probably much modified tribes as the Wedda of Ceylon, the Toala of Celebes and the Kubu of Sumatra. These must have spread over the island world at a period when the sea offered no obstacles, or at least much less formidable obstacles to their migrations than at present, for all authorities agree in claiming that Australia must have been populated from the north-west.[3] Dr. Volz thinks that this race was the first to take possession of these regions and he divides this hypothetical race into a northern (North Australia, Melanesia), southern (South Australia) and Tasmanian branch.[4] This immigrant race or rather the northern branch of the race, according to the view of Dr. Volz must have had a low form of stone culture, paleolithic weapons, burial in caves or under cairns, and a consequent association between the dead fathers and rocks or stones. The Wedda believe that the spirits of the dead live in hills, caves, and rocks.[5] At Omuni, the "Nae Yaku" (spirits of the dead) are believed to be associated with rocks.[6] There must have been a contact of some sort between these people and the so-called "stone-using immigrants" of Indonesia, the nature of which contact we can, however, hardly even attempt to guess. Perhaps the very rude stone culture of this Australian population was influenced by the immigrants and, as often happens in such cases, it was the receptive and not the inventive race which preserved

[1] *The Australasian Anthropological Journal*, 1897, 121, quoted by Hagen, *Unter den Papuas*, 1899, 146, 147. Cf. also W. Volz, *Süd und Ostasien*, in Buschan, *Illustrierte Voelkerkunde*, 1909, 226: (On the racial strata in Indonesia: first the Negritos, then the Indonesians, who are probably related to the Dravidas, and through them to the European race); 249 (on the age of wood); 260 (on boomerangs in Celebes: a connecting-link between the boomerangs of Southern India and Australia). (Cf. in the new edition, the contribution of Heine-Geldern, Vol. II.)

[2] With regard to the relationship with Dravidians, or pre-Dravidians, Howitt justly remarks that such a connexion must be considered only as the "relationship of two tribes co-descendant from a common and distant ancestral stock."—A. C. Howitt, op. cit., 30.

[3] B. Hagen, op. cit., 1899, 144.

[4] Volz, "Beiträge zur Anthropologie der Südsee," *Archiv f. Anthropologie*, XXIII. 97.

[5] C. G. Seligmann, *The Veddas*, 1911, 151.

[6] Id., ibid., 167.

the cultural and religious elements in their more archaic form. Or perhaps the extremely primitive elements which we have found at the bottom of stone-beliefs in Australia and Indonesia were developed independently in both groups, in which case only a few specific resemblances would be due to culture-contact. At any rate, we must regard the Central tribes as later immigrants than those which have the two-class system and maternal descent, and try if we can ascertain anything with regard to the nature of relations between these two groups.

Tribes on the verge of the two culture areas. The Euahlayi.

We shall best be able to demonstrate the psychological and ethnological relations of the two-culture areas by taking a few tribes that are on the verge of the two systems. The Euahlayi have the Kumbo-Murri-Hippi-Kubee four-class system,[1] like the Kamilaroi, Wirradhuri and other eastern tribes.[2] They have tooth-evulsion, and they call the Initiation rite Bora ;[3] so do the Kamilaroi amongst whom the Northern Kamilaroi have evidently dropped the knocking out of the teeth, which, however, still survives in another section of the tribe.[4] Again, they share the belief in Baiamai with the Kamilaroi and Wiradjuri.[5] That they have the same or similar beliefs as the Arunta about the origin of children has been pointed out by A. Lang[6] and detailed above. But I do not know that anybody has pointed out the existence of Intichiuma ceremonies amongst them, which according to our theory should go hand in hand with the childbirth beliefs. K. L. Parker says : "Every totem has its own special corroboree and a time for having it, as the Beewees or iguanas, when the pine pollen is falling and the red dust-storms come. And if you abused the dust to a Beewee black you would insult him ; it is not dust, it is the pollen off the pines and so a multiplex totem of his, and the rains are claimed by the totem whose wind was that blew it up." "If a storm comes without wind it belongs to Bohrah, the kangaroo." "Away to the north-west a tribe of Blacks have almost a monopoly in wind-making, holding great corroborees to sing these hurricanes up."[7] Totemic corroborees that are performed at fixed seasons, and evidently exercise a magical influence on the totem or multiplex totem, are exactly what we call Intichiumas.

Similarly the Tully River tribes, who have a four-class system (not the Panunga-Bulthara type),[8] and whose incarnation beliefs we have already commented on, have magical ceremonies that

[1] Parker, *Euahlayi*, 12.
[2] N. W. Thomas, *Kinship*, 42. R. W. Schmidt, "Gliederung," *Anthropos*, 1912, 238.
[3] Parker, l.c., 75.
[4] Howitt, l.c., 594, 595.
[5] Howitt, l.c., 494. Parker, l.c., 4. Ridley, *J. A. I.*, 1871, II. 257.
[6] Introduction to K. L. Parker.
[7] Parker, l.c., 81, 82. Cf. the Intichiuma of the Murawari: A. R. Brown, *J. R A. I.*, 1923, 440.
[8] Cf. Map 11, "Class Organizations."

13. SUCCESSION OF ETHNIC STRATA IN AUSTRALIA.

I. PROTO-AUSTRALIAN.
II. DUAL PEOPLE (LEFT WHITE).
III. POSITIVE TOTEMISM.
IV. SURVIVALS OF DUAL CULTURE (TRACES OF MATRILINEAR DESCENT, TOOTH AVULSION) IN POSITIVE TOTEMISTIC AREA.
V. POSITIVE TOTEMISTIC INFLUENCE IN DUAL CULTURE AREA.
VI. RECENT INFLUENCE FROM NEW GUINEA OR MELANESIA.

(Bamboo tube, conch, masks, leaf-garments like Duk-Duk in use at initiation.)

1, 2, 4, 8, 17, 18, 19 (Sp. III, 92), 32 (Sp. II, 705), 52 (Str. IV, 15), 76 (*Globus*, 97, 53), 198, 199, 200, 202, 203, 204, 205, 213, 332 (Roth: *Bull.*, IV, 23, 24), 351 (*F.L.*, XIV, 345), 373 (Roth: *Bull.*, IV, 23, 24).

VII. LOCAL ORGANIZATION.

(*a*) With paternal descent.
87 (H. 130), 89 (H. 131), 108–111 (H. 133), 272 (H. 129).

(*b*) With uterine descent.
1, 2, 12 (Sp. 369).

(*c*) With purely totemic descent.
4, 6, 13, 17, 18, 19, 20 (Sp. III, 179, 277).

VIII. FINGER-JOINTS MUTILATED.

3, 5, 10, 111, 155, 156, 157, 159, 163, 192, 206, 207, 223, 229, 292, 308, 315, 318, 319, 320, 327, 333, 336, 359, 360 (p. 443).

IX. ABSENCE OF BOOMERANG ACCORDING TO SARG.[1]

[1] Francis C. A. Sarg: "Die Australischen Bumerangs im städtischen Völker Museum," *Veröffentl. Frankfurt*, 1911, III.

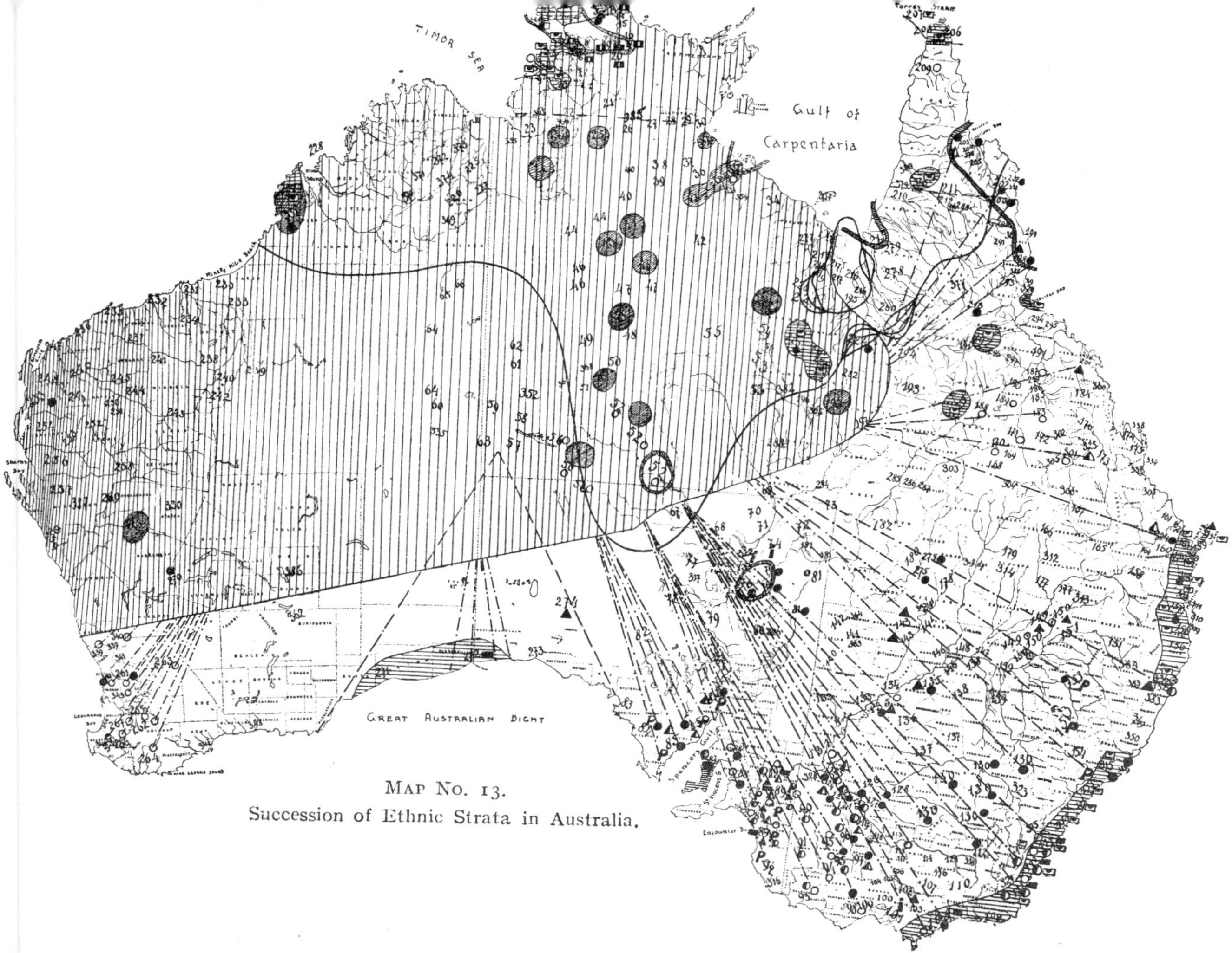

MAP NO. 13.
Succession of Ethnic Strata in Australia.

Frazer[1] has with full right compared to the Central Australian Intichiuma. At the Tully River whenever somebody goes to sleep or gets up he mentions in more or less of an undertone the name of the animal, etc., after which he is called or belonging to his group division, prefixing it with wintcha? wintcha? (where? where?). If there is any particular noise, call, or cry connected with such name he may mimic it. The object aimed at in carrying out this practice is that they may be lucky and skilful in hunting, and be given full warning as to any danger that might otherwise befall them from the animal after which they are named.[2] If a man named after a fish thus regularly calls upon it, he will be successful in catching plenty on some future occasion should he be hungry. If an individual called after the thunder, rain, etc., neglects to call them, he will lose the power of making them. Snakes, alligators, etc., will never interfere with their namesakes, provided they are always thus called upon, without giving a warning—a "something" which the aboriginal feels in his belly, tingling in his ear, thighs or legs, etc. If an individual neglects to do so, it is his own fault that he is bitten or caught.[3] On the Proserpine River the natives call on one of the animals connected with their particular subclass.[4] People who are named after the rain can make it come, the proceeding usually adopted is to hang a whirler into certain pools. If lightning and thunder are to accompany rain he will in addition throw chips of the Sarcocephalus cordatus into the pool.[5] On the Georgina River at Roxburgh Downs a piece of quartz crystal (rain-stone) is crushed and hammered to powder. Some very straight-stemmed tree is chosen and saplings are ranged all round it in the form of a bell-tent, forming a sort of shed. A small space of ground is cleared, a portion scooped out and some water placed in it. The men come out of the shed, and dancing and singing all around the artificial water-hole, break out with the sounds and imitate the antics of various aquatic birds and animals, ducks, frogs, etc. Then they form into Indian file and gradually encircle the women, over whom they throw the crushed and pulverized stone. The women at the same time hold wooden troughs, shields and pieces of bark over their heads and pretend that they are protecting themselves from a heavy downpour of

Traces of Intichiuma rites among Queensland tribes, who also possess the childbirth beliefs of the Central Australians.

[1] Frazer, *T. & E.*, I. 533.

[2] The danger dreaded from the totem animal is (like the dread of ghosts) a projection of their own repressed animosity towards the animal as a father-symbol.

[3] Cf. above, 169–171, the way the Arumburinga warns his double of approaching danger. That the warning should be in causal connexion with the constant calling on the namesake is, if considered psychologically, strictly true. Anybody whose mind is constantly occupied with the crocodile will not forget to call on it, and in consequence of the constant innervation of this attitude he is also most likely to apprehend the presence of his dangerous namesake.

[4] Roth, *S. M. M.*, 20, 21.

[5] Id., ibid., 9.

rain. While this ceremony reminds us of the imitative and perhaps also (throwing stones at the women!) of the procreative element in Intichiuma, other elements are found amongst the Kalkadoon; in their rain-making ceremony the feather down of the emu is stuck with blood over the body of the performer. At Devoncourt a sort of "soap-stone" rubbed with fat is brought into requisition.[1]

The Dieri.

The intermingling of the cultural elements of the two waves of immigration may be studied with especial profit in the case of the Dieri. They have a two-class system of the Kararu-Matteri type and their language belongs to the South Australian languages.[2] However, they have undergone considerable modification from tribes such as the Arunta, and their neighbours the Urabunna who belong to the second wave of migration. To begin with they have, as we have seen, Intichiuma ceremonies, and their Mura-Muras, who change into trees, are very similar to the Alcheringa beings and Nanja trees of their northern neighbours.[3] In one legend the female Mura-Mura Wari-in-luna is said to have come forth from the earth and given birth to her many children, the various Murdus (totems), who ran away to different districts and settled themselves there. Howitt remarks that this is an equivalent to the Alcheringa ancestors giving birth to spirit-children.[4] The Dieri have no Churinga, but tribes who stand very near to them such as the Urabunna, the Ngameni and Karanguru have got Wolkadara, which are the equivalent of the Arunta Churinga.[5] They share with the Arunta the inapertwa myth,[6] which is psychologically not far removed from the Churinga belief. At the circumcision ceremony every individual gets a name taken from the boys Mura-Mura, which, as Howitt remarks, is similar to the relation supposed to exist between an individual and his Alcheringa ancestor.[7] The Dara-ulu, that is the two Dara, are the usual dual heroes of Australian myth. They are strangled by the unanimous decision of the people. Their bodies were rolled up and it was decided that the first child born should be the guardian of the Dara.[8] This is exactly like a true Central Australian myth—the ancestors lie down on the ground and turn into Churinga. The first child born after their death is naturally a reincarnation of their person, and the proper guardian of their body. The Dieri show two heart-shaped stones, which are carefully wrapped up in feathers and fat as the Dara-ulu, to scratch which would, as they say, cause the whole people to suffer perpetual hunger. The Dara-ulu are believed to be the senders of rain, and in the rain-making ceremonies these stones which

[1] Roth, *S. M. M.*, 10.

[2] Howitt, *N. T.*, 175. Schmidt, *Anthropos*, 1912, 293.

[3] Howitt, l.c., 482.

[4] Id., l.c., 806.

[5] Siebert, "Sagen und Sitten," *Globus*, 97, 49. A. W. Howitt and O. Siebert, "Legends of the Dieri and Kindred Tribes of Central Australia," *J. A. I.*, 1904, 108.

[6] Howitt, l.c., 476.

[7] Id., l.c., 657, 658.

[8] Id., l.c., 799.

represent them are rubbed with fat.[1] Thus the Dara-ulu legend presents decided evidence of the influence of tribes with a Churinga culture on the Dieri, their southern neighbours. Here we have an Alcheringa ancestor who is turned into a stone Churinga, which is smeared with fat at the Intichiuma ceremonies. The child born shortly after the death of the two Dara-ulu seems to be a reincarnation of theirs, notwithstanding the fact that our principal authorities on the Dieri (Siebert, Gason, Howitt) know nothing about a reincarnation doctrine of this tribe. However, Spencer seems to have positive information on this subject which must outweigh the negative evidence of the other authors. He enumerates the Dieri as one of the tribes which believe in spirit-children inhabiting definite localities and entering the women, and he says that the Dieri hold the belief that sex changes at each successive reincarnation.[2]

The Mura-Muras and ancestral trees.

We must devote a few lines to the problems suggested by the Mura-Mura of the Dieri. The word Mura means holy ones, the Ancestors.[3] They are evidently offshoots of the Central area with patrilinear descent for the Dieri and —in character with their intermediate position—have a twofold system of totemism. The totems which are inherited from the mother are called madu, and are divided between the two classes Kararu-Matteri. The Dieri is also connected with his mother's Mura-Mura, and this relation is called maduka, but his allegiance to his father's Mura-Mura seems to be the more important one. Everybody inherits from his father a Mura-Mura that is a legend, an Intichiuma ceremony, and a country which is regarded as the place where his father's Mura-Mura lived. A father will tell his child, " This is your country. My Mura-Mura created it. My Mura-Mura lived here." [4] Occasionally the Mura-Mura seem to be turned into rocks, yet the general rule is that they were turned into trees, which they inhabit at the present time and which therefore are held sacred.[5]

The Mulligan River tribe will tell us that the first Black was Bitabetta, and after him came a woman called Cullabonna; a water-hole and the district bear her name. Both were created by a log of wood called " Moora," which is still found in the water-

[1] Howitt, *N, T.*, 799, 800.

[2] Spencer, *N. T. N. T. A.*, 23, 24. It is possible, however, that Spencer does not mean the Dieri tribe, but the Urabunna, who are included in the Dieri nation and undoubtedly hold these beliefs.

[3] Leonhardi, " Der Mura und die Mura-Mura der Dieri," *Anthropos*, 1909, 1067.

[4] Siebert, " Sagen und Sitten der Dieri," *Globus*, 97, 98.

[5] Howitt, l.c., 482. " There are places covered by trees, held very sacred, the larger ones being supposed to be the remains of their fathers metamorphosed. The natives never hew them; and should the settlers require to cut them down, they earnestly protest against it, asserting that they would have no luck, and might themselves be punished for not protecting their ancestors."—Gason-Curr, II. 69.

hole in a state of good preservation and reverenced.[1] Another analogy with the existence of totemic ancestors in trees is found in the "Coombangree" tribe. Each totem or family has some property peculiarly its own in the way of a water-hole or mountain in their district, and each formerly had its Camborra or ghost in the shape of an animal; others have birds, reptiles or fishes. These Camborra, or animal-shaped ghosts, live in certain trees,[2] which reminds us both of the Dieri Mura-Muras and the Arunta Nanja tree, whilst the mountain or water-hole belonging to a totem would be the equivalent of the oknanikilla.

Although we have got plenty of Nanja trees and wooden churingas besides the Nanja rocks and the stone churingas in the Arunta tribes, yet the predominance of wood (trees) as the materialization of the Mura-Muras seems to be of some importance. The same name is found scattered over the area occupied by the Central tribes, and it is perhaps possible to see traces of another wave of migration in which stone culture did not predominate, and which was still in the age of wood or on the verge between the two ages in these mythical beliefs. The Warramunga, who have not got the stone churinga of the Arunta, call their bullroarer murtu-murtu.[3] The spirit of the man Murtu-murtu was in certain trees, and now the Warramunga make the churinga called Murtu-murtu out of the wood of these trees.[4] The Binbinga call the sacred sticks wata-murra,[5] and each Anula boy is presented at initiation with a sacred stick called mura-mura.[6] Father Schmidt has pointed these facts out as well as the inference to be drawn from them; he regards them "as remnants of an old substratum."[7] Perhaps the legends which mention the use of a fire-stick for initiation previous to the introduction of the stone knife refer to the same cultural stratum of people. This may have been a population which lived in the age of wood, and their initiation ceremonies seem to have been of a much fiercer kind than those of their successors. However, we must affirm that we are far from regarding the interpretation as certain for the fire-stick, and the practice of killing youths at puberty may very well be a historical tradition which refers to the ancestors of the stone-using tribes in a more primitive phase of evolution.

The possibility of interpreting data either according to "evolutionary" or "historical" principles seems to present itself if we investigate the question of matrilinear survivals in the patrilinear

[1] W. Fraser, "Tradition of the Blacks on the Mulligan River," *Science of Man*, 1899, II. 40.

[2] McDougall, "Manners, Customs and Legends of the Coombangree Tribe," *Science of Man*, 1901, IV. 46, 63.

[3] Spencer and Gillen, *Nor. T.*, 275.

[4] Id., ibid., 279.

[5] Id., ibid., 280.

[6] Id., ibid., 373.

[7] P. W. Schmidt, "Die Stellung der Aranda," *Z. E.*, 1908, 892, 901.

area of the Centre. We find an allegiance to the mother's totem side by side with the conceptional totem amongst the Luritja and Arunta.[1] The case of a group of tribes in the north-western part of the territory drained by the Victoria River (Waduman, Mudbura, Ngainman and Bulinara) in which the totem groups are divided between the two moities, and in which the class name is counted in the paternal and the totem name in the maternal line,[2] seems, however, to indicate that maternal descent in Central Australia is symptomatic of the presence of a separate ethnic element. The Waduman tell us that in the far past there were two old men called Idakulgwan and Imumdadul. They were brothers and came from the north-east. As they travelled along they met an old woman named Ibangalma or Tjoral, who had no husband, and who came from the salt-water country. She had no husband, and her totem was sugar-bag. As they came along the two men made country, creeks, yams, kangaroos, snakes, sugar-bags, and many other things that the natives now feed on. They also carried "Ngaidjan," that is spirit-children, with them, and gave some of them to the old woman, telling her to take them away to other parts of the country and leave them there. This she did, and when leaving the spirit-children behind she gave them their totems. They grew up and became the first blackfellows, and when they died their spirits became Ngaidjan and were born again. Each spirit knows which is the right lubra to enter, and each of them has a special place called Poaridju, the equivalent of the Arunta Nanja, which is its normal stopping-place. Before going into a lubra each spirit enters and stays for a time in its mother's totemic animal or plant. Ibangalma finally went to a place called Hayward Creek, where the two brothers came after her. She married Idakulgwan, and they lived there together and had children, who are still reincarnated. The two brothers remained at Hayward Creek, where they are now represented by two stones, whilst another at the head of the Flora Creek represents the old woman.[3]

Matrilinear survivals in the patrilinear area.

If we remember that this legend is told by a tribe which counts descent of the class in the male, but descent of the totem in the female line, we cannot fail to see the piece of history which it contains. It tells us how an immigrant people which counted descent in the male line and was probably (as Rivers has shown with regard to similar migrations in Melanesia) composed principally of males, met another stock which came from the salt-water country and had female descent. The tribe, or rather horde, which

[1] Strehlow, II. 58. Cf. on the relationship between a man and his mother's totem among other Central and Northern tribes.—Spencer and Gillen, *Nor. T.*, 166, 171, 173.

[2] Spencer, *N. T. N. T. A.*, 16.

[3] Id., ibid., 268, 269.

came from the North-east formed marriage alliances with the women of the tribe which inhabited these territories before them, and it was only after this had taken place that the present race of blackfellows came into existence. The northern immigrants certainly had the class system or descent would not be counted in the male line. They must have been organized on the principles of the brother horde, or we should not find them represented by the typical dual heroes of Australian legend. But they also brought spirit-children with them, that is the belief in conceptional totemism, which is either an open (Warramunga, etc.) or a veiled, repressed (localized) patrilinear totemism (Arunta, etc.). The race which formed the other element of the mixture was also totemic, but counted the descent of the totem in the female line, like the Dieri and other tribes of South Australia. The northern immigrants with conceptional totemism were, of course, the same wave of population represented by the peculiar type of totemism which we have studied in Central Australia; witness the final petrifaction of these Alcheringa heroes and the existence of local totem-centres. The latter, taken by themselves, seem to indicate immigrant origin, for in this system each individual has two birth places, one real and one mythical, that is the ancestors whom he represents in the present generation were born somewhere else in the mythical age. The matrilinear population must have been dispersed over the continent in varying numbers, leaving large uninhabited areas between each of these small groups. In some places these groups were more numerous, in others they were totally absent, hence the varying degree of impression which they left on the tribes coming after them.

It is in the extreme north of the continent, on Melville Island and amongst the Iwaidja, that we again find tribes who reckon descent of the totem in the female line.[1] There are other reasons for connecting these with a previous population akin to the present inhabitants of South Australia. Spear-throwers are found amongst all the Northern tribes, except on Melville and Bathhurst Islands, where they are unknown[2]; they are equally conspicuous by their absence amongst the Dieri and other tribes with the dual organization and uterine descent.[3] Moreover, this Northern group, extending in this case beyond the Melville and Bathhurst Islanders to the tribes which form the Kakadu "nation," is remarkable by the absence of another custom which is very characteristic of the immigrant tribes with positive totemism; they have neither circumcision nor subincision.[4] They can be distinguished by having cicatrices as tribal marks, and the nearest approach to this custom

[1] Spencer, *N. T. N. T. A.*, 200, 201.

[2] Id., ibid., 378. W. Gregory, *The Dead Heart of Australia*, 1906, 190.

[3] Cf. Gräbner, *Z. E.*, 1905. See Map 12.

[4] Spencer, *N. T. N. T. A.*, 89.

is found in the Dieri tribe.[1] Perhaps we may even connect the grave-posts of the Melville Islanders with the marked trees of burial in New South Wales. Now the Kakadu tribe, whose totemism is next kin to that of the Arunta and who therefore have been taken by us as representing the first migration wave of the Central tribes, shows traces of this intermixture in its legends. Besides a male ancestor, Wuraka, remarkable for his large penis and for the fact that he is turned into a rock, the Kakadu have an ancestress Imberombera, who seems to be the more important of the two,[2] and who probably represents a matrilinear population.

The inter-relation between the tribes with positive and negative totemism.

If thus we have sufficient reason for reckoning with the interaction of two waves of culture in Central Australia, it is a problem of some difficulty to gain insight into the relative position of these two principal currents. Are we to regard these as totally unrelated to one another, the tribes with positive totemism, paternal descent and circumcision representing an immigrant people, those with negative totemism, uterine descent and other initiation ceremonies being the aboriginals, the children of the soil? If we refer to myth as our authority, we shall be informed that Wuraka came to the Coburg Peninsula from the West, walking through the sea. Now Imberombera, who evidently stands for the matrilinear population, also walked through the sea and landed at Wungaran (Malay Bay).[3] If we stick to the words of the legend we shall be compelled to assume that both the patrilinear and the matrilinear populations are immigrants, but the former evidently represent the second wave of migration. This conclusion seems to be confirmed by what we know of the distribution of tooth-evulsion.

The distribution of the two principal types of initiation ceremonies.

Howitt distinguishes the two principal types of initiation ceremonies mentioned above, the eastern type with evulsion of the tooth, and the western type with circumcision.[4] The Dieri are again on the border-line between the two types; they practise circumcision, but before circumcision the two lower middle front teeth are knocked out.[5] If we remember that the same tribes who have the negative type of totemism also have the expulsion of teeth as an initiation ceremony, whilst those that practise circumcision (and subincision) have what we called positive totemism,

[1] Spencer, *N. T. N. T. A.*, 43. [2] Id., ibid., 276. [3] Id., ibid., 276, 277.

[4] Some "Bora" ceremonies seem to be a still further repressed form of the Kuringal type, where even the knocking out of the tooth has disappeared, and only depilation has survived. Schmidt regards depilation as the initiation ceremony of the tribes with local, patrilinear organizations.—P. W. Schmidt, "Gliederung der australischen Sprachen," *Anthropos*, XII–XIII. 774.

[5] Howitt, *N.T.*, 655, 656. They also have subincision, but it is not compulsory.

we cannot fail to see that both our ethnological and psychological conclusions are corroborated in a striking way. That we have to do with two separate waves of migration is very probable, since in an analogous case the importance of initiation rites as keys of differentiation has not disappeared from the consciousness of the Blacks. The natives who are circumcised only are called Banapa, those who are both circumcised and subincised are the Bida. The Bidas look upon themselves as being superior in race to the Banapas, which probably shows that they represent a later conquering stock of tribes.[1] The tribes who practise circumcision only are evidently an intermediate stage between those with subincision and those with tooth-evulsion ; as the tribes with subincision are the latest arrivals of the three, it is the difference between these and their neighbours that has been retained by tradition. It is equally remarkable that the three groups of tribes form a series with regard to the degree of repression. We have ample proofs to show that initiation is a symbolic castration of the younger men. Now the further removed the mutilation practised at present is from the original, the more symbolic it is, the greater must be the influence of repression with the tribes that practise the rite. Knocking the teeth out is more symbolic than circumcision, and subincision, a still greater modification of the male member than the former, is still nearer to castration.[2] The same tribes that have the positive aspect of totemism have also much less symbolic, less neurotic forms of the initiation ceremony, and what is still more remarkable and contrary to what we should expect to find, it is the tribes that are the more recent arrivals in Australia that have conserved the more pristine forms of totemism and initiation. The question only is whether in these tribes repression has not come into play yet, or whether we have to do with a return of repressed elements ? The rite of teeth-evulsion proves an excellent test to decide this question. The tribes which mutilate the penis have also survivals of the tooth operation, while the tribes that have the latter form of initiation do not practise any operations concerned with the penis. For instance, in the Boulia district and amongst the Yaroinga we have circumcision as an initiation rite.[3] The evulsion of the incisors is a practice they

[1] Howitt, *N. T.*, 643, 644. The Muliarra undergo both circumcision and subincision, and a hostile feeling exists between them and the coastal tribes who do not practise these rites. Lord Gifford, Curr, I. 377. "They call the tribes which circumcise Buerdoppa, and those which do not Jalara." Curr, II. 176. "Of the Kalkatongo, or circumcised, who are more numerous than themselves, the Oonamurra are much afraid, as the former make raids into their country, killing their men and carrying off their women." MacGillivray, Curr, II. 342.

[2] Indeed there has been considerable discussion in literature whether the hypospadia artificialis, which is the result of the cut into the urethra, does not incapacitate the men for procreation, and although this is not the case, the discussion shows that the Europeans who held this view unconsciously understood the original meaning of the rite.

[3] Roth, *Studies*, 170, 172.

undergo voluntarily which is not in any way connected with initiation. "That it has been in vogue for ages past is probable from the fact that in none of the languages of these districts are there *a*, *th*, *v*, *s* sounds which require these teeth for their proper enunciation." [1] In the case of the Arunta tribe knocking out of teeth is a rite to which individuals of both sexes must sooner or later submit if they happen to belong to one or other of the local groups which inhabit what is called the Kartwia Quatcha, or rain country occupied by the Arunta tribes. It is usually but not always done before marriage, although it has nothing to do with initiation. The operation always takes place after the Water Intichiuma ceremony has been performed, and in case of a fully grown man it is performed on the Intichiuma ground.[2] The mother of the man who is operated upon must provide food for the operator, who in his turn gives food to the man he operated on. Spencer acutely suggests that this may be a survival of the food-giving rites at the Jeraeil (tooth-evulsion initiation) ceremony of the Kurnai. We are also told that the girl, when her tooth is knocked out, fills a small pitchi with sand and agitates it as if she were winnowing seed,[3] and we may go on to suggest that in the long-past times when knocking out of teeth was an initiation rite, this had a definite meaning now lost; it represented the girl practising her future duties of womanhood. Spencer goes on to show that amongst the tribes who practise tooth-evulsion as an initiation rite in the South-East the tooth is given to the lad's mother; in the Arunta tribe "we find that the tooth is thrown in the direction of the camp of the Alcheringa mother, which may perhaps be explained as indicating that in the Alcheringa, or rather the early times to which this name is given, the mother was entitled to the tooth." [4] This is undoubtedly the right explanation; we may carry it a step further by saying that "in the Alcheringa" tooth-evulsion was an initiation rite. In the Kaitish tribe the tooth is also thrown in the direction of the mother's Alcheringa camp.[5] Amongst the Warramunga the woman who has knocked the girl's tooth out pounds it up and places the remains in a small piece of flesh, which has to be eaten by the girl's mother. In the case of the men, the ceremony is always performed after the fall of heavy rain, when they have had enough and do not want any more rain to fall. The man's tooth is pounded up and put into meat, which is given in this case to his mother-in-law to eat.[6] The Tjingilli throw the tooth into a water-hole towards the close of the rainy season in the belief that it will drive the rain away. The Gnanji always perform the operation in the rainy season;

[1] Roth, *Studies*, 111.
[2] Spencer and Gillen, *N. T.*, 450, 451.
[3] Id., ibid., 452, 453.
[4] Id., ibid., 455, 456.
[5] Id., *Nor. T.*, 589.
[6] Id., ibid., 593.

the tooth is given to the mother, who in return presents the operator with food and red ochre. She has to bury it by the side of some water-hole, the object of this being both to stop the rain and to bring about an increase of the number of water-lilies growing in the pool.[1] If we suppose that the rite is the survival of an antiquated form of initiation ceremony, it is not difficult to explain its connexion with the rainy season and the Water totem. The symbol of initiation, the bullroarer, is a thunder-charm : initiation ceremonies are more or less intimately connected with the rainfall, growth and vegetation.[2] In the Dieri tribe it is the father who keeps the lad's foreskin as a rain-charm[3]; in other cases either the foreskin or the tooth serves to establish a magical relation between a man and a tree,[4] which points to the equivalence of these symbols. Probably certain elements of the initiation ceremony were split off as a Rain Intichiuma and took the rite of tooth-evulsion along with them. Besides, as I have shown elsewhere, knocking out the tooth is a symbolic castration,[5] and hence it must originally have been an initiation ceremony wherever it is found. In the Binbinga tribe a man's tooth is given to his brother-in-law ; it is from him that he is taking a woman (his wife) away and the tooth is a sort of symbolic penis offered in atonement for the one the brother-in-law would really like to cut off. In the case of the women, the rite is equally connected with the castration complex. Here it is again the man who is afraid of castration as the punishment for forbidden intercourse ; hence the myth of the vagina dentata. This vagina dentata is transposed upwards ; that is a tooth must be knocked out before a woman is fit to be married.[6] With the Binbinga the woman's tooth is given to her mother, she gives it to the woman's brother, and he hands it to her husband[7] as a token that he can make use of his right without the infantile dread of the vagina. If we could succeed in showing that the rite of tooth-expulsion is the pristine form of initiation common to both " waves " of immigrants supplanted in the second " wave " first by circumcision and then by subincision, we should be inclined to draw two further inferences. One of these might be that the greater degree of " openness " in the totemic and initiation rites of the second wave is not the result of an absolutely archaic state of things but is to be attributed to a return of repressed elements. But we are here confronted by another problem. The customs we have been investigating are certainly survivals of a type of initiation ceremony earlier than circumcision or subincision, but it still remains an open question whether they represent the

[1] Spencer and Gillen, *Nor. T.*, 593–95.
[2] Cf. above, p. 271.
[3] Siebert, " Dieri," *Globus*, 97, 55.
[4] Róheim, *Spiegelzauber*, 1919, 11. Id., *Imago*, VII. 500.
[5] Róheim, l.c.
[6] Mathews, op. cit., 108.
[7] Spencer and Gillen, *Nor. T.*, 596.

original initiation ceremonies of the immigrants or whether they were adopted by them from tribes they found in possession of the soil. There seems to be a close connexion between the survivals of tooth-evulsion (in "circumcision territory") and the female sex, a connexion which is explicable if we assume that the tribes who practise the rite are descendants of a mixed population. If a tribe were formed by immigrant hordes killing the men and taking possession of the women of the aboriginals, it stands to reason that the latters' initiation ceremonies would survive in connexion with the female sex. The fact that the immigrants had patrilinear descent and the aboriginals matrilinear, and moreover that the latters' initiation ceremony was applicable to both sexes whilst the former performed an operation on the male member, would tend to operate in the same direction. Here we must recall our view that the Arunta and Kakadu represent the first wave of these immigrants, which was split into two principal groups by the wedge of the Warramunga and allied tribes. If this assumption is correct, we must suppose that the representatives of the first wave must have come into closer contact with the aboriginals and hence have been more profoundly modified by them than those of the second. This modifying influence is very evident in the case of the Kakadu and other tribes of the Northern coast, and is perhaps represented by the mother totem altjirra and the emu-footed sky being Altjirra in the Arunta nation.

There is reason to believe that the Waduman and Mudburra represent a spreading movement of this wave to the South-west (reckoned from the Kakadu), for they alone share with the Arunta that type of Intichiuma ceremony which involves eating the totem. We have shown above that it is just these tribes which have preserved the clearest evidence of a double origin and of a matrilinear population in these areas. As the tribes of the East have, together with radically different languages, matrilinear descent and evulsion of the teeth, and as these customs are found like erratic blocks in the Centre, especially amongst those tribes who must be regarded as the first immigrants, there seems reason to regard them as evidence of the former existence of a population of the "Eastern" type in the Centre. The tribes born of this wedlock can hardly have developed all aspects of their culture in an harmonious manner, "progress" on one side being probably followed by "regression" on the other. From a strictly scientific point of view (apart from technical culture, where we have a reliable standard of what can be called "progress" and what the reverse) it is necessary to relinquish the evaluation involved in these expressions. It is safer to speak only of the modifications of social phenomena. These modifications are either in the direction of increased repression or in that of a return of repressed elements.

Both movements occurred amongst our Central tribes; the social structures grew more complex (eight-class system), whilst ritual and ideas showed clearly the operation of the return of the repressed elements (subincision, conceptional totemism).

The historical school and the psychological origin of institutions.

Although an investigation of the whole complex of Australian culture is quite beyond the scope of this book, certain phenomena must be pointed out which seem to confirm the conclusions we have arrived at. We accept the position of the modern ethnological schools represented by Gräbner in Germany, Rivers in England, and Schmidt in Austria, in so far as we see reason for assuming the complex character of Australian culture. Our next task is to attempt to lay bare the strata which are superposed on each other and the interaction of which forms our present subject of investigation. But we think it would be a great mistake to start from a supposed original culture, and then to construe the history of the latter migrations. We must take the latest important movement as our starting-point, and then see what is beneath it and so on as far as we can get. The further we go back from the present day (the last migration) the more we shall be groping in the dark, for it is evident that the customs of the invaders have obscured the social and religious structure of those who were there before them, and that we shall have an abundance of detail when dealing with the ceremonial, etc., life of the last wave, and only meagre general ideas on the customs of the tribes which have been assimilated by them. But, and this is usually overlooked by the advocates of the "modern" school, it is a different thing to trace the historical sequence of races in the Pacific and to explain the psychological origin of institutions. Head-hunting may be late in a given island and yet early in the history of mankind; there is no proof whatever for the view that the invaders may not have been in general, or in certain particulars, more "primitive," that is nearer to the animal stage than the invaded. Thus we shall as often as not find more primitive elements in the customs of the tribes that came later to a given area; one reason for this is that we can see back into the past much better when we have an abundance of details to argue from. This is just what we have found in our case, it is Central Australian totemism which has enabled us to go back to the pre-human roots of the institution.

It is certainly a very important ethnological problem to investigate the geographical distribution of customs and to point out the difference between two contiguous areas which must be accounted for by historical events. But if we have made a difference of custom a test for different origins, it is just as well to go one step further and to say that an equal distribution of important customs or ethnographical phenomena (provided that the agreement goes beyond the limits of the universally human[1]) over a certain area proves a unity behind the diversity. In other words, if the central tribes differ from the southern ones in certain aspects of life, proving a different past for the two groups, it proves that they have been separated for a certain period, each of them leading its own life, then the agreement in certain other customs proves a period of contact. But it will always be difficult to decide if this period of contact is recent, that is shows how two cultures acted and reacted on each other, how customs spread to the neighbour, were lent and borrowed; or whether the period is archaic, showing that the two cultures in question have been in contact at a prehistoric time, then separated and later re-united, or perhaps pointing to the two divergent types of custom as two branches of the same stem, carried into the arena of history by two migrating sections of the same race. For instance, although we have got initiation ceremonies with various mutilations (depilation, finger-joints cut off, tooth knocked out, circumcision, subincision, scars), there are certain elements which are found in all variants of the ceremony—the animal pantomimes and the removal of food taboos which the boys were compelled to observe up to that age (see Map 10). It is true that parallel lines of evolution will probably lead to animal pantomimes and food taboos (or removal of taboos) without any common origin or contact of tribes, but there is an agreement in details which makes it safest to assume a common root, an initiation ceremony observed before the ancestors of the whole race swarmed off into separate tribes.

Uniform distribution of certain customs over a given area can be accounted for in various ways.

For instance, the Yuin call the final act of the initiation rites (immersion in water) "catching fish."[2] The same cryptic expression, "let us go and fish,"[3] is found in connection with initiation ceremonies in the Larrakia tribe at the northern end of the continent.[4] Then there is a peculiar method of removing a taboo which seems to belong to the primitive inheritance of the Australian race. Anybody to whom a certain food, for instance emu or kangaroo, is forbidden, can be "made free" of its flesh if an old man takes him unawares and stealthily rubs a bit of fat or flesh on his mouth,[5] or if it is thrown at him.[6]

Certain mourning rites, the custom of organizing an expedition

[1] I, for instance, would never ascribe "magic" or even "sympathetic magic" to a given area, for we know very well that it is not absent in any race, tribe or nation.

[2] Howitt, *N. T.*, 554, 556.

[3] Spencer, *N. T. N. T. A.*, 161.

[4] In the Rockhampton district one of the older men will drop a piece of wood and tell the novice: "See the fine fish I caught."—W. E. Roth, "On Certain Initiation Ceremonies," *N. Q. E. Bull.* 12, 1909, 185.

[5] Howitt, *N. T.*, 561.

[6] Spencer, *N. T. N. T. A.*, 132.

against foreign tribes to obtain blood revenge after every death, the belief in the magical importance of human fat,[1] and in murderers who take the kidney fat out through an invisible wound,[2] are all Australian peculiarities that are well-nigh universal on this continent. The myths which are connected with the Eagle-hawk (what we have designated as the proto-totemic-complex) are especially prominent amongst the tribes with the class organization Eagle-hawk and Crow, and with the parallel two-class system of Kararu and Matteri; survivals are also found in the Central group of tribes, and if we find that these myths point to the North and North-west, the regions whence these Central tribes started on their migrations, we shall have to assume the same origin for the Southern tribes. Indications of the peculiarly south-eastern sex-totems are found in the North and even at Torres Straits, so that even these must have been imported from other latitudes to their present home by the B-wave of migration and lost afterwards by the latter immigrants.[3]

Two-class systems with male descent.

Both Gräbner and Rivers regard the two-class system as the peculiar characteristic of a certain cultural wave or stratum. It has, of course, not escaped the notice of Gräbner that we have definite evidence of the former prevalence of a two-class system in the Central area, and indeed he explains the origin of the eight-class system as the result of an interaction between tribes with the four-class and local tribes with the dual organization.[4] But there is a grave difficulty which has been completely overlooked in this solution. The occasions at which the dual organization of the tribes become specially prominent are ceremonies like the Engwura and especially the Intichiuma, which cannot in any case be regarded as inherited by the Central tribes from an aboriginal population. These ceremonies are intimately bound up with conceptional totemism, and hence we must assume an original two-class organization for our A-wave of migration. In fact, this two-class organization is still in existence amongst the Binbinga and Anula. It is true that these tribes have four classes, but the generations do not alternate between the classes; they have direct instead of indirect male descent. A(m) marries B(f): children A. C(m) marries D(f): children C. This looks like a couple of two-class systems with male descent superficially united in one tribe, and

[1] Róheim, "Das Selbst," *Imago*, VII. 22.

[2] Id., ibid., 20.

[3] See Map No. 2. Schmidt, "Sociologische und religiös-ethische Gruppierung der Australier," *Z. E.*, 1910, 376, regards sex-totems as characteristic of "nigritian" culture, and as extremely primitive. The distribution of this institution shown in the map makes its alleged "nigritian" character improbable, whilst the degree of its primitivity is discussed above from a mythological point of view.

[4] Gräbner, "Wanderung u. Entwicklung sozialer Systeme in Australien," *Globus*, 90, 221.

this is probably the real origin of the system.[1] Thus we should have to assume that our Central tribes, which represent a very primitive offshoot of that great migration which introduced clan totemism into Oceania and Australia, were also organized on the basis of a two-class system. Then another conclusion would follow; the "kava people" were also "dual" only at a very primitive phase of their social evolution which had been left behind by the other "waves" of this migration and only retained by this primitive offshoot.[2] Then we should perhaps remember the connexion of cross cousin marriage and the two-class organization and accept Frazer's view that the dual organization was a phase through which mankind in general passed. However, the dual organization is normally connected with uterine descent, that is, A(m)......B(f) : children B(m, f). This system does not prevent a father from marrying his daughter, but it prevents a man from espousing his mother. For B(m) the only possible wife is A(f), who must be his father's mother, that is his own grandmother. Thus the system contains in itself the germs both of the four-class system with its alternating generations and of the gerontocratic organization—the old men get the young women and the young men have to content themselves with old hags.[3] If, on the other hand, A(m) marries B(f) and the children are A(m, f) this would not permit a father to marry his daughter (father and daughter both A), but would allow a son to marry his mother (A(m) marries B(f)). The surprising conclusion is that the two-class system was in all branches of mankind the result of a compromise between the generations, but while a two-class system with male descent looks very much like a victory of the Son, with uterine descent the conditions of peace are those which would be made by a group of victorious Fathers.

In both cases the two-class system prohibits brother and sister union, and this prohibition is evidently a survival of the primitive patriarchal type of family. But besides this, the dual organization with female descent makes the mother taboo for the son but not the daughter for the father. A "class" is a group of people amongst whom no intercourse may take place, so that if the son belongs to the mother's class, this is really but another expression for the cardinal prohibition of sex-life. It must have been a group of victorious brothers who formed this type of society, but not till a considerable time after their victory, when they were more afraid of their coming sons than desirous of wedding their mothers. A dual organization with male descent is a society in which the

[1] Spencer and Gillen, *Nor. T.* Spencer, *N. T. N. T. A.*

[2] But this dual organization may have been the form of society of the Pre-Dravidians, who, again, may have been influenced by the race which was responsible for totemism and stone culture.

[3] J. G. Frazer, *F. O. T.*, 1919, II. 94–362.

fundamental law is: fathers may not marry their daughters, but sons have free access to their mothers. This also must be a creation of the brothers, but at the moment which followed their victory, this legislation being all in favour of the son and against the father. Thus the patrilinear bisection was destined to disappear in the course of evolution, leaving in its place patrilinear descent associated with other forms of social organization. But the fact that their first legislation was conceived in a revolutionary spirit has left its trace in the psychic disposition of this half of mankind, in a more plastic mould of their psyche, in a better adaptation to progress. The races with patrilinear descent have climbed to the top of the mountain called "civilization," whilst those who reckon descent through the mother have remained at the bottom. Movement was the leading principle in the one case, re-suppression of the next generation in the other.

Now we shall understand why we have been able to penetrate more deeply into the wish-fulfilment attitude which is behind totemic repression amongst the tribes who have descent in the male line, for the psychological difference between the two groups is the result of a different *dénouement* of the primeval Oedipus drama. If the Father, the Government Party, is victorious, repression will be the dominant feature of society, whilst the Party of the Revolutionary Son is all for wish-fulfilment, for a return of repressed elements. But repression is a very necessary element of social life and an organization which does not contain this element in a satisfactory degree will not be permanent, it is weakened constitutionally and apt to perish.[1] This is what we actually find; the dual organization with uterine descent was a successful variant in the "struggle for life" between social institutions—it has maintained itself and the people who were organized on this basis over large areas and many generations. The two-class system with male descent did not function so well; it had a short lease of life, and we can only find it as a survival overlaid by other social structures amongst the tribes who once possessed it. This is what we find amongst much more advanced races even in our own days; organizations which are conceived in a revolutionary spirit are usually short-lived, for this attitude of

[1] Naturally in all cases the conflict must, sooner or later, have led to the victory of the Young Males. But in the case of the patrilinear two-class system the law was made according to their own infantile wishes: they might marry their mothers, but the father was not allowed to touch his daughter. On the other hand, the two-class system, with matrilinear descent, is actuated by the fear of the coming generation. The former sees life and society from the point of view of the son, the latter from that of the father: a father may marry his daughter, but a son is not permitted to have access to his mother. In the first case, the sons must have made the law shortly after their victory, when wish-fulfilment was the chief thing: in the second case a longer period must have elapsed between their triumph and legislation, and in this period they had identified themselves with the father whom they had killed.

mankind thrives better in ideology (in dream-life: the Oedipus wish-fulfilment in conceptional totemism!) than in sober, hard reality.

The origin of the two-class system.

As to the connexion between the bisection of the tribe and the Oedipus complex, we have already brought some evidence in the Eagle-hawk and Crow myths of Australia. If we only remember the close connexion of this bisection with initiation myths and with totemism, we shall be inclined to regard this as symptomatic of a derivation from the Oedipus attitude.

In the very districts of Melanesia whence, according to Gräbner, the Australian tribes with the two-class system and maternal descent are to be derived, we find the two phratries represented by totem animals. For marriage purposes the people of New Britain are separated into two divisions—one of them is called Maramara and the other Pikalaba. On New Britain proper the two classes are named To Kabinana and To Kovuvuru. The totems of these classes are two insects. That of Maramara is the Kogila le "leaf of the horse-chestnut tree," so named because being about the length and size, and resembling very much in other respects the leaf of that tree. The Pikalaba totem is the Kam, which is probably the mantis religiosus. The Maramara class will on no account injure or allow to be injured with impunity their totem, the Kogila le, but they have not the slightest compunction in abusing the Kam. The Pikalaba class reverence the Kam, but they do not hesitate to destroy the Kogila le if they can do so secretly. Both classes believe that their ancestors descended from their own particular totem, which they call "Takun miat," i.e. our relative. Any evil or abuse inflicted on one class by the other's totem is considered as a *casus belli* to avenge.[1] The two matrilinear and exogamous classes are represented by the Hintubuhet, a word which means "our ancestress." The idea of the invisible Hintubuhet is materialized each time in a couple of beings who stand for the two divisions and correspond to each other. These are the two hawks *Pandion leucocephalus* and *Haliaetus leucogaster*, Sun and Moon, and the two large butterflies Talgomalgo and Heba. "Von je zwei zusammengehörenden Bildern sagen sie a hintubuhet dir, die Ahnen, unsere die beiden." The Taragau (*Pandion leucocephalus*), the Sun, and the Talgomalgo (the two last are masculine) represent the Tarago class, the Malaba (*Haliaetus leucogaster*), the Moon, and the Heba symbolize the class Pikalaba. The ending laba evidently means "big," and as "ma" is still used in the sense of bird, it seems that the class name Malaba must

[1] B. Danks, "Marriage Customs of the New Britain Group," *J. A. I.*, XVIII, 1889, 281–83. Frazer, *T. & E.*, II. 119–122. Brown, *Melanesians and Polynesians*, 1910, 27, 28.

be translated "big bird"; in point of fact the *Haliaetus leucogaster* is the largest bird of the South Sea, so that the names of the two marriage classes, tarago and malaba, are really the bird names taragau and malaba. The same is the case in the Gazelle Peninsula; here we have the taragau and maniqulai or miniqulai classes. In New Ireland Pakilaba is often used both for the *Haliaetus leucogaster* and the marriage class Malaba, or one of its members; this word originally means "big land."[1] The coincidence that two hawks represent the two marriage classes is really remarkable when we come to think of Kilparra, Mukwarra, Eaglehawk and Crow, of the part played by the Hawk in Australian and Indonesian mythology, and it decidedly points to a common origin. But it also tells against the attempt to separate the origin of totemism from that of the two-class system; the hawk and similar birds are carrion-eaters, they are totems because they have devoured the murdered father.

We can go even further; a myth from Vuatom shows us the connexion of the Dual Heroes with the two-class system and the Oedipus complex; it also shows, exactly like the Australian material, the Hawk as the Paternal Tyrant. According to the legend on the South-eastern Coast of Vuatom, people wandered from there to the North Coast of the Gazelle Peninsula, and Peekel has heard about a former immigration from Vuatom in Namatanai,[2] so that we have good reason to connect the legend that follows with the two-marriage classes as reported by Peekel. In bygone days the fish-hawk killed all the people (like Mullyan, Welu, etc., in Australia) except a woman who was enceinte and lived in a stone-cave (uterine symbol). The fish-hawk is the *Pandion leucocephalus*, the totem of one of the marriage classes, but in the course of the tale he is confounded with the sea-hawk (*Haliaetus leucogaster*),[3] the totem of the other class. The woman gives birth to twins, who climb up to the eagles' eyrie and kill the bird, exactly the same way that the two heroes kill the Eagle-hawk. The woman is proud of her two sons, and when the people out of gratitude wish to buy wives for them, she does not let them, and says "No, the two sons belong to me alone"[4]; so that her jealousy proves the correctness of our solution when we point out that the Oedipus complex lies at the root of the conflict with the giant bird.

The variants of this myth are of considerable interest; they have been treated by Gräbner in comparison with Australian

[1] G. Peekel, "Religion und Zauberei auf dem mittleren, Neu Mecklenburg," I. 3, *Anthropos. Bibl.*, 1910, 7, 8, 77; a sort of mutual food taboo of the two classes.

[2] Cf. O. Meyer, "Mythen und Erzählungen von der Insel Vuatom," *Anthropos*, 1910, 729.

[3] Id., ibid., 729.

[4] Id., ibid., 727–29.

material, and it is only his unpsychological attitude and his unfortunate addiction to "astral mythology" that hinders him in seeing their real import. In a variant from Aurora, the women live underground and the man-devouring monster is a snake.[1] In another variant, the two heroes who kill the wild boar are born of the blood of an old woman, and their names are To Kabinana and To Karvuvu,[2] the names of the two exogamous classes. Everything is as it ought to be according to our hypothesis that has been derived exclusively from Australian material: the Monster-animal is the Paternal Tyrant, the motive of the conflict is that of Atkinson's "primal law," and the Dual Heroes represent the victorious band of brothers. We have explained the two-class system as a result of a compromise between this Generation of Brothers and the next Generation, so that we shall be prepared for an intimate connexion between the Dual Heroes and the Dual Division of the Tribe: indeed, it is not too much to say that the Dual Heroes represent the two-class system. So that Gräbner, in a certain sense, is even more in the right in connecting these myths with his "Zweiklassenkultur" than he thinks, only this connexion is not a matter of historic "chance" but of evolutionary and psychological necessity. These Melanesian Dioscurs, one of whom is represented as wise and well-meaning, whose plans, however, are usually frustrated by his stupid brother, are regularly brought into connexion with the origin of the two-class system. The heroes are called Takaro and Mueragbuto in the New Hebrides, and it is Takaro who divides humanity into the two marriage classes, Takaro and Mueragbuto.[3] In the Gazelle Peninsula the two classes are connected with To Kabinana and To Karvuvu. Whilst in some instances (as we have already noted) their names are identical with those of the mythical heroes, in other cases they are simply called class "we" and "they" (cf. the "Mulyanuka" of the Arunta). At Kininigunan, and from here on the coast right to Birar, the class symbols are the *Haliaetus leucogaster* (a miniqulai) and the *Pandion leucocephalus* (a taragau).[4] In one myth To Kabinana takes the shape of the *Monarcha chalybeocephala* and his brother that of the *Poecilodryas aethiops*.[5] If we can judge by the name of the latter a black bird is meant, and black and white, dark and light are in Australia often found in the names of the two divisions. The Rev. J. Mathew, Rivers and others have taken this as an indication of the mixture of two races, and have referred to cases in which the members of one class were said

[1] Codrington, *The Melanesians*, 1891, 403.

[2] J. Meier, *Mythen und Erzählungen der Küstenbewohner der Gazellehalbinsel*, 1909, 25–7.

[3] Suas, "Mythes et Légendes des Indigènes des Nouvelles Hebrides," *Anthropos*., 1912, 47.

[4] Meier, l.c., 21.

[5] Meier, l.c., 29.

to be different in hair, skin, colour, character, etc., from members of the other; but according to the law of exogamy both races must be represented in equal proportions in both sides of the tribe.[1] There really seems to be good reason for interpreting the colour contrast in this sense, though it also typifies the contrast between the two generations of males which is projected into a contrast of character of the two heroes, while the Dual Heroes in their union represent the Generation of Brothers which set an end to endless strife about the women by the compromise expressed in the institution of the two-class system.[2] At Matupit, Valaur, Tavui and Rakunai, the two classes are represented by the light-coloured and the dark coco-nuts. To Kabinana told To Karvuvu to bring two light nuts, but he brought a light and a dark one. The light one changed into a woman, whom To Karvuvu wanted to marry, but To Kabinana did not allow it, telling him she was their mother. This evidently shows the incest wish behind the exogamous taboo, all the more so as To Kabinana deplores having been compelled (by his brother bringing a black nut) to create a black woman and so divide mankind into two classes. He says that this is why people will be mortal:[3] which is as much as to say that the absence of exogamy, incestuous wish-fulfilment, would have meant perpetual life; indeed, there is an intimate connexion between the neurotic inhibition of the primary impulse and the dread of death.[4] I think it very probable that the legends of the Dual Heroes, the Two Women, etc., taken together with the survivals of the Primary Division in the ceremonies, indicate the former extension of the two-class system, which I am inclined to regard as the most primitive form of exogamy, and the animal symbols (probably hawks) as the most primitive instance of exogamic totemism.[5] Those people who have actually conserved this archaic type of society must once have been separated together from a common stock, leaving behind other tribes who were organized on the basis of a patrilinear dual system and continued to develop four- and eight-class systems or others. But this does not in any way prove that the tribes with the two-class systems must be in all things more primitive than those with more complicated social structure.

[1] Mathews: *Eagle-hawk and Crow*, 1899. Id., *Two Representative Tribes*, 1910. Rivers, *H. M. S.*, 1914, II. 5–60. Although, of course, the institution of exogamy makes it impossible that such a colour contrast should actually exist at the present day, it may still contain a traditional element of a period when a race of a lighter hue intermarried with the aboriginals. Thus Manubada, the hawk, marries a human girl.—A. Ker: *Papuan Fairy Tales*, 1910, 57.

[2] To Kabinana was the first to invite To Karvuvu to sleep in his hut: this is the origin of the "Männerhaus" institution (Meier: l.c. 43).

[3] J. Meier, l.c., 21–23.

[4] As to the contrast of white and black as the origin of death, cf. Meier, "Mythen und Sagen der Admiralitäts Insulaner," *Anthropos.*, 1908, 194.

[5] Which is, however, far later than endogamic totemism. Cf. above, p. 96, on the Alcheringa myths.

Arrested development of one function may very well be compensated by the additional development of another; or, to put the same thing in another fashion, the hypertrophy of one side of life (class system) may easily lead to regression ("degradation") in other particulars.

In the case of the natives of the south-east these probably entered Australia from the Cape York Peninsula, with birds as representative of the two classes (Eagle-hawk and Crow; Cockatoo), which they developed into various four-class systems. They were probably more primitive in certain respects than the tribes with positive totemism, and it may have been these tribes pressing behind them that compelled them to continue their wandering to the southern limits of the Continent. But when the tribes with negative totemism reached these well-watered districts, their material culture began to develop, and here they left their former conquerors far behind them. "For example, whereas the tribes of Central Australia appear not to have conceived the idea of making any kind of clothing as a protection against cold, but huddle naked round their fires on frosty nights, though they might easily clothe themselves in the skins of kangaroos and wallabies, the tribes who inhabit the coast of South Australia make excellent warm rugs out of opossum, kangaroo, wallaby and other furs." "The Narrinyeri make durable mats; whilst in Central Australia we find only shelters of shrubs placed so as to screen their occupants from the wind, in South-Western Victoria the aborigines build permanent houses of wood or stone large enough to accommodate a dozen persons."[1] The improved conditions of food-supply must naturally have led to the disappearance of such primitive characteristics as the last survivals of the rutting season, and the ubiquitous nature of the Libido, on the other hand, leads to a corresponding strengthening of Repression. But Repression is a merely functional expression; we can also point out the psychical content from which repression takes its starting point. The greater the respect paid to the Father-Imago the greater is repression, since it was the jealousy of the Sire that, in the Primeval Horde, was the only check on the sexual activity of the young males. Spencer and Gillen have pointed out that the Warramunga, who live in a better-watered country than the Arunta, have as Intichiuma ceremonies only the dramatic performances in which the wanderings of the Alcheringa ancestors are reacted, whilst the "magical" or "procreative" elements, like hammering the cairn, blood-letting, etc., which symbolize not only identification with, but also rebellion against the Father, are absent. The rite that represents the typical rebellion against the Father, totemic incest, the custom of eating the totem, disappears equally as we proceed from South to North,

[1] Frazer, *T. & E.*, I. 320, 321.

from the Arunta to the Warramunga.[1] We can point out the reason of these differences in another difference between the Alcheringa-legends of these two tribes. In the Arunta each totem has a plurality of Alcheringa ancestors who wander about together, in the Warramunga there is one great Alcheringa father for each totem-kin.[2] The Arunta have conserved the phase of Rebellion, that of the Brother-Clan, in their myths and ceremonies, the Warramunga represent the Patriarchal Epoch and the function of Repression. The relative position of central and southern tribes is very similar to this state of things. Successful repression in the south has obliterated the survivals of the Oedipus complex and the rutting season: the beliefs in a mythical origin of children and the Intichiuma ceremonies. However, they have not disappeared without leaving some traces of their former presence, which at the same time may also be regarded as indicative of the original unity of the two waves of immigration. The child-birth myths we have demonstrated to exist in a modified form among some Southern and Victorian tribes; at the same time we must call attention to a system of naming which is probably a rudiment of these beliefs.

Naming system.

If an Arunta woman feels pregnant near an Emu totem-centre, then it is an Emu ratapa that is being re-born through her, and the child belongs to the totem. Its personal name is derived from that of its totem: it may, for instance, be called ilia-kurka (small emu) or iliapa (emu feather).[3] In south-west Australia the personal totem (oobaree) is not inherited and does not regulate marriage. Like amongst the Arunta, it depends on some circumstance attendant on the birth of the child. Beyoo means swollen; Beyooran (a woman) was called so because her father found a kangaroo he had killed all swollen from the heat: her personal totem was the kangaroo.[4] Baaburgurt's name was given from his father observing a sea-mullet leaping out of the water and making a noise like "brrrbaabur." Accordingly, the sea-mullet was his totem. One girl's totem was the wallaby, which her father was about to kill when it disappeared.[5] Again, in the Encounter Bay tribe, the child's name is often that of the totem or a part of it: for instance, "pouch of a pelican," or the child, gets a name derived from some circumstance which occurred at its birth.[6] The animal which appeared at birth was probably

[1] Survivals of it, however, are still in existence, so that it cannot be a recent relaxation of the taboo.

[2] Spencer and Gillen, *Nor. T.*, 161, 297, 317.

[3] Strehlow, *A. & L.*, II. 53, 60.

[4] Cf. p. 146, the pre-natal duel of Child and Parent in north-west Australia.

[5] Frazer, *T. & E.*, I. 564. Bates, *Victorian Geographical Journal*, XXIII–XXIV. 49.

[6] H. E. A. Meyer, *Manners and Customs of the Aborigines of the Encounter Bay Tribe.* Woods, 1879, 186.

regarded as the child's mythical father, as a sort of Alcheringa-ancestor, and hence the derivation of the name; the identity of the name amongst savages always meaning an identity of personality. In the Western districts of Victoria we find that the father, if requested, names children after one of his friends. This creates a bond between the man and the child—the man is kind to it, calling it his "namesake" ("laing," cf. the wororu, p. 146). When children are not thus called after a friend their names are taken from something in a neighbouring swamp, rivulet, water-hole, hill or animal.[1]

On the Pennefather River children may be called "Tree-Rock" or Freshwater infants, according to the place where their choi were held captive before birth.[2] In New South Wales we have names derived from some bird, beast or fish.[3] Children were named after their birthplace, after animals that turned up, or other events at their birth.[4] On the Darling, the children are named after animals.[5] In New South Wales, if the scream of an eagle was heard at the moment of birth, or the hoot of an owl, or if a bandicoot or kangaroo was seen to pass by, the name of that animal with some derivative termination added is applied to the child; one child was named from fire because the hut caught fire when he was born.[6]

The Lower Murray natives derive their names either from the spot where they were born or from a natural object seen by the mother soon after the birth of the child.[7] This naming system seems to be universal all over Australia, thus pointing to a time when the belief upon which it rests was equally prevalent. As to the other principal feature of positive totemism, the Intichiuma ceremonies, we may regard their connexion with the animal-dances at initiation as hypothetical, but the southern myths which tell us how all animal species were multiplied from the body of one giant animal, most evidently refer to Intichiuma. The hero who tears these animals into bits is one of great antiquity: it is Bundjil, the Eagle-hawk. It is remarkable that Bundjil is associated with other myths of rather Central Australian aspect. In Victoria, it is said that at creation a number of young men in an unfinished state were sitting on the ground in darkness (womb) when Bundjil, an old man, at the request of his good daughter, Karakarook, held up his hand to the Sun, who then warmed the earth and made

[1] J. Dawson, *Australian Aborigines*, 1881, 41.

[2] Roth, *S. M. M.*, 1903, 18.

[3] Collins, *An Account of the English Colony in New South Wales*, 1804, 364.

[4] R. Brough-Smyth, *The Aborigines of Victoria*, 1878, I. 56.

[5] F. Bonney, "On some Customs of the Aborigines of the River Darling," *J. A. I.*, XIII. 127.

[6] Fraser, *Aborigines of New South Wales*, 4.

[7] Günther, "Report on Australian Languages and Traditions," *Journ.*, II. 1872, 278.

it open like a door.[1] The opening of the door is birth; the legend is a close parallel to that on the origin of the Lake Perigundi. Perhaps the deep basaltic glen where he lived when on earth may be compared with the Ertnatulunga, in which case we should have to remove the date of the "Bundjil complex" far back in the abyss of time, back to the original unity of the race. The survival of the birth legend in a corroboree is equally suggestive of Intichiuma rites. Howitt says that one of the legends about Bundjil in the Woeworung tribe is perpetuated in a corroboree which was witnessed in the early forties by Richard Howitt. The legend is that Bundjil held out his hand to the sun and warmed it—the sun warmed the earth, which opened; blackfellows came out and danced this corroboree, which is called Gayipo. At it images curiously carved in bark were exhibited.[2]

It is possible that the differences between the two waves of immigration would be still further reduced if the southern tribes had been observed under equally favourable opportunities as those of the Central Plain; but that there would still be a difference in the degree of repression to account for seems to me sufficiently established by the difference in the initiation ceremonies. With the tribes who have the more repressed form (tooth-expulsion) substituted for mutilation of the penis, the "High God," the representative of the Father-Imago, the God of Initiation, is far more prominent, so that we again find the same connexion between Repression and the Father-Imago as with the Warramunga.[3]

But other Supreme Beings of the South present similar features, which (as in the case of Bundjil) seem to point to the Centre, and beyond that to the cradle of the race. Myth speaks of a giant being, Nurundure or Baiamai, who comes from the North and finally ascends to the sky.[4] This gigantic being made everything on earth—indeed, like the Alcheringa beings of the Dieri,[5] Baiamai

[1] Th. H. Braim, *History of New South Wales*, 1846, 244. W. Howitt, *Abenteuer in den Wildnissem von Australien*, 1856, 292. Thomas Günther, "Report on Australian Languages and Traditions," *J. A. I.*, II. 278. Western Port.

[2] Howitt, l.c., 492.

[3] When we read that the Murray River natives possess a being with supreme attributes called Nourelle, who lives in the sky, and is surrounded by children born without the intervention of a mother, we are reminded of the well-known attitude of European children, with whom repression often takes the shape of stoutly denying that their father could ever have done such a thing (as cohabitation), although they are ready to believe in the normal way of procreating children so far as others are concerned. (For the Murray legend see *J. A. I.*, II. 275, "Report on Australian Languages." Cf. Dillalee, son or brother of Baiamai, born without the intervention of woman.—Parker, l.c., 66.)

[4] The Supreme Being of the Wathi-wathi and Ta-ta-thi came from the far North and now dwells in the sky.—A. L. P. Cameron, "Notes on Some Tribes of New South Wales," *J. A. I.*, XIV. 364.

[5] A. W. Howitt and O. Siebert, "Legends of the Dieri and Kindred Tribes of Central Australia," *J. A. I.*, 1904, 108, 109.

is still believed to make the grass grow.[1] There is a permanent association between him and large stone-works,[2] as well as natural rocks and legends of petrifaction, which forcibly reminds us of the association between sky beings and stone culture in the Centre and in Indonesia. These Supreme Beings are deities of initiation—nevertheless, they are often brought into contrast with another being, the real spirit of the bullroarer. But there is another feature of these initiation ceremonies which attracts our interest; here we find a rivalry between two "Central Mysteries," the bullroarer and the quartz crystal. The bullroarer is regularly associated with the deities of the Daramulun type, who come into conflict with the Supreme Beings, the Conquerors of the Eagle-hawk, or themselves the Eagle-hawk. Just as regularly the Supreme Being is connected with the quartz crystal.[3] The bullroarer is directly affirmed to be the ancestor of the tribe, the Supreme Being existed in the beginning; he is the "father" but not in the sense of being a relative. The obvious conclusion seems to be that the Supreme Beings represent an immigrant race, that the myths which refer to them represent the beliefs of these immigrants. These can have been no other than the tribes with the two-class system, tooth-evulsion and negative totemism. They brought with them a culture which was on the verge between the age of wood and that of stone. Their Alcheringa ancestors turned into trees and they buried the dead in, or near, or under trees. But stone already played an important part in their religious life, although this was stone in its natural state, the quartz crystal.

Here we have another way of sublimation which played a part in the technical advance of mankind; the stone on the grave represents the Oedipus complex and the quartz crystal is a symbol of the analerotic component of the libido.[4] It is certain that the tribes with the two-class system and matrilinear descent did not find the country entirely uninhabited; they met with

[1] Honery, "Wailwun (Upper Hunter River)," *J. A. I.*, VII. 249.

[2] "There is a large stone fish-trap at Brewarrina, on the Barwon River. It is said to have been made by Byamee and his gigantic sons."—K. L. Parker, *The Euahlayi Tribe*, 1905, 8. R. H. Mathews, *E. N.*, 138. K. L. Parker, *Australian Legendary Tales*, 1897, 97.

[3] Cf. K. L. Parker, Howitt, etc.

[4] "The novices are taken to the goonambang (excrement place). Some old men perform feats of jugglery, and exhibit white stones (quartz crystals) to the novices. These quartz crystals are believed to be the excrement of Goign."—R. H. Mathews, "The Burbung of the Wiradthuri Tribes," *J. A. I.*, 1896, 329. The "Mundie" which is given to the youths at initiation is a crystal believed by the natives to be an excrement issued from the Deity and held sacred. It is worn concealed in the hair, tied up in a packet, and is never shown to the women, who are forbidden to look at it under pain of death.—G. F. Angas, *Savage Life and Scenes in Australia*, 1847, II. 227. Cf. the belief in the origin of the "boollia" (the magic force which dwells in the quartz crystal) from the anus.—A. Oldfield, "The Aborigines of Australia," *Trans. Ethnol. Soc.*, III. 235.

resistance on the part of a dark, curly-haired race of Melanesian Negrito affinity. This race had Supreme Beings of their own—the dead Father, the spirit of the bullroarer.[1] Amongst the tribes which arose out of the interaction of these two elements, the Father-God of the immigrants was raised into the sky with his quartz crystal; the Father-God of the aboriginals lived on, like early man in general, in trees, represented by the wooden bullroarer. It is as if the tribes who were descended from the union of these two, or rather three, elements were acknowledging the superiority of the immigrants by raising the deities which are their representatives into the sky, but yet they affirm themselves to be akin in blood with the vanquished, for the bullroarer is their ancestor.

This racial conflict revives a still older and universally human one, the conflict in the Primeval Horde between Father and Son. The more powerful of the two deities is said to have "made" the other, and "making" must here be interpreted in the physical sense—as generation, fatherhood. This is the key to the possibility of interpreting similar legends in a double sense; racial conflicts, wars for foreign women (exogamy), become superposed on the old Oedipus conflict (endogamy), and both are condensed in the legends which account for the origin of the two-class system; this first arose out of a tribal fission, but afterwards served to facilitate many fusions.[2]

If we have thus some grounds to assume a hypothetical aboriginal race which inhabited Australia before the advent of our B-wave, we are in partial accord with Gräbner's view. Our wave A is his "western Papuans," and wave B his "eastern Papuans," and he is probably right in assuming a "Nigritian" element which occupied the country before these waves arrived. It seems that the coastal tribes contain a larger proportion of this proto-Australian race than others; these have certain features in common at the Northern and Southern coast; such as absence

[1] The two-class system brought from Melanesia had two species of hawks as totems. But a darker aboriginal population was found in Australia, and when they became assimilated by the conquerors a bird, which might well represent them (and was probably specially reverenced by them), replaced what must have been a young eagle-hawk in the original conflict-myth and in the phratric organization. The crow is still regarded as the symbol of the Kurnai (Howitt, *N. T.*, 134), who, at any rate, are more like representatives of this aboriginal population than the typical dual tribes.

[2] We know that there is a blood division which co-exists with class-divisions in Australia. (Cf. Parker, l.c., 11. Mathews, *E. N.*, 7. Mathew, *Two Tribes*, 32.) Thus we should have dichotomies of intra- and extra-racial origin which may be confounded with each other in the course of evolution. I think this way of interpreting these myths is in accordance both with the principles of psycho-analysis, which regards every psychic phenomenon as the condensation of a series of complexes amongst which the Oedipus attitude, usually the basic complex, is buried beneath a mass of others, and with the views of Rivers, who allows for other factors of a psychological and evolutionary kind having had a share in the formation of those phenomena which he attributes to the interaction of cultures.

of the boomerang,[1] this peculiarly Australian weapon, the ligature of the finger-joints as an initiation rite of women,[2] local organization,[3] which make it possible to refer to a special ethnic element to account for them. But we must not forget that the coastal tribes, if they represent the aboriginals, represent them not in their pristine conditions, but in a highly modified state; they possess only fossil rudiments of these aboriginals covered under the layers or waves of A and B in the North and South. Some of these, like the Kurnai, were the first to come into contact with white men at a period before Australian ethnology was born, when we did not know what to look for. This explains the lack of reliable information with regard to these tribes, and it is too late to fill these gaps in our knowledge. Whatever racial elements they are made of, they have made considerable advance or undergone considerable modification in culture, and it is more than hazardous to build theories on the origin of social institutions on the scanty descriptions of these tribes which we possess. At any rate, we are not concerned with them in discussing totemism, for we have shown that the phenomena of "individual" and "sex" totemism which are ascribed to them by Father Schmidt and hence regarded as "primitive," are organic developments of a common totemic root.

We must next try and explain how the return of repressed elements in the Central Tribes is to be accounted for. When the tribes with patrilinear organization and positive totemism came under conditions that made accommodation to environment more difficult, their first reaction against the circumstances which threatened the equilibrium of repression and libido was to overdo repression still more: an eight-class system was evolved which means that seven out of eight women are taboo, seven out of eight copulations are incestuous, seven out of eight women are mothers.[4] As sexuality is to such an extraordinary degree under the influence

[1] F. A. Sarg, "Die Australischen Bumerangs im städtischen Völker-museum," *Veröffentlichungen aus dem städtischen Völker Museum, Frankfurt-am-Main*, III, 1911, 7, and Map, No. 13.

[2] Two first joints of little finger cut off the left hand of women.—G. B. Barton, *History of New South Wales*, 1889, 119, 283, 284, 342. "Den Mädchen werden in der Kindheit zwei Glieder von dem kleinen Finger der rechten Hand abgelöst. Diese Glieder werden durch starkes Unterbinden abgenommen und dann in das Meer geworfen, damit das Kind nachher im Fischfange glüklich sei."—J. Turnbull, *Reise um die Welt eigentlich nach Australien*, 1806, 57. T. L. Mitchell, *Three Expeditions into the Interior of Eastern Australia*, 1838, II. 346. The Prince of Wales Islanders have a curious mourning custom. They cut off a joint of the mother's finger to mark the loss of every child that dies.—A. C. Bicknell, *Travel and Adventure in Northern Australia*, 1895, 30.

[3] Howitt, l.c., 86, 129, 130, 135. Taplin, *The Narrinyeri*, 1879, 63. Fison and Howitt, *Kamilaroi*, 1880, 285. Curr, l.c., I. 402. *Spencer, N. T. N. T. A.*, 43–52.

[4] It makes no difference if we accept Gräbner's view and derive the eight-class system from the fusion of a four with a two-class system. The effect will be, in any case, to restrict the number of eligible women, and hence to increase repression.

of the Oedipus complex, the repression against the latter touches all that has to do with sexuality, and this explains the famous "nescience" of the Arunta. But the very myths that have been substituted for the natural explanation of birth are veiled accounts of incest; they affirm no less (in a symbolic form) that every human being is born out of incestuous wedlock, or in other words, that the incestuous libido is the prototype of all other erotic relations. This return of repressed elements makes it possible to attempt a reconstruction of the Phases of Evolution that preceded that of successful repression, so that we shall attempt to sketch the Prehistoric Evolution of the Totemic Complex in Australia as follows:

(1) Adaptation to environment and the ontogenetic pre-natal recapitulation of phylogenetic evolution.

(2) The initial phase in the movement series of the rutting season develops into an independent rite with "magical" aim. Uterine symbolism of environment. The feeling of unity with environment, the first projection of totemism as a survival of actual organic adaptation (phase 1) and a repetition of the proto-narcissistic attitude of the embryo. Totemism is purely positive, without any inhibitions.

(3) Repression and Libido, the dichotomy of the psyche, replace the two periods of Non-rut and Rut as they exist in Animal Life. Victory of the Brothers over the Father of the Primeval Horde, and subsequent projection of the Father-Imago into the totem. The totem is originally a theriomorphic ghost of the murdered father, the animal which haunts his grave. Eating the murdered father and then the totem-animal; Intichiuma ceremonies as survivals of the battles and the coitus of the rutting period.

(4) Identification with the murdered father who is mourned for in the Intichiuma rites regresses into the archaic identification with environment; the projection of the Father-Imago into the Totem is a regression to what we have called the protototemic projection. This calls forth a secondary narcissism and regresses to the narcissistic attitude of the embryo (phase 2) development of belief in doubles: Iruntarinia.

(5) Successful repression (in the Southern Tribes) with growing importance of the Father-Imago. Survivals of phases 1 and 2 disappear, leaving hardly recognizable rudiments.

(6) A second return of repressed elements in the Individual and Sex totem.

From an ethnological point of view we must observe that the series of totemic origins given above refers chiefly to the prehistoric evolution of the totemic complex in the tribes of the Centre (phases 1 to 4). Nevertheless we can, with a certain degree of probability, attribute the same pre-history to the totemic elements of our wave B for two reasons. First, because, taking the central tribes as our starting-point, we have penetrated into prehistoric strata long antecedent to the period of racial differentiation, and secondly, because a secondary infusion of "Central" elements into the east and south seems very probable. The tribes with dual organization and matrilinear descent had, at the time when they entered Australia, a phratric totemism with birds of prey as totems which was a reaction-formation against the Oedipus complex (the Proto-totemic Complex).

They probably developed clan totems in addition to the phratric totems partly through intermixture with two other culture areas (one of these being the immigrants from the Centre and the other a third stratum of population with no class-system, but in possession of a local organization), and partly from internal reasons which led to the formation of a series (Eagle-hawk as class totem, clan totem, subtotem) with the original pattern continually being repeated. Before these eastern tribes other patrilinear elements were in possession of the Continent. It seems that the totemism of our wave B, and of these tribes whom we will call C, was dominated by repression, though the development of these earlier groups still remains obscure in its details. Since nothing less than a complete analysis of Australian culture would suffice us here, demanding a book in itself, we cannot here deal further with this point.

From a methodological point of view, we have learnt that cultural phenomena must be studied both in isolation from their cultural environment—this in order to obtain a general insight into their psychic structure—and in connexion with the ethnological history of the tribes who possess them, before we can obtain adequate details of the transformations and distortions to which the original contents were subjected. In this study I have made an attempt in the first direction; I have been able merely to cast a glance here and there at the other half of the problem.

NOTES AND ADDENDA

Page 42.

Old feuds are settled at the fights connected with the Turrbal initiation ceremonies, and a man who was killed in this fighting was eaten.[1] The Arunta represent "Oruncha men . . . engaged in baking a man in an earth oven" at initiation.[2] Boys who open their eyes when forbidden to do so are killed by opening their veins at the Euahlayi ceremonies. "Stooping over two boys they opened veins in each, out flowed the blood, and the other men all raised a death cry. The boys were lifeless. The old wirreenuns, dipping their stone knives in the blood, touched with them the lips of all present." [3] Those who are considered stupid and generally incapable are killed and their bodies burnt.[4] "The youths believed that one of the party was going to be killed, not knowing on whom the fatal blow would fall." [5]

The idea of sacrificing and eating an old man at initiation is hardly Australian; but it is probably the prototype of the idea that the young men (retribution!) are eaten at this festival by a demon, and of the actual carrying out of this idea in special cases.

Page 46.

Urethral origin of flood myths. A supernatural monster in serpent form made all the rivers as he travelled inland from the sea, which is his home. He camped for a long time at the lake into which Sturt Creek empties, and it is owing to his urine that the water there is salt. The saltness of other lakes is ascribed to a similar cause.—R. H. Mathews, "Some Aboriginal Tribes of Western Australia," *Roy. Soc. of N.S.W.*, 1901, 219 (between Fitzroy, Margaret and Ord Rivers).

Page 66.

Bullroarer as sex-totem. When the women (Kamilaroi) hear the sound of the moonibear they think it is a spirit-woman congratulating them upon having their sons admitted to the degree of manhood.—R. H. Mathews, "Notes on the Aborigines of New South Wales," 17.

[1] Howitt, *N. T.*, 599.
[2] Spencer and Gillen, *N. T.*, 351.
[3] K. L. Parker, *The Euahlayi Tribe*, 1905, 72.
[4] Parker, l.c. 73.
[5] A. Meston, Description of a Bora at Mt. Milbirriman, *Science of Man*, I. 10.

Page 73.

Totemic taboo.—Brown, *J. R. A. I.*, 1923, 432, 439.

Page 77.

Totem called " his flesh." The object of marriage classes was to prevent marriage between those of "one flesh" (Tow'wilyerr).—J. Dawson, *Australian Aborigines*, 1881, 26. " A man or woman may freely eat of the totemic animal, and, indeed, a man calls his totem his wil'i, this word being apparently the common word in this language for meat or flesh food."—A. R. Brown, " Notes on the Social Organization of Australian Tribes," *J. R. A. I.*, 1923, 439 (Murawari).

Page 78.

Omens. According to the belief of the Kamilaroi the totem forewarns everybody of the designs of his enemies. If any of his friends are away in a different part of the tribal territory and sickness and death overtakes them, or they meet with a serious accident, his totem appears in sight, by which they know there is something wrong.—R. H. Mathews, " The Kamilaroi Division," *Science of Man*, I. 155. Id., " The Totemic Divisions of Australian Tribes," *Journal and Proceedings of R. S. N. S. W.*, 1897, XXXI. 157

Page 79.

On personal totems.—A. R. Brown, *J. R. A. I.*, 1923, 432, 442.

Page 131.

Dragon-slaying and initiation. The astral-symbolism and the connexion between initiation and dragon-slaying are notable features of following rites. Seven fires were lighted round an oval ring. At the south end stood a blackfellow threatening a huge clay figure of a crocodile with a spear. The seven fires represent the Pleiades, who were seven young men dancing to a song sung by three young women in Orion's belt. The clay figure in the middle of the ring was a giant crocodile frequenting the dark river in the Milky Way, and the boys are told that this fierce saurian would swallow them if they displayed any weakness in passing through the initiation ceremony.—Meston, " Description of a Bora at Mount Milbirriman, *Science of Man*, I. 10. For other representations of the Kurreah (giant crocodile) at initiation ceremonies, cf. R. H. Mathews, " Aboriginal Initiation Ceremonies," *Science of Man*, I. 79 ; Id., " Initiation Ceremonies of the Wiradjuri Tribes," *American Anthropologist*, *N. S.*, III. 339. Cf. also F. E. Williams, " The Pairama Ceremony," *J. R. A. I.*, 1923, 361.

Page 134.

Phallic nature of Alcheringa beings. The culture-heroes and ancestors of the Kagaba are called Kalguašīža—a word undoubtedly derived from "kalguákala" (penis).—K. Th. Preuss, "Die höchste Gottheit bei den kulturarmen Völkern," *Psychologische Forschungen*, 1922, II. 171.

Page 177.

Aboriginal tradition regards subincision as a mitigated form of castration.—J. G. Edge, "The Mika Ceremony, Wallwarra (Waloo-kera) Tribe," *Science of Man*, II. 105.

Page 194.

Fish as embryo-symbol. Protective deity holding up a fish in right hand.—W. D. Campbell, "Aboriginal Carvings of Port Jackson and Broken Bay," *Memoirs of the Geological Survey of New South Wales Ethnological Series*, No. 1. 41.

Page 196.

Island other-world.—Cf. E. Jones, *Essays on Applied Psycho-Analysis*, 1923, "The Island of Ireland"; and Id., "Psycho-Analysis and Anthropology," *J. R. A. I.*, 1924, 65.

Page 196.

Soul as little child. The soul goes to a pit in the west and lives there as a child of eight years.—F. Gerstäcker, Reisen IV, *Australien*, 1854, 364.

Page 207.

For some further conclusions with regard to mortuary ceremonies, cf. Róheim, "Nach dem Tode des Urvaters," *Imago*, IX. 83.

Page 217.

No imitation of human coitus in Central Australian ritual. It seems that ceremonial coitus forms a part of the Kangaroo Intichiuma, although Strehlow denies all "obscene" details (Strehlow, *Die totemistischen Kulte der Aranda und Loritja-Stämme*, 1910, p. xvii) in ritual, and Spencer and Gillen do not mention them. In describing a waninga used at the Kangaroo Intichiuma ceremony, Missionary Liebler remarks (with reference to the ceremony) "endet leider mit Hurerei."—*Cat.* VI. 35, 544. Published by kind permission of the Berlin Ethnographical Museum.

Page 225.

Blood given to sick to strengthen them. Seminal fluid is used for the same purpose. In an extreme case of disease, mulierem ob juventutem firmitatemque corporis lectam, sex vel plures viri in locum haud procul a castris remotum deducunt. Ibique omnes deinceps in illa libidinem explent. Tum mulier ad pedes surgere iubetur, quo facilius id quod maribus excepit, effluere possit. Quod in vase collectum ægrotanti ad bibendum præbent.—P. Beveridge, *The Aborigines of Victoria and Riverina*, 1889, 53. The magical use of semen is prominent in New Guinea.—Cf. Wirz, *Die Marind-anim von Holländisch Süd Neu Guinea*, 1922; Landtmann, "The Magic of the Kiwai," *J. R. A. I.*, 1916, 324.

Page 230.

Blood-letting at initiation, blood as substitute for seminal fluid. Old men let blood flow from subincised penis on boy's chest. —Donner, "Aboriginal Traditions and Rock Carvings," *Science of Man*, 1900, III. 115. From wounds.—R. H. Mathews, "Aboriginal Customs in North Queensland," *Science of Man*, I. 263. They form a ring, commit mutual onanism, making the emission go on the boy, then all go up in the trees around like flying foxes.—G. R. Brown, "Birripi Language of the Hastings and Wilson Rivers," *Science of Man*, 1898, I. 89.

Page 235.

Primitive forms of ritual to be found in west and north-west. What we call return of repressed elements is regarded as a symptom of degeneracy by A. A. Goldenweiser, "Reconstruction from Survivals in West Australia," *Am. Anthr.* XVIII. 478. According to Goldenweiser, the Kariera are degenerate from Arunta conditions because women participate in totem ceremonies; but Arunta traditions mention this custom as the original state of things in the Alcheringa.

Page 235.

According to a recent publication of Mjöberg on phallic objects, some of these at least (Kimberley, Upper Levarynga) are connected with the subincision ceremony. The Kamilaroi, however, have images of their first ancestor with erected penis, and a corresponding representation of the first woman. They perform sexual dances round these images.—Cf. intichiuma, E. Mjöberg, "Vom Phalluskult in Nordaustralien," *Archiv für Anthropologie*, 1923, XIX. 86.

Page 324.

Australia and New Guinea.

The evidence for Central Australian migrations through New Guinea and for the increase of repression during these migrations (or the return of repressed elements in New Guinea ?) would be incomplete without reference to the Bánaro.

Here the girl has intercourse with the "mundū"[1] of her future father-in-law in the spirit-house at initiation. The cohabitation must be carried out in presence of the long ceremonial flutes, the "mundū" acts the part of a spirit in cohabiting with the girl, and these flutes are regarded as vehicles of the spirit's voice. The husband is not allowed to have access to the woman till the first child procreated by the "mundū" as spirit is born. This child is distinguished from children born of normal intercourse between human beings, and called a spirit-child. When the child is born the mother asks: "Who had intercourse with me?" and the husband answers: "I am not the child's father; it is a spirit-child."[2]

Now, with the Arunta every child is a spirit-child procreated by the ancestral spirit as representative of the father. We tried to show that "throwing"[3] as a supernatural method of producing children was merely a symbolic expression for coitus, and here we actually find "spirit-children" procreated by "spirits" in a very human fashion. The denial of the woman shows repression at work, and even the very words used agree with those of the Arunta woman Kaltia, who, after having been "thrown" by the Alcheringa ancestor, protests her innocence—"Although I saw him I had nothing to do with him."[4]

In Australia we could prove that repression was directed against the Oedipus wish, and the procreative part played by the mythical ancestor appeared to be a hallucinatory wish-fulfilment of the female incest phantasy. If we follow Thurnwald into the details of the Bánaro custom, we find that the moieties were originally normal exogamous moieties, and that even to-day the father-in-law has formally to abdicate his *ius primæ noctis* in favour of his "mundū."[5] The custom must have been for the woman to commence sexual life with her father-in-law, who again is the natural substitute for the father. The present organization with the double system of "ghostly" and natural relationships provides for a curious half imaginary and half real gratification of the Oedipus situation.[6] The men with whom a woman in the course of her

[1] The Bánaro are divided into endogamous moieties. The "mundū" institution breaks through the taboo on exogamy involving the mutual *ius primæ noctis* between a man and his "mundū's" daughter-in-law.

[2] R. Thurnwald, *Die Gemeinde der Bánaro*, 1921. (*S. A. Zeitschrift für vergleichende Rechtswissenschaft* XXXVIII–XXXIX) 21, 22.

[3] In Australia the bullroarer thrown at the woman is a penis symbol, the equivalents of which are the sacred flutes of the Bánaro. Cf. the case of the Monumbo; the youths have intercourse with the chief's wife after having introduced the sacred flute into her vagina. F. Vormann, Tänze und Tanzfestlichkeiten der Monumbo-Papua, *Anthropos*, 1911, VI. 427.

[4] Strehlow, *A. & L.*, II. 54. Cf. Thurnwald, l.c., 39.

[5] Thurnwald, l.c., 21, 94.

[6] Thurnwald tells us that "the first person who has connexion with the girl is her mother's husband, possibly even her father," ibid. 184. He can only mean the mother's "spiritual" husband, and in this case there is a special prohibition against what might mean incest with the father.—Ibid., 39.

life regularly has intercourse are a father, his son (by another woman), and that son's grandchild. The father-in-law and the "spiritual" father are both called mitjoin, a survival of the period when the father-in-law was a "spiritual" father. In a wider sense the word is used to designate the generation of paternal grandfathers; this would be correct when used by a "normal" child with regard to his brother's "ghost-father," who would also be his own father's father. The problem only begins to interest us when we are told what the word means. The translation is "the little one," and therefore the child. If, then, the ghost-father is the child, this can only mean that he has been reborn by cohabitation—that the child partakes of the "spirit" nature of the spirit-father. This would serve to explain why his second father (really his half-brother) calls him "old son," [1] as a reborn grandfather. If we remember the universal opinion of the Central Australians as to the identity of the procreating ancestor with the infant, this view gains in probability. For that we are here treading on familiar ground is shown by the fact that these tribes—and no others outside Australia—have the peculiarly Central Australian institution of subincision.[2]

We must briefly consider the Melanesian parallels to the Central Australian belief in "spirit-children," both from the point of view of historical ethnology and from the unconscious side of these concepts. It is difficult (till we have further publications of Malinovski) to determine the exact cultural position of the Trobriand Islands. Certain traces in the disposal of the dead point towards betel and kava influence. Graves were dug in the village; a small house was built above the grave, in which they slept for three nights.[3] After some time the body of a chief would be exhumed, the skull made into a lime pot, and the fibula into lime spatulæ.[4] The following account of what happens after the death of a chief looks like a survival of "second burial." The bones are distributed to people of all the totems, except that of the dead man. It was said that these bones would finally be placed in the grave of a near relative of each recipient, who would "take the bone to Tuma." [5] If delayed burial goes with the idea of communion with the dead, this again would not be too far removed from the idea of the dead re-entering the maternal womb [6] and becoming reincarnated.

[1] Thurnwald, l.c., 100. Cf. C. G. Seligman on reciprocity in relationship terms. —*Man*, 1924, 81.

[2] Id., ibid. 27, 28.

[3] C. G. Seligmann, *The Melanesians in British New Guinea*, 1910, 715.

[4] Seligmann, l.c. 719.

[5] C. G. Seligmann, l.c., 718.

[6] Ideas and customs ascribed by Rivers, *History of Melanesian Society*, 1914, II. 258, 279, 376, etc., to the Kava people. The positive totemism of the members of the Tamate society would also agree with the idea of totem communion as found in Central Australia.—Rivers, l.c., II. 367.

We are told that "when the baloma (soul) [1] has grown old his teeth fall out, his skin gets loose and wrinkled, he goes to the beach and bathes in the salt water, then he throws off his skin just as a snake would do and becomes a young child again, really an embryo, a wai-waia, a term applied to children *in utero* and immediately after birth.[2] The wai-waia is the exact equivalent of the Arunta ratapa; thus confirming our view that the latter, and hence also the Churinga, is an embryo. The allusion to the serpent as a phase of transition between the old baloma and the embryo will easily be understood if we refer to Ferenczi's theory on the regressive nature of the genital act. According to this view the male in coitus effects, by the medium of the genital organ, "the serpent," and the spermatozöon (the wai-waia—the embryo), a return into the female womb [3] . . . represented in our case by salt water, a symbol of the amniotic fluid.[4] What follows is the well-known feature of duplication; besides the earthly father and mother, a "spirit-" father and mother and a spirit-birth, which is the prelude to real birth. "A baloma woman sees this wai-waia, she takes it up and puts it in a basket, or a plaited and folded coco-nut leaf (second womb-symbol). She carries it to Kiriwina and places it in the womb of some woman, inserting it per vaginam." "The real cause of pregnancy is always a baloma, who enters the body of a woman, and without whose existence a woman could not become pregnant."

"All babies are made or come into existence in Tuma" [5] (the nether-world, a womb-symbol!). When we go into further details we find a hazy idea of another stage of existence, as transition between death and the intrauterine life represented by the "spirit-children" or embryos. The dead become a sort of blood (buiai) in Tuma [6] before they turn into wai-waia. As the latter is the embryo, the "blood" can only be the seminal fluid. "Another

[1] Balum = the monster who swallows the youths at initiation.—Zahn, *Die Jabim. Neuhauss; Deutsch Neu Guinea*, 1911, III. 297. The bullroarer ancestor St. Lehner.—Bukaua, ibid., 410.

[2] Br. Malinovski, "The Spirits of the Dead in the Trobriand Islands," *Journal of the Royal Anthr. Inst.*, 1916, XLVI. 403. These childbirth beliefs are probably far more prevalent than we should suppose, as they seem not to be very easy to discover. Bellamy says with reference to these islands: "Intercourse is recognized as the cause of children, although single girls who become pregnant have a curious habit of blaming some portion of their diet."—Seligmann, l.c., 704.

[3] The Kagaba seem to be quite conscious of what the primeval lake means, they say it is the water in the mother's womb.—K. Th. Preuss, "Die höchste Gottheit," *Psychologische Forschungen*, II. 171.

[4] From the biological point of view the amniotic fluid is the "survival" of the phylogenetic salt-water environment.—Ferenczi, *Versuch einer Genitaltheorie* 1924, 61. The choice of the "symbol" frequently represents a deeper regression from the repressed towards the organic unconscious.—Cf. Róheim, "Die Sedna-Sage," *Imago*, X.

[5] Malinovski, "The Spirits of the Dead in the Trobriand Islands," *Journal*, 1916, 403.

[6] Malinovski, l.c., 404.

cycle of beliefs and ideas about reincarnation implies a pronounced association between the sea and the spirit-children." "After being transformed, the spirit goes into the sea and dwells there for a time." Girls must therefore be cautious when they go bathing. The spirit-children are supposed to be concealed in the popewo, the floating sea scum,[1] and also in some stones called dukupui." "If a married woman wants to conceive she may hit these stones to induce the concealed wai-waia to enter her womb."[2] (Cf. the belief of the Warramunga, striking the tree releases spirit-children. —Spencer and Gillen, *Northern Tribes*, 162.) There is a general belief in a close connexion between bathing and conception. A woman, for instance, will feel that something has touched or hurt her in the water. She will say, "A fish has bitten me," but really it is the wai-waia being inserted into her. Ceremonial bathing in the sea takes place about the fourth or fifth month of pregnancy "to make the skin white," or to "facilitate childbirth." "But at the coastal village of Kavataria a very different statement was volunteered, to the effect that the ceremony is connected with the incarnation of the spirit-children." It is at this stage of pregnancy that the "spirit-child" enters the woman.[3] A characteristic difference between the Arunta and Trobriand pregnancy dream seems to be that the Arunta, who trace descent in the male line, derive the child from a male ancestral being, while in the other case we have totems and names derived from the mother,[4] and the apparition of the dead mother or maternal aunt in the pregnancy dream.[5] The contradictory nature of the statements received by Malinovski as to the physiological or "psychological" causation of pregnancy clearly points to an infantile repression of sexual knowledge, the point being that the "supernatural" faculty of procreating children is attributed only to the "baloma," who represent the father and mother imago.[6]

Another account comes from the Morehead and Wassi-kussa Rivers in Western Papua. It proves beyond a doubt the correctness of some of our views.

The natives here believe that an invisible "something," which

[1] Besides the foam-born Aphrodite and Lakshmi, we find a nearer relation of these sea-scum children in the Polynesian Maui—an abortion thrown into the foam of the surf and nursed by seaweed.—G. Grey, *Polynesian Mythology*, 1855, 18. White, *Ancient History of the Maori*, 1880, II. 65.

[2] Malinovski, "The Spirits of the Dead in the Trobriand Islands," *Journal*, 1916, 404.

[3] Malinovski, l.c., 405. On bathing and conception, cf. E. S. Hartland, *The Legend of Perseus*, 1894, I. 133. P. Saintyves, *Les Vierges Mères et les Naissances Miraculeuses*, 1908, 39.

[4] Seligmann: l.c. 705.

[5] Malinovski, l.c., 405. As a rule it is a female baloma, but at any rate a member of the mother's kindred.

[6] Cf. Malinovski, l.c., 407. 408. See also "Spirit-children," by Malinovski, in Hastings' *Encyclopædia of Religion and Ethics*.

they call "Birumbir," is the animating principle of human beings. This Birumbir is the embryo from which the material body develops in the uterus. It comes into the uterus by way of the vulva in the form of junga (semen).[1] But here natural history comes to an end and myth begins. Against the evidence of their senses they are capable to declare that the semen (Birumbir) is inserted into the vulva by an "eel-like creature called Tombabwir." Tombabwir's haunts are rivers, creeks and waterholes. If a married woman enters one of these places when Tombabwir is there she will become pregnant, but this can only occur when the physical act has opened the passage for Birumbir to enter the uterus.[2]

This corresponds fairly closely to the Trobriand's belief (bathing, serpent), and shows that we were not mistaken in interpreting the "serpent, or eel-like creature," as the penis. These data show how repression is only directed against the part played by the male member in procreation, and thus agree absolutely with the data obtained by recent research in child psychology.[3] Here, however, we are concerned with other questions. We have interpreted the spirit-child (and hence also the Churinga) as an embryo, and here we are told the same thing by the natives themselves, in an area that must have been traversed by the ancestors of the Arunta.[4] But we went even one step further and explained Arunta belief and ritual by the assumption of a deeper regression; the down flying about, the minute spirit-child, is also the spermatozoön. Our natives seem to know this (unconsciously) when they talk about the life-giving being (Birumbir) in the semen.

Here we have the belief in the spirit-children; in Melanesia[5] and Fiji[6] we have what looks like conceptional totemism, in Central Australia we have both elements together.

Page 328.

On Walaga feast, cf. H. Newton, *In the Far East*, 1914, 151.

Page 337.

Cf. the remark of Wallace. "The islands eastward from Celebes and Lombok exhibit almost as close a resemblance to Australia

[1] Cf. A. P. Lyons, "Animistic and other spiritualistic beliefs of the Bina Tribe, Western Papua," *J. R. A. I.*, 1921, 432.

[2] A. P. Lyons, "Paternity Beliefs and Customs in Western Papua," *Man*, 1924, 44.

[3] M. Klein, "Eine Kinderentwicklung," *Imago*, VIII. 289.

[4] The Morehead River natives are the neighbours of the Marind (Kaia-Kaia) and frequently suffer from their raids.—Beaver, *Unexplored New Guinea*, 1920, 106, 126. I intend to discuss the close connexion between the Marind and the Central Australians in a separate paper.

[5] W. H. R. Rivers, "Totemism in Polynesia and Melanesia," *Journal*, 1909, 173.

[6] De Marzan, *Anthropos*, II. 402. Cf. for reincarnation C. E. Fox, "Social Organization in San Cristoval," *J. R. A. I.*, 1919, 432.

and New Guinea as the western islands do to Asia."—A. R Wallace, *The Malay Archipelago*, 1869, 25.

Page 332.

On cultural connexion between New Guinea and Indonesia, M. Uhle, "Holz und Bambusgeräthe aus Nordwest Neu Guinea," *Kngl. Ethn. Mus. zu Dresden*, 1886, VI. 4. On migration of stone culture from Indonesia to New Guinea, E. W. P. Chinnery, "Stone Work and Goldfields in British New Guinea," *Journ. R. A. I.*, 1919, XLIX. 271 (with a note on the stone circles in Australia, p. 277).

Page 372.

Incestuous origin of Kalangs. The inhabitants of Nicobar are immigrants from Indonesia. Origin myth ; a man married a female dog on the island. His son killed his father and married his dog-mother.—A. van Gennep, *L'état actuel du Problème totémique*, 1920, 303, from Brailowski in *Shivaia Starina*, 1901, II.

Page 384.

Post-mortal search for soul as animal. The first animal which alights on a mat where death had occurred contains the soul.—S. Percy Smith, "Futuna," *Journal of the Polynesian Society*, 1892, I. 40.

Page 397.

Petrified Supreme Being. J. Manning, "Notes on the Aborigines of New Holland," *Journal and Proceedings of R. S. N. S. W.*, XVI. 155. (See also p. 351 above.)

Page 401.

Ornamental patterns of Churinga.—Cf. H. Basedow, "Aboriginal Rock Carvings" in *J. R. A. I.*, 1914, 210. Fuhrmann sees connexion between Australia and New Guinea, interprets ornaments as symbols of vulva.—E. Fuhrmann, Neu Guinea (*Kulturen der Erde*, XIV.), 1922, 23.

Page 409.

Euahlayi Intichiuma ceremonies.

The Murawari are the south-western neighbours of the Euahlayi. A. R. Brown has recently published some very important information on their totemic ceremonies.

The members of the totem clans performed sacred totemic dances and recited certain songs at the initiation ceremonies. These sacred animal dances were called tonba.[1]

[1] A. R. Brown, "Notes on the Social Organization of Australian Tribes," *J. R. A. I.*, LIII. 1923, 439.

Just as in Central Australia, we have two groups of totemic ceremonies, the second, of "non-sacred character," i.e. not reserved to the initiates, being what we call Intichiuma ceremonies. These are connected with the different animal species, and a man who was powerful in totemic magic would sing the song of his own totem animal in such a way that he could draw all the animals of that species away from the neighbouring countries into his own country. The song of the Opossum totem refers to a certain famous legend of the tribe without which its contents are incomprehensible. The legend runs as follows:

There is a spot in the Baderi country called Bulpain, famous in myth as the place where the ancestors were turned into animals, giving rise to the species which still exist, while certain others were turned into stones still visible at the place.

The great transformation was the consequence of the incest of Kiwi (native cat) with his uncle's wives. His uncle was Bindelain (bat), a great magician who killed his faithless wives. When he had killed them he cut off small pieces of their skin and tied them in his beard. This was enough for his brothers-in-law, they knew what had happened. They decided to avenge their sisters' death, but they wished to catch the great magician unawares. One after another the ancestors danced before Bindelain, grotesquely painted, striving with every absurdity in posture to make him laugh, but none succeeded. Then came Diràn (black cockatoo with red tail), and when he turned his rump to him, all bedaubed with red as it was, and moved it up and down from side to side, Bindelain no longer could keep from laughing, and in his laughter he forgot danger and rolled from side to side. The men seized him and threw him on the fire; he was burnt and transformed into a bat.

A great fight followed, in which many of the ancestors were turned to stone, while others became the ancestors of the animal species. The opossum song, like many others, refers to marks of the burns received by the totemic ancestors on this occasion.[1]

We may as well begin by pointing out that a narrative which relates how, in the days of yore, young men tampered with the wives of their uncles, how the Great Magician of the Horde punished these evil-doers, and was in his turn killed by the united forces of the young men of the horde for what he had done to the women, looks very much like an account of incest and revolt against the Sire of the Primeval Horde. From the son's point of view it is the old man who is having illicit intercourse with his daughters[2] in the gerontocratic version, as in our myth the blame is put upon

[1] A. R. Brown, l.c., 440–442.

[2] Cf. Mandra-mankana, Howitt, *N. T.*, 781. In our myth it is the cut-off skins, in the Dieri version it is the cut-off breasts of the women, which lead to recognition in the same way. Both are accounts of primeval incest, both explain the origin of Intichiuma ceremonies.

the son. However, there seems reason to believe that the bat was originally the young man, the aggressor; for we have the Kokominni version of the bat's incest with his mother-in-law, of his subsequent search for honey in a hollow tree and the loss of eyesight as a punishment for incest which followed.[1] Now the bat is the sex-totem of many Australian tribes—a fact that goes far to prove our conjecture that he originally played the part of the son in this myth, and justifies us in using the key of sexual symbolism to explain the details of our narrative. To begin with, we notice that here also Bindelain "calls his two wives and Kiwi to come and take honey. When they came he pointed out to them the holes he had cut, and all three of them drew near and put each an arm into one of the holes. Then, by the power of his magic, he caused the holes to become smaller, imprisoning by their arms the three guilty ones."[2] If searching for honey is a symbolic equivalent of incest (penetrating into the hollow tree is coition with the mother), the loss of eyesight must be the usual talion-punishment, castration displaced upwards.[3] The secondary elaboration of the myth has extended the scope of this episode; originally it refers to the young men only. We should say, the young men did not dare to have intercourse with the father's wives, because they dreaded the magical bite of the hollow tree (vagina dentata). From their infantile-sadistic point of view they regarded coitus as killing, and this is why the old man is represented as having killed his wives. What follows is the often told tale of the Great Revolt, and now we begin to understand why Kiwi does not die in the tree-hole. The narrators felt that he must be among the aggressors, and hence he must survive this test. He manages to free himself because this part of the myth corresponds, not to a historic event, but to a psychic reality; he did not put his "arm" into the hole, and the episode only represents the castration-dread from which the brothers manage to free themselves before the Great Revolution.

But why does Bindelain laugh? What does this laughter mean? We shall consult some parallel versions of this episode.

Bootoolgah, the Crane, married Goonur, the Kangaroo Rat (Euahlayi). They discover how to make fire by rubbing two pieces of wood together, and decide to keep the art secret from all the tribes. Night Owl and Parrot watch them preparing fish, and it is decided that the two must be surprised, so that they forget to guard the bag with the fire-stick in it. A great corroboree was arranged, and all the animal ancestors came to the dance. All goes well with our heroes till the Brälgahs (Native Companion)

[1] Roth, *S. M. M.*, 15. Cf. A. R. Brown, *J. R. A. I.*, 1913, 169.

[2] A. R. Brown, *J. R. A. I.*, 1923, 441.

[3] Cf. the contributions of Eder, Ferenczi and Reitler in *Internationale Zeitschrift für Psychanalyse*, I. 157, 159, 161, on eye-symbolism. On the frequent use of phallic amulets against the evil-eye, cf. Seligmann, *Der böse Blick*, 1910.

appear. These looked very tall and dignified as they held up their red heads, which contrasted with their grey bodies, but they danced faster and faster, replacing their dignity with such grotesqueness as to make their large audience shake with laughter. Bootoolgah and Goonur rolled about helpless with laughter. The Hawk seized bag and fire-stick, fired the grass with the stick, and thus made fire the common property of the tribes.[1]

The next version accounts for the origin of water instead of fire. According to the aborigines of Lake Tyers, all water was contained in the body of a huge frog, and it was agreed that they must make the frog laugh, then the water would run out of his mouth and there would be plenty everywhere. They all try their dances, at last the remarkable contortions of the eel produced the desired effect. Many died in the flood, some were rescued by the Pelican. But he quarrelled with them about a woman and was turned into stone.[2]

The fourth variant comes from the Narrinyeri. The ancestors were assembled for a corroboree at Mootabarringar. They sent Kuratje and Kanmare (two small fish) as messengers to Kondole, a large powerful man who was the sole possessor of fire, and kept it for himself. Rilballe threw a spear and wounded him on the neck. This caused a great laughing and shouting, and nearly all were transformed into different animals. Kondole ran to the sea and became a whale, and ever after blew water from the wound which he received in his neck.[3]

The peculiar feature of this last version is that it connects the elements of fire and water with the flight towards the sea, a combination of elements which we have explained as symbolizing the urethral erotic impulse. This again seems to be merely an infantile version of the genital striving, and we shall thus endorse the view of our narrator that the quarrel between the Pelican and the others was "about a woman." There are two non-Australian versions of our episode, and in both the divine laughter is provoked by the exposure of the genitalia.[4] Now, the Black Cockatoo showing his rump bedaubed with red under the tail and moving it up and down from side to side (Murawari version) is suspicious, to say the least of it. This looks like a theriomorphic transcription of the indecent gesture of Usume and Baubo. When we remember that according to the Kakadu the women who originally possessed fire hid it up their vulvas,[5] while the Arunta believe it to have been contained

[1] K. L. Parker, *Australian Legendary Tales*, 1897, 24.

[2] R. Brough-Smyth, *Aborigines of Victoria*, 1878, I. 429, 430. Cf. A. Lang, *Myth, Ritual and Religion*, 1906, I. 43.

[3] H. E. A. Meyer, *Manners and Customs of the Aborigines of the Encounter Bay*. Woods, *Native Tribes of South Australia*, 1879, 203. Taplin, *Narrinyeri*, 59.

[4] Cf. Ed. Hahn, *Demeter und Baubo*, 1896, 77. K. Florenz, *Die historischen Quellen der Shinto Religion*, 1919, 40.

[5] Spencer, *N. T. N. T. A.*, 305.

in the penis of an euro,[1] our suspicion amounts to a certainty.[2] This explains the eel in the Lake Tyers version ; like the eel Tombabwir in Western Papua, he is the penis, and his contortions mean coitus. We shall therefore say that the laughter of all these divine beings which solves a difficult situation is merely a substitute for another relief from restraint, and this other relief is the sexual act.[3] Voyeurism and exhibitionism are merely inhibited substitutes of coitus.[4] This is demonstrated in our case by the fact that it needs an eel (male symbol) to make a frog (female symbol, womb) "laugh," while the father laughs when the red spot that must be explained as the vulva is exhibited. If we explain Bindelain as the father and the others as his children, "laughter" between them amounts to incest, and the myth would then relate how the brothers succeeded in killing the Jealous Sire when he was helpless, because caught red-handed in the midst of incestuous cohabitation.[5]

What follows is decisive for our views. It is from this moment of the Rutting Season (great corroboree) and the Primal Conflict that the animal species originate (i.e. Intichiuma ceremonies are performed), and petrifaction is the lot of the first heroes. The fact that the Intichiuma ceremonies of the Murawari refer to this myth of incest and petrifaction is so significant that it needs no further explanation.[6]

For the spread of the Central Australian type of totemism towards the southern and eastern coast the totemism of the Kumbaingerri is significant. "Each totem, gal, or family has some property peculiarly its own in the way of a water-hole or mountain in their district or hunting-ground, and each formerly had its Cambora, ghost--some in the shape of animals, birds, reptiles, or fishes. Moreover, we are told that these Cambora lived in certain trees."[7] Here we have the totem-centre, reincarnation (metempsychosis) and the Nanja tree.

Page 418.

Loss of tooth as death and castration.—C. G. Seligman, "Anthropology and Psychology," *J. R. A. I.*, 1924, 43.

[1] Spencer and Gillen, *N. T.*, 446.

[2] The red head of the Brälgah (Euahlayi version) is displaced upwards.

[3] There is a reversal here ; the father laughs at the coitus of the children. As a matter of fact, children frequently mimic or deride their elders, probably as a means of abreaction for the anxiety called forth in them by the " Urszene " (witnessing coitus of parents). Cf. Freud, " Aus der Geschichte einer infantilen Neurose," *Kleine Schriften, Vierte Folge*, 1918. This explains the "laughter" connected with childbirth beliefs in Central Australia.

[4] Cf. E. Jones, *Papers on Psycho-Analysis*, 1918, 30, 142, 158, 621.

[5] We do not mean to say that this actually took place in the Primeval Horde. As a myth, the father killed in the act of coitus merely means that he is killed on account of coitus.

[6] Cf. W. E. Armstrong, " Rossell Island Religion," *Anthropos*, 1923/24, p. 1.

[7] McDougall, " Manner, Customs and Legends of the Coombangree Tribe," *Science of Man*, 1901, IV. 46, 63.

Page 451.

Tree in tooth-evulsion ritual.—Cohen, " The Gaboora," *Science of Man*, 1898, I. 8.

In his recent publications (obtained by the author of this book after having read the proofs), W. J. Perry has taken the step which follows from his former investigations, and connected Central Australian culture-heroes with Indonesian stone-culture.—Cf. W. J. Perry, *The Children of the Sun*, 1923, 125, 176 ; *The Origin of Magic and Religion*, 1923, 102, 139 ; *The Growth of Civilization*, 1924, 120. By accepting Perry's view on this question, we do not commit ourselves to his general unpsychological attitude. His explanation of Australian totemism leaves everything unexplained (cf. *The Children of the Sun*, 1923, 332 ; *The Origin of Magic and Religion*, 1923, 142). The magical value of gold, quartz-crystals (ibid., 162), etc., plays a great part in the theories of Elliot Smith and Perry ; in this question, for instance, it is quite obvious that by taking account of the unconscious (anal-erotic) sources of such ideas the aspect of the vexed problem, independent origin *versus* migration, is considerably modified. In his theoretical zeal Perry sometimes overlooks facts ; a glance at our map No. 4, " the Alcheringa and the All-Father," will show that the "All-Father " in Australia is *not* specially connected with patrilinear, nor the dual heroes with matrilinear institutions (Perry, *Sun.* 249). To state that " the Australians do not use stone for their magic " (Perry, l.c. 307) is rather remarkable : what about Churinga and Naja ?

INDEX

LIST OF AUTHORITIES

ABBOTT, G. F. " Macedonian Folk-Lore." 1903.

ABRAHAM, K. " Untersuchungen über die früheste prägenitale Entwickelungsstufe der Libido." I.Z. Pa. IV.

Account respecting Beliefs of Australian Aborigines. Journal of American Folklore, IX. 1896,

ANDREE, R. " Votive und Weihegaben." 1904.

ANGAS, G. F. " Savage Life and Scenes in Australia and New Zealand." 1847.

ANKERMANN, B. " Das Problem des Totemismus." Korrespondenzblatt, 1910.

ANKERT, H. " Der Mond im Glauben des nordböhmischen Landvolkes." Zeitschrift f. östereichische Volkskunde, I. 1889.

ARMSTRONG, W. E. " Rossell Island Religion." Anthropos. 1923–1924.

ATKINSON, J. J. " Primal Law." 1903. (See LANG, A.)

Australasian " Anthropological Journal," 1897.

BACKHOUSE, J. " Narrative of a Visit to the Australian Colonies." 1843.

BALDWIN, J. M. " Mental Development in the Child and the Race." 1911.

BÁLINT, A. " Die mexikanische Kriegshieroglyphe atl-tlachinolli." Imago IX.

BARTON, G. B. " History of New South Wales." 1889.

BASEDOW, H. " Anthropological Notes made on the South Australian Government North-West Prospecting Expedition." Trans. Roy. Soc. S.A. XXVIII. 1904.

" Anthropological Notes on the Western Coastal Tribes of the Northern Territory of South Australia." Trans. Roy. Soc. S.A. XXXI. 1907.

" Über Felsgravierungen in Zentral Australien." Z. f. E. 1907.

" Notes on the Natives of Bathurst Island." J.A.I. 1913.

" Aboriginal Rock Carvings." J.R.A.I. 1914.

BASTIAN, A. " Indonesien." 1884.

" Der Papua des dunklen Inselreichs." 1885.

" Die samoanische Schöpfungssage." 1894.

BATES, DAISY M. " The Marriage Laws and some Customs of the Western Australian Aborigines." Victorian Geographical Journal, XXIII–XXIV.

BAUER, W. " Aberglaube der Macateca Indianer." Z.E. 1908.

BEARDMORE, E. " The Natives of Mowat, Daudai, New Guinea." J.A.I. XIX.

BEAVER, W. N. " Unexplored New Guinea." 1920.

BENNETT, G. " Wanderings in New South Wales." 1834.

BENNETT, J. F. " Historical and Descriptive Account of South Australia." 1843.

BERKUSKY, L. " Totengeister und Ahnenkultus in Indonesien." Arch. für Religionswissenschaft, 1915.

BEVERIDGE, P. " The Aborigines of Victoria and Riverina." 1889.

" Of the Aborigines Inhabiting the Great Lacustrine and Riverine Depression of the Lower Murray." Journal of the Roy. Soc. of N.S.W. XVII.

BEYER, H. O. "Origin Myths among the Mountain Peoples of the Philippines." The Philippine Journal of Science, VIII. 1913.

BICKNELL, A. C. "Travels and Adventures in Northern Queensland." 1895.

BLAND, R. H. "Aborigines of Western Australia." J.A.I. XVI.

BOAS, F. "Indianische Sagen von der Nord-Pazifischen Küste Amerikas." 1895.

"The Origin of Totemism." American Anthropologist, XVIII.

BONNEY, F. "On some Customs of the River Darling Natives talking the Weyneubulckoo Language, especially Bungyarlee and Parkungi." J.A.I. XIII.

BRAIM, TH. H. "History of New South Wales." 1846.

BRETON, W. "Excursions in New South Wales, Western Australia and Van Diemen's Land." 1833.

BRIDGEMANN, F., and REV. H. BUCAS. "Port Mackay and its Neighbourhood," in CURR, "The Australian Race," III.

BRITTON, A. "History of New South Wales." 1899.

BROCKMAN, FRED S. "Report on Exploration of North-West Kimberley." Perth, 1902.

BROTHERS, ROBERT. "Travelling Teeth, an Aboriginal Custom." The Australian Anthropological Journal. 1896.

BROWN, A. R. "Beliefs Concerning Childbirth in some Australian Tribes." Man, 1912.

"Three Tribes of Western Australia." J.A.I. 1913.

"Note on Systems of Relationship in Australia." J.A.I. 1913.

"Notes on the Social Organization of Australian Tribes." J.R.A.I. LIII. 1923.

BROWN, G. "Melanesians and Polynesians." 1910.

"Birippi Language of the Hastings and Wilson Rivers." Science of Man, 1898.

BROWN, J. M. "Maori and Polynesian." 1907.

BROWN, R. "Description of the Natives of King George's Sound (Swan River Colony)." J.R.G.S.I.

BRYNE, J. C. "Twelve Years' Wanderings in the British Colonies." 1848.

BUSCHAN, G. "Illustrierte Völkerkunde." (First edition 1913, Second edition 1923.)

CALVERT, A. F. "The Aborigines of Western Australia." 1894.

Cambridge Anthropological Expeditions to Torres Straits, Reports of, V. VI.

CAMERON, A. L. P. "Notes on some Tribes of New South Wales." J.A.I. 1885.

"Notes on a Tribe speaking the Boontha Murra." Science of Man, 1903.

"Traditions and Folk-Lore of the Aborigines of New South Wales." Science of Man, 1903.

"On Two Queensland Tribes." Science of Man, 1904.

CAMPBELL, D. "Aboriginal Carvings of Port Jackson and Brocken Bay." Memoirs of the Geological Survey of New South Wales, Ethnological Series, No 1.

CARNEGIE, W. "Spinifex and Sand." 1898.

CHALMERS, T. "Notes on the Bugilai, British New Guinea." J.A.I. XXXIII. 1903.

CHAMBERLAIN, B. H. "Aino Folk Tales." Folk-Lore Soc. XXII. 1888.

CHINNERY, E. W. P. "Stone Work and Goldfields in British New Guinea." J.R.A.I. XLIX. 1919.

CLEMENT, E. "Ethnographical Notes on the Western Australian Aborigines." Internationales Archiv für Ethnographie, XVI. 1904.

CODRINGTON, R. H. "The Melanesians." 1891.
COHEN. "The Gaboora." Science of Man, I. 1898.
COLLINS, D. "An Account of the English Colony in New South Wales." 1804.
CRAWLEY, E. "The Mystic Rose." 1902.
CREED, DR. "Notes on the Aborigines of the Northern Coast." J.A.I. VII. 1877.
CROOKE, W. "The Popular Religion and Folk-Lore of Northern India." 1896.
CUNNINGHAM, P. "Zwei Jahre in Neu Süd Wales." 1829.
CUNOW, H. "Die Verwandschaftorganisationen der Australneger." 1894.
CURR, E. M. "Recollections of Squatting in Victoria." 1883.
"The Australian Race." 1886.

DANKS, B. "Marriage Customs of the New Britain Group." J.A.I. XVIII. 1889.
DARWIN, CH. "The Descent of Man." 1898. (Second edition.)
DAWSON, J. "Australian Aborigines." 1881.
DAWSON, J. W. "The Island of Formosa." 1903.
DIXON, R. B. "Notes on the Achomawi and Atsugewi Indians of Northern California." American Anthropologist, 1908.
DOBIE, W. W. "Recollections of a Visit to Port-Phillip." 1857.
DONNER. "Aboriginal Traditions and Rock Carvings." Science of Man, III. 1900.
DORSEY, G. A. "The Mythology of the Wichita." 1904.
DORSEY, G. A., and A. L. KROEBER. "Traditions of the Arapaho." Field Columbian Museum, Anthropological Series, V. 1903.
DOUGALL, MC. "Manner, Customs and Legends of the Coombangree Tribe." Science of Man, IV. 1901.
DOUTTÉ, E. "Magie et Religion dans l'Afrique du Nord." 1908.
DUBOIS, E. "The Proto-Australian Man of Wadjak, Java." Proc. R.A. Amsterdam, XXIII. 1920.
DUNDAS, KENNETH R. "The Wawanga and other Tribes of the Elgon District." J.R.A.I. 1913.
DUNLOP, W. "Australian Folk-Lore Stories." J.A.I. XXVIII.
DURKHEIM, E. et M. MAUSS. "De quelques formes primitives de classification." L'Année Sociologique, VI.
DURKHEIM, E. "Les Formes Elémentaires de la Vie Religieuse." 1912.

EARL, WINDSOR G. "On the Aboriginal Tribes of the Northern Coast of Australia." J.R.G.S. XVI.
EDER, M. D. "Augenträume." Int. Zeitschrift für ärztliche Psychoanalyse, I.
EDGE, J. G. "The Mika Ceremony, Wallwara (Walookera) Tribe." Science of Man, II.
EERDE, J. C. VAN. "De Kalang Legende op Lombok." Tijdschrift voor Indische Taal Land en Volkenkunde, XLV. 1902.
EISLER, R. "Kuba-Kybele." Philologus, LXVIII.
"Weltenmantel und Himmelszelt." 1910.
EITREM, S. "Opferritus und Voropfer der Griechen und Römer." 1915. (Videnskapsselskapets Skrifter, II, Hist. Filos, Kl. 1914, 1.)
ELLIS, HAVELOCK. "The World of Dreams." 1911.
ELLIS, W. "Polynesian Researches." 1830.
ERLAND, P. A. "Die Marshall-Insulaner." 1914.
ESCHLIMANN, P. H. "L'enfant chez les Kuni." Anthropos VI. 1911.

ETHERIDGE, R. " Geological and Ethnological Observations in the Valley of the Wollondilly River." Records of the Australian Museum, II. 1892, 96.

" Ethnological Notes made at Copmanhurst, Clarence River." Records of the Australian Museum, V.

" Ancient Stone Implements from the Yodda Valley Goldfield, Nord-East British New Guinea." Records of the Australian Museum, VII.

" The Dendrolyphs or Carved Trees of N.S. Wales." Mem. Geol. Survey, N.S.W. Ethnological Series, No. 3.

EWENS. " Moorundee Tribe in Taplin." F.L. 1897.

EYLMANN, K. " Die Eingeborenen der Kolonie Süd Australien." 1908.

EYRE, E. J. " Journals of Expeditions into Central Australia." 1845.

FAWCETT. " Notes on the Customs and Dialects of the Wonnah-Rua Tribe." Science of Man, I.

FEDERN, P. " Über zwei typische Traumsensationen." Jahrbuch VI. 1914.

FERENCZI, S. " Zur Augensymbolik." I.Z. Pa. I. 1913.

" Contributions to Psycho-Analysis." 1916.

" Hysterie und Pathoneurosen." 1918.

" Ideges tünetek." 1919. (Second edition.)

" Versuch einer Genitaltheorie." 1924.

FIELD, Baron. " Geographical Memoirs on New South Wales." 1825.

FINSCH, O. " Neu Guinea und seine Bewohner." 1865.

FISON, L., and HOWITT, A. W. " Kamilaroi and Kurnai." 1880.

FLORENZ, K. " Die historischen Quellen der Shinto-Religion." 1919.

FLOWER, W. H., and LYDEKKER, H. " An Introduction to the Study of Mammals, Living and Extinct." 1891.

FOELSCHE, P. " The Larrakia Tribe," in CURR, " The Australian Race," I.

FORBES, J. F. S. " British Burma and its People." 1878.

FOUNTAIN, P., and TH. WARD. " Rambles of an Australian Naturalist." 1907.

FOX, C. E. " Social Organization in San Cristoval." J.R.A. I. 1919.

FOY, W. " Melanesien." Archiv für Religionswissenschaft, X.

" Fadenstern und Fadenkreux." Ethnologica, II. 1913.

" Baumstumpfsymbole und Zeremonialplattformen in Ozeanien." Ethnologica, II.

FRASER, J. " The Aborigines of New South Wales." 1892.

FRASER, W. " Tradition of the Blacks on the Mulligan River." Science of Man, II. 1899.

FRAZER, Sir J. G. " On some Ceremonies of the Central Australian Tribes." Austr. Ass. Adv. of Science, V. 1901.

" Totemism and Exogamy." 1910.

" The Golden Bough, A Study in Magic and Religion." Third edition. 1911, *seq.*

" The Belief in Immortality." 1913, *seq.*

" Folklore in the Old Testament." 1919.

FREUD, S. " Der Witz und seine Beziehung zum Unbewussten." 1921. (Third edition.)

" Sammlung kleiner Schriften zur Neurosenlehre." Erste bis Vierte Folge, 1912–1918.

" Zur Einführung des Narcissmus." Jahrbuch VI.

" Totem and Taboo." 1919.

" The Psychopatology of Everyday Life." 1914.

" The Interpretation of Dreams." 1913.

" Das Unheimliche." Imago V. 1919.

FREUD, S. " Group Psychology and the Analysis of the Ego." 1922.
" Beyond the Pleasure Principle." 1922.
FRITSCH, G. " Über die Verbreitung der östlichen Urbevölkerungen und ihre Beziehungen zu den Wandervölkern." Globus, XCI. 1907.
FROBENIUS, L. " Die Weltanschauung der Naturvölker." 1898.
" Und Afrika Sprach." 1913.
" Volksmärchen der Kabylen." 1921.
FUHRMANN, E. " Neu Guinea." Kulturen der Erde. XIV. 1922.

GARBUTT, H. W. " Native Witchcraft and Superstition in South Africa." J.R.A.I. 1909.
GASON, S. " The Dieyerie Tribe of Australian Aborigines," in CURR, " The Australian Race," II.
" Of the Tribes, Dieyerie, Auminie, Yandrawontha, Yarawuarka, Pilladapa." J.R.A.I. XXIV.
GENNEP, A. VAN. " Tabou et Totémisme à Madagascare." 1904.
" Mythes et Légendes d'Australie." 1905.
" Religions, Mœurs et Légendes." 1908, *seq.* I–V.
" Les Rites de Passage." 1909.
" L'État actuel du Problème totémique." 1920.
GERLAND, G. " Der Mythus von der Sintflut." 1912.
GERSTÄCKER, F. " Reisen IV. Australien." 1854.
GIFFORD, LORD. " The Kakarakala Tribe," in CURR, " The Australian Race," Vol. I.
GILES, E. " Geographic Travels in Central Australia." 1875.
" Australia Twice Traversed." 1889.
GILL, W. W. " Myths and Songs from the South Pacific." 1876.
GILLEN, F. J. " Notes on some Manners and Customs of the Aborigines of the McDonnell Ranges." Horn Scientific Expedition, IV. 1896,
GOLDENWEISER, A. A. " Totemism, an Analytical Study." J.A.F.L. 1910.
" Reconstruction from Survivals in West Australia." Am. Anth. XVIII.
" Form and Content in Totemism." Am. Anthr. XX. 1918.
GOMES, E. H. " Seventeen Years among the Sea Dyaks of Borneo." 1911.
GOODRICH-FREER, A. " Folk-Lore from the Hebrides." Folk-Lore, XIII.
GRÄBNER, FR. " Kulturkreise in Oceanien." Z. f. E. 1905.
" Wanderung und Entwickelung socialer Systeme in Australien." Globus, 90, 1906.
" Zur australischen Religionsgeschichte." Globus, 96, 1909.
" Kulturgeschichte der Melville Insel." Ethnologica, II. 1913.
" Totemismus als kulturgeschichtliches Problem." Anthropos, X–XI. 1915–1916.
GRANT, A. C. " Bush Life in Queensland, or John West's Colonial Experiences." 1881.
GREGORY, J. W. " The Dead Heart of Australia." 1906.
GREY, G. " Journals of Two Expeditions to North-West and Eastern Australia." 1841.
" Vocabulary of the Dialects of South-Western Australia." 1841.
" Polynesian Mythology." 1855.
GRIBBLE. " The Initiation Rites of the Goonganja Tribe." Science of Man, I.
GRUBAUER, A. " Unter Kopfjägern in Zentral Celebes." 1913.
GÜNTHER. " Grammar and Vocabulary of the Aboriginal Dialect called Wirradhuri," in THRELKELD, " An Australian Language as Spoken by the Awabakal." 1840.
" Report on Australian Languages and Traditions." J.R.A.I. II. 1872.

HABERLANDT, A. "Trinkwassersorgung primitiver Völker." Erg. Heft. 174. Petermanns, Mitteilungen, 1912.

HADDON, A. C. "The Decorative Art of British New Guinea." 1894.
"Head-Hunters, White, Black and Brown." 1901.
Proceedings of the British Association. 1902.
"Migrations of Cultures in British New Guinea." 1920.

HAECKEL, ERNST. "Anthropogenie." 1910.

HAGEN, B. "Unter den Papuas." 1899.
"Die Orang Kubu." 1908.

HAGENAUER, F. A. "The Story of Twenty-Five Years' Work at Ramahyuck." 1888.
"Report of the Aboriginal Mission at Ramahyuck for the year 1885."

HAHL, A. "Das mittlere Neumecklenburg." Globus, XCI. 1907.

HAHN, ED. "Demeter and Baubo." 1896.

HAHN, TH. "Die Bushmänner." Globus, XVIII.
"Tsuni Goam." 1881.

HALE, H. "United States Exploring Expedition." 1846.

HAMLYN-HARRIS. "Mummification." Memoirs of the Queensland Museum, 1912.

HARDMAN, E. T. "Habits and Customs of the Natives of the Kimberley District." Proc. Roy. Soc. Aust. I. Sec. III.

HARLEY, TH. "Moon-Lore." 1885.

HARTLAND, E. S. "The Legend of Perseus." 1894.
"Primitive Paternity." 1909.
"Ritual and Belief." 1914.

HAYGARTH, H. W. "Recollections of Bush Life in Australia." 1848.

HEAPE, W. "Sex Antagonism." 1913.

HEINE-GELDERN, R. "Südostasien," in BUSCHAN, Illustrierte Völkerkunde. (Second edition, II. 1923.)

HENDERSON, J. "Observations on the Colonies of New South Wales and Victoria." 1832.

HENNING. "Der Traum." 1914.

HERTZ, R. "Contribution à l'étude d'une représentation collective de la mort." Année Sociologique, X. 1907.

HESSE, R. and DOFFLEIN, F. "Tierbau und Tierleben." 1914.

HIRZEL, R. "Die Strafe der Steigung." Abh. d. sächs. Ges. d. Wiss. XXVII.

HOBLEY, C. W. "Ethnology of Akamba and other East African Tribes." 1910.

HOCART, A. M. "Notes on Fijian Totemism." Anthropos, 1914.

HODSON, T. C. "The Naga Tribes of Manipur." 1911.

HOEWELL, BARON VAN. "Leti Eilanden." Tijdschrift voor Indische Taal Land en Volkenkunde, XXXIII, 1889.

HOLDEN, R. W. "The Maroura Tribe," in G. TAPLIN, F.L., etc. 1879.

HOLZMAYER, J. B. "Osiliana." Verh. Gel. Estn. Ges. zu Dorpat, VII. 1872.

HONERY, TH. "Australian Languages and Traditions; Wailwun." J.A.I. 1877.

HOPKINS, E. WASHBURN. "The Background of Totemism." Smithsonian Report. 1918.

Horn Scientific Expedition to Central Australia. London, 1896.

HORNE, G. and AISTON, G. "Savage Life in Central Australia." 1924.

HOWITT, A. W. "On Australian Medicine Men." J.A.I. XVI.
"Australian Group Relations." Smithsonian Report. 1883.
"The Jeraeil or Initiation of the Kurnai Tribe." J.A.I. XIII. 1884.
"Further Notes on Australian Class Systems." J.A.I. XVIII. 1889.
"The Dieri and other Kindred Tribes of Central Australia." J.A.I. XX. 1891.
"The Native Tribes of South-East Australia." 1904.

HOWITT, A. W., and L. FISON. "From Mother-right to Father-right." J.A.I. 1882.
HOWITT, A. W., and O. SIEBERT. "Legends of the Dieri and Kindred Tribes of Central Australia." J.A.I. 1904.
HOWITT, W. "Abenteuer in den Wildnissen von Australien." 1856.
HOSE, CH., and W. MCDOUGALL. "Pagan Tribes of Borneo." 1912.
HOUSÉ et JAQUES. "Les Australiens du Musée du Nord." Bulletin de la Soc. Anthr. de Bruxelles, III.
HUBERT, H. et M. MAUSS. "Mélanges de l'Histoire des Religions." 1909.

JENKS, A. J. "The Bontoc Igorot." 1905.
JESSOP, W. R. H. "Flindersland and Sturtland." 1862.
JEVONS, F. B. "An Introduction to the History of Religion." 1911.
JONES, E. "Papers on Psycho-Analysis." 1918.
"Essays on Applied Psycho-Analysis." 1923.
"Psycho-Analysis and Anthropology." J.R.A.I. 1924.

KAHLE, R. "Über Steinhaufen insbesondere auf Island." Z. d. V. f. Vk. 1902.
KAINDL, R. FR. "Die Huzulen." 1894.
KENNEDY, E. B. "Four Years in Queensland." 1870.
"Blacks and Bushrangers." 1892.
KENNETH, R. DUNDAS. "The Wawanga." J.A.I. 1913.
KERR, A. "Papuan Tales." 1910.
KEYSSER, CH. "Aus dem Leben der Kaileute, Neushauss, Deutsch New Guinea." III. 1911.
KIDD, DUDDLEY. "The Essential Kaffir." 1904.
KING, PH. P. "Narrative of a Survey of the Intertropical and Western Coasts of Australia." 1827.
KLAATSCH, H. "Schlussbericht über seine Reise nach Australien." Z.E. 1907.
"Die Anfänge von Kunst und Religion in der Urmenschheit." 1913.
"Der Werdegang der Meschheit und die Entstehung der Kultur." 1920.
KLEIN, M. "Eine Kinderentwickelung." Imago, VIII.
KLEINTITSCHEN, P. A. "Die Küstenbewohner der Gazellenhalbinsel." 1906.
KNABENHANS, ALFRED. "Die politische Organisation bei den australischen Eingeborenen." 1919.
KOCH-GRÜNBERG, TH. "Zwei Jahre unter den Indianern." 1910.
KRAUSS, F. S. "Sagen und Märchen der Südslaven." 1883–84.
"Volksglaube und religiöser Brauch der Südslaven." 1890.
KROEBER, A. L. "The Religion of the Indians of California." Univ. Cal. Publ. Am. Arch. Ethn. IV. No. 16.
"Totem and Taboo." American Anthropologist, 1920.
KRUIJT, A. C. "Het Animisme in den Indischen Archipel." 1904.
KUEHN, T., in FISON and HOWITT, "Kamilaroi and Kurnai."

LANDOR, E. W. "The Bushman, or Life in a New Country." 1847.
LANDTMAN, G. "The Magic of the Kiwai." J.R.A.I. 1916.
"Papuan Magic in the Building of Houses." Acta Arbœnsis Humaniora, I. Abo. 1920.
"Folk-Tales of the Kiwai Papuans." Acta Soc. Sc. Fennicæ, 1917.
LANG, A., and J. J. ATKINSON. "Social Origins and Primal Law." 1903.
LANG, A. "The Secret of the Totem." 1905.
"Myth, Ritual and Religion." 1906.
"The Historicity of Arunta Traditions." Man, 1910.

LANG, J. D. W. "Cooksland in North-Eastern Australia." 1847.
"Phillipsland." 1847.
"Queensland." 1861.
LAUTERER, K. "Australien und Tasmanien." 1900.
LAWSON, R. "Padthaway Tribe," in TAPLIN, F.L. 1897.
LEHNER, ST. "Bukaua" in NEUHAUSS, "Deutsch Neu Guinea." III. 1911.
LEICHARDT, L. "Briefe an seine Angehörigen." 1881.
LEONHARDI, M. VON. "Der Mura und die Mura-Mura der Dieri." Anthropos, 1909.
"Über einige religiöse und totemistische Vorstellungen der Aranda und Loritja." Globus, XCI.
LEVY, L. "Sexualsymbolik in der biblischen Paradiesgeschichte." Imago, V.
LIEBRECHT, F. "Zur Volkskunde." 1879.
LIVINGSTONE, H. "Grammar and Vocabulary of the Minyung People" (Wimmera) joined to THRELKELD, An Australian Language as spoken by the Awabakal. 1892.
LOWIE, R. H. "The Northern Shoshone." Anthropological Publications of the Am. Mus. Nat. Hist. II. 1909.
"A New Conception of Totemism." American Anthropologist, 1913.
LUMHOLTZ, K. "Unter Menschenfressern." 1892.
LUSCHAN, F. VON. "Das Wurfholz in Neu Holland und Ozeanien." Bastian Festschrift. 1896.
LYONS, A. P. "Animistic and Spiritualistic Beliefs of the Bina Tribe, Western Papua." J.R.A.I. 1921.
"Paternity Beliefs and Customs in Western Papua." Man, 1924.

MACDONALD, A. "Mode of Preparing the Dead among the Natives of the Upper Mary River." J.A.I. II.
"The Aborigines of the Page and the Isis." J.A.I. VII.
MACDONALD, J. "Manners, Customs, Superstitions and Religions of South African Tribes." J.A.I. XX.
MACGILLIVRAY, ALEXANDER. "The Flinders and Cloncurry Rivers," in CURR, "The Australian Race," II.
MACKILLOP, DONALD. "Anthropological Notes on the Aboriginal Tribes of the Daly River." Trans. Roy. Soc. S. Aust. XVII. 1893.
MAJOR, R. H. "Early Voyages to Terra Austalis, now called Australia." 1859.
MALINOVSKI, B. "The Family among the Australian Aborigines." 1913.
"Spirit Children," in HASTINGS, "Encyclopaedia of Religion and Ethics."
"The Spirits of the Dead in the Trobriand Islands." J.R.Anthr.Inst. XLVI. 1916.
MANN, J. F. "Notes on Australian Aborigines." Science of Man, 1904.
MANNING, J. "Notes on the Aborigines of New Holland." Journ. and Proc. of Roy. Soc. N.S.W. XVI.
MARETT, R. R. "The Threshold of Religion." 1909.
MARZAN, J. DE. "Le Totemisme aux Isles Fiji." Anthropos, II. 1907.
MATHEW, J. "Eaglehawk and Crow." 1899.
"Two Representative Tribes of Queensland." 1910.
MATHEWS, R. H. "The Bora or Initiation Ceremonies of the Kamilaroi." J.A.I. XXIV, XXV.
"The Burbung of the Wiradthuri Tribes." J.A.I. XXV, XXVI.
"The Keepara Ceremony of Initiation." J.A.I. XXVI. 1896.
"The Bunan Ceremony of New South Wales." Journal of American Folk Lore, 1896.
"Bullroarers used by Australian Aborigines." J.A.I. XXVII. 1897.

"The Totemic Divisions of Australian Tribes." Journ. and Proc. of Roy. Soc. N.S.W. XXXI. 1897.
"The Burbung or Initiation Ceremony of the Murrumbudgee." Journn. Roy. Soc. N.S.W. 1897.
"Group Divisions and Initiation Ceremonies of the Burkunjee." Journ. Roy. Soc. N.S.W. 1898.
"Folklore of the Australian Aborigines." 1899.
"The Wombya Organization of the Australian Aborigines." American Anthropologist, 1900.
"Marriage and Descent among Australian Aborigines." Journ. Roy. Soc. N.S.W. 1900.
"Some Aboriginal Tribes of Western Australia." Journ. Roy. Soc. N.S.W. 1901.
"The Kamilaroi Division." Science of Man, I.
"Aboriginal Customs in North Queensland." Science of Man, I.
"Aboriginal Initiation Ceremonies." Science of Man, I.
"Die Multyerra Initiations Zeremonie." Mitt. d. Anthr. Ges. in Wien. 1904.
"Ethnological Notes on the Aboriginal Tribes of N.S.W. and Victoria." 1908.
"Notes on some Tribes in Australia." Journ. Roy. Soc. N.S.W. 1906.
"Bemerkungen über die Eingeborenen Australiens." Mitt. d. Anthr. Ges. in Wien, XXXVI.
"Beiträge zur Ethnographie der Australier." Mitt. d. Anthr. Ges. in Wien, 1907.
"Notes on the Aborigines of New South Wales." 1907.
"Notes on some Aboriginal Tribes." Journ. Roy. Soc. N.S.W. 1907.
"Notes on the Arranda Tribe." Journ. Roy. Soc. N.S.W. 1907.
"Notes on the Aboriginals of the Northern Territory, Western Australia and Queensland." Proc. Trans. Roy. Geog. Soc. of Australasia, XXII.
"Vocabulary of the Ngarrugu Tribe." Journ. Roy. Soc. N.S.W. 1908.
"The Sociology of the Arranda and Chingalee Tribe." F.L. XIX. 1908.
"Some Curious Stones used by the Aborigines." Journ. Roy. Soc. N.S.W. XLV. 1911.
"Ethnological Notes on the Aboriginal Tribes of the Northern Territory." Proc. and Trans. Geog. Soc. of Australasia, XVI.
"Ethnological Notes on the Aboriginal Tribes of the Northern Territory." Trans. Roy. Soc. S.A. XIV.
"Initiation Ceremonies of Australian Tribes." Proc. Amer. Phil. Soc. XXXVII.
"Initiation Ceremonies of the Wiradjuri Tribes." Amer. Anthropologist, N.S. III.
MATHEWS, R. H., and EVERITH, M. M. "The Organization, Language, etc., of the Aborigines of the S.E. Coast of N.S.W." Journ. Roy. Soc. N.S.W. 1900.
MEIER, P. J. "Mythen und Sagen der Admiralitäts-Insuluaner." Anthropos. 1908.
"Mythen und Erzählungen der Küstenbewohner der Gazellenhalbinsel." 1909.
MESTON, A. "Description of a Bora at Mt. Milbirriman." Science of Man, I.
MEYER, H. E. A. "Manners and Customs of the Aborigines of the Encounter Bay Tribe," in J. D. WOOD'S "Native Tribes of South Australia," 1879.
MEYER, O. "Mythen und Erzählungen der Insel Vuatom." Anthropos, 1910.

MITCHELL, T. L. "Three Expeditions into the Interior of Eastern Australia." 1838.

MJÖBERG, E. "Phalluskult unter den Ureinwohnern Australians." Anthropos, 1913.

"Vom Phalluskult in Nordaustralien." Archiv für Anthropologie, XIX. 1923.

MOORE, G. F. "Diary of an Early Settler in Western Australia, with a Vocabulary of the Language of the Aboriginals." 1884.

MOORHOSE, M. "South Australia." Papers ordered by the House of Commons. 1844.

MORIARTY, T. "The Goolwa Clan of the Narrinyeri Tribe," in TAPLIN, F.L. 1897.

MUIRHEAD, J. "Belyando River," in CURR, The Australian Race, III.

MÜLLER, W. "Ergebnisse der Hamburger Südsee Expedition," 1908–10. Jap. 1917.

MUNDY, G. C. "Wanderungen in Australien." 1856.

NEGELEIN, J. VON. "Die Reise der Seele ins Jenseits." Zeitschrift des Vereins für Volkskunde, XI.

NELSON, J. E. "The Eskimo about Berlin Straits." XVIII Rep. Bureau, Am, Ethn. 1899.

NIEUWENHUIS, A. W. "Quer durch Borneo." 1904.

"Die Wurzeln des Animismus." 1917.

NILSSON, K. "Griechische Feste von religiöser Bedeutung." 1906.

NORDENSKÖLD, E. "Indianerleben." 1912.

OBERLÄNDER, R. "Die Eingsborenen der Australischen Kolonie Victoria." Globus, IV.

OLDFIELD, A. "On the Aborigines of Australia." Trans. Ethn. Soc. 1865.

PALMER, E. "Notes on some Australian Tribes." J.A.I. XIII. 1884.

"The Cloncurry River," in CURR, II.

Papers, Aborigines, Australian Colonies. Ordered by the House of Commons. 1844.

PARKER, K. L. "Australian Legendary Tales." 1897.

"More Australian Legendary Tales." 1898.

"The Euahlayi Tribe." 1905.

PARKINSON, R. "Dreissig Jahre in der Südsee." 1907.

PEEKEL, G. "Religion und Zauberei auf dem Mittleren Neu-Mecklenburg." I. Anthropos, Bibl. 1910.

PEGGS, A. J. "Notes on the Aborigines of Roebuck Bay, Western Australia." Folk-Lore XIV. 1903.

PERRY, W. J. "The Megalith Culture of Indonesia." 1918.

"The Children of the Sun." 1923.

"The Origin of the Magic." 1923.

"The Growth of Civilization." 1924.

PETRIE, TOM. "Reminiscences of Early Queensland." 1904.

PETTAZONI, R. "Mythologie Australienne du Rhombe." Revue de L'Histoire des Religions, LXV. 1912.

PFEIFER, S. "Ausserungen infantil-erotischer Triebe in Spiele." Imago, V.

PITTS, H. "Children of Wild Australia." 1917.

PLANERT, W. "Aranda Grammatik." Z.E. 1907.

PLUTARCH. De Iside et Osiride (ed. Parthey).

PÖCH, R. "Studien an Eingeborenen von Neu-Südwales und an australischen Schädeln." 1915.

Preuss, K. Th. " Die Höchste Gottheit bei den kulturarmen Völkern." Psychologiscge Forschungen, II. 1922.
" Die Begräbnisarten der Amerikaner und Nordostasiaten." 1894.
Provis, Ch. " The Kukatha Tribe," in G. Taplin, F.L., etc., 1879.

Rand, S. T. " Legends of the Micmacs." 1894.
Rank, O. " Die Symbolschichtung im Wecktraum." Jahrbuch, IV.
" Psychoanalytische Beiträge zur Mythenforschung." 1919.
" Der Mythus von der Geburt des Helden." 1922. (II edition.)
Rawling, C. G. " The Land of the New Guinea Pygmies." 1913.
Read, Carveth. " No Paternity." J.R.A.I. 1918.
" The Origin of Man and his Superstitions." 1920.
Reik, Th. " Völkerpsychologisches." Zeitschrift für Psycho-analyse. III.
" Die Pubertätsriten der Wilden." Imago, IV.
" Die Bedeutung des Schweigens." Imago, V.
" Das Kainszeichen." Imago, V, 1919.
" Probleme der Religionspsychologie." 1919.
" Oedipous und die Sphinx." Imago, VI.
Reitler, R. " Zur Augensymbolik." J.Z. Psa. I.
Reitzenstein, Ferd. von. " Kausalzusammenhang zwischen Geschlechtsverkehr und Empfängnis in Glaube und Brauch der Natur und Kulturvölker." Z.E. 1909.
Reuterskiöld, E. " Die Entstehung der Speisesakramente." 1912.
Richards, C. " The Marran Warree Tribes," in Taplin, F.L. 1897.
Ridgeway, W. " The Origin of the Tragedy." 1910.
' The Dramas and Dramatic Dances of Non-European Races." 1915.
Ridley, W. " Kamilaroi, Dippil and Turrubul." 1867.
" Report on Australian Languages and Traditions." J.R.A.I. II.
Riedel, J. G. F. " De Sluik en Kroeshaarige Rassen Tuschen Selebes en Papua." 1886.
Rienzi, Domeny dë. ' Ozeanien." 1839.
Rivers, W. H. R. " Totemism in Polynesia and Melanesia." J.R.A.I. 1909.
" Sociological Significance of Myth." F.L. 1912.
" The Disappearance of Useful Arts." Festskrift tillegnad Edward Westermarck. 1912.
' The History of Melanesian Society." 1914.
" Dreams and Primitive Culture." Bulletin of the John Rylands Library, 1918.
Róheim, G. " Drachen und Drachenkämpfer." 1912.
" Zwei Gruppen von Igesagen." Z.d.V.f.Vk. 1913.
" Spiegelzauber." 1919.
" St. Nikolaus im Volksbrauch und Volksglauben." Pester Lloyd, 1919.
" Das Selbst." Imago, VII.
" Adalékok a magyar néphithez." (Contributions to Hungarian Folk-Lore) 1920.
" Die Bedeutung des Überschreitens." I.Z. Pa. VI.
" Primitive Man and Environment." I.J.P.A. II. 1921.
" Nach dem Tode des Urvaters." Imago, IX.
" Die Sedna-Sage." Imago, X.
Romilly, H. E. " From My Verandah in New Guinea." 1889.
Roscoe, J. " The Baganda." 1911.
Roscher, W. H. R. " Hermes der Windgott." 1878.
" Selene und Verwandtes." 1890.
" Lexikon der Griechischen und Römischen Mythologie " (Various papers).

ROTH, H. LING. "The Natives of Sarawak and British North Borneo." 1896.
"The Aborigines of Tasmania." 1899.

ROTH, W. E. "Ethnological Studies." 1897.
"Games, Sports and Amusements." N. Queensland Bull. No. 4, 1902.
"Superstition, Magic and Medicine." N. Queensland Ethnography Bull. 5. 1903.
"Notes on Government, Morals and Crime." N. Queensland Bull. No. 8. 1906.
"Burial Ceremonies and Disposal of the Dead." N. Queensland Ethnography Bull. No. 9.
"Marriage Ceremonies and Infant Life." N. Queensland Ethnography Bull. No. 10, Records of Australian Museum VII.
"On Certain Initiation Ceremonies." N. Queensland Ethnography Bull. No. 12. 1909.
"Social and Individual Nomenclature." N. Queensland Ethnography Bull. No. 18. 1910.

RUDDER, E. F. "Cannibalism in Queensland." Science of Man, II.

SAINTYVES, P. "Les Vierges Mères et les Naissances Miraculeuses." 1908.

SALVADO, RUDESINDO. "Memorie storiche dell' Australia." 1851.

SAPIR, E. "Religious Ideas of the Takelma Indians." Journ. Am. F.L. 1907.

SARG, F. A. "Die Australischen Bumerangs in Städtischen Völkermuseum." Veröffentlichung aus dem städtischen Völkermuseum Frankfurt am Main, III. 1911.

SAWYER, F. H. "The Inhabitants of the Philippines." 1900.

SCHIFFER, E. "Alltagglauben galizischer Juden." Am Urquell. 1893.

SCHIRREN, E. "Die Wandersagen der Neuseeländer und der Mauimythos." 1856.

SCHMIDT, W. "Die Thaten Bogda Geser Chans." 1839.

SCHMIDT, P. W. "Die sociologischen Verhältnisse der südaustralischen Stämme." Globus. XCVII.
"Die Stellung der Atanda." Z. f. E. 1908.
"Sociologische und religiös-ethische Gruppierung der Australier." Z.E. 1909.
"L'Origine de l'Idée de Dieu." Anthropos. 1909 *seq.*
"Grundlinien der Vergleichung der Religionen und Mythologien der Austronesischen Völker." Denkschrift d. Kais. Ak. d. Wiss. LIII. 1910.
"Ursprung der Gottesidee." 1912.
"Die Gliederung der Australischen Sprachen." Anthropos. 1912 *seq.*
"Die Personalpronomina in den australischen Sprachen." Ak. d. Wiss. in Wien, Denkschriften 64. 1919.

SCHNEIDER, H. G. "Missionsarbeit der Brüdergemeinde in Australien." 1882.

SCHULZE, LOUIS. "The Aborigines of the Upper and Middle Finke River, their Habits and Customs." Trans. and Proc. Roy. Soc. of. S.A. XIV. 1891.

SCHURTZ, H. "Alterklassen und Männerbünde." 1902.

SCHÜRMAN, C. W. "The Aboriginal Tribes of Port Lincoln in South Australia," in J. D. WOODS' "The Native Tribes of South Australia." 1879.

SCHWARTZ and ADRIANI. "Tontemboansche Teksten." 1907.

SCHWENK, K. "Die Mythologie der Slaven." 1850.

SEARCY, A. "In Australian Tropics." 1907.
SEBILLOT, P. "The Worship of Stones in France." American Anthropologist, IV. 1902.
"Le Folk-Lore de France." 1904 *sq.*
SELIGMAN, C. G. "The Melanesians in British New Guinea." 1910.
"The Weddas." 1911.
"Anthropology and Psychology." J.R.A.I. 1924.
SELIGMANN, S. "Der Böse Blick und Verwandtes." 1910.
SEMON, R. "Im Australischen Busch." 1896.
SHAKESPEARE, J. "The Lushei-Kuki Clans." 1912.
SHAW. "Overland Corner Tribe, River Murray, Ranbirit," in TAPLIN, F.L. 1897.
SHORTLAND, E. "Maori Religion and Mythology." 1882.
SIEBERT, O. "Sagen und Sitten der Dieri und Nachbarstämme in Zentralaustralien." Globus 197. 1910.
SILBERER, H. "Lekanomantische Versuche." Zentralblatt für Psychoanalyse, II.
"Zur Frage der Spermatozoönträume." Jahrbuch, IV.
SKEAT, W. "Malay Magic." 1900.
SMALL, JOHN F. "Customs and Traditions of the Clarence River Aboriginals." Science of Man, I.
SMITH, A. "Futuna." Journal of the Polynesian Society, I. 1892.
SMITH, ELLIOT G. "On the Significance of the Geographical Distribution of Mummification." Manchester Memoirs, LIX. 1915.
"The Migrations of Early Culture." 1915.
SMITH, H. O. "The Nimbalda Tribe," in G. TAPLIN, F.L. 1879.
SMITH, J. "The Booandik Tribe of South Australian Aborigines." 1880.
SMYTH, R. BROUGH. "The Aborigines of Victoria." 1878.
SOLLAS, W. J. "Ancient Hunters." 1911.
SOUEF, LE. "Wild Life in Australia." N.D.
SPECK, F. G. "Ethnology of the Yuchi Indians." 1909. (Univ. Penns. Anthr. Publ. I. No. 1.)
SPEISER, R. "Südsee, Urwald, Kannibalen." 1913.
SPENCER, B., and GILLEN, F. J. "The Native Tribes of Central Australia." 1899.
"The Northern Tribes of Central Australia." 1904.
SPENCER, B. "The Native Tribes of the Northern Territory of Australia." 1914.
STAIR, J. B. "Old Samoa." 1879.
STANBRIDGE, W. E. "General Characteristics of the Tribes of Victoria." Trans. of the Ethnological Society, I.
STECKEL, W. 'Die Sprache des Traumes." 1911.
STEINEN, VON DEN K. "Unter den Naturvölkern Zentralbrasiliens." 1897.
STIRLING, A. W. "The Never Never Land." 1884.
STIRLING, E. C. "Anthropology." Report on the Work of the Horn Scientific Expedition to Central Australia, 1896.
STOKES, J. LORT. "Discoveries in Australia." 1846.
STOW, G. W. "The Native Races of South Africa." 1905.
STOW, J. P. "South Australia." 1883.
STRAUSZ, A. "Bolgar néphit" (Bulgarian Folk-Beliefs). 1897.
STREHLOW, C., and LEONHARDI, VON M. "Die Aranda und Loritjastämme in Zentralasien," Veröffentlichungen des Frankfurter Museums für Völkerkunde. 1908 *seq.*
STRELECKI, P. L. DE. "Physical Description of New South Wales and Van Diemen's Land." 1845.

STRETTON, W. G. "Customs, Rites and Superstitions of the Aboriginal Tribes of the Gulf of Carpentaria." Roy. Geog. Soc. of Australia. 1893.
STUART, CH. "The Milka or Kulpi." Journal of the Roy. Soc. of N.S.W. XXX.
STURT, CH. "Two Expeditions into the Interior of Southern Australia. 1833.
SUAS, J. BT. "Mythes et Légendes des Indigènes des Nouvelles Hébrides." Anthropos. 1912.
SWANTON, J. R. "The Social and Emotional Element in Totemism." Anthropos. 1914.

TAPLIN, G. "The Folklore, Manners, Customs and Languages South Australian Aborigines." 1879.
"The Narrinyeri, an Account of the Tribes of South Australian Aborigines." 1878.
TAUNTON, H. "Australind, Wanderings in Western Australia and the Malay East." 1903.
TEICHELMANN, G., and SCHÜRMAN, C. W. "Outlines of a Grammar Vocabulary and Phraseology of the Aboriginal Language of South Australia." 1840.
TEIT, J. "The Lillooet Indians." Jesup North Pacific Expedition, V.
TENCH, W. "A Complete Account of the Settlement at Port Jackson in N.S.W." 1793.
TESSMANN, G. "Die Pangwe." 1913.
THOMAS, N. W. "Baiame and the Bell-bird." Man, 1905.
"Natives of Australia." 1906.
"Kinship Organizations and Group Marriage in Australia." 1906.
"Disposal of the Dead in Australia." F.L. XIX. 1908.
THOMSEN, P. "Palästina und seine Kultur in fünf Jahrtansenden." 1909.
THOMSON, B. "The Fijians." 1908.
THORNTON, R. "Notes on the Aborigines of New South Wales." 1892.
THRELKELD, L. E. "An Australian Language as Spoken by the Awabakal." 1892.
THURNWALD, R. "Forschungen auf den Salomo Inseln." 1912.
"Die Gemeinde der Bánaro, 1921." S.A. Zeitschrift für vergleichende Rechtwissenschaft, XXXVIII-XXXIX.
TÓTH, J. "Kiskunfélegyháza vidéki néphiedelmek." Ethnographia, 1906.
TOWSEND, J. PH. "Rambles and Observations in New South Wales." 1849.
TREGEAR, E. "Maori-Polynesian Comparative Dictionary." N.D.
TREMEARNE, A. I. N. "Notes on some Nigerian Head Hunters." J.A.I. 1912.
TREVELYAN, M. "Folk-Lore and Folk-Stories of Wales." 1908.
TRILLÉS, R. P. "Le Totémisme chez les Fân." 1912.
TROTTER, W. "Instincts of the Herd in Peace and War." 1919.
TUCKEY, J. H. "An Account of a Voyage to Port Phillip in Bass's Straits." 1805.
TURNBULL, J. "Reise um die Welt eigentlich nach Australien." 1806.
TURNER, G. "Samoa a Hundred Years Ago." 1884.
TYLOR, E. B. "On a Method of Investigating the Development of Institutions." J.R.A.I. XVIII. 1889.
"Remarks on Totemism, with Special Reference to some Modern Theories respecting it." J.A.I. XXVIII.

UHLE, M. "Holz und Bambusgeräthe aus Norwest Neu Guinea." Kngl. Ethnl. Mus. zu Dresden, VI. 1886.

VOLD, MOURLY. " Uber den Traum." 1912.
VOLZ, W. " Beiträge zur Anthropologie der Südsee." Archiv f. Anthropologie, XXIII.
" Süd und Ostasien," in BUSCHAN, Illustrierte Völkerkunde. 1909. (First edition.)
VORMANN. " Tänze in Tänzfestlichkeiten der Monumbo-Papua." Anthropos, VI. 1911.

WAITZ, TH., und GERLAND, G. " Anthropologie der Naturvölkerm." 1872.
WALLACE, A. R. " The Malay Archipelago." 1869.
WARD, A. " The Miracle of Mapoon." 1908.
WARNECK, J. " Die Religion der Batak." 1909.
WEBSTER, H. " Primitive Secret Societies." 1908.
" Totem Clans and Secret Associations in Australia and Melanesia." J.A.I. 1911.
" Rest-Days." 1916.
WENIGER, L. " Feralis Exercitus." A.R.W.IX.
WERNER, H. " Die Urspünge der Metapher." 1919.
WESTERGARTH, W. " Australia Felix." 1848.
WESTERMARCK, E. " History of Human Marriage." 1901.
" The Origin and Development of the Moral Ideas." 1908.
WESTERWELT, W. D. " Legends of Maui." 1910.
WHEATLEY, H. B. " Folk-Lore of Shakespeare." Folk-Lore, 1916.
WHEELER, G. C. " The Tribe and Intertribal Relations in Australia." 1910.
" Sketch of the Totemism and Religion of the People of the Islands in Bougainville Straits." Archiv. für Religonswissenschaft, XV. 1912.
" Totemismus in Buin." Z.E. 1914.
WHITE, J. " Ancient History of the Maori." 1880.
WHITE, A. " Psycho-analytic Parallels." The Psycho-analytic Review, II. 1915.
WIEDEMANN, F. " Aus der Inneren und Ausseren Leben der Ehsten." 1876.
WILHELMI, CH. " Manners and Customs of the Australian Natives." Roy. Soc. Trans. 1862.
WILLIAMS, F. E. " The Pairama Ceremony." J.R.A.I. 1923.
WILLIAMS, TH. " Fiji and Fijians." 1858.
WILKEN, G. A. ' De Verspreide Geschriften." 1912.
WIRZ, P. " Die Marind-anim von Holländisch Süd-Neu Guinea." 1922. (Abhandlungen aus dem Gebiete der Auslandskunde Bd. 10. Hamburg.)
WITHNELL, J. G. " The Customs and Traditions of the Aboriginal Natives of N.W.A." 1901.
WLISLOCKI, H. VON. " Volksglaube und religiöser Brauch der Zigeuner." 1891.
WOODS, J. D. " The Native Tribes of South Australia." 1879.
WORSNOP, TH. " The Prehistoric Arts, Manufactures, Weapons, etc., of the Aborigines of Australia." 1897.
WUTTKE, A. " Der Deutsche Volksaberglaube." 1900.
WYATT, W. " Some Account of the Manners and Superstitions of the Adelaide and Encounter Bay Aboriginal Tribes," in J. D. WOODS " The Native Tribes of South Australia." 1879.

ZAHN, H. " Die Jabim." Neuhauss, Deutsch Neu Guinea, III. 1911.